México
ESTADOS UNIDOS
Río Colorado
Río Gila
Tijuana
Mexicali
Nogales
Nogales
El Paso
Ciudad Juárez
Río Grande
Río Mississippi
Houston
San Antonio
Hermosillo
Chihuahua
BAJA CALIFORNIA
Golfo de California
SIERRA MADRE OCCIDENTAL
SIERRA MADRE ORIENTAL
Laredo
Nuevo Laredo
Brownsville
Reynosa
Matamoros
Torreón
Monterrey
Saltillo
Golfo de México
La Paz
Ciudad Victoria
Trópico de Cáncer
Mazatlán
Cabo San Lucas
Tula
Zacatecas
Tampico
San Luis Potosí
Aguascalientes
Canal de Yucatán
León
Guanajuato
Tizimín
Cancún
Mérida
Chichén Itzá
Cozumel
OCÉANO PACÍFICO
Puerto Vallarta
Guadalajara
Bahía de Campeche
Uxmal
Campeche
YUCATÁN
Teotihuacán
Morelia
México, D.F.
Jalapa
Veracruz
Toluca
Cuernavaca
Puebla
Orizaba
Uruapan
Islas Revillagigedo
Taxco
Río Balsas
Villahermosa
Belmopan
BELICE
Lago Petén Itzá
Tlapa
Oaxaca
ISTMO DE TEHUANTEPEC
Acapulco
Lago Isabel
GUATEMALA
San Pedro Sula
HONDURAS
Copán
Tegucigalpa
Golfo de Tehuantepec
Guatemala
San Salvador
EL SALVADOR
0 100 200 300 400 Km.
0 100 200 300 400 Mi.

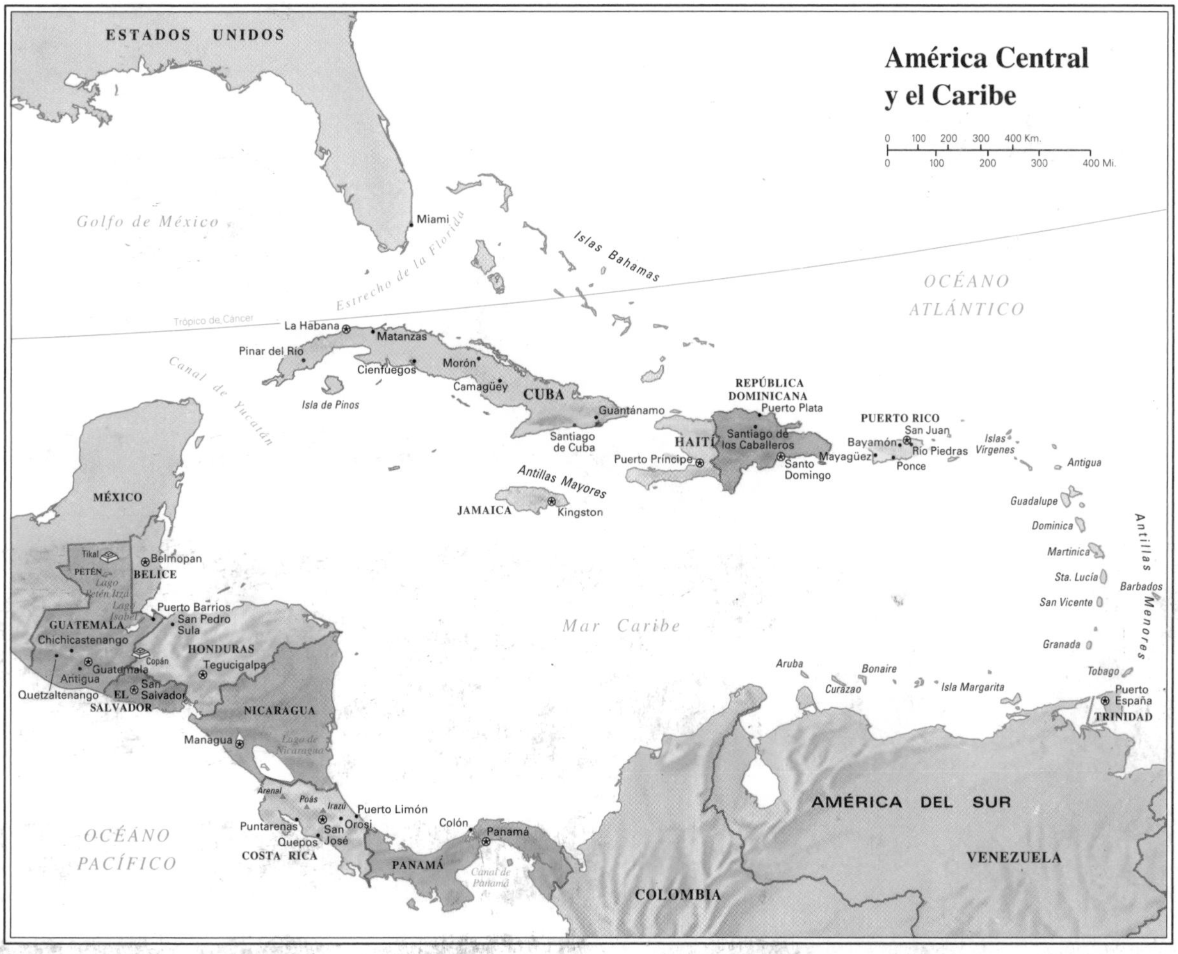
ESTADOS UNIDOS
América Central y el Caribe
0 100 200 300 400 Km.
0 100 200 300 400 Mi.
Golfo de México
Miami
Estrecho de la Florida
Islas Bahamas
OCÉANO ATLÁNTICO
Trópico de Cáncer
La Habana
Matanzas
Pinar del Río
Morón
Cienfuegos
Camagüey
CUBA
Isla de Pinos
Canal de Yucatán
REPÚBLICA DOMINICANA
Puerto Plata
Guantánamo
PUERTO RICO
San Juan
Santiago de Cuba
HAITÍ
Santiago de los Caballeros
Bayamón
Río Piedras
Mayagüez
Ponce
Islas Vírgenes
Puerto Príncipe
Santo Domingo
Antigua
Antillas Mayores
MÉXICO
JAMAICA
Kingston
Guadalupe
Dominica
Antillas Menores
Martinica
Tikal
PETÉN
Belmopan
BELICE
Lago Petén Itzá
Sta. Lucía
Barbados
San Vicente
Lago Isabel
GUATEMALA
Puerto Barrios
San Pedro Sula
Chichicastenango
HONDURAS
Mar Caribe
Granada
Copán
Tegucigalpa
Guatemala
Antigua
Aruba
Bonaire
Tobago
Quetzaltenango
San Salvador
EL SALVADOR
Curazao
Isla Margarita
Puerto España
TRINIDAD
NICARAGUA
Managua
Lago de Nicaragua
Arenal
Poás
Irazú
AMÉRICA DEL SUR
Puerto Limón
Puntarenas
Orosi
Colón
San José
Panamá
Quepos
OCÉANO PACÍFICO
COSTA RICA
PANAMÁ
Canal de Panamá
VENEZUELA
COLOMBIA

Hispanos en Estados Unidos

What is VAK?

YOU CAN APPROACH the topic of learning styles with a simple and powerful system—one that focuses on just three ways of perceiving through your senses:

- Seeing, or *visual learning*
- Hearing, or *auditory learning*
- Movement, or *kinesthetic learning*

To recall this system, remember the letters VAK, which stand for **v**isual, **a**uditory, and **k**inesthetic. The theory is that each of us prefers to learn through one of these sense channels. To reflect on your VAK preferences, answer the following questions. Circle the answer that best describes how you would respond. This is not a formal inventory—just a way to prompt some self-discovery.

When you have problems spelling a word, you prefer to

1. Look it up in the dictionary.
2. Say the word out loud several times before you write it down.
3. Write out the word with several different spellings and then choose one.

You enjoy courses the most when you get to

1. View slides, videos, and readings with plenty of charts, tables, and illustrations.
2. Ask questions, engage in small-group discussions, and listen to guest speakers.
3. Take field trips, participate in lab sessions, or apply the course content while working as a volunteer or intern.

When giving someone directions on how to drive to a destination, you prefer to

1. Pull out a piece of paper and sketch a map.
2. Give verbal instructions.
3. Say, "I'm driving to a place near there, so just follow me."

When planning an extended vacation to a new destination, you prefer to

1. Read colorful, illustrated brochures or articles about that place.
2. Talk directly to someone who's been there.
3. Spend time at that destination on a work-related trip before vacationing there.

You've made a commitment to learn to play the guitar. The first thing you do is

1. Go to a library or music store and find an instruction book with plenty of diagrams and chord charts.
2. Listen closely to some recorded guitar solos and see whether you can sing along with them.
3. Buy a guitar, pluck the strings, and ask someone to show you a few chords.

You've saved up enough money to lease a car. When choosing from among several new models, the most important factor in your decision is

1. The car's appearance.
2. The information you get by talking to people who own the cars you're considering.
3. The overall impression you get by taking each car on a test drive.

You've just bought a new computer system. When setting up the system, the first thing you do is

1. Skim through the printed instructions that come with the equipment.
2. Call up someone with a similar system and ask her for directions.
3. Assemble the components as best as you can, see if everything works, and consult the instructions only as a last resort.

You get a scholarship to study abroad next semester in a Spanish-speaking country. To learn as much Spanish as you can before you depart, you

1. Buy a video-based language course on DVD.
2. Download audio podcasts that guarantee basic fluency in just 30 days.
3. Sign up for a short immersion course in which you speak only Spanish.

Name ______________________________________ Date ______________________________

Now take a few minutes to reflect on the meaning of your responses. The number of each answer corresponds to a learning style preference.

1 = visual **2 = auditory** **3 = kinesthetic**

	Number of **Visual** responses	Number of **Auditory** responses	Number of **Kinesthetic** responses
My totals			

My dominant Learning Style(s): ____

____

Do you see a pattern in your own answers? A pattern indicates that you prefer learning through one sense channel over the others. It's also possible that your preferences are fairly balanced.

Whether you have a defined preference or not, you can increase your options for success by learning through *all* your sense channels. For example, you can enhance visual learning by leaving a space in your class notes to add your own charts, diagrams, tables, and other visuals later. You can also type your handwritten notes into a computer file and use software that allows you to add colorful fonts and illustrations.

To enhance auditory learning, reinforce your memory of key ideas by talking about them. When studying, stop often to summarize key points and add examples in your own words. After doing this several times, dictate your summaries into a voice recorder and transfer the files to an iPod or similar device. Listen to these files while walking to class or standing in line at the store.

For kinesthetic learning, you've got plenty of options as well. Look for ways to translate course content into three-dimensional models that you can build. While studying grammar, for example, create a model of a sentence using different colors of clay to represent different parts of speech. Whenever possible, supplement lectures with real-world audio and video input and experiences, field trips to Spanish-speaking neighborhoods, and other opportunities for hands-on activity. Also recite key concepts from your courses while you walk or exercise.

These are just a few examples, and in your path to mastery of learning styles, you can create many more of your own. In addition to the suggestions above, the Enhanced Edition offers new, interactive grammar practice activities for *all learning styles* that are available on iLrn.

ENHANCED TENTH EDITION

¿Cómo se dice...?

Ana C. Jarvis
Chandler-Gilbert Community College

Raquel Lebredo
California Baptist University

Francisco Mena-Ayllón
University of Redlands, Emeritus

CENGAGE Learning®

Australia • Brazil • Japan • Korea • Mexico • Singapore • Spain • United Kingdom • United States

CENGAGE
Learning®

¿Cómo se dice... ? Enhanced Tenth Edition
Jarvis | Lebredo | Mena-Ayllón

Product Director: Beth Kramer

Senior Product Manager: Heather Bradley Cole

Managing Developer: Katie Wade

Content Coordinator: Joanna Alizio

Product Assistant: Daniel Cruse

Associate Media Developer: Patrick Brand

Executive Brand Manager: Ben Rivera

Market Development Manager: Courtney Wolstoncroft

Rights Acquisition Specialist: Jessica Elias

Manufacturing Planner: Betsy Donaghey

Art and Design Direction, Production Management, and Composition: PreMediaGlobal

Cover Image: ©Nick Dolding/Getty Images; ©istockphoto.com/JordiDelagado; ©istockphoto .com/Maliketh; istockphoto.com/chuwy

Library of Congress Control Number: 2013946578

Student Edition:
ISBN-13: 978-1-285-73862-8
ISBN-10: 1-285-73862-4

Loose-leaf Edition:
ISBN-13: 978-1-285-73867-3
ISBN-10: 1-285-73867-5

Cengage Learning
200 First Stamford Place, 4th Floor
Stamford, CT 06902
USA

Cengage Learning is a leading provider of customized learning solutions with office locations around the globe, including Singapore, the United Kingdom, Australia, Mexico, Brazil, and Japan. Locate your local office at **www.cengage.com/global.**

Cengage Learning products are represented in Canada by Nelson Education, Ltd.

To learn more about Cengage Learning Solutions, visit **www.cengage.com.**

Purchase any of our products at your local college store or at our preferred online store **www.cengagebrain.com**

Instructors: Please visit login.cengage.com and log in to access instructor-specific resources.

Printed in the United States of America
1 2 3 4 5 6 7 17 16 15 14 13

Estimados estudiantes,

¿Cómo se dice…?, Enhanced Tenth Edition, is designed to present the fundamentals of Spanish in order to achieve its goal of helping you attain linguistic proficiency. The Enhanced Tenth Edition involves you in activities that require the communicative use of all four language skills (listening, speaking, reading, and writing). Special care has been devoted to providing practical insights into the cultural diversity of the Spanish-speaking world, because it is as essential to successful communication as linguistic competence. Do you have a dominant learning preference? Be sure to take the self-assessment quiz to find out and develop your skills in a new way.

As you embark on your journey to discovering the Spanish language, allow us to be your guides, together with your instructor, in offering you these tips to make the journey more productive, more interesting, and more enjoyable.

- Take every opportunity to hear, speak, read, and write Spanish.
- Try to relate everything you learn to your own experience and to the people around you, thinking of what you might say in different situations to express your ideas, opinions, needs, wants, and to ask for information or give directions or instructions.
- Try to be aware of the Spanish-speaking community around you: businesses, social organizations, and Spanish-speaking people in all walks of life.
- Create mental images of what you hear and read, always going from concept to Spanish and vice versa.
- Watch Spanish programs on TV, including the news, and yes, soap operas, or learn some songs in Spanish, because exposure to spoken Spanish will help you internalize the language.
- Remember that learning is not a passive pursuit, but an active one. It is the practice that will help you learn. Do not worry if you make mistakes. Your ability to understand and speak Spanish correctly will develop and improve as you practice it.

Lastly, don't forget that learning Spanish takes time, but with commitment, enthusiasm, and dedication, you will achieve your goal.

Un cordial saludo y los mejores deseos de,

Ana C. Jarvis   Raquel Lebredo   Francisco Mena-Ayllón

SCOPE AND SEQUENCE

SCOPE AND SEQUENCE

LECCIÓN	SITUACIONES	VOCABULARIO
4 **COSTUMBRES Y TRADICIONES** p. 102	**¡Bienvenido!** p. 104 **¡Ubíquelos!** p. 104	› weekend activities and festivities › needs and preferences › states of mind **Pronunciación:** The Spanish **b, v, d,** and **g** (before **a, o,** or **u**) p. 109
5 **LAS COMIDAS** p. 132	**¿Qué comemos...?** p. 134 **¡Ubíquelos!** p. 134	› restaurants, menu › ordering meals › paying the bill › the weather **Pronunciación:** The Spanish **p, t, c** (in the combinations **ca, co, cu**), and **q** p. 139
6 **LOS QUEHACERES DE LA CASA** p. 164	**¡Tocan a la puerta!** p. 166 **¡Ubíquelos!** p. 166	› household chores › family relationships › parts of a house **Pronunciación:** The Spanish **j, g** (before **e** or **i**), and **h** p. 171

SCOPE AND SEQUENCE

LECCIÓN	SITUACIONES	VOCABULARIO
10 BUSCANDO APARTAMENTO p. 282	**Dos amigos** p. 284 **¡Ubíquelos!** p. 284	› renting an apartment › parts of a house › home furniture and appliances **Pronunciación:** Pronunciation in context p. 289
11 EN UNA AGENCIA DE VIAJES p. 310	**Planes para una luna de miel** p. 312 **¡Ubíquelos!** p. 312	› planning a trip › at the airport, in the airplane **Pronunciación:** Pronunciation in context p. 317
12 EL AUTOMÓVIL p. 336	**Necesitamos otro coche** p. 338 **¡Ubíquelos!** p. 338	› automobiles › service station › road emergencies **Pronunciación:** Pronunciation in context p. 343

SCOPE AND SEQUENCE

LECCIÓN	SITUACIONES	VOCABULARIO	
13 EN UN CENTRO COMERCIAL p. 362	**De compras** p. 364 **¡Ubíquelos!** p. 364	› clothing › shopping **Pronunciación:** Pronunciation in context p. 369	
14 LAS CARRERAS UNIVERSITARIAS p. 388	**¿Qué carrera me interesa?** p. 390 **¡Ubíquela!** p. 390	› college activities › careers **Pronunciación:** Pronunciation in context p. 395	
15 LA SALUD p. 416	**Síntomas** p. 418 **¡Ubíquelos!** p. 418	› health problems › parts of the body **Pronunciación:** Pronunciation in context p. 423	

SCOPE AND SEQUENCE

LECCIÓN	SITUACIONES	VOCABULARIO
16 LAS ACTIVIDADES AL AIRE LIBRE p. 444	**¡Que se diviertan!** p. 446 **¡Ubíquelos!** p. 446	› sports › outdoors activities **Pronunciación:** Pronunciation in context p. 451
17 EL MUNDO DE LOS NEGOCIOS p. 470	**¿Asistente... o víctima?** p. 472 **¡Ubíquelas!** p. 472	› business › job interviews › job-related technology **Pronunciación:** Pronunciation in context p. 477
18 TEATRO... CINE... TELEVISIÓN p. 498	**La futura actriz** p. 500 **¡Ubíquelos!** p. 500	› media › the arts › communications **Pronunciación:** Pronunciation in context p. 505

ESTRUCTURAS	ASÍ SOMOS	EL MUNDO HISPÁNICO Y TÚ
1 The imperfect subjunctive p. 452 2 Some uses of the prepositions **a, de,** and **en** p. 454 3 The present perfect subjunctive p. 456 **Autoprueba** ¿Cuánto sé ahora? p. 468	**¡Vamos a ver! Ramón no es muy atlético** p. 458 **¡Vamos a escuchar!** Identifying word boundaries practice I p. 460 **¡Vamos a conversar!** Transitioning between ideas p. 460 **Rincón literario** ***Tres cartas... y un pie*** by Horacio Quiroga p. 462 **Estrategia:** Skimming; Predicting p. 462 **¡Vamos a escribir!** Exchanging ideas and experiences p. 465	› Uruguay p. 466 › Brasil p. 467
1 The pluperfect subjunctive p. 478 2 *If* clauses p. 479 3 Summary of the uses of the subjunctive p. 482 **Autoprueba** ¿Cuánto sé ahora? p. 496	**¡Vamos a ver! Dos entrevistas** p. 486 **¡Vamos a escuchar!** Guessing meaning practice II p. 488 **¡Vamos a conversar!** Giving a presentation p. 488 **Rincón literario** ***El tiempo y el espacio*** by Julio Camba (Esp.) p. 490 **Estrategia:** Interacting with a reading p. 490 **¡Vamos a escribir!** Writing to persuade p. 493	› España (I) p. 494
1 Uses of some prepositions after certain verbs p. 506 2 Uses of **por** and **para** in certain expressions p. 508 3 Some idiomatic expressions p. 509 **Autoprueba** ¿Cuánto sé ahora? p. 522	**¡Vamos a ver! El futuro director** p. 512 **¡Vamos a escuchar!** Identifying word boundaries and punctuating sentences practice II p. 514 **¡Vamos a conversar!** Expressing idiomatic language p. 514 **Rincón literario** ***Los deseos*** by Fernán Caballero (Esp.) p. 516 **Estrategia:** Using prior knowledge p. 516 **¡Vamos a escribir!** Writing a dialogue p. 519	› España (Cont.) p. 520 **Appendix A Spanish Sounds A-1** **Appendix B Verbs A-7** **Appendix C Glossary of Grammatical Terms A-17** **Appendix D Answer Key to ¿Cuánto sé ahora? A-18** **Appendix E Professions and Trades A-23** **Vocabulary V-2** **Index I-2**

ACKNOWLEDGMENTS

We wish to express our appreciation to the following colleagues for the many valuable suggestions they have offered in reviews of several editions of ***¿Cómo se dice...?***

Robert L. Adler, *University of Alabama, Birmingham*
Iris Allocati, *Citrus College*
Jon Amastae, *University of Texas, El Paso*
Richard Auletta, *Long Island University, Brookville, NY*
Ann Bachman, *Seminole Community College*
Ann Baker, *University of Evansville*
Clayton Baker, *Indiana University, Indianapolis*
Deborah Baldini, *University of Missouri, Saint Louis*
Alejandra Balestra, *University of New Mexico*
Thomas Bente, *Temple University*
Mayra E. Bonet, *Lehman College, CUNY*
Paul Budofsky, *New York University*
Renatta Buscaglia, *East Los Angeles College*
Graciela Buschardt, *St. Louis Community College, Meramec*
Ezequiel Cardenas, *Cuyamaca College*
Malcolm Compitello, *Michigan State University*
Humberto Delgado-Jenkins, *DeKalb College*
Diana Diehl, *University of Delaware*
Mario L. D'Onofrio, *Cuyahoga Community College*
Martin H. Durrant, *Mesa Community College*
Deborah Edson, *Tidewater Community College*
Kenneth Eller, *University of Nebraska, Omaha*
María Enrico, *Mercy College*
Barbara P. Esquival-Heinemann, *Winthrop University*
Robert Fedorchek, *Fairfield University*
Ronna Feit, *Nassau Community College*
José Feliciano, *University of South Florida*
Roger Fernández, *Los Angeles City College*
Rosa Fernández, *University of New Mexico*
Rachel Finney, *Richard Bland College*
Carmen Forner, *College of Southern Nevada, Las Vegas*
Mark Forrester, *Burlington County College*
Walter Fuentes, *College of Charleston*
Brian Gilles, *Pasadena College*
Yolanda Guerrero, *Grossmont College*
Peg Haas, *Kent State University*
Janet J. Hampton, *University of the District of Columbia*
Paul Jacques, *Grossmont College*
Larry King, *University of North Carolina*
Lincoln Lambeth, *College of the Ozarks*
Fidel de León, *El Paso Community College*
Roxana Levin, *St. Petersburg Junior College*
Mark Littlefield, *Buffalo State College*
Christopher Maurer, *Harvard University*
Ornella Mazzuca, *Dutchess Community College*
Li McCleod, *University of Saskatchewan*
Kathy McConnell, *Point Loma Nazarene University*
Virginia M. McCready, *Pasadena City College*
Dawn Meissner, *Anne Arundel Community College*
Virginia Morris, *Broward Community College*

Karen-Jean Muñoz, *Florida Community College at Jacksonville*
Oliver T. Myers, *University of Wisconsin, Milwaukee*
Eileen Nelson, *Brookhaven College*
Verónica Mejía Noguer, *Chaffey College*
Joanne de la Parra, *Queen's University*
Loknath Persaud, *Pasadena City College*
George Pesacreta, *Palomar College*
Vernon L. Peterson, *Missouri Southern State College*
Alcibiades Policarpo, *The University of Missouri, St. Louis*
Alvin L. Prince, *Furman University*
Joy Renjilian-Burgy, *Wellesley College*
Duane Rhodes, *University of Wyoming*
Wendy L. Rolph, *University of Toronto*
Jeff Ruth, *East Stroudsburg University*
José Angel Sainz, *Mary Washington College*
José Alejandro Sandoval Erosa, *Des Moines Area Community College*
Ruth E. Smith, *Northeast Louisiana University*
Montserrat Solá-Solé, *University of the District of Columbia*
William N. Stivers, *Pepperdine University*
Octavio de la Suarée, *William Paterson College*
Alice K. Taub, *St. Louis University*
Edda Temoche-Weldele, *Grossmont College*
Charles P. Thomas, *University of Wisconsin*
Matthew Tornatore, *Truman State University*
Alfredo Torrejón, *Auburn University*
Margarita Vargas, *SUNY, Buffalo*
Maurice Westmoreland, *SUNY, Albany*

The publication of the enhanced tenth edition of ***¿Cómo se dice...?*** could not have been accomplished without the contribution of many people. We would first like to thank Heinle Cengage Learning and P.J. Boardman, Editorial Director, and Publisher Beth Kramer for their support. We would also like to acknowledge Judith Bach for her guidance and support throughout the developmental stage of this edition. Our special thanks go to Heather Bradley Cole, Harold Swearingen, and Esther Marshall. Our thanks also go to all the other people involved with the marketing, editorial, and production stages, and to Harry Druding, the head of the Nesbitt composition service as well as to their project manager Karen Stocz, Peggy Hines the copyeditor, and Lupe Ortiz the proofreader. We would also like to thank Heather Robles for her invaluable assistance.

LECCIÓN 1

SALUDOS Y DESPEDIDAS

¡Hola!

OBJETIVOS COMUNICATIVOS

You will learn some greetings and farewells, how to introduce yourself and say where you are from, how to get and give phone numbers, and how to talk about days of the week and dates.

SITUACIONES

Estudiantes y profesores

ESTRUCTURAS

1 The alphabet

2 Cardinal numbers 0–39

3 Colors

4 Days of the week

5 Months and seasons of the year

6 Subject pronouns

7 Present indicative of **ser**

ASÍ SOMOS

¡Vamos a ver!
Watching and understanding situations

¡Vamos a escuchar!
Listening for the main idea

¡Vamos a conversar!
Speaking for basic communication

¡Vamos a leer!
Recognizing cognates

¡Vamos a escribir!
Generating ideas by brainstorming

EL MUNDO HISPÁNICO Y TÚ

› Los mexicoamericanos

› Los Estados Unidos hispánicos y el español en el mundo

AUTOPRUEBA

You will review what you learned in this lesson.

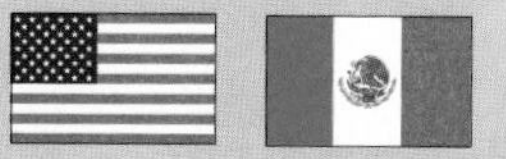

LOS MEXICOAMERICANOS

En los Estados Unidos (*United States*) hay unos 40 millones de hispanos. El 64 por ciento (*percent*) son de origen mexicano. La mayoría de ellos están (*are*) concentrados principalmente en Arizona, California, Tejas, Colorado, Nevada y Nuevo México.

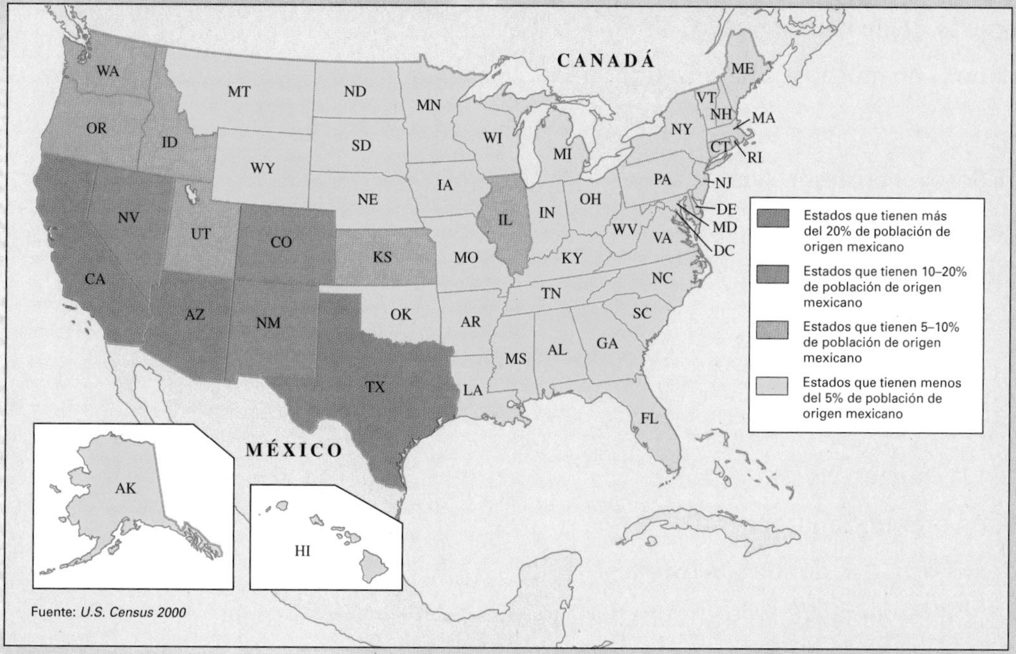

Fuente: *U.S. Census 2000*

Recursos iLrn video audio web playlist

Estudiantes y profesores

CD1-2

© Cengage Learning

¡Ubíquelos!

Fernando is from San Antonio, Texas. Watch the video about Mexican Americans to get a sense of the beautiful sights of the city of San Antonio.

© Diego Cervo/Shutterstock

© Phil Date/Shutterstock

Dos estudiantes

Sergio: ¿Cómo te llamas?

Marisol: Me llamo Marisol, ¿y tú?

Sergio: Me llamo Sergio.

Dos amigos y una estudiante

Luis: Hola, Marité, ¿cómo estás?

Marité: Bien, gracias, ¿y tú?

Luis: Muy bien, gracias. ¿Qué hay de nuevo?

Marité: Nada. Bueno… no mucho… Chau. Saludos a Eva.

Tres profesores

Dr. Vega: Doctora Soto: el profesor Viñas.

Dra. Soto: Mucho gusto.

Prof. Viñas: El gusto es mío.

Dr. Vega: La señora Marta Ruiz.

Dra. Soto: Encantada, señora.

Sra. Ruiz: Igualmente.

Tres estudiantes en la clase de inglés

Marcelo: ¿De dónde eres tú, Sandra?

Sandra: Yo soy de México. ¿De dónde son ustedes?

Marcelo: Nosotros somos de Texas. Yo soy de Dallas y Fernando es de San Antonio.

Fernando: (*A Marcelo*) Oye, ¿qué fecha es hoy?

Marcelo: Hoy es el siete de septiembre.

Fernando: ¡Caramba! ¡Hoy es mi cumpleaños!

Marcelo y Sandra: ¡Feliz cumpleaños!

En la cafetería

Ana María: Buenos días, Carlos. ¿Qué tal?

Carlos: Bien, Ana María. ¿Cómo te va?

Ana María: Muy bien, gracias. ¡Siéntate!

Carlos: Gracias. Oye, ¿cuál es tu número de teléfono?

Ana María: Tres-siete-dos-cuatro-ocho-seis-cinco.

Un estudiante en la oficina de la doctora Mena

Sr. Paz: Buenas tardes, profesora.

Dra. Mena: Buenas tardes, señor Paz. Pase. Tome asiento, por favor.

Sr. Paz: Gracias. Perdón, profesora. ¿Hay clase hoy? Hoy es martes, ¿no?

Dra. Mena: No, hoy es lunes.

Sr. Paz: ¡Ay, no! ¡La clase es mañana!

Dra. Mena: Sí, nos vemos mañana.

Sr. Paz: Hasta mañana, profesora.

© Design Pics RF/age fotostock

LEARNING TIP
Many social variables are at play when deciding whether to address people formally **(Ud.)** or informally **(tú)**. At work, a superior is addressed as **Ud.**, whereas peers are addressed as **tú.** In social situations, consider the speakers' relative ages, their level of acquaintance, and shared commonalities. When in doubt, use **Ud.**

1. Hablemos With a partner, take turns asking and answering the following questions. Base your answers on the dialogue and on your own circumstances.

En el diálogo

1. ¿Cómo está Marité?
2. ¿De dónde es Sandra?
3. ¿Cuándo (*When*) es el cumpleaños de Fernando?
4. ¿Cuál es el número de teléfono de Ana María?
5. ¿La doctora Mena es profesora o estudiante?

¿Y tú?

1. ¿Cómo estás tú?
2. ¿De dónde eres tú?
3. ¿En qué mes es tu cumpleaños?
4. ¿Cuál es tu número de teléfono?
5. ¿Tú eres profesor(a) o estudiante?

¿Lo sabía Ud.? (*Did you know?*)

María es un nombre (*name*) muy popular en España y en Latinoamérica. Frecuentemente se usa con otros nombres: Ana María, María Teresa, etcétera. Se usa también como segundo nombre (*middle name*) para hombres: José María, Carlos María, etcétera.

› **¿Mary es un nombre muy popular en este país? ¿Se usa con otros nombres?**

HINT: For a list of months, go to page 17.

VOCABULARIO

En el diálogo

Cognados (*Cognates*)[1]

la cafetería	*cafeteria*
la clase	*class*
el (la) estudiante	*student*
mucho	*much*
no	*no, not*
la oficina	*office*
septiembre[2]	*September*
el teléfono	*telephone*
la universidad	*university*

Nombres (*Nouns*)

el (la) amigo(a)	*friend*
el cumpleaños[3]	*birthday*
la despedida	*farewell*
el día	*day*
la fecha	*date*
el inglés[4]	*English (language)*
el lunes[5]	*Monday*
el martes	*Tuesday*
el número	*number*
_____ de teléfono	*telephone number*
el saludo	*greeting*

Verbo (*Verb*)

ser	*to be*

Adjetivos (*Adjectives*)

bueno(a)	*good*
feliz	*happy*
mi	*my*
nuevo(a)	*new*
tu	*your*

Títulos (*Titles*)

doctor, doctora[6] **(Dr., Dra.)**	*doctor (Dr.)*
profesor, profesora	*professor*
señor (Sr.)	*mister (Mr.), sir, gentleman*
señora (Sra.)	*madam, (Mrs.), (Ms.), lady*
señorita (Srta.)	*Miss, young lady (unmarried)*

Saludos y despedidas (*Greetings and farewells*)

adiós, chau	*good-bye*
buenas tardes[7]	*good afternoon*
buenos días	*good morning*
hasta mañana	*see you (until) tomorrow*
hola	*hello, hi*
Nos vemos.	*(I'll) See you.*

Preguntas y respuestas (*Questions and answers*)

¿Cómo estás?[8]	*How are you?*
¿Cómo te va?[9]	*How is it going (for you)?*
¿Qué tal?	*How is it going?*
Bien.	*Well., Fine.*
Muy bien.	*Very well.*
¿Cómo te llamas?[10]	*What's your name?*
(Yo) Me llamo...	*My name is . . .*

Otras palabras y expresiones (*Other words and expressions*)

a	*to*
¡Ay, no!	*Oh, no!*
bueno...	*well . . .*
¡caramba!	*gee, gosh!*
¿cómo?	*how?*
Con permiso.	*Pardon me.*
¿cuál?	*what?, which?*
_____ es tu número de teléfono?	*What's your phone number?*
de	*from, of*
¿dónde?	*where?*
El gusto es mío.	*The pleasure is mine.*
en	*in, at*
Encantado(a).	*Charmed.*
gracias	*thanks, thank you*
hay	*there is, there are*
hoy	*today*
Igualmente.	*Likewise. Same here.*
mañana	*tomorrow*
Mucho gusto.	*How do you do? (Glad to meet you.) (lit., Much pleasure.)*

[1] Cognates are words that are very similar in both languages.
[2] Names of months are not capitalized in Spanish, except in letterheads or in newspapers' upper lines, which is optional.
[3] The word **cumpleaños** is always used in the plural form.
[4] Names of languages are not capitalized in Spanish.
[5] Names of days are not capitalized in Spanish.
[6] Titles are not capitalized, unless they are abbreviated.
[7] **buenas noches** *good evening (It may also mean "good night")* [8] *Formal*: ¿Cómo está usted? ¿Cómo están Uds.? (*How are you [all]?*) [9] *Formal:* ¿Cómo le va?
[10] *Formal:* ¿Cómo se llama Ud.?

muy	*very*
nada	*nothing*
nosotros	*we*
¡Oye!	*Listen!*
Pase.	*Come in.*
Perdón.	*Pardon me. (Excuse me.)*
por favor	*please*
¿qué?	*what?*
¿Qué fecha es hoy?	*What's today's date?*
¿Qué hay de nuevo?	*What's new?*
Saludos a...	*Say hi to . . .*
sí	*yes*
Siéntate.[1]	*Sit down.*
Tome asiento.	*Have a seat.* (*formal*)
tú	*you*
y	*and*
yo	*I*

Más sobre el tema (*More about the topic*)

Expresiones de cortesía

¿Lo sabía Ud.?

Se usa **hola** con personas conocidas (*known*), no con extraños (*strangers*).

› **¿Cómo saludan ustedes (*do you greet*) al profesor (*a la profesora*)?**

LEARNING TIP

Use your powers of visualization and association to aid your language learning. Think of real (or funny) images to associate with words you learn in context. Take a moment to create a mental image in which you associate several vocabulary words; then describe the image aloud. For example: **"En la universidad hay clases con (*with*) diez estudiantes." "La fiesta de cumpleaños es hoy."**

[1] Formal: Siéntese.

Práctica

2. Saludos With a partner, take turns providing what is missing.

1. ______________ El gusto es mío.
2. ¿Cómo está Ud.? ______________
3. Encantado(a), señorita. ______________
4. ______________ Carlos es de México.
5. Hoy es mi cumpleaños. ______________
6. ______________ Nada... Bueno..., no mucho.
7. Muchas gracias. ______________
8. Hasta la vista. ______________
9. ______________ Me llamo José Díaz.
10. Buenos días, ¿qué tal? ______________

3. El profesor Vargas Complete the following dialogues.

1. Professor Vargas greets a new student.

Prof. Vargas: Buenas tardes, señorita. Pase y tome asiento.

Estudiante: ______________________

Prof. Vargas: ¿De dónde es Ud., señorita?

Estudiante: ______________________

Prof. Vargas: La clase es el lunes.

Estudiante: ______________________

Prof. Vargas: Hasta el lunes, señorita.

2. Raúl talks with Silvia at the university. Supply what Silvia says.

Raúl: Hola, Silvia. ¿Cómo estás?

Silvia: ______________________

Raúl: Muy bien, gracias. ¿Qué hay de nuevo?

Silvia: ______________________

Raúl: Hoy es el 5 de mayo.

Silvia: ______________________

Raúl: Dos, siete, cinco, ocho, tres, nueve, seis.

Silvia: ______________________

Raúl: Hoy es martes.

Silvia: ______________________

Raúl: No, hoy no hay clase. Nos vemos mañana en la cafetería.

Silvia: ______________________

Raúl: Adiós. Saludos a Teresa.

Para conversar

4. ¿Qué dicen estas personas? (*What are these people saying?*) With a partner, take turns creating exchanges between the people in the illustrations. Then join another group and compare your ideas with theirs.

A.

Modelo —*Mucho gusto, soy Eva Pasos.*
—*Encantado. Soy Luis Díaz.*

B.

C.

D.

E.

F.

Pronunciación

CD1-3 **A. The Spanish *a***

The Spanish **a** is pronounced like the *a* in the English word *father*. Listen to your teacher and repeat the following sentences.

Hola, **A**manda.

Encantada, señora Paz.

Hasta mañana, **A**na.

Hasta la vista, Marta.

Hasta la vista, **A**na.

CD1-4 **B. The Spanish *e***

The Spanish **e** is pronounced like the e in the English word *eight*. Listen to your teacher and repeat the following sentences.

Buenas noches, Teresa.

¿De dónde eres?

¿**E**s el señor Pérez?

¿**E**s de Los Ángeles?

ESTRUCTURAS

1 The alphabet (*El alfabeto*)

Letter	Name	Letter	Name	Letter	Name
A	a	K	ka	S	ese
B	be[1]	L	ele	T	te
C	ce	M	eme	U	u
D	de	N	ene	V	ve[2]
E	e	Ñ	eñe	W	doble ve[3]
F	efe	O	o	X	equis
G	ge	P	pe	Y	i griega[4]
H	hache	Q	cu	Z	zeta
I	i	R	ere		
J	jota	RR	erre		

[1]be larga
[2]ve corta
Note: Official names of these letters are: "b=be", "v=uve", [3]"w=doble uve", and [4]"y=ye", according to the *Real Academia de la Lengua Española.*

LEARNING TIP
Spell out names of people in your family and your circle of friends.

Práctica

5. Siglas (*Acronyms*) Spell these well-known acronyms in Spanish.

1. DNA ______________
2. FBI ______________
3. NFL ______________
4. CBS ______________
5. UCLA ______________
6. IBM ______________
7. Now you and your partner will give each other one acronym to spell.

6. Apellidos (*Last names*) Here are some last names that you have to spell out.

Modelo Douglas: de - o - u - ge - ele - a - ese

1. Wilson: ____________________
2. Taylor: ____________________
3. Jackson: ____________________
4. Fisher: ____________________
5. Ziegler: ____________________
6. García: ____________________
7. López: ____________________
8. Matos: ____________________

Para conversar

7. **¿Cómo se escribe?** A Spanish-speaking person may not know how to spell your name. If that person wants to write it, he or she might ask, **¿Cómo se escribe?**[1] (*How do you write it?*). Learn how to spell your name in Spanish. Ask five classmates what their last name is **(¿Cuál es tu apellido?),** and how to spell it. Then spell your last name for them to write it.

2 Cardinal numbers 0–39 (*Los números cardinales del 0 al 39*)

0 **cero**	6 **seis**	12 **doce**	18 **dieciocho**
1 **uno**	7 **siete**	13 **trece**	19 **diecinueve**
2 **dos**	8 **ocho**	14 **catorce**	20 **veinte**
3 **tres**	9 **nueve**	15 **quince**	21 **veintiuno** (*and so on*)
4 **cuatro**	10 **diez**	16 **dieciséis**	30 **treinta**
5 **cinco**	11 **once**	17 **diecisiete**	31 **treinta y uno** (*and so on*)

¡Atención! **Uno** changes to **un** before a masculine singular noun: **un profesor** (*one professor*).
Uno changes to **una** before a feminine singular noun: **una profesora** (*one professor*).

LEARNING TIP
Count from 0 to 30 first by twos, then by threes, by fours, and by fives.

Práctica

8. **Números de teléfono** In Los Angeles there are many businesses that are owned by Mexican Americans. Take turns with your partner reading the telephone numbers that a Spanish-speaking person would call, according to his/her needs.

1. Carlos wants to have his picture taken.
2. Sergio wants to send flowers to his wife.
3. Elena is having car trouble.
4. Lupe needs to have a prescription filled.
5. Fernando needs to make a dinner reservation.
6. Silvia wants to know what time the jewelry store closes.
7. Eva and Luis need an apartment.
8. Antonio wants to know if a bookstore is open on Sundays.

[1]Also **¿Cómo se deletrea?** (*How do you spell it?*)

CD1-5

9. Una canción (*A song*) Count along in Spanish! Listen to the song, then try to sing it by heart.

Canción infantil (*Children's song*)

Dos y dos son cuatro,
cuatro y dos son seis;
seis y dos son ocho
y ocho dieciséis.

10. Números With a partner, take turns reading the following numbers aloud.

1. 13 ________
2. 27 ________
3. 15 ________
4. 30 ________
5. 12 ________
6. 18 ________
7. 35 ________
8. 11 ________
9. 22 ________
10. 14 ________
11. 38 ________
12. 17 ________
13. 20 ________
14. 33 ________
15. 19 ________

Para conversar

11. ¿Cuál es tu número de teléfono?[1] Ask four members of the class what their name and phone number is and write down the information. The other person will ask what your number is.

Modelo S1: —¿Cuál es tu número de telefóno?
S2: —Mi número de teléfono es siete-cero-cinco-dos-nueve-cuatro-dos.

S1 writes 7-0-5-2-9-4-2.

12. Una clase de aritmética You and your partner are tutoring some Spanish-speaking children. Prepare addition and subtraction problems along with an answer key. The children only deal with numbers up to thirty.

+	:	más
–	:	menos
=	:	son
16 + 8 =		
3 – 2 =		
25 – 12 =		

Modelo Tú: *¿Cuánto es diez menos dos?*
Tu compañero(a): *Diez menos dos son ocho.*

[1]Say **"¿Cuál es *su* número de teléfono?"** when addressing someone as **usted** (formal).

3 Colors (*Los colores*)

› Everywhere you go, there are colors! Learn to say them in Spanish.

Práctica

13. Colores Match the items in column A with the corresponding colors in column B.

A		B
1. snow	____	a. rojo
2. coffee	____	b. verde
3. blood	____	c. azul
4. a banana	____	d. negro
5. an elephant	____	e. marrón
6. a violet	____	f. rojo, blanco y azul
7. grass	____	g. rosado
8. coal	____	h. morado
9. an orange	____	i. gris
10. the sky	____	j. anaranjado
11. rosy cheeks	____	k. blanco
12. the American flag	____	l. amarillo

14. Los colores de la ropa (*clothes*) With a partner, take turns naming the people in the illustration (people in the cafeteria) and telling what colors they are wearing.

Modelo S1: *Eva*
S2: *anaranjado y verde*

15. Una pintura This is a painting by Mexican-American painter Leo Tanguma. With a partner, take turns naming the colors that you see, in Spanish. You can add the following words to the colors:

claro *light*
oscuro *dark*
(e.g., **azul claro** *or* **azul oscuro**)

Modelo —Esto es (*This is*) de color azul claro.
—Mira (*Look*), morado oscuro.
—Y mira... aquí hay algo (*something*) amarillo.

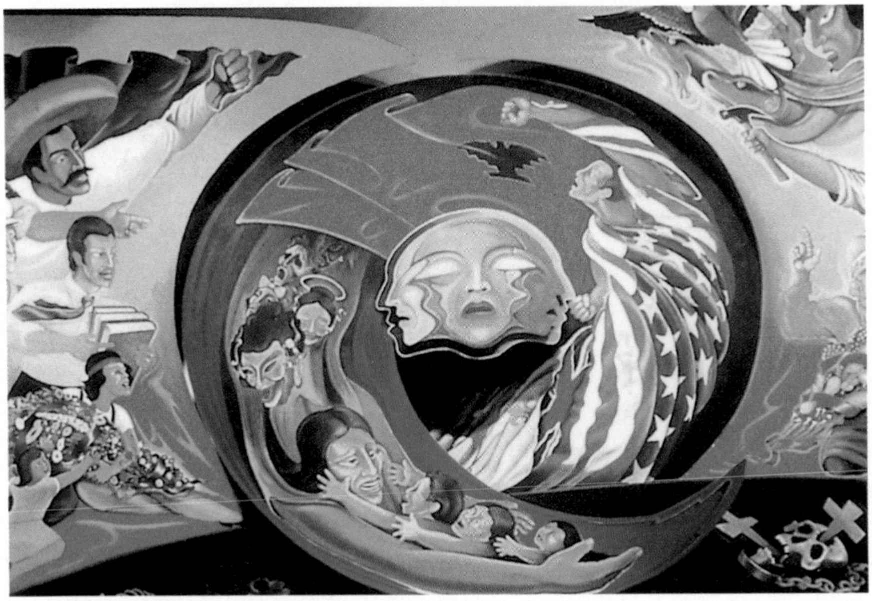

Leo Tanguma, **La antorcha de Quetzalcoatl**

Para conversar

16. ¿Qué color te gusta? (*What color do you like?*)
Conduct a survey of your classmates to find out which color is the most popular.

Modelo S1: *¿Qué color te gusta?*
S2: *Me gusta el color...*
S1: El color más popular es el ______.

17. ¡Somos pintores! (*We are painters!*) See if your partner knows what colors can be formed by mixing the primary colors.

Modelo S1: ¿Qué color forman el ______ y el ______?
S2: Forman el color ______.

LEARNING TIP
As you look at the world around you, try to name, in Spanish, the colors you see. Remember that it is always best to go from the concept to the target language (Spanish) and vice versa.

4 Days of the week *(Los días de la semana)*

—¿Qué día es hoy? **¿Sábado?**	*What day is today? Saturday?*
—No, hoy es **viernes.**	*No, today is Friday.*

› In Spanish-speaking countries, the week starts on Monday (although in some calendars it is common to see Sunday as the first day).

› The days of the week are not capitalized in Spanish.

› The days of the week are masculine in Spanish. The masculine definite articles **el** and **los** are often used with them to express *on*.

› All the days of the week use the same form for the singular and plural **(el lunes – los lunes)**. The only exceptions are **sábado** and **domingo** **(el sábado – los sábados).**

LEARNING TIP
Every day, when you get up, tell yourself: "**Hoy es...** (+ the day of the week)."

Práctica

18. ¿Qué día es? Knowing that **mañana** means *tomorrow* and **pasado mañana** means the *day after tomorrow*, give information following the model.

Modelo Hoy es lunes.
Mañana es martes y pasado mañana es miércoles.

1. Hoy es sábado.
2. Hoy es miércoles.
3. Hoy es viernes.
4. Hoy es domingo.
5. Hoy es jueves.
6. Hoy es martes.

19. En agosto Using the calendar on page 15, take turns asking a classmate what day a certain date falls on.

Modelo S1: *¿Qué día es el dos de agosto?*
S2: *Es martes.*

Para conversar

20. La guía de televisión With a partner, take turns naming different programs from **el canal 27,** saying on what days they are shown. Then keep asking questions about programs that you watch regularly.

Modelo S1: *¿¡Fútbol!?*
S2: *Los sábados.*

canal 27
Su canal hispano

Programación de la mañana 9:00–12:00

	9:00–10:00	10:00–11:00	11:00–12:00
LUNES	Buenos días, Los Ángeles	Programa educativo	Telenovela *María*
MARTES	Hospital General	Música latina	Tenis
MIÉRCOLES	Música y arte	Ciudades latinoamericanas	Programa político
JUEVES	Una clase de ejercicio	Jueves con Marisol	Noticias internacionales
VIERNES	Las aventuras de un tigre	Problemas sociales	Telenovela *Tú y Yo*
SÁBADO	Programa infantil	Música de México	Fútbol
DOMINGO	Religión	Gimnasia	Béisbol

5 Months and seasons of the year (*Los meses y las estaciones del año*)

A. Los meses

ENERO

L	M	M	J	V	S	D
					1	2
3	4	5	6	7	8	9
10	11	12	13	14	15	16
17	18	19	20	21	22	23
24/31	25	26	27	28	29	30

FEBRERO

L	M	M	J	V	S	D
	1	2	3	4	5	6
7	8	9	10	11	12	13
14	15	16	17	18	19	20
21	22	23	24	25	26	27
28						

MARZO

L	M	M	J	V	S	D
	1	2	3	4	5	6
7	8	9	10	11	12	13
14	15	16	17	18	19	20
21	22	23	24	25	26	27
28	29	30	31			

ABRIL

L	M	M	J	V	S	D
				1	2	3
4	5	6	7	8	9	10
11	12	13	14	15	16	17
18	19	20	21	22	23	24
25	26	27	28	29	30	

MAYO

L	M	M	J	V	S	D
						1
2	3	4	5	6	7	8
9	10	11	12	13	14	15
16	17	18	19	20	21	22
23/30	24/31	25	26	27	28	29

JUNIO

L	M	M	J	V	S	D
		1	2	3	4	5
6	7	8	9	10	11	12
13	14	15	16	17	18	19
20	21	22	23	24	25	26
27	28	29	30			

JULIO

L	M	M	J	V	S	D
				1	2	3
4	5	6	7	8	9	10
11	12	13	14	15	16	17
18	19	20	21	22	23	24
25	26	27	28	29	30	31

AGOSTO

L	M	M	J	V	S	D
1	2	3	4	5	6	7
8	9	10	11	12	13	14
15	16	17	18	19	20	21
22	23	24	25	26	27	28
29	30	31				

SEPTIEMBRE

L	M	M	J	V	S	D
			1	2	3	4
5	6	7	8	9	10	11
12	13	14	15	16	17	18
19	20	21	22	23	25	24
26	27	28	29	30		

OCTUBRE

L	M	M	J	V	S	D
					1	2
3	4	5	6	7	8	9
10	11	12	13	14	15	16
17	18	19	20	21	22	23
24/31	25	26	27	28	29	30

NOVIEMBRE

L	M	M	J	V	S	D
	1	2	3	4	5	6
7	8	9	10	11	12	13
14	15	16	17	18	19	20
21	22	23	24	25	26	27
28	29	30				

DICIEMBRE

L	M	M	J	V	S	D
			1	2	3	4
5	6	7	8	9	10	11
12	13	14	15	16	17	18
19	20	21	22	23	25	24
26	27	28	29	30	31	

› To ask for the date say:

—¿Qué fecha es hoy? — *What's the date today?*

› When giving the date, always begin with the phrase **"Hoy es el..."**

—Hoy es el cuatro de julio. — *Today is the fourth of July.*

› Begin with the number, followed by the preposition **de** (*of*), and then the month.

el seis de agosto — *August sixth*

—¿Qué fecha es hoy? ¿El treinta de abril? — *What's the date today? April thirtieth?*
—No, hoy es el primero de mayo. — *No, today is May first.*

› The article **el** is omitted when the day of the week is expressed.

Hoy es jueves, 20 de abril. — *Today is Thursday, April 20.*

¿Lo sabía Ud.?

Cuando en español damos (*we give*) una fecha como 10-8, no es el 8 de octubre sino (*but*) el 10 de agosto.

LEARNING TIP

Think of the birthdays of your friends and the members of your family. What are the dates? **"El cumpleaños de** (name) **es el** (day) **de** (month)."

B. Las estaciones del año

© Michael Thornton/Design Pics/Photolibrary

La primavera

© Mauritius/Photolibrary

El verano

© Luis Castaneda Inc./Riser/Getty Images

El otoño

© Chad Riley/Age Fotostock

El invierno

Un poema

CD1-6

Treinta días trae° noviembre,
con abril, junio y septiembre.
De veintiocho solo° hay uno,
y los demás,° de treinta y uno.

brings

only

los... *the others*

Práctica

21. El calendario With your partner, look at the dates circled on the calendar on page 17 and take turns saying them in Spanish.

22. ¿Qué estación te gusta? Conduct a survey of your classmates to find out which is their favorite season.

Modelo S1: *¿Cuál es tu estación favorita?*
S2: *Me gusta el (la)...*

23. Cumpleaños Imagine that these friends of yours live in the southern hemisphere. Knowing that the seasons are reversed there, can you indicate in which season their birthdays fall?

1. Mirta: 14 de febrero ________
2. Carlos: 25 de mayo ________
3. Marta: 7 de julio ________
4. Luis: 10 de marzo ________
5. Alina: 15 de octubre ________
6. Sara: 13 de agosto ________

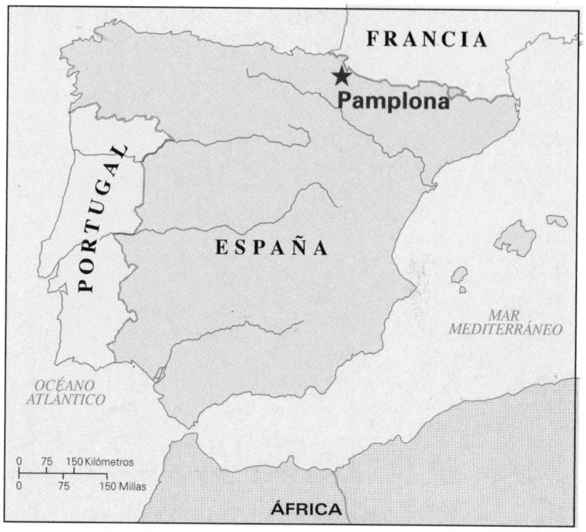

24. Una canción Listen to a folk song you would hear during the Feast of San Fermín in northern Spain. This feast is famous for bulls being let loose to chase people through the narrow streets of the old city of Pamplona. After listening to the song a couple of times, try to sing it.

CD1-7

Uno de enero,
dos de febrero,
tres de marzo,
cuatro de abril,
cinco de mayo,
seis de junio,
siete de julio,
San Fermín.

© Danny Lehman/Corbis

Celebración de San Fermín, en España (*Spain*)

ESTRUCTURAS

Para conversar

25. Oye, ¿cuál es tu signo? (*Listen, what's your sign?*) Survey your classmates to find out when everybody's birthday is and what sign everyone belongs to. For help, use the chart with the Zodiac and the corresponding dates.

Modelo —*¿Cuándo es tu cumpleaños?*
—*Es el dos de abril.*
—*¿Cuál es tu signo?*
—*Mi signo es Aries.*

Aries  21 de marzo a 19 de abril	**Tauro**  20 de abril a 20 de mayo	**Géminis**  21 de mayo a 21 de junio
Cáncer  22 de junio a 22 de julio	**Leo**  23 de julio a 22 de agosto	**Virgo**  23 de agosto a 21 de septiembre
Libra  22 de septiembre a 22 de octubre	**Escorpión**  23 de octubre a 21 de noviembre	**Sagitario**  22 de noviembre a 21 de diciembre
Capricornio  22 de diciembre a 19 de enero	**Acuario**  20 de enero a 19 de febrero	**Piscis**  20 de febrero a 20 de marzo

6 Subject pronouns (*Pronombres personales usados como sujetos*)

Singular		Plural	
yo	*I*	**nosotros** **nosotras**	*we* (*masc.*) *we* (*fem.*)
tú	*you* (*familiar*)	**vosotros** **vosotras**	*you* (*masc., familiar*) *you* (*fem., familiar*)
usted	*you* (*formal*)	**ustedes**	*you* (*formal*)
él	*he*	**ellos**	*they* (*masc.*)
ella	*she*	**ellas**	*they* (*fem.*)

› The **tú** form is used as the equivalent of *you* to address a friend, a coworker, a relative, or a child. The **usted** form is used in general to express deference or respect. In most Spanish-speaking countries today, young people tend to call each other **tú** even if they have just met. If in doubt, use **usted.**

› The plural form of **tú** is **vosotros(as)**, which is used only in Spain. In Latin America, the plural form **ustedes** (abbreviated **Uds.**) is used as the plural form of both **usted** (abbreviated **Ud.**) and **tú.**

› The masculine plural forms can refer to the masculine gender alone or to both genders together.

—¿De dónde son Diego y sus amigos? — *Where are Diego and his friends from?*
—Ellos son de Arizona. — *They are from Arizona.*
—¿Anita es de San Diego? — *Is Anita from San Diego?*
—Sí, ella es de San Diego. — *Yes, she is from San Diego.*
—¿De dónde son ustedes? — *Where are you from?*
—Nosotros somos de Texas. — *We are from Texas.*
—¿Tú eres estudiante? — *Are you a student?*
—Sí, yo soy estudiante de la Universidad de California. — *Yes, I am a student at the University of California.*

LEARNING TIP

Think of yourself talking to some of the people you know. What is your relationship to them? Formal? Informal? Whom would you call **tú**? Whom would you call **usted**? When would you use **ustedes**? Now picture yourself talking about them. What pronoun would you use to refer to a man? A woman? Two men? Two women? One of them and yourself?

¿Lo sabía Ud.?

En la cultura hispánica, los sobrenombres (*nicknames*) son muy populares. Por ejemplo, Anita es el sobrenombre de una persona que se llama Ana. Otros ejemplos: Carlos: Carlitos; Luis: Luisito. Otros sobrenombres no son diminutivos del nombre: Enrique: Quique; Dolores: Lola; José: Pepe; Mercedes: Mecha.

› **¿Qué sobrenombres son populares en inglés?**

ESTRUCTURAS

Práctica

26. ¿Quiénes somos? Identify the personal pronoun that corresponds to each picture below.

27. Pronombres Say what pronouns would be used to refer to the following people.

1. La doctora Soto ________
2. Carlos y yo (*masc.*) ________
3. Marcelo y Fernando ________
4. Ud. y Marité ________
5. Marité y sus amigas ________
6. Sara y yo (*fem.*) ________
7. un niño ________

28. **¿Tú, Ud., Uds.?** With your partner, take turns saying whether you would use **tú, usted,** or **ustedes** to address the following people.

1. Adriancito
2. your parents' elderly friend
3. two strangers
4. your math professor
5. your best friend
6. an older lady you just met
7. a twelve-year-old girl
8. three gentlemen you just met

Para conversar

29. **Habla con tu compañero(a)** With a partner, take turns asking and answering these questions in the affirmative. Use the appropriate subject pronouns.

1. ¿Ana es estudiante?
2. ¿Luis es de San Antonio?
3. ¿Olga y Eva son profesoras?
4. ¿Marcos y Sergio son de Texas?
5. ¿Sara y Juan son de México?

7 Present indicative of *ser* (*Presente de indicativo del verbo* **ser**)

ser ***to be***		
Singular		
yo	**soy**	*I am*
tú	**eres**	*you are (fam.)*
Ud.	**es**	*you are (form.)*
él	**es**	*he is*
ella	**es**	*she is*
Plural		
nosotros(as)	**somos**	*we are*
vosotros(as)	**sois**	*you are (fam.)*
Uds.	**son**	*you are (form.)*
ellos	**son**	*they are (masc.)*
ellas	**son**	*they are (fem.)*

ESTRUCTURAS

› The verb **ser**, *to be*, is irregular. Its forms, like the forms of other irregular verbs, must be memorized.

› The verb **ser** is commonly used to express identity, place of origin, occupation, characteristic, and nationality.

—¿De dónde **son** ustedes?	*Where are you from?*
—Nosotros **somos** de México.	*We are from Mexico.*
—¿Ud. **es** estudiante?	*Are you a student?*
—No, yo **soy** profesora.	*No, I am a professor.*

¡Atención! The indefinite article **(un, una)** is not used after the verb **ser** when describing profession, nationality, religion, or party affiliation, unless an adjective follows the noun.

La doctora Mena **es profesora.**

BUT: La doctora Mena **es una profesora excelente**.

LEARNING TIP
Say where several people that you know are from, including yourself and your family. Think of people individually and in pairs.

Un dicho *(A saying)*
El tiempo es oro (*gold*). Equivalent: *Time is money.*

Práctica

30. Minidiálogo Complete this conversation between two students, using the present indicative of the verb **ser**.

—¿El doctor Vega ________ profesor?
—Sí, él ________ profesor de español.
—¿De dónde ________ él?
—Él ________ de Colombia. ¿De dónde ________ Uds.?
—Nosotros ________ de Perú. ¿Marité y Sara ________ de California?
—No, ellas ________ de Colorado. ¿De dónde ________ tú?
—Yo ________ de Arizona.

31. ¿De dónde somos? Write a sentence to say where these people are from, using the information in the illustration on page 25.

1. ellos ____________________
2. tú ____________________
3. Juan, Mario y José ____________________
4. Carlos y yo ____________________
5. yo ____________________
6. nosotras ____________________
7. Teresa ____________________
8. ustedes ____________________

¿Lo sabía Ud.?

En los Estados Unidos, la influencia hispánica se nota en nombres de estados (*states*) como Colorado (*red*), Texas (*tiles*), Nevada (*snowed*), Montana (*mountain*), y ciudades (*cities*) como Sacramento, San Francisco, Santa Bárbara y El Paso (*the pass*). En Canadá, un ejemplo es el de la Península de El Labrador (*the farmer*).

› **En su (*your*) estado, ¿hay ciudades o calles (*streets*) con nombres en español? ¿Cuáles?**

Para conversar

32. **¡Habla con tu compañero(a)!** (*Speak with your partner!*) Ask each other information about yourselves, your friends, and your relatives. Use the verb **ser,** paying atention to the correct conjugation. You should ask at least four questions. Then join another pair of students and tell them about yourselves.

Modelo —*¿Quién* (Who) *eres tú?*
—*Soy Eduardo.*
—*¿De dónde son tus padres* (parents)*?*
—*Mis padres son de Ecuador...*

¡Vamos a ver!

Antes de ver el video *(Before watching the video)*

33. Preguntas With a partner, take turns responding to the following statements or questions.

1. Hola. Tú eres ____________,[1] ¿verdad?
2. ¿Cómo te llamas (tú)?
3. ¡Mucho gusto!
4. ¿Cómo te va?
5. ¿Qué hay de nuevo?
6. ¿De dónde eres tú?
7. ¿De dónde es tu papá?, ¿Y tu mamá?
8. ¡Encantado(a)!
9. ¿Cuál es tu número de teléfono?
10. ¿Hay una fiesta (*party*) hoy?
11. Hoy es mi cumpleaños.
12. Nos vemos el ____________.[2]

El video: Un día con María Inés

© Cengage Learning

—¿Cómo se llama, señorita?

—Me llamo María Inés Hidalgo.

© Cengage Learning

—Hasta mañana. Saludos a Teresa.

—Gracias.

© Cengage Learning

—Hola, ¿cómo te llamas?

—Carlitos.

© Cengage Learning

—Yo soy de Los Ángeles, ¿y ustedes?

—Nosotros somos de Arizona.

[1]your partner's name
[2]the day you'll see your partner again

Después de ver el video *(After watching the video)*

María Inés

el Dr. Trujillo

la señora

Rodolfo

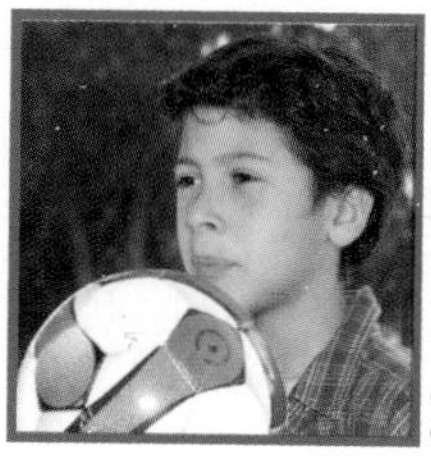
Carlitos

el Sr. Paz

34. ¿Quién lo dice? (*Who says it?*) Identify the person who said the following in the dialogues.

1. Sí... es mi cumpleaños.
2. Oye..., ¿hay una fiesta hoy?
3. Tres-ocho-seis-nueve-cuatro-siete-dos.
4. Nosotros somos de Arizona. Usted es estudiante, ¿verdad?
5. Hasta mañana. Saludos a Teresa.
6. Tome asiento, por favor.

35. Hablemos With a partner, take turns asking and answering the following questions. Base your answers on the dialogues.

1. ¿El doctor Trujillo es profesor o estudiante?
2. ¿De dónde es María Inés?
3. ¿De dónde es el papá de María Inés?
4. ¿Es el cumpleaños de María Inés o el cumpleaños de Carlitos?
5. ¿La fiesta es hoy o mañana?
6. ¿De dónde son el señor Paz y sus (*his*) amigos?
7. ¿La mamá de María Inés es mexicana o norteamericana?
8. ¿María Inés es estudiante de la Universidad de California o de la Universidad de Arizona?

36. ¿Qué pasa después? You and a partner, use your imagination to write exchanges that will take place the next day between the following people.

1. Dr. Trujillo and Miss Hidalgo
2. María Inés and Rodolfo
3. María Inés and Sergio
4. Rodolfo and Sergio
5. Dr. Trujillo, Rodolfo, and Sergio
6. Rodolfo and the lady at the cafeteria
7. Mr. Paz and Dr. Trujillo
8. Sergio and Carlitos
9. Now compare the exchanges you wrote with those of another group.

Así somos. = *This is the way we are.*

¡Vamos a escuchar!

ESTRATEGIA **Listening for the main idea** Learning to listen in a foreign language takes practice. Throughout the course, you will practice a variety of techniques to help make the process easier. When you listen for the main idea, focus on getting the general idea of what you hear. Don't worry about understanding every word; just try to grasp what a conversation or passage is about.

CD1-8 **37. Una llamada de teléfono** Rosalía calls Jorge to check on some information. Listen to their phone call and, in one or two words, jot down what the subject of the conversation is.

¡Vamos a conversar!

ESTRATEGIA **Speaking for basic communication** Throughout your study of Spanish, you will be learning to express yourself orally, first with very basic ideas and gradually with greater sophistication. As you start to speak Spanish, remember the following tips.

Keep it simple. Use the vocabulary and structures you already know.

Try to speak clearly and accurately, but don't be afraid to make mistakes.

Use short sentences or phrases to convey what you want to say until you feel more comfortable using Spanish.

Talk to yourself and others whenever you can, using the Spanish you learn in each class.

38. Hola, ¿qué tal? Greet a classmate you don't know well and use the following questions to get to know him or her. Introduce yourself and ask questions. Then answer your classmate's questions in short form using the right conjugation.

Modelo —*¿Cómo te llamas?*
—*Me llamo Bernardo.*
—*¿De dónde eres?*
—*Soy de Argentina...*

39. ¿Cómo somos? Using the appropriate forms of the verb **ser**, describe the following people, using the characteristics below. Then, with a partner, talk about yourselves and your loved ones.

yo
mi mamá
mi papá
mis amigos
mis amigos y yo
tú

cómico(a)
realista
optimista
pesimista
estudioso(a)
paciente (impaciente)
atlético(a)
inteligente
conservador(a)
liberal
romántico(a)
tímido(a)

HINT: If the subject is plural, add an **-s** to the adjective if it ends in a vowel. Add **-es** if it ends in a consonant.

40. **¿Qué dice Ud.?** (*What do you say?*) What would you say in the following situations? What might the other person say? Act out scenes with a partner. Take turns playing each role.

1. You greet your instructor in the morning and ask how he/she is.
2. Someone comes to see you. You tell this person to come in and offer him/her a seat.
3. You ask a lady what her name is and then you ask her ten-year-old daughter what her name is.
4. Someone is introduced to you.
5. You greet a friend and ask him how he is and what's new.
6. You ask some new acquaintances where they are from and tell them where you are from.
7. You ask a classmate what his/her phone number is.
8. You are not sure what day today is. You also ask the date.

41. **Para conocernos mejor** (*To get to know each other better*) Work with a classmate whom you would like to get to know better. Take turns asking each other these questions.

1. Hola, ¿cómo estás?
2. ¿Cómo te llamas?
3. ¿De dónde eres?
4. ¿Cómo eres? ¿Eres optimista, pesimista o realista?
5. ¿Cuál es tu número de teléfono?
6. ¿En qué mes es tu cumpleaños?
7. ¿Cuál es tu signo?
8. ¿Qué color te gusta?

42. **Una encuesta** (*A survey*) Interview your classmates to identify who fits the following descriptions. Include your instructor, but remember to use the **Ud.** form when addressing him/her. After finishing the survey, get together with two or three classmates and discuss the results.

1. Es de otro estado. ____________	6. Es conservador(a). ____________
2. Es pesimista. ____________	7. Es atlético(a). ____________
3. Es estudioso(a). ____________	8. Es inteligente. ____________
4. Es romántico(a). ____________	9. Es del signo de Virgo. ____________
5. Es paciente. ____________	10. Es liberal. ____________

43. **Para crear** In groups of three, look at this photo and use your imagination to create a story about the people in the picture. Who are they? Give them names. Are they students? Where are they from? What might they say to each other? In general, what's the story behind the photo?

¡Vamos a leer![1]

Antes de leer *(Before reading)*

ESTRATEGIA **Recognizing cognates** Many times Spanish words that look like English ones also have the same or very similar meanings. These words are cognates **(cognados)**. You have seen numerous cognates in this lesson, for example, **color, programa, alfabeto,** and the months of the year.

¡Atención! Although Spanish-English cognates look alike, they are pronounced differently.

44. Cognados Look over the following reading and make a list of all the cognates you find. Use your knowledge of common academic subjects in English to help you.

45. Comprensión As you read the information about the five professors, find the answers to the following questions.

1. ¿De dónde es el profesor Vargas? ¿Qué enseña (*teaches*)?
2. ¿De qué estado (*state*) es la doctora Díaz? ¿Qué clase enseña?
3. ¿De qué país (*country*) es el profesor de música? ¿Cómo se llama?
4. ¿Quién enseña literatura?
5. ¿Qué profesores son de Colombia?
6. ¿Qué enseña Jorge Pérez?
7. ¿Qué días enseña el Dr. Vargas?
8. ¿Qué días no enseña la doctora Ana Díaz?
9. ¿Quién enseña los sábados?
10. ¿Qué enseña la profesora Rojas?
11. La profesora Rojas probablemente enseña literatura argentina, ¿no?
12. ¿El Dr. Pérez enseña solamente (*only*) por la mañana y por la tarde?

UNIVERSIDAD CENTRAL • Nuevos profesores

©Layland Masuda/Shutterstock

Dr. Luis Vargas
de Lima, Perú
Profesor de español
Enseña los lunes, miércoles y viernes.

©Lisa F. Young/Shutterstock

Dra. Ana Díaz
de San Diego, CA
Profesora de historia
Enseña todos los días excepto el viernes.

©Jack Hollingsworth/PhotoDisc/Getty Images

Sergio Álvarez
de Santiago, Chile
Profesor de música
Enseña una clase los sábados.

©Huntstock/Getty Images

Dra. Eva Rojas
de Medellín, Colombia
Profesora de literatura
Enseña literatura hispanoamericana.

©Monkey Business Images/Shutterstock

Dr. Jorge Pérez
de Bogotá, Colombia
Profesor de economía.
Enseña una clase por la noche.

[1] Let's read!

Después de leer… desde tu mundo *(from your world)*

46. Información Give some information about yourself.

NOMBRE Y APELLIDO: ______
SOY DE: ______
ESTUDIO: ______
VIVO[1] EN: ______
ESTUDIO LOS DÍAS: ______
TRABAJO LOS DÍAS: ______

As a class, create your own class directory with five students with whom you may share study time, including this and any other useful information you wish to include.

¡Vamos a escribir!

Antes de escribir *(Before writing)*

ESTRATEGIA **Generating ideas by brainstorming** Before beginning to write, you need to generate ideas about a topic. Brainstorming is like thinking aloud. Allow your mind to wander and write down all of your thoughts and ideas about your topic. When brainstorming, avoid censoring your ideas. You can discard the least useful or interesting ideas later before you actually write.

¡A escribir!

47. Un mensaje electrónico (*An e-mail*) You will be exchanging e-mails with a Spanish-speaking student from another state. Before writing your e-mail, brainstorm the types of information and questions you can include.

1. Jot down information that you can provide about yourself. Include name, origin, nationality, where you are a student, characteristics, etc.
2. Write the questions you want to ask him or her.
3. Now organize your thoughts and the ideas from your brainstorming and write a draft **(borrador)** of the e-mail. Begin your e-mail with **Hola** and close with a farewell phrase.

Después de escribir

48. A revisar Before writing the final version of your e-mail, your instructor might want you to exchange your first draft with that of a classmate and peer edit each other's work. Use the following two guidelines.

- correct use of subject pronouns
- formation and agreement (with subject) of the verb **ser**

[1] I live.

EL MUNDO HISPÁNICO Y TÚ

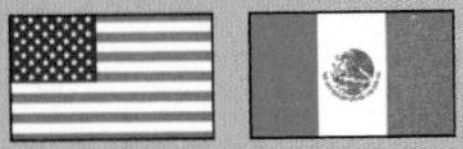

Los mexicoamericanos

Tú probablemente conoces (*know*) a muchos mexicoamericanos. Están (*They are*) en las escuelas, en las universidades, en los lugares de trabajo (*places of work*) y en las iglesias. La mayoría se ha adaptado a la cultura norteamericana, pero conserva su lengua, su música, su comida (*food*) y su unidad familiar. Muchos se destacan (*stand out*) en la educación, en la política, en las artes y en la literatura.

La política

© AP Photo/Nick Ut

Antonio Villaraigosa: Alcalde (*Mayor*) de Los Ángeles, California. Es el tercer (*third*) mexicoamericano elegido (*elected*) alcalde de esa ciudad.

© AP Photo/William Faulkner

Susana Martínez, mexicoamericana, es la primera gobernadora hispana de un estado americano: Nuevo México.

Las artes plásticas

El muralismo mexicoamericano

© Leo Tanguma

La antorcha de Quetzalcoatl de Leo Tanguma

El pensamiento y la literatura

La imaginación literaria mexicoamericana

© Ulf Andersen/Getty Images

Sandra Cisneros: escritora mexicoamericana famosa por escribir novelas sobre la cultura chicana, como *La casa en Mango Street.*

Las celebraciones y diversiones con amigos mexicoamericanos

© Danita Delimont / Alamy

El Cinco de Mayo es una fiesta tradicional de los mexicanos en Estados Unidos. Celebran la victoria de los mexicanos sobre los franceses en Puebla, México.

Los Estados Unidos hispánicos y el español en el mundo

Más (*More*) del 5% de los habitantes del mundo (*world*) hablan (*speak*) español. En los Estados Unidos, hay unos 40.000.000 de hispanos y la mayoría hablan este idioma (*language*) como primera (*first*) lengua. La influencia hispana se nota también (*also*) en otros aspectos de la vida (*life*), como en la comida, la arquitectura y la música. En las universidades y en las escuelas secundarias de este país (*country*), miles (*thousands*) de estudiantes estudian español.

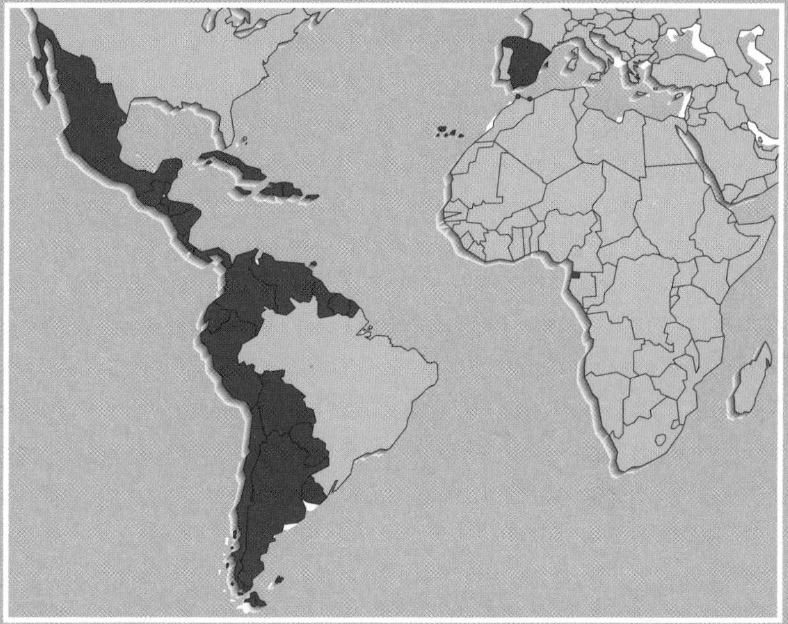

© Cengage Learning

Se habla español en España, todos los países de Hispanoamérica, Ceuta y Melilla (territorios españoles en África) y en Guinea Ecuatorial (África).

Ahora, dime... (*Now, tell me . . .*)

With a partner, take turns asking and answering the following questions.

1. ¿Qué otros políticos mexicanoamericanos conoces tú?
2. ¿Tú celebras el 5 de mayo?
3. ¿Te gusta la comida mexicana?
4. ¿Hay muchas personas de habla hispana (*Spanish speaking*) en tu ciudad (*city*)?
5. ¿Te gusta la música mexicana?

iLrn™

To learn more about Hispanic communities in the United States, watch the cultural footage in the Media Library.

AUTOPRUEBA

¿Cuánto sé ahora?

Take this test. When you have finished, check your answers in the answer key provided in Appendix D. Then use a red pen to correct any mistakes you may have made. Are you ready?

A. The alphabet Spell out these last names in Spanish. Add the names of the missing consonants.

1. Fox: ________ o ________
2. Wilson: ________ i ________ ________ o ________
3. Kurt: ________ u ________ ________
4. Jackson: ________ a ________ ________ ________ o ________
5. Budge: ________ u ________ ________ e
6. Hill: ________ i ________ ________
7. McDevit: ________ ________ ________ e ________ i ________
8. Perry: ________ e ________ ________
9. Quentin: ________ u e ________ ________ i ________
10. Zeller: ________ e ________ ________ e ________

B. Cardinal numbers (0–39) Write the following numbers in Spanish.

1. 0 ________________
2. 11 ________________
3. 20 ________________
4. 14 ________________
5. 10 ________________
6. 7 ________________
7. 12 ________________
8. 30 ________________
9. 13 ________________
10. 15 ________________
11. 38 ________________
12. 25 ________________

C. Colors What colors come to mind when you think of the following?

1. a banana ________________
2. a pumpkin ________________
3. coal ________________
4. a leaf ________________
5. coffee ________________
6. a plum ________________
7. rosy cheeks ________________
8. an elephant ________________
9. the American flag ________________
10. an apple ________________

D. Days of the week Complete the following list of days in order.

________, lunes, ________, miércoles, ________, viernes, ________

E. Months of the year Write the dates of the following celebrations.

1. Halloween: ________________
2. Independence Day: ________________
3. The first day of the year: ________________
4. Valentine's Day: ________________
5. Christmas: ________________
6. Veteran's Day: ________________

F. Seasons of the year In what season do the following months fall in this country?

1. agosto: ______________________
2. abril: ______________________
3. enero: ______________________
4. noviembre: ______________________

G. Subject pronouns and the present indicative of *ser* Complete the following dialogue, using the present indicative of the verb **ser**.

—¿Ustedes ________ de California?

—Sí, nosotros ________ de California. ¿De dónde ________ tú?

—Yo ________ de Colorado. ¿De dónde ________ Eva y Luis?

—Eva ________ de Arizona y Luis ________ de Nuevo México.

H. Just words . . . Complete the following, using vocabulary from Lesson 1.

1. —________ días, señora. ¿Cómo ________ usted?

   —________, gracias. ¿Qué hay de ________?

   —No ________.

2. —________ tardes. ¿Usted es estudiante de la ________ de California?

   —Sí, señor. ________ gusto.

   —El gusto es ________. ________ asiento, por ________.

3. —Hola, Gloria. ¿Qué ________?

   —________ bien, gracias. ¿Y ________?

   —Bien, gracias. ¡Oye! ¿Qué ________ es hoy?

   —Hoy es el trece de agosto. ________ mi cumpleaños.

   —________ cumpleaños!

   —Gracias. Bueno, nos ________ mañana.

   —Sí, ________ mañana. ¡________ a Marisa!

I. Cultura

1. Answer the following questions, based on information from the **¿Lo sabía usted?** sections.
   a. ¿Cuál es un nombre de mujer muy popular en España y en Latinoamérica?
   b. ¿Cuál es el sobrenombre de Dolores?
   c. ¿Y de Enrique?
2. Answer the following questions, based on the information found in the **El mundo hispánico y tú** section.
   a. ¿Cuántos millones de hispanos hay en los Estados Unidos aproximadamente?

   b. ¿Quién es Sandra Cisneros?

J. Un dicho Do you remember the Spanish saying about the importance of time? Find it in this lesson.

LECCIÓN 2

EN LA UNIVERSIDAD

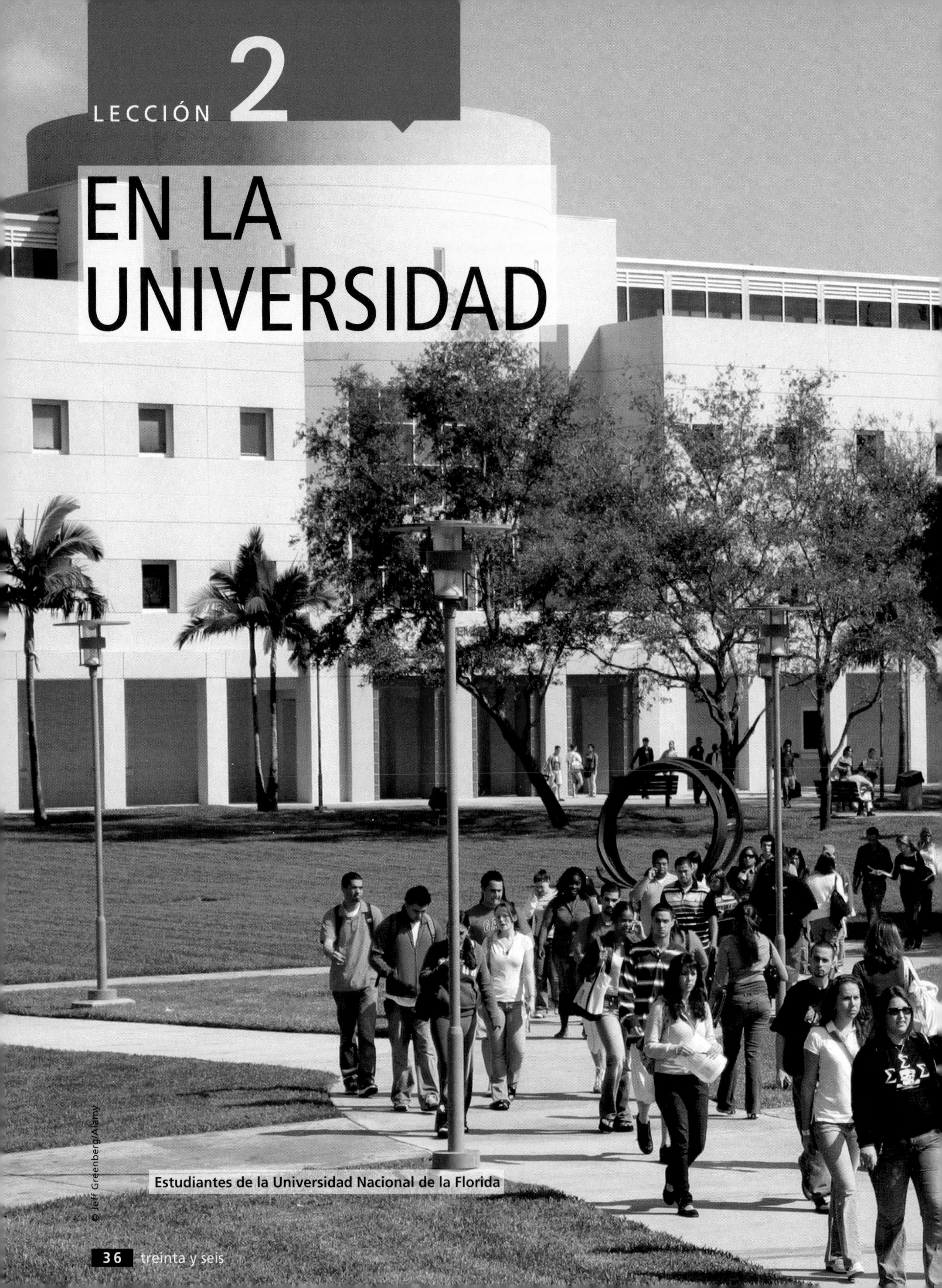

Estudiantes de la Universidad Nacional de la Florida

OBJETIVOS COMUNICATIVOS

You will learn vocabulary related to the classroom, useful questions and answers, and some polite expressions.

SITUACIONES

Si necesitas ayuda...

ESTRUCTURAS

1 Gender and number
2 Definite and indefinite articles
3 Cardinal numbers 31–100
4 Telling time
5 Present indicative of regular **-ar** verbs
6 Negative and interrogative sentences
7 Possession with **de**

ASÍ SOMOS

¡Vamos a ver!
Watching and understanding situations

¡Vamos a escuchar!
Listening for specifics and guessing intelligently

¡Vamos a conversar!
Asking for repetition

¡Vamos a leer!
Guessing the meaning of unknown words

¡Vamos a escribir!
Conducting and reporting an interview

EL MUNDO HISPÁNICO Y TÚ

› Los cubanoamericanos

AUTOPRUEBA

You will review what you learned in this lesson.

LOS CUBANOAMERICANOS Más de medio (*a half*) millón de cubanos viven en Miami, donde ejercen una gran influencia cultural y económica. Antes de la llegada (*arrival*) de los cubanos en 1959, Miami era (*was*) fundamentalmente un centro turístico. Hoy es un centro industrial y comercial de primer orden (*first-class*) y el puente (*bridge*) que une la economía de los Estados Unidos con la de Latinoamérica y con la de España (*Spain*).

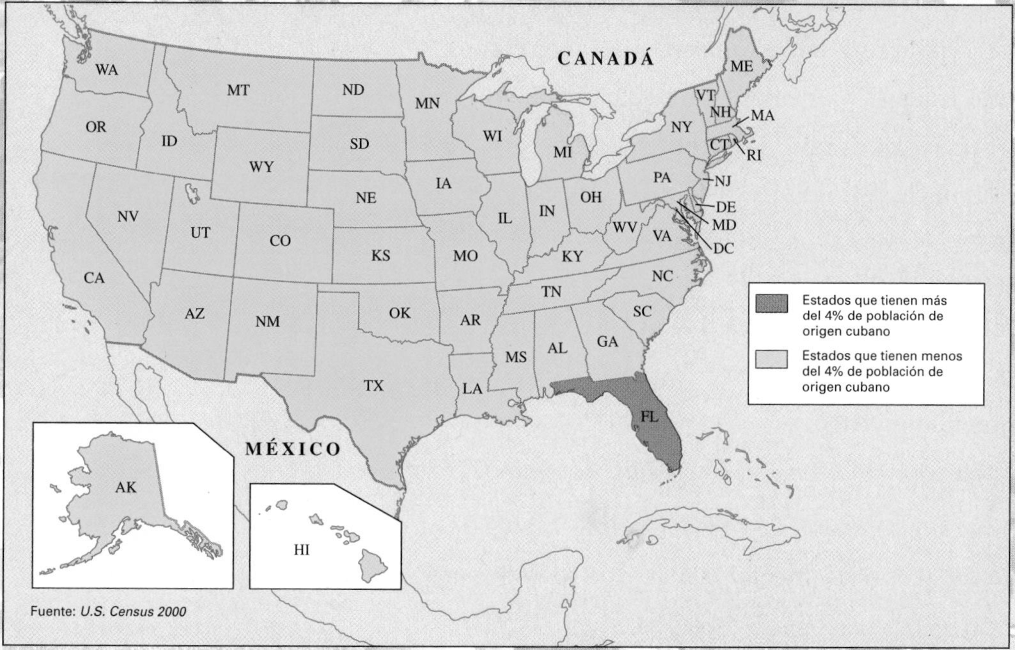

Recursos iLrn video audio web playlist

Si necesitas ayuda...

CD1-9

© Cengage Learning

¡Ubíquelos!

Carmen and Sergio study at the Universidad Internacional de la Florida. Watch the Miami video to get a sense of their surroundings.

© Stephen Coburn/Shutterstock

Sergio, un chico cubanoamericano, conversa con Carmen, una chica de Guadalajara, México. Los dos son estudiantes de la Universidad Internacional de la Florida, en Miami, y toman una clase de matemáticas juntos.

SERGIO: ¿Cuántas clases tomas tú, Carmen?

CARMEN: Yo tomo solamente tres clases, porque trabajo treinta horas por semana.

SERGIO: Yo tomo seis clases este semestre, pero no trabajo tanto.

CARMEN: Yo necesito trabajar, y además... no hablo muy bien el inglés. Es un idioma difícil...

SERGIO: ¡No, chica! ¡El inglés es fácil! Si necesitas ayuda...

CARMEN: ¿En serio? ¡Sí! Necesito practicar todos los días, y mis padres solamente hablan español.

SERGIO: Yo trabajo en el hospital por la mañana y estudio por la noche. ¿Deseas estudiar conmigo el sábado por la tarde?

CARMEN: ¡Perfecto! ¿A las dos? ¿En mi casa o en la biblioteca?

SERGIO: En tu casa. ¿Cuál es tu dirección?

CARMEN: Calle Siete, número cien.

SERGIO: (*Anota la dirección de Carmen.*) Muy bien. Nos vemos el sábado a las dos de la tarde.

El sábado, Sergio llega a la casa de Carmen a las dos y media.

SERGIO: ¿Qué hora es? ¿Las dos y media? ¡Lo siento! Yo llego tarde a todas partes. ¡No soy muy puntual!

CARMEN: ¡No hay problema! ¿Deseas una taza de café?

SERGIO: Sí, por favor.

Carmen: Siéntate. Oye, ¿cómo se dice "química" en inglés?

Sergio: Se dice "*chemistry*". ¿Por qué?

Carmen: Porque necesito tomar una clase de química el semestre próximo.

Sergio: ¡Yo también! ¡Pero la química es difícil!

Carmen: No, es fácil. Si necesitas ayuda...

Sergio: ¡Sí! ¿Estudiamos juntos?

Carmen: ¡Buena idea! ¿Otra taza de café... ?

¿Lo sabía Ud.?

Una expresión muy común entre (*among*) cubanos es **chico(a)** (*young man/girl*), equivalente a las expresiones "*dude*" y "*girl*".

› **¿Son muy populares estas expresiones en este país?**

1. **Hablemos** With a partner, take turns asking and answering the following questions. Base your answers on the dialogues and on your own circumstances.

En el diálogo

1. ¿Sergio es americano?
2. ¿Cuántas clases toma Carmen?
3. ¿Sergio trabaja o no trabaja?
4. ¿Carmen habla bien o no habla bien el inglés?
5. ¿Carmen y Sergio estudian juntos?
6. ¿Cuál es la dirección de Carmen?
7. ¿Sergio es puntual o no es puntual?
8. ¿Qué desea tomar Sergio?

¿Y tú?

1. ¿Tú eres americano(a)?
2. ¿Cuántas clases tomas tú?
3. ¿Tú trabajas o solo estudias?
4. ¿Tú hablas bien el español?
5. ¿Dónde estudias tú?
6. ¿Cuál es tu dirección?
7. ¿Tú eres puntual o no eres puntual?
8. ¿Tú deseas tomar café?

¿Lo sabía Ud.?

Cuando los hispanos dan (*give*) una dirección, usan primero la palabra **calle** o **avenida**, luego (*then*) dan el nombre de la calle o avenida y luego el número: Calle Quinta #120.

› **Además (*Besides*) de la palabra "*street*", ¿qué otras palabras usan en este país cuando dan (*they give*) una dirección?**

VOCABULARIO

En el diálogo

Cognados

cubanoamericano(a)[1]	*Cuban American*
el hospital	*hospital*
la idea	*idea*
internacional	*international*
las matemáticas	*mathematics, math*
perfecto(a)	*perfect*
el problema	*problem*
puntual	*punctual*
el semestre	*semester*

Nombres

la ayuda	*help*
la biblioteca	*library*
el café	*coffee*
la calle	*street*
la casa	*house*
la chica, muchacha	*girl*
el chico, muchacho	*young man, boy*
la dirección, el domicilio	*address*
el español	*Spanish (language)*
la hora	*hour, time (of day)*
el idioma, la lengua	*language*
la mañana	*morning*
la noche	*evening, night*
los padres	*parents*
la química	*chemistry*
la semana	*week*
la tarde	*afternoon*
la taza	*cup*

Verbos

anotar	*to write down*
conversar, platicar	*to talk, to converse*
desear	*to wish, to want*
estudiar	*to study*
hablar	*to speak*
llegar	*to arrive*
necesitar	*to need*
practicar	*to practice*
tomar	*to take (e.g., a class)*
trabajar	*to work*

Adjetivos

difícil	*difficult*
fácil	*easy*
juntos(as)	*together*
mis	*my*
otro(a)	*other, another*
próximo(a)	*next*
todos(as)	*all, every*

Otras palabras y expresiones

a todas partes, a todos lados	*everywhere*
además	*besides*
¿Cómo se dice… ?[2]	*How does one say . . . ?*
con	*with*
conmigo	*with me*
¿cuántos(as)?	*how many?*
de la tarde[3]	*in the afternoon*
¿En serio?	*Seriously?*
este semestre	*this semester*
llegar tarde	*to be late*
Lo siento.	*I'm sorry.*
los (las) dos	*both (of them)*
No hay problema.	*(There's) no problem.*
o	*or*
pero	*but*
por la mañana	*in the morning*
por la noche	*in the evening*
por la tarde	*in the afternoon*
¿por qué?	*why?*
por semana	*per week*
porque	*because*
se dice…	*one says . . .*
si	*if, whether*
solamente, solo	*only*
también	*also, too*
todos los días	*every day*
un (una)	*a, an*

[1] **cubano(a)** *Cuban;* **americano(a)** *American* (Names [and adjectives] of nationalities are not capitalized in Spanish.)

[2] **¿Qué quiere decir __?** *What does __ mean?*

[3] When speaking of specific time: **las *tres de* la tarde**.

Más sobre el tema

Vocabulario para la clase

Otros idiomas

alemán	*German*
chino	*Chinese*
francés	*French*
italiano	*Italian*
japonés	*Japanese*
portugués	*Portuguese*
ruso	*Russian*

LEARNING TIP

You may want to rewrite the words that you're learning in a way that they appear grouped or rearranged under specific categories or themes. For instance, words about the classroom (**la mochila, la ventana, el escritorio, la computadora,** etc.), parts of the day (**la tarde, la noche**), languages (**el español, el francés, el chino**), adjectives of nationality (**español[a], francés [francesa], chino[a]**), etc. Write down all thematically related words under the specific core theme or category of meaning (semantic field).

Práctica

2. ¿Qué es? Write the word or phrase from the vocabulary that corresponds to the following.

1. seis meses ________
2. lugar (*place*) donde vivimos (*we live*) ________
3. domicilio ________
4. Necesito una para tomar café. ________
5. opuesto de **difícil** ________
6. Nunca (*Never*) llega tarde. ________
7. solo ________
8. persona de Cuba ________
9. lugar donde hay muchos libros ________
10. lengua ________
11. platicar ________
12. chico ________
13. siete días ________
14. opuesto de **por la mañana** ________

3. En la clase Review the words referring to people and objects you see in the classroom, then name the numbered items below.

4. Para completar Complete the following sentences, using appropriate vocabulary.

1. Mi domicilio es: ____________ Ocho, número 98.
2. Sandra es una ____________ cubanoamericana y Julio es un ____________ de El Salvador.
3. El chino es un ____________ muy difícil.
4. ¿Cómo se ____________ *backpack* en español? Se dice "mochila".
5. Tú necesitas ____________ el español todos los ____________, de lunes a viernes.
6. Sandra ____________ con otros estudiantes en español para practicar.
7. Julio ____________ cinco clases este semestre.
8. ¿Tú hablas cinco idiomas? ¡Caramba! ¿En ____________?

Para conversar

5. **Para conocernos mejor** You need to complete the following card with information about a classmate. First, write the questions that would elicit the appropriate information. Then interview someone in your class and fill out the card. You may also ask additional questions.

> **Mi compañero(a) se llama:** ____________________
>
> **Es de:** ____________________
>
> **Dirección:** ____________________
>
> **Número de teléfono:** ____________________
>
> **Estudia los días:** ____________________
>
> **Trabaja en:** ____________________

6. **Una escuelita** (*A little school*) With a partner, play the roles of two people who are in charge of opening a small school for about 50 children. Take turns saying what you need for two classrooms. (Necesitamos...)

7. **Idiomas** With a partner, take turns saying what languages they speak in the following capitals. Then add other cities from different parts of the world.

Modelo *—¿Qué idioma hablan en Beijing?*
—En Beijing hablan chino.

Washington	Brasilia	San Salvador	Moscú
Madrid	Lima	París	Bogotá
Roma	Tokio	Berlín	

Pronunciación

CD1-10 **A. The Spanish *i***

The Spanish **i** is pronounced like the double e in the English word *see*. Listen to your teacher and repeat the following sentences.

El chino es difícil. Es el domicilio de Mimí.
El inglés es fácil.

CD1-11 **B. The Spanish *o***

The Spanish **o** is a short, pure vowel. It corresponds to the *o* in the English word *no*, but without the glide. Listen to your teacher and repeat the following sentences.

Yo no tomo. Hablo un poco de chino.
Trabajo con Rodolfo.

CD1-12 **C. The Spanish *u***

The Spanish **u** is shorter in length than the English *u*. It corresponds to the *ue* sound in the English word *Sue*. Listen to your teacher and repeat the following sentences.

Mucho gusto, Julio. Estudia en la universidad.
Laura usa uniforme.

ESTRUCTURAS

1 Gender and number (*Género y número*)

A. Gender

- In Spanish, all nouns—including those denoting nonliving things—are either masculine or feminine.
- Most nouns that end in **-o** are masculine, while most nouns that end in **-a** are feminine.

el escritorio

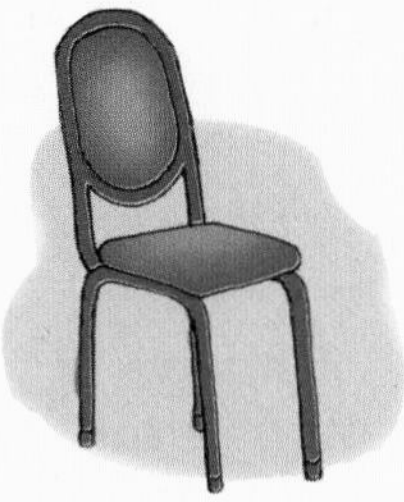

la silla

el libro

la ventana

- Nouns that denote males are masculine and nouns that denote females are feminine.

el hombre

la mujer

¡Atención! Some common exceptions include the words **el día** (*day*) and **el mapa** (*map*), which end in **-a** but are masculine, and the word **la mano** (*hand*), which ends in **-o** but is feminine.

Here are some helpful rules to remember about gender.

- Some masculine names ending in **-o** have a corresponding feminine form ending in **-a: el secretario / la secretaria.**
- When a masculine noun ends in a consonant, the corresponding feminine noun is often formed by adding **-a: el profesor / la profesora.**
- Many nouns that refer to people use the same form for both genders: **el estudiante / la estudiante.** In such cases, gender is indicated by the article **el** (masculine) or **la** (feminine).
- Nouns ending in **-sión, -ción, -tad, -dad,** and **-umbre** are feminine.

  la televisión *television*
  la conversación *conversation*
  la libertad *liberty, freedom*
  la universidad *university*
  la muchedumbre *crowd*

- Many words that end in **-ma** are masculine.[1]

  el poema *poem*
  el programa *program*
  el sistema *system*
  el idioma *language*
  el problema *problem*
  el tema *subject, theme*
  el clima, *climate*

- You must learn the gender of nouns that have other endings and that do not refer to male or female beings.

  la pared *wall*
  el lápiz *pencil*
  el borrador *eraser*
  el reloj *clock, watch*
  la luz *light*

LEARNING TIP
Remember that it is helpful to memorize each noun with its corresponding article.[2]

Práctica

8. ¿El o la? Read the following words aloud, adding **el** or **la** to the words, as appropriate.

_____ mapa	_____ pared
_____ luz	_____ silla
_____ marcador	_____ papel
_____ idioma	_____ ciudad
_____ sociedad	_____ tarde
_____ día	_____ señora
_____ mujer	_____ mano
_____ profesor	_____ dirección
_____ libertad	_____ señor
_____ problema	_____ certidumbre (*certainty*)

B. Plural forms

- The plural of nouns is formed by adding **-s** to words ending in a vowel and **-es** to words ending in a consonant.

señora ⇒ señora**s**	reloj ⇒ reloj**es**
silla ⇒ silla**s**	borrador ⇒ borrador**es**
libro ⇒ libro**s**	lección ⇒ leccion**es**

¡Atención! Note that the plural form of **lección** does not have a written accent. See Appendix A.

[1]Some feminine words end in **-ma,** such as **la cama** (*bed*) and **la rama** (*branch*).
[2]**el** = the (*masc.*); **la** = the (*fem.*)

› When a noun ends in **-z,** change the **-z** to **c** and add **-es**.

lápi**z** ⇒ lápi**ces**
lu**z** ⇒ lu**ces**

› When the plural is used to refer to two or more nouns of different genders, the masculine form is used.

dos secretari**as** y un secretari**o** ⇒ tres secretari**os**

Práctica

9. **¿Cuántos hay?** You and a partner, take turns asking about the number or the quantities of the items listed below that you see in your classroom. Use the words **cuántos (cuántas)** in your questions.

Modelo estudiantes
S1: *¿Cuántos estudiantes hay en la clase?*
S2: *Hay veinte estudiantes.*

1. ventana
2. puerta
3. pupitre
4. cesto de papeles
5. borrador
6. lápiz
7. silla
8. chico
9. chica
10. mapa

2 Definite and indefinite articles (*Artículos determinados e indeterminados*)

A. The definite article

› Spanish has four forms that are equivalent to the English definite article *the*.

	Masculine	Feminine	English article
Singular	el	la	*the*
Plural	los	las	

el profesor — **los** profesores
la profesora — **las** profesoras
el lápiz — **los** lápices

B. The indefinite article

› The Spanish equivalents of *a* (*an*) and *some* are as follows.

	Masculine	Feminine	English
Singular	un	una	*a* (*an*)
Plural	unos	unas	*some*

un libro — **unos** libros
una silla — **unas** sillas
un profesor — **unos** profesores

LEARNING TIP
Language learning is a cumulative process, so you should connect what you are studying with what you have already learned. For instance, in the first **Estructuras** point in this lesson you learned that a noun and its accompanying adjective are either masculine or feminine. You will now find out that a third class of words in Spanish (articles) are also either masculine or feminine.

Práctica

10. ¿Qué es? Identify the following objects or people using the appropriate definite article.

1. ______________ 2. ______________ 3. ______________

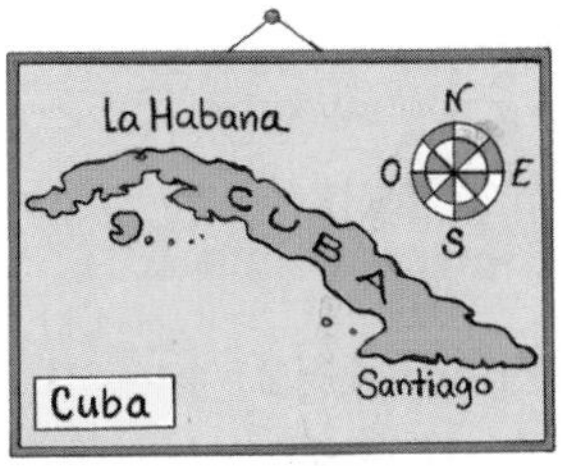

4. ______________ 5. ______________ 6. ______________

11. En la clase With a partner, take turns asking each other questions about the items or people that can be found in the classroom, according to the illustrations. Follow the model.

Modelo —*¿Hay un cuaderno?*
—*No, pero hay un libro.*

1. ______________
____
2. ______________
____
3. ______________
____
4. ______________
____
5. ______________
____
6. ______________
____

1. 

2. 

3. 

4. 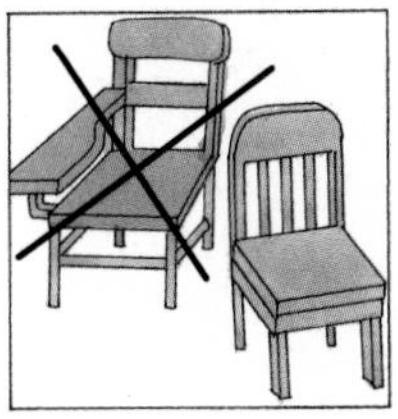

5. 

6. 

Para conversar

12. **¿Qué necesito?** With a partner, talk about what you need. Your partner should answer by using a noun and an indefinite article.

    Modelo —*¿Qué necesitas?*
    —*Yo necesito un libro.*

13. **¿Qué hay en tu mochila?** Working in groups, take turns asking each other whether or not there are certain items in your backpacks.

    Modelo —*¿Hay una pluma en tu mochila?*
    —*No. Hay un lápiz en mi mochila.*

3 Cardinal numbers 31–100 (*Números cardinales 31–100*)

31 **treinta y uno**	53 **cincuenta y tres**	80 **ochenta**
32 **treinta y dos** (*and so on*)	60 **sesenta**	84 **ochenta y cuatro**
40 **cuarenta**	68 **sesenta y ocho**	90 **noventa**
41 **cuarenta y uno** (*and so on*)	70 **setenta**	95 **noventa y cinco**
50 **cincuenta**	77 **setenta y siete**	100 **cien (ciento)**

› **Note** that **y** appears only in numbers between 31 and 99.

Un dicho

Más vale pájaro en mano que cien volando.
Equivalent: *A bird in the hand is worth two in the bush.*

LEARNING TIP

Count from 30 to 100 first by twos, then by fives, then by tens.

Práctica

14. **Especialistas** When saying phone numbers, people in many Spanish-speaking countries tend to say the first number alone and the rest of the numbers in pairs. Using this system, give the names and phone numbers of the specialists the following people would call for each situation.

    1. Your nephew has a bad case of acne.
    2. Mrs. Vega thinks she is pregnant.
    3. Your grandmother has blurred vision.
    4. Your friend's child is sick.
    5. Your neighbor has frequent chest pains.

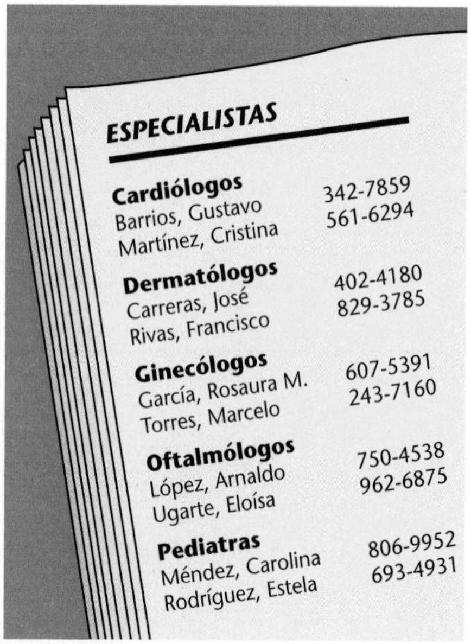

Para conversar

15. ¿Cuánto necesitamos? (*How much do we need?*) You and your partner are in charge of buying school supplies. See what items you need and how much each item costs. First read the price of each item and then take turns indicating how much money you need to buy the items.

Modelo —*¿Cuánto necesitamos para comprar tres mapas?*

— *Necesitamos 75 dólares para comprar tres mapas.*

Artículos	Precio	Total
3 mapas	$25,00	
40 bolígrafos	$1,50	
200 (doscientos) marcadores	$0,50	
45 borradores	$2,00	
2 tablillas de anuncios	$34,00	
10 cestos de papeles	$3,50	
4 relojes	$10,00	
83 cuadernos	$1,00	

4 Telling time (*La hora*)

› To ask what time it is, say, **"¿Qué hora es?"** To tell the time in Spanish, the following word order is used.

Es la				**y**		
or	+	*hour*	+	or	+	*minutes*
Son las				**menos**		

› **Es** is used with **una**.

Es la una.

› **Son** is used with all the other hours.

Son las cuatro.

› The feminine definite article is always used before the hour, since it refers to *la* **hora.**

Es **la** una y media.

Son **las** diez y cuarto.

› The hour is given first, then the minutes.

Son las **once** menos **veinte.**

› The equivalent of *past* or *after* is **y.**

Es la una **y** veinticinco.

› The equivalent of *to* or *till* is **menos**. It is used with fractions of time up to a half hour.[1]

Son las ocho **menos** cinco.

¡Atención! The equivalent of *at* + *time* is **a** + **la(s)** + *time*.

—¿Qué hora es?	*What time is it?*
—Son las dos y cuarto.	*It's a quarter past two.*
—¿A qué hora es la clase?	*What time is the class?*
—La clase es a las dos y media.	*The class is at two-thirty.*

› To specify whether the time is A.M. or P.M., use **de la mañana, de la tarde,** or **de la noche,** respectively.

—¿La clase es a las 8 **de la mañana?**	*Is the class at 8 A.M.?*
—No, ¡es a las 8 **de la noche!**	*No, it's at 8 P.M.!*

› To indicate that an activity takes place at an undefined time in the morning or in the afternoon, use **por la mañana, por la tarde,** or **por la noche,** respectively.

—¿Estudiamos **por la mañana?**	*Shall we study in the morning?*
—No, **por la tarde.**	*No, in the afternoon.*

Práctica

16. ¿Qué hora es? With a partner, take turns giving the time indicated on the clocks in the illustration. Start with clock number one.

¿Lo sabía Ud.?

Para los horarios (*schedules*) de aviones (*planes*), autobuses, trenes, televisión y algunas (*some*) invitaciones, se usa el sistema de 24 horas. Por ejemplo, las cuatro de la tarde son las dieciséis horas.

› **¿Se usa el sistema de 24 horas en este país?**

¡Atención! When we refer to after-midnight hours, for example **0:30,** we still use **horas,** in plural.

El programa empieza (starts) *a las 0:15 horas.*

17. Un mensaje telefónico Based on the information provided in the phone message, read the notes and complete the statements.

1. El mensaje es para ______________.
2. El Sr. Vega trabaja en el ______________.
3. El mensaje es de parte de[1] ______________.
4. El Sr. Ibarra trabaja para el ______________.
5. El número de teléfono del hotel es el ______________.
6. El mensaje es: ______________.
7. El Sr. Ibarra llamó (*called*) a las ______________ del ______________.
8. En el hotel hay problemas con ______________.

Hospital El Samaritano

MENSAJE PERSONAL

Para Carlos Vega
De parte de Jorge Ibarra
De la compañía Hotel Plaza
Teléfono 3-86-41-97
Llamó por teléfono a la(s) 10:30
☑ de la mañana ☐ de la tarde ☐ de la noche
MENSAJE
Desea hablar con usted mañana por la tarde.
ASUNTO
Problemas con las reservaciones del hotel para la convención
Día miércoles 24

18. ¿A qué hora es...? With a partner, take turns asking each other what time the programs in the listing are on and what programs are on at different times.

Modelo —*¿A qué hora* es Telediario?
—*Es a las seis.*
—*¿Qué hay a las siete y media?*
—Música Latina.

Programación del Canal 36

Viernes

6:00	Telediario	**9:00**	Noticiero Televisa
6:50	Noticias Internacionales	**9:30**	Música
7:00	Religión	**10:00**	Fútbol
7:30	Música Latina	**10:30**	Noticias de última hora
8:00	"María" (Telenovela)		

[1]***de parte de*** = *person who is calling*

Para conversar

19. Horario de clases This is María Elena's schedule. With a classmate, carry on a conversation to figure out when her classes are.

HORA	LUNES	MARTES	MIÉRCOLES	JUEVES	VIERNES	SÁBADO
8:00-9:00	Psicología		Psicología		Psicología	
9:00-10:00	Biología		Biología		Biología	Tenis
10:00-11:30		Historia		Historia		
12:15-1:00			ALMUERZO[1]			
1:00-2:00	Literatura		Literatura		Literatura	Laboratorio de Biología
5:00-6:30		Educación Física		Educación Física		
7:00-8:30	Arte		Arte			

Modelo —*¿Cuándo es la clase de tenis?*
—*La clase de tenis es los sábados.*
—*¿A qué hora?*
—*A las nueve.*

20. Mi horario With the help of a dictionary and/or your instructor, work with a classmate to make up each other's schedules.

Modelo *¿Qué clases tienes* (do you have) *los lunes?*
¿A qué hora es tu clase de…?

5 Present indicative of regular *-ar* verbs

(*Presente de indicativo de los verbos regulares terminados en* ***-ar***)

- Spanish verbs are classified into three main patterns of conjugation, according to the infinitive ending. The three infinitive endings are **-ar**, **-er**, and **-ir**.
- The infinitive of Spanish verbs consists of a stem (such as **habl-**) and an ending (such as **-ar**).
- The stem **habl-** does not change. The endings change with the subject.

[1] lunch

hablar *to speak*			
Singular			
yo	hablo	Yo **hablo** español.	*I speak Spanish.*
tú	hablas	Tú **hablas** francés.	*You* (inf.) *speak French.*
Ud.	habla	Ud. **habla** alemán.	*You* (form.) *speak German.*
él	habla	Él **habla** italiano.	*He speaks Italian.*
ella	habla	Ella **habla** portugués.	*She speaks Portuguese.*
Plural			
nosotros(as)	habl**amos**	Nosotros **hablamos** español.	*We speak Spanish.*
vosotros(as)	habl**áis**	Vosotros **habláis** francés.	*You* (inf.) *speak French.*
Uds.	habl**an**	Uds. **hablan** alemán.	*You* (form.) *speak German.*
ellos	habl**an**	Ellos **hablan** italiano.	*They* (masc.) *speak Italian.*
ellas	habl**an**	Ellas **hablan** portugués.	*They* (fem.) *speak Portuguese.*

—¿Qué idiomas **hablas tú?**	*What languages do you speak?*
—Yo **hablo** inglés y español.	*I speak English and Spanish.*
—¿Y Pierre?	*And Pierre?*
—Él **habla** francés.	*He speaks French.*

› Regular verbs ending in **-ar** are all conjugated as **hablar,** in the chart. Some other common **-ar** verbs are:

desear *to want, wish*
estudiar *to study*
tomar *to take*
necesitar *to need*
regresar *to return*
trabajar *to work*

—¿Uds. **estudian** por la noche?	*Do you study in the evening?*
—No, nosotros **estudiamos** por la tarde.	*No, we study in the afternoon.*
—¿Qué **necesitas** tú?	*What do you need?*
—Yo **necesito** un libro.	*I need a book.*

¡Atención! Notice that the verb forms for **Ud., él,** and **ella** are the same. In addition, **Uds., ellos,** and **ellas** share common verb forms. This is true for all verbs in all tenses.

› The Spanish present tense is equivalent to three English forms.

	I speak English.
Yo **hablo** inglés.	*I do speak English.*
	I am speaking English.

LEARNING TIP

In **Lección 1** you were introduced to the verb **ser.** Realize now that the **-ar** verbs *conjugate* those same persons (**yo, tú/Ud.,** and **él/ella**) and number (the singular or plural forms of each person). In fact, all verbal tenses in Spanish (present, past, future) conjugate according to the very same categories: person and number.

› Because the verb endings indicate who is performing the action, the subject pronouns are frequently omitted.

Necesito un lápiz.	*I need a pencil.*
Estudiamos inglés.	*We study English.*
Hoy **trabajo**.	*I work today.*

› Subject pronouns can, however, be used for emphasis or clarification.

—¿**Ellos** hablan inglés?	*Do they speak English?*
—**Ella** habla inglés y **él** habla alemán.	*She speaks English, and he speaks German.*

› In Spanish, as in English, when two verbs are used together, the second verb remains in the infinitive.

—¿Con quién necesita **hablar** Ud.?	*With whom do you need to speak?*
—Necesito **hablar** con el Sr. Vega.	*I need to speak with Mr. Vega.*

¿Lo sabía Ud.?

El español es el idioma vernáculo (*native*) de más de 430.000.000[1] de personas.

› **¿Cuántas personas cree Ud. que hablan inglés en el mundo (*world*)?**

Práctica

21. ¡Habla con tu compañero(a)! With a partner, take turns asking and answering the following questions to indicate what people do.

1. Yo estudio francés. ¿Qué idioma estudias tú?
2. Carlos trabaja por la noche. ¿Tú trabajas por la mañana, por la tarde o por la noche? (¿O no trabajas?)
3. Amanda y su familia regresan el domingo. ¿Cuándo regresan ustedes?
4. Los chicos practican el español todos los días. ¿Qué días practicas tú?
5. Nosotros hablamos inglés. ¿Qué idioma hablan los mexicanos?
6. Yo necesito un libro. ¿Qué necesitas tú?
7. Las chicas toman cuatro clases. ¿Cuántas clases toman ustedes?
8. Yo llego a casa (*home*) a las cuatro de la tarde. ¿A qué hora llegas tú a tu casa?
9. Delia anota la dirección de Sergio. ¿Qué anotan ustedes?
10. Nosotros deseamos estudiar francés. ¿Qué idioma desean estudiar ustedes?

Un dicho

El trabajo dignifica.
Equivalent: *Work dignifies.*

[1] *430 million.* Note that, in Spanish numbers, a period is used instead of a comma to indicate thousands.

22. **¿Qué pasa aquí?** With a partner, talk about what is going on in these drawings, using the subject pronouns given and the verbs **trabajar, hablar, necesitar, regresar, tomar,** and **estudiar**.

1. ________________.

2. ________________.

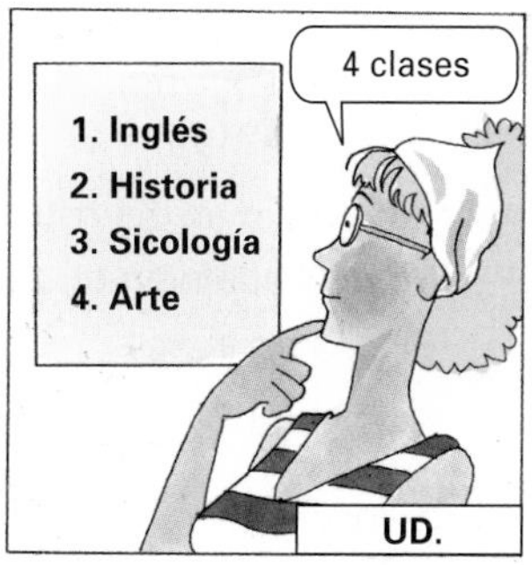

3. ________________.

4. ________________.

5. ________________.

6. ________________.

23. **¿Qué idioma hablan?** Indicate what language these people speak.

1. Jean-Pierre, que (*who*) es de París. ____________.
2. Mao, que enseña (*teaches*) en la Universidad de Beijing. ____________.
3. María Mercedes, que trabaja en la Pequeña Habana. ____________.
4. Vittorino y Gina, que estudian en Florencia. ____________.
5. Carolyn, que es de Toronto, Canadá. ____________.
6. João, que trabaja en Río de Janeiro, Brasil. ____________.

Para conversar

24. **Dos estudiantes conversan** With a partner, have a conversation about where you work, what days you work, what languages you speak, how many classes you take, and what you need. Take notes.

Modelo —*¿Dónde trabajas?*
—*Trabajo en un hospital.*
—*¿Qué días trabajas?*
—*Trabajo los lunes, miércoles y viernes.*

25. **Mi compañero(a)...** Now each student will share some information about his/her partner with the rest of the class.

Modelo (Sam) *trabaja en el hospital. Él trabaja los lunes, miércoles y viernes.*

6 Negative and interrogative sentences *(Oraciones negativas e interrogativas)*

A. Negative sentences

› To make a sentence negative, simply place the word **no** in front of the verb.

Yo trabajo en el hospital.	*I work at the hospital.*
Yo **no** trabajo en el hospital.	*I don't work at the hospital.*
Ella habla inglés.	*She speaks English.*
Ella **no** habla inglés.	*She doesn't speak English.*

› If the answer to a question is negative, the word **no** will appear twice, at the beginning of the sentence, as in English, and in front of the verb.

—¿Habla Ud. francés?	*Do you speak French?*
—**No**, yo **no** hablo francés.	*No, I don't speak French.*

The subject pronoun may be omitted.

—**No, no** hablo francés.	*No, I don't speak French.*

Un dicho

El saber no ocupa lugar.

Equivalent: *One can never know too much.*

B. Interrogative sentences

› In Spanish, there are several ways of asking a question to elicit a *yes* or *no* answer.

¿**Ud.** habla francés?

¿Habla **Ud.** francés? — **Sí,** yo hablo francés. (No, yo no hablo francés).

¿Habla francés **Ud.**?

› These three questions ask for the same information and have the same meaning. The subject may be placed at the beginning of the sentence, after the verb, or at the end of the sentence.

¡Atención! When speaking, the difference between a statement and a question is intonation. When asking *yes* or *no* questions, the voice goes up at the end of the last word.

¿Ud. habla francés?

› Note that written questions in Spanish begin with an inverted question mark.

› Another common way to ask a question in Spanish is to add tag questions such as **¿no?** and **¿verdad?** at the end of a statement.

Ud. habla español, **¿verdad?**	*You speak Spanish, don't you?*

LEARNING TIP

Stress and intonation in Spanish (just like in English) help to signal certain information about the function (purpose) or even the meaning of what you are hearing. Continue to pay attention to this aspect of speech and start to aim at recognizing specific functions of stress and intonation in spoken Spanish.

› Questions that ask for information begin with an interrogative word, and the verb, not the subject, is placed after the interrogative word.

¿Dónde **trabajas** tú?	*Where do you work?*
¿Cuándo **regresan** ellos?	*When do they return?*
¿Qué **necesita** Ud.?	*What do you need?*
¿Quién **es** el profesor?	*Who is the professor?*

¡Atención! Spanish does not use an auxiliary verb, such as *do* or *does*, in negative or interrogative sentences.

Práctica

26. ¿Qué preguntan? (*What do they ask?*) In the cafeteria, you overhear some conversations, but you miss all the questions. Supply them.

1. ______________________ Estudio matemáticas.
2. ______________________ Sí, trabajo en el hospital.
3. ______________________ No, no trabajo por la mañana. Trabajo por la tarde.
4. ______________________ Somos de California.
5. ______________________ Estudiamos en la biblioteca.
6. ______________________ Estudiamos los sábados.
7. ______________________ Necesito el libro de español y, además, necesito una pluma.
8. ______________________ No, Carlos no es profesor. Él es estudiante.
9. ______________________ Se dice *idioma*.
10. ______________________ Deseamos tomar café.

27. ¡No! With a partner, take turns answering the following questions in the negative and add the correct answer.

Modelo *¿Tú eres profesor?*
No, no soy profesor. Soy estudiante.

1. ¿Tú trabajas los sábados?
   Trabajo __________.
2. ¿Tú necesitas una pluma?
   Necesito un __________.
3. ¿Tú tomas cuatro clases?
   Tomo __________ clases.
4. ¿Tú regresas a tu casa a las tres?
   Regreso __________.
5. ¿Tú estudias matemáticas?
   Estudio __________.
6. ¿Uds. son de Perú?
   Somos de __________.

ESTRUCTURAS

Para conversar

28. Un nuevo amigo With a partner, read the following information about David Rojas. Then form ten questions about him. Your partner should answer in complete sentences.

Me llamo David Rojas. Soy cubanoamericano y estudio en la Universidad Internacional de la Florida. Tomo cuatro clases por la mañana, trabajo por la tarde y estudio por la noche; los sábados y los domingos no trabajo. Hablo tres idiomas: español, inglés y un poco de francés, y ahora deseo estudiar portugués. Trabajo mucho porque necesito dinero (*money*).

HINT
Be aware of these interrogative words.
¿Dónde? (*Where?*)
¿Qué? (*What?*)
¿Cuándo? (*When?*)
¿Cuántos(as)? (*How many?*)
¿Quién(es)? (*Who?*)
¿Por qué? (*Why?*) (porque = *because*)

© Bill Jarvis

David Rojas

Some of the questions may require a "yes" or "no" answer. After completing the questions, join another group to ask your questions and answer theirs.

7 Possession with *de* (*El caso posesivo*)

› The **de** + *noun* construction is used to express possession or relationship. Spanish does *not* use the apostrophe.

Rosa 's *address*
la dirección de Rosa
(*the address of Rosa*)

la clase **de la Dra. Peña**	*Dr. Peña's class*
el libro **de Dora**	*Dora's book*

© Ana C. Jarvis

Irene, la hermana de Carmen (*Carmen's sister*).

¡Atención! Note the use of the definite article before the words **dirección, clase,** and **libro.**

—¿Quién es Francisco Acosta?	*Who is Francisco Acosta?*
—Es **el profesor de Carmen.**	*He is Carmen's professor.*
—¿Cuál es **la dirección de Irene?**	*What is Irene's address?*
—Calle Magdalena, número seis.	*Six Magdalena Street.*

Práctica

29. Deseamos saber... (*We want to know ...*) With a partner, look carefully at the illustrations and then take turns answering the questions that follow.

1. ¿Quiénes son las amigas de Sergio?

_______________________________.

2. ¿Qué necesita Olga?

_______________________________.

3. ¿Qué necesita Luis?

_______________________________.

4. ¿Quién es el Sr. Soto?

_______________________________.

5. ¿Quién es de Cuba?

_______________________________.

6. ¿Quiénes son Pedro y José?

_______________________________.

Para conversar

30. ¿Lo necesita o no? (*Do you need it or not?*) Take turns asking other members of the class if they need certain things.

Modelo —*¿Necesitas el reloj de Raúl?*
—*No, yo no necesito el reloj de Raúl. / Sí, yo necesito el reloj de Raúl.*

Un dicho

En casa del herrero, cuchillo de palo.
Equivalent: *The shoemaker's son always goes barefoot.*

LEARNING TIP

If a certain concept such as a grammar point is giving you difficulty after having been "with it" for a while, take a break, relax, and after five or ten minutes, resume your language study afresh. As you find out what points become more challenging for you, try to make these the first points you go over during your next study session.

¡Vamos a ver!

Antes de ver el video

31. ¡Habla con tu compañero(a)! You and a partner, take turns asking and answering the following questions.

1. ¿A qué hora es la clase de español?
2. ¿Tú estudias en la biblioteca o en tu casa? ¿Estudias por la mañana, por la tarde o por la noche?
3. ¿Tú trabajas o estudias esta noche?
4. ¿Estudias solo(a) (*by yourself*) o con un(a) amigo(a)?
5. ¿Necesitas más tiempo para estudiar o para trabajar?
6. ¿Cómo se dice "*backpack*" en español?
7. ¿El español es un idioma fácil o difícil?
8. ¿Tú practicas el español todos los días? ¿Necesitas practicar más (*more*)?
9. ¿Tú hablas otros idiomas?
10. ¿Tú deseas estudiar otro idioma? ¿Cuál?

El video: El primer día de clases

Julio anota la dirección y el número de teléfono de Gloria.

—¿Tú hablas otros idiomas?
—Sí, hablo francés y un poco de portugués.

Después de ver el video

© Cengage Learning

Gloria

© Cengage Learning

Julio

© Cengage Learning

Sandra

32. ¿Quién lo dice? Identify the person who said the following in the dialogues.

1. Yo trabajo en el hospital por la noche.
2. ¡Necesitas más tiempo para estudiar!
3. ¡Ay, chica! ¡En ese caso yo hablo chino!
4. Oye, ¿deseas estudiar conmigo el sábado por la mañana?
5. Yo hablo italiano.
6. ¿Cómo se dice *backpack* en español?
7. ¡Sí! ¿Estudiamos en mi casa? Y por la tarde vamos a la Calle Ocho.
8. El español es un idioma difícil.
9. ¡Perfecto! Nos vemos el sábado.

33. Hablemos With a partner, take turns asking and answering the following questions. Base your answers on the dialogues.

1. ¿Gloria es cubanoamericana?
2. ¿A qué hora es la clase de inglés?
3. ¿Julio y Olga estudian esta noche?
4. ¿Julio trabaja en el hospital por la mañana o por la noche?
5. ¿Cuántas clases toma Julio?
6. ¿Qué necesita Julio?
7. ¿Cuál es la dirección de Gloria?
8. ¿Gloria habla otros idiomas?

34. ¿Qué pasa después? You and a partner, use your imagination to talk about what the characters do the next day. In Spanish, discuss the following.

1. Whether Julio works or studies in the morning.
2. Whether Olga and José Luis study in the library.
3. Whether José Luis writes down Olga's phone number or Olga's address.
4. Whether or not Sandra practices Spanish.
5. Whether or not Gloria speaks French with a friend.
6. Whether or not Sandra wishes to study other languages.

Now compare your statements with those of another group.

¡Vamos a escuchar!

ESTRATEGIA **Listening for specifics and guessing intelligently**
Often, when listening, you have specific information in mind that you want to know or that you expect to hear. Concentrating on these specifics helps your understanding and allows you to "discard" unrelated information. For example, if your Spanish-speaking housemate wants you to buy some things on your way home, you automatically listen for the items you need to buy. If he or she asks you to pick up **café, pan, leche y huevos,** by guessing intelligently you know you're expected to buy **leche** and **huevos** even if you aren't sure what they are.

CD1-13 **35. Necesitamos muchas cosas** Julio and Carmen need to make some classroom-related purchases. Listen to their conversation and mark only the items they need to buy. Read the list before listening. If you hear an unknown word, make an intelligent guess about it.

________ tablilla de anuncios	________ tiza
________ cesto de papeles	________ calculadora
________ mochila	________ carpetas
________ reloj	________ sacapuntas
________ mapas	________ bolígrafos
________ archivo	________ pizarras

¡Vamos a conversar!

ESTRATEGIA **Asking for repetition** Conversing is a negotiating process. Be ready to ask the person you are speaking with, for instance, to repeat whenever there's something important you didn't understand or didn't hear well. Here are some phrases you can use in these situations.

- **¿Cómo?** *(What?)* or **¿Perdón?** *(I beg your pardon?)*
- **Repite, por favor** *(informal)* or **Repita, por favor** *(formal). (Please repeat.)*
- **Más despacio, por favor.** *(More slowly, please.)*
- **Otra vez, por favor.** *(Once more, please.)*

36. ¿Cómo? With a partner, take turns asking about each other's classes. Find out which classes he or she takes, on what days, and who the professor is. Use the phrases you've just learned to ask for repetitions when necessary.

37. ¿Qué dice Ud.? What would you say in the following situations? What might the other person say? Act out scenes with a partner. Take turns playing each role.

1. You ask a friend if he/she wishes to study with you in the library. Ask at what time.

2. Tell a friend when you study and when you work and also the days you don't work. Ask him/her about his/her schedule.

3. Ask your professor how to say, in Spanish, a word that you don't know.
4. Ask a classmate what his/her address is.
5. Ask your professor if he/she speaks other languages.
6. You confess that you are not punctual, and add that you are late everywhere.

38. Para conocernos mejor To do this activity, work with a classmate whom you would like to get to know. Take turns asking each other these questions.

1. ¿Qué idiomas hablas tú? ¿Deseas estudiar otro idioma? ¿Cuál?
2. ¿Cuántas clases tomas? ¿A qué hora es tu primera clase? ¿Es una clase fácil o difícil?
3. ¿Tú estudias en la biblioteca o en tu casa? ¿Cuántas horas estudias?
4. ¿Dónde trabajas? ¿Trabajas los sábados y los domingos?
5. ¿Necesitas dinero? ¿Cuánto?
6. ¿Cuál es tu dirección? ¿Cuál es tu número de teléfono?
7. ¿Tú practicas el español todos los días? ¿Con quién? ¿Necesitas practicar más tiempo?
8. ¿Necesitas más tiempo para estudiar o para trabajar?
9. ¿Qué hora es?
10. ¿A qué hora regresas a tu casa hoy? ¿Y mañana?

39. Una encuesta Interview your classmates to identify who fits the following descriptions. Include your instructor, but remember to use the **Ud.** form when addressing him/her. After finishing the survey, get together with two or three classmates and discuss the results.

1. Trabaja en la universidad.	________________
2. Trabaja los sábados.	________________
3. Necesita dinero.	________________
4. Estudia por la noche.	________________
5. Necesita estudiar más.	________________
6. Desea estudiar otro idioma.	________________
7. Habla con sus amigos en la cafetería.	________________
8. Regresa a su casa por la noche.	________________

40. Para crear In groups of three, look at this photo and use your imagination to create a story about the person in the picture. Who is she? Give her a name. Is she a student? Where is she from? Does she work? What is her address? What might she be saying to the other person on the phone? In general, what's the story behind the photo?

ASÍ SOMOS

¡Vamos a leer!

Antes de leer

> **ESTRATEGIA** **Guessing the meaning of unknown words**
> When you read, you can often guess the meaning of some of the words you don't know by paying attention to the context. Look at the words surrounding the unknown word. Are there cognates, familiar words, or explanation or information that give clues to the meaning of the word? If a word seems important to the general meaning of a passage, try to make logical guesses about its meaning based on context before you consult a dictionary.

41. ¿Qué significa? Read the following sentences and choose the definition that best fits the context.

1. El profesor Griego enseña ciencias políticas en la universidad.
   a. learns   b. teaches   c. supervises
2. La señora Jiménez es profesora de literatura española en el departamento de lenguas.
   a. languages   b. humanities   c. arts
3. El estudiante ayuda a sus amigos a estudiar para el examen de cálculo porque las matemáticas son fáciles para él.
   a. helps   b. tests   c. demands

¡A leer!

©William Casey/Shutterstock

ORGANIZACIÓN DE ESTUDIANTES HISPANOS

La profesora del año

La Dra. Isabel Junco, de La Habana, Cuba, es profesora de literatura española y latinoamericana en el departamento de Lengua y Literatura. Este semestre ella enseña un seminario sobre° la poesía de Rubén Darío. Además de enseñar literatura, la profesora Junco enseña dos clases de francés en la sección de la noche. Ella habla cuatro idiomas: español, inglés, francés y portugués. La Dra. Junco acaba de publicar° un libro sobre la poesía° del famoso poeta y patriota cubano José Martí. La Dra. Junco es una profesora excelente y es muy respetada y admirada por todos sus estudiantes. Además de enseñar, trabaja como voluntaria con "Cuba Libre°", una organización dedicada a ayudar a los refugiados cubanos.

about

acaba... *has just published / poetry*

free

42. Comprensión Now, as you read the article about Dra. Isabel Junco again, find the answers to the following questions.

1. ¿Quién es la profesora del año?
2. ¿De dónde es la Dra. Junco?
3. ¿Qué enseña?
4. ¿En qué departamento trabaja?
5. ¿Qué enseña este semestre?

6. ¿Qué idioma enseña?
7. ¿Qué idiomas habla?
8. ¿Qué acaba de publicar?
9. ¿Quién es José Martí?
10. La Dra. Junco, ¿es una buena profesora?
11. ¿Con qué organización trabaja Isabel Junco?
12. ¿A quiénes ayuda "Cuba Libre"?

Después de leer… desde tu mundo

43. **Mi profesor(a) favorito(a)** In groups of three, talk about your favorite professor, whom you want to select as professor of the year.

Include information such as what his/her nationality is, what languages he/she speaks, what days he/she teaches, etc.

¡Vamos a escribir!

Antes de escribir

ESTRATEGIA **Conducting and reporting an interview**
To prepare an effective interview, use your knowledge of the person you plan to interview and what readers might want to know about the person or the subject the interviewee will talk about.

› Include questions that ask for information.

› Prepare more questions than you think you need, and organize them in a logical sequence.

44. **Una entrevista** (*An interview*) You write a column about new students for the school paper and must interview a Spanish-speaking student for your next article. Brainstorm eight to ten questions you might ask and organize them in a logical sequence.

¡A escribir!

45. **Informe** Now write a draft (**borrador**) of your interview article. Sequence the information you obtained so that it flows smoothly.

Después de escribir

46. **A revisar** Before writing the final version of your interview, exchange your first draft with that of a classmate and peer edit each other's work. Use the following guidelines.

› noun-adjective and noun-article agreement (in gender and number)

› subject-verb agreement (in person and number)

› logical sequence of information

Los cubanoamericanos

¿Sabes qué tienen en común las famosas actrices Eva Mendes y Cameron Díaz, la política Ileana Ros-Lehtinen, el célebre cantante (*singer*) Jon Secada, el diseñador de moda Narciso Rodríguez y Jeff Bezos, fundador de la empresa Amazon? ¡Todos son cubanoamericanos!

Hay innumerables personas que pertenecen (*belong*) a este grupo y se encuentran en numerosas profesiones y ocupaciones o son dueños (*owners*) de negocios.

La política

Los cubanos son el 4% de los hispanos de este país, y como buena parte de ellos vinieron (*came*) por razones políticas y no económicas, son los inmigrantes hispanos más conservadores, con mayor nivel de escolaridad (*education*) y de mayor ingreso (*income*) per capita.

Ileana Ros-Lehtinen (1952–) es la primera mujer hispana elegida (*elected*) al Congreso de Estados Unidos (1989–presente).

Marco Rubio, cubanoamericano, es el nuevo senador por la Florida.

El entretenimiento

Jon Secada canta en español y en inglés. Tiene dos Grammys.

Cameron Díaz actúa en muchas películas (*movies*), como *My Best Friend's Wedding* y *Charlie's Angels.*

© Jack Messler/DDB Stock Photography

En la Pequeña Habana, un barrio (*neighborhood*) cubano de la ciudad de Miami, muchos de los bancos, cafés, restaurantes, mercados y tiendas son de propiedad cubana, y el español es el idioma más hablado (*spoken*).

Anualmente se celebra el Festival de la Calle Ocho, que es parte de la celebración del Carnaval.

Los negocios[1] y el mundo de la moda[2]

© Gary Gershoff/WireImage/Getty Images

Narciso Rodríguez, famoso diseñador de ropa (*clothing*). Entre sus clientas están las actrices Salma Hayek y Sara Jessica Parker.

© David Samuel Robbins/Corbis/SYGMA

Jeff Bezos, presidente fundador (*founder*) de la empresa (*company*) Amazon, se identifica como cubanoamericano.

Ahora, dime...

In groups of three, take turns asking and answering the following questions.

1. ¿Te gusta Cameron Díaz? ¿Es una buena actriz?
2. ¿Hay otros políticos cubanoamericanos? ¿Cuáles?
3. ¿Deseas visitar la Pequeña Habana?
4. ¿Compras (*Do you buy*) libros, discos compactos o películas en Amazon?
5. ¿Qué celebraciones hay en tu ciudad? ¿Hay desfiles (*parades*)?

iLrn

To learn more about Hispanic communities in the United States, watch the cultural footage in the Media Library.

[1]business
[2]fashion

AUTOPRUEBA

¿Cuánto sé ahora?

Take this test. When you have finished, check your answers in the answer key provided in Appendix D. Then use a red pen to correct any mistakes you may have made. Are you ready?

A. Gender and number and definite articles Write **el, la, los,** or **las** before each noun.

1. ________ matemáticas
2. ________ problema
3. ________ muchacha
4. ________ dirección
5. ________ idiomas
6. ________ marcador
7. ________ decisión
8. ________ pupitres
9. ________ ciudades
10. ________ libertad
11. ________ solución
12. ________ muchedumbre
13. ________ luces
14. ________ días

B. Gender and number and indefinite articles Write **un, una, unos,** or **unas** before each noun.

1. ________________ universidad
2. ________________ mochila
3. ________________ libros
4. ________________ mapa
5. ________________ manos
6. ________________ programa
7. ________________ relojes
8. ________________ pared
9. ________________ hombres
10. ________________ mujer
11. ________________ conversación
12. ________________ poemas

C. Cardinal numbers (31–100) Write the following numbers in Spanish.

1. 42 ________________
2. 100 ________________
3. 53 ________________
4. 61 ________________
5. 80 ________________
6. 79 ________________
7. 90 ________________
8. 86 ________________
9. 50 ________________
10. 60 ________________

D. Telling time Use the cues given to say at what time the following classes are.

1. la clase de español / 9:10 A.M.
2. la clase de inglés / 1:15 P.M.
3. la clase de literatura / 8:25 P.M.

E. Present indicative of *-ar* verbs and negative and interrogative sentences
Complete the following dialogues, using the present indicative of the verbs given.

1. —¿Uds. _______ (tomar) matemáticas?
   —No, nosotros no _______ (tomar) matemáticas. Roberto _______ (tomar) matemáticas.
2. —Yo _______ (practicar) los lunes y viernes.
   —Tú _______ (necesitar) practicar todos los días.
3. —¿A qué hora _______ (llegar) Uds.?
   —Sergio _______ (llegar) a las cuatro. Luis y yo _______ (llegar) a las cuatro y media.
4. —¿_______ (Estudiar) Uds. en la biblioteca?
   —No, nosotros no _______ (estudiar) en la biblioteca.
5. —¿Qué _______ (desear) Ud., señora?
   —Yo _______ (desear) otra taza de café.

F. Possession with *de* Give the Spanish equivalent of the words in parentheses.

1. _______________ es Calle Quinta, número 456. (The girls' address)
2. _______________ son por la mañana. (Carmen's classes)
3. _______________ son de Cuba. (Alina's parents)

G. Just words . . . Match the questions in the first column with the answers in the second column.

1. ¿Qué deseas?	_______	a. No, siempre llega tarde.
2. ¿Qué clase tomas?	_______	b. Sí, a las nueve de la noche.
3. ¿Dónde trabaja?	_______	c. Reloj.
4. ¿Es puntual?	_______	d. A las ocho de la mañana.
5. ¿Estudias en tu casa?	_______	e. Solamente una.
6. ¿A qué hora llegan?	_______	f. Ruso.
7. ¿Cómo se dice "clock"?	_______	g. No, es fácil.
8. ¿Con quién estudia Nora?	_______	h. En un hospital.
9. ¿Qué idioma hablan?	_______	i. Sí, veinte horas por semana.
10. ¿Cuántas clases tomas?	_______	j. ¡Sí! ¡Yo necesito ayuda!
11. ¿Tú trabajas?	_______	k. Otra taza de café.
12. ¿El portugués es difícil?	_______	l. Conmigo.
13. ¿Nos vemos el sábado?	_______	m. No, en la biblioteca.
14. ¿Estudiamos juntos?	_______	n. Química.

H. Culture

1. Complete the following, based on information in the **¿Lo sabía Ud.?** sections.
   a. Cuando los hispanos dan una dirección, usan primero la palabra _______ o _______.
   b. Para los horarios de aviones, autobuses, televisión y algunas invitaciones, se usa el sistema de _______ horas.
2. Complete the following, based on information found in the **El mundo hispánico y tú...** sectíon.
   a. Buena parte de los cubanos vinieron por razones políticas, no _______.
   b. En la Pequeña Habana, el _______ es el idioma más hablado.

I. Un dicho Do you remember the Spanish saying about the importance of knowledge? Find it in this lesson.

LECCIÓN 3

POR TELÉFONO

Una chica habla por teléfono.

OBJETIVOS COMUNICATIVOS

You will learn vocabulary used to describe people and activities and to make and receive phone calls.

SITUACIONES

Dos compañeros de cuarto

ESTRUCTURAS

1 Possessive adjectives
2 Cardinal numbers 101–1000
3 Descriptive adjectives: Forms, position, and agreement with articles and nouns
4 Present indicative of regular **-er** and **-ir** verbs
5 Present indicative of the irregular verbs **tener** and **venir**
6 The personal **a**

ASÍ SOMOS

¡Vamos a ver!
Watching and understanding situations

¡Vamos a escuchar!
Taking a phone call

¡Vamos a conversar!
Using stock phrases

¡Vamos a leer!
Activating background knowledge

¡Vamos a escribir!
Analyzing writing models

EL MUNDO HISPÁNICO Y TÚ

› Los puertorriqueños en los Estados Unidos

AUTOPRUEBA

You will review what you learned in this lesson.

LOS PUERTORRIQUEÑOS Los puertorriqueños son el segundo grupo más grande (*largest*) de hispanos en los Estados Unidos. Como Puerto Rico es un Estado Libre Asociado a este país, los puertorriqueños son ciudadanos estadounidenses y no necesitan pasaporte ni visa para entrar en el país.

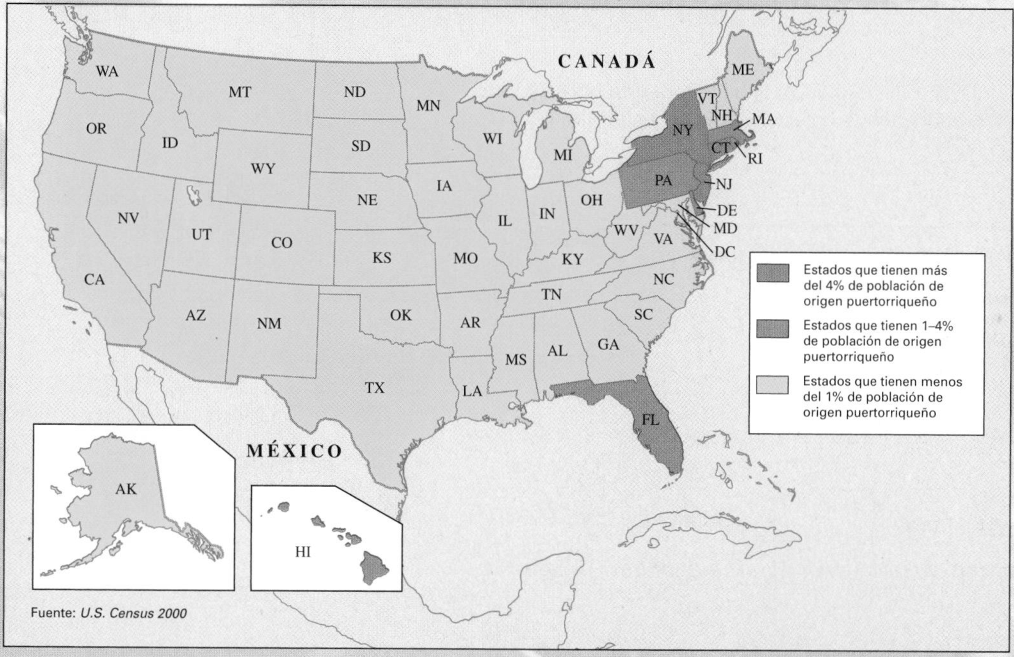

Fuente: *U.S. Census 2000*

Recursos iLrn video audio web playlist

SITUACIONES

Dos compañeros de cuarto

CD1-14

© Cengage Learning

¡Ubíquelos!

Carlos and David live and study in New York, where there are more Puerto Ricans than in San Juan, the capital of Puerto Rico. Watching the video will give you a sense of these two young men's surroundings: "La Gran Manzana" (The Big Apple).

Carlos Saldaña y David Cortés son compañeros de cuarto y viven en un apartamento muy pequeño en Nueva York. Carlos es moreno, de estatura mediana y muy simpático. David es alto, guapo y muy inteligente. Los dos son puertorriqueños y asisten a la universidad.

Carlos: ¿Tienes el periódico? Necesito leer los anuncios.

David: Sí, aquí está. ¡Ah! Hay un mensaje electrónico de tu novia.

Carlos lee el mensaje.

A: Carlos@amigo.com
De: Silvia@pr.com
Asunto: Examen
Mi amor: Tengo que llevar a mi hermano a la biblioteca esta noche y después tengo que estudiar porque mañana tengo un examen parcial en mi clase de literatura.
Nos vemos mañana.
Silvia

Carlos: Silvia no viene esta noche… Bueno, yo tengo que llenar una solicitud de empleo porque necesito ganar dinero…

David: Sí, tienes problemas económicos, pero no tienes mucha experiencia…

Carlos: ¡Es verdad!

Carlos come un sándwich, bebe café y después llama a su novia.

Al teléfono

Carlos: Hola. ¿Está Silvia?

Teresa: Sí, un momento, por favor. (*Llama a Silvia.*) ¡Silvia!

Silvia: Hola.

Carlos: ¿Silvia?

Silvia: Sí, con ella habla. ¿Carlos? ¿Cómo estás, mi amor?

CARLOS: No muy bien. ¡Tú no vienes esta noche!

SILVIA: No, mi vida. Tengo mucho que hacer.

CARLOS: ¿Deseas beber algo en el café San Juan?

SILVIA: No, lo siento. Tengo que estudiar. ¿Y tú? ¿No tienes que llenar una solicitud de empleo?

CARLOS: Sí... y también tengo que escribir un informe para mi clase de historia...

SILVIA: Entonces... Hasta mañana, mi amor.

CARLOS: Hasta mañana...

Carlos habla con David.

DAVID: ¿Silvia estudia con Fernando esta noche?

CARLOS: ¿Quién es Fernando?

DAVID: Es un amigo de Teresa. Él y Silvia tienen una clase juntos. Según Silvia, es un muchacho encantador...

CARLOS: ¡Ajá! !Con razón no viene esta noche y no acepta mi invitación! ¡Chau! ¡Me voy!

DAVID: ¿Adónde?

CARLOS: ¡A la casa de Silvia!

¿Lo sabía Ud.?

Para contestar el teléfono (*To answer the phone*):
En España (*Spain*): "Diga", "Dígame", "¿Sí?"
En Cuba y en otras regiones del Caribe: "Oigo"
En México: "Bueno"
En Argentina: "¿Sí?", "Hable", "Hola", "Aló"

› **¿Cómo se contesta el teléfono en este país (*this country*)?**

1. Hablemos With a partner, take turns asking and answering the following questions. Base your answers on the dialogue and on your own circumstances.

En el diálogo

1. ¿Dónde viven Carlos y David?
2. ¿Carlos es muy alto?
3. ¿Cómo es David?
4. ¿Qué lee Carlos en el periódico?
5. ¿Qué recibe Carlos de su novia?
6. ¿Qué tiene Silvia mañana?
7. ¿Qué tiene que hacer Silvia?
8. ¿Qué tiene que escribir Carlos mañana?
9. ¿Con quién estudia Silvia?
10. ¿Acepta Silvia la invitación de Carlos?

¿Y tú?

1. ¿Dónde vives tú?
2. ¿Tú eres alto(a)?
3. ¿Cómo eres tú?
4. ¿Tú lees el periódico todos los días?
5. ¿Tú recibes muchos mensajes electrónicos?
6. ¿Cuándo tienes exámenes tú?
7. ¿Qué tienes que hacer tú?
8. ¿Qué tienes que escribir tú?
9. ¿Con quién estudias tú?
10. ¿Tú recibes muchas invitaciones?

¿Lo sabía Ud.?

"Español" y "castellano" son equivalentes.

› **¿Hay mucha diferencia entre el inglés que hablan en Inglaterra (*England*) y el que se habla en este país?**

VOCABULARIO

En el diálogo

Cognados

el apartamento	*apartment*
el café	*café (coffee shop)*
el examen	*exam*
la experiencia	*experience*
la historia	*history*
inteligente	*intelligent*
la invitación	*invitation*
la literatura	*literature*
el mensaje	*message*
el momento	*moment*
puertorriqueño(a)	*Puerto Rican*
el sándwich	*sandwich*

Nombres

el anuncio, aviso	*advertisement*
el (la) compañero(a) de cuarto	*roommate*
el dinero	*money*
el empleo, el trabajo	*job*
el examen parcial	*midterm exam*
la hermana	*sister*
el hermano	*brother*
el informe	*report*
el mensaje (correo) electrónico	*e-mail*
la novia	*girlfriend*
el novio	*boyfriend*
el periódico, diario	*newspaper*
la solicitud	*application*
la solicitud de empleo	*job application*
la verdad	*truth*

Verbos

aceptar	*to accept*
asistir (a)	*to attend*
beber, tomar	*to drink*
comer	*to eat*
escribir	*to write*
ganar	*to earn*
leer	*to read*
llamar	*to call*
llenar	*to fill out*
llevar	*to take (someone or something someplace)*
tener	*to have*
venir	*to come*
vivir	*to live*

Adjetivos

alto(a)	*tall*
económico(a)	*financial*
encantador(a)	*charming*
guapo(a)	*handsome, good-looking*
moreno(a)	*dark*
pequeño(a)	*small*
simpático(a)	*likable*

Otras palabras y expresiones

¿adónde?	*where (to)?*
¡ajá!	*aha!*
al teléfono	*on the phone*
aquí	*here*
Aquí está.	*Here it is.*
beber algo[1]	*to have something to drink*
Con ella habla.[2]	*This is she. (Speaking.)*
con razón	*no wonder*
de estatura mediana	*of medium height*
después	*afterwards*
entonces	*then, in that case*
Es verdad.	*It's true.*
¿Está... ?	*Is . . . (name) there?*
esta noche	*tonight*
Me voy.	*I'm leaving.*
mi amor	*my love*
mi vida	*my love (life)*
para	*for*
¿quién? (¿quiénes?)	*who?*
según	*according to*
tener mucho que hacer	*to have a lot to do*
tener que + infinitivo	*to have to + infinitive*

[1] **comer algo** *to have something to eat*
[2] **Con él habla.** *This is he. (Speaking.)*

Más sobre el tema

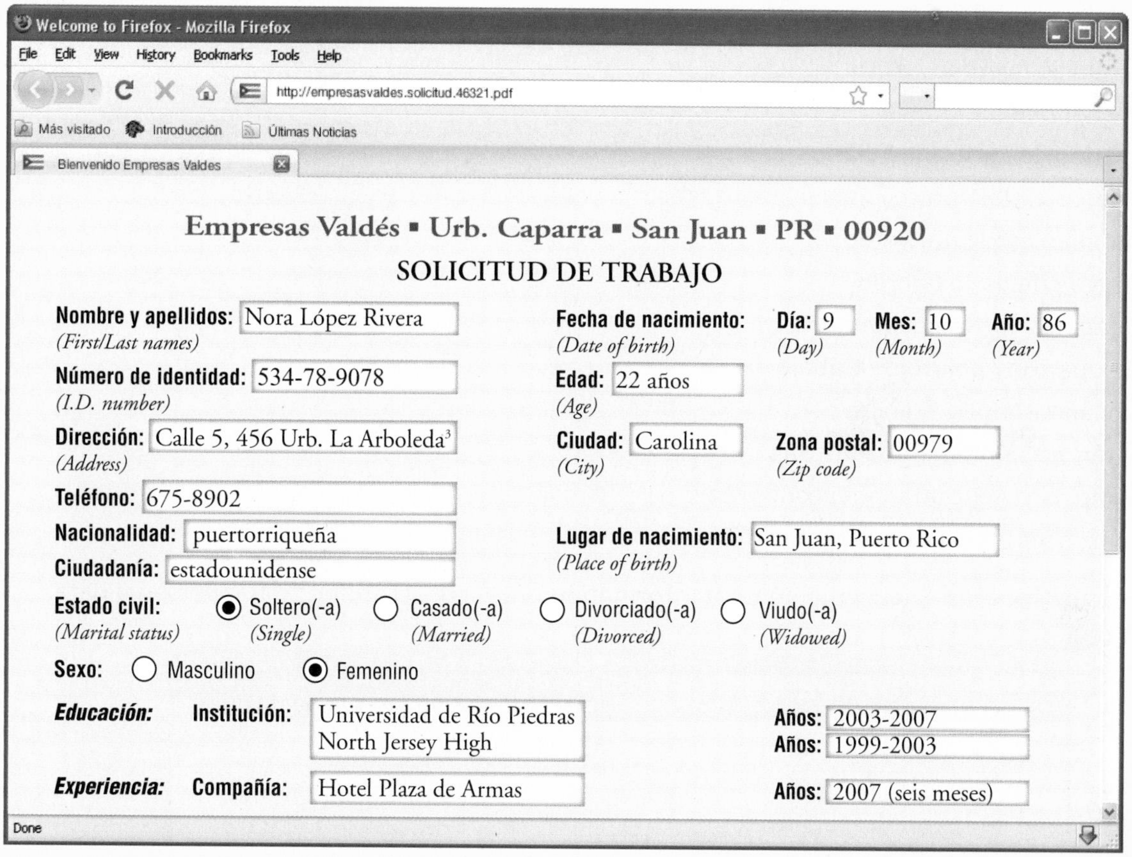

Empresas Valdés ▪ Urb. Caparra ▪ San Juan ▪ PR ▪ 00920

SOLICITUD DE TRABAJO

Nombre y apellidos: Nora López Rivera *(First/Last names)*
Fecha de nacimiento: *(Date of birth)* **Día:** 9 *(Day)* **Mes:** 10 *(Month)* **Año:** 86 *(Year)*
Número de identidad: 534-78-9078 *(I.D. number)*
Edad: 22 años *(Age)*
Dirección: Calle 5, 456 Urb. La Arboleda[3] *(Address)*
Ciudad: Carolina *(City)*
Zona postal: 00979 *(Zip code)*
Teléfono: 675-8902
Nacionalidad: puertorriqueña
Lugar de nacimiento: San Juan, Puerto Rico *(Place of birth)*
Ciudadanía: estadounidense
Estado civil: *(Marital status)* ◉ Soltero(-a) *(Single)* ○ Casado(-a) *(Married)* ○ Divorciado(-a) *(Divorced)* ○ Viudo(-a) *(Widowed)*
Sexo: ○ Masculino ◉ Femenino
Educación: **Institución:** Universidad de Río Piedras — **Años:** 2003-2007; North Jersey High — **Años:** 1999-2003
Experiencia: **Compañía:** Hotel Plaza de Armas — **Años:** 2007 (seis meses)

Características

amable, cortés	*polite, courteous*
antipático(a)	*unpleasant*
bajo(a)	*short*
bonito(a), lindo(a)	*pretty*
delgado(a)	*thin, slender*
encantador(a)	*charming*
feo(a)	*ugly*
gordo(a)	*fat*
optimista[4]	*optimist*
pelirrojo(a)	*red-headed*
pesimista[4]	*pessimist*
realista[4]	*realist*
rubio(a)	*blond(e)*
terco(a)	*stubborn*

Datos personales *(Personal data)*

lugar donde trabaja	*place of employment*
número de la licencia de conducir	*driver's license number*
número de seguro social	*social security number*
ocupación	*occupation*
profesión	*profession*
solicitud electrónica	*online application form*

[3] Given that the postal system in Puerto Rico is that of the United States, there have been trends toward reversing the street name and number so as to conform to American conventions. Remember, though: this is just in the case of Puerto Rico.
[4] The ending of this kind of adjective (**-ista**) does not change, regardless of gender: **un chico optimista; una chica optimista.**

VOCABULARIO

Práctica

2. **Palabras** Circle the word or phrase that does not belong in each group.

   1. anuncio / verdad / aviso
   2. beber / llenar / tomar
   3. periódico / informe / diario
   4. mensaje electrónico / apartamento / casa
   5. empleo / solicitud / después
   6. terco / delgado / gordo
   7. amable / cortés / pequeño
   8. ocupación / pelirrojo / trabajo
   9. mi amor / novia / dinero
   10. literatura / momento / historia
   11. simpático / encantador / económico
   12. entonces / alto / de estatura mediana

3. **Datos personales** Supply the items of information required, according to the personal data provided.

SOLICITUD DE EMPLEO

______________________: Ana Alicia Vega Ruiz

______________________: 13 de agosto de 1983

______________________: calle Bértoli, número 103

______________________: Ponce

______________________: puertorriqueña

______________________: San Juan, Puerto Rico

______________________: casada

______________________: femenino

______________________: Compañía Lux

4. **Minidiálogos** Complete the following exchanges, using vocabulary from this lesson.

   1. —¿Alicia es simpática?
      —No, es muy ______________.
   2. —¿Deseas tomar algo?
      —No, pero deseo ______________ algo.
   3. —Necesito el número de su ______________ de conducir.
      —¿Necesita también el número de mi ______________ social?
      —No, señorita.
   4. —¿Tú tienes un examen ______________ hoy?
      —Sí, esta tarde.

5. —¿Cuál es la ______________ de Ricardo?
   —Él es profesor.
6. —¿Qué necesitan ______________ ellos aquí?
   —La solicitud de empleo. Es una solicitud ______________.
7. —¿Quién es tu ______________ de cuarto?
   —Carlos Pérez.
8. —¿Tú tienes una hermana?
   —No, tengo un ______________.

5. ¿Qué es? Write the word or phrase that corresponds to the following.

1. clase en la que estudiamos a Shakespeare ______________
2. persona de Puerto Rico ______________
3. opuesto de **rubio** ______________
4. trabajo ______________
5. clase en la que estudiamos a Lincoln ______________
6. opuesto de **guapo** ______________
7. bonito ______________
8. opuesto de **gordo** ______________
9. anuncio ______________
10. opuesto de **pesimista** ______________
11. cortés ______________
12. beber ______________
13. lo que llenamos para solicitar algo ______________
14. día después de **hoy** ______________
15. diario ______________
16. tipo de mensaje que recibimos en la computadora ______________

Para conversar

6. ¿Sí o no? With a partner, take turns asking each other at least six questions starting with **¿Deseas...** ? or **¿Necesitas... ?,** and using the vocabulary presented in this lesson as much as possible. You should answer with complete sentences.

Modelo *¿Deseas tomar café?* *Sí, deseo tomar café.*

¿Necesitas el periódico? *No, no necesito el periódico.*

Pronunciación

CD1-15

Linking

- In Spanish, a final consonant is always linked with the next initial vowel sound.
  Es el‿amigo de Rafael.
- When two identical consonants are together, they are pronounced as one.
  Ellos‿son‿nativos.
- When two identical vowels are together, they are pronounced as one long vowel.
  ¿Está‿Ana‿Acosta?
- The final vowel of one word is linked with the initial vowel of the following word to form one syllable.
  La‿amiga de‿Olga‿es rubia.

ESTRUCTURAS

1 Possessive adjectives (*Los adjetivos posesivos*)

Forms of the Possessive Adjectives		
Singular	**Plural**	
mi	mis	*my*
tu	tus	*your* (*fam.*)
		his
		her
su	sus	*your* (*form.*)
		its
		their
nuestro(a)	nuestros(as)	*our*
vuestro(a)	vuestros(as)	*your* (*fam.*)

› Possessive adjectives always precede the nouns they introduce. They agree in number with the nouns they modify.

Yo necesito mi libro. / pluma.

Yo necesito mis libros. / plumas.

› **Nuestro** and **vuestro** are the only possessive adjectives that have the feminine endings **-a** and **-as**. The others take the same endings for both genders.

Nosotros necesitamos nuestro libro. / nuestra pluma.

Nosotros necesitamos nuestros libros. / nuestras plumas.

› Possessive adjectives agree in gender with the thing possessed and *not* with the possessor. For example, two male students referring to their female professor will say ***nuestra* profesora**.

› Because **su** and **sus** each has several possible meanings, the form **de él** (or **de ella, de ellos, de ellas, de Ud., de Uds.**) can be substituted to avoid confusion. The "formula" is: *article* + *noun* + **de** + *pronoun*.

sus plumas → las plumas **de él (ella, Ud.**, etc.)
su libro → el libro **de él (ella, Ud.**, etc.)

—¿De dónde son **tus** amigos?	*Where are your friends from?*
—**Mis** amigos son de Puerto Rico.	*My friends are from Puerto Rico.*
—¿Quién es la profesora **de Uds.**?	*Who is your professor?*
—**Nuestra** profesora es la doctora Paz.	*Our professor is Dr. Paz.*

Práctica

7. **Minidiálogos** Complete the following exchanges, using the corresponding possessive adjectives. Then act them out with a partner.

   1. —Inés, ¿a qué hora es ______________ clase de español?
      —______________ clase de español es a las 9.
      —¿Y la clase de inglés de Ana?
      —______________ clase (La clase de ella) es a las 10.
   2. —¿De dónde es la profesora de Uds.?
      —______________ profesora es de San Juan; es puertorriqueña.
   3. —Anita, ¿______________ hermanos hablan inglés?
      —Sí, ______________ hermanos hablan inglés.
      —¿Y las hermanas de Raúl?
      —No, ______________ hermanas (las hermanas de él) no hablan inglés.
   4. —Sr. Vega, ¿______________ clases son por la mañana o por la tarde?
      —______________ clases son por la tarde.
   5. —Sergio, ¿dónde trabaja la compañera de cuarto de Rita?
      —______________ compañera de cuarto (La compañera de cuarto de ella) trabaja en el hospital.
   6. —¿Dónde viven los amigos de Uds.?
      —______________ amigos viven en California.

8. **Respuestas negativas** (*Negative answers*) Answer the following questions *in the negative*, using the appropriate possessive adjectives.

   1. ¿Lorena es la novia de Alberto?
   2. ¿Necesitas tu libro de español?
   3. ¿La profesora de Uds. es de México?
   4. ¿Carlos y Daniel son tus amigos?
   5. ¿El Dr. Paz y la Dra. Ruiz son profesores de Uds.?
   6. ¿Tú necesitas mis cuadernos?
   7. ¿Tú necesitas la dirección de los chicos?
   8. ¿Marisa y Olga son amigas de Claudia?

Para conversar

9. **Deseamos saber...** (*We want to know . . .*) With a classmate, prepare six questions you want to ask Carlos and David about their apartment, their friends, their classes, etc. Some of the questions should be addressed to both of them, and some to one of them. Make sure you use the appropriate possessive adjectives.

2 Cardinal numbers 101–1000 (*Los números cardinales 101–1000*)

101	**ciento uno** (*and so on*)	600	**seiscientos**
200	**doscientos**	700	**setecientos**
300	**trescientos**	800	**ochocientos**
400	**cuatrocientos**	900	**novecientos**
500	**quinientos**	1000	**mil**

› When counting beyond 100 (101 to 199), **ciento** is used.

› **Y** appears only in numbers between 16 and 99. It is not used to separate thousands, hundreds, and tens from each other: **mil quinientos ochenta y seis.**

› In Spanish, one does not count in hundreds beyond 1000; thus, 1100 is expressed as **mil cien**. After 1000, thousands are counted **dos mil, tres mil,** and so on. Note that Spanish uses a period rather than a comma to indicate thousands.

—¿Cuál es su fecha de nacimiento? — *What is the date of your birthday?*
—El tres de abril de mil novecientos ochenta y dos. — *April third, nineteen (hundred and) eighty-two.*

› When modifying a feminine noun, the feminine form is used: **doscientas sillas**.

› To ask how much a single item costs, say, **"¿Cuánto cuesta?"** For multiple items, use **"¿Cuánto cuestan?"**

—¿Cuánto cuesta el escritorio? — *How much does the desk cost?*
—Cuesta **ciento cincuenta** dólares. — *It costs a hundred and fifty dollars.*
—¿Cuánto cuestan las ventanas? — *How much do the windows cost?*
—Cuestan **mil cien** dólares. — *They cost eleven hundred dollars.*

Práctica

10. Números With a partner, take turns writing and reading the following numbers aloud.

1. 348 ____________________
2. 575 ____________________
3. 815 ____________________
4. 213 ____________________
5. 937 ____________________
6. 1725 ____________________
7. 4120 ____________________
8. 8438 ____________________
9. 12 300 ____________________
10. 28 645 ____________________

11. **De compras** (*Shopping*) With a partner, look at the illustrations and ask how much each item costs.

Modelo —*¿Cuánto cuesta el sofá?*
—*El sofá cuesta novecientos noventa dólares.*

Hint: el cuadro = *picture*

el auto = *car*

Para conversar

12. **En el año...** (*In the year . . .*) Mention different historic events from the list below to different classmates. Your classmates should say the year in which that event took place. If you need help, refer to the year in the box.

1492	1969
1776	2001
1861	2010
1914	

1. Los Juegos Olímpicos de Canadá.
2. La Primera Guerra Mundial (*World War I*).
3. El descubrimiento de América.
4. La independencia de los Estados Unidos.
5. La Guerra Civil en Estados Unidos.
6. La llegada del hombre a la luna (*moon*).
7. El ataque a las torres gemelas de Nueva York.
8. Las fechas de nacimiento de Uds.

Estatua de Cristóbal Colón, Barcelona, España

13. **Buscamos apartamento.** (*We're looking for an apartment.*) In groups of three or four, try to figure out how much a one-room, two-room, and three-room apartment costs. Discuss different locations.

Modelo *Yo creo que un apartamento de una habitación en Manhattan debe costar tres mil dolares por mes.*

HINT:
- de una habitación
- de dos habitaciones
- de tres habitaciones

3 Descriptive adjectives: Forms, position, and agreement with articles and nouns (*Adjetivos calificativos: formas, posición y concordancia con artículos y nombres*)

A. Forms of adjectives

› Descriptive adjectives identify characteristics or qualities such as color, size, and personality. In Spanish, these adjectives agree in gender and number with the nouns they modify. Adjectives ending in **-o** are made feminine by changing the **-o** to **-a.**

el muchach**o** cuban**o**	la muchach**a** cuban**a**
el chic**o** rubi**o**	la chic**a** rubi**a**
el lápiz roj**o**	la pluma roj**a**

> **Un dicho**
> **A palabras necias, oídos sordos.**
> Equivalent: *Take no notice of the stupid things people say.*

› Adjectives ending in **-e** or in a **consonant** have the same form for the masculine and the feminine.

el chico inteligent**e**	la chica inteligent**e**
el esposo feli**z** *(happy)*	la esposa feli**z**
el libro fáci**l**	la clase fáci**l**

› Adjectives of nationality that end in a consonant add an **-a** in the feminine.

el muchacho españo**l**	la muchacha españo**la**
el señor inglé**s**	la señora ingle**sa**

› Adjectives ending in **-or, -án, -ón,** or **-ín** add an **-a** in the feminine.

el alumno trabajad**or**
la alumna trabajad**ora**
} *the hardworking student*

¡Atención! Adjectives that have an accent in the last syllable of the masculine form drop it in the feminine: **inglés → inglesa.**[1]

[1] For rules on accent marks, see Appendix A.

- To form the plural, adjectives follow the same rules as nouns. Adjectives ending in a vowel add **-s**; adjectives ending in a consonant add **-es**; adjectives ending in **-z** change the **-z** to **c** and add **-es**.

norteamerican**a**	norteamerican**as**
españo**l**	españo**les**
feli**z**	feli**ces**

B. Position of adjectives

- Descriptive adjectives generally follow the noun.

Miguel es un chico **inteligente.**	*Miguel is an intelligent boy.*
Necesito dos plumas **rojas.**	*I need two red pens.*

- Adjectives denoting nationality always follow the noun.

  El profesor **mexicano** trabaja en la universidad.

C. Agreement of articles, nouns, and adjectives

- In Spanish, the article, noun, and adjective agree in gender and number.

un muchach**o** **alto**	**una** muchach**a** **alta**
los muchach**os** **altos**	**las** muchach**as** **altas**

- When an adjective modifies two or more nouns, the plural form is used.

  la sill**a** y la mes**a** **rojas**

- If two nouns described together are of different genders, the masculine plural form of the adjective is used.

  la chic**a** puertorriqueñ**a**
  el chic**o** puertorriqueñ**o**
  } la chic**a** y el chic**o** **puertorriqueños**

Dos cantantes puertorriqueños: Jennifer López y Chayanne

Práctica

14. Nacionalidades You are acquainted with these famous people. With a partner, take turns matching them with their nationalities. Be sure to use the verb **ser** and to make any necessary changes to the adjectives.

mexicano (*Mexican*)
norteamericano (estadounidense)
dominicano
colombiano
español
cubano
inglés
puertorriqueño

1. David Beckham ____________
2. Shakira ____________
3. el presidente Felipe Calderón ____________
4. Gloria Estefan y Andy García ____________
5. Penélope Cruz y Antonio Banderas ____________
6. Hillary Clinton ____________
7. Jean Paul Sartre y Albert Camus ____________
8. Sammy Sosa y Juan Luis Guerra ____________

La actriz Penélope Cruz

15. ¡Al contrario! (*On the contrary!*) With a partner, take turns asking and answering the following questions. In your answers, contradict what is stated.

Modelo —*¿Rosaura es alta?*
—*No, es baja.*

1. ¿Rita y Sara son delgadas?
2. ¿La hermana de Diego es fea?
3. ¿El novio de Marisa es guapo?
4. ¿Tú eres impaciente?
5. ¿Las amigas de Graciela son antipáticas?
6. ¿El hermano de Olga es moreno?
7. ¿Los muchachos son bajos?
8. ¿Mario es pesimista?

16. ¿Cómo son? (*What are they like?*) With a partner, take turns describing the following people, using as many descriptive adjectives as possible.

1. Salma Hayek
2. Antonio Banderas
3. Roseanne
4. Brad Pitt
5. Sandra Bullock
6. las chicas de la clase
7. los chicos de la clase
8. tu mejor amigo(a)

LEARNING TIP
Empower yourself by asking for help any time you feel you need it, by using the following questions: **¿Cómo se dice... ?** and **¿Qué quiere decir... ?** (*What does . . . mean?*)

Para conversar

17. Características Get together in groups of three or four and, with the characteristics listed for all the signs of the zodiac, decide whether or not they correspond to your personalities. Then each person in the group will think of someone he or she knows and check out that person's sign. Do the characteristics fit that person?

Aries: valientes, dinámicos, interesantes y un poco impacientes

Tauro: prácticos, pacientes, leales (*loyal*) y un poco tercos

Géminis: inteligentes, enigmáticos, no muy religiosos y un poco superficiales

Cáncer: amistosos, afectuosos, hogareños (*family oriented*) y muy sensibles (*sensitive*)

Leo: optimistas, románticos, divertidos y un poco egoístas

Virgo: inteligentes, eficientes, generosos y un poco inseguros

Libra: amables, diplomáticos, idealistas y un poco indecisos

Escorpión: valientes, leales, trabajadores y un poco sarcásticos

Sagitario: lógicos, optimistas, encantadores y un poco egoístas

Capricornio: maduros, disciplinados, trabajadores y muy reservados

Acuario: compasivos, independientes, un poco excéntricos y un poco tercos

Piscis: creativos, espirituales, compasivos y un poco indecisos

18. El hombre ideal... la mujer ideal With a classmate, list ten characteristics that make a man or a woman the ideal partner. When you have finished, join another group and compare your lists. How are they the same? How do they differ? Then each person tells one characteristic they find most important in a man or a woman.

Modelo *¿Cómo es tu mujer ideal?* or *¿Cómo es tu hombre ideal?*
El hombre ideal es... ; La mujer ideal es...

4 Present indicative of regular *-er* and *-ir* verbs (*Presente de indicativo de los verbos regulares que terminan en* ***-er*** *y en* ***-ir***)

comer ***to eat***		**vivir** ***to live***	
yo	com**o**	yo	viv**o**
tú	com**es**	tú	viv**es**
Ud. / él / ella	com**e**	Ud. / él / ella	viv**e**
nosotros(as)	com**emos**	nosotros(as)	viv**imos**
vosotros(as)	com**éis**	vosotros(as)	viv**ís**
Uds. / ellos / ellas	com**en**	Uds. / ellos / ellas	viv**en**

› Other verbs conjugated like **comer:**

aprender *to learn*
creer *to believe, to think*
leer *to read*
correr *to run*
beber *to drink*
vender *to sell*
deber *must, should*

—¿Dónde **comen** ustedes?	*Where do you eat?*
—Eva y yo **comemos** en la cafetería y Anabel **come** en su apartamento.	*Eva and I eat in the cafeteria and Anabel eats in her apartment.*
—¿Tú **crees** que Marcos es simpático?	*Do you think Marcos is nice?*
—Sí, yo **creo** que es muy simpático.	*Yes, I think that he's very nice.*
—¿Qué periódico **lee** Ud., señorita?	*What newspaper do you read, miss?*
—Yo **leo** *El New York Times.*	*I read* The New York Times.

› Other verbs conjugated like **vivir**:

asistir *to attend*
abrir *to open*
escribir *to write*
decidir *to decide*
recibir *to receive*

—¿Dónde **viven** Uds.?	*Where do you live?*
—Nosotros **vivimos** en la Calle Seis.	*We live on Sixth Street.*
—¿Tú **escribes** con lápiz o con pluma?	*Do you write with a pencil or with a pen?*
—**Escribo** con bolígrafo.	*I write with a ballpoint pen.*

Un proverbio
No solo de pan vive el hombre.
Equivalent: *Man does not live by bread alone.*

Práctica

19. ¿Y los demás? (*And the others?*) The following is what David does. With a partner, use your imagination to indicate what other people do differently.

Modelo David come a las seis. (Nosotros)
Nosotros comemos a las ocho.

1. **David** come en su apartamento. (Nosotros)
2. ...vive en la calle Quinta. (Yo)
3. ...recibe mensajes electrónicos de sus amigos. (Tú)
4. ...lee el periódico *New York Times.* (Mi papá)
5. ...vende sus libros de historia. (Mis amigos)
6. ...bebe café. (Nosotras)
7. ...debe estudiar por la mañana. (Eva y Dora)
8. ...escribe en español. (Tú)
9. ...corre por la noche. (Mi hermano)
10. ...cree que el español es fácil. (Los estudiantes)
11. ...asiste a clases los martes y jueves. (Nosotros)
12. ...abre su ventana por la noche. (Yo)

20. **Deseo saber...** With a partner, take turns turning the statements on page 86 into questions to ask each other.

Modelo —*¿Tú comes en tu apartamento?*
—*No, yo no como en mi apartamento; como en la cafetería.*

21. **¿Qué hacemos?** (*What do we do?*) With a partner, complete the following sentences by describing what one or both of you do or don't do. Use regular **-er** and **-ir** verbs in your answers.

Modelos _______ el diario por la mañana.
Yo (no) leo el diario por la mañana.
or *Nosotros (no) leemos el diario por la mañana.*

1. _______ mucho (*a lot of*) café.
2. _______ en la cafetería de la universidad.
3. _______ mucho dinero.
4. _______ a la universidad.
5. _______ en Arizona.
6. _______ estudiar más (*more*).
7. _______ español.
8. _______ en Santa Claus.
9. _______ por la mañana.
10. _______ en el cuaderno.
11. _______ la puerta de la clase.
12. _______ en un apartamento.

Un dicho
Debes comer para vivir, no vivir para comer.
Equivalent: *You should eat to live, not live to eat.*

Para conversar

22. **Dime...** (*Tell me . . .*) With a partner, take turns asking and answering the following questions in complete sentences.

1. ¿Dónde vives? ¿Vives en una casa o en un apartamento?
2. ¿Dónde comes? ¿A qué hora comes? ¿Comes con un(a) amigo(a) o comes solo(a)?
3. ¿Tú y tus amigos comen sándwiches? ¿Comen comida (*food*) mexicana?
4. ¿Tú bebes refrescos o café?
5. ¿Aprendes mucho en la clase de español? ¿Debes estudiar más?
6. ¿Tú lees periódicos en español?
7. ¿Lees bien el español?[1] ¿Escribes en español o en inglés?
8. ¿Vendes tus libros? ¿Los estudiantes reciben mucho dinero por (*for*) sus libros?
9. ¿Debes trabajar mañana o debes estudiar?
10. ¿Recibes muchos mensajes electrónicos por día? ¿Cuántos?

[1] The definite article is used with names of languages except after the prepositions **en** and **de,** or after the verbs **hablar** and usually **estudiar**.

23. ¿Estás de acuerdo? (*Do you agree?*) In groups of three, express your opinion about each of the following (**Yo creo que...**). The others agree (**Estoy de acuerdo**) or disagree (**No estoy de acuerdo**). Use the hints and other descriptive words that you already know.

Hint:	caro	*expensive*	bueno	*good*
	barato	*inexpensive*	malo	*bad*

1. la clase de español
2. el presidente
3. los programas de TV en español
4. Nueva York
5. Christina Aguilera
6. el Hotel Hilton
7. los profesores de la universidad
8. la universidad

Christina Aguilera

5 Present indicative of the irregular verbs *tener* and *venir*

(*Presente de indicativo de los verbos irregulares* tener *y* venir)

tener ***to have***		**venir** ***to come***	
yo	**tengo**	yo	**vengo**
tú	**tienes**	tú	**vienes**
Ud. / él / ella	**tiene**	Ud. / él / ella	**viene**
nosotros(as)	**tenemos**	nosotros(as)	**venimos**
vosotros(as)	**tenéis**	vosotros(as)	**venís**
Uds. / ellos / ellas	**tienen**	Uds. / ellos / ellas	**vienen**

—¿Cuántas clases **tienen** Uds.?	*How many classes do you have?*
—**Tenemos** dos. ¿Cuántas **tienes** tú?	*We have two. How many do you have?*
—Yo **tengo** cuatro.	*I have four.*
—¿A qué hora **vienen** Uds. a la universidad?	*What time do you come to the university?*
—Yo **vengo** a las ocho y Teresa **viene** a las diez.	*I come at eight and Teresa comes at ten.*
—¿Las chicas **vienen** los sábados?	*Do the girls come on Saturdays?*
—Sí, y nosotras **venimos** con ellas.	*Yes, and we come with them.*

¡Atención! Tener que means *to have to*, and it is followed by an infinitive: Olga **tiene que** trabajar hoy. *Olga has to work today.*

Práctica

24. Compañeros de estudio (*Study partners*) Using the present indicative of **tener** and **venir**, complete the following paragraph about what Rafael says he will do next Saturday.

Yo no ________________ a la universidad el sábado porque no ________________ clases. Mis compañeros de cuarto y yo ________________ que estudiar este (*this*) sábado porque ________________ un examen muy difícil el lunes. Mis amigos ________________ a mi casa por la tarde para estudiar conmigo. Mi amigo Luis no ________________ examen el lunes. Por eso él no ________________ a mi casa a estudiar.

25. ¿Qué tienes que hacer? You and a partner talk about nine things you have to do this week.

1. trabajar / ¿cuántas horas?
2. estudiar / ¿qué días?
3. escribir / ¿qué?
4. llamar / ¿a quién?
5. llenar / ¿qué?
6. asistir / ¿adónde?
7. practicar / ¿qué?
8. aceptar / ¿qué?
9. hablar / ¿con quién?

¿Tienes que estudiar?

Join another group and compare your responses to theirs.

Para conversar

26. Entrevista With a partner, take turns asking and answering these questions.

1. ¿Tú tienes mi número de teléfono? ¿Tienes mi dirección?
2. ¿El (La) profesor(a) tiene tu número de teléfono? ¿Tiene tu número de seguro social?
3. ¿Tú y tus amigos vienen a la universidad los sábados? ¿Vienen los domingos?
4. ¿Tú tienes problemas económicos? ¿Tienes que trabajar más?
5. ¿A qué hora vienes tú a tu primera clase?
6. ¿Qué días vienes a la universidad?
7. ¿Tienes compañero(a) de cuarto o vives solo(a)?
8. ¿Cuándo tienen exámenes parciales tú y tu compañero(a) de cuarto?

ESTRUCTURAS

6 The personal *a* (*La* a *personal*)

› The preposition **a** is used in Spanish before a direct object[1] referring to a specific person or persons. It is called "the personal **a**" and has no equivalent in English.

Yo llamo **a** mi amiga.	Nosotros llamamos **a** los estudiantes.
D.O.	D.O.
I call my friend.	*We call the students.*
D.O.	D.O.

› The personal **a** is *not* used when the direct object is not a person.

Yo llamo un taxi.	*I call a taxi.*
Nosotros llevamos los libros a la biblioteca.	*We take the books to the library.*

› The verb **tener** generally does not take the personal **a**, even if the direct object is a person.

Yo tengo muchos amigos.	*I have many friends.*
—¿Tú llevas **a** tu novia a la universidad?	*Do you take your girlfriend to the university?*
—Yo no tengo novia. Llevo **a** Jorge y **a** Luis.	*I don't have a girlfriend. I take Jorge and Luis.*

¡Atención! When there is a series of direct object nouns referring to people, the personal **a** is repeated:

Llevo *a* Jorge y *a* Luis.

Práctica

27. Preguntas y respuestas Match the items in column A with the ones in column B. Add the personal **a** to the items in column B when needed.

A			B
1. Nosotros tenemos	________	a. ________	el informe para mi clase de historia.
2. Miguel llama	________	b. ________	su mamá.
3. Yo escribo	________	c. ________	su mamá a la biblioteca.
4. Mi novio lleva	________	d. ________	muchos mensajes electrónicos.
5. Yo debo llamar	________	e. ________	un taxi.
6. Los niños (*kids*) necesitan	________	f. ________	sus pacientes (*patients*).
7. El profesor Paz tiene	________	g. ________	cien estudiantes en su clase.
8. Yo recibo	________	h. ________	muchos amigos puertorriqueños.
9. El doctor Peña debe llamar	________	i. ________	nuestros amigos a la fiesta.
10. Nosotros invitamos	________	j. ________	su novia por la tarde.
11. Luis tiene	________	k. ________	mi papá por la noche.
12. Yo llamo	________	l. ________	tu invitación.
13. Yo acepto	________	m. ________	mi novia a su casa.
14. Yo llevo	________	n. ________	una novia muy bonita.

[1] See **Lección 6** for further explanation of the direct object.

28. Minidiálogos Use the personal **a** when needed to complete the following exchanges. Then act them out with a partner.

1. —¿Cuántos hermanos tienes tú?
   —Yo no tengo ________ hermanos. Tengo dos ________ hermanas.
2. —¿A quién llevas tú a la universidad?
   —Yo llevo ________ mi hermana y ________ mis amigos.
3. —¿Tú llamas ________ tu compañero de cuarto?
   —Sí, necesito hablar con él.
4. —¿Adónde llevas los ________ cuadernos?
   —A la clase.
5. —¿Qué escribe Ud.?
   —Escribo ________ un informe para mi clase de historia.
6. —¿Tú llamas ________ un taxi?
   —No, llamo ________ mi amigo Raúl.
7. —¿Tú visitas ________ Nora los domingos?
   —No, visito ________ Carlos y ________ Maribel.
8. —¿Tú necesitas ver (*to see*) ________ tus amigos?
   —No, necesito ver ________ mis padres.

Para conversar

29. ¡Una fiesta! (*A party!*) With a partner, decide which members of the class you want to take or invite **(invitar)** to the party next Saturday. Give reasons for your choices.

© Dmitriy Shironosov/Shutterstock.com

¡Vamos a ver!

Antes de ver el video

30. Antes de ver el video With a partner, take turns responding to the following.

1. si viven en un apartamento o en una casa
2. si comen en la cafetería de la universidad
3. si beben mucho café
4. dónde trabajan
5. cómo son sus padres
6. si necesitan estudiar más o ganar más dinero
7. si tienen conocimiento (*knowledge*) de computadoras
8. si leen los anuncios en el periódico
9. si reciben muchos mensajes electrónicos de sus amigos
10. si tienen exámenes parciales en sus clases
11. si tienen que escribir un informe
12. si desean comer algo después de la clase

El video: Dos puertorriqueñas en Nueva York

—Tengo que llenar la solicitud de empleo de la compañía Sandoval.

—Hola. ¿Está Mariana?
—Sí, con ella habla.

—Tengo que escribir un informe para mi clase de literatura, pero acepto tu invitación...

Después de ver el video

© Cengage Learning
Mariana

© Cengage Learning
Olga

© Cengage Learning
Rafael

31. ¿Quién lo dice? Identify the person who said the following in the dialogues.

1. Oye, mañana tenemos el examen parcial en la clase de historia. ________________
2. Pero recibo mensajes electrónicos de mi amiga de Brasil. ________________
3. ¡Acepto tu invitación! ________________
4. Pero tú no tienes conocimiento de computadoras. ________________
5. Tengo que llenar la solicitud de empleo de la compañía Sandoval. ________________
6. Buena idea. Nos vemos a las seis. Oye... ¿está Olga? ________________
7. ¿Deseas beber algo en el café París? ________________
8. Tú no hablas portugués. ________________
9. ¡Ajá! ¡Con razón Rafael viene a estudiar conmigo! ________________

32. Hablemos With a partner, take turns asking and answering the following questions. Base your answers on the dialogue.

En el diálogo

1. ¿Quién es la compañera de cuarto de Olga?
2. ¿Dónde conversan las chicas?
3. ¿Cómo es Olga? ¿Cómo es Mariana?
4. ¿Mariana tiene dinero o tiene problemas económicos?
5. ¿Mariana tiene conocimiento de computadoras?
6. ¿Qué recibe Mariana de Brasil?
7. ¿Qué tienen Rafael y Mariana mañana?
8. ¿Qué tiene que escribir Olga?
9. ¿Acepta Olga la invitación de Rafael?
10. ¿Rafael viene o no a estudiar con Mariana?

33. ¿Qué pasa después? You and a partner use your imagination to talk about what happens to the characters after they leave the café. In Spanish, discuss the following.

1. what time the girls return to their apartment
2. whether Mariana fills out the job application
3. whether Mariana receives another e-mail from her friend from Brazil
4. whether Olga reads a book or the paper
5. whether Rafael calls Olga again (*otra vez*) or he comes to the girls' apartment
6. whether Mariana studies for the history exam
7. whether Olga writes the report for her literature class or watches TV (*mira la tele*)
8. if Rafael calls another girl when he arrives at his apartment

Now compare your statements to those of another group.

¡Vamos a escuchar!

ESTRATEGIA **Taking a phone call** In a very broad sense, most listening has a purpose, whether to get specific information such as movie times or store hours, follow a lecture for the important points, or simply to provide an ear for a friend. When you get a phone call, you generally expect the caller to let you know the reason for the call, which then tells you how to respond and what specific information to listen for or ask about as the conversation continues.

CD1-16 **34. Hola** Javier calls his friend Marta. Listen to their conversation and answer the first question to identify the reason for his call. Then listen a second time for the specifics and answer the remaining questions.

1. ¿Por qué llama a Marta?
2. ¿Qué hay mañana?
3. ¿Dónde estudian Javier y Marta? ¿A qué hora?
4. ¿Para qué clase tiene que escribir un informe Marta?

¡Vamos a conversar!

ESTRATEGIA **Using stock phrases** Having a repertoire of phrases that you can use in particular situations can help take the pressure off speaking, especially when you are beginning to learn a language. It also lets you concentrate on listening and understanding. Here are some phrases you can use.

To show agreement: **Buena idea.** (*Good idea.*) **Es verdad.** (*It's true.*) **Por supuesto.** (*Of course.*) **Está bien.** (*That's fine/good.*)
To apologize: **Lo siento.** (*I'm sorry.*)
To decline or make an excuse: **No puedo.** (*I can't.*) **Tengo que...**

35. ¿Estudiamos el lunes? With a partner, agree on a day, time, and place to study Spanish together. Use some of the preceding phrases in your conversation as you try to find a day and time that's convenient for both of you.

36. ¿Qué dice Ud.? What would you say in the following situations? What might the other person say? Act out the scenes with a partner. Take turns playing each role.

1. Describe your best (*mejor*) friend as completely as possible. Add any pertinent information about him/her you deem important.
2. You have agreed to pick up a classmate on your way to school. Inform him/her at what time you come to class in the morning and get the following information:
   a. where he/she lives
   b. at what time he/she returns home in the evening
3. Your phone rings and you answer it. The call is for you. You and the caller, a friend, make plans for him/her to come to your house to study.
4. You tell a friend three things you have to do tomorrow afternoon.
5. Ask your friend if he/she wants to have something to drink after studying.

37. Para conocernos mejor To do this activity, work with a classmate whom you would like to get to know. Take turns asking each other these questions.

1. ¿Vives en una casa o en un apartamento pequeño? ¿Vives con tu familia o con unos(as) amigos(as)?
2. ¿Qué días asistes a la universidad? ¿Tus clases son por la mañana, por la tarde o por la noche? ¿Cuál es tu clase favorita?
3. ¿A qué hora estudias? ¿Estudias solo(a) o con tu compañero(a) de clase? ¿Él (Ella) es muy inteligente? ¿Tienes que escribir muchos informes para tus clases? ¿Son fáciles?
4. ¿Tienes problemas económicos? ¿Necesitas trabajar? ¿Tienes experiencia? ¿Cuánto dinero deseas ganar en tu trabajo? ¿Lees los anuncios en los periódicos todos los días? ¿Qué periódico lees?
5. ¿Qué tienes que hacer mañana?
6. ¿Tienes novio(a)? ¿Cómo es?

38. Una encuesta Interview your classmates to identify who fits the following descriptions. Include your instructor, but remember to use the **Ud.** form when addressing him/her. After finishing the survey, get together with two or three classmates and discuss the results.

1. Tiene un(a) amigo(a) puertorriqueño(a).	___________
2. Asiste a la universidad los sábados.	___________
3. No tiene novio(a).	___________
4. Necesita empleo.	___________
5. Necesita ganar más dinero.	___________
6. Lee los anuncios en el periódico los domingos.	___________
7. Recibe muchas invitaciones.	___________
8. Tiene mucho que hacer mañana.	___________

39. Para crear Get together in groups of three and "create" the scenario for this photo. Who are the people? Give them names. What is the relationship they have with each other? Where are they from? What might they say to each other? What plans might they make?

© Maria Teijeiro/PhotoDisc/Getty Images

¡Vamos a leer!

Antes de leer

ESTRATEGIA **Activating background knowledge** Bringing your own experiences to a new reading helps prepare you for the kinds of information you may encounter. By thinking about what you know of a topic before reading, you will be better able to anticipate the content of a text and understand more of what you read.

40. Un mensaje electrónico Aurora Paz and Sergio Guzmán have recently met in a chat room. Before reading an e-mail from Aurora to Sergio, discuss with a partner what information you would give about yourself to a new cyberfriend and what questions you would ask to get to know someone.

¡A leer!

El mensaje de Aurora

Send Mail: Message Composition

A: Sergio

De: Aurora

Asunto: Cómo soy

Sergio:

Tú deseas una descripción de mi persona.° ¡Aquí va!

Soy morena, alta y delgada. Muchos dicen° que soy bonita. Creo que soy inteligente, trabajadora y muy disciplinada. Y ahora... lo negativo: soy impaciente. Mi mamá dice que soy muy terca.

Asisto a la universidad por la mañana, trabajo por la tarde y estudio por la noche. Los sábados salgo° con mis amigos. Vamos° a la playa,° a una discoteca, a un concierto o al teatro.

¿Y tú? ¿Cómo eres? ¿Alto o de estatura mediana? ¿Trabajas o solo estudias? ¿Tus clases son fáciles o difíciles? ¿Vives en San Juan o en Santurce? ¿Vives en una casa con tu familia o vives en un apartamento?

¿Vives solo° o tienes un compañero de cuarto? ¿Tienes hermanos? ¿Cuántos? Mándame° un mensaje mañana.

de... *of myself*
Muchos... *Many say*
I go out / We go / beach
alone
Send me

41. Comprensión As you read the e-mail, find the answers to the following questions.

1. ¿Qué desea Sergio?
2. ¿Aurora es rubia?
3. ¿Qué características positivas tiene?
4. ¿Qué dice la mamá de Aurora?
5. ¿Qué actividades tiene Aurora todos los días?
6. Los sábados, ¿trabaja o sale con sus amigos?
7. ¿Adónde va (*goes*) con sus amigos?
8. ¿Qué pregunta (*asks*) Aurora sobre las clases de Sergio?
9. ¿Qué ciudades puertorriqueñas menciona Aurora?
10. ¿Qué pregunta ella sobre la familia de Sergio?

Después de leer... desde su mundo

42. Caracteristicas In groups of three or four discuss your positive and negative traits. Then describe the positive and negative characteristics of your best friend.

LEARNING TIP
As with speaking and pronunciation, paying attention to the words and structures used by the writer of a Spanish text will help you to improve your ability to communicate when you speak or write in Spanish.

¡Vamos a escribir!

Antes de escribir

ESTRATEGIA **Analyzing writing models** A model or written sample is often an excellent aid for your development as a writer in Spanish. By examining how a letter, an article, or other piece of writing is organized and what words are used, you can gain helpful ideas about how to construct your own writing.

43. Organización Look at the e-mail in **¡A leer!** and ask yourself the following questions.

1. What is the main idea that groups together the sentences in each paragraph?
2. How does Aurora describe herself? How would you describe yourself?
3. What activities does she talk about in the second paragraph?
4. What questions does she ask Sergio in the third paragraph? What questions would you ask?

¡A escribir!

44. Mensaje electrónico You have a new cyberacquaintance. Write the first draft **(primer borrador)** of an e-mail to send to this person, following the organization of Aurora's e-mail to Sergio. You may want to use some of the questions that you brainstormed for the pre-reading activity in **¡A leer!**

Después de escribir

45. A revisar Before writing the final version of your e-mail, exchange your first draft with a classmate's and peer edit each other's work using the following guidelines:

- noun-adjective-article agreement (in gender and number)
- subject-verb agreement (in person and number)
- clear organization and use of the model

If students do not have Spanish-speaking pen pals, have them exchange e-mails with a classmate and respond to their partner's e-mail.

EL MUNDO HISPÁNICO Y TÚ

Los puertorriqueños en los Estados Unidos

Aproximadamente 3.000.000 de puertorriqueños viven en los Estados Unidos, el 70% de ellos en Nueva York y Nueva Jersey. En la ciudad de Nueva York viven más puertorriqueños que en San Juan, la capital de Puerto Rico. El desfile puertorriqueño de Nueva York es uno de los más coloridos y espectaculares de esta ciudad, y unos tres millones de personas asisten a él (*attend it*). Tiene lugar (*It takes place*) el segundo domingo de junio.

La mayoría de los puertorriqueños llegaron (*arrived*) a los Estados Unidos después de la Segunda Guerra Mundial (*Second World War*) y, para muchos, fue (*it was*) muy difícil adaptarse a la vida de la gran ciudad. En las últimas décadas, han llegado de Puerto Rico miles de profesionales, artistas y gente de negocios (*business people*). Algunos ejemplos de puertorriqueños exitosos son Sonia Sotomayor, jueza (*judge*) de la Corte Suprema de los Estados Unidos; Nydia Velázquez y José Serrano, congresistas; Ricky Martin y Chayanne, cantantes; Rosalyn Sánchez y Benicio del Toro, artistas de Hollywood, y Félix "Tito" Trinidad, ex triple campeón de boxeo.

© Picture Partners/Alamy

© Philip Scalia/Alamy

Nuyorican Poets Café, una de las instituciones neoyorquinas dedicadas a la poesía, la música, las artes visuales, la comedia y el teatro.

La música y el baile

© Bryan Bedder/Getty Images Entertainment / Getty Images

Los dos son puertorriqueños; los dos cantan y bailan (*dance*). Además, ella es actriz de cine y él actuó en algunas películas (*movies*). ¿Sabes (*Do you know*) quiénes son?[1]

© Scott Gries/Getty Images

Daddy Yankee, ganador del premio "Artista del Año" del MTV latino.

[1] Marc Anthony y Jennifer López

El cine y la televisión

© Gerard Julien/AFP/Getty Images

Benicio del Toro, famoso actor y productor de cine puertorriqueño. Es ganador (*winner*) de varios premios (*awards*), incluyendo un Óscar.

© Gary Gershoff/WireImage/Getty Images

Geraldo Rivera tiene varias profesiones: abogado (*lawyer*), reportero, escritor y comentarista. Su programa actual (*current*) es *Geraldo at large*. Muchos opinan que algunas (*some*) de sus ideas son controversiales.

Los beisbolistas puertorriqueños

El béisbol es el deporte nacional de Puerto Rico, a diferencia de otros países latinoamericanos donde el fútbol es el deporte popular.

© Associated Press

Carlos Beltrán es jardinero (*outfielder*) del equipo (*team*) los Cardenales de San Luis.

Ahora, dime...

In groups of three, take turns asking and answering the following questions.

1. ¿En qué ciudad de los Estados Unidos hay mayor población puertorriqueña?
2. ¿Qué evento histórico marca la llegada de los puertorriqueños a los Estados Unidos?
3. ¿Qué ciudad cerca de donde tú vives tiene mucha población hispana?
4. Geraldo Rivera tiene ideas controversiales.¿Qué otros comentaristas tienen ideas controversiales?
5. ¿Qué deporte prefieres, el béisbol, el fútbol americano o el fútbol (*soccer*)? ¿Por qué?

iLrn™

To learn more about Hispanic communities in the United States, watch the cultural footage in the Media Library.

AUTOPRUEBA

¿Cuánto sé ahora?

A. Possessive adjectives Complete these sentences with the appropriate possessive adjectives. Make sure they agree with the subjects.

1. Yo necesito _______ libro y _______ bolígrafos.
2. Nosotros hablamos con _______ profesora y ellos hablan con _______ profesor.
3. ¿Tú vives con _______ padres (*parents*)?
4. Jorge come con _______ amigos.
5. Nosotros vivimos en _______ casa con _______ padres.
6. ¿ _______ computadora es nueva, Srta. Mejías?

B. Cardinal numbers (101–1000) Write the following numbers in Spanish.

1. 195
2. 286
3. 371
4. 460
5. 553
6. 644
7. 732
8. 827
9. 918
10. 1000

C. Descriptive adjectives Give the Spanish equivalent of the words in parentheses.

1. Mi compañera de cuarto es _____________________. (*a very pretty girl*)
2. La señorita Vega es _________________. (*a charming woman*)
3. Los muchachos son _________________. (*tall, dark, and handsome*)
4. ¿Helen es _______ o _________? (*English / German*)

D. Present indicative of regular *-er* and *-ir* verbs Complete each sentence using the appropriate verb in the list in the correct form.

deber	abrir
aprender	creer
vender	leer
comer	recibir
escribir	beber

1. Nosotros __________ mucho en la clase de español.
2. ¿Tú ________ en la cafetería?
3. Yo ______ que Elena habla portugués.
4. ¿Ustedes _______ muchos libros?
5. Carlos _______ café.
6. Usted ________ estudiar más.
7. Ellos ________ sus libros por (*for*) treinta dólares.
8. Yo ______ las ventanas.
9. Ellos ________ mensajes electrónicos.
10. Nosotros ________ con lápiz.

E. The verbs *tener* and *venir* Complete the following sentences using the present indicative of **tener** or **venir**.

1. Yo no ________ a la universidad los viernes porque no ________ clases.
2. ¿Tú ________ la dirección de Julio? Él no ________ a clase los lunes.
3. Nosotros ________ a la biblioteca con Amanda porque no ________ auto (*car*).
4. Rogelio ________ a las ocho y ellos ________ a las diez.
5. ¿Ellos ________ tu número de teléfono?

F. The personal *a* Give the Spanish equivalent of the words in parentheses.

1. Yo ____________ todos los domingos. (*call my friends*)
2. Elena ____________ a la universidad. (*takes her brother*)
3. Nosotros ______________ los lunes. (*call Nora and Alicia*)

G. Just words . . . Circle the word or phrase that does not belong in each group.

1. anuncio	solicitud	aviso
2. informe	empleo	trabajo
3. periódico	diario	mensaje
4. ganar	beber	tomar
5. leer	escribir	llenar
6. bonita	linda	alta
7. mi amor	mi escritorio	mi vida
8. Con ella habla.	Me voy.	Chau.
9. rubio	pequeño	bajo
10. Trabajo mucho.	Tengo mucho que hacer.	Bebo mucho.

H. Cultura

1. Answer the following questions, based on information from the **¿Lo sabía usted?** sections.
   a. ¿Cómo contestan el teléfono en México? ________
   b. ¿Cuál es un equivalente de **español?** ________
2. Complete the following, based on the information found in the **El mundo hispánico y tú** section.
   a. El _______ es el deporte nacional de Puerto Rico.
   b. Benicio del Toro es un famoso __________ puertorriqueño.

I. Un dicho Do you remember the Spanish saying that discourages overeating? Find it in this lesson.

LECCIÓN 4

COSTUMBRES Y TRADICIONES

Una fiesta de quinceañera

OBJETIVOS COMUNICATIVOS

You will learn vocabulary related to planning weekend activities, needs and preferences, and states of mind.

SITUACIONES

¡Bienvenido!

ESTRUCTURAS

1 Pronouns as objects of prepositions

2 Contractions

3 Present indicative of the irregular verbs **ir, dar,** and **estar**

4 **Ir a** + *infinitive*

5 Present indicative of **e:ie** stem-changing verbs

6 Expressions with **tener**

ASÍ SOMOS

¡Vamos a ver!
Watching and understanding situations

¡Vamos a escuchar!
Listening to voice mail

¡Vamos a conversar!
Asking for additional information

¡Vamos a leer!
Identifying text formats

¡Vamos a escribir!
Writing an e-mail

EL MUNDO HISPÁNICO Y TÚ

› México

AUTOPRUEBA

You will review what you learned in this lesson.

MÉXICO, con más de cien millones de habitantes, ocupa por su población el primer lugar entre los países del mundo hispano, y tiene casi tres veces el área de Texas. Su capital, la Ciudad de México, D.F. (Distrito Federal), con unos 24 millones de habitantes, es el centro urbano más grande del mundo.

Recursos iLrn video audio web playlist

SITUACIONES

¡BIENVENIDO!

CD1-17

© Cengage Learning

¡Ubíquelos!

Gabriela is a native of Mexico City, and Luis, who is from Ecuador, now resides there. Watch the video and you will see "plazas", museums, and monuments that reflect Mexico's diverse history, and are part of the two young people's lives.

© Orange Line Media/Shutterstock.com

Gabriela Alvarado y su amigo Luis Junco están en el Zócalo, en la Ciudad de México. Luis va a pasar la Navidad y el Año Nuevo con la familia de Gabriela porque él es de Ecuador y este año no va a su país para las fiestas. Luis acaba de hablar por teléfono con su mamá.

GABRIELA: ¿Cómo está tu mamá? ¿Está triste porque tú no estás en Quito? ¿O está preocupada? Tú eres su hijo favorito, ¿no?

LUIS: ¡No, no! Mi mamá está muy ocupada con los preparativos para la fiesta de quinceañera[1] de Gloria, mi hermanita. Ella cumple quince años el veinte de diciembre.

GABRIELA: ¿Van a tener muchos invitados?

LUIS: Sí, van todos los parientes, los amigos, los vecinos... Ella baila el primer vals con mi papá y después con uno de los muchachos. ¡Y mi mamá va a preparar mucha comida! ¡Ah! Y mi hermano va a sacar muchas fotos.

GABRIELA: ¿Y tú no piensas ir?

LUIS: No... no tengo dinero para el viaje... ¡Yo soy muy pobre! Prefiero ir para el cumpleaños de mi mamá, que es en febrero.

GABRIELA: Pues aquí vas a ver las posadas, que empiezan el dieciséis de diciembre. ¡Ah! y este fin de semana es el santo de mi tío Rodolfo y damos una fiesta. ¡Y tú estás invitado!

LUIS: ¡Gracias! ¿La fiesta es en tu casa o en la casa de don Rodolfo?

GABRIELA: Esta vez es en la casa de mi abuela.

LUIS: Ah, sí. Doña Nieves. Oye, son las doce. ¿Quieres ir a comer algo? ¿No tienes hambre?

GABRIELA: No, pero tengo mucha sed y estoy un poco cansada. ¿Por qué no vamos a mi casa? Tomamos una soda y charlamos un rato...

LUIS: Sí, pero esta noche vamos al cine ¿no? ¿O prefieres ir a una discoteca?

GABRIELA: Bueno... yo no bailo muy bien...

LUIS: ¡Magnífico! Vamos al cine, entonces, porque yo como bailarín, ¡soy un desastre!

[1] the party to celebrate a girl's fifteenth birthday

¿Lo sabía Ud.?

En España y en Latinoamérica, no existe tanta (*as much*) separación entre (*among*) generaciones como en los Estados Unidos. Los niños, los padres y los abuelos frecuentemente van juntos a fiestas y celebraciones.

› **¿Qué celebraciones tienen las familias de este país?**

¿Lo sabía Ud.?

En México, durante la época de Navidad, celebran las posadas, que representan el viaje de María y José desde Nazaret a Belén y su búsqueda (*search*) de alojamiento (*lodging*). Empiezan el 16 de diciembre y terminan el 24 de diciembre.

› **¿Celebran las posadas en algún barrio mexicano en la ciudad donde Ud. vive?**

1. Hablemos With a partner, take turns asking and answering the following questions. Base your answers on the dialogue and on your own circumstances.

En el diálogo

1. ¿Dónde va a pasar Luis la Navidad?
2. ¿La mamá de Luis está triste?
3. ¿Quién cumple 15 años?
4. ¿Con quién va a bailar Gloria el primer vals?
5. ¿Por qué no va a ir Luis a la fiesta?
6. ¿Gabriela tiene hambre o tiene sed?
7. ¿Adónde van a ir Luis y Gabriela?
8. ¿Gabriela baila bien?

¿Y tú?

1. ¿Dónde vas a pasar tú la Navidad?
2. ¿Tú estás triste?
3. ¿Cuántos años cumples tú?
4. ¿Con quién bailas tú?
5. ¿Tú tienes mucho dinero?
6. Cuando tienes sed, ¿bebes agua (*water*) o bebes una soda?
7. ¿Adónde vas a ir tú hoy?
8. ¿Tú eres buen bailarín (buena bailarina)?

¿Lo sabía Ud.?

Los hispanos generalmente celebran el cumpleaños y también el día de su "santo", que corresponde al santo de su nombre en el calendario católico. Por ejemplo, si un niño nace (*is born*) en junio, y sus padres lo llaman Miguel, celebra su cumpleaños en junio y celebra el día de su "santo" el 29 de septiembre, que es el día de San Miguel.

› **En este país, ¿celebran el día de San Patricio?**

¿Es el día de su cumpleaños o de su santo?

VOCABULARIO

En el diálogo

Cognados

el desastre	*disaster*
la discoteca	*discotheque*
la familia	*family*
favorito(a)	*favorite*
la foto, la fotografía	*photo, photograph*
invitado(a)	*invited*
el parque	*park*
la soda[1]	*soda*
el vals	*waltz*

Nombres

la abuela	*grandmother*
el abuelo	*grandfather*
el año	*year*
el Año Nuevo	*New Year*
el bailarín (la bailarina)	*dancer*
el cine	*movie theater*
la comida	*food*
la fiesta	*party*
las fiestas	*holidays*
el fin de semana	*weekend*
la hermanita	*little sister*
la hija	*daughter*
el hijo	*son*
el (la) invitado(a)	*guest*
la mamá, la madre	*mom, mother*
la Navidad	*Christmas*
el país	*country, nation*
el papá, el padre	*dad, father*
los parientes	*relatives*
los preparativos	*preparations*
el santo	*saint's day*
la tía	*aunt*
el tío	*uncle*
el (la) vecino(a)	*neighbor*
la vez	*time (in a series)*
el viaje	*trip*

Verbos

bailar	*to dance*
charlar	*to chat*
cumplir	*to turn (years old)*
dar	*to give*
empezar (e:ie), comenzar (e:ie)	*to begin, to start*
estar	*to be*
ir	*to go*
pasar	*to spend (time)*
pensar (e:ie)	*to think*
pensar + *infinitive*	*to plan (to do something)*
preferir (e:ie)	*to prefer*
preparar	*to prepare*
querer (e:ie)	*to want, to wish*
ver (yo veo)	*to see*

Adjetivos

bienvenido(a)	*welcome*
cansado(a)	*tired*
este(a)	*this*
magnífico(a)	*great, magnificent*
muchos(as)	*many*
ocupado(a)	*busy*
pobre	*poor*
preocupado(a)	*worried*
primero[2] **(a)**	*first*
triste	*sad*

Otras palabras y expresiones

acabar de + *infinitive*	*to have just (done something)*
don	*a title of respect, used with a man's first name*
doña	*a title of respect, used with a woman's first name*
esta vez	*this time*

[1]also *la gaseosa* (Colombia, Cuba), *el refresco*

[2]Primero drops the **o** before masculine singular nouns: el primer año.

pues...	*well . . .*
que	*that, which*
sacar (tomar) una foto	*to take a picture*
tener hambre	*to be hungry*
tener sed	*to be thirsty*
un poco	*a little*
un rato	*a while*
Vamos.	*Let's go.*

Más sobre el tema

Actividades para un fin de semana

ir a un baile	*to go to a dance*
ir a un concierto	____ *concert*
ir a un partido (o juego) de...	____ *game*
ir a la montaña	____ *the mountains*
ir a la playa	____ *beach*
ir al museo	____ *museum*
ir al parque de diversiones	____ *amusement park*
ir al teatro	____ *theater*
ir al zoológico	____ *zoo*

Para describir cómo estamos

aburrido(a)	*bored*
alegre	*joyful*
animado(a)	*animated*
aturdido(a)	*dazed*
contento(a)	*happy, content*
enfermo(a)	*sick*
enojado(a), enfadado(a)	*angry*
entusiasmado(a)	*enthusiastic*
furioso(a)	*furious*
nervioso(a)	*nervous*

¿Lo sabía Ud.?

La celebración familiar más importante para los hispanos es la Nochebuena (*Christmas Eve*), no la Navidad, el día 25.

Práctica

2. Palabras Choose the word or phrase that best completes each sentence.

1. Quiero beber una soda porque tengo (hambre, sed, invitados).
2. Doña Elisa es mi abuela. Es la (hermana de mi mamá, hija de mi tío, mamá de mi papá).
3. Hoy doy una fiesta porque es mi (pariente, año, santo).
4. Yo no bailo muy bien. Soy un (invitado, país, desastre).
5. Este fin de semana vamos a ir (a los preparativos, al cine, a los vecinos).
6. Elsa está un poco (nerviosa, entusiasmada, alegre) porque hoy tiene un examen difícil.
7. No tengo nada (*nothing*) que hacer. Estoy muy (animada, aburrida, enferma).
8. La Navidad y el Año Nuevo son mis (comidas, vecinas, fiestas) favoritas.

3. ¿Qué es? Write the words or phrases that correspond to the following.

1. opuesto de **alegre** ______________
2. enojado ______________
3. Mount Everest, por ejemplo ______________
4. lugar (*place*) donde vamos a bailar ______________
5. Disneylandia, por ejemplo ______________
6. que tiene mucho entusiasmo ______________
7. partido ______________
8. lugar donde hay muchos animales ______________
9. el Louvre, por ejemplo ______________
10. empezar ______________

4. Para completar Complete the following sentences logically, using vocabulary from this lesson.

1. Yo soy el hijo ______________ de mi mamá.
2. En la fiesta de mi abuelo, yo voy a ______________ muchas fotografías de la familia.
3. ¿De qué ______________ son ______________ Manuel y su hijo? ¿De México?
4. Un brindis: ¡______________!
5. ¿Uds. acaban de llegar? ¡______________!
6. En la fiesta de Año ______________ vamos a bailar y a cantar. Yo voy a ______________ mucha comida y vamos a tener muchos ______________.
7. Diego no tiene dinero. Es muy ______________.
8. Aquí en México vas a ______________ las posadas.
9. ¿Deseas ir al cine? ¡Magnífico! Entonces ______________ al cine.
10. Esta ______________ vamos a ______________ el día en el parque.

Para conversar

5. Planes With a partner, ask each other about what you plan to do at different times in the near future.

Modelo E1: *¿Vas a ir a...?*
E2: *(No) Pienso ir a...*

6. Una fiesta You and a partner play the roles of two friends who are planning a party and cannot agree on anything: the day, the time, the place, whom to invite, what to serve, etc.

Modelo —*¿Damos una fiesta el sábado?*
—*No... el domingo.*

Pronunciación

CD1-18

A. The Spanish *b* and *v*

The Spanish **b** and **v** are pronounced exactly alike. Both sound like a weak English *b*, as in the word *Abe*. In Spanish, they are even weaker when pronounced between vowels. The lips don't quite touch. Never pronounce these consonants like the English *v*. Listen to your instructor and repeat the following words.

Beto **v**i**v**e en **B**ogotá. Don Gusta**v**o es mi a**b**uelo.
Bien**v**enida a **B**oli**v**ia.

1-19

B. The Spanish *d*

The Spanish **d** is slightly softer than the *d* in the English word *day*. When pronounced between two vowels or at the end of a word, it is similar to the *th* in the English word *they*. Listen to your instructor and repeat the following words.

Doña **D**elia es **d**e Colora**d**o. **D**avi**d** está invita**d**o.
¿Uste**d**es están cansa**d**os?

1-20

C. The Spanish *g* (before *a*, *o*, or *u*)

› When followed by **a**, **o**, or **u**, the Spanish **g** is similar to the *g* in the English word *guy*. Listen to your instructor and repeat the following words.

Gustavo es **g**ordo.

› When pronounced between vowels, the Spanish **g** is much softer. Repeat after your instructor.

Mi ami**g**o es uru**g**uayo.

› In the combinations **gue** and **gui**, the **u** is silent. Repeat after your instructor.

Guillermo **G**uevara toca la **g**uitarra.

ESTRUCTURAS

1 Pronouns as objects of prepositions

(*Pronombres usados como objetos de preposición*)

› The object of a preposition is the noun or pronoun that immediately follows it: **La fiesta es para María (ella). Ellos van con nosotros.**

Singular		Plural	
mí	*me*	**nosotros(as)**	*us*
ti	*you* (fam.)	**vosotros(as)**	*you* (fam.)
Ud.	*you* (form.)	**Uds.**	*you* (form.)
él	*him*	**ellos**	*them* (masc.)
ella	*her*	**ellas**	*them* (fem.)

Un dicho

Hoy por ti, mañana por mí.
Equivalent: *One hand washes the other.*

› Only the first and second-person singular, **mí** and **ti**, are different from regular subject pronouns.

› **Mí** and **ti** combine with **con** to become **conmigo** *(with me)* and **contigo** *(with you)*, respectively.

—¿Hablan de **mí**? — *Are you talking about me?*
—No, no hablamos de **ti**; hablamos de **ella**. — *No, we are not talking about you; we're talking about her.*

—¿Estudias **conmigo** o con Carlos? — *Are you studying with me or with Carlos?*
—No estudio **contigo**; estudio **con él.** — *I'm not studying with you; I'm studying with him.*

Práctica

7. Minidiálogos Complete the following dialogues, using the Spanish equivalent of the words in parentheses. Then act them out with a partner, adding a sentence or two to each dialogue.

1. —¿Vas al concierto ______________ o ______________? (*with me / with him*)
   —Voy al concierto ______________, pero voy a la playa ______________. (*with you / with her*)
2. —¿Para quién es el vino? ¿______________ o ______________? (*for you / for them*)
   —Es ______________. (*for me*)
3. —¿Para quién es el ponche? ¿______________ o ______________? (*for her / for us*)
   —Es ______________. (*for you, pl.*)

Para conversar

8. **¡Habla con tu compañero(a)!** Interview a classmate, using the following questions and two questions of your own. When you have finished, switch roles. Use the appropriate prepositions and pronouns in your responses. Answer in complete sentences.

   1. ¿Hablas con tus amigos en la clase?
   2. ¿Deseas estudiar español conmigo?
   3. ¿Trabajas para tus padres?
   4. ¿Vives cerca de (*near*) tus abuelos?
   5. ¿Hablas mucho con tus amigos por teléfono?
   6. ¿Tus amigos vienen a la universidad contigo?

2 Contractions (*Contracciones*)

› There are only two contractions in Spanish: **al** and **del**. Both the preposition **a** (*to, toward*) and the personal **a** followed by the article **el** contract to **al**.

Llamo	**a**	+	**el**	profesor.
Llamo		**al**		profesor.

› The preposition **de** (*of, from*) followed by the article **el** contracts to **del**.

Tiene los libros	**de**	+	**el**	profesor.
Tiene los libros		**del**		profesor.

—¿Llevas **al** amigo de Ana?	*Are you taking Ana's friend?*
—No, llevo **a las** primas de Eva.	*No, I'm taking Eva's cousins.*
—¿La casa es **de la** Sra. Vega?	*Is it Mrs. Vega's house?*
—No, es **del** Sr. Parra.	*No, it's Mr. Parra's.*

¡Atención! **A** + **el** and **de** + **el** must always be contracted to **al** and **del**. None of the other combinations **(de la, de las, de los, a la, a las, a los)** is contracted: **Llaman a los hijos de los profesores.**

LEARNING TIP
Practice "seeing" yourself coming from and going to certain places: **Vengo del hotel; voy al cine.**

Práctica

9. **Minidiálogos** Complete the following dialogues, using **de la, de las, del, de los, a la, a las, al,** or **a los.** Then act them out with a partner.

   1. —¿Adónde van Uds. hoy?
      —Yo voy ______________ cine y Eduardo va ______________ discoteca. ¿Adónde vas tú?
      —Yo voy ______________ montaña.
   2. —¿De qué hablan Uds.?
      —Hablamos ______________ viaje a México.
   3. —¿El equipo estereofónico es ______________ amigos de Alicia?
      —No, es ______________ hijas de la señora Gómez.
   4. —¿A quién llamas?
      —Llamo ______________ hermano de mi amiga Sandra.
   5. —¿Adónde llevas ______________ muchachos?
      —Llevo ______________ muchachos ______________ fiesta ______________ hermano de Ana.

Un dicho

Al pan, pan y al vino, vino.
Equivalent: *To call a spade a spade.*

10. Preguntas y respuestas With a partner, take turns asking and answering the following questions, using the cues provided. Pay special attention to the use of contractions.

1. ¿De quién es el árbol de Navidad? (amigo de mi tío)
2. ¿De quién son los discos compactos? (señorita Vargas)
3. ¿A quiénes llevas a la fiesta? (chicos)
4. ¿A quién piensan invitar (*to invite*) Uds.? (señor Robles)
5. ¿De dónde vienen Uds.? (concierto)
6. ¿Adónde llevan Uds. a sus hijos? (teatro)
7. ¿Las fotos son de los muchachos? (no, las muchachas)
8. ¿De quién hablan Uds.? (estudiantes)

Para conversar

11. ¿Qué pasa aquí? In a hotel lobby, you and your partner observe what is going on. Take turns asking each other who is calling whom, where people are coming from, how they relate to each other, etc. Use prepositions, contractions, and pronouns.

3 Present indicative of the irregular verbs *ir, dar,* and *estar*

(*Presente de indicativo de los verbos irregulares* ***ir, dar*** *y* ***estar***)

	ir *to go*	dar *to give*	estar *to be*
yo	**voy**	**doy**	**estoy**
tú	**vas**	**das**	**estás**
Ud. / él / ella	**va**	**da**	**está**
nosotros(as)	**vamos**	**damos**	**estamos**
vosotros(as)	**vais**	**dais**	**estáis**
Uds. / ellos / ellas	**van**	**dan**	**están**

—Susana **da** una fiesta hoy. ¿Tú **vas**?	*Susana is giving a party today. Are you going?*
—No, no **voy** porque **estoy** muy cansada.	*No, I'm not going because I am very tired.*
—Entonces **voy** con Ana y Beto. ¿Dónde **están** ellos?	*Then I'm going with Ana and Beto. Where are they?*
—**Están** en la universidad. Vienen a las tres.	*They're at the college. They're coming at three.*

¿Lo sabía Ud.?

En los países hispanos, las chicas y los muchachos generalmente van en grupos a fiestas, al teatro y a conciertos.

› **En este país, ¿los chicos prefieren salir en grupos o en parejas** (*couples*)**?**

› The verb **estar,** *to be*, is used here to indicate current condition (**Estoy muy cansada.**) and location (**Están en la universidad.**). **Ser,** another equivalent of the English verb *to be*, has been used up to now to refer to origin (**Él es de México.**), nationality (**Ellas son mexicanas.**), characteristics (**Jorge es rubio.**), profession (**Elsa es profesora.**), and time (**Son las doce.**).

› Other frequent uses of **dar** are **dar un examen, dar una conferencia** (*lecture*), and **dar una orden** (*order*).

Práctica

12. Unos y otros Using the present indicative of **ir, dar,** or **estar**, as appropriate, write statements combining elements from columns A and B. Several combinations are possible. When you have finished, join one or two of your classmates and compare your statements.

A	B
1. Yo	a. fiestas los sábados
2. Tú	b. en la biblioteca.
3. Mi papá	c. al cine o al teatro los sábados.
4. La profesora	d. muy contento(a).
5. Mis amigos y yo	e. exámenes difíciles.
6. Los estudiantes	f. a la playa en el verano.
	g. al zoológico.
	h. muy cansado(a).
	i. dinero para los pobres.
	j. en la universidad.

13. ¿Y los demás? Complete the following statements in a logical manner, by using the verb given in the sentence.

1. Roberto está en el parque y nosotros...
2. Yo doy una fiesta esta noche y tú...
3. Tú vas al museo y yo...
4. Yo estoy muy enojado(a) y ellos...
5. Nosotros damos una fiesta de Navidad y él...
6. Ellos van hoy y nosotros...
7. Ella está nerviosa y su novio...
8. Julia está aburrida y yo...

Para conversar

14. ¡Habla con tu compañero(a)! Interview a classmate, using the following questions. When you have finished, switch roles. You both should answer in complete sentences.

1. ¿Cómo estás? ¿Estás preocupado(a)? ¿Por qué?
2. ¿Dónde están tus amigos hoy?
3. ¿Estás muy ocupado(a) hoy? ¿Qué tienes que hacer?
4. ¿Tus amigos dan una fiesta de Navidad? ¿Dónde?
5. ¿Tú vas a muchas fiestas?
6. En tu familia, ¿quién da muchas fiestas?

15. ¿Adónde vamos? Imagine that you or you and one classmate are walking around town and walk around the classroom. You will bump into several of your classmates. Ask them where they are going now. Here is a list of places that people go to.

la playa	el cine	el parque
el parque de diversiones	el concierto	el zoológico
el teatro	el museo	la tienda (*store*)

Modelo —*¡Hola! ¿Adónde vas?*
—*Voy al cine. ¿Y tú?*
—*Yo voy a la tienda.*

After everyone sits down, the instructor will ask where everyone is going.

4 *Ir a* + infinitive (*Ir a + infinitivo*)

› **Ir a** + *infinitive* is used to express future action. It is equivalent to the English expression to be going (*to*) + *infinitive*. The "formula" is as follows.

ir (*conjugated*)	+ **a** +	*infinitive*
Voy	**a**	**trabajar.**
I am going		*to work.*

—¿Con quién **vas a bailar** en la fiesta? — *With whom are you going to dance at the party?*
—**Voy a bailar** contigo. — *I'm going to dance with you.*
—¿Uds. **van a cantar?** — *Are you going to sing?*
—No, **vamos a bailar.** — *No, we're going to dance.*

Práctica

16. Lo que va a pasar What do you think these people are going to do? Consider where they are and what time of day it is.

Modelo *José / en el hospital / por la tarde*
José va a trabajar en el hospital por la tarde.

1. yo / en mi casa / por la noche
2. los estudiantes / en la clase / por la mañana
3. nosotros / en la discoteca / por la noche
4. tú / en la cafetería / a las doce
5. Susana / en su casa / por la mañana
6. Uds. / en la fiesta / por la noche
7. mis amigos / en la biblioteca / el sábado
8. el profesor / en la universidad

ESTRUCTURAS

Para conversar

17. ¡Habla con tu compañero(a)! Interview a classmate, using the following questions. Your classmate should answer in complete sentences. When you have finished, switch roles.

1. ¿Cuántas horas vas a estudiar hoy? ¿Con quién vas a estudiar? ¿Dónde?
2. ¿Vas a comer en tu casa o en la cafetería? ¿A qué hora vas a comer? ¿Tú y tu familia van a comer juntos?
3. ¿Qué vas a hacer este fin de semana? ¿Vas a ir a un baile?
4. ¿Adónde van a ir tus amigos el sábado? ¿Qué van a hacer? ¿Van a ir a un concierto?
5. ¿Tú y tu familia van a dar una fiesta? ¿Cuándo? ¿Dónde? ¿A quiénes van a invitar?

18. ¿Qué van a hacer? What are these people going to do? With a partner, take turns asking and answering questions, using the information in the illustrations.

Modelo *—¿Con quién va a bailar Marisol?*
—Va a bailar con Tito.

Marisol

1. Roberto

2. Elisa

3. Julio y Estrella

4. Daniel

5. Eduardo

6. Graciela

5 Present indicative of *e:ie* stem-changing verbs

(*Presente de indicativo de los verbos que cambian en la raíz* e:ie)

› Some Spanish verbs undergo a stem change in the present indicative. For these verbs, when **e** is the last stem vowel and it is stressed, it changes to **ie** as follows.

preferir ***to prefer***			
yo	pref**ie**ro	nosotros(as)	preferimos
tú	pref**ie**res	vosotros(as)	preferís
Ud. / él / ella	pref**ie**re	Uds. / ellos / ellas	pref**ie**ren

—¿A qué hora **piensas** ir a la fiesta? *What time are you planning to go to the party?*
—**Prefiero** ir a las diez. ¿Y tú? *I prefer to go at ten. And you?*
—Yo **no quiero** ir. Estoy cansado. *I don't want to go. I'm tired.*

—¿A qué hora **empiezan** a[1] estudiar Uds.? *What time do you start to study?*
—**Empezamos** a las tres. *We start at three.*

› Note that the stem vowel is not stressed in the verb forms used with **nosotros(as)** and **vosotros(as);** therefore, the **e** does not change to **ie.**

› Stem-changing verbs have the same endings as regular **-ar, -er,** and **-ir** verbs.

› Some verbs that undergo this change are:

cerrar *to close*
comenzar *to begin, to start*
empezar *to begin, to start*
entender *to understand*
pensar *to think*
pensar (+ *infinitive*) *to plan* (*to do something*)
perder *to lose*
querer *to want, to wish, to love*

Un dicho

Ojos que no ven, corazón que no siente.
Equivalent: *Out of sight, out of mind.*

[1]The preposition **a** is used after **empezar** and **comenzar** when they are followed by an infinitive.

Práctica

19. ¿Tú lo sabes...? With a partner, complete each statement with the correct form of the verb in parentheses, and by answering the questions that follow it.

1. Yo (preferir) comer...	¿qué?	¿dónde?	¿con quiénes?
2. Nosotros (preferir) ir...	¿adónde?	¿con quiénes?	¿qué días?
3. Tú (querer) bailar...	¿qué?	¿con quién?	
4. Nosotros (querer) charlar...	¿con quiénes?	¿cuándo?	
5. Mi papá (pensar) leer...	¿qué?	¿cuándo?	
6. Nosotros (cerrar)...	¿qué?	¿cuándo?	
7. Mis amigos (perder)...	¿qué?	¿dónde?	
8. Ellos (empezar)...	¿qué?	¿en qué mes?	
9. Yo (comenzar) a...	¿qué?	¿a qué hora?	
10. Tú no (entender)...	¿qué?		

20. Orientación You have just enrolled at a new university, and some current students are helping to orient you. Compare their routines and preferences with your own.

1. Comenzamos las clases a las nueve.
2. No entendemos inglés.
3. Pensamos trabajar mañana.
4. Queremos ir al zoológico.
5. Preferimos beber ponche.
6. No cerramos las ventanas por la noche.

Para conversar

21. ¡Habla con tu compañero(a)! Interview a classmate, using the following questions. Your classmate should answer in complete sentences. When you have finished, switch roles.

1. ¿Tienes sed? ¿Qué quieres beber?
2. ¿Dónde quieres comer hoy? ¿Qué quieres comer?
3. ¿Tú prefieres comer en un restaurante o en la cafetería de la universidad?
4. ¿A dónde piensas ir este fin de semana?
5. ¿Qué prefieres hacer, ir al zoológico o ir a un parque de diversiones?
6. ¿Tú entiendes una conversación en español?

¿ Lo sabía Ud.?

Muchos productos norteamericanos, como las sodas y los chicles, son muy populares en los países hispanos.

› **¿Qué productos extranjeros (*foreign*) son populares en este país?**

6 Expressions with *tener* (*Expresiones con* tener)

› Many useful idiomatic expressions that use *to be* + *adjective* in English are formed with **tener** + *noun* in Spanish.

tener (mucho) frío	*to be (very) cold*
tener (mucha) sed	*to be (very) thirsty*
tener (mucha) hambre	*to be (very) hungry*
tener (mucho) calor	*to be (very) hot*
tener (mucho) sueño	*to be (very) sleepy*
tener (mucha) prisa	*to be in a (great) hurry*
tener (mucho) miedo	*to be (quite) afraid, scared*
tener (mucho) cuidado	*to be (very) careful*
tener razón	*to be right*
no tener razón[1]	*to be wrong*
tener... años (de edad)	*to be . . . years old*

—**¿Tienes calor?**	*Are you hot?*
—Sí, y también **tengo** mucha **sed.**	*Yes, and I'm also very thirsty.*
—¿Deseas comer pollo?	*Do you want to eat chicken?*
—No, gracias, no **tengo hambre.**	*No, thank you, I'm not hungry.*
—¿Cuántos **años tienes?**	*How old are you?*
—**Tengo** diecinueve **años.**	*I'm nineteen years old.*
—Tenemos que trabajar más.	*We have to work harder (more).*
—**Tienes razón...**	*You're right . . .*

¡Atención! Note that Spanish uses **mucho(a)** (*adjective*) + *noun* (as in **mucha hambre**) the way English uses *very* + *adjective* (as in *very hungry*).

© Alexander Sysoev/Shutterstock.com

¿Tienes frío?

[1]Incorrectness is also conveyed by the expression **estar equivocado(a)** (*to be wrong*).

Práctica

22. ¿Qué tienen? Using expressions with **tener**, indicate how these people feel.

1. José

2. Yo

3. Tú

4. La profesora

5. Ud.

6. Felipe

7. Marisa y Elena

8. Ella

23. ¡Siete problemas y un cumpleaños! Which expression with **tener** would you use in each of the following situations?

1. You are in the Sahara desert in the middle of summer.
2. A big dog is chasing you.
3. You have only a minute to get to your next class.
4. You are in Alaska in the middle of winter.
5. You haven't eaten for an entire day.
6. You got up at 4 A.M. and it is now midnight.
7. You just ran for two hours in the sun.
8. You are blowing out twenty candles on your birthday cake.

Para conversar

24. ¡Habla con tu compañero(a)! Interview a classmate, using the following questions. When you have finished, switch roles.

1. ¿Qué bebes cuando tienes sed? ¿Y cuando tienes frío?
2. ¿Qué comes cuando tienes hambre?
3. ¿Cuántos años tienes?
4. ¿Cuántos años tiene tu mamá? ¿Y tu papá?
5. En tu familia, ¿quién tiene razón siempre? ¿Y en la clase?
6. ¿Tienes miedo a veces (*sometimes*)?

25. Tenemos huéspedes. (*We have guests.*) Imagine that Mr. and Mrs. Vega and their two children, Anita and Luisito, are staying with you and your partner. Take turns asking them individually and/or collectively whether they are hungry, thirsty, etc. When possible, ask them also if they want a drink, etc.

¿Lo sabía Ud.?

En español se dice "¡Salud!" (*Cheers*) para brindar. En España también dicen "Salud, amor y pesetas[1]" (*Health, love, and money*).

[1]**Pesetas** were the monetary unit in Spain before the use of the Euro.

¡Vamos a ver!

Antes de ver el video

26. Habla con tu compañero(a) You and a partner, take turns asking and answering the following questions.

1. ¿Tú vas a veces a la casa de tus tíos? ¿Tienes muchos primos (*cousins*)?
2. ¿Tú vas a pasar el Año Nuevo con tus amigos o con tu familia? ¿Y la Navidad?
3. ¿Tienes hambre? ¿Tienes sed? ¿Tienes sueño?
4. ¿Prefieres beber una soda o un vaso de agua?
5. ¿Estás cansado(a)? ¿Estás contento(a) o triste?
6. ¿Vas al parque con tus amigos a veces?
7. ¿Piensas ir a la tienda (*store*) mañana?
8. ¿Qué vas a hacer pasado mañana (*the day after tomorrow*)?
9. ¿Tú vas a dar una fiesta el viernes?
10. ¿Tú celebras (*celebrate*) el día de tu santo? ¿Celebras el día de San Patricio?
11. ¿Tú y tu familia tienen mariachis cuando dan fiestas?
12. Cuando das una fiesta, ¿muchas chicas (muchos chicos) quieren bailar contigo?
13. ¿Vas a dar una fiesta la semana que viene? ¿Vas a bailar este fin de semana? ¿Invitas a tus vecinos cuando das una fiesta?
14. ¿Quieres platicar un rato más?

El video: Julia visita la Ciudad de México

¡Bienvenida, hijita! ¡Ay! ¡Dame un abrazo!

—¿Cuándo empiezan las posadas?

—La semana que viene. Este fin de semana pensamos ir a una discoteca de la Zona Rosa.

Después de ver el video

© Cengage Learning

Doña Luz

© Cengage Learning

Lupita

© Cengage Learning

Julia

© Cengage Learning

Don Rodolfo

27. ¿Quién lo dice? Identify the person who said the following in the dialogues.

1. Pasado mañana damos una fiesta aquí en casa.
2. Entonces quiero sacar muchas fotos.
3. Mario, una soda para tu prima.
4. ¡Pero no tengo sueño! Quiero platicar un rato más.
5. ¡Bienvenida, hijita! ¡Ay! ¡Dame un abrazo!
6. ¡La pobre Julia está aturdida!
7. ¡Mamá! ¡Una pregunta a la vez!
8. ¿Cómo estás, sobrina? ¿Qué tal el viaje?
9. Y su hermano está bien, también.

28. Hablemos With a partner, take turns asking and answering the following questions. Base your answers on the dialogues.

1. ¿Dónde va a pasar Julia la Navidad?
2. ¿Julia tiene hambre o tiene sed?
3. ¿Qué quiere beber Julia?
4. ¿Adónde van a ir Julia y Lupita mañana?
5. ¿Es el santo o el cumpleaños del abuelo de Lupita?
6. ¿Quiénes van a venir a la fiesta?
7. ¿Cuándo empiezan las posadas?
8. ¿Julia tiene sueño?

29. ¿Qué pasa después? You and a partner, use your imagination to say what the characters do. In Spanish, discuss the following.

1. Whether or not doña Luz calls Julia's father.
2. Whether or not Julia is still **(todavía)** tired.
3. Whether Julia converses with her uncle.
4. Whether Julia and Lupita eat a lot of food at the party.
5. Whether or not Julia dances with Mario.
6. Whether or not Julia takes pictures of don Gustavo.
7. With whom Julia dances when she goes to the discotheque.
8. Whether or not Julia and Lupita take part **(toman parte)** in the **posadas.**

Now compare your statements to those of another group.

¡Vamos a escuchar!

ESTRATEGIA **Listening to voice mail** When you listen to recorded announcements, such as a voice mail message or an announcement about an upcoming event or a sale at a store, it's important to grasp the basic information: the *who, what, when,* and *where*. As you listen, try to focus on the main facts rather than trying to understand everything you hear.

CD1-21 **30. Un mensaje telefónico** A relative of your Spanish-speaking housemate has left a voice mail on your phone system. Listen to the message and make a note of the specifics of the call for your housemate. Listen to the message as many times as necessary.

1. ¿Quién llama?
2. ¿Quiénes vienen?
3. ¿Cuándo vienen?
4. ¿Dónde van a estar?
5. ¿Qué quieren hacer el sábado?

¡Vamos a conversar!

ESTRATEGIA **Asking for additional information** When conversing, you often ask questions to learn more about a topic or statement. Asking questions also lets the person you are talking with know that you are interested in what he or she is saying. Here are some question words you can use when you want more information.

¿qué?	**¿con quién?**	**¿para qué?** (*what for?*)	**¿cuál?**
¿cuándo?	**¿dónde?**	**¿por qué?**	**¿cuánto?**

31. ¿Y qué más? For each of the following statements, write two or three questions you might ask to get more information.

1. Ana viene.
2. Necesito dinero.
3. Quiero libros.

32. ¿Qué dice Ud.? What would you say in the following situations? What might the other person say? Act out the scenes with a partner. Take turns playing each role.

1. Someone offers you something to eat. Decline, saying that you are not hungry because you have just been eating.
2. You are planning a weekend with a friend. Ask where he/she wants to go; offer as many choices as possible.
3. A friend of yours is obviously upset. Try to find out what's wrong by asking him/her whether he/she is angry, nervous, etc.
4. You have three days off. Tell a friend what you are going to do for fun and ask him/her what he/she is going to do.
5. You are talking to an acquaintance from Mexico. Tell him/her what you and your friends do when you give a party.

33. Para conocernos mejor To do this activity, work with a classmate whom you would like to get to know. Take turns asking and answering these questions.

1. ¿Cuántos años tienes? ¿Cuándo es tu cumpleaños?
2. ¿Estás invitado(a) a una fiesta? ¿Asistes a muchas fiestas?
3. En una fiesta, ¿prefieres bailar o charlar con un amigo? ¿Bailas bien o eres un desastre como bailarín (bailarina)?
4. ¿Dónde vas a pasar el Año Nuevo? ¿Vas a dar una fiesta?
5. ¿Qué piensas hacer este fin de semana? ¿Adónde piensas ir?
6. ¿Prefieres ir a un museo o a un parque de diversiones? ¿A la playa o a la montaña?
7. ¿Tienes hambre o acabas de comer? ¿Quieres beber algo?
8. ¿Tú eres el hijo (la hija) favorito(a) de tus padres?
9. ¿Estás contento(a) o triste hoy? ¿Estás cansado(a)?
10. ¿Dónde vas a estar mañana por la mañana? ¿Y por la tarde?

34. Una encuesta Interview your classmates to identify who fits the following descriptions. Include your instructor, but remember to use the **Ud.** form when addressing him/her. After finishing the survey, get together with two or three classmates and discuss the results.

1. Va a ir a un baile este domingo.	______________
2. Va al cine los sábados.	______________
3. Piensa hacer (*to take*) un viaje este verano.	______________
4. Pasa mucho tiempo con sus amigos(as).	______________
5. Va a estar muy ocupado(a) este fin de semana.	______________
6. Tiene muchos invitados cuando da una fiesta.	______________
7. Saca muchas fotografías.	______________
8. Cumple años en agosto.	______________

35. Para crear Get together in groups of three or four and "create" the scenario for this photo. Who are the people in it? Give them names and describe them. What is their relationship to each other? What kind of party is it? Add any other pertinent details.

¡Vamos a leer!

Antes de leer

ESTRATEGIA **Identifying text formats** Before reading a text, it is useful to look at the title, subtitles, photos or illustrations, and format to get a general idea of the nature of the text. For example, is it an informative article, a calendar of events, an advertisement, or an interview? Recognizing formats can help orient you to the type of information to expect.

36. ¿De qué habla? Look at the reading that follows. Have you come across similar types of texts? Where did this reading possibly appear? What is the title? Who is featured? Why? What might be said about them? Use this information to help you decipher the specifics of this reading.

¡A leer!

SOCIALES

© Ana C. Jarvis

La señorita María Isabel Paz Roldán va a dar una fiesta el sábado, 20 de agosto, para celebrar su cumpleaños. La fiesta va a tener lugar° en la residencia de sus padres. ¡Feliz cumpleaños, María Isabel!

take place

© michaeljung/Shutterstock.com

La señora Delia Maldonado va de vacaciones a la ciudad de Guadalajara, donde piensa pasar las fiestas de Navidad en compañía de sus hermanos. Después de las fiestas piensa visitar las hermosas° playas de Cancún. Le deseamos un buen viaje.

beautiful

© Chawalit S./Shutterstock.com

El matrimonio Peña-Mirabal anuncia la llegada de su hijo Juan Carlos, nacido° el 18 de agosto. El niño va a ser bautizado° el mes próximo. ¡Felicitamos a los nuevos papás!

born
baptized

© Beryl Goldberg

En la Basílica de Guadalupe celebran su boda el doctor Raúl Valverde y la bellísima° señorita Alina Carreras. La feliz pareja° va a pasar su luna de miel° en Acapulco. ¡Muchas felicidades al nuevo matrimonio!

beautiful
happy couple/honeymoon

37. Comprensión As you read the **Sociales** section of the newspaper, find the answers to the following questions.

1. ¿Qué día va a dar una fiesta María Isabel? ¿Qué va a celebrar?
2. ¿Dónde va a tener lugar la fiesta?

3. ¿A qué ciudad va de vacaciones la Sra. Maldonado?
4. ¿Qué fiestas va a pasar allí (*there*)? ¿con quiénes?
5. ¿Adónde va a ir después?
6. ¿Qué anuncia el matrimonio Peña-Mirabal? ¿Cuándo va a ser bautizado el niño?
7. ¿Quién es la esposa del doctor Valverde?
8. ¿Adónde va a ir de luna de miel la pareja?

Después de leer... desde tu mundo

38. **Celebraciones** In groups of three or four, talk about your plans for several holidays in the year.

HINT: Día de Acción de Gracias = *Thanksgiving*

¡Vamos a escribir!

Antes de escribir

ESTRATEGIA **Writing an e-mail** Although e-mails are more informal than letters, they follow a similar pattern.

- Greeting: **Querido(a)...: Hola...:** (Use a colon after the name.)
- Body: one or more paragraphs that include the purpose of the message, the information you want to convey, and questions you want to ask
- Closing: **Bueno, nos vemos el día..., Besos *(Kisses)*, Tu amigo(a)...**

LEARNING TIP
Don't ever feel shy about asking for correction. That's how learning takes place.

39. **Una invitación** You will write an e-mail in which you invite a friend to spend a weekend with you. Before writing, jot down the information you want to include.
    - When will it be? When should your friend arrive?
    - What are the general plans and schedule of activities for the weekend? What are you going to do each day?
    - Ask your friend if he or she prefers or wants to do one activity or another.

¡A escribir!

40. **Una invitación** Write your **primer borrador** of the message. Remember to use an appropriate greeting and closing.

Después de escribir

41. **A revisar** Before writing the final version, exchange your first draft with a classmate and peer edit each other's work using the following guidelines.
    - use of **ir a** + *infinitive*
    - formation of **e:ie** stem-changing verbs
    - form of the e-mail: greeting, body, and closing

EL MUNDO HISPÁNICO Y TÚ

México

México es tu país vecino. ¿Te interesan sus bellezas (*beauties*) naturales? ¿Sus reliquias históricas? ¿Sus centros turísticos? ¿Sus museos de arte? ¿Quieres conocer solamente la capital o quieres ver también ciudades como Guadalajara, Guanajuato y San Miguel Allende?

- Quizás (*Perhaps*) quieres estudiar en México para perfeccionar tu español o seguir una carrera específica.
- ¡México lo tiene todo! Playas famosas como Acapulco, Cancún y Puerto Vallarta. Su música es popular en todo el mundo, y las obras (*works*) de sus escritores están traducidas a muchas lenguas. Sus telenovelas se ven en muchos países, incluyendo aquellos (*those*) donde no se habla español. Su comida ya es internacional, ¡y en los Estados Unidos, la salsa mexicana se vende (*is sold*) más que el "ketchup"!

Ruinas arquitectónicas y edificios coloniales

Un ejemplo de arquitectura mesoamericana, producida en las culturas y civilizaciones precolombinas de Mesoamérica. Esta arquitectura es notable por sus pirámides, que son las más grandes fuera de Egipto.

En la Ciudad de México está el Palacio Nacional (la sede del gobierno), situado en El Zócalo, la plaza más grande de Latinoamérica. Este palacio es una muestra de la arquitectura colonial española.

Ciudades de interés turístico

Guadalajara, la segunda ciudad más grande del país, origen del mariachi y del tequila. En esta ciudad hay un gran número de firmas internacionales, y está considerada como "la ciudad del futuro".

La Ciudad de México —la más grande del país— es también el Distrito Federal, que los mexicanos llaman "el D.F.". La Ciudad de México tiene la mayor población de las Américas.

Las artes plásticas y la literatura

"Diego y yo", por Frida Kahlo. Ella y Diego Rivera son dos famosos pintores mexicanos. Frida es la pintora más famosa de México.

Octavio Paz (1914–1998), pensador e intérprete de la cultura mexicana, Premio Nobel de Literatura, 1990. Su obra *El Laberinto de la Soledad* es un estudio de la identidad mexicana.

Dos grandes universidades

La UNAM[1], fundada en 1553, es la segunda universidad más antigua de Norteamérica y está considerada una de las mejores (*best*) instituciones educacionales de Latinoamérica. La UNAM ofrece cursos para estudiantes extranjeros (*foreign*) durante todo el año.

Otra universidad importante es la Universidad Autónoma de Guadalajara, una universidad privada. Estudiantes de muchos países (incluyendo los Estados Unidos) estudian en la UAG.

Ahora, dime...

In groups of three, take turns asking and answering the following questions.

1. Si visitas México, ¿cuánto tiempo quieres pasar allí? ¿Qué te interesa?
2. ¿Cuánto tiempo quieres pasar en la Ciudad de México? ¿Quieres visitar Guadalajara, Guanajuato...?
3. En cuanto a la arquitectura de México, ¿quieres ver ejemplos de la arquitectura precolombina, de la colonial o de la ultramoderna? ¿Por qué?
4. ¿Prefieres ver un mural de Diego Rivera o algunas (*some*) pinturas de Frida Kahlo?
5. ¿Te gusta la idea de leer la versión inglesa de *El Laberinto de la Soledad*?
6. Si quieres estudiar en México, ¿cuál de las dos universidades presentadas aquí prefieres? ¿Por qué?

iLrn™

To learn more about México, watch the cultural footage in the Media Library.

[1] Universidad Nacional Autónoma de México

AUTOPRUEBA

¿Cuánto sé ahora?

Take this test. When you have finished, check your answers in the answer key provided in Appendix D. Then use a red pen to correct any mistakes you may have made. Are you ready?

A. Pronouns as objects of prepositions Complete the following sentences, using the Spanish equivalent of the words in parentheses.

1. En la fiesta, yo quiero bailar ________. Mañana ... ¿quieres ir a un concierto ________? (*with you / with me*)
2. El ponche es para ________, Carlitos; el vino es para ________. (*you / me*)
3. ¿Vas a ir a la montaña con ________ o con ________? (*him / her*)
4. Don Carlos quiere hablar con ________, doña Ana, no con ________. (*you / us*)
5. Mi hija siempre (*always*) habla de________, Anita. (*you*)

B. Contractions Complete the following sentences, using the Spanish equivalent of the words in parentheses.

1. Nosotros venimos ___________ y ellos vienen ___________. (*from the zoo / from the beach*)
2. ¿Quieres ir ________________ o ___________. (*to the Christmas party / to the theater*)
3. Nosotros llevamos ___________ a la universidad. (*Mr. Vega's son*)
4. Yo quiero ver _______________. (*my neighbor's children*)

C. Present indicative of the irregular verbs *ir, dar,* and *estar* Complete the following sentences, using the present indicative of **ir**, **dar**, or **estar**, as appropriate.

1. Yo no ________ al concierto con mis amigos.
2. Nosotros ________ una fiesta aquí hoy.
3. Mi hermana ________ en su casa.
4. ¿Dónde ________ el ponche?
5. Las chicas ________ a la fiesta con sus amigos.
6. Tus primos no ________ mucho dinero para los pobres (*poor*).
7. Yo ________ cansado.
8. ¿Adónde ________ tus padres hoy?
9. ¿Dónde ________ tú ahora?
10. Yo no ________ mi número de teléfono.

D. *Ir a* + infinitive Form sentences that tell what is and is not going to happen. Use the given elements.

1. yo / no hablar / con mi mamá / hoy
2. mis hijos / estudiar / en Guadalajara
3. mi amiga / leer / libro
4. Uds. / traer / los discos compactos
5. tú / bailar / en la fiesta
6. nosotros / no beber / vino

E. Present indicative of *e:ie* stem-changing verbs Complete the following sentences, using the present indicative of the verbs in the list, as necessary.

entender	cerrar	empezar	preferir
pensar	querer	perder	comenzar

1. ¿Uds. ________ ir al partido conmigo? ¡Vamos!
2. Las posadas ______________ el 16 de diciembre.
3. ¿Tú ________ bailar salsa o bailar un vals?
4. ¿Tu tía Sandra ________ una conversación en español, David?
5. Mi abuelo ________ mucho dinero en los casinos de Las Vegas.
6. Yo ________ pasar el Año Nuevo con mi familia.
7. Nosotros ________ la ventana por la noche.

F. Expressions with *tener* Write the Spanish equivalent of the words in parentheses.

1. Mis primos ________. (*are in a hurry*)
2. Yo ____________, pero ____________. (*am not hungry / am very thirsty*)
3. Nosotros vamos a abrir la ventana porque ____________. (*we are hot*)
4. Las chicas ____________. (*are very sleepy*)
5. ¿Tú __________, Anita? (*are afraid*)
6. Ud. __________, Srta. Peña. María __________. (*are right / is ten years old*)

G. Just words . . . Choose the word or phrase that best completes each sentence.

1. Yo estoy (aturdido, contento, aburrido) porque mi novia está conmigo. ¡Ella es una chica encantadora!
2. Quiero comer algo porque tengo (sueño, miedo, hambre).
3. Voy a (sacar, charlar, pensar) muchas fotos.
4. Voy a pasar el (fin de semana, viaje, vecino) con mi abuela.
5. ¡Un brindis! (¡Semana!, ¡Salud!, ¡Árbol!)
6. Yo estoy muy (preocupado, bienvenido, ocupado) porque mi tío está enfermo.
7. Ana está (enojada, cansada, entusiasmada) porque su novio no está invitado a la fiesta.
8. Ellos bailan y (comienzan, ven, cantan) en la fiesta.
9. Nora va a tomar algo porque tiene (prisa, sed, cuidado).
10. Nosotros (pensamos, queremos, acabamos) de hablar con Eva.

H. Culture

1. Complete the following, based on the information found in the **¿Lo sabía Ud.?** sections.
   a. Las posadas representan el viaje de María y ________ desde Nazaret a Belén.
   b. Los hispanos generalmente celebran el cumpleaños y también el día de su ________.
2. Complete the following, based on information found in **El mundo hispánico y tú** section.
   a. ________ es la segunda ciudad más grande de México.
   b. La Universidad ________ de Guadalajara es una universidad privada.
   c. Frida Kahlo es una famosa ________ mexicana.

I. Un dicho Do you remember the Spanish saying that is equivalent to "Out of sight, out of mind"? Find it in this lesson.

LECCIÓN 5

LAS COMIDAS

© Bill Bachmann/Alamy

Un restaurante cubano en Antigua, Guatemala

OBJETIVOS COMUNICATIVOS

You will learn vocabulary related to restaurants, menus, ordering meals, and paying the bill. You will also learn to talk about the weather.

SITUACIONES

¿Qué comemos...?

ESTRUCTURAS

1 Comparative forms
2 Irregular comparative forms
3 Present indicative of **o:ue** stem-changing verbs
4 Present progressive
5 Uses of **ser** and **estar**
6 Weather expressions

ASÍ SOMOS

¡Vamos a ver!

Watching and understanding situations

¡Vamos a escuchar!

Listening for details I

¡Vamos a conversar!

Providing supporting details

¡Vamos a leer!

Expanding your vocabulary through reading

¡Vamos a escribir!

Solidifying and repurposing what you learn

EL MUNDO HISPÁNICO Y TÚ...

› Guatemala
› El Salvador

AUTOPRUEBA

You will review what you learned in this lesson.

Guatemala es uno de los países centroamericanos que fue (*was*) parte del imperio maya. Aunque el español es el idioma oficial, solo lo habla el 60% de la población; el resto habla alguna lengua maya.

Guatemala es un país de volcanes, montañas y bellos paisajes. Su clima es muy agradable y por eso se conoce como "el país de la eterna primavera".

El Salvador es el país más pequeño de Centroamérica, pero es el más densamente poblado. Tiene más de seis millones de habitantes en un área aproximadamente del tamaño (*size*) del estado de Massachusetts.

En El Salvador hay gran número de volcanes, y por eso lo llaman "la tierra (*land*) de los volcanes".

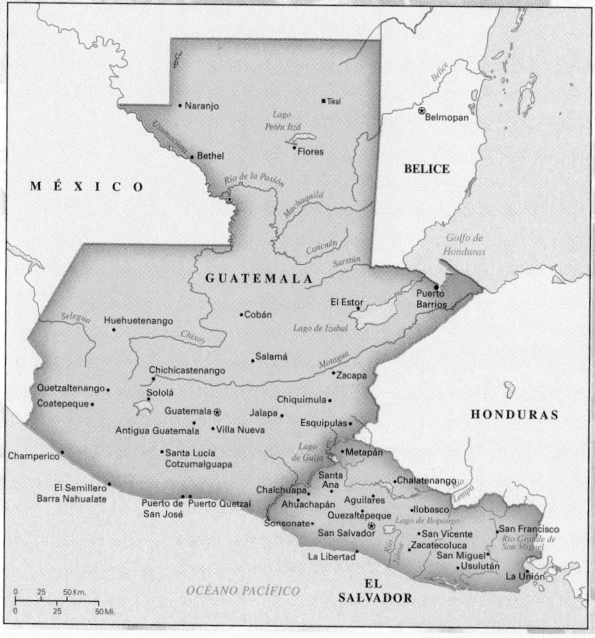

Recursos iLrn video audio web playlist

SITUACIONES

¿Qué comemos...?

CD1-22

© Cengage Learning

¡Ubíquelos!

Rogelio and Maribel are visiting the city of Antigua. They see churches and visit markets. Watch the video, and enjoy the sights. You will also "visit" Maribel's home town of El Salvador.

© Holger Scheibe/Corbis

© John Mitchell/DDB Stock Photo

Rogelio Silva y su esposa Maribel están de vacaciones en la ciudad de Antigua. Rogelio es alto y bastante guapo. Es moreno, de ojos castaños. Maribel es de estatura mediana; no es muy bonita, pero es muy simpática. Rogelio es dos años mayor que su esposa.

En este momento están en el restaurante del hotel, y van a desayunar. Los dos están leyendo el menú.

Rogelio: Yo quiero jamón con huevos revueltos y pan tostado. Para beber, jugo de frutas y chocolate caliente.

Maribel: Yo voy a pedir yogur, y para beber... té helado y un vaso de leche. Estoy contando calorías; además, yo no tengo tanta hambre como tú.

El camarero trae la comida.

Rogelio: ¡Mmm! ¡El jamón está muy sabroso!

Maribel: (*Está mirando su yogur.*) ¿Por qué no pruebas el yogur? ¡Y yo pruebo el jamón y los huevos... !

Al mediodía, Rogelio y Maribel están en un restaurante que tiene comida internacional. Van a almorzar.

Rogelio: (*Al camarero*) Tráigame biftec y langosta con puré de papas y sopa de fideos. Para beber, vino tinto. De postre... flan con crema y helado.

El mozo anota el pedido.

Maribel: Tráigame pescado, una papa al horno y una ensalada. Para beber, agua con limón.

Rogelio y Maribel están conversando.

Rogelio: Tenemos un correo electrónico de mi hermano. Está furioso, porque está en El Salvador, que tiene algunas de las playas más hermosas del mundo, y no puede hacer surfing porque llueve todos los días.

Maribel: ¡Por supuesto! ¡Están en la estación de las lluvias! ¿Y... qué está haciendo tu cuñada?

Rogelio: Siempre está mirando telenovelas en el hotel. ¡Ella lo está pasando muy bien!

El mozo trae la comida.

Maribel: ¿Por qué no pruebas la ensalada...? Yo quiero un pedazo de tu biftec... y un poco de flan y de helado...

Cuando terminan de comer, los dos beben café. Rogelio paga la cuenta y deja una buena propina.

Por la noche, los dos están cenando en su habitación, porque están muy cansados.

Rogelio: (*Mirando la comida.*) A ver... pollo frito, sopa de verduras, ensalada de camarones... y torta de chocolate.

Maribel: Yo tengo un pedazo de pollo a la parrilla, ensalada... y un refresco de dieta.

Maribel "prueba" el pollo frito, toma la sopa y come un pedazo de la torta.

Rogelio: Maribel, voy a salir un rato. ¡Y voy solo! En seguida vuelvo.

Maribel: Pero... ¿no estás cansado? ¿Qué pasa, mi amor? ¿Estás enojado...?

Rogelio: No. ¡Estoy muerto de hambre!

1. Hablemos With a partner, take turns asking and answering the following questions. Base your answers on the dialogues and on your own circumstances.

En el diálogo

1. ¿Rogelio es bajo?
2. ¿Rogelio es menor (*younger*) que su esposa?
3. ¿Cómo es Maribel?
4. ¿Qué desayuna Rogelio?
5. ¿Cuándo van a almorzar Rogelio y Maribel?
6. ¿Qué va a almorzar Rogelio?
7. ¿Por qué está furioso el hermano de Rogelio?
8. ¿Qué está haciendo la cuñada de Rogelio en el hotel?
9. ¿Dónde cenan Rogelio y Maribel?
10. Cuando almuerzan, ¿por qué no pide postre Maribel?
11. ¿Qué beben Maribel y Rogelio cuando terminan de comer?
12. ¿Qué problema tiene Rogelio? ¿Está cansado?

¿Y tú?

1. ¿Tú eres alto(a) o bajo(a)?
2. ¿Tú eres mayor (*older*) o menor que tu mejor amigo(a)?
3. ¿Tu mejor amiga es muy bonita?
4. ¿Qué desayunas tú generalmente?
5. ¿A qué hora almuerzas tú?
6. ¿Tú comes langosta o prefieres comer pescado?
7. ¿Tú haces *surfing*?
8. ¿Tú miras mucha televisión? ¿Miras telenovelas?
9. Cuando estás en un hotel, ¿tú prefieres cenar en el restaurante o en tu habitación?
10. ¿Tú comes postre o no? ¿Qué postre te gusta?
11. ¿Qué bebes tú después de la comida?
12. ¿Tú estás muerto(a) de hambre ahora? ¿Qué quieres comer?

VOCABULARIO

En el diálogo

Cognados

las calorías	*calories*
el chocolate	*chocolate*
la crema	*cream*
la ensalada	*salad*
la fruta	*fruit*
el hotel	*hotel*
el limón	*lemon*
el menú	*menu*
el restaurante	*restaurant*
la sopa	*soup*
el té	*tea*
las vacaciones[1]	*vacation*
el yogur	*yogurt*

Nombres

el agua *(fem.)*	*water*
el biftec, bistec	*steak*
el (la) camarero(a), el mozo	*waiter, waitress*
los camarones	*shrimp*
la cuenta	*bill, check*
la cuñada	*sister-in-law*
la esposa, la mujer	*wife*
el esposo, el marido	*husband*
la estación	*season*
los fideos	*noodles*
el flan	*caramel custard*
la habitación, el cuarto	*room*
el helado	*ice cream*
el huevo	*egg*
el jamón	*ham*
el jugo de frutas	*fruit juice*
la langosta	*lobster*
la leche	*milk*
la lluvia	*rain*
el mundo	*world*
el pan	*bread*
_____ tostado, la tostada	*toast*
la papa	*potato*
_____ al horno (asada)	*baked potato*
el pedazo, trozo	*piece*
el pedido	*order*
el pescado	*fish*
el pollo	*chicken*
la propina	*tip*
el puré de papas	*mashed potatoes*
el refresco	*soft drink, soda pop*
la telenovela	*soap opera*
la torta	*cake*
la verdura, la legumbre	*vegetable*
el vaso	*glass*

Verbos

almorzar (o:ue)	*to have lunch*
cenar	*to have dinner*
contar (o:ue)	*to count*
dejar	*to leave (behind)*
desayunar	*to have breakfast*
hacer (yo hago)	*to do, to make*
llover (o:ue)	*to rain*
mirar	*to look at, to watch (e.g., TV)*
pagar	*to pay*
pedir[2] **(e:i)**	*to order*
poder (o:ue)	*to be able (to)*
probar (o:ue)	*to taste*
salir (yo salgo)	*to go out*
terminar (de)	*to finish, to end*
traer (yo traigo)	*to bring*

© Holger Scheibe/Corbis

[1] **Vacaciones** is always used in the plural in Spanish.
[2] This stem-changing verb will be studied in Lesson 6.

Adjetivos

algunos(as)	*some*
caliente	*hot*
frito(a)	*fried*
helado(a)	*iced*
hermoso(a)	*beautiful*
mayor	*older*
revueltos(as)	*scrambled*
sabroso(a), rico(a)	*tasty*
solo(a)	*alone, by oneself*
tinto	*red (when referring to wine)*

Otras palabras y expresiones

a la parrilla	*grilled*
A ver.	*Let's see.*
al mediodía	*at noon*
bastante	*quite*
cuando	*when*
de dieta, dietético(a)	*diet*
de ojos castaños	*with brown eyes*
de postre	*for dessert*
en este momento	*at this moment*
en seguida, enseguida	*right away*
En seguida vuelvo.	*I'll be right back.*
estar de vacaciones	*to be on vacation*
estar muerto(a) de hambre	*to be starving*
hacer surfing	*to surf*
más	*more*
para beber	*to drink*
pasarlo bien	*to have a good time*
¡por supuesto!	*of course!*
¿Qué pasa?	*What's the matter?, What's happening?*
siempre	*always*
terminar de comer	*to finish eating*
tomar sopa[3]	*to eat soup*
tráigame	*bring me*

Más sobre el tema

Para comer

el arroz con leche	*rice pudding*
el arroz con pollo	*chicken and rice*
el cordero	*lamb*
los frijoles	*beans*
la hamburguesa	*hamburger*
las papas fritas	*French fries*
el pastel	*pastry, pie*
el pavo	*turkey*
el perro caliente	*hot dog*
el queso	*cheese*

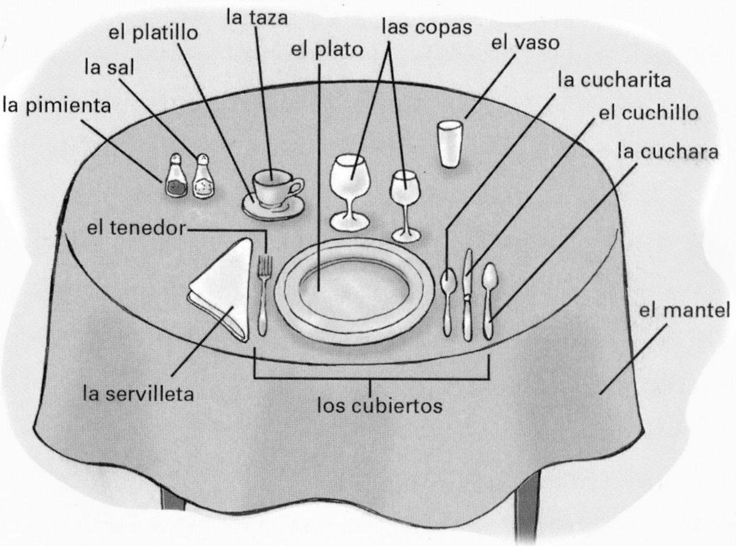

Bebidas (*Drinks*)

el agua mineral	*mineral water*
la bebida alcohólica	*alcoholic beverage*
la cerveza	*beer*
el champán	*champagne*
la sidra[4]	*cider*

¿Lo sabía Ud.?

En los países hispanos el café se sirve después del postre. Generalmente es café tipo espreso, y se sirve en tazas muy pequeñas.

› **¿Se bebe mucho café en este país? ¿Qué tipo de café es muy popular aquí ahora?**

LEARNING TIP

To organize your Spanish study sessions, create standard checklists that will provide a habitual structure. What categories should you include? These will depend on your style of learning. Pay attention to how you approach specific aspects of language learning and build your own studying strategies on those.

[3] **tomar helado** *to eat ice cream*

[4] In Spanish-speaking countries, **sidra** is an alcoholic beverage.

VOCABULARIO

Práctica

2. Completa la oración Choose the word or phrase that best completes each sentence.

1. Para beber quiero (cordero, cerveza, queso).
2. De postre queremos (pavo, fideos, arroz con leche).
3. Necesito (un cuchillo, una cuchara, un tenedor) para tomar la sopa.
4. Voy a poner la mesa. ¿Dónde está (el mantel, la cocina, el camarero)?
5. Quiero comer (leche, papa, torta) asada.
6. Voy a tomar (un plato, una copa, una taza) de café.
7. Quiero probar (el pedido, la lluvia, la sidra).
8. ¿Prefieres vino blanco o vino (rojo, delgado, tinto)?
9. Quiero un sándwich de (jamón, pastel, frijoles) y queso.
10. Necesito la sal y la (servilleta, pimienta, cucharita) para el biftec.

3. ¿Qué es? Write the words or phrases from the vocabulary that correspond to the following.

1. universo
2. pedazo
3. legumbre
4. esposa
5. lo que cuenta una persona que está a dieta
6. mozo
7. pan tostado
8. comer al mediodía
9. sabroso(a)
10. las doce del día
11. banana, por ejemplo
12. tipo de bebida, como el champán o el vino

¿Lo sabía Ud.?

Después de comer, los hispanos se quedan sentados (*remain seated*) alrededor de la mesa y conversan. A esto se le llama "hacer la sobremesa".

› **¿Se hace la sobremesa en este país?**

4. Minidiálogos Complete the following exchanges, using vocabulary from this lesson.

1. —¿Deseas comer ahora?
   —Sí, estoy ______________ de hambre.
2. —¿Vas a comer huevos fritos?
   —No, ______________, con jamón.
3. —¿Deseas tomar café?
   —Sí, con ______________.
4. —En un restaurante, ¿quién trae el menú?
   —El ______________.
5. —¿Qué desea Ud. para cenar?
   —Deseo pollo ______________, ______________ de camarones y, de ______________, arroz con leche.
6. —¿Vas a tomar ______________ mineral?
   —No, agua con ______________.
7. —¿Quién va a pagar la ______________, Elsa o tú?
   —Elsa ______________ la cuenta y yo dejo la ______________.

8. —¿Elsa no quiere comer postre?

—No, porque está contando ______________.

9. —¿Qué estás mirando?

—La ______________ "Todos mis hijos".

10. —¿Te gusta ir a California?

—Sí, porque lo ______________ muy bien allí (*there*).

Para conversar

5. **Tráigame...** With a partner, take turns playing a customer and a waiter (waitress). The waiter (waitress) recommends things to eat, things for dessert, and things to drink **(Yo le recomiendo...)**. The customer has other ideas and orders something else **(No, tráigame...)**.

¿Lo sabía Ud.?

En los países hispanos, la propina generalmente es del 10%. Con frecuencia la propina está incluida en la cuenta. Si Ud. no está seguro de esto, debe preguntar (*ask*): ¿Está incluido el servicio?

› **Generalmente, ¿cuánto se deja de propina en un restaurante en este país?**

Pronunciación

CD1-23 **A. The Spanish *p***

The Spanish **p** is pronounced like the English *p* in the word *sparks*, but with no expulsion of air. Listen to your instructor and repeat the following phrases.

Paco **p**refiere **p**apas fritas. Mi es**p**osa está un **p**oco **p**reocu**p**ada.

CD1-24 **B. The Spanish *t***

The Spanish **t** is pronounced by placing the tongue against the upper teeth, as in the English word *stop*. Listen to your instructor and repeat the following phrases.

Cris**t**ina es**t**á en Gua**t**emala. **T**ambién **t**ienen **t**or**t**a.

CD1-25 **C. The Spanish *c***

The Spanish sound for the letter **c** in the combinations **ca**, **co**, and **cu** is /k/, pronounced as in the English word *car*, but with no expulsion of air. Listen to your instructor and repeat the following phrases.

Carlos **c**ome **c**amarones. ¿**C**uánto **c**uesta el **c**afé?

CD1-26 **D. The Spanish *q***

The Spanish **q** is always followed by a **u**; it is pronounced like the *c* in the English word *come*, but without any expulsion of air. Listen to your instructor and repeat the following phrases.

¿**Q**ué **q**uiere **Q**ui**q**ue? Ro**q**ue **Q**uintana come **q**ueso.

ESTRUCTURAS

1 Comparative forms (*Formas comparativas*)

A. Comparisons of inequality

› In Spanish, the comparative of inequality of most adjectives, adverbs, and nouns is formed by placing **más** (*more*) or **menos** (*less*) before the adjective, the adverb, or the noun and **que** (*than*) after it.

		adjective		
más (*more*)		or		
	+	*adverb*	+	**que** (*than*)
menos (*less*)		or		
		noun		

—¿Tú eres **más alta que** Ana? — *Are you taller than Ana?*
—Sí, ella es mucho **más baja que** yo. — *Yes, she is much shorter than I.*

¡Atención! De is used instead of **que** before a numerical expression of quantity or amount.

Luis tiene **más de** treinta años. — *Luis is over thirty years old.*
Hay **menos de** veinte estudiantes aquí. — *There are fewer than twenty students here.*

B. Comparisons of equality

› To form comparisons of equality with adjectives, adverbs, and nouns, use the adverb **tan** or the adjective **tanto(a, os, as)** and **como**.

When comparing adjectives or adverbs:

tan (*as*) bonita / tarde **+ como**

When comparing nouns:

tanto (*as much*) dinero
tanta bebida
tantos (*as many*) libros
tantas plumas
+ como

—Luis es **tan** inteligente **como** Sergio. — *Luis is as intelligent as Sergio.*
—Sí, pero él no es **tan** guapo **como** Sergio. — *Yes, but he is not as handsome as Sergio.*

—Carol habla muy bien el español. — *Carol speaks Spanish very well.*
—Tú hablas **tan** bien **como** ella. — *You speak as well as she (does).*

—Tú tomas mucho café. — *You drink a lot of coffee.*
—Sí, pero no tomo **tanto** café como tú. — *Yes, but I don't drink as much coffee as you (do).*

Un dicho

No es tan fiero el león como lo pintan.
Equivalent: *His bark is worse than his bite.*

C. The superlative

› The superlative construction is similar to the comparative. It is formed by placing the definite article before the person or thing being compared.

				más				
definite	+	(*noun*)	+	or	+	*adjective*	+	**de**
article				**menos**				

—¿Quieres ir a Antigua? — *Do you want to go to Antigua?*

—Sí, es **la ciudad más hermosa de** Guatemala. — *Yes, it's the most beautiful city in Guatemala.*

—Juan no es muy inteligente. — *Juan is not very intelligent.*

—No, es **el**[1] **menos inteligente de** la familia. — *No, he is the least intelligent* (*one*) *in the family.*

¡Atención! Note that the Spanish **de** translates to the English *in* after a superlative.

Es la ciudad más hermosa **de** Guatemala. — *It's the most beautiful city in Guatemala.*

Es la chica más bonita **de** la clase. — *She is the prettiest girl in the class.*

Un dicho

Amigo y vino, el más antiguo.

Equivalent: *Old friends and old wine are best.*

Práctica

6. **¿Cómo son?** With a partner, compare the people in the picture to each other.

1. María es ________________ Rosa.
2. Rosa es ________________ María.
3. Carlos es ________________ Rosa y que María.
4. Carlos es ________________ Juan.
5. Juan es ________________ Carlos.
6. Juan es ________________ María.
7. Juan es ________________ de todos.
8. Carlos es ________________ de todos.

[1]As in English, the noun may be omitted.

7. **Comparando** Establish comparisons between the following people, places, and things using the adjectives provided and adding any necessary words.
   1. Michael Jordan / Danny DeVito (alto)
   2. El Salvador / Canadá (pequeño) (*small*)
   3. La clase de español / inglés (difícil)
   4. Jessica Alba / Penélope Cruz (bonita)
   5. Argentina / Guatemala (grande) (*big*)
   6. Antonio Banderas / Johnny Depp (guapo)

   Now find a partner and take turns comparing more people, places, and things.

8. **Comparaciones y más comparaciones** Complete the following, using the appropriate comparative forms.
   1. El Hotel Hilton es ________ caro (*expensive*) que el Motel 6.
   2. Yo tengo ________ libros como tú.
   3. El jamón está ________ sabroso como el pollo.
   4. Alicia estudia ________ horas como Elsa.
   5. Dora no es bonita. Ella es la ________ bonita de su familia.
   6. Diego tiene ________ prisa como yo.

Para conversar

9. **¡A conocernos mejor!** With a partner, take turns asking each other comparative questions. Start with the following questions, then add five more of your own. Answers should be given in complete sentences.
   1. ¿Tú eres tan inteligente como tus padres? ¿Quién es el (la) más inteligente de la familia? ¿Tú eres más inteligente que tu mejor (*best*) amigo(a)?
   2. ¿Tú eres más alto(a) que yo? ¿Tú eres más alto(a) que tu mamá? ¿Quién es el más alto de la familia?
   3. ¿Tú bailas tan bien como Ricky Martin? ¿Cantas tan bien como él?
   4. ¿Tú eres tan guapo como Brad Pitt? (¿Tan bonita como Jennifer López?) ¿Quién es el más guapo de tus amigos? ¿La más bonita de tus amigas?
   5. ¿Tú tienes tanto dinero como tus padres?

10. **¡Vamos a comparar!** (*Let's compare!*) In groups of three or four, make comparisons between each one of you and other members of the class. You might want to include the instructor. Decide who is the tallest, the most intelligent, the most charming, etc.

2 Irregular comparative forms (*Formas comparativas irregulares*)

› The following adjectives and adverbs have irregular comparative and superlative forms in Spanish.

Adjective	Adverb	Comparative	Superlative
bueno	bien	mejor	el (la) mejor
malo	mal	peor	el (la) peor
grande		mayor	el (la) mayor
pequeño		menor	el (la) menor

—El restaurante El Dorado es muy **malo**. — *The El Dorado Restaurant is very bad.*
—Sí, pero la cafetería de la universidad es **peor.** — *Yes, but the university's cafeteria is worse.*

—Eva es una **buena** estudiante. — *Eva is a good student.*
—Sí, es **la mejor** de la clase. — *Yes, she's the best in the class.*

› When the adjectives **grande** and **pequeño** refer to size, the regular forms are generally used.

Tu casa es **más grande** que la de Carolina. — *Your house is bigger than Carolina's.*

› When these adjectives refer to age, the irregular forms are used.

Ella es **mucho mayor** que yo. — *She is much older than I.*
Teresa es **menor** que Carlos. — *Teresa is younger than Carlos.*
Ella es **la menor** de todos. — *She is the youngest of all.*

Práctica

LEARNING TIP
Think of hotels and restaurants in your city. Which ones are the best? The worst? Compare some of your friends and relatives to you. Who is older? Who is younger?

11. Dime... (*Tell me . . .*) Answer the following questions with complete sentences.

1. Mi sobrina tiene siete años y mi sobrino tiene cinco. ¿Quién es mayor? ¿Quién es menor?
2. Mi tío tiene cuarenta años y mi tía tiene treinta y ocho. ¿Quién es menor? ¿Quién es mayor?
3. ¿Quién habla mejor el español, tú o el profesor (la profesora)?
4. Pedro tiene una "B" en inglés; Antonio tiene una "C"; y José tiene una "F". ¿Quién es el peor estudiante? ¿Quién es el mejor estudiante?

Now write three original comparative situations, using the ones you have just completed as models. When you have finished, take turns giving and responding to situations with a partner.

Para conversar

12. ¡Habla con tu compañero(a)! Interview a classmate, using the following questions. When you have finished, switch roles.

1. ¿Tú eres mayor o menor que tu mejor amigo(a)?
2. ¿Tu mamá es menor que tu papá?
3. ¿Quién cocina (*cooks*) mejor, tú o tu mamá?
4. ¿Quién crees tú que es el (la) mejor estudiante de la clase?
5. ¿Cuál crees tú que es la mejor película (*film*) del año? ¿Y la peor?
6. De los restaurantes de la ciudad donde vives, ¿cuál es el mejor? ¿Y el peor?
7. ¿Cuál crees tú que es la mejor universidad de tu país?
8. ¿Quiénes crees tú que manejan (*drive*) mejor: los hombres o las mujeres?
9. ¿Cuál crees tú que es el mejor programa de la televisión? ¿Y el peor?
10. ¿Cuál crees tú que es la mejor estación del año y cuál es la peor? ¿Por qué?

Now, change the *tú* form to the *Ud.* form, and ask your instructor the same questions.

3 Present indicative of *o:ue* stem-changing verbs (*Presente de indicativo de los verbos que cambian en la raíz* ***o:ue***)

› Some verbs undergo a stem change in the present indicative. For these verbs, when **o** is the last stem vowel and it is stressed, it changes to **ue.**

poder *to be able*	
puedo	podemos
puedes	podéis
puede	pueden

—¿**Puedes** ir conmigo al restaurante? — *Can you go with me to the restaurant?*
—No, no **puedo**. No tengo dinero. — *No, I can't. I don't have (any) money.*

› Other verbs that undergo this change:[1]

almorzar	*to have lunch*	**llover**	*(impersonal) to rain*
contar	*to tell, to count*	**morir**	*to die*
costar	*to cost*	**recordar**	*to remember*
dormir	*to sleep*	**volar**	*to fly*
encontrar	*to find*	**volver**	*to return*

—¿A qué hora **vuelven** Uds.? — *At what time are you returning?*
—**Volvemos** a las doce. — *We'll return at twelve o'clock.*
—Entonces **almorzamos** a las doce y media. — *Then we'll have lunch at twelve-thirty.*

Note that the stem vowel is not stressed in the verb forms used with **nosotros(as)** and **vosotros(as);** therefore, the **o** does not change to **ue.**

[1]For a complete list of stem-changing verbs, see Appendix B.

Práctica

13. **¿Con quién habla Marité?** Marité is talking to her roommate, who is sound asleep. Complete the story, supplying the missing (**o:ue**) verbs. Think logically before filling in the blanks. Then read it aloud.

Marité: ¡Teresa, me voy! No __________ mis libros. ¿Dónde están? No __________ ir a mi clase sin *(without)* mis libros. ¡Oye! Hoy __________ con Pedro en la cafetería; no tengo dinero y los sándwiches en la cafetería __________ tres dólares. ¡Ay, Teresa!, hoy tengo que llamar a Marta y no __________ su número de teléfono. ¡Teresa!, ¿tú __________ el número de Marta? ¡Oye! ¿Roberto __________ a San Salvador hoy? ¿Vas al aeropuerto con él? *(Mira por la ventana.)* ¡Ay, cómo __________ ! Necesito tu impermeable *(raincoat).* ¡Ah!, hoy __________ a casa a las cinco. *(Abre la puerta de Teresa.)* ¡Teresa! ¡Teresa! ¿Por qué no contestas *(answer)?*

Teresa: (Mmm...) Nunca __________ dormir cuando tú estás en casa.

Marité: Tú __________ mucho. No necesitas dormir más. Me voy. Nos vemos.

14. **Preguntas** Arnaldo is very nosy and is always asking questions. Here are the answers. What are his questions?

1. ¿____________________? Mi computadora cuesta $500.
2. ¿____________________? Yo siempre almuerzo a las doce.
3. ¿____________________? No, nosotros no volvemos a la universidad hoy.
4. ¿____________________? Yo duermo ocho horas.
5. ¿______________________________? No, no recuerdo el número de teléfono del profesor (de la profesora).
6. ¿____________________? Vuelo a México el domingo.
7. ¿________________________? No, hoy no puedo estudiar en la biblioteca.
8. ¿____________________? No, yo no cuento calorías.

15. **Uds. preguntan** With a classmate, prepare four or five questions to ask a member of another group, using stem-changing (**o:ue**) verbs.

Para conversar

16. **¡Habla con tu compañero(a)!** Interview a classmate, using the following questions. When you have finished, switch roles.

1. ¿Dónde almuerzas generalmente, en la cafetería o en tu casa? ¿A qué hora almuerzas? ¿Almuerzas solo(a) o con tus amigos(as)?
2. En la cafetería, ¿cuánto cuestan las hamburguesas? ¿Cuánto cuesta un sándwich de jamón y queso? ¿Y uno de ensalada de pollo?
3. ¿Te gusta la comida de la cafetería? ¿Es buena? ¿Es muy cara (*expensive*)?
4. Cuando comes en un restaurante muy bueno, ¿cuentas las calorías o comes mucho?
5. Cuando vas a salir, ¿siempre encuentras las llaves (*keys*) de tu casa o no recuerdas dónde están?
6. ¿A qué hora vuelves a tu casa hoy? ¿Vuelves muy tarde (*late*) o vuelves temprano (*early*)? ¿Vuelves a la universidad los sábados?
7. ¿Llueve mucho en tu ciudad? ¿En qué meses llueve más? ¿Tú vienes a la universidad cuando llueve mucho o prefieres no salir de tu casa?
8. ¿Recuerdas la dirección del profesor (de la profesora)? ¿Y la de tu mejor amigo(a)?

17. **Compañeros de cuarto** You are interviewing a prospective roommate. Your roommate asks how much the apartment costs, what he can do and cannot do in the apartment, etc. Tell him/her how much the apartment costs and ask pertinent questions about his/her schedule and routine. Give details about yours.

4 Present progressive (*Estar + gerundio*)

› The present progressive describes an action that is in progress. It is formed with the present tense of **estar** and the **gerundio,** which is equivalent to the English present participle (the *-ing* form of the verb).

Gerundio		
hablar	***comer***	***escribir***
habl **-ando**	com **-iendo**	escrib **-iendo**
speaking	*eating*	*writing*

—¿Qué **estás tomando**?	*What are you drinking?*
—**Estoy tomando** chocolate caliente. Y tú, ¿qué **estás comiendo?**	*I am drinking hot chocolate. And you, what are you eating?*
—**Estoy comiendo** un pedazo de pastel.	*I'm eating a piece of pie.*
—¿Qué **están haciendo** los niños?	*What are the children doing?*
—**Están escribiendo.**	*They are writing.*

› The following forms are irregular.

pedir:	**pidiendo**	dormir:	**durmiendo**
decir:	**diciendo**	traer:	**trayendo**
servir:	**sirviendo**	leer:	**leyendo**

—¿Daniel **está leyendo**?	*Is Daniel reading?*
—No, **está durmiendo**.	*No, he's sleeping.*
—¿Qué **está sirviendo** el camarero?	*What is the waiter serving?*
—**Está sirviendo** las bebidas.	*He's serving the drinks.*
—¿José **está pidiendo** champán?	*Is José ordering champagne?*
—No, porque el champán cuesta 70 quetzales.	*No, because champagne costs 70 quetzales.*

› Note that as shown with **traer** and **leer,** the **i** of **-iendo** becomes **y** between vowels.

¡Atención! In Spanish, the present progressive is never used to indicate a future action. The present tense is used in future expressions that would require the present progressive in English.

Trabajo mañana. *I'm working tomorrow.*

Some verbs, such as **ser, estar, ir,** and **venir,** are rarely used in the progressive construction.

¿Lo sabía Ud.?

El **quetzal** es la unidad monetaria de Guatemala. Argentina, Chile, Colombia, Cuba, México, República Dominicana y Uruguay usan el **peso.** Otras unidades monetarias de los países de habla hispana son: el **boliviano** en Bolivia, el **colón** en Costa Rica y El Salvador[1], el **dólar** en Ecuador, Panamá y Puerto Rico, el **lempira** en Honduras, el **córdoba** en Nicaragua, el **nuevo sol** en Perú, el **guaraní** en Paraguay, el **bolívar** en Venezuela y el **euro** en España. El valor de estas monedas no es estable y su equivalencia con el dólar varía frecuentemente.

› **¿Cuál es la unidad monetaria de este país?**

Práctica

18. **¿Qué están haciendo?** With a partner, take turns asking each other what the following people are doing **(haciendo).**

Tú...

Yo...

Raúl y Sara...

Eva...

La profesora...

Nosotros ... y el chico...

[1]The dollar is legal tender in this country.

19. **¿Cuál es la pregunta?** With a partner, take turns supplying the questions that prompted the following answers. Make sure you use the present progressive.

1. Estoy comiendo papas fritas.
2. Estamos leyendo el menú.
3. El camarero está sirviendo las bebidas.
4. Ellos están diciendo que quieren camarones.
5. Anita está durmiendo en mi cuarto.
6. Estamos bebiendo vino tinto.
7. Estoy haciendo puré de papas.
8. Los niños están pidiendo perros calientes.
9. Rosa está desayunando con José Luis.
10. Estamos anotando la dirección del restaurante.

20. **Según[1] donde están** With a partner, discuss what you think these people are doing. Give two or three possibilities for each situation.

1. la secretaria / en la oficina
2. los estudiantes / en la clase
3. los chicos / en la cafetería
4. el profesor / en la universidad
5. los muchachos y las muchachas / en la fiesta
6. el Sr. Vega / en su cuarto
7. el camarero / en el restaurante
8. la Srta. Barrios / en su apartamento

Para conversar

21. **Chicos** The instructor will play the role of house-parent in a dorm. He/She will leave the classroom for one minute, then return and ask each student what he/she is doing. Each person will claim to be doing something worthwhile and accuse another student of doing something naughty. That student will deny it and say he/she is doing something else.

HINT: fumar *to smoke*

5 Uses of *ser* and *estar* (*Usos de* **ser** *y* **estar**)

The English verb *to be* has two Spanish equivalents, **ser** and **estar**. As a general rule, **ser** expresses *who* or *what* the subject is *essentially*, and **estar** indicates *state* or *condition*. **Ser** and **estar** are *not* interchangeable.

A. Uses of *ser*

Ser expresses a fundamental quality and identifies the essence of a person or thing.

› It describes the basic nature or character of a person or thing. It is also used with expressions of age that do not refer to a specific number of years.

Amanda **es** hermosa y muy inteligente. **Es** joven *(young)*, pero **es** muy madura.

[1]According to

- It is used to denote nationality, origin, and profession or trade.
  Amanda **es** guatemalteca. **Es** de la ciudad de Guatemala. **Es** estudiante.
- It is used to indicate relationship or possession.
  Amanda **es** la sobrina del Sr. Álvarez. Los discos compactos **son** de Amanda.
- It is used with expressions of time and with dates.
  Son las cuatro y cuarto de la tarde. Hoy **es** miércoles, cuatro de abril.
- It is used with events as the equivalent of *taking place*.
  La fiesta **es** en la casa de Amanda.
- It describes the material that things are made of.
  La mesa **es** de metal.

Un dicho

No todo lo que brilla es oro.
Equivalent: *All that glitters is not gold.*

Práctica

22. **¡Habla con tu compañero(a)!** Interview a classmate, using the following questions and two of your own. When you have finished, switch roles.

1. ¿Eres norteamericano(a)? ¿De dónde eres?
2. ¿De qué ciudad eres?
3. ¿Cómo es tu mamá? ¿Cómo es tu papá?
4. ¿De dónde son tus abuelos?
5. ¿Quién es tu mejor amigo(a)? ¿Cómo es?
6. ¿Eres optimista o pesimista?
7. ¿Dónde son tus clases? ¿Tienes clases hoy?
8. ¿Qué fecha es hoy?
9. ¿Qué hora es?
10. ¿Tu reloj es de oro *(gold)*?

B. Uses of *estar*

Estar is used to express more transitory qualities and often implies the possibility of change.

- It indicates place or location. Mi marido no **está** aquí. ¿**Está** en el restaurante?
- It is used to indicate condition. Mis amigos **están** muy cansados. El profesor **está** enfermo.
- With personal reactions, it describes what is perceived through the senses—that is, how a person or thing seems, looks, tastes, or feels. El ponche **está** muy sabroso.
- It is used in the present progressive tense. Yo **estoy** estudiando y Ana **está** leyendo.

LEARNING TIP
Remember to "stay" with **each use**, creating as many examples as possible and always personalizing them. (Yes it's all about you!) For example: ***Yo estoy* en la universidad, mi mamá *está* en casa, mis amigos *están* en la cafetería,** etc.

Práctica

23. **En el club** Imagine that you and a friend are at a party at a club, and answer the following questions. Work with a partner.
   1. ¿En qué calle está el club?
   2. ¿Los amigos de Uds. están en el club?
   3. ¿Sus amigos están contentos o tristes?
   4. ¿Cómo está la comida? ¿Rica?
   5. ¿Quiénes están bailando?
   6. ¿Tu mamá está en la fiesta?
   7. ¿Tú estás conversando?
   8. ¿Lo estás pasando bien?

24. **Minidiálogos** Complete the following dialogues, using the appropriate forms of **ser** or **estar.** Then act them out with a partner.
   1. —¿De dónde _______ tus padres?
      —Mi papá _______ de México y mi mamá _______ de Chile; pero ahora ellos _______ viviendo en Guatemala.
      —¿Tu papá _______ profesor?
      —Sí, él _______profesor, y ahora _______ trabajando en la universidad.
   2. —¿Carlos _______ tu novio?
      —No, él _______ mi hermano.
      —¿Cómo _______ él?
      — _______ alto, rubio, de ojos castaños y _______ muy simpático.
      —¿Dónde _______ trabajando él ahora?
      —No _______ trabajando. _______ estudiando en la universidad.
   3. —¿Qué _______ bebiendo Uds.?
      —Yo _______ bebiendo té helado, y Rosa _______ bebiendo un refresco de limón.
   4. —¿Dónde _______ la fiesta de Maricela?
      — _______ en su casa. Yo no voy porque _______ muy cansado(a).

5. —¿Qué _______ comiendo?
   — _______ comiendo flan.
   —¿ _______ sabroso?
   —Sí, _______ muy rico.
6. —¿De quién _______ ese (*that*) reloj?
   — _______ de María.
   —¿ _______ de oro?
   —No, _______ de plata (*silver*).

25. **En un restaurante** Answer the following questions according to what you see in the illustration. Take turns responding with a partner.

1. ¿Qué día es hoy? ¿Qué fecha es hoy? ¿Qué hora es?
2. ¿Luis es casado o soltero?
3. ¿Tú crees que Eva es la esposa o la mamá de Luis?
4. ¿Eva es bonita o fea? ¿Cómo es Luis?
5. ¿Dónde están Eva y Luis?
6. ¿Qué está comiendo Luis? ¿Está sabrosa la langosta?
7. ¿Quién es José?
8. ¿Qué está sirviendo José?
9. ¿En qué está pensando José? ¿Dónde es la fiesta?
10. ¿Isabel está contenta o triste?

Para conversar

26. **¿Quién es?** With two or three other students, prepare a description of a famous person. Include as much information as possible (nationality, profession, physical characteristics, etc.). Read your description to the rest of the class and see who can identify your subject.

¿Lo sabía Ud.?

En la mayoría de los países hispanos, los restaurantes no sirven la cena hasta las nueve de la noche. A las cuatro de la tarde, la gente merienda (*have an afternoon snack*).

› **¿A qué hora empiezan a servir la cena los restaurantes en este país?**

6 Weather expressions (*Expresiones para describir el tiempo*)

› In the following expressions, Spanish uses the verb **hacer,** *to make*, followed by a noun.

Es el 13 de agosto. Eva está en Phoenix, Arizona.

Hace sol y **hace** mucho **calor**.

Es el 20 de enero. Luis está en Alaska. **Hace** mucho **frío**.

Ana y Raúl están en Chicago en octubre. Hoy **hace** mucho **viento.**

› To ask about the weather, say, **"¿Qué tiempo hace?"** (*What's the weather like?*).

—**¿Qué tiempo hace** hoy?	*What's the weather like today?*
—**Hace** buen (mal) tiempo.	*The weather is good (bad).*
—**¿Hace frío** en Guatemala?	*Is it cold in Guatemala?*
—No, Guatemala es el país de la eterna primavera.	*No, Guatemala is the country of eternal spring.*

› The following words used to describe the weather do not combine with **hacer;** they are impersonal verbs used only in the infinitive, present participle, past participle, and third person singular forms of all tenses.

llover (o:ue) *to rain*	**Llueve**. *It rains.*
nevar (e:ie) *to snow*	**Nieva**. *It snows.*

› Other weather-related words are **lluvia** (*rain*) and **niebla** (*fog*).

—¿Vas a volar hoy a San Salvador?	*Are you going to fly to San Salvador today?*
—No, porque **hay niebla.**	*No, because it's foggy.*

Práctica

27. **Minidiálogos** Study the words in the following list, then complete the dialogues.

el paraguas *umbrella*	**el sombrero** *hat*	**el suéter** *sweater*
el impermeable *raincoat*	**el abrigo** *coat*	

1. —¿Necesitas un paraguas?
   —Sí, porque ____________ mucho. También necesito un abrigo porque ____________.
2. —¿Por qué no quieres llevar el suéter?
   —¡Porque ____________, ____________!
3. —¿Vas a llevar el sombrero?
   —Sí, porque ____________.
4. —¿Necesitas un suéter y un abrigo?
   —Sí, porque ____________.
5. —¿Un impermeable? ¿Por qué? ¿Está lloviendo?
   —No, pero ____________.
6. —¡Qué lluvia! Necesito un ____________ y un ____________.
   —¡Yo también!

28. **¿Qué tiempo hace?** Say what the weather will be like in different locations at different times of the year.

1. Portland, Oregón—el 2 de enero
2. Anchorage, Alaska—el 25 de diciembre
3. Phoenix, Arizona—el 13 de agosto
4. Londres (*London*)—el 5 de febrero
5. Chicago—el 6 de marzo

Un dicho

A mal tiempo, buena cara.
Equivalent: *Keep a stiff upper lip.*

LEARNING TIP
Note that when talking about weather conditions, the normal Spanish sentence structure is modified. Instead of the general *subject + verb + object* structure, one uses **Hace** or **Hay** (impersonal forms of **hacer** and **haber**—that is, in this construction the verb is not conjugated) + the particular weather expression, or just the impersonal weather-related verb such as **Llueve** or **Nieva.** The repertory of sentence structures in Spanish, just as in English, goes beyond the basic one you know. Start recognizing any variant structure (syntactic) patterns.

Para conversar

29. **De visita** (*Visiting*) A visiting professor from Guatemala is planning a weekend visit to your hometown. What questions is he or she likely to ask about the weather there and what clothes to bring? How will you respond? Act out the scene with a partner. Say at least three lines each.

30. **¿Dónde quiero vivir?** In groups of three, talk about the places where you want to live and those where you don't want to live. Keep in mind the kind of weather in said places.

31. **El pronóstico del tiempo** (*The weather forecast*) You and a classmate are in charge of preparing the weather report for a local TV station. Discuss the weather in your area today.

ASÍ SOMOS

¡Vamos a ver!

Antes de ver el video

32. Prepárate To prepare to watch the video, you and a partner talk about the following.

1. si almuerzan en restaurantes frecuentemente
2. si tienen un restaurante favorito (¿Cuál?)
3. si prefieren papas fritas o puré de papas
4. si creen que la langosta es más cara (*expensive*) o más barata (*inexpensive*) que el pescado
5. si prefieren beber vino tinto o agua mineral
6. si prefieren comer un pedazo de torta o tomar un helado
7. si pasan más tiempo durmiendo, estudiando o mirando la tele
8. si hoy hace calor o hace frío y si hace sol o llueve
9. si lo pasan bien cuando van de vacaciones
10. si reciben muchos mensajes electrónicos

El video: En un restaurante

Cristina está leyendo el menú.

El mozo anota el pedido.

Cristina llama a su mamá.

Fernando y Cristina están conversando.

Después de ver el video

© Cengage Learning

Cristina

© Cengage Learning

Fernando

© Cengage Learning

Camarero

33. ¿Quién lo dice? Identify the person who said the following in the dialogues.

1. Tráigame biftec con papas fritas y sopa de verduras. ________
2. Mañana vuelvo a mi dieta. ________
3. Voy a llamar a mamá para ver qué están haciendo los niños. ________
4. Las papas fritas tienen más sabor que las papas asadas. ________
5. Yo a veces almuerzo aquí. Preparan una ensalada de camarones muy rica. ________
6. ¡Están bien! ¡Eres imposible! ________
7. ¿Qué desean comer? ________
8. Pollo a la parrilla con ensalada y una papa al horno. ________
9. Tengo que contar calorías. ________
10. Estamos solos... podemos conversar. ________

34. Hablemos With a partner, take turns asking and answering the following questions. Base your answers on the dialogue.

En el diálogo

1. ¿De dónde es Fernando?
2. ¿Fernando es contador[1] o profesor?
3. ¿De dónde es Cristina?
4. ¿Dónde trabaja Fernando?
5. ¿Cómo es Fernando?
6. ¿Qué está leyendo Cristina?
7. ¿Cuánto cuesta la langosta?
8. ¿Qué va a comer Cristina y qué va a beber?
9. ¿A quién va a llamar Cristina?
10. ¿Qué está haciendo la mamá de Cristina?

35. ¿Qué pasa después? You and a partner use your imagination to talk about what happens to the characters in the video after Cristina and Fernando leave the restaurant. In Spanish, discuss the following:

1. The time when Fernando and Cristina return home.
2. What the weather is like.
3. What the children are doing. (Hint: **jugar** = *to play*)
4. Whether the grandmother is watching another soap opera or sleeping.
5. Whether they have another e-mail (from whom?).
6. Whether they watch TV for a while or talk in the living room.
7. Where they have dinner that evening and what they eat and drink.
8. Whether or not Cristina goes back to her diet.

Now compare your statements to those of another group.

[1]contador: *accountant*

¡Vamos a escuchar!

ESTRATEGIA **Listening for details I** In the preceding lessons, you have practiced listening for the main idea and for specific information in different types of oral texts. When listening for details, draw on the strategies you've already learned and concentrate on the specific information you want to obtain, such as the what, where, and when. Also use your knowledge of the topic and format (voice mail, ad, public service announcement, etc.) to anticipate the kind of information you will hear. This will help you understand more of the details.

CD1-27 **36. Un anuncio de radio** You hear a commercial about a new restaurant that has just opened near where you live. You want to know what it's like, its menu, the hours, specific location, prices of dishes, etc. Listen attentively and jot down the following information. Listen a second time for any details you missed.

nombre del restaurante ________________

dirección ________________

tipo de comida ______________________________

horas del almuerzo ________________

horas de la cena ________________

cómo son los precios ________________

¡Vamos a conversar!

ESTRATEGIA **Providing supporting details** To express a point of view effectively, give an explanation, or inform others about a topic, you need to include details or information that make the topic interesting to your listener, help him or her understand it, and support and expand on your basic idea.

37. Un restaurante nuevo You're interested in going to the new restaurant you have just heard about (or your favorite restaurant). Tell two friends about it, giving as much information as you can about the restaurant to explain why it's a good choice. Answer their questions about the food, the specialties **(especialidades)**, the prices, etc., and find out if they want to try it.

38. ¿Qué dice Ud.? What would you say in the following situations? What might the other person say? Act out the scenes with a partner. Take turns playing each role.

1. You describe your mother and a friend describes his/hers. Make comparisons between them.
2. You and a friend are at a restaurant. Order a complete meal, including drinks and dessert. Then, ask for the check.
3. You tell your dining companion that you can pay the bill and ask if he/she can leave the tip.
4. You are cooking a gourmet dinner. Ask your roommate to set the table. Name the utensils and other items you want. Your roommate doesn't know where things are.
5. You are hosting a party at your home. Some of your guests have brought children. Offer a selection of beverages.

39. Para conocernos mejor To do this activity, work with a classmate whom you would like to get to know. Take turns asking and answering these questions.

1. En el desayuno, ¿prefieres tomar café, chocolate caliente o leche? ¿Prefieres comer huevos fritos o revueltos? ¿Comes frutas o tomas jugo de frutas?
2. En la cafetería, ¿comes hamburguesas o perros calientes? ¿Qué bebes?
3. Generalmente, ¿almuerzas en tu casa o en la cafetería? ¿Almuerzas solo(a)? ¿Vives en un apartamento o en tu casa, con tu familia?
4. ¿Cómo es tu mamá? ¿Y tu papá? ¿Quién es mayor? ¿Tienes hermanos? ¿Cuántos? ¿Son mayores o menores que tú?
5. ¿Quién es tu mejor amigo(a)? ¿Cómo es? ¿Dónde está ahora?
6. ¿Qué tiempo hace hoy? ¿Qué usas cuando llueve? ¿Y cuando hace frío?
7. En el lugar donde vives, ¿hace mucho frío en el invierno? ¿Nieva? ¿Prefieres vivir en un lugar donde hace frío o en un lugar donde hace calor?
8. En la ciudad donde viven tus padres, ¿generalmente hace buen tiempo o mal tiempo?

40. Una encuesta Interview your classmates to identify who fits the following descriptions. Include your instructor, but remember to use the **Ud.** form when addressing him/her. After finishing the survey, get together with two or three classmates and discuss the results.

1. Siempre almuerza en la cafetería. ________________.
2. Bebe café con las comidas. ________________.
3. Toma bebidas alcohólicas. ________________.
4. Toma refrescos de dieta. ________________.
5. Cuenta calorías. ________________.
6. Come mucho pescado. ________________.
7. No come papas fritas. ________________.
8. No come frijoles. ________________.
9. Come arroz con pollo. ________________.
10. No come postre. ________________.

41. Para crear Get together in groups of three and "create" the scenario for this photo. Who are the people in it? Are they celebrating? What? What are they eating? What do you see on the table? What are they ordering for dessert? What are they going to drink after dessert? What are they going to do later?

¡Vamos a leer!

Antes de leer

ESTRATEGIA **Expanding your vocabulary through reading** Just as in English, a purpose of reading in any language is to increase your vocabulary. Some ways of doing this are by looking for cognates, for word families **(comer-comida-comedor)**, and for words that pertain to topics of interest to you.

42. **Cómo mantenernos saludables (*healthy*)** The following reading about healthful eating habits contains numerous words that are unfamiliar to you. As you answer these questions, make it a goal to learn at least five new words.

¡A leer!

Tácticas y estrategias para tener buena salud (*health*)

Es mejor…

1. ...comer muchas verduras y frutas.
2. ...cocinar (*to cook*) la carne, el pollo y el pescado al horno o a la parrilla (*grilled*).
3. ...cocinar las verduras al vapor (*steam*).
4. …beber mucha agua.
5. …tomar leche sin grasa (*fat free*).
6. …comer alimentos (*foods*) bajos en grasa y en azúcar (*sugar*).
7. …hacer ejercicio (*exercise*) por lo menos tres veces por semana, por 30 minutos.

No es una buena idea…

1. ...tener alimentos con muchas calorías en el refrigerador y en la despensa (*pantry*).
2. ...comer mucha comida frita.
3. ...comer mucho por la noche.
4. ...beber mucha cerveza y muchos refrescos.
5. ...beber mucho café.
6. ...tener una vida (*life*) sedentaria.

El Dr. Rafael Mirabal siempre da muy buenos consejos (*advice*). Su filosofía es "mente sana en cuerpo sano".

43. Comprensión As you read the article, find the answers to the following questions.

1. ¿Qué alimentos debemos preferir?
2. ¿Cómo debemos cocinar la carne y el pescado?
3. ¿Cómo debemos cocinar las verduras?
4. ¿Debemos beber mucha o poca agua?
5. ¿Qué tipo de leche debemos preferir?
6. ¿Debemos comer alimentos que tienen mucha grasa?
7. ¿Cuántas veces a la semana debemos hacer ejercicio? ¿Por cuánto tiempo?
8. ¿Qué alimentos no debemos tener en la casa?
9. ¿Debemos comer mucha comida frita?
10. ¿Es una buena idea comer mucho por la noche?
11. ¿Qué no debemos beber en exceso?
12. ¿Qué tipo de vida debemos evitar (*avoid*)?

Después de leer...

44. Desde su mundo In groups of three or four, discuss your preferences for specific dishes and foods. Do you have good eating habits?

¡Vamos a escribir!

Antes de escribir

ESTRATEGIA **Solidifying and repurposing what you learn** You were asked to use the reading activity for the goal of increasing your vocabulary on the basic subjects of food and health. To add new words to those you already use, you need to practice and reuse them whenever you can.

45. ¿Qué comes? In preparation for inviting your classmates to dinner, interview two classmates about their food preferences and general eating habits to find out about the kinds of food and drinks they like. Be sure to use some of the words you learned from the reading and don't forget to ask about dessert! Take notes.

46. Un menú sabroso You are planning to invite two classmates to an evening of fine and healthy dining at your place! Before writing an e-mail invitation, use your notes from the preceding activity to plan the menu. Also, organize the paragraphs of your e-mail according to what you will communicate in each, including the occasion, comments about the menu, day, time, and place.

¡A escribir!

47. Una invitación a una comida Write your **primer borrador** of the e-mail invitation. Remember the greetings and closings presented in **Lección 4.** You may want to begin by saying: **Quiero invitarlos** (*invite you*) **a cenar en mi casa...**

Después de escribir

48. A revisar Before writing the final version, exchange your first draft with that of a classmate and peer edit each other's work, using the following guidelines.

- spelling of foods
- formation and subject-verb agreement of verbs, especially stem-changing and irregular verbs
- completeness of information (when, what time, where)

EL MUNDO HISPÁNICO Y TÚ

Guatemala

¿No te gustan los inviernos muy fríos, ni los veranos muy calurosos (*hot*)?

Entonces puedes visitar un país donde la primavera parece (*seems*) eterna: Guatemala. Además, el país tiene mucho más que ofrecer al visitante: sus paisajes, sus playas, sus selvas tropicales, sus centros arqueológicos y su artesanía (*arts and crafts*).

La economía

Guatemala es un país agrícola. Sus productos principales son café, bananas, algodón (*cotton*) y madera. La moneda guatemalteca es el *quetzal*, nombre del pájaro que es el símbolo de Guatemala.

Tradiciones

En Guatemala se mezclan las tradiciones, los mitos y las costumbres mayas con la cultura europea y universal. Esto se ve en su religión, su artesanía, sus vestidos y su música.

Guatemala turística

Tikal es la mejor muestra de la cultura precolombina, y el más grande de sus centros ceremoniales.

Antigua, capital de Guatemala hasta el año 1776, es una de las principales atracciones turísticas de Guatemala.

La literatura

Antes de Colón

Dos libros que se conservan son *el Popol Vuh,* que recoge las creencias mayas sobre el origen del mundo y una historia de su civilización, y los *Libros de Chilán Balam,* que incluyen historia, mitología y profecías.

Reciente

Los autores más conocidos son Miguel Ángel Asturias (Premio Nobel de Literatura, 1967), Rafael Arévalo, Augusto Monterroso y Rigoberta Menchú (Premio Nobel de la Paz, 1992).

El Salvador

Si quieres ver volcanes, debes visitar El Salvador, llamado "la tierra de los volcanes".

El Salvador es el más pequeño de los países de Centroamérica y uno de los más bellos (*beautiful*). Tiene unos 300 kilómetros de costa, y sus playas están entre las más hermosas de América.

© cassiede alain/Shutterstock.com

La capital de El Salvador es San Salvador, la ciudad más industrializada de Centroamérica. Los principales productos industriales del país son textiles y artículos de cuero, madera y metal. La agricultura también es importante en El Salvador; entre los productos agrícolas que exporta el país están el café y las bananas.

El "surfing" es el deporte que más se practica en las playas de El Salvador.

El Salvador turístico

© Stefano Paterna/Alamy

El **Volcán de Izalco** es el más joven del país. Su última erupción fue (*was*) en 1966.

© Stefano Paterna/Alamy

La **Joya de Cerén** es un pueblo maya del siglo (*century*) VII. El pueblo se mantiene en perfectas condiciones, porque estaba (*it was*) cubierto por la ceniza (*ash*) de un volcán.

Ahora, dime...

In groups of three, discuss the following.

1. Guatemala es el país de la eterna primavera. ¿Les gusta la idea de tener un clima así, o prefieren experimentar las cuatro estaciones? Den razones.
2. ¿En qué playas de este país se practica el "surfing"? ¿Qué hacen Uds. cuando van a la playa? ¿Van a menudo?

iLrn

To learn more about Guatemala and El Salvador, watch the cultural footage in the Media Library.

AUTOPRUEBA

¿Cuánto sé ahora?

Take this test. When you have finished, check your answers in the answer key provided in Appendix D. Then use a red pen to correct any mistakes you may have made. Are you ready?

A. Comparative forms Complete the following sentences, using the Spanish equivalent of the words in parentheses.

1. El pollo frito es ________________ el cordero. (*much tastier than*)
2. El pescado cuesta ________________ dólares. (*more than twenty*)
3. Sergio cree que su esposa es ________________ Salma Hayek. (*as beautiful as*)
4. Yo tengo ________________ tú. (*as many problems as*)
5. Mi marido es ________________ la familia. (*the most intelligent in*)
6. Eva toma ________________ Silvia. (*as much ice cream as*)

B. Irregular comparative forms Complete the following sentences, using the Spanish equivalent of the words in parentheses.

1. Mi esposo es ____________ yo. (*much older than*)
2. El Hotel Hilton es ____________ el Hotel Miramar; es ____________ la ciudad. (*better than / the best in*)
3. El restaurante Colina es malo, pero el restaurante Don Pepe es ____________. (*much worse*)
4. Anita es ____________ la familia. (*the youngest in*)

C. Present indicative of *o:ue* stem-changing verbs Complete the following sentences, using the present indicative of the verbs in the list, as appropriate.

recordar	almorzar	costar	dormir
contar	volver	poder	llover

1. ¿Cuánto ________ el libro?
2. Ellos no ________ ir hoy.
3. ¿________ Ud. cuál es el número de teléfono de Claudia?
4. Yo ________ de uno a veinte en francés.
5. Tengo hambre. ¿A qué hora ________ (nosotros)?
6. ¿Cuándo ________ tú a Guatemala?
7. En Oregón ________ mucho.
8. ¿________ usted bien, señora?

D. Present progressive Write sentences saying what *is happening,* using the verbs in the list.

pedir	estudiar	comer	servir	hablar	leer	decir	dormir

1. ella / que nosotros necesitamos más dinero ________________________
2. yo / con mi abuela en español ____________________
3. nosotros / un libro muy bueno ____________________
4. ¿qué / tú? / ¿Biftec? ________________
5. Luis / en su cuarto ________________
6. los chicos / dinero ________________
7. el camarero / la comida ________________
8. ¿Uds. / en la biblioteca? ________________

E. Uses of *ser* and *estar* Form sentences, using the elements provided and the appropriate forms of **ser** or **estar.** Add the necessary connectors.

1. Elsa / mamá / Marcela ____________________
2. restaurante Miramar / calle Siete ______________________________
3. ¡Mmmm! / el pollo / delicioso ____________________
4. Roberto / de México / pero ahora / en Guatemala ___________________________________
5. café / frío ____________
6. escritorio / metal __________________
7. hoy / lunes __________
8. Elvira / profesora de español ______________________
9. fiesta / casa / Armando _________________________
10. Mariana / muy inteligente ____________________
11. ellos / cansados _________________
12. mi suegra / salvadoreña ____________________

F. Weather expressions Complete the following sentences appropriately.

1. Necesito un paraguas. __________ mucho en este momento.
2. ¿No te vas a poner el abrigo? ¡Brrr! __________.
3. No necesito el suéter. ¡__________!
4. En Alaska __________ mucho en el invierno.
5. Necesitas el sombrero. Hoy __________.
6. No quiero vivir en Oregón porque allí llueve mucho y no me gusta la __________.

G. Just words . . . Choose the word or phrase that does not belong in each group.

1. copa	vaso	plato	__________
2. servilleta	cuchillo	tenedor	__________
3. camarones	cordero	langosta	__________
4. desayunar	almorzar	volver	__________
5. leche	torta	helado	__________
6. cuenta	pescado	propina	__________
7. mantel	sal	pimienta	__________
8. a la parrilla	al mediodía	frito	__________
9. sabroso	tinto	rico	__________
10. pedazo	trozo	verdura	__________

H. Culture

1. Complete the following, based on the information found in the **¿Lo sabía Ud.?** sections.
   a. En los países hispanos, la __________ frecuentemente está incluida en la cuenta.
   b. El __________ es la unidad monetaria de España.
2. Answer the following questions, based on the information found in **El mundo hispánico y tú...** section.
   a. ¿Qué pájaro es el símbolo nacional de Guatemala? __________
   b. En Guatemala, ¿qué ciudad es la mejor muestra de la arquitectura colonial? __________

I. Un dicho Do you remember the Spanish saying that is equivalent to "Keep a stiff upper lip"? Find it in this lesson.

LECCIÓN 6

LOS QUEHACERES DE LA CASA

Este hombre ayuda a su esposa con los trabajos de la casa.

OBJETIVOS COMUNICATIVOS

You will learn vocabulary related to household chores, family relationships, and various parts of a house.

SITUACIONES

¡Tocan a la puerta!

ESTRUCTURAS

1 Demonstrative adjectives and pronouns
2 Present indicative of **e:i** stem-changing verbs
3 Affirmative and negative expressions
4 Verbs with irregular first-person forms
5 **Saber** vs. **conocer**
6 Direct object pronouns

ASÍ SOMOS

¡Vamos a ver!

Watching and understanding situations

¡Vamos a escuchar!

Listening for details II

¡Vamos a conversar!

Reporting

¡Vamos a leer!

Skimming

¡Vamos a escribir!

Sequencing steps for a recipe

EL MUNDO HISPÁNICO Y TÚ

- Honduras
- Nicaragua

AUTOPRUEBA

You will review what you learned in this lesson.

Honduras debe su nombre a que cuando Colón llegó a estas costas de Centroamérica, quedó sorprendido por la profundidad (*depth*) de las aguas junto a la tierra, así que llamó al lugar Honduras (de **hondo** = deep). Aquí floreció el gran imperio maya unos 500 años antes de la llegada de los conquistadores.

Nicaragua, con un área un poco mayor que la del estado de Nueva York, es el país más extenso de Centroamérica, pero menos de una décima parte de su territorio es cultivable.

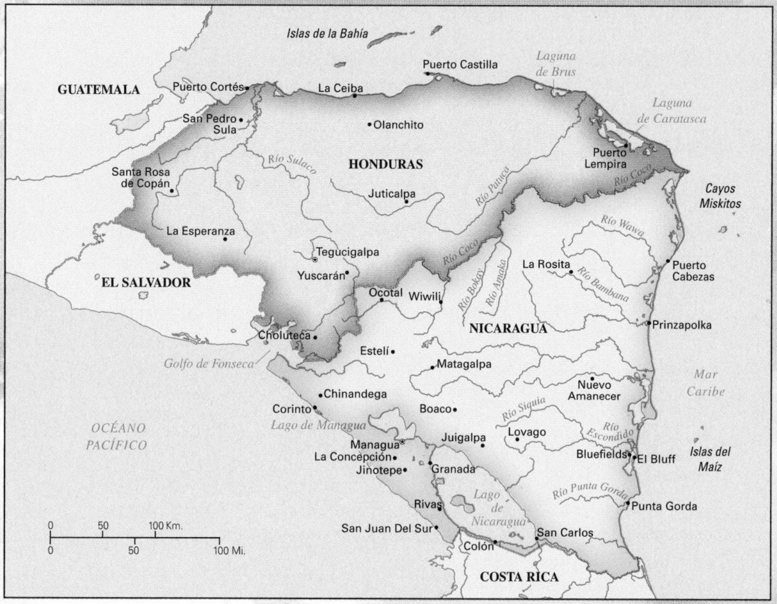

Recursos iLrn video audio web playlist

SITUACIONES

¡TOCAN A LA PUERTA!

CD1-28

¡Ubíquese!

Beatriz and Guillermo live in Tegucigalpa, the capital of Honduras. Watch the video to see many places of historical interest. You will also see Managua, the capital of Nicaragua, where Beatriz's mother lives.

Beatriz y su esposo Guillermo viven en Tegucigalpa, Honduras. Hoy es viernes y tienen mucho que hacer porque mañana llega la mamá de Beatriz, que viene a visitarlos.

GUILLERMO: ¿Dónde está mi camisa azul? La necesito para ir al mercado.

BEATRIZ: Estoy planchándola. ¿Por qué no barres el garaje? Aquí está la escoba.

GUILLERMO: Estoy leyendo una revista. Hay un artículo muy interesante...

BEATRIZ: ¡Tienes que ayudar con los quehaceres de la casa! ¡Tú nunca haces nada!

GUILLERMO: (*Suspira*) ¡Tú siempre dices eso! Pero yo a veces lavo los platos... Y cuando necesitamos algo del mercado, yo lo compro... Y a veces cocino...

BEATRIZ: Sí, es verdad que a veces haces las compras... y a veces recoges tus revistas y las pones debajo de la cama...

GUILLERMO: Y mañana... ¿tu mamá va a tomar un taxi? Si no, ¿quién va a ir a la parada de autobuses a buscarla?

BEATRIZ: ¡Tú! ¡Ya lo sé! ¿Puedes arreglar el cuarto de huéspedes? Necesitamos cambiar las sábanas y después tienes que comprar carne.

GUILLERMO: No, tú siempre dices que yo nunca consigo carne buena. ¡Yo no estoy de acuerdo! Y... ¿qué vas a hacer tú?

BEATRIZ: Pues... yo voy a llamar por teléfono a alguien.

GUILLERMO: Bueno. Ahora salgo para el mercado. Quiero traer algunas revistas.

Beatriz llama a una agencia de empleos.
Tres horas después, tocan a la puerta. Guillermo esconde un montón de revistas debajo del sofá y mira por la ventana.

GUILLERMO: Es una mujer… ¿quién es? No la conozco.

BEATRIZ: ¿Puedes abrir la puerta, por favor? ¡Rápido! Y después puedes leer el artículo… ¡Tenemos criada!

¿Lo sabía Ud.?

En una guía telefónica en español, alfabetizan los nombres según los dos apellidos, por ejemplo:
Núñez Arzuaga, Pedro
Núñez Lara, Inés

› **¿Cómo alfabetizan los nombres en una guía telefónica en este país?**

1. Hablemos With a partner, take turns asking and answering the following questions. Base your answers on the dialogue and on your own circumstances.

En el diálogo

1. ¿En qué país viven Beatriz y Guillermo?
2. ¿Por qué tienen ellos mucho que hacer hoy?
3. ¿Para qué necesita Guillermo su camisa azul?
4. ¿Qué está haciendo Beatriz?
5. ¿Qué está leyendo Guillermo?
6. ¿Qué dice Beatriz que Guillermo tiene que hacer?
7. ¿Dónde pone Guillermo las revistas?
8. ¿Qué tiene que arreglar Guillermo?
9. ¿Qué necesitan cambiar?
10. ¿Qué tiene que comprar Guillermo?
11. ¿Adónde llama Beatriz?
12. ¿Qué tienen Guillermo y Beatriz?

¿Y tú?

1. ¿En qué estado (*state*) o provincia vives tú?
2. ¿Tú tienes mucho que hacer? ¿Por qué?
3. ¿Te gusta el color azul?
4. ¿Qué estás haciendo tú?
5. ¿Tú estás leyendo? ¿Qué?
6. ¿Tú haces los trabajos de la casa?
7. ¿Dónde pones tú las revistas?
8. ¿Tu casa tiene cuarto de huéspedes?
9. ¿Qué días cambias las sábanas de tu cama?
10. ¿Tú tienes que comprar algo? ¿Qué?
11. ¿A quién llamas tú?
12 ¿Tú tienes criada en tu casa?

¿Lo sabía Ud.?

Actualmente muchos hombres hispanos, especialmente los más jóvenes, ayudan a sus esposas con los trabajos de la casa. Esto se debe a que a menudo los dos trabajan fuera de la casa.

› **Generalmente, ¿ayudan los hombres norteamericanos a sus esposas con los quehaceres de la casa?**

Esta empleada doméstica hace todos los trabajos de la casa, excepto uno. ¿Qué creen Uds. que ella no hace?

VOCABULARIO

En el diálogo

Cognados

la agencia	*agency*
el artículo	*article*
el autobús, el bus, el ómnibus	*bus*
el garaje	*garage*
interesante	*interesting*
el sofá	*sofa*
el taxi	*taxi*

Nombres

la agencia de empleos	*employment office*
la cama	*bed*
la camisa	*shirt*
la carne	*meat*
la criada, la empleada doméstica	*maid*
el cuarto de huéspedes	*guest room*
la escoba	*broom*
el mercado	*market*
la parada de autobuses	*bus stop*
los quehaceres (trabajos) de la casa	*housework*
la revista	*magazine*
la sábana	*sheet*

Verbos

arreglar	*to tidy up, to fix*
ayudar	*to help*
barrer	*to sweep*
buscar	*to get, to pick up, to look for*
cambiar	*to change*
cocinar	*to cook*
comprar	*to buy*
conocer (yo conozco)	*to know, to be acquainted with*
conseguir (e:i)	*to get, to obtain*
decir (e:i) (yo digo)	*to say, to tell*
esconder	*to hide*
lavar los platos, fregar (e:ie)	*to wash dishes*
planchar	*to iron*
poner (yo pongo)	*to put*
recoger	*to pick up*
saber (yo sé)	*to know (a fact; how to)*
suspirar	*to sigh*
tomar	*to take (e.g., a taxi or a bus)*
visitar	*to visit*

Otras palabras y expresiones

a veces	*sometimes*
ahora	*now*
algo	*something, anything*
alguien	*someone, somebody*
debajo (de)	*under*
eso	*that (neutral)*
estar de acuerdo	*to agree, to be in agreement*
hacer las compras	*to do the shopping*
mirar por la ventana	*to look out the window*
¡Rápido!	*Quick!*
tocar a la puerta	*to knock on the door*
un montón de	*a bunch of*
¡Ya lo sé!	*I know it!*

¿Lo sabía Ud.?

En los países hispanos, muchas familias de la clase alta y de la clase media tienen criadas. Frecuentemente la criada vive en la casa donde trabaja. Cuando lleva muchos años trabajando en la misma casa, es considerada prácticamente como un miembro de la familia.

› **En general, ¿las familias de este país tienen criadas?**

Más sobre el tema

cortar el césped	*to cut (mow) the grass*
doblar la ropa	*to fold clothes*
lavar la ropa	*to wash the clothes (do laundry)*
limpiar (el cuarto de baño)	*to clean (the bathroom)*
pasar la aspiradora	*to vacuum*
sacar la basura	*to take out the trash*
sacudir los muebles	*to dust the furniture*
secar (los platos)	*to dry (the dishes)*
trapear el piso	*to mop the floor*

LEARNING TIP

Especially when learning concrete actions (verbs) such as **arreglar, barrer, recoger, cocinar, lavar, planchar,** etc., you might want to reinforce their meaning in your mind by stating which ones you do and what is done by other people. For example: **Yo arreglo mi cuarto. Mi mamá plancha la ropa.**

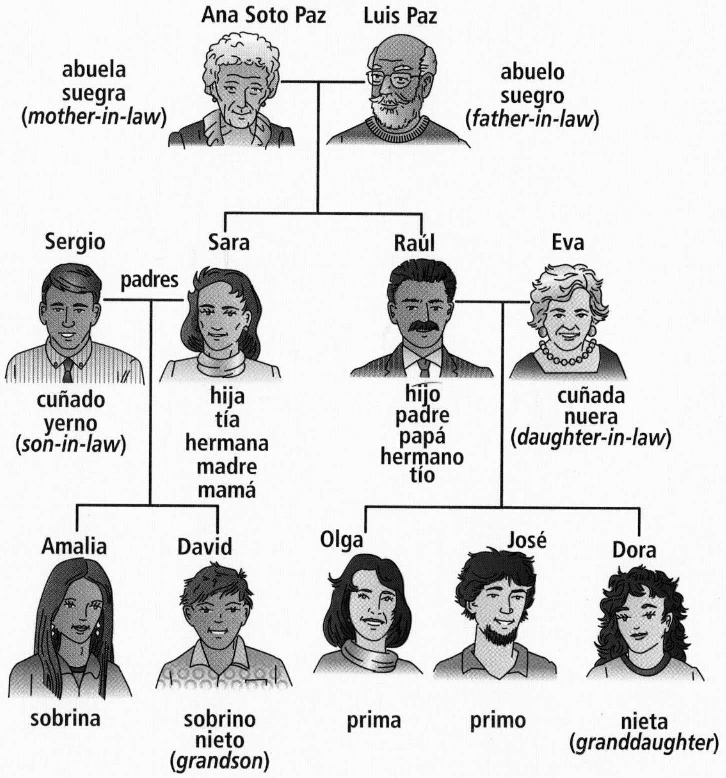

La casa

la cocina	*kitchen*	**el (cuarto de) baño**	*bathroom*
el comedor	*dining room*	**la sala**	*living room*
el dormitorio, la recámara (*Méx.*), la pieza	*bedroom*	**la sala de estar**	*family room*
		el sótano	*basement*

¿Lo sabía Ud.?

En los países de habla hispana, el concepto de familia es más amplio e incluye a todos los parientes: tíos, primos, sobrinos, etcétera. Generalmente, la relación entre ellos es muy estrecha (*close*).

› **Generalmente, ¿con qué miembros de la familia tienen los norteamericanos una relación estrecha?**

VOCABULARIO

Práctica

2. **Preguntas y respuestas** Match the questions in column A with the responses in column B.

A		B
1. _____	¿Qué está haciendo Rosa?	a. Debajo del sofá.
2. _____	¿Qué vas a comprar?	b. En la sala de estar.
3. _____	¿Qué no te gusta hacer?	c. De lo que tiene que hacer.
4. _____	¿Beto está en la parada de autobuses?	d. Sí, desde las seis.
5. _____	¿Dónde escondes las revistas?	e. Los quehaceres de la casa.
6. _____	¿Cuándo viene tu cuñado?	f. Sí, aquí tengo la lista.
7. _____	¿De qué está hablando Ana?	g. Está arreglando su cuarto.
8. _____	¿Dónde vas a poner el sofá?	h. La semana próxima.
9. _____	¿Felipe está aquí?	i. Sí, está esperando a Nora.
10. _____	¿Vas a ir al mercado?	j. Carne.

3. **¿Qué es?** Write the words or phrases that correspond to the following.
   1. ómnibus __________
   2. la hermana de mi esposo __________
   3. *Newsweek,* por ejemplo __________
   4. comprar __________
   5. opuesto de **llevar** __________
   6. opuesto de **siempre** __________
   7. parte de la casa donde comemos __________
   8. recámara __________
   9. lavar los platos __________
   10. la usamos para barrer __________

4. **Oraciones incompletas** Complete the following sentences, using vocabulary from this lesson.
   1. Yo voy a arreglar el cuarto de __________ y también voy a __________ las sábanas. ¿Tú puedes __________?
   2. Necesitamos una __________. Voy a llamar a la agencia de __________.
   3. Tocan a la __________. Voy a __________ por la ventana antes de *(before)* __________.
   4. Tú y yo nunca estamos de __________.
   5. ¿Dónde vas a __________ esas sábanas? ¿En mi __________?
   6. Hoy tengo que hacer un __________ de cosas. Doblar la __________, limpiar el __________ de baño y la sala, sacar la __________ y __________ los muebles.
   7. Carlos, ¿tú puedes ir a __________ a mi prima a la __________ de autobuses? Ella no quiere tomar un __________.
   8. Elba va a trapear el __________ de la sala y va a barrer el sótano.

Para conversar

5. **Relaciones familiares** With a partner, look at the family tree on page 169 and ask each other questions about the relationships of the people in the illustration.

   HINT: ¿Cuál es la relación que existe entre _______ y _______?

6. **¿Quién puede ayudarme?** With a partner, take turns asking for help and saying that you can't help. Say what you have to do.

   Modelo —*¿Puedes ayudarme a...?*
   —*No puedo; tengo que...*

7. **Prefiero hacer otra cosa** (*I prefer to do something else*) With a partner, take turns indicating what you frankly *hate* to do, and stating what you *would rather* do.

   Modelo *Francamente, yo odio pasar la aspiradora; prefiero sacudir los muebles.*

Pronunciación

CD1-29 A. **The Spanish *j***

The Spanish **j** sounds somewhat like the *h* in the English word *hit*. It is never pronounced like the English *j* in *John* or *James*. Listen to your instructor and repeat the following phrases.

Julia y **J**avier traba**j**an hoy. **J**uana de**j**a a su hi**j**o aquí.

Juan **J**osé viene el **j**ueves.

CD1-30 B. **The Spanish *g* (before *e* or *i*)**

When followed by **e** or **i**, the Spanish **g** sounds like the Spanish **j** mentioned above. Listen to your instructor and repeat the following phrases.

Gerardo reco**g**e a **G**enaro. El **g**eneral **G**inés está en Ar**g**entina.

Eva **G**il es inteli**g**ente.

CD1-31 C. **The Spanish *h***

The Spanish **h** is always silent. Listen to your instructor and repeat the following phrases.

Humberto **H**ernández **H**errera es de **H**onduras.

Tu **h**ermano está en el **h**otel.

Hilda es la **h**ija de **H**ugo.

¿Lo sabía Ud.?

En la mayoría de los países de habla hispana, cuando una mujer se casa (*gets married*) retiene su apellido de soltera (*maiden name*). Puede también añadir (*add*) el apellido de su esposo. Por ejemplo, Ana Soto está casada con Luis Paz y su nombre completo es Ana Soto (de) Paz. La mayoría de los hispanos usan dos apellidos: el del padre y el de la madre, en ese orden. Por ejemplo, el nombre completo de Raúl (el hijo de Ana y Luis) es Raúl Paz Soto.

› **Cuando las mujeres de este país se casan, ¿usan el apellido del esposo? ¿Usan su apellido de soltera?**

ESTRUCTURAS

1 Demonstrative adjectives and pronouns (*Los adjetivos y los pronombres demostrativos*)

A. Demonstrative adjectives

› Demonstrative adjectives point out persons or things. Like all other adjectives, they agree in gender and number with the nouns they modify. The forms of the demonstrative adjectives are as follows.

Masculine		Feminine		
Singular	***Plural***	***Singular***	***Plural***	
este	**estos**	**esta**	**estas**	*this, these*
ese	**esos**	**esa**	**esas**	*that, those*
aquel	**aquellos**	**aquella**	**aquellas**	*that, those* (at a distance in space or time)

—¿Qué vas a fregar?
—**Este** plato, **esas** tazas y **aquellos** vasos.

What are you going to wash?
This dish, those cups, and those glasses (over there).

B. Demonstrative pronouns

› The forms of the demonstrative pronouns are as follows.

Masculine		Feminine			
Singular	***Plural***	***Singular***	***Plural***	Neuter	
éste	**éstos**	**ésta**	**éstas**	esto	*this* (one), *these*
ése	**ésos**	**ésa**	**ésas**	eso	*that* (one), *those*
aquél	**aquéllos**	**aquélla**	**aquéllas**	aquello	*that* (one), *those* (*at a distance*)

› The masculine and feminine demonstrative pronouns are the same as the demonstrative adjectives, except that they generally have a written accent.[1]

[1]Recently, the Real Academia accepted the use of demonstrative pronouns without written accents. In the chart above, we are keeping the written accents.

› Each demonstrative pronoun has a neuter form. They are **esto, eso,** and **aquello.** The neuter forms, which do not change in number or gender, are used to refer to situations, ideas, and nonspecific objects or things, equivalent to the English ***this, that matter; this, that business;*** and ***this, that stuff.***

—¿Entiendes **eso**?	*Do you understand that?*
—No, es muy difícil.	*No, it's very difficult.*
—¿Qué es **esto**?	*What's this?*
—¿Quién sabe?	*Who knows?*

LEARNING TIP
Pronouns refer to something already mentioned. Their use is especially useful when, in conversation or writing, you need to refer again to something or someone that you have already talked about.

Práctica

8. **Los quehaceres de la casa** Two roommates, Amalia and Celia, are doing a lot of housework today. With a partner, complete their conversation, using demonstrative adjectives. Then play the roles of the two girls.

Amalia: Celia, ¿tú necesitas ________ (*these*) sábanas que están aquí?

Celia: Sí, y también ________ (*those*) camisas.

Amalia: Tienes que fregar ________ (*these*) vasos (*glasses*) y ________ (*those*) platos.

Celia: Y tú tienes que sacudir ________ (*this*) mesa y ________ (*this*) escritorio.

Amalia: ¿Dónde vamos a poner ________ (*that over there*) sofá?

Celia: En la sala de estar. Y ________ (*this*) vez, Daniel tiene que ayudar.

Amalia: Es verdad. ¡Ah! ¿Dónde quieres poner ________ (*those over there*) revistas?

Celia: En ________ (*that over there*) mesa. Oye... ¿qué es ________ (*that*) que está debajo del sofá?

Amalia: ¿Quién sabe? *(Who knows?)*

9. **Este, ese y aquel** With a partner, play the roles of two friends. Take turns asking and answering the questions. The one who answers always rejects the objects indicated and wants the ones far away from both.

   1. ¿Vas a leer estas revistas? ____________________
   2. ¿Vas a lavar esta ropa? ____________________
   3. ¿Vas a secar estos platos? ____________________
   4. ¿Vas a comprar en este mercado? ____________________

Para conversar

10. **¡Habla con tu compañero(a)!** With a partner, take turns asking each other who the other students in the class are. Respond, using the appropriate demonstrative adjectives, and a description.

Modelo *—¿Quién es Sandra?*
—Es aquella chica rubia.

2 Present indicative of *e:i* stem-changing verbs (*Presente de indicativo de los verbos que cambian en la raíz* **e:i**)

servir *to serve*	
sirvo	servimos
sirves	servís
sirve	sirven

› Some **-ir** verbs undergo a special stem change in the present indicative. For these verbs, when **e** is the last stem vowel and it is stressed, it changes to **i.**

—¿Qué **sirven** Uds. en sus fiestas? *What do you serve at your parties?*
—**Servimos** champán. *We serve champagne.*

› Note that the stem vowel is not stressed in the **nosotros(as)** and **vosotros(as)** verb forms; therefore, the **e** does not change to **i.**

› Other verbs that undergo this change:[1]

conseguir	*to get, to obtain*	**pedir**	*to ask for, to request, to order*
decir	*to say, to tell*	**seguir**	*to follow, to continue*

› The verb **decir** undergoes the same change, but in addition it has an irregular first-person singular form: **yo digo**.

› Note that in the present tense **seguir** and **conseguir** drop the **u** before **a** or **o: yo sigo, yo consigo.**

Summary of the present indicative of stem-changing verbs

e:ie	*o:ue*	*e:i*
cerrar	almorzar	conseguir
comenzar	contar	decir
empezar	costar	pedir
entender	dormir	seguir
pensar	encontrar	servir
perder	llover	
preferir	morir	
querer	mostrar	
	poder	
	probar	
	recordar	
	volar	
	volver	

Add to this list as you learn other stem-changing verbs.

[1]For a complete list of stem-changing verbs, see Appendix B.

Práctica

11. ¿Qué hacemos y qué decimos? Form complete sentences by combining the words in the three columns in sequence, starting with A. Use each subject and each verb at least once.

A	B	C
yo	decir	la comida
nosotros	servir	un cuarto
Amalia y Celia	pedir	que necesitamos un sofá nuevo
mis padres	conseguir	revistas
tú	seguir	información sobre Honduras
mi cuñado		a mis amigos
		estudiando español

12. Beatriz y nosotros With a partner, use your imagination to compare what Beatriz does to what the other people mentioned do. Take turns! Beatriz...

1. ... consigue carne buena en el mercado. (Mi mamá)
2. ... dice que es más difícil planchar que limpiar el baño. (Yo)
3. ... sirve cerveza en sus fiestas. (Mis amigos)
4. ... pide tamales cuando va a un restaurante mexicano. (Tú)
5. ... siempre sigue la moda (*fashion*). (Nosotros)
6. ... consigue frijoles en un mercado mexicano. (Yo)
7. ... dice que ella no quiere sacar la basura. (Mi papá)
8. ... sirve el café después de la comida. (Tú)
9. ... pide ravioles cuando va a un restaurante italiano. (Mis amigos y yo)
10. ... sigue en su clase de literatura. (Yo)

Para conversar

13. ¡Habla con tu compañero(a)! Interview a classmate, using the following questions. When you have finished, switch roles.

1. En tu cuidad, ¿hay muchos restaurantes que sirven comida china? ¿mexicana? ¿Cuál prefieres tú? ¿Qué platos pides? ¿Con la comida, siempre pides café? Generalmente, ¿qué pides de postre? ¿Y para beber?
2. Cuando tú invitas a tus amigos a comer a tu casa, ¿qué sirves para comer? ¿Qué sirven tus amigos cuando vas a su casa? ¿Y tus parientes?
3. ¿Tú compras revistas en español? ¿Dónde las consigues? ¿Es fácil conseguir libros en español en la biblioteca?
4. ¿Tú dices que el español es fácil? ¿Qué dicen tus amigos del español? ¿Qué dicen de los otros idiomas?
5. ¿Tú siempre sigues los consejos (*advice*) de tus padres?

14. Yo digo... In groups of three, discuss what you think the worst chores are when you have to do housework.

Modelo *Yo digo que lo peor* (the worst thing) *es doblar la ropa.*

Now one person in each group reports to the class: ______ *dice que lo peor es...* *y* ______ *dice que...*

Is there a chore that most people agree is the worst?

3 Affirmative and negative expressions (*Expresiones afirmativas y negativas*)

Affirmative	Negative
algo *something, anything*	**nada** *nothing, not anything*
alguien *someone, somebody, anyone*	**nadie** *nobody, no one, not anyone*
alguno(a), algún *any, some*	**ninguno(a), ningún** *no, none, not any*
a veces *sometimes* / **siempre** *always*	**nunca, jamás** *never*
también *also, too*	**tampoco** *neither, not either*
o *or*	
o... o *either . . . or*	**ni... ni** *neither . . . nor*

—¿Necesitas **algo** más? — *Do you need anything else?*
—No, no necesito **nada** más. — *No, I don't need anything else.*
—¿Tienes **algunos** amigos de Nicaragua? — *Do you have any friends from Nicaragua?*
—No, no tengo **ningún** amigo nicaragüense.[1] — *No, I don't have any Nicaraguan friends.*
—¿Hay **alguien** en tu recámara? — *Is there anybody in your room?*
—No, no hay **nadie.** — *No, there's no one.*
—¿Quieres café **o** té? — *Do you want coffee or tea?*
—Yo no bebo **ni** café **ni** té. — *I don't drink either coffee or tea.*

¡Atención! Note that **alguno(a)** may be used in the plural forms, but **ninguno(a)** is not pluralized.

› **Alguno** and **ninguno** drop the **-o** before a masculine singular noun: ***algún*** **niño,** ***ningún*** **niño**; but ***alguna*** **niña,** ***ninguna*** **niña.**

¡Atención! **No** is never used as an adjective, as it sometimes is in English (*No person could do all that.*).

› Spanish sentences frequently use a double negative form to express a degree of negation: the adverb **no** is placed before the verb and the second negative word either follows the verb or appears at the end of the sentence. If, however, the negative word precedes the verb, **no** is never used.

No hablo español **nunca.**
or: **Nunca** hablo español. — *I never speak Spanish.*

No compro **nada nunca.**
or: **Nunca** compro **nada.** — *I never buy anything.*

› Note that Spanish often uses several negatives in one sentence.

Yo **no** quiero **nada tampoco.** — *I don't want anything either.*

[1] In some cases before an **e** or **i**, the **u** is not silent. To indicate this, a **diéresis** (two dots) is added over the **u** (**pingüino, Mayagüez**).

Práctica

15. No estoy de acuerdo Change the following statements to express the opposite.

1. Diego nunca corta el césped los sábados.
2. Mi mamá necesita comprar algo en el mercado.
3. Nadie va a ir a recoger a mi suegra.
4. Mi sobrina pasa la aspiradora a veces.
5. Mireya seca o los platos o las tazas.
6. Aquí no hay ningún lugar interesante.
7. Rita va a ir a Honduras y yo voy a ir también.
8. Nosotros tenemos algunos amigos de Honduras.

Para conversar

16. ¡Habla con tu compañero(a)! Interview a classmate, answering the following questions in the negative. Use the expressions you have just learned. When you have finished, switch roles and create new questions.

1. ¿Quieres ir a Nicaragua o a Honduras?
2. ¿Tienes algunos amigos en Managua?
3. Yo no hablo portugués. ¿Y tú?
4. ¿Siempre vas a restaurantes chinos?
5. ¿Siempre vienes con alguien aquí?
6. ¿Compras algo cuando vas de vacaciones?

17. Siempre... a veces... nunca With a partner, tell each other four things that you always do, four things that you sometimes do, and four things that you never do. Compare notes.

Modelo Yo siempre leo libros en Internet. A veces compro libros en la librería. Nunca voy a la biblioteca.

18. Quejas (*Complaints*) With a partner, write a list of complaints frequently heard on campus. Use the expressions you have just learned.

Modelo *Nunca podemos comer nada en la cafetería.*

Un dicho

Nadie es profeta en su tierra.
Equivalent: *A prophet is not recognized in his own land.*

4 Verbs with irregular first-person forms *(Verbos irregulares en la primera persona)*

The following verbs are irregular in the first-person singular of the present tense.

Verb	*yo* form	Regular forms
salir (*to go out*)	**salgo**	sales, sale, salimos, salís, salen
hacer (*to do, make*)	**hago**	haces, hace, hacemos, hacéis, hacen
poner (*to put, place*)	**pongo**	pones, pone, ponemos, ponéis, ponen
traer (*to bring*)	**traigo**	traes, trae, traemos, traéis, traen
conducir (*to drive*)	**conduzco**	conduces, conduce, conducimos, conducís, conducen
traducir (*to translate*)	**traduzco**	traduces, traduce, traducimos, traducís, traducen
conocer (*to know*)	**conozco**	conoces, conoce, conocemos, conocéis, conocen
caber (*to fit*)	**quepo**	cabes, cabe, cabemos, cabéis, caben
ver (*to see*)	**veo**	ves, ve, vemos, veis, ven
saber (*to know*)	**sé**	sabes, sabe, sabemos, sabéis, saben

—¿Qué haces los domingos? — *What do you do on Sundays?*
—No **hago** nada. — *I don't do anything.*

—¿Estás mirando por la ventana? — *Are you looking out the window?*
—Sí, pero no **veo** nada. — *Yes, but I don't see anything.*

Práctica

19. Celia y yo Compare this information about Celia to what you do, by completing the following sentences.

1. Celia sale de su casa a las siete y yo...
2. Celia conduce un Ford y yo...
3. Celia ve a sus amigos los sábados y yo...
4. Celia conoce a muchos estudiantes y yo...
5. Celia trae a su hermana a la universidad y yo...
6. Celia cabe en un coche (*car*) muy pequeño y yo...
7. Celia sabe hablar portugués y yo...
8. Celia no hace nada los domingos y yo...

20. De viaje Read this paragraph about Amalia's preparations for her trip to Nicaragua and then rewrite it as if you were Amalia, starting with **Yo**...

Amalia sale para Nicaragua esta noche. Va con su amiga Susan. Conduce al banco para comprar cheques de viajero (*travelers' checks*), regresa a su casa, pone todos los documentos en su bolso de mano (*handbag*) y después hace las maletas (*packs*). Como sabe que hay mucho tráfico, sale de su casa a las cinco para ir al aeropuerto. Cuando llega al aeropuerto, ve que Susan está esperando.

Para conversar

21. ¡Habla con tu compañero(a)! Your classmate is traveling to Tegucigalpa. Here is a list of questions you want to ask in order to help him/her prepare for the trip. Your classmate should conjugate the verb correctly and answer in complete sentences. Then create new questions with the same verbs, focusing on a trip to Honduras.

1. ¿Conoces Tegucigalpa? ¿Sabes a qué distancia está de aquí?
2. ¿Sabes cuál es la moneda (*currency*) de Honduras? ¿Sabes a cómo está el cambio de moneda (*rate of exchange*)?
3. ¿Haces la reservación del hotel antes de salir de viaje? ¿Dónde pones el pasaporte?
4. El día del viaje, ¿sales de casa con tiempo? ¿Conduces tu coche para ir al aeropuerto?
5. ¿Conoces a alguien en Tegucigalpa?
6. ¿Traes muchas cosas para tu familia? ¿Compras algo para ti?

5 *Saber* vs. *conocer*

Spanish has two verbs that mean *to know*, ***saber*** and ***conocer***.

A. *Saber* means:

- to know something by heart.
  Yo **sé** un poema de Rubén Darío.
- to know a fact.
  Yo **sé** que Rubén Darío es un poeta nicaragüense.
- to know how to do something.
  Yo **sé** bailar salsa.

B. *Conocer* means:

- to be familiar or acquainted with a person.
  Nosotros **conocemos** a Ester Núñez.
- to be acquainted with a place.
  Ellos **conocen** Honduras.
- to be acquainted with an artist's or writer's work.
  ¿Tú **conoces** la poesía de Rubén Darío?

Práctica

22. *¿Saber o conocer...?* With a partner, tell what these people know, using **saber** or **conocer**.

1. Natalia __________ al suegro de Mirta. Ella __________ dónde vive él, pero no __________ su número de teléfono.
2. David __________ muchas ciudades de España, pero no __________ hablar español.
3. Estela __________ muchos poemas de ese poeta, pero no __________ ninguno de memoria.
4. Roberto __________ a la familia que da la fiesta de Año Nuevo, pero no __________ dónde es la fiesta.
5. Yo __________ que Lorca es un poeta español.

Para conversar

23. ¡Habla con tu compañero(a)! Interview a classmate, using the following questions as a guide. When you have finished, switch roles and create five new questions with **saber** and five with **conocer.**

1. ¿Cuántos idiomas sabes hablar? ¿Cuáles son?
2. ¿Conoces a los padres de tu mejor amigo(a)?
3. ¿Sabes dónde viven?
4. ¿Qué sabes hacer?
5. ¿Sabes tocar (*play*) el piano? ¿la guitarra? ¿el violín?
6. ¿Sabes cocinar?
7. ¿Conoces un buen restaurante? ¿Dónde está?
8. ¿Conoces a un actor famoso? ¿Quién es? ¿Cómo es?
9. ¿Conoces las novelas de Hemingway? ¿Cuáles?
10. ¿Sabes bailar salsa? ¿Qué sabes bailar?

24. ¿Qué sabes? o ¿Qué conoces? With a partner, talk about the places you are familiar with and the ones you want to know, some people you know, facts you know about your college, city or state, and things you know how to do. Compare notes!

6 Direct object pronouns (*Pronombres usados como complemento directo*)

A. The direct object

› In addition to a subject, most sentences have an object that directly receives the action of the verb.

Ellos	compran	el libro.
S.	V.	D.O.

In the preceding sentence, the subject (**Ellos**) performs the action, while **el libro**, the direct object, directly receives the action of the verb. The direct object of a sentence may be either a person or a thing.

› The direct object can be easily identified as the answer to the questions *whom?* and *what?* about what the subject is doing.

Ellos compran **el libro**.	*What are they buying?*
Pepe visita a **su primo**.	*Whom does Pepe visit?*
Yo llamo a **mis padres**.	*Whom do I call?*

› Direct object pronouns may be used in place of the direct object.

Un dicho
El que la sigue, la consigue.
Equivalent: *If at first you don't succeed, try, try again.*

B. Forms of the direct object pronouns

Singular		Plural	
me	*me*	**nos**	*us*
te	*you (fam.)*	**os**	*you (fam.)*
lo	*you (form., masc.)* *him, it (masc.)*	**los**	*you (form., masc.)* *them (masc.)*
la	*you (form., fem.)* *her, it (fem.)*	**las**	*you (form., fem.)* *them (fem.)*

—¿Tú tienes **la lista?** *Do you have the list?*
—Sí, yo **la** tengo. *Yes, I have it.*

—¿Seca Ud. **los platos?** *Do you dry the dishes?*
—Sí, yo **los** seco. *Yes, I dry them.*

C. Position of direct object pronouns

› In Spanish, object pronouns are normally placed before a conjugated verb.

Spanish (D.O.)	English (D.O.)
Ellos sirven **la comida.**	*They serve the meal.*
Ellos **la** **sirven.**	*They serve it.*

› In negative sentences, the **no** must precede the object pronoun.

Spanish (D.O.)	English (D.O.)
Ellos sirven **la comida.**	*They serve the meal.*
Ellos **la** sirven.	*They serve it.*
Ellos **no** **la** sirven.	*They don't serve it.*

› When an infinitive is used with a conjugated verb, the direct object pronoun may either be attached to the infinitive or be placed before the conjugated verb. The same principle applies with the present participle in progressive constructions.

Yo puedo leer**lo.**
Yo **lo** puedo leer. *I can read it.*

Yo estoy leyéndo**lo.**
Yo **lo** estoy leyendo. *I am reading it.*

¡Atención! When a direct object pronoun is attached to a present participle **(leyéndolo)**, an accent mark is added to maintain the correct stress.

Un dicho
A quien madruga, Dios lo ayuda.
Equivalent: *The early bird catches the worm.*

Práctica

25. ¿Qué quiere Julio? Complete the following dialogue, using the appropriate direct object pronouns. Then act it out with a partner.

JULIO: ¿Tú me puedes llevar a casa hoy?

DELIA: Sí, _______ puedo llevar a las tres.

JULIO: ¡Ah! Necesito la maleta *(suitcase)* de mamá. ¿Tú _______ tienes?

DELIA: Sí, yo _______ tengo. ¿Tú quieres llevar _______ a Tegucigalpa?

JULIO: Sí. También necesito comprar cheques de viajero *(travelers checks)*...

DELIA: Podemos comprar _______ esta tarde.

JULIO: Rosa y yo tenemos que estar en el aeropuerto a las ocho de la noche. ¿Tú _______ puedes llevar?

DELIA: Sí, yo _______ puedo llevar...

JULIO: ¡Ah! Las sobrinas de Rosa quieren ir al aeropuerto con nosotros. ¿Tú _______ puedes traer a mi casa a las siete?

DELIA: ¡No! ¡Yo no tengo un servicio de taxi!

LEARNING TIP
Save a small part of your study sessions to learn things through repetition. This will help embed the material in your long-term memory.

26. Yo lo hago You and your roommates are doing chores. Volunteer to do the following tasks yourself.

Modelo —¿Quién lava las sábanas?
—Yo las lavo.

1. ¿Quién barre el garaje?
2. ¿Quién friega los platos?
3. ¿Quién limpia el cuarto de baño?
4. ¿Quién corta el césped?
5. ¿Quién pasa la aspiradora?
6. ¿Quién sacude los muebles?
7. ¿Quién lava la ropa?
8. ¿Quién prepara la comida?

27. Nadie hace lo mismo With a partner, take turns answering the following questions. Use direct object pronouns and the cues provided to indicate what people do differently.

Modelo —Yo pongo las revistas en la mesa (Teresa / en su escritorio)
—Teresa las pone en su escritorio.

1. Don Manuel consigue la carne en el supermercado.
(nosotros / en la carnicería)
2. Yo voy a llevar a Tito a su casa.
(Elena / a la parada de autobuses)
3. Yo plancho las camisas en la cocina.
(Julio / en su dormitorio)
4. Nosotros hacemos las compras los viernes.
(mis padres / los sábados)
5. Elisa trapea el piso dos veces por semana.
(tú / todos los días)
6. Nosotros sabemos el número de teléfono de Irene.
(yo / no)

28. ¿Tú lo sabes...? With a partner, take turns answering the questions below, basing your answers on the illustrations. Use direct object pronouns in your responses.

1. ¿A qué hora llama Sara a Luis?
2. ¿Cuándo tiene que llamar Luis a Sara?
3. ¿Pepe puede llevar a los chicos a casa?
4. ¿Dónde tiene Pepe los libros?
5. ¿Quién abre la puerta?
6. ¿Quién sirve el café?
7. ¿Quién bebe el refresco?
8. ¿Quién tiene las cartas?

Para conversar

29. ¡Habla con tu compañero(a)! You and your partner play the roles of two roommates who are planning their weekend activities. Take turns answering the following questions, using appropriate direct object pronouns.

1. ¿Quieres dar la fiesta el viernes o el sábado?
2. ¿Vamos a invitar a los chicos de la clase?
3. ¿Tú puedes comprar las bebidas?
4. Mi auto no funciona. ¿Puedes llevarme al mercado?
5. Vamos a tener que limpiar la casa. ¿Quién puede ayudarnos?
6. ¿Quién va a preparar el postre?
7. Yo no puedo ir contigo a la iglesia (*church*) el domingo. ¿Alguien puede llevarte?
8. Mis amigos y yo queremos ver el partido de fútbol por la tarde. ¿Y tú?

30. ¿Quién lo hace? With a partner, ask each other who does what around the house, with other members of the family, etc. Use the appropriate direct object pronouns in the answers.

Modelo —*¿Quién friega los platos?*
—*Mi mamá los friega.*

¡Vamos a ver!

Antes de ver el video

31. Preguntas You and a partner take turns asking and answering the following questions.

1. ¿Tú tienes un hermano o hermana mayor?
2. Cuando tú haces los quehaceres de la casa, ¿prefieres lavar los platos o barrer la cocina?
3. ¿Tú haces todo el trabajo, ayudas a tu mamá o nunca haces nada?
4. ¿Tú haces la cama todos los días? ¿Qué días cambias las sábanas de tu cama?
5. Cuando tú arreglas tu cuarto, ¿pones todas las cosas en su lugar?
6. ¿Qué días haces las compras en el mercado? ¿Consigues carne buena?
7. ¿Siempre tienes una lista o sabes lo que tienes que comprar?
8. Si tú sabes que alguien va a visitarte, ¿limpias tu casa o apartamento?
9. ¿Qué ciudad quieres conocer tú?
10. Cuando tu familia quiere visitar una ciudad, ¿tú estás de acuerdo?
11. Si tú tomas el ómnibus, ¿tienes que ir a la parada de autobuses?
12. Cuando tocan a la puerta, ¿tú miras por la ventana para ver quién es?

El video: Hoy llega tía Nora

¡Amalia! Yo estoy cocinando. Tú tienes que lavar los platos y barrer la cocina.

Para él, arreglar su cuarto es esconderlo todo debajo de la cama.

¡Pedro! Tienes que ir al Mercado Municipal. Y a ver si esta vez consigues carne buena...

¡Daniel! ¡Rápido! ¡Todo esto va debajo de la cama!

Después de ver el video

Ester

Celia

Amalia

Pedro

32. ¿Quién lo dice? Identify the person who said the following in the dialogues.

1. Yo sé lo que tengo que comprar. ________
2. Y a ver si esta vez consigues carne buena. ________
3. ¿Y qué va a hacer Celia mientras yo hago todo el trabajo? ________
4. ¡Pedro! Tienes que ir al Mercado Municipal. ________
5. ¿Papá va a ir a buscar a tía Nora a la parada de autobuses? ________
6. Yo estoy planchando las camisas de papá. ________
7. No, ella dice que es mejor tomar un taxi. ________
8. ¿Quién va a hacer las compras en el mercado? ________
9. ¡Qué trabajo tenemos cuando mi cuñada viene a visitarnos! ________

33. Hablemos With a partner, take turns asking and answering the following questions. Base your answers on the dialogue.

En el diálogo

1. ¿De dónde es la familia Núñez Arzuaga?
2. ¿Qué están haciendo Ester y sus hijos?
3. ¿Qué tiene que hacer Amalia?
4. ¿Qué está haciendo Celia?
5. ¿Qué va a hacer Celia después?
6. ¿Dónde va a dormir Nora? ¿Y Daniel?
7. ¿Quién va a hacer las compras en el mercado?
8. ¿Qué ciudad quiere conocer Amalia?
9. ¿Pedro va a ir a la parada de autobuses a buscar a Nora?
10. ¿Dónde va a poner Daniel las revistas?

34. ¿Qué pasa después? With a partner, use your imagination to say what the characters do. In Spanish, discuss the following.

1. Whether or not doña Nora does any cooking the day after she arrives. What does she prepare? Or do they all go to a restaurant?
2. While she is visiting, does doña Nora help with any housework? What does she do? Does she tell Daniel that he has to help?
3. Does Daniel sleep on the sofa every night or does doña Nora sleep on the sofa sometimes?
4. Does doña Nora go to the market sometimes? Does she pay for (*por*) anything?
5. Where do they take doña Nora while she is visiting? Name three or four places.
6. Do they tell doña Nora that they want to visit Managua next year? Does she think it's a good idea?
7. Does doña Nora tell Daniel that he shouldn't hide his magazines under the bed?
8. Are they sad or happy when doña Nora returns to Managua? Give reasons.

Now compare your statements to those of another group.

¡Vamos a escuchar!

ESTRATEGIA **Listening for details II** Remember what you have learned in preceding lessons about focusing your listening. Anticipate the kinds of information you will hear, concentrate on listening for the details you want to know, and ignore extraneous information.

CD1-32 35. **Propaganda de televisión** Everybody in your household has been discussing the need for extra cleaning help as you are all very busy. You hear a TV commercial on cleaning services. Listen once and make notes of the following details so that you can report to your housemates in the **A conversar...** activity.

1. nombre del servicio
2. dos servicios que ofrece
3. el número de teléfono

ESTRATEGIA **Reporting** When you tell something you hear to another person, you can use **decir (Ramón dice que va a limpiar)** or you can simply report the information without specifying the source. When restating what you hear, use the language you know.

¡Vamos a conversar!

36. **Un servicio fenomenal** Get together with two classmates. Today they happen to be your housemates, too! You all heard a TV commercial for a cleaning service and now take turns telling the others what you recall about the services offered and what cleaning help you think you need. Decide what help you most need and who's going to call for prices.

37. **¿Qué dice Ud.?** What would you say in the following situations? What might the other person say? Act out the scenes with a partner. Take turns playing each role.

1. You and your roommate are trying to divide household chores. Volunteer for those chores that you want to do.
2. Talk about some members of your family and indicate with whom you always agree and with whom you never agree.
3. You complain about chores that certain people in your family never do.
4. You are trying to sell or rent your house or apartment. Describe it to a prospective buyer, by giving as many details as possible.

38. Para conocernos mejor To do this activity, work with a classmate whom you would like to get to know. Take turns asking and answering these questions.

1. ¿Te gusta hacer los quehaceres de la casa? ¿Cuáles no te gusta hacer?
2. En tu casa, ¿quién friega los platos? ¿Quién barre la cocina? ¿Quién saca la basura?
3. ¿Te ayuda alguien a arreglar tu cuarto (*room*)? ¿Quién? ¿Siempre pones las cosas en su lugar?
4. ¿Te gusta hacer las compras en el mercado? ¿Qué días las haces?
5. ¿Prefieres pasar la aspiradora o trapear el piso?
6. ¿Prefieres cortar el césped o limpiar el baño?
7. ¿Algunos de tus parientes viven en otras ciudades? ¿Vas a visitarlos? ¿Ellos te visitan?
8. ¿Tienes primos? ¿Tienes sobrinos? ¿Tienes cuñados?
9. ¿Tú sabes tocar (*play*) algún instrumento musical? ¿Te gusta el piano o prefieres la guitarra?
10. ¿Qué ciudades de este país conoces? ¿Cuáles quieres conocer?

39. Una encuesta Interview your classmates to identify who fits the following descriptions. Include your instructor, but remember to use the **Ud.** form when addressing him/her. After finishing the survey, get together with two or three classmates and discuss the results.

1. *Hace su cama todos los días.*	________________
2. *Cambia las sábanas de su cama una vez por semana.*	________________
3. *Arregla su cuarto los fines de semana.*	________________
4. *Sacude los muebles de su cuarto.*	________________
5. *Tiene un montón de revistas en su cuarto.*	________________
6. *Plancha su ropa.*	________________
7. *Hace las compras en el mercado los sábados.*	________________
8. *Cocina muy bien.*	________________

40. Para crear In groups of three or four, look at the photo and use your imagination to create a story about the people in the picture. Give them names and ages. What is their relationship to each other? What are they doing? What are they going to do later?

¡Vamos a leer!

Antes de leer

ESTRATEGIA **Skimming** When skimming, you look over a text quickly to get the gist or general idea of its content. Scanning is a similar technique often used along with skimming; however, when scanning, you look for very specific information. For example, you might scan a TV listing to locate a basketball game you know is on.

41. La receta You will be reading a recipe for **flan,** one of the most popular desserts in the Spanish-speaking world. Imagine that you have promised to make a dessert for dinner at a friend's. You don't have a lot of time so you first skim the recipe to decide whether it's relatively easy and quick to make.

1. ¿Hay muchos o pocos ingredientes? ¿Son fáciles o difíciles de encontrar?
2. ¿Cuánto tiempo tiene que estar en el horno (*oven*)?
3. ¿Vas a preparar un flan? ¿Por qué sí o por qué no?

¡A leer!

Sección de cocina

Flan casero

Ingredientes:

1 taza de azúcar
4 huevos
2 latas de leche evaporada
1 cucharadita (*tsp*) de esencia de vainilla (*vanilla extract*)
caramelo líquido

© Cindy Miller Hopkins/DanitaDelimont.com

Preparación:

1. Poner[1] los huevos en un bol. Agregar el azúcar y revolver con una cuchara de madera.
2. Agregar la leche lentamente. Agregar la esencia de vainilla.
3. Para hacer el caramelo, poner azúcar y un poco de agua en el fuego. Cuando la mezcla tenga color dorado, sacarla del fuego.
4. Poner el caramelo líquido en el molde y, cuando ya está frío, poner la preparación.
5. Cocinar en el horno a baño María (*double boiler*) a 350° por una hora.
6. Ponerlo en el refrigerador.
7. Servirlo frío, solo o con crema.

[1]In Spanish the infinitive is often used as a command to give instructions or directions.

42. Comprensión As you read the recipe, find the answers to the following questions.

1. ¿Cuáles son los ingredientes del flan?
2. ¿Qué hacemos con el azúcar (*sugar*) para hacer el caramelo? ¿Qué color va a tener el azúcar?
3. Después de batir los huevos, ¿qué agregamos (*add*)?
4. ¿Cómo debemos cocinar el flan? ¿A qué temperatura y por cuánto tiempo?
5. ¿Qué debemos hacer después de sacarlo del horno?
6. ¿Qué podemos hacer antes de servirlo?

Después de leer... desde su mundo

43. ¿Te gusta...? In groups of three or four, find out who likes to cook and what types of food your classmates like to make. Do they have a favorite recipe?

¡Vamos a escribir!

Antes de escribir

ESTRATEGIA **Sequencing steps for a recipe** When following a recipe, the preparation process generally requires a precise order of steps. The sequence of a well-written recipe can save preparation time as well as ensure a tasty final result. Here are some sequencing words you can use: **primero, luego, después, finalmente.**

44. Tu receta favorita You will be sharing with the class how you make one of your favorite dishes. First, make a list of the steps to follow in the order in which they should be completed. With the help of a bilingual dictionary, look up only the words you absolutely need. Here are some verbs commonly used in recipes.

agregar to add	**revolver (o:ue)** to mix	**freír**[1] to fry
batir to beat	**cocinar** to cook	**hervir (e:ie)** to boil

¡A escribir!

45. Receta Write your **primer borrador** of the recipe, using the **flan** recipe as a model and being sure to sequence the steps carefully.

Después de escribir

46. Mi receta Before writing the final version, exchange your first draft with a classmate and peer edit each other's work using the following guidelines.

- use of infinitives in cooking instructions
- subject-verb agreement
- clear and logical sequence of steps

47. Del libro de cocina de... ¡la clase de español! Prepare a cookbook with the recipes from the entire class. You might want to confer as a class to set aside a day or an evening to gather socially and cook recipes from your class cookbook! Take the opportunity to mingle and chat in Spanish.

[1]**Present indicative: frío, fríes, fríe, freímos, freís, fríen**

Honduras

Honduras es uno de los países más grandes de América Central, y las famosas ruinas de Copán son su mayor atracción turística. ¿Qué te parece la idea de hacer una excursión a este país?

Puntos de interés turístico

La mayor atracción turística del país es Copán, una de las ciudades más importantes de la civilización maya.

La biosfera del río Plátano fue (*was*) nominada como una de las maravillas naturales del mundo moderno.

Economía

La economía del país se basa en la agricultura. Sin embargo, Honduras es el único país centroamericano que no tiene volcanes. Esto no es favorable para la agricultura, pues las tierras volcánicas generalmente son fértiles. Honduras tiene muchos problemas políticos y sociales.

Población

Honduras tiene una población principalmente mestiza, de indios, españoles y africanos. La influencia africana se ve en el folclore del país.

Ciudades importantes

Tegucigalpa es la capital, el centro administrativo y la ciudad más grande **y con mayor población.**

San Pedro Sula es el centro industrial y comercial más importante del país. Es la ciudad más grande.

Nicaragua

Nicaragua, el más grande de los países centroamericanos y uno de los más pobres de todo el continente, tiene algo que hay en muy pocos países: un lago de agua dulce (*fresh water lake*)—el mayor de Centroamérica—, donde hay tiburones (*sharks*) y peces que, generalmente, solo viven en agua salada.

La economía

La economía nicaragüense se basa en la agricultura. El país exporta café, mariscos, algodón, tabaco, bananas, carne, azúcar y oro.

La literatura

El más famoso de los escritores nicaragüenses es Rubén Darío, principal creador del modernismo en la lengua española.

Turismo

Sus playas, lagos, volcanes y bosques (*forests*) hacen de Nicaragua el paraíso natural de centroamérica.

Ciudades importantes

Managua, la capital de Nicaragua desde (*since*) 1851, está situada en la costa sur del lago Managua.

Granada es la ciudad más antigua del país y una de las ciudades más hermosas de Nicaragua.

Ahora dime...

In groups of three, take turns asking and answering the following questions.

1. En Honduras, la agricultura es importante. ¿Qué zonas de este país son buenas para la agricultura?
2. Muchas frutas de América Central se exportan. ¿Has comido *(Have you eaten)* bananas de Nicaragua?¿De dónde viene la fruta que comes?
3. ¿Cuál de estos dos países quieren visitar ustedes? ¿Qué quieren ver allí?

iLrn

To learn more about Honduras and Nicaragua, watch the cultural footage in the Media Library.

AUTOPRUEBA

¿Cuánto sé ahora?

Take this test. When you have finished, check your answers in the answer key provided in Appendix D. Then use a red pen to correct any mistakes you may have made. Are you ready?

A. Demonstrative adjectives and pronouns Complete the following sentences, using the appropriate demonstrative adjectives and pronouns.

1. Yo necesito ________ escritorio, ________ silla y ________ mapas. (*this / this / those*)
2. ________ señor es el profesor de inglés y ________ chicas son sus estudiantes. (*That over there / those over there*)
3. Ellas estudian tres horas por día. ________ es muy importante. (*That*)

B. Present indicative of *e:i* stem-changing verbs Complete the following sentences, using the present indicative of the verbs in the list, as needed.

decir (2)	servir (2)	seguir	pedir	conseguir

1. Mi cuñada está en Guatemala, pero mi hermano ________ en Honduras.
2. Yo siempre ________ que mi sobrina Susana es la favorita de sus abuelos, pero ella ________ que eso no es verdad.
3. Eva y yo ________ el postre y mi nieta ________ el café.
4. Yo generalmente ________ carne buena.
5. ¿Qué ________ Uds. cuando van a un restaurante mexicano?

C. Affirmative and negative expressions Answer the following questions in the negative.

1. ¿Tú trapeas el piso a veces?
2. ¿Uds. limpian el baño o la cocina?
3. ¿Hay algunas revistas españolas en tu casa?
4. ¿Hay alguien en la casa de tus suegros?

D. Verbs with irregular first-person forms Complete the following sentences, using the present indicative of the verbs in the list, as needed.

traducir	hacer	conocer	saber	salir
poner	caber	ver	traer	conducir

1. Yo ____________ un Ford, modelo 2008.
2. Yo no ____________ dónde está el hotel.
3. Yo no ____________ en este taxi. ¡Hay ocho personas!
4. Yo siempre ____________ de mi casa a las siete de la mañana.
5. Yo ____________ las lecciones del inglés al portugués.
6. Yo no ____________ los pasaportes. ¿Dónde están?
7. Yo no ____________ nada los domingos.
8. Yo nunca ____________ las sillas aquí.
9. Yo no ____________ California.
10. Yo ____________ a mi amigo Carlos a la universidad.

E. *Saber* vs. *conocer* Form sentences, using **saber** and/or **conocer**.

1. nosotros / que ella es su novia
2. yo / a Teresa / pero / no / dónde vive

3. Peter / Madrid / pero / no / hablar español
4. los chicos / no / los poemas / de memoria

F. Direct object pronouns Answer the following questions in the affirmative. Substitute direct object pronouns for the direct objects.

1. ¿Tú conoces a la cuñada de Amalia?
2. ¿Tus tíos saben tu número de teléfono?
3. ¿Sus abuelos los llevan a Uds. al teatro?
4. ¿Tus primos te llaman por teléfono?
5. ¿Tú puedes llevarme a la parada de autobuses?
6. ¿Tú escondes las revistas en tu cuarto?
7. ¿Tú lavas los platos?
8. ¿Uds. sacan la basura todos los días?

G. Just words . . . Complete the following, using vocabulary from Lesson 6.

1. Yo voy a pasar la _________, Ana va a _________ los muebles, Julio va a cortar el _________ y mamá va a doblar la _________.
2. Tocan a la puerta; voy a _________. Yo no _________ quién es.
3. Voy a barrer. ¿Dónde está la _________? Elena va a arreglar el cuarto de _________.
4. ¿Tu prima está en el comedor o en la _________ de estar? ¿Tú crees que ella puede _________ las camisas de Tito?
5. ¿Tú vas a ir en autobús o vas a tomar un _________? ¿Vas a llamar a la _________ de empleos?
6. Yo _________ de mi casa a las siete y vuelvo a las once.
7. Raúl es mi _________; es el hermano de mi esposo.
8. Tengo un _________ de revistas en español. Muchas tienen _________ muy interesantes que yo quiero leer.

H. Culture

1. Complete the following sentences, based on information found in the **¿Lo sabía Ud.?** sections.
   a. Actualmente, muchos hombres hispanos, especialmente los más jóvenes, ayudan a su esposa con los _________ de la casa.
   b. En la mayoría de los países de habla hispana, cuando una mujer se casa, retiene su apellido de _________.
2. Answer the following questions, based on the information found in the **El mundo hispánico y tú** section.
   a. ¿Cuál es la capital de Honduras? _________
   b. ¿En qué se basa la economía de Nicaragua? _________

I. Un dicho Do you remember the Spanish saying that states that a prophet is not recognized in his own land? Find it in this lesson.

LECCIÓN 7

EN UN HOTEL

Un hotel en Costa Rica

OBJETIVOS COMUNICATIVOS

You will learn vocabulary related to checking in at a hotel and asking about accommodations and tourism.

SITUACIONES

De vacaciones en Costa Rica

ESTRUCTURAS

1 Indirect object pronouns
2 Constructions with **gustar**
3 Time expressions with **hacer**
4 Preterit of regular verbs
5 Ordinal numbers

ASÍ SOMOS

¡Vamos a ver!
Watching and understanding situations

¡Vamos a escuchar!
Listening to authentic language

¡Vamos a conversar!
Simplifying ideas through paraphrasing

¡Vamos a leer!
Guessing meaning from context

¡Vamos a escribir!
Summarizing and organizing the information

EL MUNDO HISPÁNICO Y TÚ

› Costa Rica
› Panamá

AUTOPRUEBA

You will review what you learned in this lesson.

COSTA RICA, llamada "la Suiza de América" por su estabilidad política, es una nación progresista y democrática. El país no tiene ejército (*army*); la educación es obligatoria y gratuita (*free*) y el analfabetismo casi no existe. La mayoría de los ticos (como se les llama a los costarricenses) es de origen español.

PANAMÁ está situado en el istmo que une Norteamérica con Sudamérica. Panamá fue (*was*) una provincia de Colombia hasta 1903 y, por lo tanto (*so*), es la república hispanoamericana de más reciente creación.

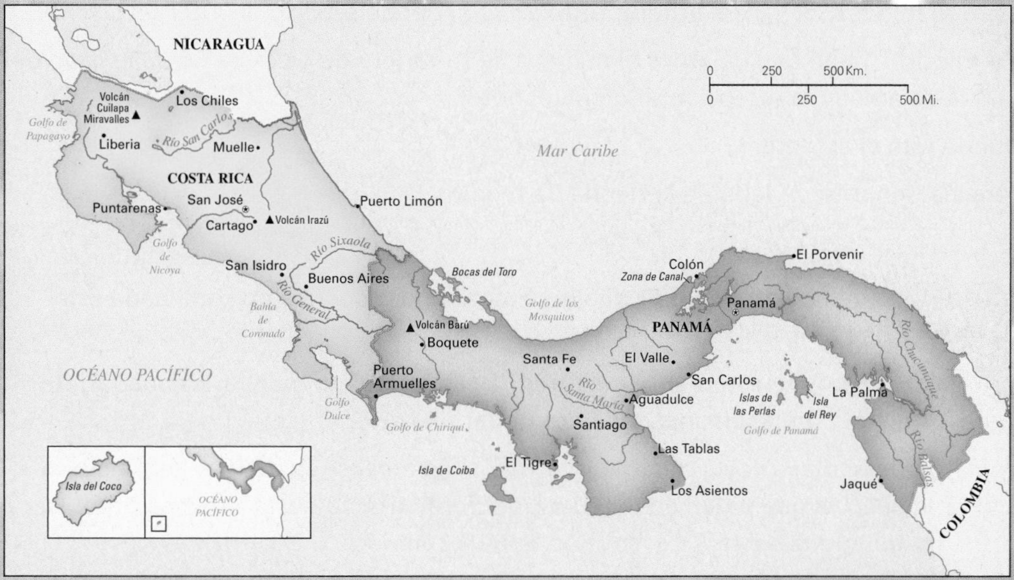

Recursos iLrn video audio web playlist

De vacaciones en Costa Rica

CD2-2

© Cengage Learning

¡Ubíquelas!

Delia and Sara are staying in a hotel in San José while they visit Costa Rica. Watching the video will give you an idea about the places that the girls can visit.

© Somos Images/Alamy

La semana pasada, Delia y Sara, dos chicas panameñas, decidieron pasar sus vacaciones juntas. Ahora están en un hotel de Costa Rica, hablando con un empleado.

Empleado: (*A Delia*) ¿En qué puedo servirle, señorita?

Delia: Buenos días. Mi amiga y yo tenemos reservación para una habitación doble. Yo llamé ayer para confirmarla. La reservación está a nombre de Delia Villalobos.

Empleado: A ver... Sí, Delia Villalobos. Su habitación está en el cuarto piso, señorita. El botones puede llevar sus maletas al cuarto.

Sara: No, no es necesario. No tenemos mucho equipaje.

Delia: ¿Los cuartos tienen televisor? ¿Aire acondicionado? Y… ¿tienen servicio de Internet?

Empleado: Sí, señorita. ¡Ah! Tiene que dejarnos el número de su tarjeta de crédito. (*Le da la llave del cuarto.*) Tienen que dejarla en la recepción si salen del hotel.

Sara: Gracias. ¿Dónde está el ascensor?

Empleado: A la derecha, señorita. Al lado de la tienda de regalos.

En el cuarto

Delia: El hotel tiene servicio de habitación. ¿Por qué no almorzamos aquí? Yo no comí nada esta mañana y estoy muerta de hambre…

Sara: ¡Ay, no! ¿Por qué no vamos al restaurante del hotel? Después quiero mandarles una tarjeta postal a mis padres. Y el hotel tiene piscina. Podemos nadar un rato…

Delia: Sara, te prometo que mañana voy a caminar y correr… Voy a hacer ejercicio… Pero hoy quiero comer, mirar la película que pasan en el canal cinco y tomar una siesta. ¡Vamos, Sara! Hace mucho tiempo que no tomo una siesta. ¡Y el colchón es muy cómodo!

SARA: No me gusta dormir cuando estoy de vacaciones. Esta noche, después de cenar, podemos mirar las noticias, y después...

DELIA: ¡Está bien! Vamos al restaurante.

Delia y Sara caminan hacia el restaurante y ven a un grupo de muchachos muy guapos cerca de la piscina.

DELIA: Sara... ¡Tengo una idea brillante! ¿Por qué no nadamos un rato después de almorzar? ¡Tenemos que usar la piscina!

SARA: Pero... ¿No estás cansada? ¿No quieres dormir?

DELIA: ¡Ya dormimos anoche! Y tú descansaste anteayer, antes del viaje... Y mañana vamos a ir al jardín Lankester y al parque Braulio Carrillo.

SARA: ¿Solas...?

DELIA: O quizás con algunos nuevos amigos...

LEARNING TIP
Take advantage of any opportunity you may have to interact in conversation with a native Spanish speaker.

¿Lo sabía Ud.?

En muchos países hispanos, especialmente en los pueblos pequeños, hay hoteles donde las habitaciones no tienen baño privado. Generalmente tienen uno o dos baños por piso.

› **¿Cuál es la situación en los *bed and breakfasts* de este país?**

1. **Hablemos** With a partner, take turns asking and answering the following questions. Base your answers on the dialogue and on your own circumstances.

En el diálogo

1. ¿Dónde están de vacaciones Delia y Sara?
2. ¿En qué piso está la habitación de las chicas?
3. ¿Las chicas tienen mucho equipaje?
4. ¿Los cuartos del hotel tienen servicio de Internet?
5. ¿Qué quiere mandarles Sara a sus padres?
6. ¿Qué quiere hacer Sara en el hotel?
7. ¿Qué quiere mirar Delia?
8. ¿Cómo es el colchón de Delia?
9. ¿Dónde van a comer Delia y Sara?
10. ¿Qué no le gusta hacer a Sara cuando está de vacaciones?

¿Y tú?

1. ¿Adónde vas tú de vacaciones?
2. En un hotel, ¿en qué piso prefieres tener tu habitación?
3. ¿Tú viajas con mucho equipaje?
4. ¿Tú tienes Internet en tu casa?
5. ¿A quiénes les mandas tú tarjetas postales?
6. ¿Tu casa tiene piscina? ¿Tú sabes nadar?
7. ¿Tú prefieres mirar las noticias o ver una película?
8. ¿Cómo es tu colchón? ¿Cómodo o incómodo?
9. En un hotel, ¿tú comes en tu habitación o en el restaurante del hotel?
10. ¿Qué te gusta hacer a ti cuando estás de vacaciones?

VOCABULARIO

En el diálogo

Cognados

brillante	*brilliant*
doble	*double*
el grupo	*group*
necesario(a)	*necessary*
panameño(a)	*Panamanian*
la reservación, la reserva	*reservation*
el servicio	*service*

Nombres

el aire acondicionado	*air conditioner*
el ascensor, el elevador	*elevator*
el botones	*bellhop*
el canal	*channel*
el colchón	*mattress*
el, (la) empleado(a)	*clerk, employee*
el equipaje	*luggage*
el (la) Internet, la Red	*Internet, World Wide Web*
el jardín	*garden*
la llave	*key*
la maleta, la valija	*suitcase*
la noticia	*piece of news*
la película	*movie, film*
la piscina, la alberca (*Méx.*)	*swimming pool*
el piso	*floor*
la recepción	*registration*
el servicio de habitación (cuarto)	*room service*
la siesta	*nap*
la tarjeta de crédito[1]	*credit card*
_____ postal	*post card*
el televisor	*TV set*
la tienda	*shop*
____ de regalos	*gift shop*

Verbos

caminar	*to walk*
confirmar	*to confirm*
descansar	*to rest*
gustar	*to like, to be pleasing to*
mandar, enviar	*to send*
nadar	*to swim*
prometer	*to promise*

Adjetivos

cómodo(a)	*comfortable*
cuarto(a)	*fourth*
pasado(a)	*last*

Otras palabras y expresiones

a la derecha[2]	*to the right*
a nombre de	*under the name of*
al lado de	*next to*
anoche	*last night*
anteayer	*the day before yesterday*
antes (de)	*before*
ayer	*yesterday*
cerca (de)	*near*
¿En qué puedo servirle?	*How may I help (serve) you?*
Hace mucho tiempo que no tomo una siesta.	*I haven't taken a nap for a long time.*
hacer ejercicio	*to exercise*
hacia	*towards*
mucho tiempo	*a long time*
pasar (dar) una película	*to show a movie*
quizá(s)	*perhaps*
¡Vamos!	*Come on!*

En el hotel

[1] tarjeta de débito *debit card*
[2] a la izquierda *to the left*

Más sobre el tema

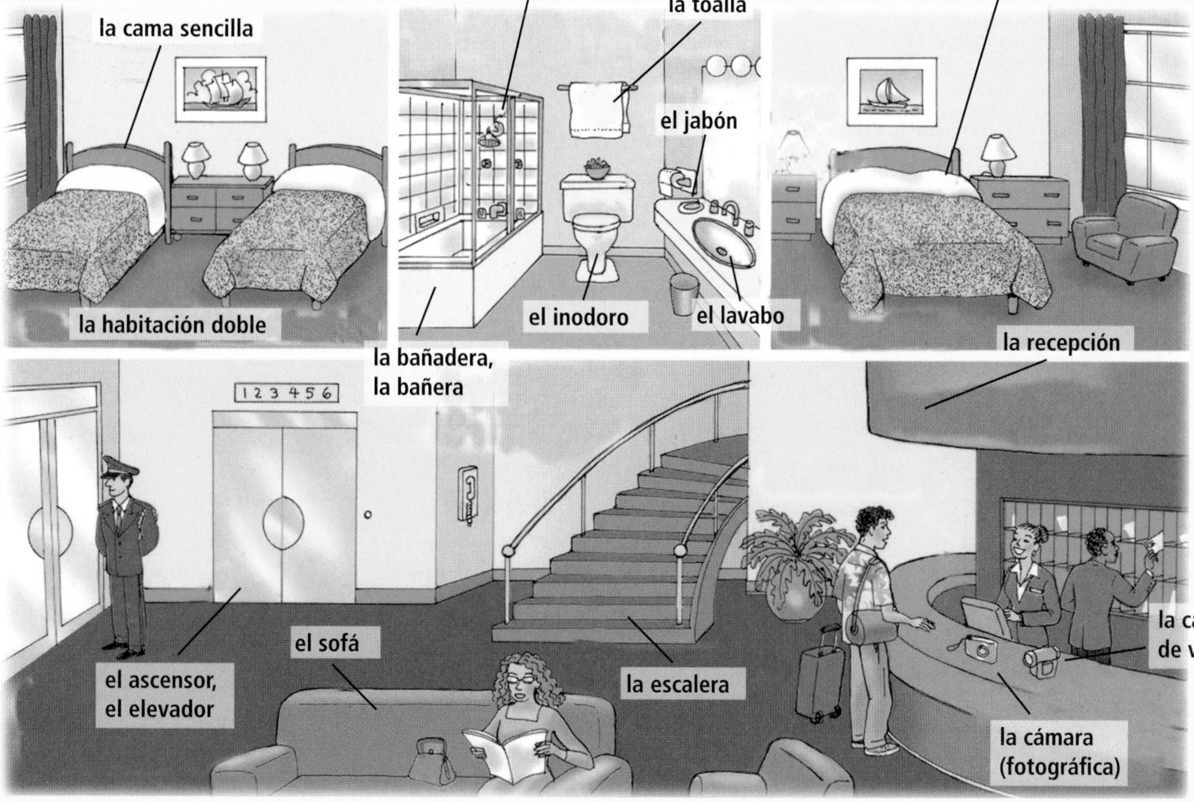

Las comidas

el desayuno	*breakfast*
el almuerzo	*lunch*
la merienda	*afternoon snack*
la cena	*dinner, supper*

Para hablar de turismo

¿A cómo está el cambio de moneda?	*What is the rate of exchange?*
la aduana	*customs*
cancelar	*to cancel*
con vista a	*overlooking*
el consulado	*consulate*
desocupar el cuarto	*to vacate the room*
la embajada	*embassy*
la escalera mecánica	*escalator*
la habitación sencilla	*single room*
libre	*vacant*
la lista de espera	*waiting list*
el mar	*sea*
el pasaporte	*passport*
pasar por la aduana	*to go through customs*
la tarjeta de turista	*tourist card*
viajar	*to travel*

¿Lo sabía Ud.?

En los países de habla hispana, el desayuno consiste en una taza de café con leche y pan con mantequilla.

› **Generalmente, ¿qué desayuna la gente en este país?**

VOCABULARIO

Práctica

2. Palabras Circle the word or phrase that doesn't belong in each group.

1. almuerzo / cena / escalera
2. jardín / empleado / botones
3. ducha / llave / bañadera
4. equipaje / jabón / toalla
5. enviar / nadar / mandar
6. recepción / reservación / inodoro
7. cama / canal / colchón
8. televisor / lavabo / película
9. brillante / doble / sencillo
10. hacer ejercicio / prometer / caminar

3. Preguntas y respuestas Match the questions in the first column with the answers in the second column.

1. ¿Tienen reservación? ________
2. ¿Miraste las noticias? ________
3. ¿Le diste la tarjeta de crédito? ________
4. ¿Vas a tomar una siesta? ________
5. ¿Vas a usar la escalera? ________
6. ¿Viste esa película? ________
7. ¿Quién lleva las maletas? ________
8. ¿Cómo es tu colchón? ________

a. El botones.
b. Sí, necesito hacer ejercicio.
c. Sí, la vi anoche.
d. No, mi cuarto no tiene televisor.
e. Muy cómodo.
f. Sí, tengo sueño.
g. Sí, yo la confirmé ayer.
h. No, solamente el número.

4. ¿Qué es? Write the words or phrases that correspond to the following.

1. reservación ________
2. elevador ________
3. valija ________
4. opuesto de **cancelar** ________
5. opuesto de **mañana** ________
6. bañera ________
7. la primera comida del día ________
8. opuesto de **trabajar** ________

5. Oraciones incompletas Complete the following sentences, using vocabulary from this lesson.

1. ¿En qué ________ servirle, señor?
2. A ver... La reservación está a ________ de Marcela Rodríguez.
3. El ascensor está a la ________, al ________ de la ________ de regalos.
4. En el hotel podemos comer en el cuarto, porque tiene servicio de ________. También tiene Internet y aire ________.
5. Ellos no van a ir al consulado. Van a ir a la ________.
6. ¿A cómo está el ________ de ________?
7. Tenemos que pasar por la ________ con el equipaje.
8. Necesitamos comprar una cámara de ________ y una cámara ________.
9. No voy a usar la escalera ________ porque necesito hacer ejercicio.
10. ¿A qué hora tenemos que ________ la habitación? ¿A las doce?

Para conversar

6. **¿En qué puedo servirle?** With a partner, take turns playing the part of a hotel employee and a customer who wants to find out about specific accommodations that the hotel has to offer. The employee's answers will determine what kind of hotel it is.

   Modelo —*Buenas tardes. Quiero una habitación sencilla.*
   —*No tenemos habitaciones sencillas. Todas son dobles y muy cómodas.*

7. **Quejas** (*Complaints*) With partners, play the roles of two guests and the concierge. The guests complain about everything when staying at a hotel. Discuss everything that you find wrong with the place and the service.

   Modelo —*No hay suficientes toallas en el baño.*
   —*Tampoco hay agua caliente.*
   —*Lo siento. Voy a darles otra habitación.*

¿Lo sabía Ud.?

La moneda (*currency*) que utilizan con más frecuencia los latinoamericanos cuando viajan fuera de su país es el dólar estadounidense, porque es fácil cambiar dólares en la mayoría de los bancos principales.

› **¿Se puede cambiar dinero de otros países en los bancos de este país?**

Pronunciación

CD2-3 **A. The Spanish *ll***

In most countries, the Spanish **ll** has a sound similar to the *y* in the English word *yes*. Listen to your instructor and repeat the following sentences.

Me **ll**amo Raúl A**ll**ende.

E**ll**os **ll**evan las **ll**aves.

El Dr. **Ll**anes vive en la ca**ll**e Porti**ll**o.

Las **ll**amas **ll**egaron del Ca**ll**ao.

CD2-4 **B. The Spanish *ñ***

The Spanish **ñ** is similar to the *ny* in the English word *canyon*. Listen to your instructor and repeat the following sentences.

El se**ñ**or Salda**ñ**a está en Espa**ñ**a.

La se**ñ**orita Nú**ñ**ez viene ma**ñ**ana.

La se**ñ**ora Pe**ñ**a tiene treinta a**ñ**os.

La ni**ñ**a sue**ñ**a con ir a la monta**ñ**a.

¿Lo sabía Ud.?

Al seleccionar un hotel en Latinoamérica, hay que tener en cuenta (*keep in mind*) que los precios que dan no incluyen los impuestos (*taxes*) que, en la mayoría de los países, son muy altos.

› **En este país, los precios que dan los hoteles, ¿incluyen los impuestos?**

ESTRUCTURAS

1 Indirect object pronouns *(Pronombres usados como complemento indirecto)*

› In addition to a subject and a direct object, a sentence may have an indirect object.

Él **te** da **el libro**.	*He gives you the book.*
I.O. D.O.	I.O. D.O.

› An indirect object describes *to whom* or *for whom* an action is done. An indirect object pronoun can be used in place of an indirect object. In Spanish, the indirect object pronoun includes the meaning *to* or *for*: **Yo *les* mando los libros (a los estudiantes)**.

› The forms of the indirect object pronouns are as follows. Notice that the indirect object pronouns are the same as the direct object pronouns, except in the third person.

Singular		Plural	
me	*(to, for) me*	**nos**	*(to, for) us*
te	*(to, for) you* (fam.)	**os**	*(to, for) you* (fam.)
le	*(to, for) you* (form.) *(to, for) him* *(to, for) her*	**les**	*(to, for) you* (form.) *(to, for) them* (masc., fem.)

› Indirect object pronouns are usually placed in front of the conjugated verb.

—¿Qué **te** está diciendo el empleado?	*What is the employee saying to you?*
—Que puedo pagar con dólares.	*That I can pay with dollars.*
—¿En qué idioma **les** hablan sus padres a ustedes?	*In what language do your parents speak to you?*
—Ellos **nos** hablan en español.	*They speak to us in Spanish.*

› In sentences with a conjugated verb followed by an infinitive, the indirect object pronoun may either be placed in front of the conjugated verb or be attached to the infinitive.

Le quiero dar dinero.
Quiero dar**le** dinero.
I want to give him money.

› When used in sentences with the present progressive, an indirect object pronoun may either be placed in front of the conjugated verb or be attached to the present participle.

Nos está diciendo que viene hoy.
Está diciéndo**nos**[1] que viene hoy.
He is telling us that he is coming today.

[1]When an indirect object pronoun is attached to a **gerundio**, an accent mark is added to maintain the correct stress.

¡Atención! The indirect object pronouns **le** and **les** sometimes require clarification when the person to whom they refer is not specified. Spanish provides clarification (or emphasis) by using the preposition **a** + *personal pronoun* or *noun*.

Le doy el pasaje.	*I am giving the ticket* . . . (to him? to her? to you?)
but: **Le** doy el pasaje **a ella**.	*I am giving the ticket to her.*

Note, however, that the prepositional phrase is optional, while the indirect object pronoun must always be used.

Le traigo un libro a **Roberto**.	*I am bringing a book to Roberto.*
¿**Les** vas a dar el dinero **a ellas?**	*Are you going to give the money to them?*

LEARNING TIP
Remember that pronouns refer to something already mentioned.

Práctica

8. **Comentarios** You are at a hotel, waiting for a friend to arrive, and you overhear some people making the following comments. Complete their sentences with the appropriate indirect object pronouns.

    1. ________ dan las llaves. (a nosotros)
    2. ________ doy el equipaje. (a ellos)
    3. ________ doy la maleta. (a él)
    4. ________ doy las tarjetas postales. (a ella)
    5. ________ traigo la cámara fotográfica. (a Uds.)
    6. ________ piden el pasaporte. (a ella)
    7. ________ traigo la cámara de video. (a ti)
    8. ________ traen el periódico. (a él)
    9. ________ decimos "gracias". (a ellos)
    10. ________ dan las bebidas. (a mí)

9. **Minidiálogos** Add the appropriate indirect object pronouns to the following exchanges, and then act them out with a partner.

    1. —¿Quién ________ va a dar los pasaportes a Ana y a mí?
    —El empleado de la embajada, y Uds. tienen que dar ________ el dinero a él.
    2. —¿A quiénes ________ vas a enviar las tarjetas postales? ¿A tus hermanos?
    —No, a mis hermanas.
    3. —¿Qué ________ vas a comprar a tu hermana?
    —Voy a comprar ________ una maleta.
    4. —¿Qué ________ va a dar el botones a ti?
    — ________ va a dar la llave de la habitación.
    5. —¿Dónde ________ dan las tarjetas de turista a Uds.?
    — ________ dan las tarjetas en el consulado.

10. ¿Qué van a hacer? With a partner, take turns asking each other what the people depicted here do or are going to do. Remember to use the appropriate indirect object pronouns in your questions and answers.

1. dar

2. dar

3. dar

4. dar

5. traer

6. traer

11. ¿Qué necesitan? The following people are going on a trip and need certain items. Say who is going to give, bring, or buy the things they need.

Modelo Óscar necesita un mapa. *El papá de Luisa le va a traer (comprar, dar) el mapa.*

tu mamá · el amigo de... · mi hermano · el novio de... · nuestros amigos · el papá de... · la abuela de... · su esposo(a) · los chicos

1. Yo necesito las maletas.
2. Teresa necesita el pasaporte.
3. Tú necesitas una valija.
4. Ana y yo necesitamos ropa.
5. Carlos necesita una cámara de video.
6. Los chicos necesitan una cámara fotográfica.
7. Olga y Pedro necesitan dinero.
8. Ud. necesita una tarjeta postal.

Para conversar

12. ¡Habla con tu compañero(a)! You are going on a trip to Panamá to visit your aunt and uncle. Discuss with a classmate what you are doing now and what you are going to do once you get there. Answer the questions in complete sentences.

1. ¿Les estás escribiendo a tus tíos de Panamá?
2. ¿Qué les estás diciendo?
3. ¿Qué les vas a llevar a tus tíos?
4. ¿Tu papá te va a dar su cámara fotográfica?
5. ¿Nos vas a escribir desde (*from*) Panamá?
6. ¿Me vas a dejar la llave de tu casa?
7. ¿Qué les vas a traer a tus padres?
8. ¿Qué me vas a traer a mí?

13. De Costa Rica You and your partner are going on a trip to Costa Rica. Ask each other what you are going to bring people as gifts. Add five more persons or group of people that will receive your gifts.

1. a tu mamá
2. a tus hermanos
3. a tu mejor amigo(a)
4. a tus compañeros de clase
5. a tus tíos favoritos

2 Constructions with *gustar* (Construcciones con *gustar*)

› The verb **gustar** means *to like* (literally, *to be pleasing to*). **Gustar** is always used with an indirect object pronoun (**me** in the following example).

Me gusta tu casa.	*I like your house.*
I.O. V. S.	S. V. D.O.
	Your house is pleasing to me.
	S. V. I.O.

› The two most commonly used forms of **gustar** are the third-person singular form, **gusta**, used if the subject is singular or if **gustar** is followed by one or more infinitives; and the third-person plural form, **gustan**, used if the subject is plural.

Indirect object pronouns

Me / Te / Le / Nos / Os / Les	gusta	esta ciudad.
		viajar en el verano.
		cantar y bailar.
	gustan	estas maletas.

› Note that the verb **gustar** agrees with the *subject* of the sentence—that is, with the person or thing being liked.

Me gusta **Lima.**	*I like Lima.*
No me gustan esas **maletas**.	*I don't like those suitcases.*

¡Atención! When what is liked is an activity, **gustar** is followed by the infinitive.

Me gusta **ir** al cine.	*I like to go to the movies.*

› The person who does the liking is the indirect object.

Me gustan los hoteles de esta ciudad.
I.O.

—¿**Te** gusta Panamá?	*Do you like Panamá?*
—Sí, **me** gusta **mucho** Panamá, pero **me** gusta **más** Guatemala.	*Yes, I like Panamá very much, but I like Guatemala better.*
—A Eva **le** gusta México y **a nosotros nos** gusta Costa Rica.	*Eva likes México and we like Costa Rica.*

LEARNING TIP
The construction with **gustar** is one of the cases in which Spanish expresses something in a way quite different from English. This structure will require some understanding on its own terms.
Spanish: **Me gusta...** (. . . *appeals to me*)

¡Atención! Note that the words **mucho** and **más** (*better*) immediately follow **gustar**.

› The preposition **a** + *noun* or *pronoun* may be used to emphasize or specify the name of the person referred to by the indirect object pronoun.

A Eva (A ella) le gusta nadar y **a mí** me gusta bailar.	*Eva (She) likes to swim and I like to dance.*

Práctica

14. Entrevista a tu compañero(a) You have used certain constructions with **gustar (me gusta, te gusta)**. To review, get together with a partner and ask each other whether or not you like the following things.

1. la comida mexicana (italiana / china)
2. la cerveza (el vino)
3. el rojo (el azul)
4. la playa (la montaña)
5. nadar (correr)
6. ir al cine (ir al teatro)
7. cantar (bailar)
8. el béisbol (el tenis)

If you address someone as **usted**, **le** is used instead of **te**. Now choose questions from the list above to ask your instructor.

15. ¿Qué nos gusta más? Rewrite the following sentences, using constructions with **gustar más**.

Modelo Ellos prefieren comer en la habitación.
A ellos les gusta más comer en la habitación.

1. Nosotros preferimos una habitación con vista al mar.
2. ¿Ud. prefiere usar el ascensor o la escalera mecánica?
3. Graciela prefiere un cuarto con aire acondicionado.
4. ¿Tú prefieres estar de vacaciones con un grupo de amigos?
5. ¿Uds. prefieren mirar las noticias o ver una película?
6. Yo prefiero tomar una siesta antes de cenar.
7. Mis padres prefieren las ciudades grandes.
8. Las chicas prefieren bailar salsa.
9. ¿Ud. prefiere pagar con tarjeta de crédito?
10. Yo prefiero las películas españolas.

16. Los fines de semana Interview a classmate to find out what the following members of his or her family like and don't like to do on weekends. When you have finished, switch roles.

Modelo *—A tu hermana, ¿qué le gusta hacer? ¿Qué no le gusta hacer?*
—A mi hermana le gusta mucho ir a bailar. No le gusta trabajar.

1. a ti
2. a tus hermanos
3. a tu padre
4. a Uds.
5. a tus primos
6. a tu mamá

17. ¿Nos gusta o no? Look at the illustrations below and say what these people like (or don't like) and what they like (or don't like) to do.

Modelo
A Juan le gusta leer.

Juan

Inés

1. ______________________________

Jorge

Mario

2. ______________________________

Yo

3. ______________________________

Nosotras

4. ______________________________

Tú

5. ______________________________

Ud.

6. ______________________________

Para conversar

18. ¡Habla con tu compañero(a)! Interview a classmate, using the following questions. When you have finished, switch roles.

1. ¿Dónde te gusta pasar tus vacaciones?
2. ¿Te gustan más las ciudades grandes o las ciudades pequeñas?
3. ¿Te gusta vivir cerca de una playa?
4. ¿Te gusta más ir a un museo o a un parque de diversiones?
5. ¿Qué les gusta hacer a tus amigos los fines de semana?
6. ¿A Uds. les gusta bailar? ¿cantar?
7. ¿A tu mejor amiga le gustan las canciones de Enrique Iglesias?
8. ¿Qué estación del año te gusta más?
9. ¿Qué día de la semana te gusta más? ¿Por qué?
10. ¿Qué te gusta hacer cuando llueve?

19. ¿Y a usted? With a partner, prepare four questions to ask your instructor about his or her likes and dislikes. Ask him/her formal questions (**usted**) and write his/her answers.

20. Para comparar Compare your likes and dislikes with those of two classmates and their relatives. Consider your tastes in food, music, weekend activities, classes, and travel.

Modelo —*A mí me gusta la música de Carlos Santana.*
—*A mis padres también les gusta Santana. A mí me gusta Green Day.*
—*A todos nos gusta Green Day. A mí también me gusta la música latina.*

3 Time expressions with *hacer* (*Expresiones de tiempo con el verbo* **hacer**)

› English uses the present perfect progressive or the present perfect tense to express how long something has been going on.

***I have been living** here **for** twenty years.*

› Spanish uses the following construction.

Hace	+	*length of time*	+	**que**	+	*verb* (in the present tense)
Hace		veinte años		que		vivo aquí.

—**¿Cuánto tiempo hace que** Ud. estudia español?	*How long have you been studying Spanish?*
—**Hace** tres meses **que** estudio español.	*I have been studying Spanish for three months.*
—¿Tienes mucha hambre?	*Are you very hungry?*
—¡Sí! **Hace** ocho horas **que** no como.	*Yes! I haven't eaten for eight hours.*

¡Atención! To ask how long something has been going on, use the expression **¿Cuánto tiempo hace que...?**

LEARNING TIP
Note that just as with some weather expressions (**hace calor, hace frío**, etc.), **hace** is used with time expressions in Spanish (**hace mucho tiempo, hace tres meses,** and so on).

Práctica

21. ¿Cuánto tiempo hace...? Tell how long each action depicted below has been going on. Use **hace... que** and the length of time specified.

1. veinte minutos

2. tres años

3. una hora

4. dos horas

5. siete horas

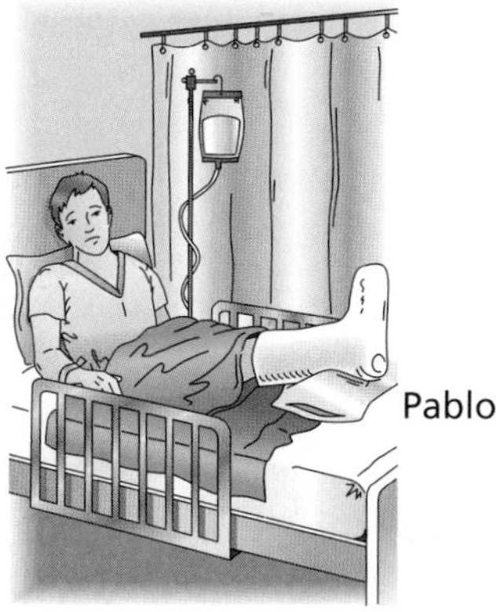

6. quince días

Para conversar

22. ¡Habla con tu compañero(a)! Interview a classmate, using the following questions, and create five more of your own. When you have finished, switch roles.

Modelo —¿Cuánto tiempo hace que vives en la misma (*same*) casa?
—Hace cinco años que vivo en la misma casa.

1. ¿Cuánto tiempo hace que estudias en esta universidad?
2. ¿Cuánto tiempo hace que trabajas en esta ciudad?
3. ¿Cuánto tiempo hace que hablas español?
4. ¿Cuánto tiempo hace que no tienes exámenes?
5. ¿Cuánto tiempo hace que conduces?

23. Queremos saber... In groups of three, prepare six questions to ask your instructor, using time expressions with **hacer**. You may want to use the verb **enseñar** (*to teach*) in your questions.

Modelo *—¿Cuánto tiempo hace que enseña español?*

4 Preterit of regular verbs (*Pretérito de verbos regulares*)

› Spanish has two simple past tenses: the preterit and the imperfect. (The imperfect tense will be studied in **Lección 10**.) The preterit tense is used to refer to actions or states that the speaker views as completed in the past.

› The preterit of regular verbs is formed as follows. Note that the endings for the **-er** and **-ir** verbs are the same.

-ar verbs	-er verbs	-ir verbs
tomar *to take*	**comer** *to eat*	**escribir** *to write*
tom**é**	com**í**	escrib**í**
tom**aste**	com**iste**	escrib**iste**
tom**ó**	com**ió**	escrib**ió**
tom**amos**	com**imos**	escrib**imos**
tom**asteis**	com**isteis**	escrib**isteis**
tom**aron**	com**ieron**	escrib**ieron**

—¿**Hablaste** con Silvia ayer? — *Did you speak with Silvia yesterday?*
—Sí, **comí** con ella en la cafetería. — *Yes, I ate with her in the cafeteria.*
—¿Le **escribió** Roberto? — *Did Roberto write to her?*
—Sí, **recibió** una tarjeta de él ayer. — *Yes, she received a card from him yesterday.*

› The first-person plural of **-ar** and **-ir** verbs is identical to the present tense forms.

—¿A qué hora salieron Uds.? — *What time did you leave?*
—**Salimos** de casa a las seis y no **llegamos** hasta las siete. — *We left home at six, and we didn't arrive until seven.*

› Verbs ending in **-gar**, -**car**, and **-zar** change **g** to **gu**, **c** to **qu**, and **z** to **c** before **-é** in the first-person singular of the preterit: **pagar → pagué; buscar** (*to look for*) **→ busqué; empezar → empecé.**

—¿A qué hora **llegaste** a la pensión? — *What time did you arrive at the boarding house?*
—**Llegué** a las ocho y **empecé** a trabajar enseguida. — *I arrived at eight, and I started to work right away.*

› Certain -**er** and **-ir** verbs with the stem ending in a vowel change **i** to **y** in the third-person singular and plural endings: **leer → leyó, leyeron; creer → creyó, creyeron.**

Él lo **leyó** en el periódico, pero no lo **creyó**.

› Verbs of the **-ar** and **-er** groups that are stem-changing in the present indicative are regular in the preterit.

Rosa **volvió** a las seis y **cerró** las puertas. — *Rosa returned at six o'clock and closed the doors.*

Un dicho
Salió de Guatemala y entró en Guatepeor.
Equivalent: *He went from bad to worse.*

¿Lo sabía Ud.?

Las pensiones son muy populares en los países de habla hispana. Son más económicas que los hoteles y generalmente el precio incluye el cuarto y las comidas.

› **Los *bed and breakfast* que hay en este país, ¿son equivalentes a las pensiones?**

› Spanish has no equivalent for the English word *did* used as an auxiliary verb in questions and negative sentences.

—¿Encontraste el dinero?	*Did you find the money?*
—No lo busqué.	*I didn't look for it.*
—¿Dejaste una buena propina?	*Did you leave a good tip?*
—Sí, dejé el 20 por ciento.	*Yes, I left 20 percent.*

Práctica

24. **Minidiálogos** Complete the following exchanges, using the verbs given. Then, act them out with a partner.

1. hablar volver

   —¿Con quién ______ Uds. por teléfono ayer?

   —______ con nuestros padres. ¿Con quién ______ tú?

   —Yo ______ con mi suegro. Él ______ de su viaje a San José anteayer.

2. pagar pasar comer

   —¿Cuánto ______ tú por la habitación en el hotel?

   —Yo ______ doscientos dólares por noche. Por eso no ______ mucho tiempo en el hotel.

   —¿______ en el restaurante del hotel?

   —No, ______ en la cafetería.

3. llegar empezar

   —¿A qué hora ______ Uds. a la oficina ayer?

   —Yo ______ a las ocho y media y ______ a trabajar a las nueve. Rosario ______ a las nueve y ______ a trabajar a las nueve y media.

4. escribir mandar recibir

   —¿A quiénes les ______ tú la semana pasada?

   —Yo les ______ a mis hermanos. Ellos me ______ unas tarjetas postales muy bonitas. Las ______ ayer.

5. leer creer

   —¿Uds. ______ las noticias en el periódico anoche?

   —Sí, las ______, pero Jorge no las ______.

6. buscar

   —¿Tú ______ las llaves?

   —No, no las ______.

25. **¿Qué compraron?** With a partner, ask each other questions about what the following people purchased and how much each item cost.

Modelo Tú —¿Qué compraste tú?
—*Compré una blusa (*blouse*).*
—¿Cuánto te costó?
—*Me costó cuarenta dólares.*

1.

2.

3.

4.

5.

Para conversar

26. **¡Habla con tu compañero(a)!** With a partner, talk about what you did this morning, yesterday, and last weekend. Focus on routine and extraordinary activities, using regular verbs in the preterit.

Modelo —*¿Qué comiste ayer?*
—*Ayer comí ensalada de papas.*

27. **¿Qué hiciste tú...?** With a partner, have a conversation about what your family and friends did yesterday using the following verbs.

Modelo —*¿Dónde almorzaste ayer?*
—*Almorcé en la cafetería.*

almorzar	escribir	mirar	trabajar	volver	conversar
cenar	leer	pagar	ver	mandar	bailar
cerrar	llegar	practicar	buscar	salir	beber

5 Ordinal numbers (*Números ordinales*)

primero(a)[1]	*first*	**sexto(a)**	*sixth*
segundo(a)[1]	*second*	**séptimo(a)**	*seventh*
tercero(a)[1]	*third*	**octavo(a)**	*eighth*
cuarto(a)	*fourth*	**noveno(a)**	*ninth*
quinto(a)	*fifth*	**décimo(a)**	*tenth*

› Ordinal numbers agree in gender and number with the nouns they modify.

el segundo **chico**	la segunda **chica**
los primeros **días**	las primeras **semanas**

› Ordinal numbers are seldom used after **décimo** (*tenth*).

Un dicho
Los últimos serán los primeros.
Equivalent: *The last shall be first.*

[1]abbreviated 1°, 2°, 3°, and so on

¡Atención! The ordinal numbers **primero** and **tercero** drop the final **-o** before masculine singular nouns.

el **primer**[1] día	el **tercer**[2] año
—Nosotros estamos en el **segundo** piso. ¿Y Uds.?	*We are on the second floor. And you?*
—Estamos en el **tercer** piso.	*We are on the third floor.*

[1]abbreviated 1er [2]abbreviated 3er

Práctica

28. Ordena los números. Match the cardinal numbers in column A with the corresponding ordinal numbers in column B.

A				**B**	
nueve	_____	cuatro	_____	a. séptimo	f. octavo
dos	_____	ocho	_____	b. décimo	g. quinto
cinco	_____	tres	_____	c. primero	h. segundo
siete	_____	seis	_____	d. sexto	i. noveno
uno	_____	diez	_____	e. tercero	j. cuarto

29. ¿Es el primero...? Complete the following sentences with the appropriate ordinal numbers.

1. Según la Biblia, Adán fue (*was*) el __________ hombre y Eva fue la __________ mujer.
2. Febrero es el __________ mes del año y mayo es el __________ mes.
3. En el calendario hispano el miércoles es el __________ día de la semana y el domingo es el __________ día.
4. El Día de Acción de Gracias es el ________ jueves de noviembre.
5. El ________ mes del año es junio y el ________ mes es octubre.

30. Concurso de belleza (*Beauty contest*) In a beauty contest, these are the ten finalists. With a partner, put their names in order, according to the points that they have accumulated.

Modelo *Maribel Fuentes es la primera; Isabel Reyes...*

1. Lucía Ayala:	450 pts.	6. Mireya Vargas:	760 pts.
2. Teresa Peñarol:	560 pts.	7. María Inés Valles:	490 pts.
3. Ana Luisa Peña:	380 pts.	8. Isabel Reyes:	800 pts.
4. Maribel Fuentes:	850 pts.	9. Marcela Vigo:	700 pts.
5. Silvia Torres:	600 pts.	10. Gloria Calderón:	500 pts.

Para conversar

31. ¿En qué piso están? Imagine that the whole class is staying at a 10-story hotel in Costa Rica. Your classmates were assigned rooms on different floors. With a partner, have a conversation about who is on what floor, where the restaurant is, where the swimming pool is, etc.

Modelo S1: ¿En qué piso está Karina?
S2: Karina está en el segundo piso.

¡Vamos a ver!

Antes de ver el video

32. **Preguntas** You and a partner, take turns asking and answering the following questions in complete sentences:

1. Cuando tú reservas una habitación en un hotel, ¿llamas para confirmarla?
2. ¿Prefieres una habitación en el octavo piso o en el primer piso? ¿Por qué?
3. Cuando tú estás en un hotel, ¿quién lleva tu equipaje a tu cuarto, tú o el botones?
4. Cuando sales del hotel, ¿llevas la llave contigo o la dejas en la recepción?
5. Generalmente, ¿hasta qué hora sirven la cena en un restaurante? Si estás en un hotel, ¿tú usas el servicio de habitación?
6. Si tu cuarto está en el tercer piso, ¿usas el ascensor o usas la escalera para hacer ejercicio?
7. Si el hotel tiene piscina, ¿nadas un rato?
8. Cuando tú miras televisión, ¿te gusta más ver las noticias o ver una película?
9. ¿Prefieres ver un drama o una comedia romántica?
10. ¿Tú prefieres mandarles mensajes instantáneos a tus amigos o prefieres mandarles tarjetas postales?

El video: Una familia panameña en Costa Rica

Me llamo Rubén Saldaña. Mi familia y yo necesitamos una habitación para cuatro personas, con dos camas dobles.

Vamos a nuestro cuarto. ¿Dónde está el ascensor? Estoy cansada.

Yo voy a usar la escalera. Necesito hacer ejercicio.

¿Por qué no miras la película con nosotras? Te prometo que te va a gustar. Es una comedia romántica...

Después de ver el video

El empleado

Rubén

Paola

Beatriz

Ariana

33. ¿Quién lo dice? Identify the person who said each of the following in the dialogues.

1. El botones puede llevar las maletas a su cuarto. __________
2. A mí me gusta más mirar las noticias. __________
3. Yo quiero mirar televisión hasta tarde. __________
4. Rubén... ya cenamos... ¡Y tú comiste muchísimo! __________
5. No me gusta la cama. El colchón no es muy cómodo. __________
6. ¿En qué puedo servirle, señor? __________
7. ¿El hotel tiene servicio de habitación? __________
8. Yo necesito mandarle un mensaje instantáneo a Carolina. __________
9. ¿Por qué no miras la película con nosotras? __________
10. Yo voy a usar la escalera. Necesito hacer ejercicio. __________

34. Hablemos With a partner, take turns asking and answering the following questions. Base your answers on the dialogue.

1. ¿Dónde están Rubén Saldaña y su familia?
2. ¿Qué pide la familia Saldaña en el hotel?
3. ¿En qué piso está la habitación de la familia Saldaña?
4. ¿A quién quiere mandarle un mensaje instantáneo Paola?
5. ¿Quién lleva las maletas al cuarto?
6. En el hotel, ¿hasta qué hora sirven la cena?
7. ¿Ariana va a usar la escalera o el ascensor? ¿Por qué?
8. ¿Qué quiere hacer Paola en la piscina?
9. ¿Qué dice Paola del colchón?
10. ¿Qué quieren mirar Beatriz y las chicas? ¿Qué quiere mirar Rubén?

35. ¿Qué pasa después...? You and a partner, use your imagination to say what the characters do. In Spanish, discuss the following.

1. Whether Paola sends Carolina a message or sends her another postcard, and what she says to her friend.
2. Whether or not they watch the movie on channel 4.
3. Whether Beatriz watches the news with her husband after the movie.
4. Whether or not they go to the Lankester Garden and to the Braulio Carrillo Park and what they do afterward.
5. Whether they go to a restaurant in the evening or whether they use room service. Does Rubén eat a lot?
6. Whether there are other teenagers at the hotel and whether the girls talk to them.

Now compare your statements with those of the members of another group.

¡Vamos a escuchar!

ESTRATEGIA **Listening to authentic language** When listening to authentic programs and commercials, listen as attentively as you can, but don't feel frustated if you don't understand everything. Seek out opportunities to listen to Spanish speakers or Spanish-language television and try to identify what the subject of conversation or discussion is; catch as many words and phrases as you can. With time and continued practice, your comprehension level *will* improve.

CD2-5 **36. Turismo local** You will listen three times to a fragment from a Costa Rican TV program on local tourism.

1. Escuche por primera vez y conteste: ¿De qué trata (*deals with*) este fragmento?
2. Escuche por segunda vez y conteste:
   a. ¿Cuántas habitaciones tiene el hotel?
   b. ¿Dónde está el hotel? ¿Cuántas personas trabajan en el hotel?
   c. ¿Qué tipos de restaurantes hay en la zona?
3. Escuche por tercera vez y conteste: ¿Hacia qué lugar dan (*overlook*) las habitaciones del hotel?

¡Vamos a conversar!

ESTRATEGIA **Simplifying ideas through paraphrasing** An important skill in conversation is to be able to bring the interaction to a manageable level so you can participate. Paraphrasing and simplifying ideas is one technique that enables you to engage with others in discussion. For instance, when talking with someone, you can demonstrate your understanding of a statement by expressing it in simpler words.

37. ¿Cómo? You will hear a series of sentences on familiar topics. Listen and express an approximation of the message of each one. Then compare your responses with those of a classmate to determine whether you've understood the essence of the message.
CD2-6

Modelo *You hear:* Para quienes les gusta la comida internacional hay un gran número de restaurantes en la zona entre los cuales escoger. *Sample paraphrase:* Si te gusta la comida internacional, hay muchos restaurantes aquí que la sirven.

38. ¿Qué dice Ud.? What would you say in the following situations? What might the other person say? Act out the scenes with a partner. Take turns playing each role.

1. You have just checked into a hotel. You want to know what time they serve breakfast, and whether they have room service.
2. You tell someone that you want to send a postcard to your best friend.
3. You tell a traveling companion that you want to go to your room for a while because they are showing a good movie on channel four.
4. You are checking in at a hotel in Costa Rica. Ask about prices and accommodations. Make sure you get a room with an ocean view.
5. You are a hotel employee and ask a guest what you can do for him/her.
6. You ask the concierge two questions: what time you have to vacate the room and where the American embassy or consulate is.

39. **Para conocernos mejor** To do this activity, work with a classmate whom you would like to get to know. Take turns asking each other these questions.

1. Cuando viajas, ¿haces reservaciones para el hotel antes de salir de viaje? ¿Prefieres una habitación interior o con vista a la calle (al mar)? ¿Cuál es tu hotel favorito?
2. ¿Prefieres un cuarto en el segundo piso o en el décimo piso? Si el cuarto no tiene baño privado, ¿lo aceptas?
3. Cuando viajas, ¿les mandas tarjetas postales a tus amigos? ¿Sacas muchas fotografías cuando viajas? ¿Prefieres llevar una cámara fotográfica o una cámara de video? ¿Compras algo en la tienda de regalos del hotel?
4. ¿Prefieres cenar en tu cuarto si el hotel tiene servicio de habitación o te gusta más ir a un restaurante? ¿Cuál es tu restaurante favorito? ¿Es muy caro?
5. Cuando estás de viaje, ¿miras televisión? ¿Qué tipos de programas te gustan más? ¿Tienes un canal favorito? ¿Cuál? ¿Viste alguna película anoche? ¿Te gustó?
6. ¿Qué lugares te gusta visitar cuando estás de vacaciones? ¿Te gusta más viajar solo(a), con tus amigos o con tu familia? ¿Cuándo son tus próximas vacaciones? ¿Adónde piensas ir? ¿Cuánto tiempo hace que no viajas?

40. **Una encuesta** Interview your classmates to identify who fits the following descriptions. Include your instructor, but remember to use the **Ud.** form when addressing him/her. After finishing the survey, get together with two or three classmates and discuss the results.

1. Siempre va de vacaciones en el verano.	______________
2. No le gusta viajar en grupo.	______________
3. Lleva mucho equipaje cuando viaja.	______________
4. Tiene un jardín en su casa.	______________
5. Siempre ve las noticias en la tele.	______________
6. Tiene piscina en su casa.	______________
7. Hace ejercicio todos los días.	______________
8. Camina una milla (*mile*) todos los días.	______________

41. **De viaje** (*Traveling*) Get together with a couple of your classmates and plan a trip to a Spanish-speaking country. Visit a Web site to obtain information about the country you are going to visit. Find out about hotels, rate of exchange, places of interest, and so on. Discuss how and when you will be leaving, how much spending money you'll bring, what cities and special sites you intend to visit, and what you will need to take with you.

42. **Para crear** Get together in groups of three and "create" the scenario for this photo. Who are the people in it? Give them names and say where they are coming from and where they are going. What places of interest are they going to visit? What kind of accommodations do they want?

¡Vamos a leer!

Antes de leer

ESTRATEGIA **Guessing meaning from context** Continue to practice guessing the meaning of unknown words by examining the surrounding context. Remember to look for clues such as cognates, other familiar words, and to make logical guesses based on what you know.

43. Los hoteles Before reading this "to do" list when making hotel reservations, try to guess the meaning of the highlighted words in these sentences:

1. Decidir el tipo y la **calidad** de los hoteles que mejor **se ajustan** a su **presupuesto** y preferencias.
2. Usar la Internet para comparar **precios** y servicios que el hotel **ofrece**.
3. Leer en la Internet los comentarios de personas que **se hospedaron** en el hotel.
4. **Averiguar** las horas de **llegada** y **salida** de la habitación.

¡A leer!

44. Comprensión As you read the "to do" list, find the answers to the following questions.

1. Además de decidir nuestras preferencias sobre los tipos de hoteles, ¿qué más debemos tener en cuenta (*keep in mind*)?
2. ¿Qué debemos recordar sobre la clasificación de los hoteles por el número de estrellas?
3. ¿Qué debemos comparar?
4. ¿Qué debemos leer en la Internet?
5. ¿Cuándo debemos hacer la reservación?
6. ¿Qué debemos especificar bien?
7. ¿Qué debemos averiguar sobre los impuestos?
8. ¿Qué debemos preguntar sobre la transportación?

Cómo reservar habitaciones de hotel

Si va a hacer una reservación en un hotel, Ud. debe…

1. …decidir el tipo y la calidad de los hoteles que mejor se ajustan a su presupuesto° y preferencias. — *budget*

2. …recordar que clasifican los hoteles por el número de estrellas°, pero que las estrellas no significan lo mismo en todos los países. — *stars*

3. …usar la Internet para comparar precios y servicios que el hotel ofrece.

4. …leer en la Internet los comentarios de personas que se hospedaron° allí. — *stayed*

5. …hacer la reservación lo antes posible°. — **lo…** *as soon as possible*

6. …especificar bien el tipo de habitación que desea.

7. …averiguar° si los impuestos° están incluidos en el precio de la habitación. — *find out / taxes*

8. …preguntar si el hotel ofrece transportación gratis desde y hasta° el aeropuerto. — **desde…** *from and to*

9. ...confirmar la reservación varios días antes de iniciar el viaje.
10. ...notificar al hotel si va a llegar tarde. En este caso, por lo general, los hoteles cobran° por adelantado°.
11. ...averiguar cuándo se puede cancelar la reservación sin tener que pagar extra.
12. ...averiguar las horas de llegada° y salida° de la habitación.

charge / in advance

check in / check out

Después de leer...

45. **Desde su mundo** In groups of three or four, discuss the following.

1. What you always do when reserving a room at a hotel.
2. What you don't do, that you should.
3. Which hotels you recommend (hint: **yo recomiendo...**)
   a. for people who have money
   b. for people who can't spend (*gastar*) much money.

¡Vamos a escribir!

Antes de escribir

ESTRATEGIA **Summarizing and organizing** When writing an e-mail, brevity and organization are important. Also, remember the words you use to indicate "To whom," "from whom," and "regarding" used in the e-mail.

¡A escribir!

46. **Un mensaje electrónico** You will be writing an e-mail to a friend who is going to be traveling for the first time. Keeping in mind the advice given on hotel reservations, ask him whether he already *(ya)* did some of the things he must do. For example:

1. ¿Ya decidiste qué tipo de hotel te gusta?
   Ask about the following numbers: 3, 4, 6, 7, 8, 9, 11, 12

Después de escribir

47. **A revisar** Before writing the final version of your e-mail, exchange your first draft with a classmate and peer edit each other's work. Notice the use of the preterit.

› formation of all verbs and subject-verb agreement
› noun-adjective agreement
› clear topic in each paragraph

Costa Rica

¿Te gusta acampar, ir a la playa, escalar (*to climb*) montañas y estar cerca de la naturaleza, pero al mismo tiempo quieres proteger el medio ambiente (*environment*)? En ese caso, debes admirar el ecoturismo, que trata (*tries*) de conservar los recursos naturales del planeta y educar a los turistas en cuestiones ambientales. Quizás puedes unirte a las millones de personas que viajan a Costa Rica, el país más visitado de Centroamérica.

Un país extraordinario

Costa Rica tiene una de las mejores economías de Centroamérica. Produce principalmente café, bananas, caña de azúcar (*sugar cane*) y flores.

San José, la capital, no es una gran ciudad, pero tiene lugares muy interesantes como el Jardín Botánico de Lankester y el Museo del Oro.

El Parque Nacional Braulio Carrillo tiene varios volcanes. Por su gran tamaño (*size*) y su variada altitud, mantiene uno de los niveles (*levels*) más altos de biodiversidad.

Un gran presidente

Óscar Arias ganó la presidencia de Costa Rica en 1986. Trabajó con los presidentes de Guatemala, El Salvador y Honduras para terminar con la guerra en Centroamérica. En 1987 recibió el Premio Nobel de la Paz.

Panamá

¿No crees que sería (*it would be*) interesante visitar el país y navegar por las aguas del famoso canal? Panamá está situado en Centroamérica entre Colombia y Costa Rica. Limita con el Mar Caribe y el Océano Pacífico. Su posición en el Istmo de Panamá es estratégica.

La principal fuente de ingreso de Panamá proviene del famoso Canal, que divide su territorio y une los Océanos Atlántico y Pacífico. Junto al Canal están las dos ciudades más grandes del país: Ciudad de Panamá, su capital, y Colón, la segunda ciudad más importante del país.

Puntos de interés turístico

© B. Franklin/Shutterstock.com

Entre las hazañas (*heroic deeds*) pacíficas realizadas por el hombre, que contribuyen significativamente al progreso mundial (*world*), la construcción del Canal es un logro (*achievement*) excepcional.

© Bradley Ireland/DanitaDelimont.com

Los turistas comienzan a descubrir las bellezas ecológicas de Panamá, especialmente sus selvas tropicales, la gran cantidad de arrecifes (*reefs*) de coral de sus costas, y la extraordinaria variedad de peces que viven en ellos.

© Gonzalo Azumendi/age fotostock

La isla Barro Colorado ubicada en la parte grande del Canal es una reserva biológica donde se realizan investigaciones científicas. Está controlada por el Instituto Smithsonian.

Un famoso cantante y actor

© STR/Reuters/Corbis

Rubén Blades es un famoso cantante y actor, que trabajó en muchas películas de Hollywood. Participa activamente en la política de su país.

Ahora dime...

In groups of three, take turns asking and answering the following questions.

1. ¿Estás de acuerdo (*Do you agree*) con las ideas y los objetivos del ecoturismo? ¿Son importantes estas ideas en este país?
2. ¿Qué parque nacional de este país crees tú que recibe la mayor cantidad de turismo?
3. ¿Existen programas de educación ambiental en tu ciudad? Nombra alguno.

iLrn™

To learn more about Costa Rica and Panamá, watch the cultural footage in the Media Library.

AUTOPRUEBA

¿Cuánto sé ahora?

Take this test. When you have finished, check your answers in the answer key provided in Appendix D. Then use a red pen to correct any mistakes you may have made. Are you ready?

A. Indirect object pronouns Give the Spanish equivalent of the words in parentheses.

1. Elsa ________ las llaves. (*gives them*)
2. Yo siempre ________ que el español es fácil. (*tell him*)
3. El botones ________ el equipaje, señora. (*is going to bring you*)
4. Él ________ el desayuno. (*serves us*)
5. Ana va a ________ una cámara de video. (*buy me*)
6. Ellos ________ en inglés, pero nosotros ________ en español. (*speak to us / speak to them*)

B. Constructions with *gustar* Indicate who likes what. Add any necessary words.

1. Elsa / tomar / una siesta
2. ellos / caminar / por jardín
3. yo / habitación / con vista al mar
4. nosotros / más / ese colchón
5. ¿tú / más / nadar / piscina?
6. ¿Uds. / viajar / el verano?

C. Time expressions with *hacer* Form sentences with the elements provided, using the expression **hace... que.** Follow the model.

Modelo una hora / él / trabajar
Hace una hora que él trabaja.

1. dos días / yo / no dormir
2. un mes / tú / no llamarme
3. media hora / nosotras / estar / aquí
4. un año / ellos / vivir / Panamá
5. doce horas / Eva / no comer
6. quince minutos / Uds. / hablar / por teléfono

D. Preterit of regular verbs Complete the following sentences, using the verbs given.

1. Anoche yo ________ (llamar) al hotel, ________ (reservar) una habitación y ________ (pagar) trescientos dólares por dos noches.
2. Yo ________ (llegar) a las ocho, y ________ (empezar) a estudiar.
3. María ________ (leer) la nota que tú ________ (dejar), pero Teresa y Jorge no la ________ (leer).
4. Rafael ________ (volver) de su viaje ayer. Le ________ (gustar) todos los lugares (*places*) que ________ (visitar).
5. Yo ________ (salir) del hotel a las doce y ________ (almorzar) en la cafetería. ________ (regresar) por la tarde y ________ (nadar) un rato. Por la noche ________ (mirar) una película en la televisión.
6. Yo ________ (buscar) las tarjetas postales que me ________ (mandar) mis padres, pero no las ________ (encontrar).

E. Ordinal numbers Complete the following sentences.

1. Marzo es el ________ mes del año.
2. Mayo es el ________ mes del año.
3. Abril es el ________ mes del año.
4. El ________ mes del año es octubre.
5. Agosto es el ________ mes del año.
6. Enero es el ________ mes del año.

F. Just words...

a. Write the words or phrases that correspond to the following.

1. valija ________
2. ascensor ________
3. enviar ________
4. bañadera ________
5. piscina ________
6. reservación ________
7. opuesto de **trabajar** ________
8. opuesto de **a la derecha** ________

b. Complete the following exchanges, using vocabulary from **Lección 7**.

1. —¿Dónde compraste la ________ de video?
   —La compré en el hotel, en la ________ de regalos que está ________ del elevador.
2. —¿En qué ________ servirles?
   —Tenemos una ________ a ________ de Isabel López. Queremos una habitación ________.
3. —¿Qué quieres hacer ahora?
   —Podemos ________ ejercicio o ________ por el jardín.
4. —¿El hotel tiene ________ de habitación?
   —Sí, mañana por la mañana podemos ________ en el cuarto.
5. —¿Cómo es el ________ de tu cama?
   —Es muy ________. Me gusta mucho.
6. —¿El baño tiene ________ o bañadera?
   —Solamente tiene bañadera.
7. —¿Uds. tienen reservación?
   —No, pero estamos en la ________ de espera.
8. —¿Vas a ir de vacaciones este verano?
   —No, no puedo ir. Voy a ________ la reservación del hotel.
9. —¿A cómo está el ________ de moneda?
   —No sé.
10. —¿Qué necesitas para viajar a Costa Rica?
    —El ________ o la ________ de turista.

G. Cultura

1. Complete the following, based on the information found in the **¿Lo sabía Ud.?** sections.
   a. Las ________ son más económicas que los hoteles y generalmente incluyen el cuarto y la ________.
   b. Generalmente, en las pensiones, el precio incluye el cuarto y las ________.
2. Complete the following, based on the information found in the **El mundo hispánico y tú** section.
   a. Costa Rica tiene una de las mejores ________ de Centroamérica.
   b. La principal fuente de ingreso de Panamá proviene del famoso ________ de Panamá.

H. Un dicho Do you remember the Spanish saying that is equivalent to *"He went from bad to worse"*? Find it in this lesson.

LECCIÓN 8

HACIENDO DILIGENCIAS

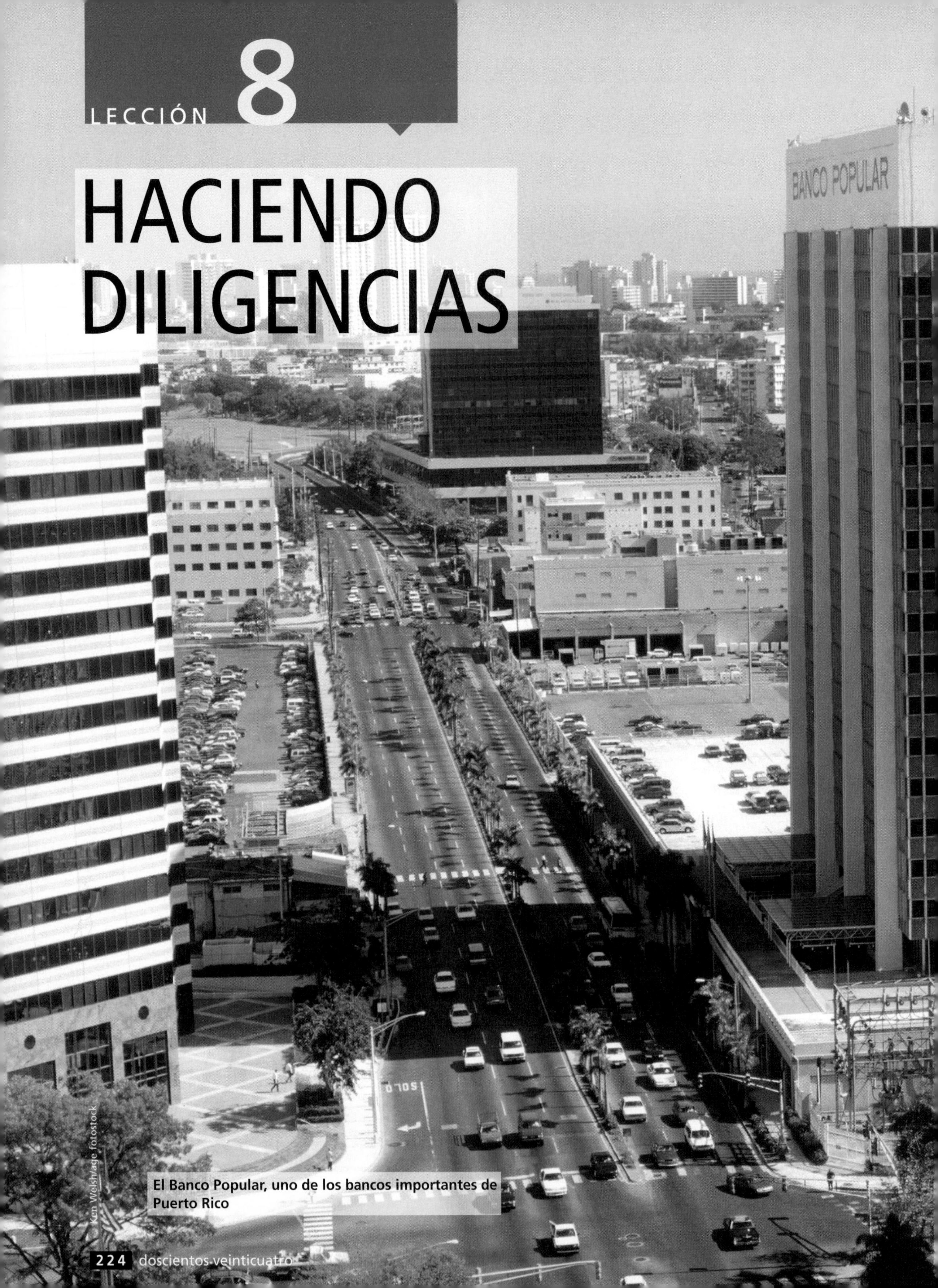

Ken Welsh/age fotostock

El Banco Popular, uno de los bancos importantes de Puerto Rico

OBJETIVOS COMUNICATIVOS

You will learn vocabulary related to banking and running errands. You will also be able to talk about flowers and pets.

SITUACIONES

¡Qué supersticioso eres!

ESTRUCTURAS

1 Direct and indirect object pronouns used together
2 Preterit of **ser**, **ir**, and **dar**
3 Preterit of **e:i** and **o:u** stem-changing verbs
4 Uses of **por** and **para**
5 Formation of adverbs

ASÍ SOMOS

¡Vamos a ver!
Watching and understanding situations

¡Vamos a escuchar!
Guessing meaning from context

¡Vamos a conversar!
Paraphrasing practice I

¡Vamos a leer!
Reading critically

¡Vamos a escribir!
Writing journal entries

EL MUNDO HISPÁNICO Y TÚ...

› Puerto Rico

AUTOPRUEBA

You will review what you learned in this lesson.

PUERTO RICO, "La isla del Encanto", es la menor de las islas que forman el archipiélago de las Antillas Mayores. Los indígenas la llamaban **Boriquén**, y aún hoy muchos la llaman así, y llaman **boricuas** a sus habitantes.

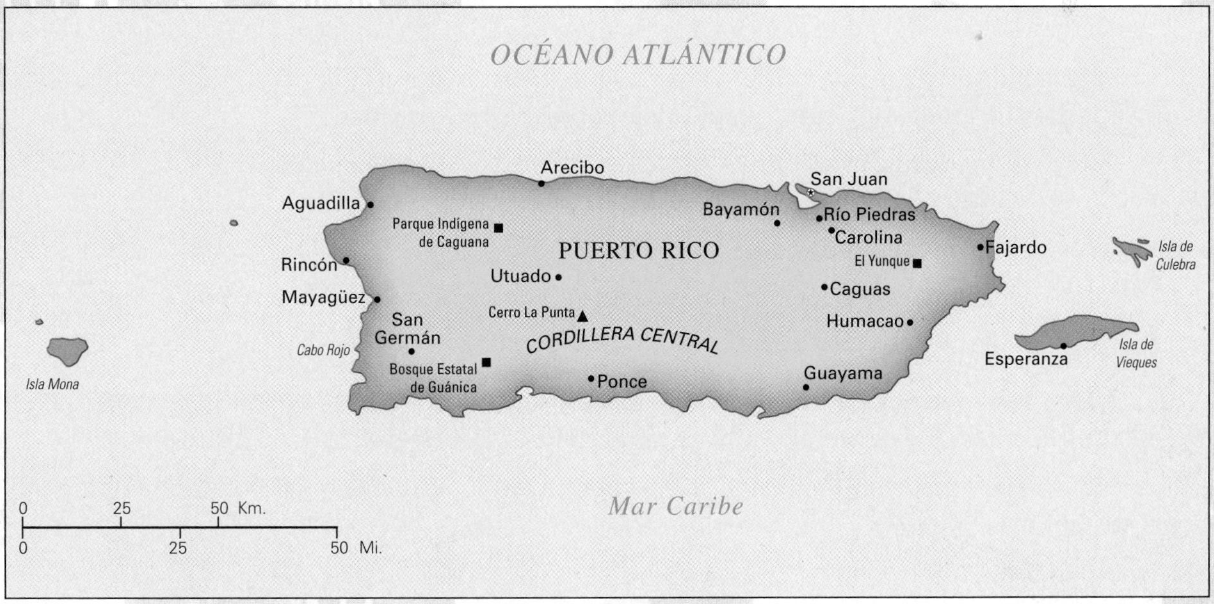

Recursos iLrn video audio web playlist

SITUACIONES

¡Qué supersticioso eres!

CD2-7

© Cengage Learning

¡Ubíquelos!

The Villegas family lives in San Juan, the capital of Puerto Rico. Watching the video will give you an opportunity to learn about the places that this family often visits.

Ocean/Corbis

Rafael Villegas, un muchacho de diecinueve años, vive con sus padres y una hermana en una casa de la avenida Ponce de León, en San Juan, la capital de Puerto Rico. Ahora está hablando con Sandra, su hermana mayor. Los dos tienen que hacer muchas diligencias, pero Rafael piensa que no deben salir de casa porque hoy es martes trece que, como todos saben, es un día de mala suerte.

SANDRA: ¿Fuiste a la tintorería a recoger tus pantalones?

RAFAEL: Sí, pero no me los dieron. No están listos. ¿Viste? ¡Martes trece!

SANDRA: ¡Eso es una tontería! Oye, yo tengo que ir al banco para depositar dinero en mi cuenta corriente y en mi cuenta de ahorros. Y voy a pedir un préstamo.

RAFAEL: Desgraciadamente, no te lo van a dar. ¡Martes trece!

SANDRA: ¡Ay, bendito![1] ¡Qué supersticioso eres! Bueno, tienes que ir a la florería y comprar un ramo de rosas para tía Estela. Hoy es su cumpleaños. Por favor, no te olvides.

RAFAEL: Estoy seguro de que es alérgica a las flores. Bueno, voy a llevar la moto.

SANDRA: Sí, pero... ¡No puedes estacionar frente a una boca de incendios! La semana pasada un policía te dio una multa. ¿Recuerdas?

RAFAEL: Sí, sí... solamente voy a comprar unos peces de colores para Robertito. No voy a tardar.

Por la noche, Rafael y Sandra están charlando en la sala.

SANDRA: ¿Qué tal te fue hoy, Rafael? ¿A dónde fuiste? ¿Pasó algo malo? ¿Te robaron la moto? ¿Tía Estela sufrió un ataque de alergia? ¿Los peces de colores se murieron? ¿Fue un día terrible?

RAFAEL: No... no pasó nada... y a tía Estela le encantaron las flores que le regalamos... En fin, fue un día casi normal...

[1] **¡Ay, bendito!** = *Oh, my goodness!* (a common phrase in Puerto Rico)

Sandra: ¡Ah! Pasé por el banco y me dieron el préstamo que solicité. Y puedo prestarte los cincuenta dólares que necesitas para comprar el regalo para tu novia.

Rafael: ¡Un momento! ¡Sandra! ¡Quizás tú y yo estamos equivocados! Según los estadounidenses, ¡el día de mala suerte es el **viernes** trece! ¿Dónde hay un calendario? ¡El próximo viernes trece no salgo de casa!

LEARNING TIP

You are learning standard Spanish for the most part. As is the case in English, different regions of the Spanish-speaking world use different words for common things. In **"Un martes trece,"** Rafael and his sister Sandra would normally use the following Puerto Rican terms: **motocicleta** = **motora, florería** = **floristería**, and **policía** = **guardia**.

¿Lo sabía Ud.?

En los países hispanos por lo general los jóvenes (*young people*) viven con su familia hasta que se casan (*get married*), pero esto está cambiando un poco, especialmente en las ciudades grandes.

› **Generalmente, ¿hasta qué edad viven con sus padres los jóvenes de este país?**

1. Hablemos With a partner, take turns asking and answering the following questions. Base your answers on the dialogue and on your own circumstances.

En el diálogo

1. ¿Qué tienen que hacer Sandra y Rafael?
2. ¿Qué dice Rafael del martes 13?
3. ¿Qué fue a recoger Rafael a la tintorería?
4. ¿En qué cuentas va a depositar dinero Sandra?
5. ¿Qué va a pedir Sandra?
6. ¿Qué va a comprar Rafael?
7. ¿Para quién son las flores?
8. ¿Por qué le dieron una multa a Rafael?
9. ¿Para qué necesita dinero Rafael?
10. ¿Qué no va a hacer Rafael el próximo viernes 13?

¿Y tú?

1. ¿Qué tienes que hacer tú?
2. ¿Tú crees que el viernes 13 es un día de buena o de mala suerte?
3. ¿Tú mandas la ropa a la tintorería o la lavas en tu casa?
4. ¿Qué cuentas tienes tú en el banco?
5. ¿Tú piensas pedir un préstamo?
6. ¿Cuál es tu flor favorita?
7. ¿Para quién compras flores tú?
8. ¿Te dieron una multa alguna vez (*ever*)?
9. ¿Para qué necesitas dinero tú?
10. ¿Tú eres supersticioso(a)?

¿Lo sabía Ud.?

En los países hispanos el día de "mala suerte" es el martes trece y no el viernes trece. Dice un dicho, "Martes trece ni te cases ni te embarques" (*Don't get married or get on a boat [travel] on Tuesday the 13th*).

› **En este país, ¿toman muy en serio la idea de que el viernes trece es un día de mala suerte?**

VOCABULARIO

En el diálogo

Cognados

la alergia	*allergy*
alérgico(a)	*allergic*
la avenida	*avenue*
el banco	*bank*
el calendario	*calendar*
la capital	*capital*
la motocicleta, la moto	*motorcycle*
normal	*normal*
el (la) policía	*police officer (policeman / policewoman)*
probablemente	*probably*
la rosa	*rose*
solamente	*only*
supersticioso(a)	*superstitious*
terrible	*terrible*

Nombres

la boca de incendios, el hidrante	*fire hydrant*
la cuenta	*account*
—corriente	*checking account*
—de ahorros	*savings account*
la flor	*flower*
la florería	*flower shop*
el incendio, el fuego	*fire*
la multa	*fine, ticket*
los pantalones	*pants, trousers*
el pez de color	*goldfish*
el préstamo	*loan*
el ramo	*bouquet*
el regalo	*present*
la suerte	*luck*
la tintorería	*dry cleaner's*
la tontería	*nonsense, foolishness*

Verbos

depositar	*to deposit*
estacionar, aparcar, parquear	*to park*
morirse (o:ue)	*to die*
pasar, ocurrir	*to happen*
prestar	*to lend*
regalar	*to give (as a gift)*
robar	*to steal*
sufrir	*to suffer*

Adjetivos

demasiado(a)	*too*
equivocado(a)	*wrong*
listo(a)	*ready*
malo(a)	*bad*
seguro(a)	*sure*

Otras palabras y expresiones

el ataque de alergia	*allergy attack*
casi	*almost*
como todos saben	*as everybody knows*
dar (poner) una multa	*to fine*
desgraciadamente, por desgracia, desafortunadamente	*unfortunately*
en fin...	*anyway . . .*
encantarle a uno	*to love*
frente a	*in front of*
hacer diligencias	*to run errands*
pedir (solicitar) un préstamo	*to apply for a loan*
¡Qué supersticioso(a) eres!	*How superstitious you are!*
salir de casa	*to leave the house*
todo	*all, everything*
todos(as)	*everybody*

© Ocean/Corbis

¿Lo sabía Ud.?

Cada nación latinoamericana tiene un banco central encargado de (*in charge of*) emitir el dinero y de controlar la actividad de los bancos comerciales. En algunos países hay también sucursales (*branches*) de bancos extranjeros.

› **En este país, ¿qué institución está encargada de emitir el dinero?**

Más sobre el tema

Animales

En el banco

a plazos	*on installments*
abrir una cuenta	*to open an account*
ahorrar	*to save (i.e., money)*
al contado	*in cash*
el cajero automático	*automatic teller (ATM)*
el cheque de viajero	*traveler's check*
cobrar un cheque	*to cash a check*
la cuenta conjunta	*joint account*
en efectivo	*in cash*
estar seguro	*to be sure*
fechar	*to date (a check, a letter, etc.)*
la firma	*signature*
firmar	*to sign*
gratis	*free of charge*
el talonario de cheques, la chequera	*checkbook*

Flores

la camelia	*camellia*
el clavel	*carnation*
el geranio	*geranium*
la lila	*lilac*
la margarita	*daisy*
la orquídea	*orchid*
el pensamiento	*pansy*
el tulipán	*tulip*
la violeta	*violet*

¿Lo sabía Ud.?

El uso de cheques no es tan común en Latinoamérica como en los Estados Unidos y en Canadá, pero muchos bancos tienen sus propias (*own*) tarjetas de crédito.

› **Generalmente, ¿cómo paga la gente de este país cuando va de compras?**

VOCABULARIO

Práctica

2. Preguntas y respuestas Match the questions in column A with the responses in column B.

A		B
1. ______	¿Cuál es tu flor favorita?	a. Del cajero automático.
2. ______	¿Vas a ir al banco?	b. Sí, y me dio una multa.
3. ______	¿Dónde estacionaste la moto?	c. No, a plazos.
4. ______	¿Hablaste con el policía?	d. Sí, se lo di anoche.
5. ______	¿Compraste el regalo para Olga?	e. No, de ahorros.
6. ______	¿Adónde llevaste los pantalones?	f. Frente a una boca de incendios.
7. ______	¿De dónde sacaste el dinero?	g. No, un canario.
8. ______	¿Tienes cuenta corriente?	h. La margarita.
9. ______	¿Lo compraste al contado?	i. A la tintorería.
10. ______	¿Tienes un loro?	j. Sí, voy a solicitar un préstamo.

3. ¿Qué es? Write the words or phrases that correspond to the following.

1. que tiene alergia
2. lugar donde venden flores
3. fuego
4. aparcar
5. pasar
6. por desgracia
7. gustarle mucho a uno
8. poner la fecha
9. chequera
10. Garfield, por ejemplo

4. Oraciones incompletas Complete the following sentences, using vocabulary from this lesson.

1. Por _________ me robaron la motocicleta. ¡Qué mala _________!
2. Hoy tengo que hacer muchas _________. Voy a salir de _________ a las ocho.
3. Mi esposa y yo vamos a _________ una cuenta _________.
4. Le regalé un _________ de rosas y unos _________ de colores.
5. Necesito 40 dólares, ¿tú me los puedes _________?
6. No va a hacer nada el martes _________ porque es muy _________.
7. Mi hermano sufrió un _________ de alergia anoche.
8. Me gustan mucho los pensamientos. ¡Me _________!
9. No debes decir eso. ¡Es una _________!
10. Voy a _________ el cheque y voy a _________ el dinero en el banco.

Para conversar

5. Problemas y más problemas With a partner, take turns indicating what these people can do about all the problems they had last week.

Modelo Anita compró dos peces de colores y los dos murieron (*died*).
Anita puede comprar otros peces de colores y preguntarle al empleado cómo cuidarlos (to take care of them).

1. Paloma solicitó un préstamo en el banco y no se lo dieron.
2. Roberto tiene que comprarle un regalo de cumpleaños a su novia y no tiene mucho dinero.
3. Beto quiere comprar un ramo de flores para una chica, pero no sabe qué flores le gustan a ella.
4. Julio quiere ahorrar dinero para comprar una motocicleta pero él gana (*earns*) muy poco.
5. A Marisa le robaron el coche el sábado pasado y ella no sabe cómo va a ir a la universidad.

6. **¡Cuántas diligencias!** With a partner, play the roles of two roommates who were supposed to run several errands yesterday. You ask each other whether or not you did certain things, including follow-up questions as much as possible (**¿Fuiste a...?**, **¿Compraste...?**, etcétera).

¿Fuiste al supermercado?

Pronunciación

CD 2-8

A. The Spanish *l*

The Spanish **l** is pronounced like the *l* in the English word *lean*. The tip of the tongue must touch the palate. Listen to your instructor and repeat the following sentences.

Laura y Si**l**via **l**e dan e**l** rega**l**o.

Luis vue**l**a a **l**a capita**l** e**l** **l**unes.

El po**l**icía **l**e dio una mu**l**ta a **L**o**l**a.

CD 2-9

B. The Spanish *r*

The Spanish **r** sounds something like the *dd* in the English word *ladder*. Listen to your instructor and repeat the following sentences.

Sa**r**a Bu**r**gos fue a la tinto**r**e**r**ía.

El teat**r**o ab**r**e a las t**r**es y cua**r**to.

Te**r**esa Ve**r**a comp**r**ó flo**r**es en la flo**r**e**r**ía.

CD 2-10

C. The Spanish *rr*

The Spanish **rr** is spelled **r** at the beginning of the word and after the letter **n** and **rr** between vowels. It is a strong trill. Listen to your instructor and repeat the following sentences.

Rosa **R**omero está abu**rr**ida.

En**r**ique **R**eyes come con **R**ita.

El a**rr**oz está **r**ico.

CD 2-11

D. The Spanish *z*

In Latin America, the Spanish **z** is pronounced like the *ss* in the English word *pressing*. In Spain, it is pronounced like the *th* in the English word *think*. Avoid using the buzzing sound of the English *z* in the words *zoo* and *zebra*. Listen to your instructor and repeat the following sentences.

La ta**z**a a**z**ul es de **Z**oila.

Zulema Pére**z** fue al **z**oológico.

El lápi**z** es del mo**z**o.

ESTRUCTURAS

1 Direct and indirect object pronouns used together (*Pronombres de complemento directo e indirecto usados juntos*)

› When an indirect object pronoun and a direct object pronoun are used together, the indirect object pronoun always comes first.

D.O.

Ana **me** da **la maleta.** → Ana **me** **la** da.

I.O.

› With an infinitive, the pronouns can either be placed before the conjugated verb or be attached to the infinitive.

I.O. D.O.

Ana **me** **la** va a dar.

Ana va a **dármela.**[1]

› With the present progressive, the pronouns can either be placed before the conjugated verb or be attached to the gerund.

I.O. D.O.

Ella **me** **lo** está diciendo.

Ella está **diciéndomelo.**[1]

› If both pronouns begin with **l**, the indirect object pronoun (**le** or **les**) is changed to **se.**

For clarification, it is sometimes necessary to add **a él, a ella, a Ud., a Uds., a ellos,** or **a ellas.**

D.O.

Ana **le** da **la cuenta.** → Ana **se** **la** da.

I.O.

—¿A quién le da la cuenta Ana?
—**Se** la da **a él.**

[1]Note the use of the written accent, which follows the rules for accentuation. See Appendix A.

Práctica

7. **Minidiálogos** Complete the following exchanges, using direct and indirect object pronouns. Then act them out with a partner, adding a sentence or two to each dialogue.

1. —¿Le vas a dar las lilas a tu novia?
   —Sí, _________ voy a dar esta tarde.
2. —¿Uds. nos van a traer el calendario?
   —Sí, _________ vamos a traer.
3. —¿Tus padres les van a comprar la tortuga a los niños?
   —No, no _________ van a comprar.
4. —¿El empleado siempre te da la libreta de ahorros?
   —Sí, él siempre _________ da.
5. —¿Me compraste los claveles?
   —Sí, _________ compré.
6. —¿Mis tíos les van a traer el perro a Uds.?
   —Sí, _________ van a traer esta tarde.

8. **Él nos ayuda** You have a friend who is always willing to help others. Explain how, using the information provided.

Modelo —Yo necesito un diccionario. (comprar) *Mi amigo* ***me lo*** *compra.*

1. Tú necesitas los cheques. (traer)
2. Yo necesito dos tarjetas. (comprar)
3. Nosotros necesitamos un préstamo. (dar)
4. Elsa necesita cheques de viajero. (comprar)
5. Mis hermanos necesitan dinero. (prestar)
6. Ud. necesita la chequera. (traer)
7. Yo quiero el talonario de cheques. (buscar)
8. Mi prima quiere unas flores. (comprar)

9. **Lo siento** With a partner, take turns asking and answering questions about what the following people want and whether you can help them. Use the verbs **mandar, dar, prestar, comprar,** and **traer.** Use direct and indirect object pronouns together.

Modelo *—¿Qué quiere Elisa?*
—Quiere dinero. ¿Tú se lo puedes mandar?
—No, lo siento. Yo no puedo mandárselo.

Elisa

1. Carlos

2. Ana y Paco

3. Javier

4. Lidia

5. Lucía

10. ¿Puedes hacerlo? You are in a bad mood, and people keep asking you to do things you don't want to do. Tell them you can't do the favors they are requesting.

Modelo —¿Puedes traerme las violetas?
—*No, no puedo traér**telas**.*

1. ¿Puedes comprarle el regalo a mamá?
2. ¿Puedes buscarme la chequera?
3. ¿Puedes llevarle las flores a Luisa?
4. ¿Puedes darle los cheques de viajero a Raúl?
5. ¿Puedes traernos los pantalones de la tintorería?
6. ¿Puedes comprarnos un perro?

11. Now repeat Activity 10, following the model below.

Modelo —¿Puedes traerme las violetas?
—*No, no **te las** puedo traer.*

Para conversar

12. ¡Habla con tu compañero(a)! Interview a classmate, using the following questions and two questions of your own. Answer the questions in complete sentences. When you have finished, switch roles. Answers should be given with indirect object pronouns.

1. Cuando tú necesitas dinero, ¿a quién se lo pides?
2. Cuando tú les pides dinero a tus padres, ¿te lo dan?
3. Si yo necesito tu libro de español, ¿me lo prestas?
4. Si Uds. no entienden algo, ¿se lo preguntan (*ask*) a su profesor(a)?
5. Si tú y yo somos amigo(as) y yo necesito tu auto, ¿tú me lo prestas?
6. Necesito tu pluma. ¿Puedes prestármela?
7. Necesito cheques de viajero. ¿Tú me los puedes conseguir?
8. Yo no tengo el número de teléfono del profesor (de la profesora). ¿Tú se lo puedes pedir?

13. ¿Qué necesitamos? In groups of three, talk about what each of you needs. Then ask a member of the group whether he/she can lend you, give you, or send you the needed item.

Modelo —Necesito dinero. ¿Puedes prestármelo?
—*Sí, cómo no* (of course). *Yo puedo prestártelo.* o
—*No, lo siento. No puedo prestártelo.*

2 Preterit of *ser, ir,* and *dar* (*Pretérito de los verbos **ser**, **ir** y **dar***)

› The preterit forms of **ser, ir,** and **dar** are irregular.

ser *to be*	**ir** *to go*	**dar** *to give*
fui	fui	di
fuiste	fuiste	diste
fue	fue	dio
fuimos	fuimos	dimos
fuisteis	fuisteis	disteis
fueron	fueron	dieron

› Note that **ser** and **ir** have identical forms in the preterit.

—Ayer **fue** el cumpleaños de Lucía, ¿no? *Yesterday was Lucía's birthday, right?*
—Sí, Ana y yo **fuimos** a su casa y le **dimos** los regalos. *Yes, Ana and I went to her house and gave her the presents.*
—¿**Fuiste** a la fiesta que **dio** Sara? *Did you go to the party that Sara gave?*
—Sí, **fui. Fue** la mejor fiesta del año. *Yes, I went. It was the best party of the year.*

Práctica

14. ¿Y los demás? With a partner, use your imagination to compare what Rafael did to what the other people mentioned did. Take turns!

1. …fue al banco y depositó quinientos dólares. (Yo)
2. …fue a la florería y compró un ramo de rosas. (Nosotros)
3. …fue al cine con sus amigos el sábado pasado. (Las chicas)
4. …fue el mejor estudiante de su clase de inglés. (Yo)
5. …fue uno de los peores estudiantes en su clase de matemáticas. (Tú)
6. …dio una fiesta para celebrar el Año Nuevo. (Nosotros)
7. …le dio un beso *(kiss)* a su novia. (Tú)
8. …fue a la casa de su tía y le dio un regalo. (Yo)

15. La última vez With a partner, talk about when the last time was that each of you . . .

1. went to a concert or to the theater (with whom?)
2. went to the bank (to do what?)
3. gave a party (to celebrate what?)
4. gave someone money (to whom and how much?)

Un dicho
Todo tiempo pasado fue mejor.
Equivalent: *Those were the good old days.*

Para conversar

16. ¡Habla con tu compañero(a)! Interview a classmate, using the following questions. Answer the questions in complete sentences, paying attention to the conjugation of the verbs **ser, dar,** and **ir.** When you have finished, switch roles.

1. ¿Quién fue tu profesor(a) favorito(a) el año pasado? ¿La clase fue fácil o difícil? ¿Tú fuiste un buen (una buena) estudiante en esa clase?
2. ¿Fuiste a la cafetería ayer? ¿A qué hora? ¿Alguien fue contigo o fuiste solo(a)?
3. ¿Adónde fuiste el sábado? ¿Alguién fue contigo?
4. ¿Tus amigos fueron a visitarte o tú fuiste a visitarlos a ellos?
5. ¿Dieron tus amigos una fiesta para celebrar tu cumpleaños? ¿Cuándo la dieron? ¿Dónde? ¿Quién te dio el mejor regalo?
6. ¿Diste una fiesta el viernes pasado? ¿Alguien dio una fiesta el sábado?
7. ¿A quién le diste un abrazo (*hug*) ayer? ¿Alguien te dio un beso (*kiss*)?
8. ¿Cuál fue tu clase favorita el semestre pasado?

3 Preterit of *e:i* and *o:u* stem-changing verbs (*Pretérito de los verbos que cambian en la raíz:* ***e:i*** *y* ***o:u***)

› Verbs of the **-ir** conjugation that have a stem change in the present tense change **e** to **i** and **o** to **u** in the third-person singular and plural of the preterit.[1]

preferir *to prefer*		**dormir** *to sleep*	
preferí	preferimos	dormí	dormimos
preferiste	preferisteis	dormiste	dormisteis
prefirió	prefirieron	durmió	durmieron

› Other verbs that follow the same pattern:

pedir	seguir
mentir (*to lie*)	conseguir
servir	morir
repetir (*to repeat*)	

—¿Cómo **durmieron** Uds. anoche? — *How did you sleep last night?*
—Nosotros **dormimos** bien, pero Paco no **durmió** muy bien. — *We slept well, but Paco didn't sleep very well.*

—¿Qué **pidieron** ellos? — *What did they order?*
—Raúl **pidió** camarones y Rosa **pidió** langosta. — *Raúl ordered shrimp and Rosa ordered lobster.*
—Eva dice que ella no comió nada. — *Eva says that she didn't eat anything*
—Te **mintió**. — *She lied to you.*

[1]Remember that the **-ar** and **-er** stem-changing verbs are regular in the preterit: **él cerró, ellos volvieron.** Exceptions are **poder** and **querer**, which are explained in **Lección 9.**

Práctica

17. Anoche With a partner, take turns describing what the following people did last night. Use the verbs given (or similar).

1. Arturo (preferir) ____________________

2. Ernesto (pedir) ____________________

3. Paco (seguir) ____________________

4. Rosa (dormir) ____________________

5. el mozo (servir) ____________________

6. Pilar (conseguir) ____________________

18. Andrés Find out what Andrés did yesterday by adding the correct form of the missing verbs.

1. Yo ________ (ir) a visitar a mi padre y le ________ (pedir) dinero.
2. ________ (Conseguir) revistas en español.
3. ________ (Salir) con otra chica y le ________ (mentir) a mi novia.
4. Nosotros ________ (ir) a un restaurante. Yo ________ (pedir) pollo frito y Ana ________ (pedir) langosta.
5. Yo ________ (volver) a mi casa y ________ (dormir) dos horas.
6. Mis padres me ________ (invitar) a una fiesta, pero yo ________ (preferir) no ir.
7. Por la noche, yo ________ (dar) una fiesta y ________ (servir) ponche.

Un dicho

El pez muere por la boca.

Equivalent: *Engage brain before putting mouth in gear.*

Para conversar

19. Queremos saber... Now, using the information in activity 18, prepare questions to ask your classmates about what Andrés did.

20. ¡Qué mala suerte! With two classmates, imagine that you have a friend who had really bad luck last Friday the 13th. Brainstorm to come up with all the bad things that happened to him. Use the verbs studied in this section.

4 Uses of *por* and *para* (*Usos de* por *y* para)

A. Uses of *por*

The preposition **por** is used to express the following concepts.

› motion or approximate location (*through, around, along, by*)

Luis salió **por** la ventana.	*Luis went out through the window.*
Enrique va **por** la calle Juárez.	*Enrique is going down Juárez Street.*
Gustavo pasó **por** el hotel.	*Gustavo went by the hotel.*

› cause or motive of an action (*because of, on account of, on behalf of*)

Llegamos tarde **por** la lluvia.	*We were late because of the rain.*
Lo hago **por** ellos.	*I do it on their behalf.*

› means, manner, unit of measure (*by, for, per*)

Siempre viajamos **por** tren.	*We always travel by train.*
Van a 100 kilómetros **por** hora.	*They're going 100 kilometers per hour.*

› *in exchange for*

Te doy 50 dólares **por** esa cámara.	*I'll give you 50 dollars for that camera.*

› period of time during which an action takes place (*during, in, for*)

Ella trabaja **por** la mañana.	*She works in the morning.*
Va a estar aquí **por** dos meses.	*He's going to be here for two months.*

› *in search of, for*

Voy a venir **por** ti a las siete.	*I'll come by for you at seven.*

Práctica

21. Entrevista a tu compañero(a) Interview a classmate, using the following questions. When you have finished, switch roles.

1. ¿Tienes una clase por la mañana? ¿y por la noche?
2. Antes de ir a clase, ¿vas por tus amigos? ¿Alguien viene por ti?
3. ¿Cuánto pagaste por tu libro de español?
4. ¿Pasaste por mi casa anoche?
5. Si tú pierdes la llave de tu casa, ¿entras por la ventana?
6. ¿Tus padres hacen mucho por ti?
7. ¿Tú les escribes a tus padres o prefieres llamarlos por teléfono?
8. ¿Prefieres viajar por ómnibus o por avión (*plane*)? ¿Por qué?

B. Uses of *para*

The preposition **para** is used to express the following concepts.

› destination

Mañana salgo **para** San Juan. — *Tomorrow I am leaving for San Juan.*
¿A qué hora hay autobuses **para** Río Piedras? — *What time are there buses for Río Piedras?*

› goal for a point in the future (*by* or *for* a certain time)

Quiero el dinero **para** el sábado. — *I want the money for Saturday.*
Debo estar allí **para** el mes de noviembre. — *I must be there by the month of November.*

› whom or what something is for

Compré una mesa **para** mi cuarto. — *I bought a table for my room.*
Compramos los libros **para** Fernando. — *We bought the books for Fernando.*

› *in order to*

Necesito mil dólares **para** pagar el viaje. — *I need a thousand dollars in order to pay for the trip.*
Vamos al teatro **para** celebrar mi cumpleaños. — *We are going to the theater (in order) to celebrate my birthday.*

› objective or goal

Mi novio estudia **para** médico. — *My boyfriend is studying to be a doctor.*

LEARNING TIP
Using **por** and **para** correctly takes time. Reading all the examples is only the first step. With *each* use, think of as many examples as possible, always *personalizing* them—that is, using them in sentences reflecting your own circumstances.

Práctica

22. Cosas que pasan Look at the illustrations and describe what is happening, using **por** or **para.**

1. Fuimos ______________ a la capital.

2. Daniel salió ______________.

3. La torta es ______________.

4. Luisa va a estar en San Juan ______________.

5. Jorge pagó 35 ______________ el vino.

6. Eva sale mañana ______________.

23. Planes Complete the following description of a trip to Mexico, using **por** or **para**.

Roberto y yo salimos __________ Cancún la semana próxima. Vamos a viajar __________ avión. Tenemos pasajes __________ el sábado __________ la mañana. Pagamos tres mil dólares __________ el pasaje, pero como pensamos pasar __________ Guatemala, donde vamos a estar __________ unos días, no es muy caro. Mañana __________ la tarde vamos a la tienda __________ comprar algunos regalos __________ nuestros amigos mexicanos. Desde Guatemala vamos a llamar __________ teléfono a nuestros amigos en Cancún y ellos van a ir al aeropuerto __________ nosotros.

24. *¿Por o para?* Use **por** or **para** to finish the following. Add the necessary words to complete the sentences. When you have finished, join one of your classmates and compare your work.

1. Llamé a mis padres…
2. Mis clases son…
3. Necesito dinero…
4. Mi mejor amigo(a) estudia…
5. No tengo la llave. Voy a entrar…
6. Mañana salgo…
7. Siempre viajo…
8. A las ocho, mis amigos vienen…
9. ¿Cuánto pagaste…?
10. Llegamos tarde a clase…
11. Los libros son…
12. ¿A qué hora son los viajes…?
13. Necesito volver de mi viaje…
14. Vamos a estar en Puerto Rico…

Para conversar

25. De viaje Plan a trip to Puerto Rico with a classmate. Using the paragraph in Activity 23 as a model, describe your travel plans.

5 Formation of adverbs *(La formación de los adverbios)*

› Most Spanish adverbs are formed by adding **-mente** (the equivalent of the English *-ly*) to the adjective.

especial	*special*	especial**mente**	*especially*
reciente	*recent*	reciente**mente**	*recently*
general	*general*	general**mente**	*generally*
probable	*probable*	probable**mente**	*probably*

› Adjectives ending in **-o** change the **-o** to **-a** before adding **-mente.**

lento	*slow*	lent**amente**	*slowly*
rápido	*rapid*	rápid**amente**	*rapidly*
desafortunado	*unfortunate*	desafortunad**amente**	*unfortunately*

› If two or more adverbs are used together, both change the **-o** to **-a,** but only the last adverb takes the **-mente** ending.

Habló clara y **lentamente.** *He spoke clearly and slowly.*

› If the adjective has an accent, the adverb retains it.

fácil **fácilmente**

Práctica

26. De adjetivos a adverbios Change the following adjectives to adverbs.

1. fácil
2. feliz
3. claro (*clear*)
4. raro (*rare*)
5. necesario
6. frecuente (*frequent*)
7. triste
8. trágico (*tragic*)
9. alegre (*merry*)
10. desgraciado

27. Sergio Complete the following sentences with appropriate adverbs.

1. Sergio entiende muy bien a la profesora, porque ella habla ______________ y claramente.
2. Sergio ______________ le trae flores a su novia: orquídeas, violetas, pensamientos, tulipanes…
3. Sergio ______________ va al teatro; él prefiere ir al cine.
4. ______________ Sergio no tiene dinero para prestarme.
5. Sergio me visita ______________; por lo menos dos veces por semana.
6. Sergio no es lento; camina ______________.
7. El pobre Sergio nos habló ______________.
8. La fiesta es ______________ para Sergio, porque hoy es su cumpleaños.
9. ___________ Sergio no va a poder firmar esos papeles hoy, porque tiene mucho trabajo.
10. La abuela de Sergio camina muy ______________ porque está cansada.

28. ¡Habla con tu compañero(a)! Interview a classmate, using the following questions and two of your own. Include adverbs in your responses. When you have finished, switch roles.

1. ¿A qué hora sales de tu casa por la mañana?
2. ¿Tú y tu familia van de compras juntos?
3. ¿Tú ves a tus abuelos a menudo (*often*)?
4. ¿Vas al teatro a menudo?
5. ¿Tú tienes mucho dinero?

Para conversar

29. Lo que hacemos With a partner, discuss what you frequently do, rarely do, and what, unfortunately, you can't do.

Modelo *Yo raramente visito a mis abuelos.*

¡Vamos a ver!

Antes de ver el video

30. Preguntas You and a partner, take turns asking and answering the following questions.

1. ¿Tú vives en una calle o en una avenida?
2. ¿Tú desayunas solo(a), con un(a) compañero(a) de cuarto o con tu familia?
3. ¿A quién le cuentas tú lo que te pasa?
4. ¿Cuándo fue la última vez (*the last time*) que fuiste a la tintorería?
5. ¿Prefieres tener un coche o una motocicleta? Si tú conduces, ¿estacionas a veces frente a una boca de incendios?
6. ¿Te dieron una multa alguna vez? ¿Por qué?
7. La última vez que fuiste al banco, ¿depositaste dinero en tu cuenta de ahorros o en tu cuenta corriente?
8. ¿Le compraste un regalo a alguien? ¿Se lo diste? ¿Le gustó?
9. Si tienes peces de colores y les das demasiada comida, ¿qué les va a pasar?
10. ¿Tú eres supersticioso(a)? ¿Piensas salir de tu casa el próximo viernes 13?

El video: Un martes 13

—¿Fuiste a la tinterоría a recoger tus pantalones?

—Sí… ese fue mi primer problema…

—Estacioné la motocicleta frente a una boca de incendios y un policía me dio una multa.

—¡Pobrecito!

—Bueno… desgraciadamente es alérgica a las flores…

—¡Ay, Edwin! ¡Qué desastre!

Después de ver el video

Mamá

Edwin

31. ¿Quién lo dice? Identify the person who said the following in the dialogue.

1. ¿Fuiste a la tintorería a recoger tus pantalones?
2. Después pedí un préstamo, pero no me lo dieron.
3. Tu papá tampoco consiguió el préstamo que pidió.
4. Después compré dos peces de colores para Martita.
5. ¿Compraste el regalo para tu novia?
6. Sí, pero su ex novio le regaló una enciclopedia.
7. En fin... fui a la florería y le compré un ramo de rosas.
8. Pero tú tienes una moto casi nueva.
9. ¡Ya sé por qué ocurrió todo eso! ¡Ayer fue martes trece!
10. ¡Pero el próximo martes trece no salgo de casa!

32. Hablemos With a partner, take turns asking and answering the following questions. Base your answers on the dialogue.

1. ¿Edwin durmió bien anoche?
2. ¿Qué le está contando Edwin a su mamá?
3. ¿Para qué fue Edwin a la tintorería?
4. ¿Por qué le dio el policía una multa a Edwin?
5. ¿En qué cuentas depositó Edwin dinero?
6. ¿Consiguió el papá de Edwin el préstamo que pidió?
7. ¿Qué compró Edwin para Martita? ¿Qué les pasó a los peces?
8. ¿Qué compró Edwin en la florería?
9. ¿Para qué tiene que ahorrar dinero Edwin?
10. ¿Qué no piensa hacer Edwin el próximo martes trece?

33. ¿Qué pasa después...? You and a partner, use your imagination to say what the characters do. In Spanish, discuss the following.

1. Three or four things that you think happened to Edwin's mother yesterday.
2. How much money you think Edwin deposited in his savings account and in his checking account.
3. How much money he applied for and whether or not he is going to apply for another loan.
4. Whether or not Edwin bought another present for his girlfriend. What?
5. Whether or not Edwin saves enough (**suficiente**) money to buy another motorcycle.
6. What you think Edwin is going to do next Tuesday the thirteenth.
7. How much he paid for the ticket and whether he ever parked in front of a fire hydrant again.

Now compare your statements with those of the members of another group.

¡Vamos a escuchar!

ESTRATEGIA **Guessing meaning from context** When you listen to speech, you can use informed guesswork to figure out the approximate meaning of an unknown word or phrase, just as you have been learning to do when reading. Use your knowledge of the topic and the words you do know to help you decipher unfamiliar words.

CD 2-12 **34. ¿Qué significa?** You will listen to three commercials on different products and services. Guess the meaning of the following words and phrases.

Commercial 1:

a. mándale
b. va a quedar encantada

Commercial 2:

a. perrito
b. gatito
c. venga
d. cuidarlos

Commercial 3:

a. bancarios
b. estamos a su disposición

ESTRATEGIA **Paraphrasing practice I** In **A conversar...** of **Lección 7,** you were introduced to the technique of simplifying statements in your own words. This helps you manage a conversation by confirming that you understand. The following is the first of four activities in which you will practice paraphrasing what you hear.

¡Vamos a conversar!

35. ¿Qué dice? Listen to the following sentences and restate them in a simpler way in your own words. Then compare your responses with those of a classmate.
CD 2-13

Modelo *You hear*: Me resulta imposible sacar dinero del cajero automático. Parece que está roto o fuera de servicio.
Simple paraphrase: No puedo sacar dinero del cajero automático porque no funciona.

36. ¿Qué dice Ud.? What would you say in the following situations? What might the other person say? Act out the scenes with a partner. Take turns playing each role.

1. Mention four transactions that people can make at a bank.
2. You ask Mrs. López if she got the loan that she asked for at the bank.
3. You work at a pet store. Tell a customer what pets you have for sale.
4. A young man wants to send flowers to his girlfriend. Make suggestions about what kind of flowers to send.
5. You are talking to a friend about your activities last week. Mention several things you did and places you went to. Mention whether or not you gave a party.

37. Para conocernos mejor To do this activity, work with a classmate whom you would like to get to know. Take turns asking each other these questions.

1. ¿A qué hora desayunaste esta mañana? ¿Qué comiste? ¿Qué tomaste? ¿Desayunaste solo(a)? ¿A qué hora almorzaste ayer?
2. ¿Fuiste a la tintorería la semana pasada? Generalmente, ¿llevas tu ropa a la tintorería o la lavas en tu casa?
3. ¿Fuiste al banco la semana pasada? ¿Depositaste dinero? ¿Sacaste dinero del cajero automático? ¿Abriste una cuenta?
4. ¿Compraste algún regalo el mes pasado? ¿Para quién? ¿Le gustó a esa persona el regalo? ¿Y tú? ¿Recibiste algún regalo?
5. ¿Compras flores frecuentemente? ¿Cuáles son tus flores favoritas?
6. ¿Tú eres alérgico(a) a los animales? ¿A las flores? ¿A algún tipo de comida?
7. ¿Te gustan los animales? ¿Tienes alguna mascota (*pet*)? ¿Qué animales prefieres?
8. ¿Te gustan las motocicletas? ¿Tienes una? Muchas personas dicen que las motocicletas son peligrosas (*dangerous*); ¿qué piensas tú?

38. Una encuesta Interview your classmates to identify who fits the following descriptions. Include your instructor, but remember to use the **Ud.** form when addressing him/her. After finishing the survey, get together with two or three classmates and discuss the results.

1. Tiene una cuenta de ahorros.	____________
2. Tiene una cuenta conjunta.	____________
3. Prefiere pagar con cheques.	____________
4. Pidió un préstamo el mes pasado.	____________
5. Siempre paga al contado.	____________
6. Es alérgico(a) a las flores.	____________
7. Tiene geranios en su jardín.	____________
8. Tiene peces de colores.	____________
9. Quiere comprar un mono.	____________
10. Es supersticioso(a).	____________

39. Para crear Get together in groups of three and "create" the scenario for this photo. Who are the people? Give them names. Talk about what the employee and the customer do and want to do. Include as many banking transactions as possible. Add any details you deem interesting or important.

¡Vamos a leer!

Antes de leer

ESTRATEGIA **Reading critically** Interacting with a reading engages you personally with the text. A reading might generate questions, as well as positive and negative reactions. When you read critically, try to think about your impressions of what you read and why a reading evokes particular thoughts. Does what you read ring true or make sense? Do you agree with the writer's point of view, ideas, or the information conveyed? Why?

40. La suerte Find out what day of the week you were born and read what the following text says about that day. In pairs, tell your partner your impression of what you read. Answer this question: **¿Es cierto lo que se dice de tu día?**

¡A leer!

El día de la semana en que nació marcó su suerte

Según el profesor Waffman, mucho de lo que sucede en su vida depende del día de su nacimiento.

Si nació un lunes…

Ella: Sus problemas se deben a hechos* anteriores, pero luego se estabilizan. Si aprende a confiar*, será feliz.

Él: Tiene excelentes posibilidades de éxito en su vida si sabe aprovecharlas* y no lo deja todo para último momento.

Si nació un martes…

Ella: Recuerde que su mejor defensa está en el cariño* que da y que recibe.

Él: Aprenda a comprender y a compartir* para vivir en armonía.

Si nació un miércoles…

Ella: Tendrá problemas en su vida conyugal, pero no van a durar si usted resuelve las tensiones diarias.

Él: Tiene posibilidades de éxito personal y profesional. Evite las situaciones que ponen en peligro su felicidad.

Si nació un jueves…

Ella: Trate de combatir la depresión y escuche los consejos* de personas realistas.

Él: Para lograr los objetivos deseados, trabaje y acepte las cosas como vienen. No se desespere, pues todo llega.

Si nació un viernes…

Ella: Usted tiene un gran poder de recuperación.

Él: Planee el futuro junto a la mujer que ama. En el plano profesional tendrá éxito si acepta la realidad como es.

Si nació un sábado…

Ella: Usted puede encontrar la felicidad si sabe aprovechar todas las oportunidades.

Él: Si quiere conseguir la felicidad, use sus habilidades para destacarse*.

Si nació un domingo…

Ella: El triunfo profesional le va a ser difícil.

Él: No se preocupe por los conflictos familiares que no están vinculados con usted.

events
trust
to take advantage of them
love
share
advice
to stand out

41. Comprensión As you read the article, find the answers to the following questions.

1. ¿Por qué es importante en su vida el día de la semana en que Ud. nació?
2. ¿Qué debe aprender a hacer una mujer que nació un lunes? ¿Y un hombre?
3. ¿Qué debe recordar una mujer que nació un martes? ¿Qué debe aprender a hacer un hombre que nació ese día?
4. ¿Qué debe hacer una mujer que nació un miércoles? ¿Y un hombre?
5. Si una mujer nació un jueves, ¿qué debe combatir? ¿Qué debe aceptar un hombre que nació ese día?
6. ¿Qué gran poder tiene una mujer que nació un viernes? ¿Qué debe aprender a aceptar un hombre que nació ese día?
7. ¿Qué deben hacer las mujeres y los hombres que nacieron un sábado?
8. ¿Qué le va a ser difícil a una mujer que nació un domingo? ¿Por qué no debe preocuparse un hombre que nació ese día?

Después de leer...

42. Desde su mundo Reread the descriptions for every day for your gender. In groups of three, discuss your impressions of the nature and validity of the descriptions. Answer these questions: **¿Son apropiadas para cualquier** (*any*) **persona? ¿Por qué?**

¡Vamos a escribir!

Antes de escribir

ESTRATEGIA **Writing journal entries** Diary or journal writing allows you to freely express yourself however you want, for however long you want. You can use a journal to record events, whether large or small, or to think about something you read or heard or a problem you're working to resolve. Whatever your purpose, just let the ideas flow. Writing frequently will help you become a better writer, and journal writing is particularly useful.

43. Querido diario Before writing journal entries, for two days jot down some ideas or events you want to write about. Will you report mainly things that happened or will you also write about your ideas or difficulties you might be facing?

¡A escribir!

44. Diario personal Write journal entries for two days. You can include whatever you like: people you saw, interesting things you did, a troublesome encounter, a special achievement, etc. Remember to let the thoughts flow.

Después de escribir

45. A revisar Review what you wrote and add any additional thoughts you might have. Because a journal is a personal rather than a formal piece of writing, you won't be asked to peer edit it for grammar. Exchange your journal entries with a classmate and comment only on general content, reacting to what your classmate wrote. Some useful phrases: **¡Qué interesante! ¡Qué bien! ¡Qué divertido** (*fun*)**! Lo siento. ¡Qué mala suerte!** (*What bad luck!*)

Puerto Rico

Puerto Rico es ideal para pasar unos días. Allí vas a necesitar un traje de baño (*swimsuit*), pero no vas a necesitar pasaporte. ¿Recuerdas? Puerto Rico es un Estado Libre Asociado (Commonwealth) de los Estados Unidos. Además, es el único país hispano donde el español y el inglés son idiomas oficiales. Sus hermosas playas, sus barrios y edificios coloniales, sus modernas ciudades, un bosque tropical y San Juan, su capital, son atracciones para el turista.

Los puertorriqueños llaman a la isla *Borinquen*, nombre que viene de los primitivos habitantes de la isla, los indios taínos. Su cultura es una mezcla de las tradiciones indígenas, españolas, africanas, y de la cultura de los Estados Unidos.

La economía y el turismo

Puerto Rico es el país hispanoamericano con mejor estándar de vida. Además, aunque los puertorriqueños son ciudadanos de los EE.UU., no pagan impuesto federal.

La economía de Puerto Rico es una de las más diversas de toda Latinoamérica. Numerosas empresas multinacionales tienen en el país industrias electrónicas, farmacéuticas, textiles y biotecnológicas.

© Maresa Pryor/Danita Delimont/Alamy

© kai hecker/Shutterstock.com

Una importante fuente de ingreso (*source of income*) del país es el turismo.

Los miles de turistas que visitan Puerto Rico todos los años, en busca de (*looking for*) su sol y sus playas, o para admirar la arquitectura colonial de El Viejo San Juan o el bosque tropical El Yunque, dejan millones de dólares en sus hoteles, restaurantes y centros de diversión.

La música

La música tradicional puertorriqueña es la **plena**, una canción que cuenta los eventos de la vida diaria, como los corridos mexicanos.

La música actual es una combinación de los ritmos puertorriqueños con la música de Cuba, Estados Unidos, Jamaica, etcétera.

La **salsa** nació (*was born*) en Nueva York entre los emigrantes de Puerto Rico y Cuba. Es muy rítmica y está hecha (*made*) para bailar.

© Angel M. Rivera/STAFF/El Nuevo Día de Puerto Rico/Newscom

En la década de los noventa, apareció el **reguetón**, un género derivado del *reggae* de Jamaica, del hip-hop norteamericano y de diferentes ritmos puertorriqueños.

© Otokimus/Shutterstock

La comida

La comida puertorriqueña es una combinación de las comidas de los taínos, de los esclavos africanos y de la comida española y americana. Algunos de los platos típicos de la cocina puertorriqueña son los asopaos (arroz con pollo, carne o pescado), el sancocho (sopa de vegetales y carne), y el mofongo (puré de plátanos verdes con carne o pollo). Por supuesto, vas a encontrar comida internacional en los muchos restaurantes de la isla.

© Townsend Dickinson/The Image Works

El Viejo San Juan

El Viejo San Juan es uno de los barrios coloniales de Hispanoamérica mejor conservados. Se identifica por sus calles de adoquines (*paving stones*), sus edificios de diferentes colores, sus plazas, museos y galerías de arte, tiendas y restaurantes.

© Fuse/Jupiter Images

El Yunque

El Yunque es un bosque tropical situado al este de San Juan. Tiene muchas caídas de agua, gran variedad de plantas, orquídeas, helechos, árboles y diferentes especies de animales. El más famoso de ellos es el **coquí**, una pequeña ranita que es el símbolo de Puerto Rico.

Otras atracciones turísticas de Puerto Rico son sus playas, sus casinos y su intensa vida nocturna.

Ahora, dime...

1. ¿Qué opinas de tener un Estado Libre Asociado? ¿Deben los puertorriqueños tener los mismos derechos que una persona de Arizona o de Massachusetts?
2. ¿Crees que la salsa es una música famosa en todo el mundo? ¿Qué músicos de salsa conoces?
3. ¿Te parece interesante visitar El Yunque? ¿Por qué? ¿Con qué lugar de Estados Unidos puedes comparar El Yunque? ¿Qué otros lugares quieres ver? ¿Te interesa la vida nocturna?

iLrn™

To learn more about Puerto Rico, watch the cultural footage in the Media Library.

AUTOPRUEBA

¿Cuánto sé ahora?

Take this test. When you have finished, check your answers in the answer key provided in Appendix D. Then use a red pen to correct any mistakes you may have made. Are you ready?

A. Direct and indirect object pronouns used together Complete the following exchanges, using direct and indirect object pronouns together.

1. —¿Le vas a dar el calendario a Sergio?
   —Sí, _________ voy a dar (voy a _________).
2. —¿Tus padres te compraron la motocicleta?
   —No, no _________ compraron.
3. —¿El policía les va a dar una multa a Uds.?
   —Sí, _________ va a dar (va a _________).
4. —¿El empleado de la tintorería le mandó los pantalones a Ud.?
   —Sí, _________ mandó.
5. —¿Tú me vas a regalar un ramo de rosas?
   —Sí, _________ voy a regalar (voy a _________).
6. —¿A quiénes les das los peces de colores?
   — _________ doy a los niños (*children*).

B. Preterit of *ir*, *ser*, and *dar* Complete the following sentences, using the preterit of **ir**, **ser**, or **dar**.

1. Nosotros _________ al banco y le _________ el dinero al empleado.
2. Ellos _________ mis estudiantes el año pasado.
3. ¿A quién le _________ tú la cuenta?
4. Ayer, yo _________ a la florería y compré rosas.
5. Ellos no nos _________ el préstamo.
6. Ellas _________ de vacaciones a México.
7. La doctora Vega _________ mi profesora.
8. Él _________ al hotel y le _________ las maletas al botones.
9. ¿Tú _________ al banco y abriste una cuenta de ahorros? ¿Quién te _________ el dinero?
10. Nosotros _________ estudiantes de la doctora Álvarez el año pasado.

C. Preterit of *e:i* and *o:u* stem-changing verbs Complete the following sentences, using the preterit tense of the verbs listed below, as needed.

mentir dormir seguir conseguir pedir repetir morir servir

1. ¿_____________ ellos en el hotel el jueves?
2. Los chicos _____________ a sus amigos a la tienda.
3. Nosotros _____________ sándwiches de jamón y queso.
4. Ella me _____________. No tiene veinte años.
5. ¿No _____________ Ud. el dinero para ir de vacaciones?
6. ¿Qué le _____________ los niños a Santa Claus?
7. El hombre _____________ en un accidente.
8. Ella me _____________ la pregunta.
9. Anoche yo _________ bien, pero Ana _________ muy mal.
10. ¿Ud. _________ un préstamo en el banco ayer?

D. Uses of *por* and *para* Complete the following, using **por** or **para** as needed.

Mañana Luis y yo salimos _________ Puerto Rico. Vamos _________ diez días. En San Juan vamos a llamar _________ teléfono a nuestra amiga Julia, que estudia allí _________ abogada. Ella va a venir _________ nosotros. Tenemos que regresar _________ el treinta de agosto _________ empezar en la universidad. _________ pagar _________ el viaje y _________ los regalos que compramos _________ nuestros padres, vamos a pedir un préstamo en el banco.

E. Formation of adverbs Give the Spanish equivalent of the adverbs in parentheses.

1. Me gustan las flores, _________ las rosas. (*especially*)
2. Yo _________ voy a conciertos. (*frequently*)
3. El profesor habló _________ y _________. (*slowly and clearly*)
4. Vino a verme _________. (*recently*)
5. _________ voy al banco los sábados. (*Generally*)
6. ______________ no tengo dinero. (*Unfortunately*)

F. Just words . . . Choose the word that best completes each sentence.

1. Voy a llevar los pantalones a la (tintorería, florería).
2. Fui al banco para pedir un (fuego, préstamo).
3. Me (pasaron, robaron) la motocicleta ayer.
4. El policía me dio (una multa, un ramo) anoche.
5. No tengo que pagar por los cheques porque son (seguros, gratis).
6. Las (margaritas, violetas) son moradas.
7. Tienes que (contar, fechar) y firmar el cheque.
8. Voy a comprarle un (incendio, regalo) para su cumpleaños.
9. Me gusta mucho ese loro. Me (encanta, solicita).
10. El viernes trece es un día de mala (flor, suerte).
11. Él (estacionó, mató) la moto frente a una boca de incendios.
12. Ellos les van a dar demasiada comida a los (peces, tulipanes) y los van a matar.
13. No tienes razón. Estás (equivocado, listo).
14. Compró la motocicleta (a plazos, al contado) y ahora tiene que pagar cincuenta dólares todos los meses.
15. Juan dice muchas (tonterías, florerías).

G. Cultura

1. Complete the following, based on the information found in the **¿Lo sabía Ud.?** sections.
   a. En los países hispanos el día de mala suerte es el _________ trece.
   b. En los países hispanos generalmente los jóvenes viven con su _________ hasta que se casan.
2. Complete the following, based on information found in the **El mundo hispánico y tú** section.
   a. El _________ es un centro de atracción turística de Puerto Rico.
   b. El Yunque es un _________ tropical situado al este de San Juan.

H. Un dicho Do you remember the Spanish saying that is equivalent to "Those were the good old days"? Find it in this lesson.

LECCIÓN 9

PREPARATIVOS PARA UNA FIESTA

Celebrando un aniversario de bodas

OBJETIVOS COMUNICATIVOS

You will learn vocabulary related to shopping for groceries, meal preparation, and daily routines.

SITUACIONES

¡Feliz aniversario!

ESTRUCTURAS

1. Reflexive constructions
2. Some uses of the definite article
3. Possessive pronouns
4. Irregular preterits
5. **Hace...** meaning *ago*

ASÍ SOMOS

¡Vamos a ver!

Watching and understanding situations

¡Vamos a escuchar!

Dealing with fast speech

¡Vamos a conversar!

Using pauses to manage a conversation

Rincón literario

Using prior knowledge to guess the meaning of new vocabulary

La liebre y la tortuga by Esopo

¡Vamos a escribir!

Sequencing steps for writing a didactic story

EL MUNDO HISPÁNICO Y TÚ...

› Cuba

› La República Dominicana

AUTOPRUEBA

You will review what you learned in this lesson.

CUBA es la mayor de las islas del archipiélago de las Antillas. Su figura es similar a la de un cocodrilo y, como es larga y estrecha (*narrow*), tiene extensas costas en las cuales hay playas de gran belleza (*beauty*). Muchos llaman a Cuba "la Perla de las Antillas".

LA REPÚBLICA DOMINICANA ocupa las dos terceras partes de la isla que Colón descubrió en su primer viaje y a la que llamó La Española. La parte occidental de la isla está ocupada por la República de Haití.

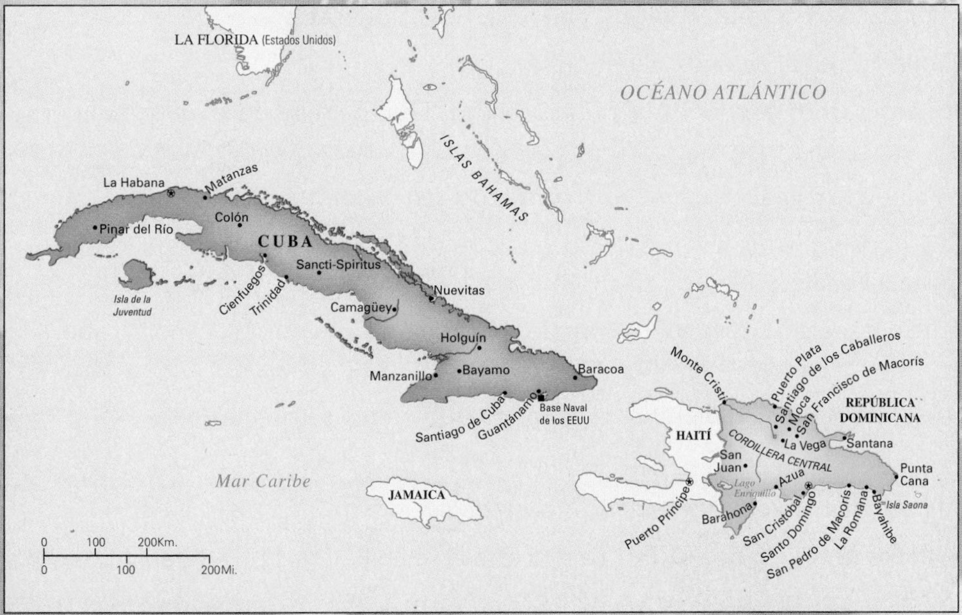

Recursos iLrn video audio web playlist

SITUACIONES

¡Feliz aniversario!

CD2-14

© Cengage Learning

¡Ubíquelos!

Don Carlos lives with his family in Santo Domingo, the capital of the Dominican Republic, but still misses his native Cuba. When you watch this video, you will get a sense of the places he remembers. You will also see places that are now part of their lives.

© Monkey Business Images Ltd/PhotoLibrary

© Monkey Business Images Ltd/PhotoLibrary

Don Carlos Ferreyra y su esposa, doña Consuelo, celebran sus bodas de oro. Ellos viven ahora en Santo Domingo, la capital de la República Dominicana, con su hija Noemí y su yerno Daniel y sus tres nietos, Graciela, Alberto y Teresa. Don Carlos y su esposa vinieron de Cuba hace más de cuarenta años, después de la revolución castrista[1]. A veces los dos extrañan los lugares donde nacieron y donde pasaron su infancia y su juventud: La Habana, Camagüey, Pinar del Río... Graciela, Alberto y Teresa están ahora en un supermercado, haciendo las compras.

Graciela: (*A Teresa*) ¿Trajiste la lista que te dio mamá?

Teresa: ¡Ay, no! ¡Me olvidé de traerla! La puse en mi otra cartera... pero me acuerdo de todas las cosas que necesitamos.

Alberto: Yo también: manzanas, naranjas, mangos, plátanos, uvas, aguacates...

Teresa: Y verduras: cebolla, lechuga, pepinos, zanahorias...

Graciela: ¡No podemos acordarnos de todo! A ver... azúcar, tres latas de salsa de tomate, pan, mantequilla...

Teresa: ¡Ay, chicos! ¡Yo tengo la culpa! ¡Y mamá está contando con nosotros!

Alberto: Yo la ayudé. Es verdad que me levanté un poco tarde, pero... fui a la pescadería y traje el pescado que le gusta a abuelo.

Graciela: ¡Yo me levanté a las seis! ¡Y tuve solamente dos horas para bañarme, lavarme la cabeza y vestirme!

Teresa: ¡Pobrecita! Yo me levanté muy temprano, ¡a pesar de que no me acosté hasta la medianoche!

Los chicos terminan de hacer las compras y están listos para pagar.

Alberto: (*a Teresa*) ¿Tú tienes tu tarjeta de crédito? La mía está en mi billetera, que está en mi cuarto.

[1]de Fidel Castro, líder de la revolución cubana

Teresa: ¡La mía está en mi otra cartera! Graciela, ¿tú tienes la tuya?

Graciela: No... ¿No te acuerdas que yo perdí la mía hace una semana?

Teresa: Vamos a tener que llamar a mamá...

Por la noche, todos se divierten en la fiesta. Alberto toca la guitarra y Graciela canta unas canciones cubanas. Don Carlos recita un poema de José Martí. A las dos de la mañana, los invitados se van.

Noemí: (*A sus tres hijos*) Todo estuvo muy bien pero, de ahora en adelante, ¡yo hago las compras en el supermercado!

¿Lo sabía Ud.?

En los países hispanos frecuentemente hay dos o más generaciones que viven en la misma (*same*) casa. Los abuelos, por ejemplo, muchas veces viven con sus hijos y contribuyen al cuidado (*care*) de los niños. Muy raramente las personas mayores viven en una casa de ancianos (*nursing home*).

› **En este país, ¿las personas mayores generalmente viven con sus hijos o en una casa de ancianos?**

1. Hablemos With a partner, take turns asking and answering the following questions. Base your answers on the dialogue and on your own circumstances.

En el diálogo

1. ¿Dónde pasaron su infancia don Carlos y doña Consuelo?
2. ¿Qué extrañan ellos?
3. ¿De qué se olvidó Teresa? ¿De qué se acuerda?
4. ¿Qué verduras va a comprar Teresa?
5. ¿Qué compró Alberto? ¿Dónde lo compró?
6. ¿A qué hora se levantó Graciela?
7. ¿Dónde tiene Alberto su tarjeta de crédito?
8. ¿Qué perdió Graciela hace una semana?
9. ¿Quién tocó la guitarra en la fiesta?
10. ¿Qué recitó don Carlos?

¿Y tú?

1. ¿Dónde pasaste tu niñez?
2. ¿Qué extrañas tú? ¿Extrañas a alguien?
3. ¿Tú te olvidas de muchas cosas o siempre te acuerdas de todo?
4. ¿Qué verduras te gustan a ti?
5. ¿Tú compras pescado a veces? ¿Dónde lo compras?
6. ¿A qué hora te levantaste tú? ¿A qué hora te acostaste anoche?
7. ¿Tú tienes tarjetas de crédito? ¿Las usas frecuentemente?
8. ¿Tú perdiste algo recientemente? ¿Qué perdiste?
9. ¿Tú tocas algún instrumento? ¿Cuál es tu favorito?
10. ¿Te gusta leer poemas? ¿Quién es tu poeta favorito?

VOCABULARIO

En el diálogo

Cognados

el aniversario	*anniversary*
la guitarra	*guitar*
la lista	*list*
el mango	*mango*
la revolución	*revolution*
el supermercado	*supermarket*
el tomate	*tomato*

Nombres

el aguacate	*avocado*
el azúcar	*sugar*
la billetera	*wallet*
la boda	*wedding*
la canción	*song*
la cartera, el bolso	*purse*
la cebolla	*onion*
la infancia, la niñez	*childhood*
la juventud	*youth*
la lata, el bote (*Méx.*)	*can*
la lechuga	*lettuce*
el lugar	*place*
la mantequilla	*butter*
la manzana	*apple*
la medianoche	*midnight*
la naranja	*orange*
el oro	*gold*
el pepino	*cucumber*
la pescadería	*fish store*
el plátano, la banana	*banana*
pobrecito(a)	*the poor thing*
la salsa	*sauce*
las uvas	*grapes*
la zanahoria	*carrot*

Verbos

acordarse (o:ue) (de)	*to remember*
acostarse (o:ue)	*to go to bed*
bañarse	*to bathe*
celebrar, festejar	*to celebrate*
divertirse (e:ie)	*to have fun, to have a good time*
extrañar	*to miss*
irse	*to leave, to go away*
levantarse	*to get up*
nacer	*to be born*
olvidarse (de)	*to forget*
recitar	*to recite*
tocar	*to play (e.g., a musical instrument)*
vestirse (e:i)	*to get dressed*

Otras palabras y expresiones

a pesar de que	*in spite of the fact that*
las bodas de oro	*golden wedding (anniversary)*
de ahora en adelante	*from now on*
hace una semana	*a week ago*
lavarse la cabeza	*to wash one's hair*
temprano	*early*
tener la culpa	*to be at fault*

Una adivinanza° *riddle*

A un naranjo° me subí;° *orange tree / I climbed*
naranjas encontré;
naranjas no comí;
naranjas no dejé.
¿Cuántas naranjas había° en el árbol?[1] *were there*

[1]*Answer*: dos naranjas

© Georgios Alexandris/Shutterstock.com

¿Lo sabía Ud.?

La palabra **salsa** (sauce, spice) se usa también para referirse a la música caribeña. Actualmente este ritmo, basado en la música afrocubana, es muy popular en muchos países.

› **¿Cuáles son los ritmos típicos de los Estados Unidos?**

Más sobre el tema

Para hacer compras

la carnicería	*meat market*
la farmacia	*pharmacy*
la ferretería	*hardware store*
la joyería	*jewelry store*
la panadería	*bakery*
la zapatería	*shoe store*

Instrumentos musicales

la batería	*drums*
el clarinete	*clarinet*
el contrabajo	*bass*
la flauta	*flute*
el órgano	*organ*
el piano	*piano*
la trompeta	*trumpet*
el violín	*violin*

¿Lo sabía Ud.?

Aunque en la actualidad los supermercados son muy populares en los países de habla hispana, todavía es costumbre comprar en pequeñas tiendas especializadas en uno o dos productos: panadería, pescadería, etc. La mayoría de los pueblos tienen un mercado central, con pequeñas tiendas. Mucha gente todavía prefiere comprar en estos mercados donde los precios son más bajos y los clientes pueden regatear (*bargain*) con los vendedores (*merchants*).

› **¿Hay en su ciudad pequeñas tiendas que se especializan en dos o más productos? ¿Hay mercados al aire libre?**

Práctica

2. ¿Qué es? Write the words or phrases from the vocabulary that correspond to the following.

1. fruta cítrica _________
2. banana _________
3. celebrar _________
4. opuesto de acordarse _________
5. durazno _________
6. lugar donde compramos pescado _________
7. lugar donde compramos carne _________
8. similar a la mantequilla _________
9. lugar donde compramos pan _________
10. lugar donde compramos medicinas _________

3. Palabras Select the word or phrase that does not belong in each group.

1. niñez / juventud / contrabajo
2. uvas / lata / sandía
3. manzana / azúcar / piña
4. olvidarse / acordarse / extrañar
5. lechuga / fresas / apio
6. canción / pepino / cebolla
7. lavarse la cabeza / bañarse / acordarse
8. levantarse / divertirse / acostarse

4. Para completar Complete the following sentences, using vocabulary from this lesson.

1. La _________ castrista empezó en Cuba en 1959.
2. Ellos _________ sus _________ de oro este año.
3. De _________ en adelante yo voy a _________ a las siete de la mañana.
4 Van a dar una fiesta para _________ su _________.
5. ¿Dónde tienes tu tarjeta de crédito: en la _________ o en la cartera?
6. Elisa siempre le pone _________ y _________ a la ensalada.
7. El instrumento que _________ en las iglesias (*churches*) es el _________.
8. Voy a comprar tres _________ de salsa de _________.
9. En el _________ yo siempre compro muchas _________: mangos, aguacates, piñas... También compro _________ como zanahorias, repollo y apio.
10. Tengo que comprar _________ higiénico para el baño.

Para conversar

5. ¿Qué te olvidaste de traer? With a partner, play the roles of two roommates who ask each other whether or not they bought certain items at the supermarket. Each one will answer saying that he/she did not buy the particular item, but another, and indicate where he/she is going to put those items: in the refrigerator, on the table, or in the pantry (**la alacena**).

Modelo *—¿Compraste...?*
—No, pero compré... Lo/La/Los/Las voy a poner en...

CD2-15

Pronunciación

La entonación

Intonation refers to the variations in the pitch of your voice when you are talking. Intonation patterns in Spanish are different from those in English. Note the following regarding Spanish intonation.

1. For normal statements, the pitch generally rises on the first stressed syllable.

Yo compré el regalo para Elena.

2. For questions eliciting information, the pitch is highest on the stressed syllable of the interrogative pronoun.

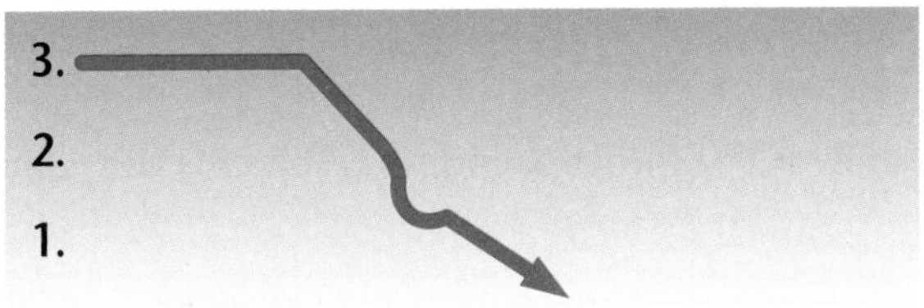

¿Cómo está tu mamá?

3. For questions that can be answered with **sí** or **no**, the pitch is generally highest on the last stressed syllable.

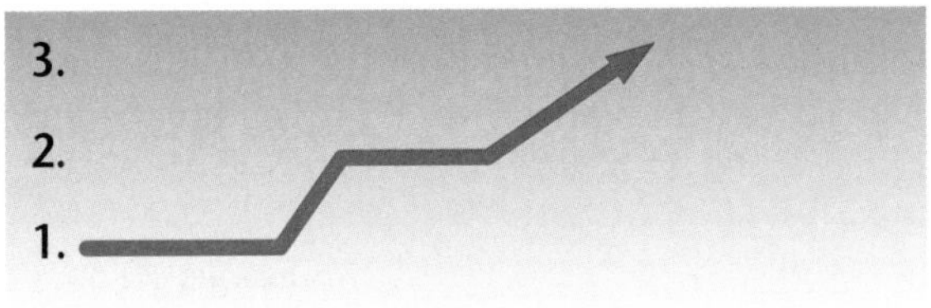

¿Fuiste al mercado ayer?

4. In exclamations, the pitch is highest on the first stressed syllable.

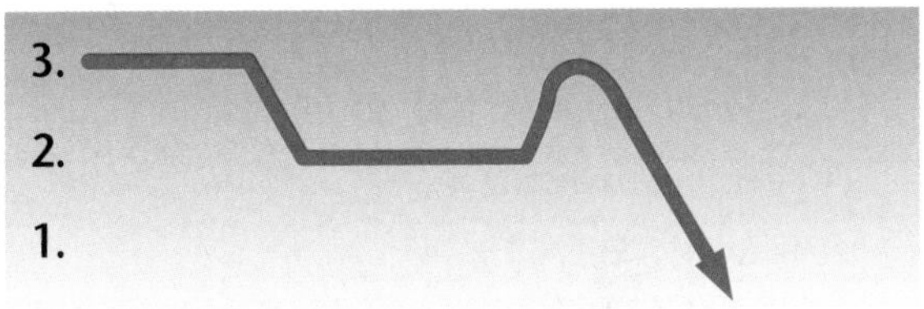

¡Qué bonita es esa chica!

ESTRUCTURAS

1 Reflexive constructions (*Construcciones reflexivas*)

A. Reflexive pronouns

Subjects		Reflexive pronouns
yo	**me**	*myself, to (for) myself*
tú	**te**	*yourself, to (for) yourself* (**tú** *form*)
nosotros(as)	**nos**	*ourselves, to (for) ourselves*
vosotros(as)	**os**	*yourselves, to (for) yourselves* (**vosotros** *form*)
Ud.	**se**	*yourself, to (for) yourself* (**Ud.** *form*)
Uds.	**se**	*yourselves, to (for) yourselves* (**Uds.** *form*)
él	**se**	*himself, to (for) himself*
ella	**se**	*herself, to (for) herself*
	se	*itself, to (for) itself*
ellos, ellas	**se**	*themselves, to (for) themselves*

› Reflexive pronouns are used whenever the direct or indirect object is the same as the subject of the sentence.

› Note that except for **se,** the reflexive pronouns have the same forms as the direct and indirect object pronouns.

› The third-person singular and plural **se** is invariable.

› Reflexive pronouns are positioned in the sentence in the same manner as object pronouns. They are placed in front of a conjugated verb—**Yo *me* levanto**—or they may be attached to an infinitive or to a present participle: **Yo voy a levantar*me*. Yo estoy levantándo*me*.**

B. Reflexive verbs

› Many verbs can be made reflexive in Spanish, that is, they can be made to act upon the subject, by the use of a reflexive pronoun.

lavarse	*to wash oneself*
Yo **me lavo.**	*I wash (myself).*
Tú **te lavas.**	*You wash (yourself)* (**tú** *form*).
Ud. **se lava.**	*You wash (yourself)* (**Ud.** *form*).
Él **se lava.**	*He washes (himself).*
Ella **se lava.**	*She washes (herself).*
Nosotros(as) **nos lavamos.**	*We wash (ourselves).*
Vosotros(as) **os laváis.**	*You wash (yourselves)* (**vosotros** *form*).
Uds. **se lavan.**	*You wash (yourselves)* (**Uds.** *form*).
Ellos **se lavan.**	*They* (masc.) *wash (themselves).*
Ellas **se lavan.**	*They (fem.) wash (themselves).*

Julia baña al perro.

Julia se baña.

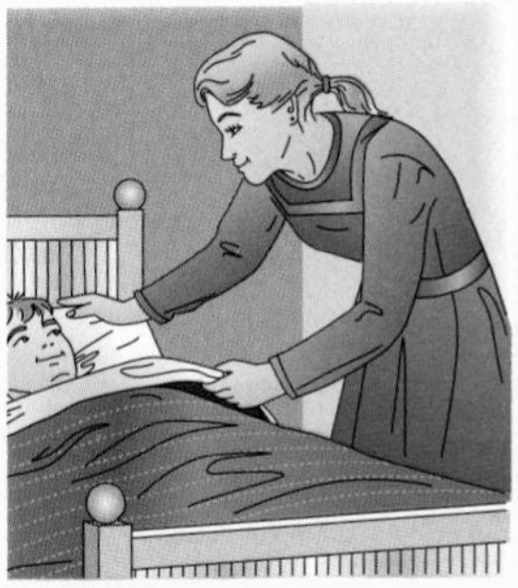

Elsa acuesta a su hijo a las siete.

Elsa se acuesta a las diez.

› In addition to the verbs included in the vocabulary list, the following verbs are commonly used in reflexive constructions.

afeitarse	*to shave*
cepillarse los dientes	*to brush one's teeth*
despertarse (e:ie)	*to wake up*
desvestirse (e:i)	*to get undressed*
peinarse	*to comb one's hair*
preocuparse (por)	*to worry (about)*
quejarse	*to complain*
sentarse (e:ie)	*to sit (down)*
sentirse (e:ie)	*to feel* (mood or physical condition)

—¿A qué hora **se acuestan** Uds.? *What time do you go to bed?*
—Yo **me acuesto** a las diez y Ana **se acuesta** a las doce. *I go to bed at ten and Ana goes to bed at twelve.*

¡Atención! The Spanish reflexives are seldom translated using the reflexive pronouns in English: **Yo me acuesto** = *I go to bed.*

› The following verbs have different meanings when they are used with reflexive pronouns.

acostar (o:ue) *to put to bed*	**acostarse** *to go to bed*
dormir (o:ue) *to sleep*	**dormirse** *to fall asleep*
ir *to go*	**irse** *to go away, leave*
levantar *to raise, lift*	**levantarse** *to get up*
llamar *to call*	**llamarse** *to be called*
poner *to put, place*	**ponerse** *to put on*
probar (o:ue) *to try; to taste*	**probarse** *to try on*
quitar *to take away*	**quitarse** *to take off*

—¿A qué hora se **levantaron** Uds.? *What time did you get up?*
—**Nos levantamos** muy temprano. *We got up very early.*
—¿Ya **te vas**? *Are you leaving already?*
—Sí, tengo que ir al mercado. *Yes, I have to go to the market.*

Summary of Personal Pronouns				
Subject	***Direct object***	***Indirect object***	***Reflexive***	***Object of prepositions***
yo	me	me	me	mí
tú	te	te	te	ti
usted (*fem.*)	la	le	se	usted
usted (*masc.*)	lo			usted
él	lo			él
ella	la			ella
nosotros(as)	nos	nos	nos	nosotros(as)
vosotros(as)	os	os	os	vosotros(as)
ustedes (*fem.*)	las	les	se	ustedes
ustedes (*masc.*)	los			ustedes
ellos	los			ellos
ellas	las			ellas

Práctica

6. La rutina diaria Say what you and your relatives normally do, by adding the correct form of the missing verbs.

1. Mis hermanos _________ (afeitarse) cuando _________ (levantarse).
2. Mi tía _________ (lavarse) la cabeza y después _________ (peinarse).
3. Mis padres ___________ (despertarse) muy temprano, pero nosotros ___________ (despertarse) tarde.
4. Ayer mis hijas no _________ (acostarse) hasta la medianoche.
5. Ayer yo _________ (levantarse) muy temprano, pero hoy _________ (levantarse) tarde.
6. Paquito _________ (bañarse) y _________ (vestirse) antes de ir a la escuela (*school*).
7. Cuando mi hijo va a la zapatería, siempre _________ (probarse) muchos zapatos.
8. En la clase yo _________ (sentarse) cerca de la pizarra.
9. Mi madre _________ (preocuparse) mucho por mí.
10. Yo _________ (desvestirse) y _________ (bañarse) antes de _________ (acostarse).

Un dicho

Yo me lavo las manos.
Equivalent: *I wash my hands* (*of this*).

› The definite article is used with abstract and generic nouns.

Me gusta **el té**, pero prefiero **el café.**	*I like tea, but I prefer coffee.*
Las madres siempre se preocupan por sus hijos.	*Mothers always worry about their children.*
La educación es muy importante.	*Education is very important.*

› The definite article is used with certain nouns, including **cárcel** (*jail*), **iglesia** (*church*), and **escuela** when they are preceded by a preposition.

—¿Vas a **la iglesia** los domingos?	*Do you go to church on Sundays?*
—No, voy a **la iglesia** los sábados.	*No, I go to church on Saturdays.*
—¿Dónde están los chicos?	*Where are the children?*
—Están en **la escuela.**	*They're at school.*
—¿Jorge está en **la cárcel**?	*Is Jorge in jail?*
—Sí, yo lo visito todas las semanas.	*Yes, I visit him every week.*

› Remember that the definite article is also used with days of the week, when indicating titles in indirect address, and when telling time.

El Sr. Vega viene **el sábado** a **las tres** de la tarde.	*Mr. Vega is coming on Saturday at three o' clock in the afternoon.*

Práctica

11. Minidiálogos Supply the Spanish equivalents of the words in parentheses. Then act out the dialogues with a partner.

1. —¿Tú vas todos los domingos a ________? (*church*)
   —No, los domingos voy a ________ a visitar a un amigo de mi hijo. (*jail*)
2. —¿Tú hablas frecuentemente con ________ Silva? (*Mr.*)
   —No, pero hablo con su esposa, ________ Álvarez. (*Dr.*)
3. —¿Qué dice ella de los problemas de ________? (*education*)
   —Ella dice que son muchos.
4. —¿Qué están haciendo ________ Gómez y ________ Díaz? (*Miss*) / (*Mrs.*)
   —Se están poniendo ________ porque hace mucho frío. (*their coats*)
5. —Luisito, ¿dónde estás?
   —Estoy en el baño. Me estoy lavando ________. (*my hands*)
6. —Amalia, ¿cuándo es tu clase de piano?
   —Es ________ ________ tres. (*on Tuesday / at three*)

Un dicho

El amor todo lo puede.
Equivalent: *Love conquers all.*

ESTRUCTURAS

Para conversar

12. ¡Habla con tu compañero(a)! With a partner, take turns asking and answering the following questions in complete sentences.

1. ¿Qué te gusta más, el pescado o la carne? ¿Te gustan más las manzanas o las uvas?
2. ¿Qué te gusta más, el café o el té? ¿El agua mineral o los refrescos?
3. ¿Te lavas la cabeza todos los días? ¿Qué champú usas?
4. ¿Te quitas los zapatos cuando llegas a tu casa? ¿Te cambias de ropa?
5. ¿Te gustan los idiomas extranjeros (*foreign*)? ¿Te gusta más el francés o el español?
6. ¿Vas a la iglesia los domingos? ¿A qué hora vas? ¿Con quién vas?
7. ¿Qué es más importante para ti, el amor o el dinero?
8. ¿Quiénes conducen mejor, los hombres o las mujeres? ¿Quiénes son más eficientes?

3 Possessive pronouns (*Pronombres posesivos*)

Singular		Plural		
Masculine	***Feminine***	***Masculine***	***Feminine***	
el mío	la mía	los míos	las mías	*mine*
el tuyo	la tuya	los tuyos	las tuyas	*yours* (fam.)
el suyo	la suya	los suyos	las suyas	*yours* (form.) / *his* / *hers*
el nuestro	la nuestra	los nuestros	las nuestras	*ours*
el vuestro	la vuestra	los vuestros	las vuestras	*yours* (fam.)
el suyo	la suya	los suyos	las suyas	*yours* (form.) / *theirs*

LEARNING TIP
Remember that pronouns are especially useful when, in conversation or writing, you need to refer again to an idea or something or someone that you have already introduced. For example: **La novia de Luis es de Perú. *La mía* es de Chile.**

In Spanish, possessive pronouns agree in gender and number with the thing possessed. They are generally used with the definite article.

—Aquí están **mis maletas.** ¿Dónde están **las tuyas**?	*Here are my suitcases. Where are yours?*
—**Las mías** están en mi cuarto.	*Mine are in my room.*
—**Nuestro profesor** es de Colombia.	*Our professor is from Colombia.*
—**El nuestro** es de Venezuela.	*Ours is from Venezuela.*
—**Mi apartamento** está en la calle Palma.	*My apartment is on Palma Street.*
—**El mío** está en la calle Estrella.	*Mine is on Estrella Street.*

¡Atención! After the verb **ser**, the definite article is frequently omitted.

—¿Estos billetes son **suyos**, señor? *Are these tickets yours, sir?*
—No, no son **míos**. *No, they're not mine.*

› Because the third-person forms of the possessive pronouns (**el suyo, la suya, los suyos, las suyas**) can be ambiguous, they can be replaced by the pronouns below for clarification.

	Ud.		
el de	él	el [libro]	de él
la de	ella	el	**de él**
los de	Uds.		
las de	ellos	Es **suyo.** (*unclarified*)	
	ellas	Es **el de él.** (*clarified*)	

—Estas maletas son de Eva y de Jorge, ¿no? *These suitcases are Eva's and Jorge's, aren't they?*
—Bueno, la maleta azul es **de ella y** la maleta marrón es **de él.** *Well, the blue suitcase is hers, and the brown suitcase is his.*
—¿El piano es **de Uds.**? *Is the piano yours?*
—No, es **de ellos**. *No, it's theirs.*

Un dicho
Lo que es tuyo es mío y lo que es mío es tuyo.
Equivalent: *What's yours is mine and what's mine is yours.*

Práctica

13. Todo es nuestro According to Eva and Luis, *everything* belongs to them. Indicate how they would answer the following questions. Keep in mind who is answering.

Modelo ¿La cartera es de Nora? (Eva)
No, no es suya; es mía.

1. ¿La billetera es de Carlos? (Luis)
2. ¿Las sábanas son de Uds.? (Eva y Luis)
3. ¿Las naranjas son mías? (Luis)
4. ¿Los regalos son tuyos? (Eva)
5. ¿Las maletas son de Marta? (Luis)
6. ¿El televisor es de Uds.? (Eva y Luis)
7. ¿El mantel es de Gloria? (Eva)
8. ¿Los cubiertos son de Uds.? (Eva y Luis)

14. Minidiálogos Complete the following dialogues using the correct possessive pronoun.

1. —Mis padres viven en Cuba. ¿Dónde viven _________, señor Suárez? *(yours)*
   —_________ viven en Costa Rica. (*mine*)
2. —Mis llaves están en la mesa. ¿Dónde están _________, María? (*yours*)
   —_________ están en mi cuarto, pero Armando no tiene _________. (*mine / his*)
3. —Yo no tengo mi equipaje en el cuarto. ¿Elsa tiene _________ en su cuarto? (*hers*)
   —Sí, y también tiene _________. (*ours*)

15. Comparaciones With a partner, make comparisons between the objects and people described and those in your own experience. Use appropriate possessive pronouns when asking each other questions.

Modelo —El hermano de Teresa tiene quince años. ¿Y el tuyo?
—El mío tiene dieciocho.

1. Los mejores amigos de Rosa son de Cuba.
2. El apartamento de Ana tiene cuatro cuartos.
3. Los padres de Ramiro viven en Pinar del Río.
4. El cumpleaños de Jorge es en septiembre.
5. Las maletas de Alina son verdes.
6. La hermana de Rafael es muy bonita.
7. El idioma de Hans es alemán.
8. Las primas de Enrique son cubanas.

Para conversar

16. Así es la vida (*Such is life*) In groups of three, compare some aspects of your lives, such as your room or apartment, relatives, classes, jobs, and so on. For example:

Modelo S1: *Mi apartamento está cerca de* (near) *la universidad.*
S2: *El mío está cerca también.*
S3: *El mío está lejos.*

4 Irregular preterits (*Pretéritos irregulares*)

› The following Spanish verbs are irregular in the preterit.

tener: tuve, tuviste, tuvo, tuvimos, tuvisteis, tuvieron

estar: estuve, estuviste, estuvo, estuvimos, estuvisteis, estuvieron

poder: pude, pudiste, pudo, pudimos, pudisteis, pudieron

poner: puse, pusiste, puso, pusimos, pusisteis, pusieron

saber: supe, supiste, supo, supimos, supisteis, supieron

hacer: hice, hiciste, hizo,[1] hicimos, hicisteis, hicieron

venir: vine, viniste, vino, vinimos, vinisteis, vinieron

querer: quise, quisiste, quiso, quisimos, quisisteis, quisieron

[1]Note that in the third-person singular form, **c** changes to **z** in order to maintain the soft sound.

decir: dije, dijiste, dijo, dijimos, dijisteis, dijeron[1]

traer: traje, trajiste, trajo, trajimos, trajisteis, trajeron[1]

conducir: conduje, condujiste, condujo, condujimos, condujisteis, condujeron[1]

traducir: traduje, tradujiste, tradujo, tradujimos, tradujisteis, tradujeron[1]

—¿Por qué no **viniste** anoche?	*Why didn't you come last night?*
—No **pude; tuve** que trabajar.	*I wasn't able to; I had to work.*
Y tú, ¿qué **hiciste**?	*And you, what did you do?*
—Yo **estuve** en casa toda la noche.	*I was home all night.*
—¿Qué me **trajeron** Uds.?	*What did you bring me?*
—Te **trajimos** una cámara.	*We brought you a camera.*
—¿Dónde la **pusieron**?	*Where did you put it?*
—La **pusimos** en tu cuarto.	*We put it in your room.*

¡Atención! The preterit of **hay** (impersonal form of **haber**) is **hubo** (*there was, there were*).

Anoche **hubo** un concierto.	*Last night there was a concert.*

Práctica

17. ¡Qué idiotas! Elsa and David are arguing. Complete their dialogue, using the preterit of the verbs given. Then act it out with a partner.

Elsa: ¿Dónde _________ (estar) (tú) anoche? ¡ _________ (Venir) muy tarde!

David: ¡Te lo _________ (decir)! _________ (Estar) en casa de mamá. _________ (Tener) que hablar con papá. No te llamé porque no _________ (poder).

Elsa: ¿No _________ (poder) o no _________ (querer)?

David: Bueno. ¿Dónde _________ (poner) tú los documentos que yo _________ (traducir) ayer en la oficina?

Elsa: ¡Tú no _________ (traer) ningún documento!

David: No... los empleados los _________ (traer) cuando _________ (venir) ayer.

Elsa: Ellos no me _________ (decir) nada. ¡Son unos idiotas!

18. Ayer Read what the following people typically do. Then, using your imagination, say what everyone did differently yesterday.

1. Yo estoy en mi casa por la mañana.
2. Tú vienes a la universidad a las diez de la mañana.
3. Paquito hace ejercicio por la tarde.
4. Julio tiene que trabajar en el mercado.
5. Nosotros traemos a nuestros hijos a la escuela.
6. Ellos traducen las lecciones al inglés.
7. María se pone el suéter azul.
8. Yo conduzco mi coche.

[1] Note that in the third-person plural ending of these verbs, the **i** is omitted.

ESTRUCTURAS

Para conversar

19. ¡Habla con tu compañero(a)! With a partner, take turns asking each other the following questions and answering in complete sentences.

1. ¿Qué tuviste que hacer ayer? ¿Tuviste mucho trabajo? ¿Estuviste muy ocupado(a)?
2. ¿Qué hicieron tú y tus amigos ayer? ¿Qué hicieron el sábado?
3. ¿Dónde estuvieron tú y tu familia anoche? ¿Qué hicieron tus padres?
4. ¿Hubo una fiesta en tu casa el mes pasado? ¿Quiénes vinieron?
5. ¿Tuviste que limpiar la casa ayer? ¿Alguien tuvo que ayudarte?
6. ¿Viniste a clase la semana pasada? ¿Viniste solo(a)? ¿Qué días viniste?
7. ¿Pudiste venir temprano a la universidad ayer? ¿A qué hora viniste? ¿Alguien vino contigo? ¿Qué te pusiste para venir a la universidad?
8. ¿Condujiste tu auto ayer o viniste en autobús?

20. ¿Qué hiciste? In groups of three, ask each other about what you did yesterday, last night, or last week. Use irregular preterit forms in your questions. Ask for as many details as possible.

Modelo —*¿Qué hicieron tú y tus amigos el fin de semana?*

—*Hicimos un viaje a Nueva York. ¿Qué hicieron el sábado?*

5 *Hace...* meaning *ago* (*Hace... como equivalente de* ago)

Hace + *preterit* indicates how long ago something took place.

In sentences using the preterit and in some cases the imperfect, **hace** + *period of time* is the equivalent of the English *ago*.

LEARNING TIP
Here is another case of an English expression that uses the impersonal form **hace** in Spanish along with weather expressions (**Lección 5**) and time expressions (**Lección 7**).

When **hace** is placed at the beginning of the sentence, the construction is as follows.

Hace + *period of time* + **que**
Hace + *dos años* + **que** la conocí.

—¿Cuánto tiempo hace que conociste a tu novia?	*How long ago did you meet your girlfriend?*
—**Hace tres años que** la conocí.	*I met her three years ago.*
—**Hace diez años que** ellos vinieron a los Estados Unidos. ¿Y tú?	*They came to the United States ten years ago. And you?*
—Yo llegué **hace cuatro años.**	*I arrived four years ago.*

¡Atención! Note that it is also possible to say: **Yo llegué hace cuatro años.**

Práctica

21. ¿Cuánto tiempo hace? Say how long ago everything happened, according to the information provided.

Modelo Mi padre viajó el martes. Hoy es viernes.

Mi padre viajó hace tres días.

1. Mi nieto nació en junio. Estamos en diciembre.
2. El Sr. Calderón compró la ferretería en el año 2010. Estamos en el año 2012.
3. Yo desayuné a las ocho. Son las once y media.
4. Mis hijos fueron a Lima el lunes. Hoy es sábado.
5. Ramiro empezó a tocar la trompeta a las doce. Son las doce y cuarto.

Para conversar

22. Dime... With a partner, take turns asking and answering these questions in complete sentences.

1. ¿Cuánto tiempo hace que llegaste a la universidad?
2. ¿Cuánto tiempo hace que conociste a tu profesor (profesora)?
3. ¿Cuánto tiempo hace que empezaste a estudiar aquí?
4. ¿Cuánto tiempo hace que tuviste un examen?
5. ¿Cuánto tiempo hace que terminaste la escuela secundaria?
6. ¿Cuánto tiempo hace que aprendiste a conducir?
7. ¿Cuánto tiempo hace que compraste tu coche?
8. ¿Cuánto tiempo hace que almorzaste?

23. ¡Hace mucho tiempo! With a partner, take turns asking each other how long ago you did each of the following things.

Modelo visitar un museo

S1: *¿Cuánto tiempo hace que visitaste un museo?*

S2: *Hace seis meses que visité un museo.*
(Visité un museo hace seis meses.)

1. ir a la playa
2. ir al dentista
3. dar una fiesta
4. ir de compras
5. ir al cine
6. empezar a estudiar
7. ver a tus padres
8. ir de vacaciones
9. llamar a tu mejor amigo(a)
10. levantarse

Now, use similar questions to interview your instructor.

24. Acontecimientos importantes With a partner, prepare two questions about how long ago an important event took place in his/her life. Then join another pair, and ask them your questions and answer theirs.

Modelo *¿Cuánto tiempo hace que empezaste a estudiar español?*

Hace un año que empecé a estudiar español.
(Empecé a estudiar español hace un año.)

¡Vamos a ver!

Antes de ver el video

25. Antes de ver el video You and a partner take turns asking and answering the following questions.

1. ¿Cuántos años vas a cumplir en tu próximo cumpleaños?
2. Para festejar tu cumpleaños, ¿das una fiesta en tu casa o lo festejas en un restaurante?
3. ¿Tú sabes dónde pasaron tus padres su infancia y su juventud? ¿Ellos extrañan esos lugares?
4. ¿Tú sabes tocar la guitarra y cantar? ¿Sabes cantar "La guantanamera"? ¿Quieres aprender a cantarla?
5. ¿Tú tuviste que levantarte temprano ayer? ¿Qué hiciste? ¿Te acostaste muy tarde anoche?
6. ¿Tú puedes bañarte, lavarte la cabeza y vestirte en veinte minutos?
7. Generalmente, ¿a qué hora es la cena en tu casa?
8. ¿Tú tienes alguna receta especial?
9. El congrí, una comida cubana típica, se hace con arroz blanco y frijoles negros. ¿Tú sabes cocinarlo?
10. ¿Tú usas lechuga, tomates, cebollas, pepinos y zanahorias para preparar una ensalada?
11. Cuando fuiste al mercado, ¿te acordaste de comprar frutas? ¿Qué frutas compraste? ¿Pusiste algunas en el refrigerador?
12. Cuando haces una ensalada de frutas, ¿le pones azúcar? ¿La sirves con crema?
13. ¿Tú sabes preparar un flan? ¿Sabes preparar dulce de leche?
14. Cuando haces espaguetis, ¿usas salsa de tomate? ¿Tú la preparas o compras una lata de salsa de tomate?

El video: Guantanamera

—¿Y tú, Mario? ¿Qué hiciste?

—Yo tuve que levantarme muy temprano para ir a la pescadería para comprar un pargo, el pescado que le gusta a abuelo.

—Extrañas Cuba, ¿verdad?

—Mucho. Extraño los lugares donde pasé mi infancia y mi juventud: La Habana, Camagüey... Pinar del Rio...

Después de ver el video

Graciela

Magali

Mario

Don Rogelio

26. ¿Quién lo dice? Identify the person who said the following in the dialogues.

1. Yo tuve que levantarme muy temprano para ir a la pescadería.
2. Extraño los lugares donde pasé mi infancia y mi juventud.
3. Tu tío César va a hacer el lechón asado.
4. Yo le pongo azúcar y la sirvo con crema.
5. ¿Qué estás haciendo, abuelo?
6. ¡Ay, pobrecito! Yo me levanté a las cinco.
7. Estoy leyendo unos poemas de José Martí.
8. Todavía tengo que bañarme, lavarme la cabeza y vestirme.

27. Hablemos With a partner, take turns asking and answering the following questions. Base your answers on the dialogue.

1. ¿Cuántos años cumple don Rogelio?
2. ¿Qué trajo Magali para preparar el congrí?
3. ¿Qué trajo Magali para la ensalada?
4. ¿A qué hora tuvo que levantarse Mario? ¿Adónde fue? ¿Qué compró?
5. ¿A qué hora se levantó Magali? ¿A qué hora se acostó? ¿Con quién estuvo hablando?
6. ¿Qué frutas necesita Mario?
7. ¿Qué se olvidó de comprar Magali?
8. ¿Dónde está don Rogelio? ¿Qué está haciendo?
9. ¿Qué extraña don Rogelio? ¿Qué ciudades recuerda?
10. ¿Qué instrumento toca don Rogelio?

28. ¿Qué pasa después...? You and a partner use your imagination to say what the characters do. In Spanish, discuss the following.

1. Whether or not everybody liked the barbecued pork that César prepared and what he served with it.
2. Whether or not everybody liked the fruit salad that Ramón prepared.
3. Whether or not Graciela was able to bathe, wash her hair, and get dressed before eight.
4. Whether Magali's grandpa played the guitar at the party and whether he and Magali sang their favorite song.
5. What Graciela and Magali bought at the supermarket a week after the party.
6. Whether Mario had to get up early the day after the party.
7. Whether Magali went to bed before eleven the night after the party.
8. Whether Mrs. Torales gave them another recipe.

Now compare your answers to those of the members of another group.

¡Vamos a escuchar!

ESTRATEGIA **Dealing with fast speech** Listening to speech when you can't ask the speaker to slow down or repeat is especially challenging in a foreign language, particularly if the language is spoken at what seems to be a fast pace. In such instances, try to listen for familiar words to understand what the topic is, or to get the gist of what is said. When dealing with fast speech in a classroom setting—with video or lab activities, for instance—you can often listen more than once and thus train yourself to become a better listener.

29. ¿Qué dijeron? Listen to a conversation between Ester and Raúl, and answer the following questions when you feel you can provide the answer or make a guess.

CD2-16

1. ¿Qué festejan hoy Ester y Raúl?
2. ¿Qué necesita Ester para la ensalada?
3. ¿Qué va a comprar Raúl en la pescadería?
4. ¿Quién va a traer el postre?
5. ¿Para qué debe ir Raúl a la joyería?

¡Vamos a conversar!

ESTRATEGIA **Using pauses to manage a conversation** In addition to asking for repetition or clarification (**Lección 2**), and restating something you hear in your own words (**Lecciones 7 and 8**), you can create pauses during a conversation in order to gain time to organize your thoughts and reply. The following words and expressions, most of which you have seen in previous lessons, are commonly used as pausing devices.

- Gaining time: **Bueno... , A ver...**
- Asking for your listener's attention: **Oye... (Óyeme...), Mira...**
- Reacting to what you hear: **¡Caramba!**
- Fillers: **Este... , Eh...** (*Uh . . ., Ummm . . .*)
- Correcting or clarifying what you are saying: **Es decir...** (*That is to say . . .*)

30. Este... Take turns telling a classmate about the last birthday you celebrated. Your goal is to describe the celebration as fully as you can. Tell whose birthday you celebrated, where, how many people attended, and talk about the food, gifts, etc. Use some of the phrases above when you need to pause or gain time to think.

31. ¿Qué dice Ud.? What would you say in the following situations? What might the other person say? Act out the scenes with a partner. Take turns playing each role.

1. You and your roommate are going to decide what you need from the grocery store. Don't forget to include fruits and vegetables.
2. You are talking to a prospective roommate and want to know about his/her daily routine. Ask him/her pertinent questions.
3. You are in Santo Domingo. Your Dominican friend is going to accompany you downtown to do some shopping. Tell him/her which stores you have to go to. You want to buy nails, shoes, a bracelet, medicine, etc. Say what time you want to leave.
4. Last night you called your friend Fernando and he wasn't home. Ask him where he was, what he had to do, whether or not he was able to speak with his parents, and what they said about the party.

32. **Para conocernos mejor** To do this activity, work with a classmate whom you would like to get to know. Take turns asking and answering these questions.

1. ¿Cuánto tiempo hace que empezaste a estudiar en esta universidad? ¿Te gusta la universidad? ¿Tienes muchos amigos aquí?
2. ¿Sabes algún poema en español? ¿Alguna canción? ¿Te gusta recitar poemas?
3. ¿Hiciste algo de interés anteayer? ¿Adónde fuiste? ¿Con quién estuviste? ¿Tuviste que trabajar? ¿Hubo una fiesta en tu casa?
4. ¿Qué hiciste anoche para cenar? ¿Tienes alguna receta (*recipe*) especial? ¿Dónde la conseguiste?
5. ¿A qué hora te despertaste hoy? ¿A qué hora te levantas generalmente? ¿Te gusta acostarte temprano o tarde?
6. Generalmente, ¿te bañas por la mañana o por la tarde? ¿Qué jabón usas? ¿Te lavas la cabeza todos los días? ¿Necesitas mucho tiempo para vestirte?
7. ¿Tomas café? ¿Le pones azúcar y crema? ¿Lo tomas después de las comidas o con las comidas?
8. ¿Dónde naciste? ¿Extrañas el lugar donde pasaste tu niñez? ¿Extrañas a tus amigos de la escuela? ¿Tú sabes dónde pasaron tus padres su juventud?

33. **Una encuesta** Interview your classmates to identify who fits the following descriptions. Include your instructor, but remember to use the **Ud**. form when addressing him/her. After finishing the survey, get together with two or three classmates and discuss the results.

1. Come muchas frutas y muchas verduras. ____________
2. Nunca le pone mantequilla al pan. ____________
3. No le pone azúcar al café. ____________
4. Le pone aceite y vinagre a la ensalada. ____________
5. Sabe tocar el piano. ____________
6. Se levanta muy temprano. ____________
7. Siempre se baña por la mañana. ____________
8. Siempre se acuerda de todo. ____________

34. **Para crear** Get together in groups of three or four and "create" the scenario for this photo. Who is this person? What is he buying? What does he like to eat? Is he going to have a party? Give details.

Rincón literario

Esopo (c. 600 A.C.[1])

Esopo, escritor de la Grecia Antigua, es famoso por sus fábulas, que llegan a nosotros a través[2] de la tradición oral y de traducciones escritas. La fábula tiene un objetivo didáctico, que se expresa en la moraleja. En muchas fábulas, los personajes son animales.

Antes de leer

ESTRATEGIA **Using prior knowledge to guess the meaning of new vocabulary** This strategy is very simple: You have heard or read Aesop's fable "The Tortoise and the Hare." Think about what takes place in this fable and what the moral of the story is. What words and expressions might you find in this narration? Which ones do you know in Spanish? You might make logical guesses about the ones with which you are not familiar, based on what you know about the story.

35. Una fábula Do the following:

1. Skim the fable, without looking at the English equivalent of the glossed words, and try to guess their meaning.
2. Find the words and expressions whose meaning you know. Also, list the reflexive verbs that you recognize.

¡A leer!

36. Comprensión As you read the selection, find the answers to the following questions.

1. ¿Por qué se está burlando la liebre de la tortuga?
2. ¿Qué dice la tortuga que puede hacer?
3. ¿La liebre acepta el reto?
4. ¿Cómo camina la tortuga hacia la meta?
5. ¿Qué hace la liebre?
6. ¿Qué ve cuando se despierta?
7. ¿Cuál es la moraleja?

La liebre y la tortuga

Cierto día, una liebre se está burlando de la tortuga que, como todos sabemos, es muy lenta. La tortuga se ríe y le contesta:

—Tú eres muy rápida y corres como el viento, pero yo sé que puedo ganarte en una competencia.

La liebre, totalmente segura de que eso es imposible, continúa burlándose de la tortuga y acepta el reto.

El día de la carrera,° las dos empiezan a correr al mismo tiempo. La tortuga camina lentamente hacia la meta.° La liebre, que se cree invencible, se acuesta y descansa° en el camino muchas veces y al final se duerme.

Cuando se despierta y empieza a correr, ve que la tortuga llega a la meta y obtiene la victoria.

Moraleja: Con paciencia y constancia siempre se triunfa.

race
goal
rests

[1] circa (*around*) 600 años antes de Cristo = *before Christ* (B.C.)
[2] *through*

Después de leer...

37. Reflexiones In groups of three, apply the moral of the story to this scenario, which is a part of student life.

> Dos estudiantes: Luis y Sergio
>
> Luis es muy inteligente y tiene dinero, de modo que no tiene que trabajar. Él raramente estudia y todo lo deja para última hora. Sergio encuentra difíciles varias de sus clases y trabaja veinte horas por semana. Él es disciplinado y estudia mucho. ¿Cuál de los dos triunfa? ¿Por qué? Den detalles sobre la rutina diaria de los dos. Comparen los hábitos de estos estudiantes con los de ustedes.

¡Vamos a escribir!

Antes de escribir

ESTRATEGIA **Sequencing steps for writing a didactic story** When telling a story that is meant to teach something, the process requires an order of steps. The following might be useful.

1. Presentation and description of the characters
2. The scenario
3. The problem or the challenge the characters face
4. The action
5. What happens at the end
6. The moral of the story

¡A escribir!

38. Narración Using the conversation you had with your partners as a guide, write a story about Luis and Sergio, providing details about their personalities and their routine. The story should illustrate the moral of the fable that you read on page 276.

Después de escribir

39. Before writing the final version, exchange your first draft with a classmate and peer edit each other's work, using the guidelines suggested in the strategy. Pay attention to the use of the reflexive construction.

EL MUNDO HISPÁNICO Y TÚ

Cuba

Hay dos Cubas: una anterior a Castro; otra, después de él. La Cuba anterior a la revolución no era (*was*) el paraíso que describen los emigrados, pero era el país con el mejor estándar de vida de Latinoamérica, después de Argentina y Uruguay. La Cuba de hoy no es tampoco el paraíso de los trabajadores que ofreció Castro, sino uno de los países más pobres del continente. Muchas cosas han cambiado (*have changed*), pero Cuba sigue siendo "La perla de las Antillas" por sus bellezas naturales.

Puntos de interés turístico

La Habana, la capital, es la ciudad más grande de las Antillas. En su parte antigua, la Habana Vieja, hay muchos edificios coloniales: la Catedral, la Plaza de Armas, el Templete... y al otro lado de la bahía, las fortalezas de El Morro y La Cabaña.

Varadero es la playa más famosa de Cuba y una de las mejores del mundo. Otras bellas playas cubanas son Santa María del Mar, en La Habana, Santa Lucía, en Camagüey, y Guardalabarca, en Holguín.

Las artes

La pintura

El más famoso de los pintores cubanos es Wifredo Lam. Su ascendencia —blanca, negra y china— se refleja en sus cuadros. Algunas de sus obras están expuestas en el Museo de Arte Moderno de Nueva York y en el Museo Reina Sofía de Madrid.

La literatura

En Cuba encontramos escritores notables en todas las épocas. De la época colonial, el más famoso es José Martí. Entre los contemporáneos sobresalen (*excel*) los novelistas Reinaldo Arenas, Zoe Valdés y Daína Chaviano.

La música

La música cubana es una combinación de la música española y de la africana. Los ritmos tradicionales son *la rumba, la conga, el son* y *el danzón*. De creación más reciente son *el bolero, el mambo* y *el cha cha chá*.

La República Dominicana

La isla que hoy conocemos como Santo Domingo fue descubierta por Colón en su primer viaje (1492). La República Dominicana ocupa las dos terceras partes de la isla. La otra tercera parte la ocupa Haití.

La capital

Santo Domingo, la capital, fue la primera ciudad europea fundada (*founded*) en América. Tiene una zona colonial con hermosas construcciones como el Hospital de San Nicolás de Bari, el Monasterio de San Francisco y la Catedral de Santa María la Menor, donde según dicen los dominicanos, están los restos de Cristóbal Colón.

© Tom Bean/Corbis

© Kimberly White/Reuters/Corbis

La música

El *merengue* es el ritmo y el baile típicos de la República Dominicana. Uno de los más famosos compositores y cantantes de *merengue es* Juan Luis Guerra.

En todos los pueblos hay discotecas donde se bailan, además del merengue, otros ritmos populares como *la bachata*.

Los deportes

El deporte nacional dominicano es el béisbol, que en el Caribe se llama "la pelota". Muchos jugadores de las Grandes Ligas de los Estados Unidos son dominicanos. Entre ellos se destacan Pedro Martínez, Alfonso Soriano y Albert Pujols.

© Aspen Photo/Shutterstock.com

La economía

La economía de la República Dominicana se basa en el turismo, las zonas francas (*duty-free zones*), la agricultura, la minería y el dinero que envían a sus familiares en el país más de un millón de dominicanos residentes en los Estados Unidos. La República Dominicana es el cuarto exportador de ropa del mundo.

Ahora dime...

In groups of three, take turns asking and answering the following questions.

1. ¿Hay en este país ciudades similares a las ciudades coloniales de La Habana y Santo Domingo? ¿Cuáles? ¿Ustedes las conocen?
2. ¿Qué ritmos latinoamericanos saben bailar ustedes? ¿Qué ritmos de este país se bailan en Latinoamérica?

iLrn

To learn more about Cuba and the Dominican Republic, watch the cultural footage in the Media Library.

AUTOPRUEBA

¿Cuánto sé ahora?

A. Reflexive constructions Complete the following sentences, using the correct form of the verbs given.

1. Mi padre _________ (afeitarse) por la mañana, pero mi hermano y yo _________ (afeitarse) por la tarde.
2. Yo _________ (levantarse) a las siete y _________ (acostarse) a las once de la noche.
3. Ayer todos _________ (divertirse) mucho en la fiesta de nuestro aniversario de bodas.
4. ¿Tú _________ (bañarse) por la mañana o por la tarde?
5. Paquito _________ (lavarse) las manos antes de comer.
6. Ayer yo _________ (olvidarse) de llevar la lista al supermercado.
7. Nosotros _________ (acordarse) de los lugares donde pasamos nuestra niñez.
8. ¿Uds. _________ (quitarse) los zapatos (*shoes*) cuando llegan a su casa? ¿Qué _________ (ponerse)?
9. ¿A qué hora _________ (despertarse) Ud.?
10. Nosotros _________ (preocuparse) por nuestros hijos.
11. En la clase, ¿tú _________ (sentarse) cerca de la puerta?
12. Yo _________ (vestirse) en diez minutos.

B. Some uses of the definite article Form sentences with the elements given, adding the necessary connectors. Use verbs in the present tense. Follow the model.

Modelo yo / ponerse / pantalones
Yo me pongo los pantalones.

1. ¿tú / quitarse / abrigo?
2. ellos / estar / escuela
3. mi mamá / lavarme / cabeza
4. Uds. / no lavarse / manos
5. padres / preocuparse / por / sus hijos
6. nosotros / preferir / café
7. educación / ser / lo más importante
8. ¿tú / ir / iglesia / hoy?
9. me / gustar / mucho / té
10. Sra. Díaz / llegar / lunes / ocho / noche

C. Possessive pronouns Give the Spanish equivalent of the pronouns in parentheses.

1. El vestido de Nora está aquí. _________ está en mi cuarto. (*Mine*)
2. Mis revistas están aquí. ¿Dónde están _________, Sr. Vega? (*yours*)
3. Ellos van a enviar sus cartas (*letters*) hoy. ¿Cuándo vamos a enviar _________? (*ours*)
4. No tengo maletas. ¿Puedes prestarme _________, Anita? (*yours*)
5. Aquí están los regalos de Jorge. ¿Dónde están _________? (*ours*)
6. Juan necesita tu cuaderno, Eva. _________ está en la universidad. (*His*)
7. La hija de Mirta nació en Cuba. _________ nació en Chile. (*Ours*)
8. Ana y Luis celebran su aniversario de bodas en febrero. ¿Cuándo celebran Uds. _________? (*yours*)
9. Su billetera está en el cuarto. ¿Dónde está _________? (*mine*)
10. Yo tengo mi guitarra. ¿Ud. tiene _________, señorita? (*yours*)

D. Irregular preterits Complete the following sentences, using the preterit of the verbs given.

1. Yo _________ (tener) una fiesta anoche y todos mis amigos _________ (estar) allí.
2. Ellos _________ (traer) las fresas y las _________ (poner) en la mesa.
3. María _________ (venir) anoche y _________ (traducir) los documentos.
4. Él no _________ (poder) ir porque _________ (tener) que trabajar.
5. Nosotros no les _________ (decir) nada.

6. ¿Cuándo lo ________ (tú) (saber)? ¿Anoche?
7. Ellos no ________ (venir) porque no ________ (querer).
8. ¿Ellas ________ (conducir) tu coche?
9. Andrés ________ (hacer) todo el trabajo.
10. ¿Qué te ________ (decir) ellos ayer?

E. *Hace...* meaning *ago* Say how long ago everything happened, according to the information provided.

1. Llegué aquí a las dos. Son las dos y media.
2. Vi a Carlos el lunes. Hoy es jueves.
3. Conocí a Eva en enero. Estamos en mayo.
4. Compré mi coche en el año 2009. Estamos en el año 2012.
5. Carlitos empezó a tocar el piano a las tres de la tarde. Son las tres y cuarto.

F. Just words...

a. Write the words or phrases that correspond to the following.

1. niñez ________
2. cartera ________
3. durazno ________
4. lata ________
5. opuesto de **mediodía** ________
6. lugar donde compramos carne ________
7. instrumento que tocan en las iglesias ________
8. fruta cítrica ________

b. Match the questions in the first column with the answers in the second column.

1. ¿Qué le pones al café?	______	a. En la joyería.
2. ¿Qué compraste para la ensalada?	______	b. En el supermercado.
3. ¿Qué instrumento tocas?	______	c. Su aniversario de bodas.
4. ¿Quieres mantequilla?	______	d. No, tarde.
5. ¿Qué extrañas?	______	e. No, margarina.
6. ¿Qué le pones a la ensalada?	______	f. No, me olvidé de traerla.
7. ¿Dónde compraste los mangos?	______	g. No, el piano.
8. ¿Él sabe tocar el violín?	______	h. Azúcar.
9. ¿Te acostaste temprano?	______	i. Aceite y vinagre.
10. ¿Trajiste la receta?	______	j. Aguacate y lechuga.
11. ¿Qué celebran ellos hoy?	______	k. La guitarra.
12. ¿Dónde compraste el reloj?	______	l. El lugar donde nací.

G. Cultura

1. Complete the following, based on the information found in the **¿Lo sabía Ud.?** sections.
   a. En los países de habla hispana todavía es costumbre comprar en tiendas especializadas en uno o dos ________.
   b. La palabra **salsa** (*sauce*) se usa también para referirse a la ________ caribeña.
2. Complete the following based on the information in the **El mundo hispánico y tú** section.
   a. Wifredo Lam es el más famoso de los ________ cubanos.
   b. La música típica de la República Dominicana es el ________.

H. Un dicho Do you remember the Spanish saying that is equivalent to *Love conquers all*? Find it in this lesson.

LECCIÓN 10

BUSCANDO APARTAMENTO

Vista de la ciudad de Caracas

OBJETIVOS COMUNICATIVOS

You will learn vocabulary related to renting an apartment, the various parts of a house, home furniture, and appliances.

SITUACIONES

Dos amigos

ESTRUCTURAS

1 The imperfect

2 The preterit contrasted with the imperfect

3 Verbs that change meaning in the preterit

4 The relative pronouns **que** and **quien**

ASÍ SOMOS

¡Vamos a ver!

Watching and understanding situations

¡Vamos a escuchar!

Training yourself to listen for units of meaning

¡Vamos a conversar!

Paraphrasing practice II

Rincón literario

Reading poetry

Solo de flauta by Nicolás Guillén

¡Vamos a escribir!

Brainstorming and organizing

EL MUNDO HISPÁNICO Y TÚ

› Venezuela

AUTOPRUEBA

You will review what you learned in this lesson.

VENEZUELA Cuando los conquistadores españoles llegaron al lago Maracaibo, las construcciones de los indígenas a orillas del lago les recordaron las de Venecia, y por eso llamaron al país "Venezuela", nombre que significa "pequeña Venecia".

Recursos iLrn video audio web playlist

Dos amigos

CD2-17

© Cengage Learning

¡Ubíquelos!

Álvaro and Mirta are two Venezuelan students who live in Caracas, the capital of Venezuela. This video will give you a sense of their surroundings and an appreciation for the "presence" of Simón Bolívar, the great liberator who was born in this city.

© Blend/Jupiter Images/Getty Images

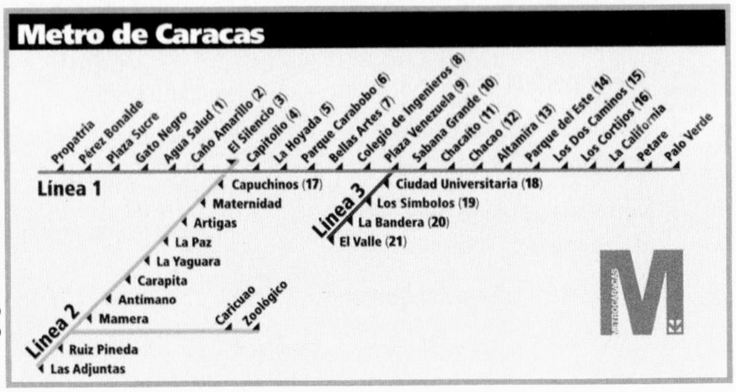

© Cengage Learning

Álvaro y Mirta, dos estudiantes venezolanos, se encuentran en un café de Caracas para tomar algo y charlar un rato. Mirta está tratando de encontrar un apartamento, que ella va a compartir con su hermana. Ahora las chicas viven en una pensión y tienen que mudarse. Álvaro conoció a Mirta el año pasado en una clase de historia y ahora son muy buenos amigos. En este momento están hablando de su niñez.

Álvaro: ¿Dónde vivías tú cuando eras niña?

Mirta: Yo vivía en un pueblo pequeño, en una casa antigua y muy grande, con habitaciones amplias, de paredes blancas. La casa de mis abuelos no quedaba lejos, y los veíamos casi todos los días. ¿Y tú?

Álvaro: Yo vivía en Caracas. Cuando tenía siete años, mis padres y yo fuimos a vivir a Bogotá, pero volvimos tres años después. Como yo era hijo único, me gustaba más vivir en Caracas, porque todos mis primos estaban aquí. Íbamos a la escuela juntos, y a veces teníamos los mismos maestros.

Mirta: Yo no sabía que eras hijo único... ¿Tus padres te malcriaban?

Álvaro: (*Se ríe.*) No, pero mi abuela, sí. ¡Y todavía me malcría! Ayer me dijo que yo necesitaba un traje nuevo, y quizás un coche...

Mirta: (*Se ríe también.*) ¡Caramba! ¡Es tarde! Tengo que encontrarme con mi hermana para ver un apartamento desocupado que yo quiero alquilar. No es muy grande, pero el alquiler no es muy caro, y está amueblado. ¡Y está cerca de la estación del metro!

Álvaro: ¿El alquiler incluye la electricidad, el agua y el teléfono?

Mirta: El teléfono, no. Yo voy a tratar de convencer a mi hermana de que el apartamento no es muy chico y de que el barrio no es malo... pero sé que se va a quejar.

Álvaro: Cuando yo me mudé a mi apartamento, no tenía muebles... Bueno, tenía una mesita de noche, una cómoda y una bolsa de dormir... pero ustedes estaban acostumbradas a vivir en una casa grande...

Mirta: Bueno... esos eran otros tiempos... ¡No es lo mismo!

Álvaro: ¿Me vas a llamar para decirme si tienes una nueva dirección?

Mirta: Sí, yo te voy a avisar.

1. **Hablemos** With a partner, take turns asking and answering the following questions. Base your answers on the dialogue and on your own circumstances.

En el diálogo

1. ¿Cuándo y dónde conoció Álvaro a Mirta?
2. ¿Dónde vivía Mirta cuando era niña?
3. ¿Mirta veía a sus abuelos frecuentemente?
4. ¿Álvaro tiene muchos hermanos?
5. ¿Quién malcría a Álvaro?
6. ¿Para qué va a encontrarse Mirta con su hermana?
7. ¿Cómo es el apartamento que quiere alquilar Mirta?
8. ¿El apartamento tiene muebles?
9. ¿Qué incluye el alquiler del apartamento?
10. Según Mirta, ¿quién se va a quejar?

¿Y tú?

1. ¿Cuándo y dónde conociste a tu mejor amigo(a)?
2. ¿Dónde vivías tú cuando eras niño(a)?
3. ¿Tus abuelos vivían cerca (*near*) o lejos de tu casa?
4. ¿Tú eres hijo(a) único(a)?
5. ¿Quién te malcriaba a ti cuando eras niño(a)?
6. ¿Tú tienes que encontrarte con alguien hoy?
7. ¿Cómo es el lugar donde tú vives?
8. ¿Qué muebles tienes tú?
9. ¿Tú pagas alquiler en el lugar donde vives?
10. ¿De qué te quejas tú?

¿Cómo es el apartamento que quiere alquilar Mirta?

VOCABULARIO

En el diálogo

Cognados

la electricidad	*electricity*
la estación	*station*
venezolano(a)	*Venezuelan*

Nombres

el alquiler	*rent*
el barrio, la vecindad	*neighborhood*
la bolsa (el saco) de dormir	*sleeping bag*
el coche, el carro, el auto, el automóvil	*car*
la cómoda	*chest of drawers*
la escuela[1]	*school*
el (la) maestro(a)	*teacher*
la mesita de noche	*night stand*
el metro, el subterráneo	*subway*
los muebles	*furniture*
el (la) niño(a)	*child*
la pensión	*boarding house*
el pueblo	*town*
el traje	*suit*

Verbos

alquilar	*to rent*
avisar	*to let know, to advise*
compartir	*to share*
conocer	*to meet (for the first time)*
convencer	*to convince*
encontrarse (o:ue)	*to meet (someone somewhere)*
incluir[2]	*to include*
malcriar	*to spoil (i.e., a child)*
mudarse	*to move (from one house to another)*
quedar	*to be located*
quejarse	*to complain*
reírse[3]	*to laugh*

Adjetivos

acostumbrado(a)	*used to*
amplio(a)	*large, ample*
antiguo(a)	*old*
amueblado(a)	*furnished*
caro(a)	*expensive*
chico(a)	*small*
desocupado(a)	*vacant*
mismo(a)	*same*
único(a)	*only*

Otras palabras y expresiones

el (la) hijo(a) único(a)	*only child*
lejos	*far*
lo mismo	*the same thing*
todavía	*still*

¿Lo sabía Ud.?

La palabra "barrio" equivale simplemente al inglés *neighborhood,* pero en muchos lugares de los Estados Unidos y en algunos países latinoamericanos tiene una connotación negativa.

› **¿Le gusta a Ud. el barrio donde vive?**

© Blend/Jupiter Images

[1] **escuela primaria** = *elementary school*; **escuela secundaria** = *secondary school*
[2] present indicative: **incluyo, incluyes, incluye, incluimos, incluís, incluyen**
[3] present indicative: **me río, te ríes, se ríe, nos reímos, os reís, se ríen**

Más sobre el tema

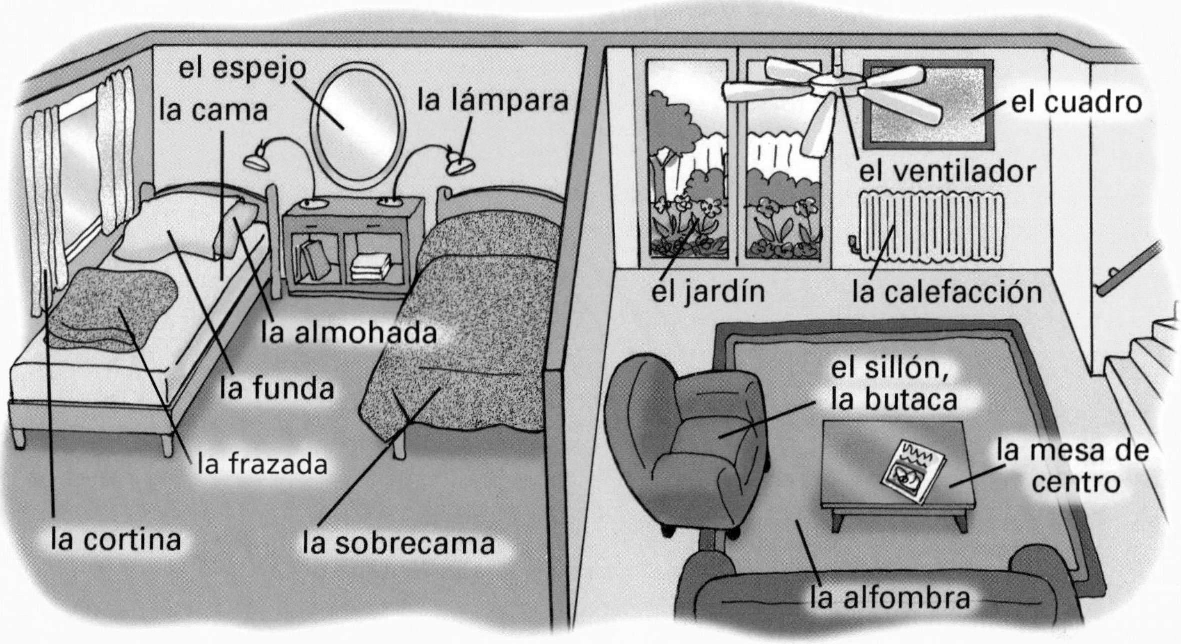

Aparatos electrodomésticos y batería de cocina *(Home appliances and cookware)*

la cacerola	*pot*
la cafetera	*coffee pot, coffee-maker*
el horno	*oven*
la lavadora	*washing machine*
la licuadora	*blender*
el microondas	*microwave* (*oven*)
la plancha	*iron*
la sartén	*frying pan*
la secadora	*clothes dryer*
la tostadora	*toaster*
la tabla de planchar	*ironing board*

LEARNING TIP

Exercise your memory so that it may aid you in learning Spanish. Think of combining several new vocabulary items in funny or otherwise memorable statements, and visualize these statements in your mind. This will help you remember the new words.

Práctica

2. Preguntas y respuestas Match the questions in column A with the responses in column B.

A	B
____ 1. ¿Qué compraste para tu cama?	a. No, en la secadora.
____ 2. ¿Qué vas a comprar para la sala?	b. No, es muy chico.
____ 3. ¿La ropa está en la lavadora?	c. No, muy cerca.
____ 4. ¿Vas a usar la cacerola?	d. Sí, porque no tengo coche.
____ 5. ¿Está lejos?	e. Sábanas y fundas.
____ 6. ¿Están en un hotel?	f. No, me voy a mudar.
____ 7. ¿El apartamento es amplio?	g. No, la sartén.
____ 8. ¿Vienes en ómnibus?	h. No, en una pensión.
____ 9. ¿No te gusta tu casa?	i. Una mesa de centro.

3. Palabras Select the word or phrase that best completes each sentence.

1. Compré (una licuadora, unas cortinas, un espejo) para la ventana de la sala.
2. Puse el pollo en (la cómoda, el horno, el ventilador).
3. La almohada está en mi (cama, microondas, tostadora).
4. Ayer compré una (estación, almohada, cacerola) para mi cama.
5. Voy a pasarle la aspiradora (al cuadro, a la sobrecama, a la alfombra).
6. El alquiler (incluye, se queja, convence) la electricidad y el agua.
7. Me voy a sentar en esa (cómoda, butaca, tabla de planchar).
8. Aquí hay muchos apartamentos (desocupados, mismos, acostumbrados).
9. ¿Vas a comprar la casa o la vas a (avisar, alquilar, convencer)?
10. Voy a poner el pan en la (cafetera, licuadora, tostadora).

4. ¿Qué es? Write the words or phrases that correspond to the following.

1. barrio ____________
2. metro ____________
3. coche ____________
4. opuesto de moderno ____________
5. opuesto de aire acondicionado ____________
6. que no está ocupado ____________
7. la usamos para planchar ____________
8. sillón ____________
9. la usamos para hacer café ____________
10. que tiene muebles ____________

5. **Para completar** Complete the following, using appropriate vocabulary.

1. Ayer compré una bolsa de ________.
2. Tengo un ________ muy viejo, pero no me ________ porque no tengo que usar el autobús para ir a la universidad.
3. Voy a comprar algunos ________ para mi cuarto: dos mesitas de ________ y una ________.
4. ¿Dónde ________ Ud. a su novio(a)?
5. No necesito comprar muebles porque el apartamento está ________.
6. Quiero ________ pero no encuentro ningún apartamento ________ cerca de aquí.
7. Creo que yo puedo ________ a mi esposo(a) de alquilar esa casa, porque está en un ________ muy bueno.
8. ¿Dónde ________ la pensión donde vives?

Para conversar

6. **Mañana nos mudamos** With a partner, play the roles of two people who are moving into a new house or apartment. Ask each other whether or not you have certain pieces of furniture, appliances, or kitchen utensils. You each answer what you have, and mention what you have to buy.

Modelo —*¿Tenemos...?*

—*Sí, tenemos..., pero tenemos que comprar...*

7. **No estamos de acuerdo** You and a partner, play the roles of two roommates looking for a new apartment. One likes everything and the other finds fault with everything.

Modelo —*Las cortinas son muy bonitas.*

—*No me gusta el color...*

CD2-18

Pronunciación

Pronunciation in context

In this lesson, there are some new words or phrases that may be challenging to pronounce. For further pronunciation practice of Spanish sounds, listen to your instructor and repeat the following sentences.

1. **Ahora** las chicas viven en una **pensión**.
2. Están hablando de su **niñez.**
3. La casa de sus abuelos no **quedaba lejos.**
4. ¿Tus padres **te malcriaban**?
5. El apartamento **está amueblado**.
6. **Incluye la electricidad** y el teléfono.
7. Voy a tratar de **convencer** a mi hermana.
8. Uds. **están acostumbradas** a vivir en una casa grande.

1 The imperfect (*El imperfecto de indicativo*)

› There are two simple past tenses in the Spanish indicative: the preterit, which you studied in **Lecciones 7, 8,** and **9**, and the imperfect.

A. Regular forms

› To form the regular imperfect, add the following endings to the verb stem.

-ar verbs		*-er* and *-ir* verbs			
hablar		***comer***		***vivir***	
habl-	**aba**	com-	**ía**	viv-	**ía**
habl-	**abas**	com-	**ías**	viv-	**ías**
habl-	**aba**	com-	**ía**	viv-	**ía**
habl-	**ábamos**	com-	**íamos**	viv-	**íamos**
habl-	**abais**	com-	**íais**	viv-	**íais**
habl-	**aban**	com-	**ían**	viv-	**ían**

› Note that the endings of the **-er** and **-ir** verbs are the same, and that there is a written accent on the first **í** of the endings of the **-er** and **-ir** verbs.

› The Spanish imperfect tense is equivalent to three English forms.

Yo **vivía** en Caracas. — *I used to live in Caracas.*
I was living in Caracas.
I lived in Caracas.

› The imperfect is used to refer to habitual or repeated actions in the past, with no reference to when they began or ended.

—¿Uds. **tenían** una casa en Caracas? — *Did you have a house in Caracas?*
—No, **vivíamos** en un apartamento. — *No, we lived in an apartment.*

› The imperfect is also used to refer to actions, events, or conditions that the speaker views as *in the process* of happening in the past, again with no reference to when they began or ended.

Veníamos para casa cuando vimos a Raúl. — *We were coming home when we saw Raúl.*

¿Lo sabía Ud.?

En las grandes ciudades españolas y latinoamericanas, la mayoría de la gente vive en apartamentos, que en España se llaman "pisos". Los apartamentos se alquilan o se compran. Muchos edificios tienen oficinas o tiendas en la planta baja y apartamentos en los otros pisos.

› **En la ciudad donde Ud. vive, ¿la mayoría de la gente vive en casas o en apartamentos?**

B. Irregular forms

› Only three verbs are irregular in the imperfect tense: **ser**, **ver**, and **ir**.

ser	ver	ir
era	veía	iba
eras	veías	ibas
era	veía	iba
éramos	veíamos	íbamos
erais	veíais	ibais
eran	veían	iban

—¿**Ibas** mucho a casa de tus abuelos cuando **eras** niño? *Did you often go to your grandparents' house when you were a child?*

—Sí, los **veía** todos los sábados. *Yes, I used to see them every Saturday.*

—¿Adónde **iban** Uds. de vacaciones cuando eran niños? *Where did you go on vacation when you were children?*

—**Íbamos** a la playa o a las montañas. *We used to go to the beach or to the mountains.*

Práctica

8. **Hace diez años** Ten years ago, María wrote this composition about herself and her family. Rewrite her composition, using the imperfect tense.

   Mi familia y yo vivimos en Caracas. Mi padre trabaja para la compañía Sandoval y mi madre enseña en la universidad. Es una profesora excelente. Mis hermanos y yo asistimos a la escuela. Generalmente pasamos las vacaciones en Isla Margarita. Allí vamos a la playa y nadamos. Mis abuelos viven en Maracaibo y no los vemos mucho, pero siempre les escribimos.

9. **Tu historia** Now write a paragraph about your own childhood, using Activity 8 as a model.

10. **Adolescentes** Compare your teenage years with those of a classmate by taking turns completing the following sentences.
    1. Cuando yo era adolescente...
    2. Mi familia y yo siempre...
    3. Mis abuelos...
    4. Mi mejor amigo(a)...
    5. Frecuentemente, nosotros...
    6. Cuando yo tenía dieciséis años...
    7. En la escuela, yo...
    8. Todos los fines de semana, mis amigos y yo...
    9. En el verano...
    10. Cuando yo quería salir con mis amigos, mis padres...

11. ¡Habla con tu compañero(a)! Interview a classmate, using the following questions and two of your own. When you have finished, switch roles.

1. ¿Dónde vivías cuando tenías diez años? ¿Vivías en una ciudad grande o en un pueblo pequeño? ¿Vivías en una casa o en un apartamento?
2. ¿A qué escuela ibas? ¿La escuela quedaba cerca o lejos de tu casa? ¿Tenías muchos(as) amigos(as) en la escuela? ¿Tenías buenos maestros?
3. ¿Te gustaba estudiar? ¿Eras un(a) buen(a) estudiante? ¿Sacabas buenas notas (*grades*)?
4. ¿Con quiénes ibas de vacaciones? Generalmente, ¿ibas a la playa o a la montaña? ¿Qué hacías durante las vacaciones?
5. ¿Preferías pasar las vacaciones en el campo (*country*) o en la ciudad?
6. Generalmente, ¿cuánto tiempo estabas de vacaciones? ¿Qué era lo que más te gustaba hacer en tus vacaciones? ¿Siempre hacías lo mismo?

12. Recuerdos Get together with a partner and compare your high school years. Ask pertinent questions.

Modelo —*¿Te gustaba la ciudad donde vivías?*
—*Sí, me gustaba mucho.*

¿Te gustaba la ciudad donde vivías?

2 The preterit contrasted with the imperfect (*El pretérito contrastado con el imperfecto*)

› The difference between the preterit and the imperfect can be visualized in the following way.

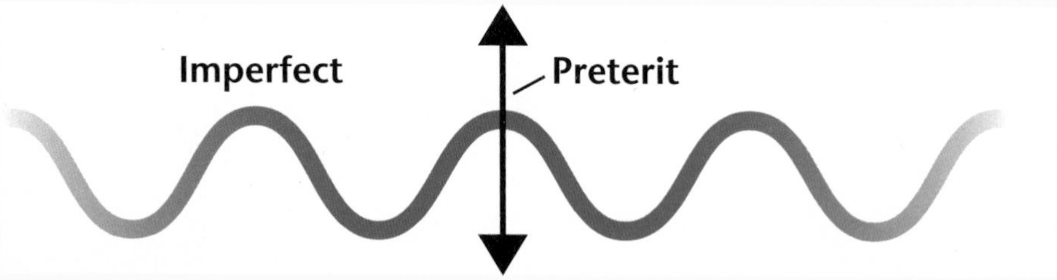

The wavy line representing the imperfect shows an action or event taking place over a period of time in the past. There is no reference to when the action began or ended. The vertical line representing the preterit shows an action or event as completed in the past.

In some instances, the choice between the preterit and the imperfect depends on how the speaker views the action or event. The following table on page 293 summarizes some of the most important uses of both tenses.

Preterit	Imperfect
1. Reports past actions that the speaker views as finished and completed. Yo **estuve** allí el año pasado. Ayer **compré** una bolsa de dormir.	1. Describes past actions in the process of happening, with no reference to their beginning or end. **Iba** a la biblioteca cuando lo vi.
2. Sums up a condition or state viewed as a whole (and no longer in effect). Me **sentí** mal todo el día.	2. Refers to repeated or habitual actions or events: *used to . . .* Cuando **era** niña **iba**[1] de vacaciones a Montevideo.
	3. Describes a physical, mental, or emotional state or condition in the past. Me **sentía** muy mal.
	4. Expresses time in the past. **Eran** las ocho de la noche cuando llegaron a su casa.
	5. Is generally used in indirect discourse. Me dijo que **podía** encontrarse con nosotras.
	6. Describes age in the past. Cuando **tenía** veinte años, vivía en Chile.
	7. Describes or sets the stage in the past. **Hacía** frío y **llovía**.

LEARNING TIP

Using the preterit and the imperfect correctly takes time. To personalize some of the uses, say what you *used to do* when you were a child. Then say what you did last week. Think of as many examples as possible.

[1]Note that this use of the imperfect also corresponds to the English *would* used to describe a repeated action in the past: *When I was a child, I used to go to Montevideo on vacation. = When I was a child, **I would go** to Montevideo on vacation.*

Preterit or Imperfect . . . ?

Práctica

13. Minidiálogos Complete the following dialogues. Then act them out with a partner.

1. —¿Cuántos años ________ (tener) tú cuando ________ (venir) a vivir a Caracas?
   —________ (Tener) doce años.
2. —¿Qué te ________ (decir) la maestra ayer?
   —Me ________ (decir) que yo ________ (deber) volver mañana.
3. —¿Qué tiempo ________ (hacer) cuando Uds. ________ (salir) de casa esta mañana?
   —________ (Hacer) frío y ________ (nevar).
4. —¿Adónde ________ (ir) Uds. de vacaciones cuando ________ (ser) niños?
   —Siempre ________ (ir) a la playa, pero un verano mis padres ________ (decidir) alquilar una casa en las montañas y esas ________ (ser) nuestras mejores vacaciones.
5. —¿Qué hora ________ (ser) cuando tú ________ (llegar) a casa ayer?
   —________ (Ser) las ocho.
   —¿________ (Ir) a la tienda?
   —Sí, ________ (ir) con Nora. Cuando nosotras ________ (ir) para la tienda, ________ (ver) un accidente en la calle Bolívar.
   —¿________ (Morir) alguien?
   —No, por suerte no ________ (morir) nadie.

14. Una entrevista This interview takes place in Caracas. With a classmate, play the role of a reporter interviewing a famous star from Spain.

—___________

—Yo nací en Sevilla, y no te digo cuándo.

—___________

—Yo tenía diez años cuando nos fuimos a vivir a Madrid.

—___________

—Cuando era niña era fea y un poco gorda.

—___________

—Sí, tenía un perro que se llamaba Chispita.

—___________

—Cuando era niña me gustaba ir a la playa y nadar.

—___________

—Estudié en la Escuela de Arte Dramático.

—___________

—Empecé a trabajar en televisión en el año 2002.

—___________

—Vine a Caracas en el año 2000.

—___________

—Sí, el año pasado estuve en París y trabajé en un club nocturno.

—___________

—Estuve allí por tres meses.

15. ¡Pobre Beto! With a partner, go to the illustration on page 294 and prepare questions about what Beto's day was like. Take turns asking and answering the questions.

16. Pretérito e imperfecto As you know, the preterit *advances* the story, while the imperfect adds information about what was happening at that moment. With a partner, create clauses using the imperfect tense to provide descriptions, to talk about what was going on when something else took place, to tell what someone was saying, etc. Be creative! Then get together with another group to compare stories.

Modelo —Me levanté a las seis y miré por la ventana.
—Estaba nevando y no había nadie en la calle.

1. Desayuné con mi familia. Comimos cereal con leche y panqueques.
2. Me bañé y me vestí. Salí de mi casa a las siete.
3. Decidí ir a la universidad a pie. Fui por el parque. En el parque vi a Marisol. Hablamos por unos diez minutos.
4. Llegué a la universidad a las ocho.
5. El profesor de historia nos dio un examen muy difícil.
6. A las once y media, almorcé en la cafetería. La comida no me gustó.
7. A la una, comencé a sentirme enfermo.
8. Volví a mi casa y hablé con mi mamá.
9. No cené. Me acosté a las nueve, pero no pude dormir en toda la noche.

Para conversar

17. ¡Habla con tu compañero(a)! Interview a classmate. Ask the following questions to practice the preterit and the imperfect. Then add four more questions of your own to practice both tenses. When you have finished, switch roles.

1. ¿Cuántos años tenías cuando conociste a tu mejor amigo(a)?
2. ¿A qué escuela ibas cuando tenías 12 años?
3. ¿Siempre ibas de vacaciones en el verano?
4. ¿Te divertías mucho en las vacaciones?
5. ¿Cómo era tu primer(a) novio(a)?
6. ¿A qué hora te levantaste ayer? ¿Qué hiciste?
7. ¿Te encontraste con algún (alguna) amigo(a)?
8. ¿Qué tiempo hacía cuando saliste de tu casa?
9. ¿Llegaste tarde a clase hoy? ¿A qué hora llegaste?
10. ¿Tuviste algún examen la semana pasada (*last*)?

18. Cuando Ud. era adolescente... In groups of four or five, prepare five to six questions to ask your instructor about his or her life as a teenager.

3 Verbs that change meaning in the preterit (*Verbos que cambian de significado en el pretérito*)

› Some Spanish verbs change meaning when they are used in the preterit. Note the usage of the verbs in the following examples.

conocer:	conocí (preterit)	*I met*
	conocía (imperfect)	*I knew (was acquainted or familiar with)*
	Anoche **conocí** a una chica muy simpática.	*(I met her for the first time.)*
	Yo no **conocía** la ciudad.	*(I wasn't familiar with the city.)*
saber:	supe (preterit)	*I found out, I learned*
	sabía (imperfect)	*I knew*
	Lo **supe** cuando él me lo dijo.	*(I found it out.)*
	Yo no **sabía** que te gustaba el golf.	*(I wasn't aware of it.)*
no querer:	no quise (preterit)	*I refused*
	no quería (imperfect)	*I didn't want*
	Raúl **no quiso** ir.	*(didn't want to and refused)*
	Rita **no quería** ir, pero después decidió ir.	*(didn't want to at the time)*

—¿Tú **conocías** al cuñado de Carmen?	*Did you know Carmen's brother-in-law?*
—No, lo **conocí** anoche.	*No, I met him last night.*
—¿Y Roberto? ¿No vino?	*And Roberto? Didn't he come?*
—No, **no quiso** venir.	*No, he refused to come.*
—Yo tampoco **quería** venir, pero vine para traer a Anita.	*I didn't want to come either, but I came to bring Anita.*

Práctica

19. Una telenovela Act out the following scene from a soap opera with a partner, providing the missing verbs.

ADRIÁN: ¿Tú ________ que Rosaura estaba embarazada (*pregnant*)?

SARA: No, lo ________ anoche.

ADRIÁN: ¡Qué horrible! Dicen que su esposo es un idiota. Los padres de ella no ________ ir a la boda (*wedding*). Ese día se fueron a Europa.

SARA: Pero, ¿dónde ________ Rosaura a Lorenzo?

ADRIÁN: En una fiesta. Rosaura no ________ ir, pero Olga la llevó.

SARA: ¿Olga ________ a Lorenzo?

ADRIÁN: Sí, Olga es la ex esposa de Lorenzo...

Para conversar

20. La próxima escena With a partner, write and act out the scene that follows the one you read in **19. Una telenovela.** Some words you might use: **divorciarse, el (la) amante** (*lover*), **irse de casa, los problemas económicos,** etc.

21. ¡Habla con tu compañero(a)! Interview a classmate, using the following questions and at least two of your own. When you have finished, switch roles. Anwer the questions in complete sentences.

1. ¿Conocías tú al profesor (a la profesora) antes de empezar esta clase?
2. ¿Cuándo lo (la) conociste?
3. ¿Sabías tú la nacionalidad del profesor (de la profesora)?
4. ¿Cuándo la supiste?
5. Yo no quería venir a clase hoy. ¿Y tú?
6. La última vez (*last time*) que no viniste a clase, ¿fue porque no pudiste o porque no quisiste?
7. ¿Cuándo conociste a tu mejor amigo(a) o novio(a)?
8. De niño(a), ¿conocías a alguien interesante? ¿A quién?
9. ¿Cuándo supiste que Santa Claus no traía los regalos?
10. De niño(a), ¿qué cosas no querías comer?

¿Ya sabías la nacionalidad de tu profesora?

4 The relative pronouns *que* and *quien* (*Los pronombres relativos* que *y* quien)

Relative pronouns are used to combine two sentences that have a common element, usually a noun or a pronoun.

A. The relative pronoun *que*

¿Dónde está **el dinero**? Trajiste **el dinero.**

common element

¿Dónde está el dinero **que** trajiste?

R.P.

La chica se llama Rosa. **La chica** vino esta mañana.

common element

La chica **que** vino esta mañana se llama Rosa.

R.P.

- The relative pronoun **que** not only helps to combine the two sentences in the examples, but also replaces the nouns **el dinero** and **la chica** in the combined sentences.
- The relative pronoun **que** is invariable and is used for both persons and things. It is the Spanish equivalent of *that, which*, and *who*. Unlike its English equivalent, the Spanish **que** is never omitted.

—¿Para quién es el sofá **que** compraste?	*For whom is the sofa that you bought?*
—Es para la señora **que** alquiló el apartamento.	*It is for the lady who rented the apartment.*

B. The relative pronoun *quien*

—¿La muchacha **con quien** hablabas es estadounidense?	*Is the girl with whom you were talking an American?*
—No, es venezolana.	*No, she's a Venezuelan.*
—¿Quiénes son esos señores?	*Who are those gentlemen?*
—Son los señores **de quienes** te habló José.	*They are the gentlemen about whom José spoke to you.*

- The relative pronoun **quien** is used only with persons.
- The plural of **quien** is **quienes. Quien** does not change for gender.
- **Quien** is generally used after prepositions, e.g., **con quien, de quienes**.
- **Quien** is the Spanish equivalent of *whom* and *that*.

Práctica

22. **Minidiálogos** Complete the following dialogues, using **que**, **quien**, or **quienes**. Then act them out with a partner.

1. —¿Quién es el muchacho ________ va a compartir el apartamento con Mario?
   —Es el hermano del chico con ________ estudio.
2. —¿Dónde pusiste el ventilador ________ traje ayer?
   —Lo puse en el cuarto de los niños.
3. —Los muchachos con ________ trabajo estuvieron aquí ayer.
   —¿Trajeron el microondas ________ les pedí?
   —Sí, y lo dejaron en la cocina.
4. —¿Vas a salir sola esta noche?
   —No, voy a salir con Roberto, el muchacho de ________ te hablé ayer.
5. —¿Esa es la chica ________ estudia contigo?
   —No, es la muchacha con ________ trabajo.
6. —¿Quién es la persona ________ todavía te malcría?
   —Mi abuela. Ayer me regaló un traje magnífico.
7. —¿Sandra es la chica ________ te invitó a su fiesta?
   —No, ella es la muchacha ________ trabaja para mi papá.

Un dicho

El que ríe último, ríe mejor.
Equivalent: *He who laughs last, laughs best.*

Para conversar

23. **¡Habla con tu compañero(a)!** Interview a classmate using the following questions. When you have finished, switch roles.

1. ¿Cómo se llama la persona a quien más admiras?
2. ¿Cómo se llama el profesor o la profesora que enseña tu clase favorita?
3. ¿Quiénes son las personas que viven contigo?
4. ¿Cómo se llaman las personas con quienes vas a salir el sábado?
5. ¿Quién es la persona que más te quiere?
6. ¿Cuál es la comida que más te gusta?
7. ¿Cuál es el color que más te gusta?
8. ¿Dónde está el banco en el que tienes tu cuenta corriente?
9. ¿Quién es el actor que más te gusta?
10. ¿Quién es la persona con quien te gusta ir al cine?

¡Vamos a ver!

Antes de ver el video

24. **Preguntas** You and a partner take turns asking and answering the following questions. Answers should be given in complete sentences.

1. ¿Cuándo y dónde conociste a tu mejor amigo(a)?
2. ¿Tú te encontraste con tus amigos la semana pasada?
3. Cuando tú das una fiesta, ¿cuántos invitados tienes, por lo general?
4. Cuando tú eras niño(a), ¿quién hacía los trabajos de la casa?
5. ¿A qué escuela asistías cuando eras niño(a)? ¿Estaba cerca o lejos de tu casa?
6. ¿Tú te quejabas de todo cuando eras chico(a)? Generalmente, ¿estabas de acuerdo con tus padres?
7. ¿Vas a tratar de convencer a tu papá de que tú necesitas más dinero?
8. ¿Te gusta tu barrio o quieres mudarte?
9. Si tú alquilas un apartamento, ¿tiene que estar amueblado o tú tienes muebles?
10. Generalmente, el alquiler incluye la electricidad y el agua. ¿Incluye también el teléfono?
11. Los edificios de apartamentos que hay en tu ciudad, ¿tienen muchos apartamentos desocupados?
12. Generalmente, ¿qué muebles hay en una sala comedor?
13. ¿Hay una cómoda en tu dormitorio? ¿Hay una mesita de noche?
14. ¿Tú duermes a veces en una bolsa de dormir? ¿Es tan cómoda como tu cama?

El video: Marísol se queja de todo

—Vamos, que es tarde. ¿Dónde pusiste la llave?

—Te la di esta mañana… ¡Ah, no! Está en mi bolso.

—Esta es la sala comedor. Como ven, es muy amplia. Tiene un sofá, una mesa y cuatro sillas.

—(*A Cristina*) Podemos tener solamente un invitado a la vez.

—Yo sé que a ti te gustó el apartamento que vimos anteayer.

—Sí, yo no quería ver este porque tampoco me gusta el barrio donde está y el otro estaba más cerca de la universidad. Este está muy lejos.

Después de ver el video

© Cengage Learning
Silvia

© Cengage Learning
Marisol

© Cengage Learning
el encargado

© Cengage Learning
Cristina

25. ¿Quién lo dice? Identify the person who said the following in the dialogue.

1. Cuando eras chica también te quejabas de todo. ______
2. Cuando veníamos para acá vi un edificio de apartamentos mucho mejor que este. ______
3. Vamos, que es tarde. ¿Dónde pusiste la llave? ______
4. Yo sé que a ti te gustó el apartamento que vimos anteayer. ______
5. Entonces, ¿no piensan alquilar el apartamento? ______
6. El apartamento tiene que estar amueblado porque no tenemos muebles. ______
7. Bueno... tenemos bolsas de dormir. ______
8. Esta es la sala comedor. Como ven, es muy amplia. ______

26. Hablemos With a partner, take turns asking and answering the following questions. Base your answers on the dialogue.

En el diálogo

1. ¿De qué ciudad vinieron Silvia, Marisol y Cristina?
2. ¿Dónde conocieron Silvia y Marisol a Cristina?
3. ¿A qué hora dijo Cristina que podía encontrarse con sus amigas?
4. ¿Cómo van a ir las chicas al apartamento?
5. ¿Dónde puso Marisol la llave?
6. ¿Qué incluye el alquiler?
7. ¿Cómo es el baño del apartamento?
8. ¿Marisol conocía a Cristina cuando las dos eran chicas?
9. ¿Qué dice Marisol del barrio donde está el apartamento?
10. ¿Qué va a hacer Silvia enseguida?

27. ¿Qué pasa después...? You and a partner, use your imagination to say what the characters do. In Spanish, discuss the following.

1. Whether Hugo took Cristina to see another apartment or whether she took a taxi.
2. Whether or not the girls had to buy (some) furniture and why or why not.
3. What the girls used to do when they were little. Name three or four things.
4. Whether the girls saw another building that had vacant apartments.
5. Whether they went to see another apartment, and whether Marisol liked it.
6. Whether or not Marisol continued to complain about everything.
7. Whether or not Silvia's father sent them more money.
8. Whether or not the super (*el encargado*) was able to rent the apartment.

Now compare your answers to those of the members of another group.

¡A escuchar!

ESTRATEGIA **Training yourself to listen for units of meaning** One of the most challenging aspects of listening to native speech as a beginning Spanish learner is telling where a word or a part of a sentence ends and the next one begins. Linking, which you read about in **Lección 3**, can contribute to the challenge of hearing words or phrases distinctly. Remember that if two adjacent letters are the same (for example, **las sopas** or **va a tomar**), they sound almost like one in speech. Be aware of this and listen for logical phrases or groups of words.

CD2-19 **28. En busca de un apartamento** You will listen to several sentences that are transcribed below without spacing between words. Listen as many times as needed and mark the divisions between the words.

1. elapartamentoquevimosenesteedificionotienecalefacción
2. nopiensanalquilareseapartamentoporquenoestáamueblado
3. megustamáselotroapartamentoporqueestácercadelmetro
4. levanaavisarmañanasipuedemudarseestasemana
5. ellosquedaronenencontrarseenlauniversidadalauna

¡Vamos a conversar!

ESTRATEGIA **Paraphrasing practice II** When paraphrasing, remember that your goal is to simplify what you hear, using words that you know. Developing this skill can be useful in conversation as well as in writing to summarize and report or explain something that you have heard or read.

CD2-20 **29. ¿Qué dijo?** You will hear five sentences. Listen and restate them in your own words. Then compare your responses with those of a classmate.

30. ¿Qué dice Ud.? What would you say in the following situations? What might the other person say? Act out the scenes with a partner. Take turns playing each role.

1. You are talking to a real estate agent. You are looking for a house in a good neighborhood, with five bedrooms, air conditioning, and a three-car garage.
2. You and your friend are going to share an apartment. Describe one that you have just seen, and tell him/her why you should take the apartment. Your friend doesn't think it is a good idea.
3. You are going to give a bridal shower for a friend who has nothing. Decide what appliances and other necessities you think that your guests can buy.
4. You ask the super of an apartment building if the rent includes electricity, water, and phone.
5. You tell someone where you lived when you were a child and where you and your family used to go on vacation.

31. Para conocernos mejor To do this activity, work with a classmate whom you would like to get to know. Take turns asking and answering these questions.

1. La escuela secundaria a la que tú asistías, ¿estaba cerca o lejos de tu casa? ¿Cómo ibas a la escuela? ¿A qué hora empezaban las clases? ¿Almorzabas en la cafetería con tus amigos? ¿A qué hora volvías a tu casa?
2. ¿Dónde te encontrabas con tus amigos los fines de semana? ¿Qué hacían? ¿Iban al cine a veces? ¿Les gustaba bailar o preferían conversar?
3. ¿Tú vives en una casa o en un apartamento? ¿Cuántos dormitorios tiene? ¿Te gusta tu barrio? ¿Vives cerca o lejos de la universidad?
4. ¿Qué muebles tienes en tu dormitorio? ¿Qué muebles hay en la sala? ¿Qué aparatos electrodomésticos hay en la cocina?
5. ¿Qué tuviste que hacer ayer? ¿Qué hora era cuando saliste de tu casa esta mañana? ¿Qué tiempo hacía? ¿A qué hora piensas volver a tu casa hoy?

32. Una encuesta Interview your classmates to identify who fits the following descriptions. Include your instructor, but remember to use the **Ud.** form when addressing him/her. After finishing the survey, get together with two or three classmates and discuss the results.

1. Vive lejos de la universidad.	____________
2. Vive en un buen barrio.	____________
3. Se mudó hace poco tiempo.	____________
4. Comparte su apartamento con un(a) amigo(a).	____________
5. Tiene una habitación muy amplia.	____________
6. Tiene alfombra en toda su casa.	____________
7. Compró un coche muy caro recientemente.	____________
8. Es hijo(a) único(a).	____________

33. Para crear Get together in groups of three or four and "create" the scenario for this photo. Imagine that the couple is talking to a real estate agent about renting an apartment. What do they want? What is everybody saying? Add any other pertinent details.

© Shelley Gazin/The Image Works

Rincón literario

Nicolás Guillén (Cuba: 1902–1989)

Nicolás Guillén es un poeta y periodista cubano de renombre internacional. En su obra se ven tres direcciones fundamentales: la de la poesía social, la neo-popular de raíz folclórica y la de la poesía negra. En esta última, muestra una gran preocupación por la raza negra y por los explotados del mundo. Su principal aportación técnica a la poesía es el poema-son, inspirado en este motivo de la música popular cubana.

Entre sus mejores libros de poemas pueden citarse *Motivos de son* (1930), *Sóngoro consongo* (1931), *Cantos para soldados y sones para turistas* (1937), *Elegías* (1958) y *Antología mayor* (1964).
El poema que presentamos a continuación es una comparación entre el sonido triste o alegre de la flauta y el canto o el llanto del hombre.

Antes de leer

ESTRATEGIA **Reading poetry** As with reading short stories and essays, the title of the work and the skimming of the poem can help the reader better understand it. When reading poetry, the rhyme, the symbols and images, the rhythm, and sometimes the repetition of certain sounds, words, or phrases give the reader what is necessary to aid comprehension and the ability to appreciate this most important literary genre.

El poema

1. The title of the poem is "Solo de flauta". What does the sound produced by a flute mean to you? How does it differ from the sound produced by other instruments?
2. What two letters are repeated throughout the poem?
3. What sentence appears in every stanza?
4. Read the poem out loud and you will "hear" how the words become musical.

¡A leer!

Solo de flauta

La flauta gemía su melancolía.
La flauta decía: no hay pena tan grande
cual la pena mía.

La flauta gemía su melancolía.
La flauta decía: si lloro, mi llanto
parece el estruendo° de loca alegría. *big noise*

La flauta gemía su melancolía.
La flauta decía: si canto, mi canto
parece suspiro° de cruel agonía. *sigh*

La flauta gemía su melancolía.
La flauta decía: no hay pena tan grande
cual la pena mía.

Yo soy cual la flauta que rima
con ritmo sonoro su fino y sonoro quebranto° *grief*
si canto parece que lloro; si lloro parece que canto…

34. Comprensión As you read the poem, find the answers to the following questions.

1. ¿Qué gemía la flauta? ¿Qué decía?
2. Según la flauta, ¿qué parece su llanto?
3. ¿Qué parece su canto?
4. ¿Con qué se compara el poeta?
5. ¿Qué pasa cuando el poeta canta? ¿Qué pasa cuando llora?

Después de leer... reflexiones

35. Preguntas In groups of three, have a conversation about the following.

1. ¿Cuáles son los instrumentos musicales que ustedes prefieren? ¿Cuáles saben tocar? ¿Cuáles quieren aprender a tocar? ¿Cuál creen que es el más difícil?
2. ¿Qué tipo de música les gusta para escuchar? ¿Esto depende a veces de su estado de ánimo (*mood*)? ¿Qué compositores (*composers*) les gustan? ¿Qué tipo de música les gusta para bailar?

¡Vamos a escribir!

Antes de escribir

ESTRATEGIA **Brainstorming and organizing** When getting ready to write, it is a good idea to think about your main topic and two or three subtopics. Jot down everything that comes to mind, and then try to organize your ideas and, if applicable, a sequence of events.

La música y mi niñez You will write three or four paragraphs about your experiences with music during your childhood: Whether or not music was an important part of your life and why; whether or not you took music lessons; whether you and your parents used to like the same type of music; what you and your friends liked when you were in high school, and any other information about this topic that you deem important or interesting.

¡A escribir!

La música y mi niñez Write the **primer borrador** of your essay.

Después de escribir

36. ¡A revisar! Before writing the final version of your essay, exchange your first draft with a classmate's and peer edit each other's work, using the following guidelines:

- correct use of the preterit and the imperfect
- organization according to ideas and events

Venezuela

Venezuela está en el norte de Sudamérica. Es uno de los diez mayores exportadores de petróleo del mundo. Más de la octava parte del petróleo importado por los Estados Unidos viene de Venezuela. El presidente del país es Nicolás Maduro, que parece (*seems*) seguir los pasos (*to follow in the footsteps*) de Fidel Castro, el dictador cubano. Si escuchas las noticias, vas a enterarte (*find out*) de los eventos que tienen lugar en Venezuela.

La industria petrolera

Estos pozos (*wells*) petroleros están en el lago Maracaibo, que es el lago más grande de Sudamérica. Desafortunadamente, sus aguas están muy contaminadas, y una de las razones es el daño (*damage*) que causa la extracción del petróleo.

Caracas, ciudad de contrastes

Caracas, la capital de Venezuela, es el centro gubernamental, financiero y cultural del país. El rápido crecimiento (*growth*) de su población ha influenciado profundamente el desarrollo (*development*) urbano de la ciudad.

En Caracas se mezclan lo ultramoderno con lo antiguo, y el lujo (*luxury*) con la pobreza (*poverty*).

Puntos de atracción turística

El Salto Ángel está en el Parque Nacional Canaima. Es el salto de agua más alto del mundo, con una altura de 3.485 pies (*feet*). Es tan grande la altura que, antes de (*before*) llegar al suelo, mucha del agua se evapora o se convierte en una fina niebla cuando hay fuertes vientos.

El turismo en la Isla Margarita crece año tras (*after*) año. Sus paisajes maravillosos, sus excelentes hoteles y su vida nocturna atraen no solamente a los venezolanos, sino (*but*) también a muchos extranjeros, especialmente a los europeos.

© ZUMA Press, INC./Alamy

Las telenovelas

Venezuela es famosa por su producción de telenovelas, que se exportan a todo el mundo. En la foto vemos a una de sus principales actrices, Gabriela Spanic, de la telenovela *Soy tu dueña*, que se ve en el canal estadounidense Univisión.

La música

© Rodrigo Varela/WireImage/Getty Images

La música venezolana no tiene fronteras ni edades. Desde el tradicional joropo, pasando por los ritmos melódicos hasta el moderno rap y reggaetón en español, Venezuela produjo una gran cantidad de artistas ganadores de premios Grammy.

© JUAN BARRETO/AFP/Getty Images

La venezolana Stefania Fernández fue coronada Miss Universo en Bahamas, en 2009. Ganó un certamen en que participaron candidatas de 83 países.

Ahora, dime...

In groups of three, take turns asking and answering the following questions.

1. ¿En qué lugares de este país hay petróleo?
2. ¿Qué opinas de la contaminación (*pollution*) por el petróleo en las aguas del Golfo de México? ¿Pueden solucionarlo?
3. En tu ciudad, ¿hay muchos contrastes entre los edificios y las casas de lujo y las casas de la gente pobre?
4. ¿Qué islas cerca de los Estados Unidos atraen a muchos turistas? ¿Conoces la Isla Margarita u otra isla? ¿Qué te parece interesante de ir de vacaciones a una isla?
5. ¿Ves programas de televisión en español o escuchas música en español? Explica.

iLrn™

To learn more about Venezuela, watch the cultural footage in the Media Library.

AUTOPRUEBA

¿Cuánto sé ahora?

Take this test. When you have finished, check your answers in the answer key provided in Appendix D. Then use a red pen to correct any mistakes you may have made. Are you ready?

A. The imperfect Complete the following exchanges, using the imperfect of the verbs in the list.

quejarse (1) vivir (3) gustar (1) ser (4) ir (1) ver (1)

1. —¿Qué hora ________ cuando tú llegaste a casa?
   —________ las dos y media.
2. —¿Dónde ________ tú cuando ________ chico?
   —Yo ________ en Lima, pero todos los años mi familia y yo ________ de vacaciones a Venezuela.
   —¿Tú ________ a tus abuelos frecuentemente?
   —No, porque ellos ________ en Chile.
3. —Cuando Rita ________ chica siempre se ________ de todo.
   —¿Por qué?
   —Porque a ella no le ________ nada.

B. The preterit contrasted with the imperfect Complete the following sentences, using the preterit or the imperfect of the verbs in parentheses.

1. Anoche Alberto me ________ (decir) que ________ (necesitar) alquilar un apartamento, pero que no ________ (poder) ser muy caro porque él no ________ (tener) mucho dinero.
2. Ayer mi hermana y yo ________ (comprar) dos bolsas de dormir para las vacaciones. Cuando nosotras ________ (ser) niñas siempre ________ (llevar) bolsas de dormir cuando ________ (ir) de vacaciones.
3. Cuando yo ________ (tener) diez años, mi familia y yo ________ (venir) a los Estados Unidos a vivir. Nosotros ________ (hablar) inglés y español y ________ (estudiar) portugués.
4. —¿Cómo te ________ (ir) anoche en la fiesta de Silvia?
   —No muy bien. (Yo) ________ (tener) que irme a las diez porque no me ________ (sentir) bien.
5. Cuando Amalia ________ (ir) a la biblioteca, ________ (ver) un accidente en la calle Quinta. Dos personas ________ (morir).
6. ________ (Ser) las ocho de la noche cuando nosotros ________ (salir) de casa. ________ (llover) y ________ (hacer) mucho frío. ________ (volver) a casa en seguida.

C. Verbs that change meaning in the preterit Complete the following exchanges, using the preterit or the imperfect of the verbs given.

1. conocer —¿Tú ________ a la profesora de español?
   —No, la ________ el primer día de clases.
2. saber —¿Uds. ________ que Marta tuvo que mudarse de la pensión?
   —No, lo ________ ayer, cuando ella nos lo dijo.
3. no querer —¿Jorge vino hoy a clase?
   —No, él no ________ venir. Decidió quedarse (*to stay*) en su casa.
   —Yo no ________ venir tampoco, pero vine porque tenía un examen.

D. The relative pronouns *que* and *quien* Give the Spanish equivalent of the words in parentheses.

1. Esa es la chica ________ de todo. (*who complains*)
2. Yo hablé con los muchachos ________ ayer. (*who moved*)
3. Esta es la butaca ________. (*that we like*)
4. El chico ________ anoche se llama Esteban. (*whom I met*)
5. La señora ________ compramos el refrigerador está aquí. (*for whom*)

E. Just words . . .

a. Write the words or phrases that correspond to the following.

1. dinero que pagamos por vivir en una casa ________
2. barrio ________
3. metro ________
4. opuesto de **cerca** ________
5. persona de Venezuela ________
6. dar aviso ________

b. Complete the following sentences, using vocabulary from **Lección 10**.

1. El alquiler ________ el agua y la ________.
2. Necesito comprar muebles porque el nuevo apartamento no está ________.
3. Ernesto no tiene hermanos. Es hijo ________.
4. Necesito una mesa de ________ para la sala y una ________ de noche para el dormitorio.
5. En este barrio no hay apartamentos ________. Todos están alquilados.
6. El apartamento no tiene aire ________, pero no vamos a tener calor porque tiene muchos ________.
7. Mi apartamento ________ cerca de la ________ del metro.
8. Saqué la ropa de la ________ y la puse en la secadora.
9. Los niños quieren pan tostado. ¿Dónde está la ________?
10. Voy a ________ de convencer a Javier de que este apartamento es el mejor.

F. Cultura

1. Complete the following, based on the information found in the **¿Lo sabía Ud.?** sections.
   a. La palabra ________ tiene una connotación negativa en algunos países.
   b. En España, los apartamentos se llaman ________.
2. Complete the following based on the information found in the **El mundo hispánico y tú** section.
   a. Venezuela es uno de los diez mayores exportadores de ________ del mundo.
   b. La música tradicional de Venezuela es el ________.

G. Un dicho Do you remember the Spanish saying that is equivalent to *He who laughs last, laughs best*? Find it in this lesson.

LECCIÓN 11

EN UNA AGENCIA DE VIAJES

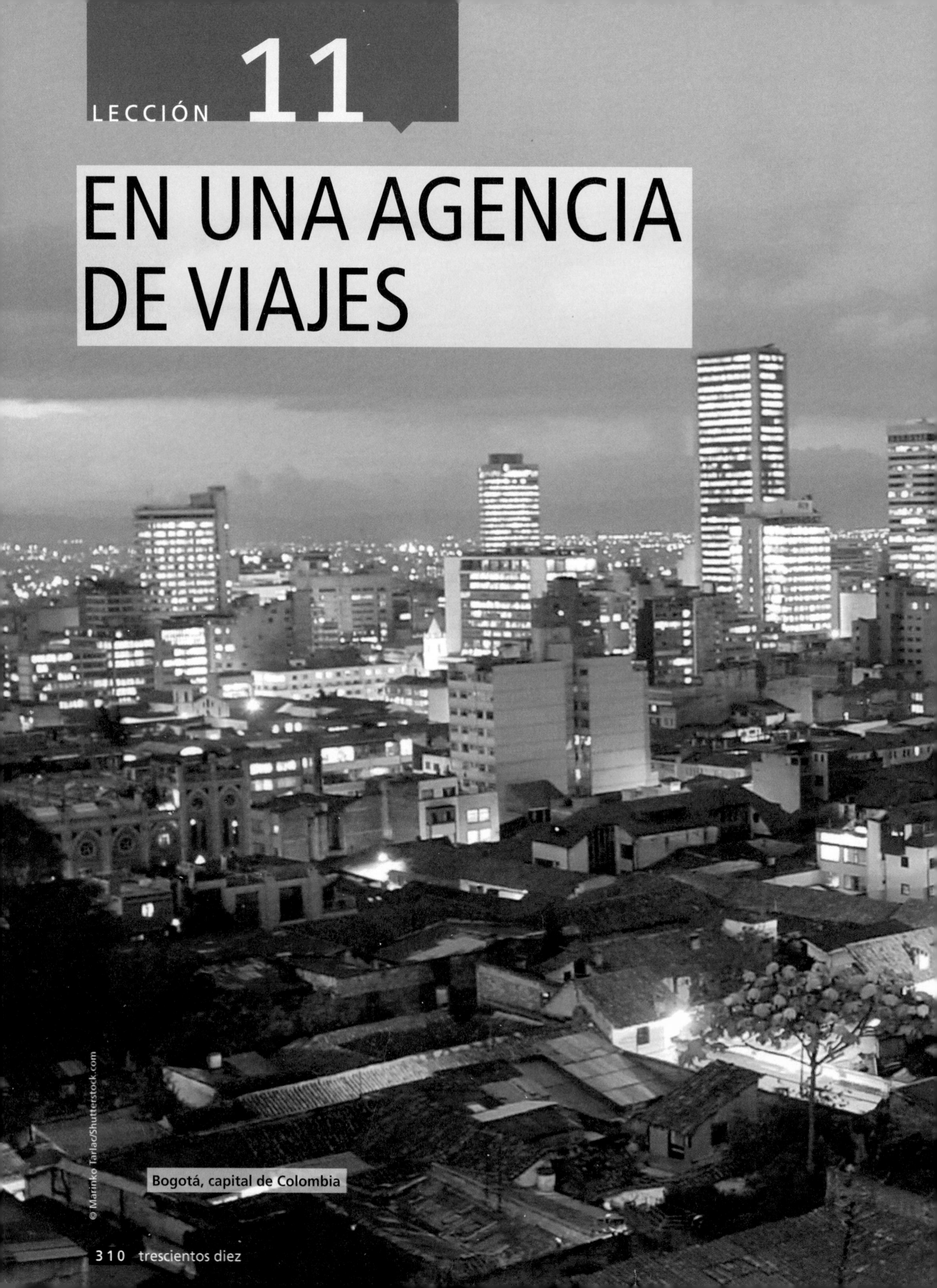

Bogotá, capital de Colombia

OBJETIVOS COMUNICATIVOS

You will learn vocabulary related to travel.

SITUACIONES

Planes para una luna de miel

ESTRUCTURAS

1 The subjunctive mood

2 The subjunctive with verbs of volition

3 The subjunctive with verbs of emotion

ASÍ SOMOS

¡Vamos a ver!

Watching and understanding situations

¡Vamos a escuchar!

Recognizing linking or transition words

¡Vamos a conversar!

Using courtesy expressions and common phrases

Rincón literario

Reading literature

Sala de espera by Enrique Anderson Imbert

¡Vamos a escribir!

Assessing your needs as a writer

EL MUNDO HISPÁNICO Y TÚ...

› Colombia

AUTOPRUEBA

You will review what you learned in this lesson.

COLOMBIA es la única nación nombrada en honor de Cristóbal Colón. Su extensión es algo mayor que las de los estados de California y Tejas juntos. Es el cuarto país sudamericano en tamaño (*size*), y es el único con costas en el océano Pacífico y en el mar Caribe.

Recursos iLrn video audio web playlist

Planes para una luna de miel

CD2-21

¡Ubíquelos!

The travel agency that Esteban visits is in Bogotá, the capital of Colombia. The video will show you many of the places that they can visit in this beautiful city, including good restaurants and excellent music clubs and theaters.

Esteban está en una agencia de viajes en Bogotá, Colombia. Él y Delia, su prometida, piensan casarse el mes que viene y están tratando de planear su luna de miel. Esteban le pide a la agente de viajes que le dé algunas ideas, que quiere compartir con Delia después. La muchacha trabaja hoy, y por eso no puede acompañarlo.

ESTEBAN: Espero que usted pueda darme algunas ideas, señorita, pero debo decirle que temo no tener mucho dinero.

AGENTE: Bueno, yo les sugiero que vayan a Costa Rica, que tiene unos bosques magníficos y excelentes hoteles.

ESTEBAN: ¿Tienen buenos precios?

AGENTE: ¡Buenísimos! Tenemos unos paquetes turísticos que incluyen el pasaje (en clase turista) y el hospedaje. Hay vuelos directos y vuelos con escalas. Mi padrino acaba de volver de Costa Rica y le encantó. Un billete de ida y vuelta en avión a San José cuesta unos ochocientos dólares. Aquí tiene unos folletos que describen el país.

ESTEBAN: Bueno... ¿tienen algo más barato? ¿Quizás aquí en Colombia? Podemos ir en tren.

AGENTE: Yo les aconsejo que hagan un crucero. Viajar por barco es muy romántico.

ESTEBAN: ¡Y muy caro! Podemos quedarnos aquí, en Bogotá, y hacer una excursión...

AGENTE: Sí... en Bogotá hay lugares muy interesantes, y hay hoteles y restaurantes excelentes.

ESTEBAN: ¡Tengo una idea brillante! Mis abuelos se van de vacaciones a Buenos Aires y su casa va a estar vacía por dos semanas; podemos quedarnos allí. Muchas gracias por su ayuda, señorita, pero creo que encontré el lugar ideal. ¡Y no me va a costar un centavo! ¡Ojalá que a Delia le guste mi idea!

Esteban sale de la agencia y la agente lo mira, frunciendo el ceño. Rita, una compañera de trabajo, se acerca a ella. Minutos después...

RITA: ¿Qué pasa, Lorena? Pareces preocupada.

AGENTE: No sé... ¡Creo que acabo de hablar con el hombre más tacaño del mundo!

¿Lo sabía Ud.?

En los países hispanos, las parejas (*couples*) generalmente están comprometidas durante años, porque no se casan hasta terminar los estudios o tener un buen puesto (*job*). Muchos esperan hasta tener un apartamento amueblado o una casa.

› **Por lo general, ¿las parejas de este país están comprometidas por mucho tiempo antes de casarse?**

1. Hablemos With a partner, take turns asking and answering the following questions. Base your answers on the dialogue and on your own circumstances.

En el diálogo

1. ¿Qué están planeando Esteban y Delia?
2. ¿Por qué no pudo acompañar Delia a Esteban?
3. ¿Adónde les sugiere la agente que vayan de luna de miel?
4. Para ir a Costa Rica, ¿solo hay vuelos directos?
5. ¿Qué le da la agente de viajes a Esteban?
6. ¿Qué dice la agente de los cruceros?
7. ¿Qué dice Esteban de viajar en barco?
8. Si Esteban se queda en Bogotá, ¿qué puede hacer?
9. ¿Por qué cree Esteban que la casa de sus abuelos es el lugar ideal para su luna de miel?
10. ¿Qué piensa la agente de viajes de Esteban?

¿Y tú?

1. ¿Qué estás planeando tú?
2. ¿Tú trabajas hoy?
3. ¿Quién te sugiere a ti adónde ir?
4. ¿Tú prefieres hacer un vuelo directo o un vuelo con escala? ¿Por qué?
5. ¿Dónde buscas tú información antes de hacer un viaje?
6. ¿Tú prefieres hacer un crucero o viajar en avión?
7. ¿Qué piensas tú de viajar en barco?
8. ¿A qué lugares de tu ciudad puedes hacer excursiones?
9. ¿Cuál crees tú que es el lugar ideal para una luna de miel?
10. ¿Tú conoces a alguien tan tacaño como Esteban?

El dos de mayo tuvo lugar la boda (*wedding*) del Dr. José Luis Villarreal y la Srta. Isabel Vera Vierci. La pareja está de luna de miel en Río de Janeiro.

VOCABULARIO

En el diálogo

Cognados

el centavo	*cent*
directo(a)	*direct*
excelente	*excellent*
la excursión	*excursion*
ideal	*ideal*
romántico(a)	*romantic*
turístico(a)	*tourist* (adj.)

Nombres

la agencia de viajes	*travel agency*
el (la) agente de viajes	*travel agent*
el avión	*plane*
el barco	*ship*
el bosque, la selva	*forest, jungle*
la clase turista	*tourist class*
el (la) compañero(a) de trabajo	*co-worker*
la escala	*stopover*
el folleto	*brochure*
el hospedaje	*lodging*
la luna	*moon*
_____ de miel	*honeymoon*
el padrino[1]	*godfather*
el paquete	*package*
el pasaje, el billete	*ticket*
_____ de ida	*one-way ticket*
_____ de ida y vuelta	*round-trip ticket*
el precio	*price*
el (la) prometido(a)	*fiancé(e)*
el tren	*train*
el vuelo	*flight*

Verbos

acercarse (a)	*to approach*
acompañar	*to accompany, to go with*
aconsejar	*to advise*
casarse	*to get married*
describir	*to describe*
esperar	*to hope*
parecer (yo parezco)	*to seem*
planear	*to plan*
quedarse	*to stay*
sugerir (e:ie)	*to suggest*
temer	*to fear, to be afraid*

Adjetivos

barato(a)	*inexpensive*
buenísimo(a)	*extremely good*
tacaño(a)	*stingy*
vacío(a)	*empty*

Otras palabras y expresiones

fruncir el ceño	*to frown*
hacer escala	*to make a stopover*
hacer un crucero	*to take a cruise*
hacer una excursión	*to go on an excursion*
irse de vacaciones	*to go on vacation*
ojalá	*I hope (God grant)*
por eso	*that's why*

© Adri Berger/Stone+/Getty Images

¿Lo sabía Ud.?

Cuando se bautiza a un hijo o a una hija, los padres invitan a dos amigos o parientes para ser los padrinos de sus hijos. Los padrinos se convierten en **compadre** y **comadre** de los padres del niño o de la niña; el niño o la niña que se bautiza es ahora el **ahijado** o la **ahijada** de sus padrinos. La relación entre los compadres, los ahijados y los padrinos es generalmente muy estrecha. Los padrinos son considerados como parte de la familia.

› **Cuando se bautiza a un niño en este país, ¿siempre tiene padrinos?**

LEARNING TIP

Remember to learn new vocabulary words in meaningful contexts. Construct sentences in which you use several related vocabulary items.

[1] **la madrina** = *godmother*

Más sobre el tema

En el aeropuerto / En el avión

De viaje

la aerolínea	*airline*
¡Buen viaje!	*Have a nice trip!*
la entrada	*entrance*
facturar el equipaje	*to check the luggage*
la fila	*row*
hospedarse	*to stay, to lodge (e.g., at a hotel)*
pagar exceso de equipaje	*to pay for excess baggage*
el paquete turístico	*vacation package*
la primera clase	*first class*
la salida	*exit, departure*
tener... de retraso (atraso)	*to be . . . behind schedule*
el (la) viajero(a)	*traveler*

Un dicho

Si la vida es un viaje...,
viajemos en primera clase.

[1]*Note*: **La azafata** is feminine only.

Práctica

2. **Palabras** Select the word or phrase that does not belong in each group.

    1. aconsejar / sugerir / temer
    2. ventanilla / tarjeta / pasillo
    3. avión / barco / folleto
    4. selva / novio / prometido
    5. hospedaje / hotel / tren
    6. viajar / acercarse / hacer un crucero
    7. bosque / casarse / luna de miel
    8. esperar / hacer escala / vuelo directo
    9. precio / centavo / luna
    10. agente de viajes / por eso / irse de vacaciones

3. **Preguntas y respuestas** Match the questions in column A with the answers in column B.

A		B
1. ¿Sabes que hoy salgo para Caracas?	_____	a. No, van a hacer un crucero.
2. ¿Qué están planeando ellos?	_____	b. No, tiene una hora de retraso.
3. ¿Llegó el avión?	_____	c. Una excursión.
4. ¿En qué aerolínea van a viajar?	_____	d. Sí, se casan en junio.
5. ¿Luis es el prometido de Eva?	_____	e. Sí. ¡Es buenísimo!
6. ¿Viajan en avión?	_____	f. Sí. ¡Buen viaje!
7. ¿Te gusta ese hotel?	_____	g. En American.
8. ¿Qué van a hacer ellos?	_____	h. Su luna de miel.

4. **¿Qué es?** Write the words or phrases that correspond to the following.

    1. hacer planes __________
    2. muy bueno __________
    3. pasaje __________
    4. hacer una descripción __________
    5. no irse __________
    6. opuesto de **caro** __________
    7. opuesto de **entrada** __________
    8. lo que le decimos a una persona que va a viajar __________
    9. auxiliar de vuelo __________
    10. persona que viaja __________

5. **Para completar** Complete the following sentences, using vocabulary from this lesson. Think logically.

   1. Trabaja en una agencia de ________.
   2. Pagué mucho por el ________ porque tengo cinco maletas.
   3. ¿Uds. viajan en primera clase o en clase ________?
   4. Quiero un billete de ida y ________, en la ________ "F", asiento de ________, no de pasillo.
   5. Tiene que darle la tarjeta de ________ a la auxiliar de vuelo.
   6. ¿En qué hotel van a ____________ Uds.?
   7. ¿Cuál es la ________ de salida?
   8. Queremos ________ un crucero porque viajar por ________ es muy ________.
   9. Mi padrino ________ Costa Rica es el ________ ideal.
   10. No quiero viajar sola. Ojalá que mi hermano me ________.

Para conversar

6. **¡Buen viaje!** With a partner, play the roles of two travelers planning every step of a trip, from going to the travel agency and deciding where they will travel, to buying the tickets, and then getting to the airport and boarding the plane. Give details.

   Modelo —*¿Vamos a viajar en primera clase?*
   —*No, vamos en clase turista.*

7. **En el avión** With a partner, play the roles of a difficult traveler and a very patient flight attendant.

   Modelo —*Azafata, estoy muy nervioso. ¿Puedo fumar?*
   —*No, señor, aquí está prohibido fumar.*

CD2-22

Pronunciación

Pronunciation in context

In this lesson, there are some new words or phrases that may be challenging to pronounce. For further pronunciation practice of Spanish sounds, listen to your instructor and repeat the following sentences.

1. Yo **les sugiero** que **vayan** a **Costa Rica.**
2. Aquí tiene **unos folletos que describen** el país.
3. Los **paquetes incluyen** el pasaje y **el hospedaje**.
4. **Viajar por barco** es muy **romántico.**
5. **Podemos quedarnos en Bogotá** y hacer **una excursión.**
6. **Mis abuelos** se van de **vacaciones a Buenos Aires.**
7. **Ojalá** que a Delia le guste **mi idea**.
8. **La agente** lo mira, **frunciendo el ceño.**

ESTRUCTURAS

1 The subjunctive mood (*El modo subjuntivo*)

A. Introduction to the subjunctive

Until now, you have been using verbs in the indicative mood. The indicative is used to express factual, definite events. By contrast, the subjunctive is used to reflect the speaker's feelings or attitudes toward events, or when the speaker views events as uncertain, unreal, or hypothetical.

- The Spanish subjunctive is most often used in subordinate or dependent clauses.
- The subjunctive is also used in English, although not as often as in Spanish. Consider the following sentence:

  *I suggest that he **arrive** tomorrow.*

The expression that requires the use of the subjunctive is in the main clause, *I suggest*. The subjunctive appears in the subordinate clause, *that he **arrive** tomorrow*. The subjunctive is used because the action of arriving is not real; it is only what is *suggested* that he do.

B. Present subjunctive forms of regular verbs

- To form the present subjunctive, add the following endings to the stem of the first-person singular of the present indicative after dropping the **o**.

-*ar* verbs		**-*er* verbs**		**-*ir* verbs**	
habl	**-e**	com	**-a**	viv	**-a**
habl	**-es**	com	**-as**	viv	**-as**
habl	**-e**	com	**-a**	viv	**-a**
habl	**-emos**	com	**-amos**	viv	**-amos**
habl	**-éis**	com	**-áis**	viv	**-áis**
habl	**-en**	com	**-an**	viv	**-an**

- Note that the endings for **-er** and **-ir** verbs are identical.
- The following table shows how to form the first-person singular of the present subjunctive. The stem is the same for all persons.

> **Un dicho**
> **Antes de casarte, abre bien los dos ojos. Después de casarte... ¡cierra uno!**
> *Before getting married, keep both eyes wide open. After marrying . . . close one!*

First-person singular			
Verb	**Present indicative**	**Subjunctive stem**	**Present subjunctive**
camin**ar**	camin**o**	camin-	**camine**
aprend**er**	aprend**o**	aprend-	**aprenda**
escrib**ir**	escrib**o**	escrib-	**escriba**
dec**ir**	dig**o**	dig-	**diga**
hac**er**	hag**o**	hag-	**haga**
tra**er**	traig**o**	traig-	**traiga**
sac**ar**	sac**o**	sac-	**saque**[1]
lleg**ar**	lleg**o**	lleg-	**llegue**[1]
empez**ar**	empiez**o**	empiez-	**empiece**[1]

Práctica

8. Formas Give the present subjunctive of the following verbs.

1. *yo*: solicitar, recibir, traer, decir, caminar, comer, ver
2. *tú*: escribir, cobrar, decidir, regresar, venir, barrer, aparcar
3. *él*: aconsejar, hacer, mandar, salir, anotar, esperar
4. *nosotros*: cocinar, depositar, leer, poner, pagar, parecer
5. *ellos*: caminar, deber, robar, conocer, vender, salir, empezar

C. Subjunctive forms of stem-changing verbs

› Verbs that end in **-ar** and **-er** undergo the same stem changes in the present subjunctive as in the present indicative.

recomendar (e:ie) *to recommend*		**recordar (o:ue)** *to remember*	
recom**ie**nde	recomend**emos**	rec**ue**rde	record**emos**
recom**ie**ndes	recomend**éis**	rec**ue**rdes	record**éis**
recom**ie**nde	recom**ie**nden	rec**ue**rde	rec**ue**rden

[1]Remember that in verbs ending in **-gar**, **-car**, and **-zar**, **g** changes to **gu**, **c** changes to **qu**, and **z** changes to **c** before **e**.

entender (e:ie) *to understand*		devolver (o:ue) *to return (something)*	
entienda	entend**amos**	dev**ue**lva	devolv**amos**
entiendas	entend**áis**	dev**ue**lvas	devolv**áis**
entienda	entiendan	dev**ue**lva	dev**ue**lvan

› In stem-changing verbs that end in **-ir**, the unstressed **e** changes to **i** and the unstressed **o** changes to **u** in the first- and second-person plural (**nosotros** and **vosotros**) forms. The other persons follow the same pattern as the indicative.

mentir (e:ie) *to lie*		dormir (o:ue) *to sleep*	
mienta	mint**amos**	duerma	durm**amos**
mientas	mint**áis**	duermas	durm**áis**
mienta	mientan	duerma	duerman

D. Verbs that are irregular in the subjunctive

› The following verbs are irregular in the subjunctive.

dar	estar	saber	ir	ser
dé	esté	sepa	vaya	sea
des	estés	sepas	vayas	seas
dé	esté	sepa	vaya	sea
demos	estemos	sepamos	vayamos	seamos
deis	estéis	sepáis	vayáis	seáis
den	estén	sepan	vayan	sean

¡Atención! The subjunctive of **hay** (impersonal form of **haber**) is **haya**.

Práctica

9. Más formas Give the present subjunctive of the following verbs.

1. *yo*: dormir, mentir, recomendar, dar, pensar, ir
2. *tú*: volver, estar, ser, preferir, recordar, morir, ver, pedir
3. *él*: cerrar, saber, perder, probar, dar, servir, seguir
4. *nosotros*: sentir, ir, dar, dormir, perder, cerrar, saber, ser
5. *ellos*: estar, ser, recordar, saber, encontrar, repetir

E. Uses of the subjunctive

There are four main concepts that call for the use of the subjunctive in Spanish.

› **Volition:** demands, wishes, advice, persuasion, and other attempts to impose will

Ella **quiere** que yo **viaje** hoy.	*She wants me to travel today.*
Te **aconsejo** que no **vayas** a esa agencia.	*I advise you not to go to that agency.*
Les **ruego** que no se **vayan**.	*I beg you not to leave.*

› **Emotion:** pity, joy, fear, surprise, hope, and so on

Espero que **lleguen** temprano.	*I hope they arrive early.*
Siento que no **puedas** ir a Costa Rica.	*I'm sorry you can't go to Costa Rica.*
Me **sorprende** que no **vayas** a Río de Janeiro.	*It surprises me that you're not going to Río de Janeiro.*

› **Doubt:** disbelief, denial, uncertainty, and negated facts

Dudo que se **casen** hoy.	*I doubt they'll get married today.*
No creo que ella sea **argentina**.	*I don't think she is Argentinian.*
No es verdad que Ana **esté** en Bogotá.	*It isn't true that Ana is in Bogotá.*

› **Unreality:** indefiniteness and nonexistence

¿**Hay alguien** que **tenga** los pasajes?	*Is there anyone who has the tickets?*
No hay nadie que **quiera** ir.	*There's nobody that wants to go.*

2 The subjunctive with verbs of volition (*El subjuntivo con verbos que indican voluntad o deseo*)

› All impositions of will, as well as indirect or implied commands, require the subjunctive in subordinate clauses. The subject in the main clause must be different from the subject in the subordinate clause.

› Note the sentence structure for this use of the subjunctive in Spanish.

Él **quiere**	que	yo **estudie.**
He wants		*me to study.*
main clause		subordinate clause

—¿Quiere que le **dé** el número de mi cuenta?	*Do you want me to give you my account number?*
—Sí, y también necesito que **firme** la tarjeta.	*Yes, and I also need you to sign the card.*
—Roberto quiere que tú **vayas** a la fiesta.	*Roberto wants you to go to the party.*
—Sí, pero yo no quiero **ir.**	*Yes, but I don't want to go.*

¡Atención! Notice that the infinitive is used after a verb of volition if there is no change of subject: **Yo no quiero *ir.***

› Some verbs of volition are:

aconsejar *to advise*	**pedir (e:i)** *to ask for, request*
desear *to want*	**querer (e:ie)** *to want*
exigir *to demand*	**recomendar (e:ie)** *to recommend*
mandar *to order*	**rogar (o:ue)** *to beg, plead*
necesitar *to need*	**sugerir (e:ie)** *to suggest*

Práctica

LEARNING TIP
Try to personalize the uses of the subjunctive. Think of people you know. What do they want you to do (or not to do)? What do you want them to do (or not to do)? Think of as many examples as possible. Remember: Practice makes perfect!

10. Yo no estoy de acuerdo Tell the following people that you want them to do something other than what they'd like to do.

Modelo Yo quiero viajar el martes. (el sábado)
Yo te sugiero que viajes el sábado.

1. Nosotros queremos ir en avión. (en tren)
2. Ellos quieren hablar con su padrino. (madrina)
3. Ana quiere casarse en mayo. (junio)
4. Uds. quieren quedarse una semana. (5 días)
5. Yo quiero hacer un crucero por el Mediterráneo. (Caribe)
6. Nosotros queremos empezar a las ocho. (a las diez)
7. Yo quiero volver en tren. (en coche)
8. Ellos quieren almorzar en la cafetería. (en un restaurante)

11. ¡Órdenes y más órdenes! With a partner, take turns describing what the following people want each person to do, using the present subjunctive.

Modelo

Anita
La mamá de Anita quiere que ella estudie.

1. Tito

2. Julia

3. Beto

4. Los estudiantes

5. Hugo

12. Mis consejos Your friends are always coming to you with their problems. Tell them what you suggest, recommend, or advise for each situation.

Modelo —Necesito comprar un pasaje a Bogotá. ¿Qué me aconsejas que haga?
—Te aconsejo que lo compres por Internet.

1. Ana y Beto no saben adónde ir de luna de miel. ¿Adónde les sugieres que vayan?
2. Luis y su prometida no saben en qué mes casarse. ¿En qué mes les sugieres que se casen?
3. Yo no tengo dinero para comprar los pasajes. ¿A quién me aconsejas que se lo pida?
4. No sé si comprar un billete de ida o un billete de ida y vuelta. ¿Qué me aconsejas que haga?
5. Eva y yo podemos ir a Boston en avión o en tren. ¿Cómo nos recomiendas que viajemos?
6. Los chicos no saben en qué hotel hospedarse. ¿Qué les recomiendas que hagan?
7. Pedro quiere viajar a Sudamérica, pero es muy tacaño. ¿A qué país le sugieres que viaje?
8. Yo no quiero pagar exceso de equipaje. ¿Cuántas maletas me sugieres que lleve?
9. Yo le voy a dar dinero a Nora para viajar a Costa Rica. ¿Cuánto me sugieres que le dé?
10. Ada y yo no tenemos mucho dinero para viajar. ¿En qué clase nos aconsejas que viajemos?

13. Excusas With a classmate, look at the list of errands that must be done tomorrow. Then take turns saying what you want each other to do, and give different reasons why you can't do it.

Modelo —comprar la medicina para Ernesto
—Yo quiero que tú compres la medicina para Ernesto.
—Yo no puedo comprarla porque tengo que estudiar.

1. llevar los pantalones a la tintorería
2. pagar los pasajes
3. depositar el cheque en el banco
4. llevar la motocicleta al taller (*shop*)
5. comprar las bebidas para la fiesta
6. llevar los discos compactos a casa de Ana
7. alquilar un video
8. comprar los billetes para la excursión
9. ir a la oficina de turismo para pedir la lista de hoteles
10. comprar el regalo para Eva

Para conversar

14. **Todos me dan órdenes** Discuss with a classmate things that important people in your life (parents, relatives, friends, professors, etc.) want you to do. List at least five things, and then compare your results with another group.

15. **Problemas y soluciones** Write two or three problems on a slip of paper. Then, form a small group with two or three classmates. Switch slips with the group and take turns offering solutions to each other's problems.

Un dicho

Si quieres que los demás te respeten... ¡empieza por respetar a los demás!
If you want others to respect you, start by respecting others.

3 The subjunctive with verbs of emotion (*El subjuntivo con verbos de emoción*)

› In Spanish, the subjunctive is always used in subordinate clauses when the verb in the main clause expresses any kind of emotion, such as fear, joy, pity, hope, pleasure, surprise, anger, regret, sorrow, likes and dislikes, and so forth.

—**Siento** que Julia no **venga** hoy.	*I'm sorry that Julia is not coming today.*
—**Espero** que **pueda** venir mañana.	*I hope she can come tomorrow.*
—Ramón no tiene dinero para comprar un coche.	*Ramón doesn't have money to buy a car.*
—**Ojalá** que **consiga** un préstamo.	*I hope that he obtains a loan.*

¡Atención! **Ojalá** is always followed by the subjunctive: **Ojalá** que él **esté** aquí.

› If there is no change of subject, the infinitive is used instead of the subjunctive.

Me alegro de estar aquí. (**Yo** me alegro—**yo** estoy aquí.)	*I'm glad to be here.*

› Some verbs and expressions that express emotion are:

alegrarse (de)	*to be glad*
esperar	*to hope*
sentir (e:ie)	*to be sorry, to regret*
sorprender	*to surprise*
temer	*to fear*
es una lástima	*it's a pity*
ojalá	*I hope*

Práctica

16. ¿Me alegro... o no? You are talking to a classmate. Say whether you are glad (**Me alegro de que...**) or sorry (**Siento que...**) about what is happening to your classmate and his or her family.

Modelo —*Me caso el mes que viene.*
—*Me alegro de que te cases.*

1. Mi hija quiere ir de vacaciones, pero no tiene dinero para pagar el viaje.
2. Mis hermanos no pueden hospedarse en ese hotel porque no hay habitaciones libres.
3. Mi novio es muy romántico.
4. Mis padres tienen que pagar exceso de equipaje porque llevan cinco maletas.
5. Mi familia y yo vamos a irnos de vacaciones.
6. Yo voy a tener que llevar las maletas conmigo porque no puedo facturar el equipaje.
7. Mis primos son muy tacaños.
8. Mis profesores son excelentes.

17. Emociones Complete the following sentences to express how you feel, using the infinitive or the subjunctive as appropriate.

1. Yo me alegro mucho de...
2. Yo me alegro mucho de que mis amigos...
3. Yo temo no...
4. Yo temo que mi papá (mamá, hijo[a]) no...
5. Yo siento...
6. Yo siento que el profesor (la profesora, los profesores)...
7. Yo espero...
8. Yo espero que mis padres (Ud.)...
9. Ojalá que...
10. Es una lástima que tú...

Para conversar

18. ¿Qué tal nos va? In groups of three, tell each other about things that are going on in your life, some positive and some negative. Everyone should react appropriately.

Modelo —*Hoy estoy contento.*
—*Me alegro de que estés contento.*

¡Vamos a ver!

Antes de ver

19. Preguntas With a partner, take turns asking and answering the following questions.

1. Cuando compras pasajes, ¿los compras por Internet o prefieres ir a una agencia de viajes?
2. Generalmente, ¿los paquetes incluyen el pasaje y el hospedaje? ¿Incluyen algunas excursiones?
3. Por lo general, ¿tú compras pasajes de ida o de ida y vuelta? ¿En primera clase o en clase turista?
4. ¿Prefieres un vuelo directo o te gusta hacer escalas?
5. ¿Prefieres viajar en avión, en tren o en barco? ¿Qué es más romántico?
6. ¿Te encantan las ciudades grandes o prefieres los pueblos pequeños?
7. ¿Tú quieres conocer los bosques de Costa Rica o prefieres visitar Canadá?
8. ¿Alguien de tu familia planea casarse pronto? ¿Cuál es el lugar ideal para pasar la luna de miel?
9. Yo quiero ir de vacaciones. ¿A dónde me sugieres que viaje? ¿Me aconsejas que viaje a otro país?
10. ¿Tú me recomiendas que haga un crucero por el Mediterráneo o por el Caribe?

El video: ¿Dónde pasamos la luna de miel?

—Mi amor, si tú quieres ir a Buenos Aires, no hay problema. A mí me encantan las ciudades grandes.

—Bueno, la verdad es que yo quiero conocer los bosques de Costa Rica.

—Yo les recomiendo que hagan un crucero por el Mediterráneo. ¡Viajar en barco es muy romántico! Y después, una semana en Italia.

—Bueno... temo que eso sea un poco caro. Mi prometida y yo preferimos quedarnos en este continente.

Después de ver el video

Victoria

Gustavo

el agente

20. ¿Quién lo dice? Identify the person who said the following in the dialogue.

1. Bueno… temo que eso sea un poco caro.
2. Les sugiero que visiten Canadá.
3. Mi prometida y yo preferimos quedarnos en este continente.
4. A mí me encantan las ciudades grandes.
5. Pueden ir en avión hasta Toronto.
6. Estos folletos describen unos paquetes buenísimos.
7. Queremos dos pasajes de ida y vuelta a San José, en clase turista.
8. Yo les recomiendo que hagan un crucero por el Mediterráneo.
9. Mi amor, si tú quieres ir a Buenos Aires, no hay problema.

21. Hablemos With a partner, take turns asking and answering the following questions. Base your answers on the dialogue.

1. ¿Cuándo planean casarse Victoria y Gustavo?
2. ¿Qué están tratando de decidir Gustavo y Victoria?
3. ¿Qué les sugieren los padrinos de Victoria?
4. ¿Qué incluyen los paquetes que describen los folletos?
5. ¿Qué espera Victoria que puedan hacer hoy?
6. ¿Qué les recomienda el agente que hagan?
7. ¿Qué decide hacer Victoria?
8. ¿Por qué prefieren Victoria y Gustavo un vuelo directo?

22. ¿Qué pasa después? You and a partner use your imagination to say what the characters do. In Spanish, discuss the following.

1. Whether or not Gustavo and Victoria were able to get a direct flight to Costa Rica.
2. Whether they liked the forests in Costa Rica.
3. Whether Gustavo and Victoria want to live in Bogotá or they want to go back to Chía.
4. Whether Gustavo plans to take Victoria to Buenos Aires next year or prefers to go to Río.
5. Whether Gustavo's mother hopes that they go to Buenos Aires next year.
6. Whether Gustavo's mother decides to travel too and where she wants to go. Does she travel first class or tourist class? What does the agent recommend to her?
7. Whether Victoria's godparents decide to go back to Costa Rica, to take a cruise, or to travel to Canada.

Now compare your statements to those of another group.

¡Vamos a escuchar!

ESTRATEGIA **Recognizing linking or transition words** Different classes of words contribute to convey different aspects of meaning orally or in writing. For example, nouns, adjectives, and verbs provide the bulk of the "picture" that is being communicated in words. There are other classes of words, such as linking or transition words, that hold the ideas together, indicate sequence, and establish transitions or relationships among the elements in the picture.

- Linking ideas: **y, también, además (de)**
- Comparing or contrasting: **pero, como** (*like*)
- Establishing sequence: **primero, luego, antes, después, finalmente**
- Expressing a result: **entonces** (*so then*), **por eso, como resultado, de modo que**

CD2-23 **23. Unas vacaciones** Raúl and Rita are talking about where to go on vacation. Listen to their conversation and try to list at least six words you hear that serve to link ideas and/or create a transition.

¡Vamos a conversar!

ESTRATEGIA **Using courtesy expressions and common phrases** Interacting with others requires being able to express your reactions and emotions in a sensitive way. Here are some common phrases for a variety of situations.

To wish a friend well

¡Que te mejores! *Get better!*
¡Que te vaya bien! *May it all go well!*
¡Que te diviertas! *Have fun!*
¡Que pases un buen fin de semana! *Have a good weekend!*

To react with certain emotions

¡Cuánto me alegro! *I'm so glad!*
Temo que no. *I'm afraid not.*
Espero que sí (no). *I hope so (not).*
¡Qué lástima! *What a pity (shame)!*
¡Qué sorpresa! *What a surprise!*

24. Situaciones With a partner, react to the following situations. Then, take turns telling your partner something about your own life and react to each other's news.

1. Una amiga te dice que sale de viaje para México mañana.
2. Un amigo perdió su vuelo para Cancún.
3. Un compañero quiere que le hagas un favor. No sabes si quieres hacerlo.
4. A tu hermana le ofrecieron el trabajo que quería para el verano.

25. ¿Qué dice Ud.? What would you say in the following situations? What might the other person say? Act out the scenes with a partner. Take turns playing each role.

1. Two of your friends are getting married and ask your advice about the wedding date, the reception, and where to spend their honeymoon. Give suggestions and recommendations.
2. At a travel agency, you ask whether the tourist packages they offer include the tickets, lodging, and excursions.
3. You tell your traveling companion that you have to check your luggage.
4. You tell a friend what you hope will happen in your life this year.

26. Para conocernos mejor To do this activity, work with a partner whom you would like to get to know. Take turns asking and answering these questions.

1. Cuando tú viajas, ¿dónde compras los pasajes? ¿Prefieres pasar tus vacaciones en una selva, en una playa o en una ciudad grande?
2. Generalmente, ¿cuánto tiempo tienes de vacaciones? ¿Prefieres tener vacaciones en el verano o en el invierno? ¿Qué te gusta hacer? ¿Adónde planeas ir en tus próximas vacaciones? ¿Vas a viajar solo(a), con tu familia o con tus amigos(as)?
3. ¿Tú prefieres hacer un crucero o pasar una semana en un balneario (*resort*)? ¿Qué es más romántico para una luna de miel?
4. Si alguien no sabe adónde ir de vacaciones, ¿adónde le sugieres que vaya? ¿Le aconsejas que compre los pasajes en una agencia de viajes o por el Internet? ¿Por qué? ¿En qué hotel le sugieres que se hospede?
5. Cuando tú viajas, ¿llevas mucho equipaje? ¿Llevas cámara fotográfica o cámara de video cuando viajas? ¿Les mandas tarjetas postales a tus amigos?

27. Una encuesta Interview your classmates to identify who fits the following descriptions. Include your instructor, but remember to use the **Ud.** form when addressing him/her. After finishing the survey, get together with two or three classmates and discuss the results.

1. No le gusta viajar en barco.	______________
2. El año pasado viajó a otro país.	______________
3. Siempre tiene que pagar exceso de equipaje.	______________
4. Prefiere un asiento de pasillo.	______________
5. Se hospeda en buenos hoteles.	______________
6. Piensa irse de vacaciones en el verano.	______________
7. Le gusta hacer escala cuando viaja.	______________
8. Lee muchos folletos antes de decidir a dónde ir de viaje.	______________

28. Para crear Get together in groups of three and "create" the scenario for this photo. Who are the people? Give them names. Where does the woman want to travel? Why is she traveling? What kind of ticket is she buying? What places of interest is she going to visit? What does the travel agent suggest to her?

Rincón literario

Enrique Anderson-Imbert (Argentina: 1910–2000)

Enrique Anderson-Imbert se conoce internacionalmente, sobre todo como cuentista y crítico. Anderson-Imbert escribió cuentos muy breves de tipo fantástico, en los que la realidad se mezcla con la fantasía. La selección que Ud. va a leer muestra ambas (*shows both*) cualidades, y es uno de sus famosos "minicuentos" de la colección *El gato Cheshire*.

Antes de leer

ESTRATEGIA **Reading literature** Predicting, guessing meaning from context, anticipating content as you read, and reading critically all contribute to understanding a text. In addition, for short stories or prose narrations, it may be important to identify who is telling the story. Is the narrator the writer or a character? Is the narration in the first or third person? This will determine whether you see a character only through his or her thoughts and speech or from the perspective of an observer and the point of view of others.

Before reading the complete story, you will look at different aspects with different goals for each.

1. Predicting: Read the first two sentences of the story. In pairs, list three possible things that could happen to Costa, the murderer.
2. Creating context by establishing key connections: Skim the story and try to figure out why it was entitled "Sala de espera."

¡A leer!

Sala de espera

[Source: Original publicado en *El gato Cheshire*, 1965]

Costa y Wright roban una casa. Costa asesina° a Wright y se queda con° la valija llena de joyas y dinero. Va a la estación para escaparse en el primer tren. En la sala de espera una señora se le sienta a la izquierda y le da° conversación. Fastidiado°, Costa finge con un bostezo° que tiene sueño y que se dispone a dormir, pero oye que la señora, como si no se hubiera dado cuenta, sigue conversando. Abre entonces los ojos y ve, sentado, a la derecha, el fantasma° de Wright. La señora atraviesa a Costa de lado a lado° con su mirada y dirige su charla al fantasma, quien contesta con gestos de simpatía. Cuando llega el tren Costa quiere levantarse, pero no puede. Está paralizado, mudo; y observa atónito° cómo el fantasma agarra tranquilamente la valija y se aleja con la señora hacia el andén°, ahora hablando y riéndose. Suben y el tren parte°. Costa los sigue con la vista. Viene un peón y se pone a limpiar° la sala de espera, que ha quedado completamente desierta. Pasa la aspiradora por el asiento donde está Costa, invisible.

murders / **se...** *keeps*

le... *engages him in*

annoyed / *yawn*

ghost

atraviesa... *looks right through Costa*

aghast

platform (train) / *leaves*

se... *starts cleaning*

29. **Comprensión** Read the story and find the answers to the following questions.

1. ¿Qué hacen Costa y Wright y qué pasa después?
2. ¿Para qué va Costa a la estación?
3. ¿Qué sucede en la sala de espera?
4. ¿Con quién conversa la señora?
5. ¿Por qué no puede Costa tomar el tren?
6. ¿Quiénes toman el tren?
7. ¿Qué hace el hombre que viene a limpiar la sala de espera?

Después de leer... reflexiones

30. **Preguntas** In groups of three or four, discuss the following.

1. ¿Qué pensaron Ud. y sus compañeros(as) que le iba a pasar a Costa?
2. ¿Alguna de sus posibilidades se acerca a lo que le ocurrió a Costa según el desenlace (*according to the ending*) del cuento? Comparta sus ideas con la clase.

¡Vamos a escribir!

Antes de escribir

ESTRATEGIA **Assessing your needs as a writer** Strategies are helpful guidelines, but in addition to all the strategies that have been presented so far, you are likely to come across specific needs that you will have to assess and find solutions to. This means tackling your projects with successful strategies you have used in the past as well as new or adapted ones.

¡A escribir!

31. **Un minicuento de ciencia ficción** You will write a story in which reality and fantasy are mixed. Use any number of strategies that you think you need (Lessons 9 and 10 give some good ideas). Start by brainstorming about a scenario where what is real could go side by side with the fantastic. How will it end? Will reality "win"? Write the *primer borrador* of your story, imitating Anderson-Imbert's style.

Después de escribir

32. **A revisar** Before writing the final version of your story, exchange your first draft with a classmate's and peer edit each other's work.

- noun-adjective agreement
- use of transition
- spelling and punctuation
- surprise ending

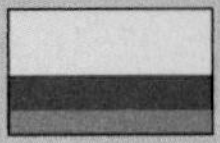

Colombia

Colombia tiene cuatro cosas famosas: el mejor café del mundo, las esmeraldas, la cumbia y Shakira. Es el único país del continente que tiene salida al Atlántico (el mar Caribe) y al Pacífico. Su territorio presenta gran variedad de regiones naturales: glaciares, montañas, selvas lluviosas, llanuras, desiertos y hermosas playas. El 90% de las esmeraldas del mundo proviene de Colombia.

Ciudades importantes

Bogotá

En Bogotá, la capital del país, se contrasta lo moderno con lo antiguo. En la ciudad hay arquitectura colonial, modernos rascacielos y muchos museos. Uno de los barrios más interesantes es La Candelaria, con sus muchas iglesias y casas coloniales.

Cartagena de Indias

La ciudad, fundada en 1533, está situada en la costa noreste del país. Durante la época colonial fue el puerto principal de donde se exportaban las riquezas del Nuevo Mundo a Europa. La parte antigua de la ciudad estaba amurallada para protegerla de los piratas.

Puntos de atracción turística

La Catedral de Sal de Zipaquirá

Al norte de Bogotá se encuentra la Catedral de Sal de Zipaquirá, una de las catedrales más grandes del mundo. Está construida en el interior de una montaña, en una antigua mina de sal convertida en catedral. Todo allí está hecho de sal.

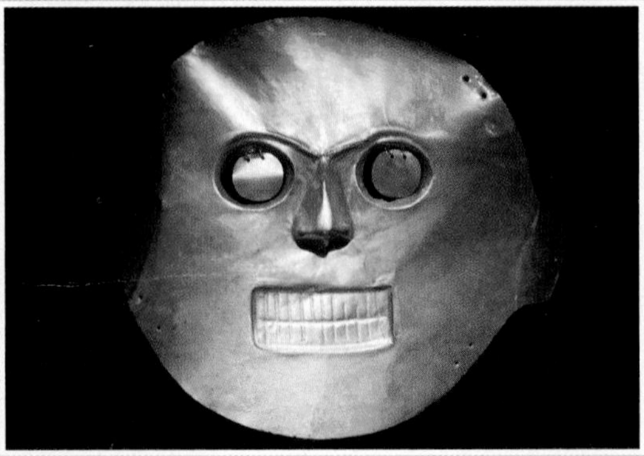

El Museo del Oro

En el Museo del Oro de Bogotá hay unas 35,000 piezas de oro y cerca de 25 mil objetos en cerámica. También hay una colección de esmeraldas que es una de las más grandes del mundo.

Las artes

Literatura

© Piero Pomponi/Liaison/Getty Images

Gabriel García Márquez es el escritor colombiano más famoso. Ganó el Premio Nobel de Literatura en 1982 por su novela *Cien años de soledad,* que ha sido traducida a 35 idiomas.

© Museum of Modern Art/Licensed by SCALA/Art Resource, NY
© Fernando Botero, courtesy Marlborough Gallery, New York

Artes plásticas

Otro artista colombiano de gran fama internacional es Fernando Botero, pintor, escultor y dibujante. Se dice que es el artista vivo originario de Latinoamérica cuyas obras han alcanzado mayor precio en todo el mundo. El estilo de pintura de Botero se caracteriza por sus formas redondeadas, infladas, hasta lo exagerado, "gordas" como él mismo las ha llamado. Esta pintura se titula "La familia presidencial".

Música

En la música colombiana se mezclan tres culturas: la indígena, la africana y la española. Entre sus ritmos más importantes están la cumbia y el vallenato. Entre los cantantes modernos más famosos están Juanes y Shakira, ambos ganadores de Premios Grammy.

© Christian Jakubaszek/Getty Images

© AP Photo/Ben Curtis

Ahora, dime...

In groups of three, take turns asking and answering the following questions.

1. ¿Tienes algunos discos compactos de Shakira? ¿Te gusta cómo canta? ¿Piensas comprar algún disco compacto de Juanes? ¿Quién es tu cantante estadounidense favorito?
2. ¿Qué contrastes se ven en Bogotá? ¿Cómo se compara tu ciudad con la capital colombiana?
3. El Museo de Oro es famoso por sus metales y piedras preciosas. ¿Conoces algún museo similar en este país?

iLrn

To learn more about Colombia, watch the cultural footage in the Media Library.

AUTOPRUEBA

¿Cuánto sé ahora?

Take this test. When you have finished, check your answers in the answer key provided in Appendix D. Then use a red pen to correct any mistakes you may have made. Are you ready?

A. The subjunctive mood Give the present subjunctive of the following verbs, according to each subject.

1. estar: nosotros ________
2. caminar: tú ________
3. sacar: yo ________
4. sugerir: ella ________
5. dar: ellos ________
6. saber: usted ________
7. volver: tú ________
8. quejarse: yo ________
9. ser: ustedes ________
10. ir: usted ________
11. recoger: él ________
12. recibir: yo ________

B. The subjunctive with verbs of volition Complete the following exchanges, using the infinitive or the present subjunctive of the verbs in parentheses.

1. —¿Tú quieres ________ (ir) a Colombia?
   —Sí, pero mi esposa quiere que (nosotros) ________ (ir) a Chile.
2. —¿A qué hora me aconsejas que ________ (venir)?
   —Yo te sugiero que ________ (estar) aquí a las dos.
3. —¿Tienes que ________ (ir) a la agencia de viajes?
   —Sí, mi madre quiere que yo ________ (comprar) los pasajes hoy.
4. —¿Qué quieres ________ (hacer) hoy?
   —Quiero que nosotros ________ (hacer) una excursión al bosque.
5. —¿Vas a viajar en avión?
   —Sí, quiero ________ (viajar) en primera clase, pero mi hermano prefiere que ________ (viajar) en clase turista porque es más barato.
6. —Nosotros queremos ________ (quedarse) en la ciudad.
   —Yo les sugiero que no ________ (quedarse) aquí. Les aconsejo que ________ (visitar) Canadá.

C. The subjunctive with verbs of emotion Rewrite the following sentences, according to the new beginnings.

1. Ellos van a hacer una excursión.
   Me alegro de que ellos...
2. Julio va a venir este verano.
   Espero que Julio...
3. Yo no sé cuánto cuesta el vuelo.
   Me sorprende que tú...
4. Ada está enferma.
   Temo que Ada...
5. Nosotros no podemos ir en ese viaje.
   Es una lástima que nosotros....
6. Ellos van a Colombia.
   Ojalá que ellos...
7. El vuelo hace escala en Panamá.
   Siento que el vuelo...

D. Just words . . .

a. Match the questions in column A with the answers in column B.

A		B
1. ¿Vas a viajar en avión?	____	a. En un hotel.
2. ¿Van a hacer escala?	____	b. Sí, tengo cinco maletas.
3. ¿Qué me sugieres?	____	c. Que hagas un crucero.
4. ¿Quieres un asiento de pasillo?	____	d. No, el vuelo es directo.
5. ¿Dónde te vas a hospedar?	____	e. No, de ventanilla.
6. ¿Tienes que pagar exceso de equipaje?	____	f. No, en barco.
7. ¿Quién te va a acompañar?	____	g. No, es muy tacaño.
8. ¿Mario gasta mucho dinero?	____	h. Mi padrino.
9. ¿Qué te dieron en la agencia de viajes?	____	i. Sí. ¡Buen viaje!
10. ¿Sabes que viajo a Costa Rica?	____	j. Unos folletos.

b. Choose the word or phrase that best completes each sentence.

1. Vamos a hacer una (excursión, luna) al bosque.
2. Mi (compañera, madrina) de trabajo y su prometido planean casarse la semana próxima.
3. Ella (espera, frunce) el ceño cuando está preocupada.
4. Los paquetes (temen, incluyen) el pasaje y el hospedaje.
5. Teresa va a pagar el viaje. A mí no me va a costar un (centavo, vuelo).
6. Estos folletos que me dieron en la agencia de viajes (describen, acompañan) el pais.
7. Mi asiento está en la (salida, fila) cuatro.
8. Le voy a dar la tarjeta de embarque a la (azafata, escala).
9. Ellos van a (aconsejar, facturar) el equipaje porque tienen muchas maletas.
10. Costa Rica tiene unos (pasillos, bosques) magníficos.

E. Culture

1. Complete the following, based on the information found in the **¿Lo sabía Ud.?** sections.
   a. En los países hispanos las parejas *(couples)* generalmente están ________________ durante muchos años.
   b. Cuando se bautiza a un hijo o a una hija, los padres seleccionan a dos personas para ser la madrina y el ________________ de sus hijos.
2. Answer the following questions, based on the information found in the **El mundo hispánico y tú** section.
   a. ¿Cuál es el museo más famoso de la ciudad de Bogotá?
   b. ¿De qué país son las mejores esmeraldas del mundo?
   c. ¿Qué cantantes colombianos son famosos?

F. Un dicho Do you remember the Spanish saying that stresses the importance of being respectful? Find it in this lesson.

LECCIÓN 12

EL AUTOMÓVIL

En el centro de Quito

Philip Lewis/Alamy

OBJETIVOS COMUNICATIVOS

You will learn vocabulary related to automobiles, service stations, and road emergencies.

SITUACIONES

Necesitamos otro coche

ESTRUCTURAS

1 The **Ud.** and **Uds.** commands
2 The subjunctive to express doubt, disbelief, and denial
3 Constructions with **se**

ASÍ SOMOS

¡Vamos a ver!

Watching and understanding situations

¡Vamos a escuchar!

Recognizing spatial markers

¡Vamos a conversar!

Paraphrasing practice III

Rincón literario

Guessing

El alquiler de una casa by Manuel Gutiérrez Nájera

¡Vamos a escribir!

Writing a "mini theatre"

EL MUNDO HISPÁNICO Y TÚ

› Perú

› Ecuador

AUTOPRUEBA

You will review what you learned in this lesson.

PERÚ Y ECUADOR

PERÚ es el tercer país más grande de Sudamérica. Su territorio es un poco menor que el de Alaska, y su población es de unos 28 millones de habitantes. La moneda del país es el nuevo sol. El Puerto del Callao es uno de los más importantes de Sudamérica.

ECUADOR debe su nombre a su posición geográfica. El país está situado justamente sobre la línea del ecuador. Su territorio, incluidas las islas Galápagos, es un poco menor que el de Nevada, y su población es de unos 13,5 millones de habitantes.

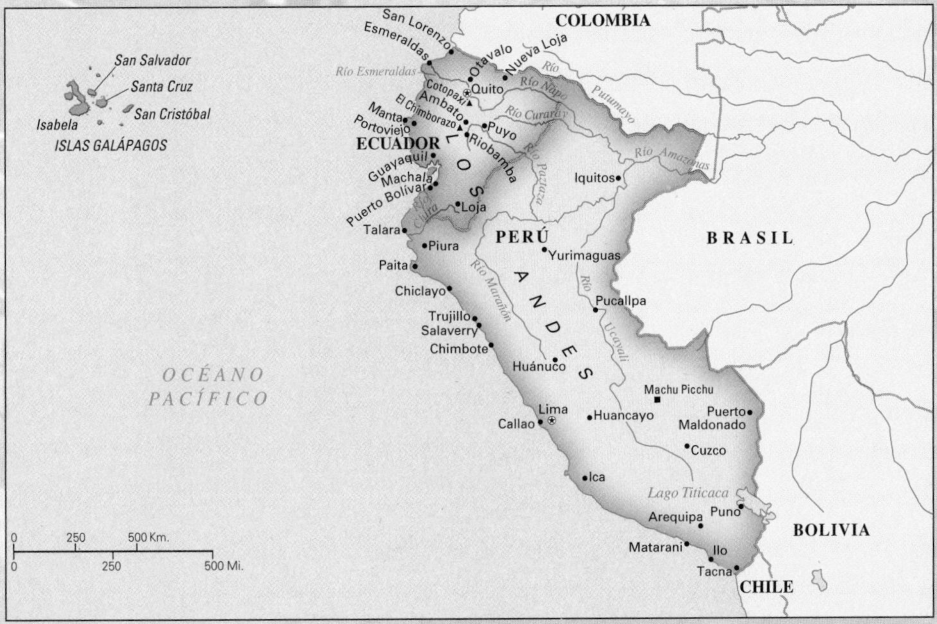

Recursos iLrn video audio web playlist

SITUACIONES

Necesitamos otro coche

CD2-24

© Cengage Learning

¡Ubíquelos!

Lidia´s parents' house is in the district of Miraflores in Lima, the capital of Perú. The video will show you several places one can visit in Lima. It will also show you Quito, the capital of Ecuador, which is Miguel´s hometown.

© Niko Guido/iStockphoto.com

Miguel Araújo y su esposa, Lidia, viven con los padres de ella, en el Distrito de Miraflores en la ciudad de Lima, la capital de Perú. Miguel es de Ecuador y Lidia es peruana. En este momento están hablando de la posibilidad de comprar un coche. Están leyendo los avisos clasificados.

Lidia: Necesitamos comprar un coche, porque el nuestro funciona muy mal y a menudo está en el taller de mecánica.

Miguel: Dudo que podamos comprar un coche, Lidia. Don Aldo me dijo que podía arreglar el que tenemos. Va a necesitar un acumulador nuevo, pero el arreglo no va a ser muy caro.

Lidia: ¡No! Ayer no arrancó y tuve que llamar una grúa. Fui a mi trabajo caminando. ¡No vale la pena arreglarlo!

Miguel: Pero Lidia, un coche nuevo cuesta un ojo de la cara.

Lidia: A lo mejor podemos comprar un buen coche usado. Lee este aviso.

Agencia Pérez y Hnos

¿Su auto funciona un día sí y otro no?

Tenemos carros nuevos y usados a los mejores precios.

Se vende al contado y a plazos.

Visítenos este fin de semana.

Estamos en la esquina de las calles Primera y Sol.

Teléfono: (555) 238-6217

© Dana E. Fry/Shutterstock.com

Lidia convence a Miguel y ahora están en la agencia donde se venden coches usados. Están hablando con uno de los vendedores.

Vendedor: Vengan por aquí, por favor. Miren este que está aquí. Es un coche compacto, de cambios mecánicos, y no gasta mucha gasolina.

Miguel: Francamente, yo prefiero los coches automáticos. Y no creo que mi esposa pueda acostumbrarse a manejar uno de cambios mecánicos.

Lidia: (*Bromeando*) ¡Ni tú tampoco! (*Al vendedor*) Dígame, ¿de qué año es este carro?

Vendedor: Es del año dos mil ocho, pero está en muy buenas condiciones.

Lidia: ¡No, no! Yo quiero uno más moderno. Creo que este se va a descomponer a menudo, como el que tenemos ahora. ¿Cuánto cuesta ese coche rojo?

Vendedor: Ese cuesta tres mil soles.[1]

Miguel: Muchas gracias, señor. Denos su tarjeta y nosotros lo llamamos la semana próxima. Adiós. (*A Lidia*) Vamos a la esquina a tomar el colectivo.

Lidia: ¿No vamos a comprar un coche?

Miguel: Bueno… Depende… ¿Cuánto podamos ahorrar al mes? A ver… si no vas a la peluquería… si nunca comemos en restaurantes… si no compramos ropa… si vamos a pie a todas partes…

Lidia: Allí viene el colectivo. Yo sé adónde vamos a ir.

Miguel: ¿Adónde? ¿Al correo? ¿A la farmacia?

Lidia: No, a un lugar donde se venden bicicletas. Espero que esté abierto.

Miguel: Ojalá que esté cerrado. No me gustan las bicicletas.

1. Hablemos With a partner, take turns asking and answering the following questions. Base your answers on the dialogue and on your own circumstances.

En el diálogo

1. ¿De qué están hablando Miguel y Lidia?
2. ¿Qué están leyendo Lidia y Miguel?
3. Según Lidia, ¿cómo funciona el coche de ellos?
4. ¿Quién dijo que podía arreglar el coche?
5. ¿Por qué tuvo Lidia que llamar una grúa ayer?
6. ¿Qué dice Miguel que cuesta un ojo de la cara?
7. ¿Cómo es el coche que les ofrece el vendedor?
8. ¿Por qué no quiere Miguel un coche de cambios mecánicos?
9. ¿Por qué no pueden comprar un coche Lidia y Miguel?
10. ¿Qué decide hacer Lidia?

¿Y tú?

1. ¿Tú tienes coche? ¿Lo compraste nuevo o usado?
2. Cuando tú vas a comprar algo, ¿dónde buscas información?
3. ¿Tu coche funciona bien o tiene muchos problemas?
4. ¿Tú sabes arreglar coches?
5. ¿Alguna vez tuviste que llamar una grúa? ¿Por qué?
6. ¿Alguna vez compraste algo que te costó un ojo de la cara? ¿Qué fue?
7. ¿Qué tipo de coche te gusta?
8. ¿Tú prefieres un coche de cambios mecánicos o un coche automático? ¿Por qué?
9. Si tú quieres comprar un coche, ¿necesitas ahorrar mucho?
10. ¿Tú tienes bicicleta? ¿Cuándo la usas?

[1] Peruvian currency

VOCABULARIO

En el diálogo

Cognados

automático(a)	*automatic*
clasificado(a)	*classified*
compacto(a)	*compact*
la condición	*condition*
francamente	*frankly*
la gasolina	*gasoline*
moderno(a)	*modern*
la posibilidad	*possibility*
peruano(a)	*Peruvian*
usado(a)	*used*

Nombres

el acumulador, la batería	*battery*
el arreglo	*repair*
la bicicleta	*bicycle*
el colectivo	*bus*
el correo, la oficina de correos	*post office*
la esquina	*(street) corner*
la grúa, el remolcador	*tow truck*
la peluquería, el salón de belleza	*beauty salon*
el taller de mecánica	*car repair shop*
el (la) vendedor(a)	*salesperson*

Verbs

acostumbrarse (a)	*to get used (to)*
arrancar	*to start (e.g., a motor)*
arreglar	*to repair*
bromear	*to kid, to joke*
descomponerse	*to break down (e.g., a motor)*
dudar	*to doubt*
funcionar	*to work, to function*
gastar	*to use, to spend*
manejar	*to drive*

Adjetivos

abierto(a)	*open*
cerrado(a)	*closed*

Otras palabras y expresiones

a lo mejor	*maybe*
a menudo, frecuentemente	*often, frequently*
a pie	*on foot*
al mes	*monthly, per month*
costar un ojo de la cara	*to cost an arm and a leg*
de cambios mecánicos	*standard shift*
depende	*it depends*
ir a pie, ir caminando	*to go on foot, to walk*
por aquí	*this way*
valer (merecer) la pena	*to be worth it*

¿Lo sabía Ud.?

En las grandes ciudades como Madrid, Bogotá, la Ciudad de México y Buenos Aires, hay muchísimos automóviles y autobuses, lo cual (*which*) está causando graves problemas de contaminación del aire. Sin embargo, en muchas zonas rurales de los países hispanos, particularmente en Hispanoamérica, hay muy pocos automóviles, ya que no hay carreteras, o las que existen están en muy malas condiciones.

› **¿En qué ciudades de este país hay mucha contaminación del aire?**

Más sobre el tema

Para hablar del coche

la autopista	*highway, freeway*
la bocina	*horn*
la bolsa de aire	*air bag*
descompuesto(a)	*out of order, not working*
el freno	*brake*
la gasolinera, la estación de servicio	*gas (service) station*
lleno(a)	*full*
la milla[1]	*mile*
el neumático pinchado, la llanta pinchada	*flat tire*
la pieza de repuesto	*spare part*
el tanque	*tank*
la velocidad máxima	*speed limit*

Un dicho

Un viaje de mil millas comienza con el primer paso.

[1]Una milla = 1.6 km.

Práctica

2. ¿Cuál no va? Select the word or phrase that does not belong in each group.

1. automático / posibilidad / cambios mecánicos
2. ir a pie / ir en coche / ir caminando
3. acostumbrarse / descomponerse / no funcionar
4. neumático / bocina / llanta
5. ventanilla / capó / parabrisas
6. bicicleta / carro / correo
7. maletero / cajuela / volante
8. costar muy caro / costar poco / costar un ojo de la cara

3. Preguntas y respuestas Match the items in column A with the ones in column B.

A		B
1. ¿Cuánto te costó el coche?	________	a. Sí, vamos a pie.
2. ¿Tu coche no arranca?	________	b. Piezas de repuesto.
3. ¿Van en coche?	________	c. El mecánico.
4. ¿Quién va a arreglar el coche?	________	d. No, en colectivo.
5. ¿El coche funciona?	________	e. En el taller de mecánica.
6. ¿Qué necesitas?	________	f. Un ojo de la cara.
7. ¿Dónde está tu coche?	________	g. No, está descompuesto.
8. ¿Vas a ir caminando?	________	h. No, necesito un remolcador.

4. ¿Qué es? Write the words or phrases that correspond to the following.

1. la chapa ____________
2. batería ____________
3. lo necesitamos para cambiar una llanta ____________
4. correo ____________
5. grúa ____________
6. peluquería ____________
7. persona de Perú ____________
8. frecuentemente ____________
9. persona que vende ____________
10. tener dudas ____________

La grúa

5. **Para completar** Complete the following sentences, using vocabulary from this lesson.

1. La ________ máxima en la autopista es de 65 ________ por hora.
2. Tengo que llevar mi coche al ________ de mecánica porque tiene un ________ pinchado. También necesito ________ las luces y los frenos.
3. Necesito llamar al vendedor. ¿Dónde está mi teléfono ________?
4. Mi coche tiene dos ________ de aire.
5. Elsa está leyendo los avisos ________ porque quiere comprar un coche usado.
6. Este coche tiene muchos problemas. No ________ la pena ________.
7. No me gustan los coches grandes. Prefiero un modelo ________.
8. No podemos comprar un coche nuevo. Tenemos que ________ a caminar.
9. Los coches de cambios ________ gastan menos ____________ que los coches ________.
10. ¿Tú tienes tu ________ para conducir?
11. La parada del ________ está en esa esquina.
12. No puedo comprar un coche nuevo. Voy a comprar un coche ________ que esté en buenas ________.

Para conversar

6. **¿Vale la pena arreglarlo?** With a partner, play the roles of two family members who are trying to decide what has to be done with a car that frequently breaks down and is very old. Decide also who can fix it, how much it's going to cost, etc.

7. **Tenemos mucho que hacer** Someone wants you and your partner to do some chores tomorrow morning. Take turns telling this person you can't help him or her, and say what you have to do and where you have to go tomorrow. Think of several excuses.

Pronunciación

CD2-25

Pronunciation in context

In this lesson, there are some new words or phrases that may be challenging to pronounce. For further pronunciation practice of Spanish sounds, listen to your instructor and repeat the following sentences.

1. **Miguel Araújo** y su esposa viven en el **distrito de Miraflores.**
2. **Don Aldo** me dijo que podía **arreglar** el coche que tenemos.
3. Ayer no **arrancó** y tuve que llamar un **remolcador.**
4. **Están hablando** con uno de los **vendedores.**
5. **Francamente** yo prefiero los coches **automáticos.**
6. Creo que este **se va a descomponer a menudo.**
7. ¿Cuánto podemos **ahorrar al mes**?
8. A ver… si no vas a **la peluquería…**

ESTRUCTURAS

1 The *Ud.* and *Uds.* commands (*Formas del imperativo para* Ud. *y* Uds.)

The command forms for **Ud.** and **Uds.**[1] are identical to the corresponding present subjunctive forms.

A. Regular forms

Endings of the Formal Commands			
		Ud.	*Uds.*
-ar verbs	cantar	cant **-e**	cant **-en**
-er verbs	beber	beb **-a**	beb **-an**
-ir verbs	vivir	viv -a	viv **-an**

LEARNING TIP
Think of as many **-ar** verbs as you can and use them to give commands: ***Estudie* más. *Cierre* la puerta.** Repeat this activity using **-er** and **-ir** verbs.

—¿Cuándo volvemos? — *When do we return?*
—**Vuelvan** mañana y **traigan** los documentos. — *Come back tomorrow and bring the documents.*
—¿Compro la batería? — *Do I buy the battery?*
—No, no **compre** la batería. — *No, don't buy the battery.*

¡Atención! To give a negative **Ud./Uds.** command, place **no** in front of the verb: **No** compre la batería.

B. Irregular forms

› The command forms of the following verbs are irregular.

	dar	**estar**	**ser**	**ir**
Ud.	dé	esté	sea	vaya
Uds.	den	estén	sean	vayan

—¿Adónde tengo que ir? — *Where do I have to go?*
—**Vaya** a la gasolinera. — *Go to the gas station.*

—¿A qué hora tenemos que estar aquí? — *At what time do we have to be here?*
—**Estén** aquí a las ocho. ¡**Sean** puntuales! — *Be here at eight. Be punctual!*

Práctica

8. Órdenes What commands would these people give?

1. Un padre a sus hijos, que piensan comprar un coche usado:
   a. leer los anuncios clasificados
   b. ir a varias agencias de venta (*sale*) de coches
   c. preguntar si el coche está en buenas condiciones
   d. preguntar cuánta gasolina gasta el coche
   e. estar seguros de que el coche funciona bien
   f. conducir el coche por un rato
   g. Llevar el coche a un mecánico para que lo revise

[1] **Tú** commands will be studied in **Lección 13.**

2. El cliente (*customer*) al mecánico:
   a. cambiar la llanta pinchada
   b. revisar el sistema de inyección
   c. pedir la pieza de repuesto
   d. poner un acumulador nuevo
   e. arreglar las luces
   f. arreglar los frenos

Para conversar

9. **¿Cómo vamos?** Claudia and Silvia, two girls from Quito, have decided to visit a few places of interest in Lima, but don't know how to get to them. Using the map, you and your partner are going to give them directions. (Note: In Peru, **jirón** = **calle**.)

HINT: doblar = *to turn* seguir derecho = *to continue straight ahead*

1. del Hotel Lima a la Plaza San Martín
2. de la Plaza San Martín a la Universidad de San Marcos
3. de la Universidad de San Marcos al Palacio de Justicia
4. del Palacio de Justicia al Centro Cívico
5. del Centro Cívico al Museo de Arte Italiano
6. del Museo de Arte Italiano a la Plaza Grau
7. de la Plaza Grau a la Embajada de los Estados Unidos
8. de la embajada al hotel

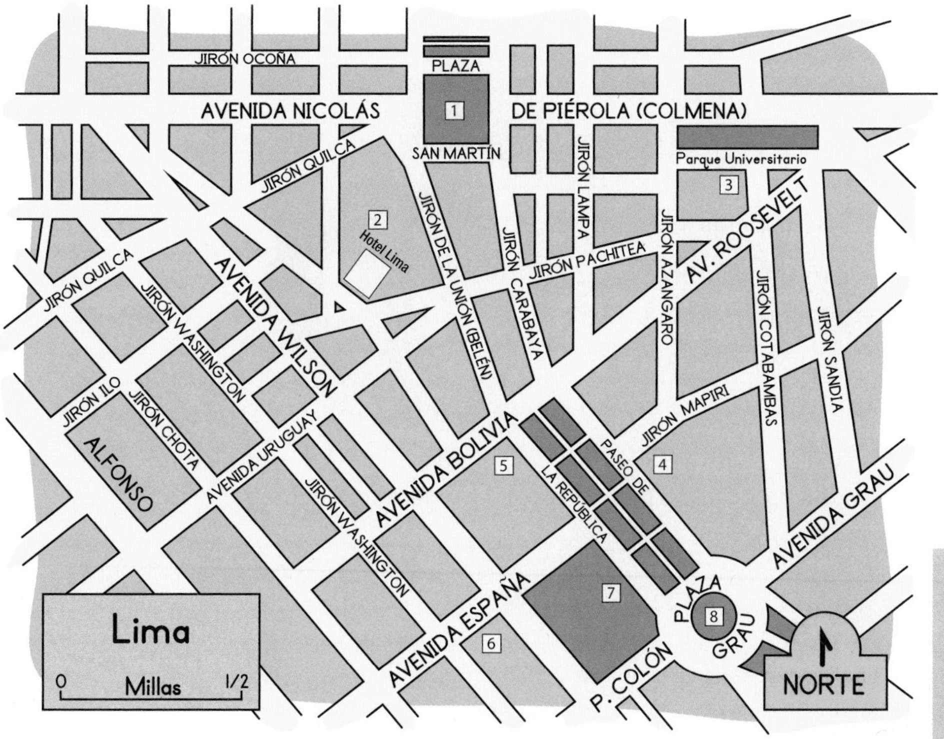

LEYENDA

1. Plaza San Martín
2. Hotel Lima
3. Universidad de San Marcos
4. Palacio de Justicia
5. Museo de Arte Italiano
6. Embajada de los Estados Unidos
7. Centro Cívico
8. Plaza Grau

Un dicho

Si toma, no maneje. Si maneja, no tome.
If you drink, don't drive. If you drive, don't drink.

C. Position of object pronouns with direct commands

› In all direct *affirmative* commands, the object pronouns are placed *after* the verb and attached to it.

Ud. form		*Uds.* form	
Hága**lo.**	*Do it.*	Cómpren**lo.**	*Buy it.*
Díga**les.**	*Tell them.*	Díganle**.**	*Tell him/her.*
Tráiga**nosla.**	*Bring it to us.*	Tráigan**selo.**	*Bring it to him/her.*
Quéde**se.**	*Stay.*	Quéden**se.**	*Stay.*

¡Atención! Note the use of the written accent, which follows the rules for accentuation. See Appendix A.

› In all *negative* commands, the pronouns are placed *in front of the verb.*

Ud. form		*Uds.* form	
No **lo** haga.	*Don't do it.*	No **lo** hagan.	*Don't do it.*
No **le** hable.	*Don't speak to him/her.*	No **le** hablen.	*Don't speak to him/her.*
No **se lo** dé.	*Don't give it to him/her.*	No **se lo** den.	*Don't give it to him/her.*

› Remember that when an indirect and a direct object pronoun are used together in the same sentence, the indirect object always precedes the direct object.

Práctica

10. A mis hermanitos Using the direct commands, tell your younger brothers to do the following.

1. Levantarse a las siete, bañarse y vestirse.
2. Hacer unos sándwiches y ponerlos en el refrigerador.
3. Escribirle una carta a su madrina.
4. Mandarle un paquete a Teresa.
5. Llamar a la Dra. Peña, pero no llamarla antes de las tres.
6. Comprarle el regalo a mamá, pero no dárselo hoy.
7. Decirle a Marta que la fiesta es mañana, pero no decírselo a Raúl.
8. No acostarse muy tarde.

¿Lo sabía Ud.?

En la mayoría de los países hispanos, la gasolina y los automóviles son mucho más caros que en los Estados Unidos. Por esta razón es muy popular la motocicleta, especialmente entre la gente joven.

› **¿Qué medio de transporte prefiere usar la gente joven en la ciudad donde Ud. vive?**

11. **¿Qué hacemos?** With a partner, take turns telling two people what to do about the items given.

Modelo los avisos clasificados *Léanlos.*

1. la grúa
2. el tanque
3. las piezas de repuesto
4. el sistema de inyección
5. los frenos
6. el gato
7. el aceite
8. el acumulador
9. el neumático pinchado
10. el coche descompuesto

12. **Mozo...** You are having dinner at a fancy restaurant. With a classmate, play the role of the waiter and the client. Ask the following questions and tell the waiter what you want or don't want him to do. Add four more questions of your own.

Modelo ¿Le traigo el menú?
Sí, tráigamelo, por favor. (*No, no me lo traiga.*)

1. ¿Le traigo la lista de vinos?
2. ¿Le sirvo la ensalada primero?
3. ¿Le pongo pimienta a la ensalada?
4. ¿Abro la botella de vino ahora?
5. ¿Le traigo el postre?
6. ¿Le sirvo el café?
7. ¿Le traigo la cuenta ahora?

Para conversar

13. **Querida Zulema...** You and your partner are going to be the "ghost" advice columnist behind Zulema. Decide what advice you are going to give each of the following people. Be sure to use commands.

Querida Zulema

1. Tengo 29 años y vivo con mis padres. Quiero comprarme un coche, pero mi padre dice que no vale la pena y no quiere prestarme el dinero. **¿Qué hago?**
Incomprendida

2. Mi esposa y yo le compramos a nuestro vecino un coche usado que funciona un día sí y otro no. ¡Siempre está en el taller! Queremos que nos devuelva *(return)* el dinero, pero él se niega. **¿Qué podemos hacer?**
Dos víctimas

3. Pienso dar una fiesta solamente para adultos. Invité a mis vecinos y ellos insisten en traer a sus dos niños. **¿Cómo les pido que no los traigan?**
Tímida

4. Yo quiero ir a pasar una semana en Lima, donde vive mi novia, pero tengo un amigo que siempre insiste en ir conmigo a todas partes. Esta vez yo prefiero ir solo. **¿Cómo se lo digo para no ofenderlo?**
Preocupado

2 The subjunctive to express doubt, disbelief, and denial

(Uso del subjuntivo para expresar duda, incredulidad y negación)

A. Doubt

› In Spanish, the subjunctive is always used in a subordinate clause when the verb of the main clause expresses doubt or uncertainty.

—Vamos al correo.	*Let's go to the post office.*
—**Dudo** que **esté** abierto a esta hora.	*I doubt that it's open at this time.*
—Estoy seguro de que abren a las ocho.	*I'm sure that they open at eight.*

¡Atención! When *no doubt* is expressed and the speaker is certain of the reality (**Estoy seguro[a], No dudo**), the indicative is used: **Estoy seguro** de que **abren** a las ocho.

B. Disbelief

› The verb **creer** is followed by the subjunctive in negative sentences, where it expresses disbelief.

—¿Uds. van a la peluquería hoy?	*Are you going to the beauty parlor today?*
—No, **no creo** que **tengamos** tiempo...	*No, I don't think we'll have time . . .*
—Yo creo que pueden ir, si salen temprano.	*I think you can go if you leave early.*

¡Atención! **Creer** is followed by the indicative when it expresses belief or conviction: **Yo creo** que **pueden** ir.

C. Denial

› When the main clause expresses denial of what is said in the subordinate clause, the subjunctive is used.

—¡Tú siempre llegas tarde!	*You always arrive late!*
—**No es verdad** que siempre **llegue** tarde. No niego que *a veces llego* un poco tarde, pero a veces soy puntual.	*It's not true that I always arrive late. I don't deny that sometimes I arrive a little late, but sometimes I'm punctual.*

LEARNING TIP
Make a list of descriptive adjectives and think of them as being applied to you. Then indicate whether each statement is true or not. For example: **Es verdad que yo soy muy alto. (No es verdad que yo sea muy alto.)**

¡Atención! When the main clause does not deny, but rather confirms what is said in the subordinate clause, the indicative is used: **No *niego* que a veces *llego* un poco tarde.**

Un dicho
Es verdad que la mejor manera de terminar algo, es empezar.

Práctica

14. ¿Verdadero o falso? Say whether the following statements are true or not. If a statement is false, correct it.

1. Texas es más grande que Maine.
2. Hace más calor en Alaska que en Arizona.
3. Quito es la capital de Perú.
4. El 25 de diciembre celebramos la independencia de nuestro país.
5. Necesitamos un documento de identidad para comprar un coche.
6. Arreglan coches en un taller de mecánica.
7. Una bicicleta es más cara que un auto.
8. Los coches modernos tienen bolsas de aire.

15. Un fin de semana You and a friend are spending the weekend in a very small town. Your friend wants to know about things to do, places to go, and so on. Answer, expressing belief or disbelief, doubt or certainty.

1. ¿Tú crees que hay habitaciones libres en el hotel?
2. ¿Tú crees que un cuarto cuesta menos de cien dólares por noche?
3. ¿Tú crees que aceptan cheques de viajero en el hotel?
4. ¿Tú crees que hay un aeropuerto internacional aquí?
5. ¿Podemos alquilar un coche?
6. Son las siete; ¿tú crees que el correo está abierto?
7. Vamos al centro. Quiero ir a una tienda elegante.
8. Tengo el pelo (*hair*) muy largo. Dicen que aquí hay peluquerías excelentes.
9. Quiero ir a cenar a un restaurante francés.
10. ¿Tú crees que vamos a volver aquí algún día?

16. Hablando de coches Complete the following sentences logically, using the subjunctive or the indicative as appropriate.

1. Yo dudo que ese coche…
2. Estoy seguro(a) de que el mecánico…
3. No creo que las piezas de repuesto…
4. Estoy seguro(a) de que la estación de servicio…
5. No es verdad que yo...
6. Yo no niego que mis padres...
7. Creo que un Cadillac...
8. No dudo que un buen mecánico...

¿Lo sabía Ud.?

En muchos países hispanos es necesario tener una cédula (*document*) de identidad como identificación y es necesario llevarla en todo momento.

› **¿Qué documento de identificación es el equivalente, en su país, a la cédula de identidad?**

Para conversar

17. ¡Habla con tu compañero(a)! With a partner, take turns asking each other the following questions.

1. ¿Tú crees que un Honda cuesta mucho más que un Chevrolet?
2. ¿Es verdad que un Cadillac cuesta un ojo de la cara?
3. ¿Tú crees que un coche automático gasta menos gasolina que un coche de cambios mecánicos?
4. ¿Crees que pronto los coches no van a necesitar gasolina o dudas que esto pueda pasar?
5. ¿Crees que las estaciones de servicio están abiertas a esta hora?
6. Si tu coche se descompone, ¿crees que puedes arreglarlo?
7. ¿Crees que tu mamá sabe cambiar una llanta?
8. ¿Es verdad que tú vienes a la universidad a pie?
9. ¿Es verdad que tú lees los anuncios clasificados todos los días?
10. ¿Es verdad que el correo está abierto (*open*) los domingos?

3 Constructions with *se* (*Construcciones con* ***se***)

› In Spanish, the pronoun **se** + *the third-person singular or plural form of the verb* is used as an impersonal construction. It is equivalent to the English passive voice, in which the person doing the action is not specified. It is also equivalent to English constructions that use the impersonal subjects *one, they, people*, and *you* (indefinite). The impersonal construction is widely used in Spanish.

LEARNING TIP
Think about different ads, instructions, or directions you see around you and express them in Spanish. Example: *For rent*: **Se alquila.**

Se habla español en Lima.	*Spanish is spoken in Lima. / They speak Spanish in Lima.*
—¿A qué hora **se abren** las peluquerías?	*What time do the beauty salons open?*
—**Se abren** a las nueve de la mañana.	*They open at nine a.m.*
—**Se dice** que la gasolina es barata aquí.	*It's said that gasoline is inexpensive here.*
—Sí, pero los coches son muy caros.	*Yes, but cars are very expensive.*

› The impersonal **se** is often used in ads, instructions, or directions.

FOR SALE

NO SMOKING

EXIT TO THE RIGHT

Práctica

18. **Letreros** In groups of three, write signs with the following information on them, using the impersonal construction.

    1. *No parking* ________________.
    2. *Exit to the left* ________________.
    3. *Spanish spoken here* ________________.
    4. *No littering* (*to litter*: **tirar basura**) ________________.
    5. *Apartments for rent* ________________.
    6. *No swimming* ________________.
    7. *Cars for sale* ________________.

19. **¡No, no, no...!** With a partner, take turns telling different people what is inappropriate, according to what they are doing.

    Modelo A teenager is using a swear word.
    ¡Eso no se dice!

    1. A child is eating spaghetti with his/her hands.
    2. A little boy is trying to eat dirt.
    3. Someone wears white after Labor Day.[1] (*to wear*: **usar**)
    4. A child is touching the salad on your plate. (*to touch*: **tocar**)
    5. Someone is about to drink mouthwash.

Para conversar

20. **El turista necesita saber...** With a partner, act out a scene between a tourist in Lima and a resident of the city who responds to the tourist's questions about the city. Use constructions with **se** in your conversation.

    1. ...el horario (*schedule*) de los bancos, del correo y de las tiendas
    2. ...qué idiomas habla la gente
    3. ...qué y dónde comen
    4. ...si venden objetos de oro (*gold*) y de plata (*silver*)
    5. ...dónde alquilan coches
    6. ...dónde venden coches usados
    7. ...dónde arreglan coches
    8. ...la hora en que abren y cierran las peluquerías

¿Lo sabía Ud.?

En Paraguay se hablan dos idiomas: español y guaraní.

› **¿Qué idiomas se hablan en Canadá?**

Un dicho

Se sufre, pero se aprende.
One suffers, but one learns.

[1] *Labor Day* = **Día del Trabajo**

¡Vamos a ver!

Antes de ver el video

21. Preguntas You and a partner take turns asking and answering the following questions.

1. ¿Tú crees que es mejor comprar un coche usado o un coche nuevo? ¿Prefieres un coche de cambios mecánicos o un coche automático?
2. Si un coche funciona un día sí y otro no, ¿tú crees que vale la pena arreglarlo?
3. ¿Qué haces tú si tu coche no arranca? ¿Llamas a un amigo o llamas una grúa?
4. ¿Cuándo fue la última vez que llevaste tu coche a un taller? ¿El arreglo te costó un ojo de la cara?
5. Generalmente, ¿cuántas veces al mes va una persona a una gasolinera para comprar gasolina?
6. ¿Es verdad que tú sabes arreglar coches? ¿Los coches modernos son complicados?
7. ¿Tu carro se descompone a menudo?
8. ¿Es verdad que tú tienes que ir a pie a todas partes?
9. ¿Vas a la peluquería (*hairdresser's*) a menudo? ¿Necesitas un corte de pelo (*haircut*)?
10. ¿Tú lees los avisos clasificados?

El video: Se venden coches usados

—Creo que voy a necesitar un carro si tengo que ir al trabajo después de mi última clase...

—Bueno... aquí dice que se venden coches usados, pero dudo que podamos comprar uno con el dinero que tenemos.

—Buenos días. ¿Están leyendo los avisos clasificados?

—Sí. Dígame, don José, ¿usted cree que necesitamos comprar un carro?

—Francamente, no creo que valga la pena.

—Vamos, Ramiro. Tenemos que acostumbrarnos a usar colectivos...

—(*Bromeando*) Si quieren, les vendo mi coche...

—No, gracias. ¡Prefiero una bicicleta!

Después de ver el video

Ramiro

Liliana

Don José

22. ¿Quién lo dice? Identify the person who said the following in the dialogue.

1. Me gustan más los carros automáticos.
2. Eso es porque Marta me obliga a ir a pie a todas partes.
3. Pero tía Marta dice que usted sabe arreglar carros.
4. No, gracias. ¡Prefiero una bicicleta!
5. ¿Usted cree que necesitamos comprar un carro?
6. Tenemos que acostumbrarnos a usar colectivos.
7. No, no es verdad que yo sepa arreglar nada.
8. ¡Ay! Tengo que ir al correo y después a la peluquería.
9. Llamé una grúa, que llevó el coche al taller de mecánica.

23. Hablemos With a partner, take turns asking and answering the following questions. Base your answers on the dialogue.

1. ¿Adónde tiene que ir Ramiro después de su última clase?
2. ¿Qué tipo de carro prefiere Ramiro?
3. ¿Don José cree que vale la pena comprar un coche usado?
4. ¿Por qué tuvo que llamar una grúa don José?
5. ¿Le costó a don José mucho dinero el arreglo del coche?
6. ¿Qué dice don José que su esposa lo obliga a hacer?
7. ¿Adónde tiene que ir Liliana?
8. ¿A qué tienen que acostumbrarse Liliana y Ramiro?

24. ¿Qué pasa después? You and a partner use your imagination to say what the characters do. In Spanish, discuss the following.

1. Whether the post office was open when Liliana got there or whether she had to go back the next day (**al día siguiente**).
2. Whether Marta went to the hairdresser's and whether she needed a haircut.
3. Whether it's true that don José´s wife makes him walk everywhere.
4. Whether don José's car started the next day.
5. Whether don José had to take his car to the repair shop again.
6. What kind of car Liliana and Ramiro bought. Give as many details as possible.
7. Whether or not Ramiro and Liliana got used to using buses.

Now compare your statements with those of another group.

¡Vamos a escuchar!

ESTRATEGIA **Recognizing spatial markers** In **Lección 11** you reviewed transition words that hold together and establish relationships between ideas in a sentence. Prepositions such as **en, entre,** and **hacia** and phrases indicating location are another category of words that serve to mark the spatial relationship of elements in a sentence. Some common phrases that indicate location are:

al lado de next to, beside **debajo de** underneath, below **detrás de** behind
cerca de near **encima de** on top of **frente a** in front of

25. Un aviso comercial You are going to hear a commercial from a car-towing business. Listen for and write the four words or phrases that indicate spatial relationships. There is one phrase that you have probably never heard. Can you identify it?
CD2-26

¡Vamos a conversar!

ESTRATEGIA **Paraphrasing practice III** You have already read that paraphrasing, in speech or writing, can be a useful tool for showing that you understand what is said, as well as for reporting or summarizing what you hear.

26. ¿Qué dijeron? You will hear a series of sentences related to everyday situations. Listen and restate each one in your own words. Then compare your responses with those of a classmate.
CD2-27

27. ¿Qué dice Ud.? What would you say in the following situations? What might the other person say? Act out the scenes with a partner. Take turns playing each role.

1. You tell someone that you are reading the classified ads because you're thinking about (**en**) the possibility of buying a used car.
2. You indicate that you doubt that the mechanic can fix the car because he does not have the spare parts that he needs.
3. You tell a friend that your car won't start and ask if he can call a tow truck.
4. You ask a friend if he prefers to drive a standard shift car or an automatic. You indicate what your preference is.
5. You ask a friend if the post office is open and add that you hope that it isn't closed.

28. Para conocernos mejor To do this activity, work with a classmate whom you would like to get to know. Take turns asking and answering these questions.

1. ¿Prefieres los coches automáticos o los coches de cambios mecánicos? ¿Los coches grandes o los compactos? ¿Los de dos puertas o los de cuatro puertas? ¿Prefieres comprar un coche nuevo o un coche usado?
2. ¿Qué haces tú cuando tu coche no arranca? Si tienes una llanta pinchada, ¿sabes cambiarla? ¿Tú crees que es fácil hacerlo? ¿Siempre llevas un gato en el maletero de tu coche? ¿Es verdad que tú sabes arreglar coches? Si un coche se descompone a menudo, ¿crees que vale la pena arreglarlo?

3. Cuando vienes a la universidad, ¿vienes en coche, en autobús o a pie? Si haces un viaje largo, ¿prefieres ir en avión o en coche?
4. ¿Cuántas veces al mes vas al correo? La oficina de correos, ¿está cerca o lejos de tu casa? ¿Tú sabes a qué hora se abre el correo? ¿A qué hora se cierra?
5. Generalmente, ¿a qué peluquería vas? ¿Vas a menudo? ¿Qué día de la semana prefieres ir? ¿Por qué? Cuando vas a la peluquería, ¿te lavan la cabeza, o solamente te peinan o te cortan el pelo (*give you a haircut*)? ¿Te cobran mucho por cortarte el pelo?

29. Una encuesta Interview your classmates to identify who fits the following descriptions. Include your instructor, but remember to use the **Ud.** form when addressing him/her. After finishing the survey, get together with two or three classmates and discuss the results.

1. Conduce desde los dieciséis años.	________________
2. Usa su teléfono celular cuando maneja.	________________
3. No le gusta conducir en la autopista.	________________
4. Vive a más de diez millas de la universidad.	________________
5. Tiene un coche que costó un ojo de la cara.	________________
6. Compra gasolina cuatro o cinco veces al mes.	________________
7. Lleva su coche al taller de mecánica a menudo.	________________
8. Va a todas partes en bicicleta.	________________

30. Para crear Get together in groups of three and "create" the scenario for this photo. Who are the people? Give them names. What kind of car do they want? What kind of car is the salesman (**vendedor**) trying to sell them? Discuss prices, colors, and so on. Finally, indicate what kind of car they bought. Give details.

Rincón literario

Manuel Gutiérrez Nájera (México: 1859–1895)
Este autor mexicano fue uno de los primeros que le dieron belleza y elegancia a la prosa. En 1894 fundó la Revista Azul, el primer periódico modernista. Publicó *Cuentos frágiles y Cuentos color de humo*, que fueron muy bien recibidos por los críticos.

Antes de leer

ESTRATEGIA **Guessing** "El alquiler de una casa", the story presented here, relates a series of conditions to which a renter must agree. Knowing this, read the first few lines of this "mini theatre", and you will soon discover what the characters are like. Try to guess how this conversation will end, taking into account the landlord's demands.

¡A leer!

31. Comprensión As you read the story, find the answers to the following questions.

1. ¿Cómo es el propietario? ¿Cómo es el inquilino?
2. ¿Qué es lo primero que quiere hacer el propietario?
3. ¿Cómo se llama el inquilino? ¿Cómo dice el propietario que debe llamarse? ¿Por qué?
4. ¿El inquilino tiene profesión? ¿A qué se dedica?
5. ¿Dónde quiere el propietario que el inquilino viva tres meses cada año?
6. ¿Cuál es la primera condición de arrendamiento? ¿Y la segunda?
7. ¿Por dónde deben entrar los artistas y los literatos que visiten al inquilino?
8. ¿Por qué dejó el inquilino su antiguo domicilio?

El alquiler de una casa (Adaptado)

El propietario: hombre gordo, bajo y de carácter alegre
El inquilino: hombre joven y flaco

Acto único

EL PROPIETARIO ¿Es usted quien desea alquilar el piso alto de la casa?
EL INQUILINO Sí, señor.

—Tome asiento. Voy a interrogarlo brevemente.
—Me había dicho el portero°... *doorman*
—¡Perdón! ¿Cómo se llama usted?
—Carlos Saldaña.
—Si alquila mi casa, debe llamarse "de Saldaña". Es más distinguido.
—Tengo treinta años. Soy soltero.
—¿Soltero? Bueno... espero que su novia no sea morena. No me gustan las morenas. ¿Tiene usted profesión?

—No, me dedico a cuidar mis intereses.

—Perfecto, Le voy a presentar a mi abogado.

—Gracias, tengo el mío.

—No importa. Puede cambiar. ¿Que tal de salud? Desnúdese°, por favor. *Take off your clothes*

—¿Qué...?

—Por un instante. No quiero que mis inquilinos sean enfermizos°. *sickly*

Humm...

No parecía usted tan flaco. ¿Hace usted ejercicio?

—Sí, todas las tardes.

—De ahora en adelante°, usted va a vivir en el campo tres meses de cada año. **De...** *From now on*

Bueno, voy a leerle mis condiciones de arrendamiento:

1°. El inquilino debe levantarse y acostarse temprano, para no turbar mi reposo.

2°. El inquilino debe invitar a comer al dueño todos los meses.

3°. Los artistas y los literatos que visiten al inquilino deben subir por la escalera de la servidumbre.

—¿Eso es todo?

—Sí. ¡Ah! ¿Por qué dejó usted su antiguo domicilio?

—¿Yo? Por nada! Porque arrojé° por el balcón al propietario... *threw*

Después de leer... reflexiones

32. Preguntas In groups of three, discuss the advantages and disadvatages of renting.

¡Vamos a escribir!

Antes de escribir

ESTRATEGIA **Writing a "mini theatre"**

- Decide how the characters relate to each other.
- Decide what the characters will say to each other, and how the conversation is going to end.

¡A escribir!

33. El inquilino y el propietario siguen hablando You will write eight or ten more exchanges between these two characters. Indicate what happens at the end. Write the **primer borrador** of your dialogue.

Después de escribir

34. Before writing the final version of your story, exchange your first draft with a classmate's and peer edit each other's work.

Perú

Perú es famoso por unos animales llamados "llamas". ¿Alguna vez viste llamas en el zoológico? ¿Leíste el cartelito (*little sign*) que decía de dónde venían? De Perú, ¿verdad? De allí también son las alpacas y las vicuñas...

Perú es el lugar ideal para los amantes de la cultura. Unos se quedan en Lima, cuyo centro histórico fue declarado Monumento Cultural de la Humanidad. Otros van a Machu Picchu, en Cuzco, la capital del Imperio Inca y una de las siete nuevas maravillas del mundo. Algunos quieren ver las enigmáticas líneas y figuras geométricas de Nazca, y a otros les interesa la amazonia peruana, el lago Titicaca o la extraordinaria diversidad de la flora y la fauna peruanas.

Puntos de atracción turística

Lima

La capital de Perú fue fundada en 1535. Allí están las mejores muestras de la arquitectura colonial, como la Catedral, el convento de San Francisco y la Universidad de San Marcos. Hay casas con hermosos balcones tallados en madera, y muchas plazas, como la de San Martín, llamada así en honor del libertador de Perú, José de San Martín.

Cuzco

La capital del Imperio Inca está situada al sureste de Lima, en los Andes. Está rodeada de ruinas preincaicas e incaicas, entre ellas el Templo del Sol, construido con piedras colocadas unas sobre otras sin nada que las mantenga unidas. El nombre de la ciudad proviene de una palabra quechua que significa "ombligo" (*navel*), porque sus fundadores creían que estaba situada en el centro del universo.

Machu Picchu

Machu Picchu, la ciudad perdida de los incas, fue construida en la cordillera de los Andes, a una altura (*height*) de 1400 pies sobre el río Urubamba. Estuvo escondida en las montañas por más de cuatro siglos, hasta que, en 1911, Hiram Bingham, un profesor de Yale, la descubrió. Se cree que fue un centro religioso y la residencia del primer emperador inca.

Ecuador

Ecuador está justo en la mitad del mundo. ¿Puedes imaginarte con un pie en el hemisferio norte y otro en el hemisferio sur? Esto puedes hacerlo en Ecuador, donde también puedes visitar una de las zonas ecológicas mejor conservadas del mundo: las islas Galápagos.

La lengua oficial del país es el español, pero la tercera parte de su población habla lenguas indígenas: la mayoría, quechua.

Ecuador es el principal exportador de bananas y uno de los mayores exportadores de petróleo, flores, camarones y cacao.

Puntos de atracción turística

© Gonzalo Azumendi/Age Fotostock /Photolibrary

Quito

Quito es la capital más antigua de Sudamérica, y todavía mantiene su aspecto colonial y sus calles estrechas (*narrow*). Está situada al pie del volcán Pichincha y tiene un clima primaveral todo el año.

© Jenny Leonard/Shutterstock.com

Mitad del Mundo:

A 22 millas de Quito, cerca de la villa de San Antonio, está el monumento La Mitad del Mundo, que marca el punto por donde hasta hace poco se creía que pasaba la línea del ecuador. Sin embargo, mediciones más recientes sitúan el ecuador 240 metros más al sur.

© McPHOTO/vario images GmbH & Co .KG/Alamy

Las Islas Galápagos

Las Islas Galápagos son de origen volcánico, y deben su nombre a sus enormes tortugas, llamadas galápagos, que pesan unos 200 kilos y viven hasta 250 años. Estas islas deben su fama a los estudios sobre la evolución de las especies que hizo allí el naturalista Charles Darwin.

Ahora dime...

1. ¿Por qué crees que la llama es un animal importante en Perú? ¿Conoces otro animal parecido a la llama?
2. La Universidad de San Marcos es una de las más antiguas de América. ¿Cuál es la universidad más antigua de este país? ¿Dónde está?
3. ¿Crees que es importante hablar un idioma indígena? ¿Por qué? ¿Qué idiomas indígenas se hablan en los Estados Unidos?

iLrn

To learn more about Perú and Ecuador, watch the cultural footage in the Media Library.

AUTOPRUEBA

¿Cuánto sé ahora?

Take this test. When you have finished, check your answers in the answer key provided in Appendix D. Then use a red pen to correct any mistakes you may have made. Are you ready?

A. The *Ud.* and *Uds.* commands

a. Complete the following sentences, using the Spanish equivalent of the words in parentheses.

1. ________ en la oficina de correos a las ocho, señoras. (*Be*)
2. Necesito el acumulador. ________ esta tarde, señor. (*Bring it to me*)
3. ________ por aquí, señoritas. (*Go out*)
4. ¿La licencia para conducir? ________ hoy, señora. (*Give it to him*)
5. ________ al salón de belleza, señorita. (*Go*)
6. ________ aquí, señor López. (*Stay*)
7. Necesitamos una grúa. ________, señor. (*Send it to us*)
8. ¿Los neumáticos? ________ allí, señor. (*Don´t put them*)
9. Señores, ________ al vendedor cuánto cuesta el coche. (*ask him*)
10. ¿Las bicicletas? ________, señoras. (*Buy them*)

b. You are talking with one of your employees. Using the command for **Ud.**, give him the following orders.

1. Ir al taller de mecánica.
2. Decirle al mecánico que haga lo siguiente:
   a. Cambiar el aceite del coche.
   b. Revisar los frenos.
   c. Arreglar el neumático pinchado.
   d. Limpiar el sistema de inyección.

B. The subjunctive to express doubt, disbelief, and denial Complete the following sentences, using the present subjunctive or the present indicative of the verbs in parentheses.

1. Yo no creo que ella ________ (ser) peruana.
2. Dudo que la gasolinera ________ (estar) abierta ahora.
3. No es verdad que Uds. ________ (necesitar) ir por la autopista.
4. Creo que Cuzco ________ (estar) a cien kilómetros de aquí.
5. Estoy seguro de que ellas ________ (encontrarse) en la peluquería.
6. Es verdad que nosotros ________ (necesitar) acostumbrarnos a usar el colectivo.
7. No dudo que el arreglo ________ (costar) un ojo de la cara.
8. Yo no niego que no me ________ (gustar) conducir.

C. Constructions with *se* Form questions with the elements given, adding the necessary connectors. Follow the model.

Modelo a qué hora / abrir / las tiendas

¿A qué hora se abren las tiendas?

1. qué idiomas / hablar / Perú
2. a qué hora / cerrar / las gasolineras
3. por dónde / salir / de aquí

4. cómo / llegar / a la estación de servicio
5. cómo / decir / **manejar** / en inglés
6. dónde / comprar / piezas de repuesto

D. Just words . . .

a. Choose the word or phrase in parentheses that best completes each sentence.

1. Voy a llamar una grúa porque mi coche no (bromea, arranca).
2. Prefiero los coches (de cambios mecánicos, abiertos).
3. Es muy caro. Me (costó, pagó) un ojo de la cara.
4. Mi coche tiene dos (bolsas, maleteros) de aire.
5. No pude parar porque (los frenos, las bocinas) no funcionaban.
6. El número de la (chapa, luz) de mi coche es SB-456.
7. Ponga el gato en (la cajuela, el volante) del coche.
8. El tanque del auto está (vacío, descompuesto).

b. Complete the following sentences, using vocabulary from **Lección 12**.

1. Yo siempre leo los avisos ________ cuando quiero comprar un coche usado.
2. No me gustan los coches grandes. Prefiero los modelos ________.
3. La oficina de ________ queda en la esquina. Podemos ir a ________.
4. Necesito comprar otro coche porque el mío siempre está ________.
5. No me gusta manejar por la ________ porque los coches van a mucha ________.
6. No necesito gasolina porque el tanque está ________.
7. Yo no conduzco muy rápido. Siempre voy a 25 ________ por hora en la ciudad.
8. No podemos ir al ________ de mecánica porque no está abierto.
9. No ________ la pena arreglar este coche.
10. Yo no voy a poder ________ a manejar un coche de ________ mecánicos.

E. Culture

1. Complete the following, based on the information found in the **¿Lo sabía Ud.?** section.
   a. En la mayoría de los países hispanos la gasolina es mucho más ________ que aquí.
   b. En muchos países hispanos es necesario tener una cédula (documento) de ________.
2. Answer these questions, based on the information found in the **El mundo hispánico y tú...** section.
   a. ¿Cuál es la principal atracción turística de Perú?
   b. ¿Cuál es una de las zonas ecológicas mejor conservadas del mundo?
   c. ¿Cuál es la capital más antigua de Sudamérica?

F. Un dicho Do you remember the Spanish saying about the fact that life´s trials can teach us good lessons? Find it in this lesson.

LECCIÓN 13

EN UN CENTRO COMERCIAL

Centro comercial en Santiago de Chile

OBJETIVOS COMUNICATIVOS

You will learn vocabulary related to clothing and shopping.

SITUACIONES

De compras

ESTRUCTURAS

1 The familiar commands (**tú**)

2 **¿Qué?** and **¿cuál?** used with **ser**

3 The subjunctive to express indefiniteness and nonexistence

ASÍ SOMOS

¡Vamos a ver!

Watching and understanding situations

¡Vamos a escuchar!

Listening for the order of events

¡Vamos a conversar!

Expressing ideas and opinions

Rincón literario

Reading poetry

Meciendo and *Piececitos* by Gabriela Mistral

¡Vamos a escribir!

Writing an advice column

EL MUNDO HISPÁNICO Y TÚ...

› Chile

AUTOPRUEBA

You will review what you learned in this lesson.

CHILE es un país largo y estrecho. El país tiene dos veces el área de Montana y su población es de unos 16 millones de habitantes. De estos, el 80% vive en las ciudades. En Santiago, la capital, vive casi la tercera parte de los habitantes del país.

Chile es famoso por sus lugares turísticos, como Viña del Mar, sus pistas de esquí y por su rica producción de vinos de exportación.

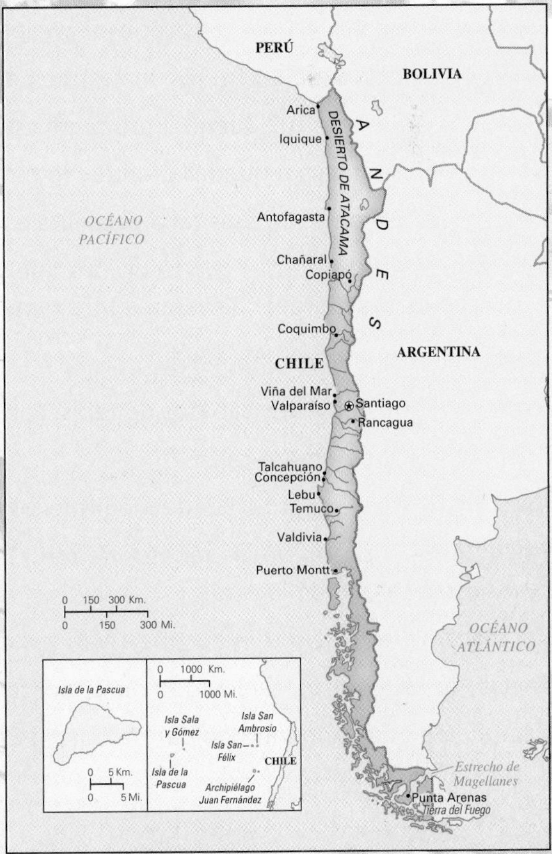

Recursos iLrn video audio web playlist

SITUACIONES

De compras

CD3-2

© Cengage Learning

¡Ubíquelos!

Fabio and Mireya and their two children live in Santiago, the capital of Chile. The video shows you many places that this family visits, generally on weekends.

© Jose Luis Pelaez Inc/Blend Images/Jupiter Images

Fabio y Mireya, un matrimonio chileno, viven en Santiago, la capital de Chile. Tienen dos hijos: Héctor, de trece años, y Nora, de catorce años. Hoy los cuatro van al centro comercial porque los chicos necesitan ropa y zapatos. Fabio va a ir de compras con Héctor y Mireya va a llevar a Nora.

Mireya y Nora, en una tienda por departamentos muy elegante.

MIREYA: Mira este vestido. ¡Es precioso! ¡Pruébatelo! ¿Dónde está el probador?

NORA: ¡Ay, no! No me gusta. ¡Es un vestido para una niñita!

MIREYA: ¿Y qué eres tú? Bueno... pruébate esta blusa y esta falda. Hacen juego con tus sandalias.

NORA: La blusa me va a quedar grande. Yo uso talla extra pequeña.

MIREYA: ¡Escúchame! Tú usas talla pequeña o mediana.

NORA: (*Casi llorando*) ¡No! ¡No te olvides que yo perdí dos kilos! Además, aquí no hay nada que me guste. Hazme un favor, llévame a otra tienda…

Fabio y Héctor, en una zapatería.

HÉCTOR: Me gustan estos zapatos de tenis. Son de buena marca.

EMPLEADO: ¿Qué número calzas?

HÉCTOR: No estoy seguro. ¿Puede medirme los pies?

FABIO: (*Mira el precio de los zapatos de tenis.*) ¡Héctor! Fíjate en el precio de estos zapatos de tenis. ¡Cuestan un ojo de la cara!

HÉCTOR: No, papá. ¡No te preocupes! Van a durar mucho tiempo...

FABIO: Por este precio, tienen que durar por lo menos diez años. ¡Y no estoy exagerando!

HÉCTOR: (*Se está probando un par de botas.*) Estas son un poco estrechas. Necesito unas que sean un poco más anchas…

Después de media hora, Fabio va a la caja y paga por los zapatos de tenis y por las botas. Después compran dos camisetas y luego van a una librería. Por fin se encuentran con Mireya y Nora, que están en un restaurante de comida rápida, cargadas de bolsas.

Fabio: Nora, no me digas que compraron todo eso. ¡Vamos a necesitar un camión!

Nora: Es que no tenía nada que ponerme. Además, tuvimos que cambiar unos zapatos que no me gustaban.

Fabio: (*A Mireya*) ¡Tengo una idea!

Mireya: ¿Sí? ¿Cuál es tu idea?

Fabio: ¿Qué te parece si nunca más volvemos al centro comercial?

Mireya: (*Se ríe.*) ¡Me parece una idea estupenda!

¿Lo sabía Ud.?

Los restaurantes de comida rápida son populares en los países hispanos. Muchos de estos restaurantes pertenecen a famosas cadenas de Estados Unidos.

› **¿Cuál de los restaurantes de comida rápida es el más popular en tu ciudad?**

1. Hablemos With a partner, take turns asking and answering the following questions. Base your answers on the dialogue and on your own circumstances.

En el diálogo

1. ¿Fabio y Mireya son un matrimonio estadounidense?
2. ¿Por qué van al centro comercial?
3. ¿Qué dice Nora del vestido que le gusta a Mireya?
4. Según Mireya, ¿qué talla usa Nora?
5. ¿Por qué quiere Nora que su mamá la lleve a otra tienda?
6. ¿Héctor sabe qué número calza?
7. ¿Qué dice Fabio de los zapatos de tenis?
8. ¿Qué dice Héctor de las botas que se prueba?
9. ¿Dónde se encuentran los cuatro?
10. ¿Qué dice Fabio que no deben hacer nunca más?

¿Y tú?

1. ¿Tú conoces a algunas personas chilenas?
2. ¿Tú vas al centro comercial frecuentemente?
3. ¿Tú te pruebas la ropa antes de comprarla?
4. ¿Qué talla usas tú?
5. ¿Tú vas a muchas tiendas cuando vas al centro comercial?
6. ¿Qué número calzas tú?
7. ¿Tus zapatos de tenis te costaron un ojo de la cara?
8. ¿Te gusta usar botas?
9. ¿Tú comes en restaurantes de comida rápida frecuentemente?
10. ¿Qué días te gusta ir al centro comercial?

En el diálogo

Cognados

la blusa	*blouse*
las botas	*boots*
chileno(a)	*Chilean*
elegante	*elegant*
estupendo(a)	*stupendous*
extra	*extra*
el kilo,[1] el kilogramo[1]	*kilogram*
el par	*pair*
las sandalias	*sandals*

Nombres

la bolsa	*bag*
la caja	*cash register*
el camión	*truck*
la camiseta	*T-shirt*
el centro comercial	*shopping mall*
la falda	*skirt*
la librería	*bookstore*
la marca	*brand*
el matrimonio	*married couple*
el número	*size (of shoes)*
los pies	*feet*
el probador	*fitting room*
la talla, la medida	*size (in clothing)*
la tienda por departamentos, el almacén	*department store*
el vestido	*dress*
los zapatos	*shoes*
____ de tenis	*tennis shoes*

Verbos

calzar	*to wear (a certain size shoe)*
cambiar	*to exchange*
durar	*to last*
escuchar	*to listen (to)*
exagerar	*to exaggerate*
fijarse	*to notice*
llorar	*to cry*
medir (e:i)	*to measure*
usar	*to wear*

Adjetivos

ancho(a)	*wide*
estrecho(a), angosto(a)	*narrow*
cargado(a)	*loaded*
mediano(a)	*medium*
precioso(a)	*pretty, beautiful*
rápido(a)	*quick, fast*

Otras palabras y expresiones

es que...	*the fact is . . .*
hacer juego (con), combinar (con)	*to match*
no tener nada que ponerse	*to have nothing to wear*
nunca más	*never again*
por fin	*at last*
por lo menos	*at least*
¿Qué te parece si...?	*What do you think about . . . ?*
quedarle chico(a) (grande) a uno	*to be too small (big) on one*
Vamos de compras.	*Let's go shopping.*

[1] 1 kilo(gramo) = 2.2 pounds

Más sobre el tema

Mirando vidrieras (*Window shopping*)

Más sobre las tiendas

el departamento de caballeros	*men's department*
el departamento de señoras	*women's department*
el descuento	*discount*
devolver (o:ue) (algo)	*to return (something)*
la ganga	*bargain*
la rebaja, la liquidación	*sale*
rebajar	*to mark down*

Tipos de tela (*material*)

el algodón	*cotton*
el cuero	*leather*
el hilo, el lino	*linen*
la lana	*wool*
el poliéster	*polyester*
el rayón	*rayon*
la seda	*silk*

Un dicho

Aunque la mona se vista de seda, mona se queda.
Equivalent: *You can't make a silk purse out of a sow's ear.*

VOCABULARIO

Práctica

2. Preguntas y respuestas Match the questions in column A with the answers in column B.

A		B
1. ¿Tú conduces un coche?	_____	a. Por lo menos mil dólares.
2. ¿Compraste botas?	_____	b. No. ¡Vamos de compras!
3. ¿Qué número calzas?	_____	c. Música clásica.
4. ¿No te gusta el vestido?	_____	d. No, de cuadros.
5. ¿Qué te gusta escuchar?	_____	e. No, sandalias.
6. ¿No tienes nada que ponerte?	_____	f. Sí, y volvimos cargadas de bolsas.
7. ¿La camisa es de rayas?	_____	g. El ocho.
8. ¿Fueron al centro comercial?	_____	h. No, un camión.
9. ¿Cuánto necesitas?	_____	i. No, de algodón.
10. ¿El vestido es de seda?	_____	j. No, lo voy a cambiar.
11. ¿Qué se puso Ana para dormir?	_____	k. Sí, y una corbata.
12. ¿Le compraste una camisa?	_____	l. El camisón rosado.

3. ¿Qué es? Write the words or phrases that correspond to the following.

1. Se usa con una falda. _____
2. mil gramos _____
3. tienda por departamentos _____
4. lugar donde se venden libros _____
5. persona de Chile _____
6. talla _____
7. estrecho _____
8. opuesto de **estrecho** _____
9. ni grande ni pequeño _____
10. hermoso _____
11. opuesto de **lento** _____
12. hacer juego _____
13. hilo _____
14. liquidación _____

Mauricio es de Chile.

4. Para completar Complete the following sentences, using vocabulary from this lesson.

1. ¡Yo tardé veinte minutos, no una hora! ¡Tú siempre _____!
2. Compré un _____ de zapatos y me dieron un _____ de 10 dólares.
3. ¿Qué número _____ Ud.?
4. Estos zapatos de _____ van a _____ mucho tiempo, porque son de muy buena marca.
5. ¿Qué te _____ si compro este vestido de _____? ¡Es muy elegante!
6. No voy a comprar estos zapatos porque me _____ chicos.
7. El Sr. Roca compra su ropa en el departamento de _____, y su esposa compra su ropa en el departamento de _____.

8. No me gustan estas botas; las voy a _________.
9. ¿El traje cuesta solamente noventa dólares? ¡Es una _________!
10. Compré ropa _________ para Paquito.
11. ¡Tu idea es magnífica! ¡___________!
12. ¿Tienes las manos frías? ¿Dónde están tus _________?
13. ¿El vestido es estampado, de rayas o de _________?
14. No sé qué número calzo. ¿Me puede _________ los pies?
15. ¿El vestido es de _________, de rayón, de algodón, de seda o de _________?
16. Los zapatos costaban cien dólares, pero ellos los _________ y me costaron solamente sesenta dólares. También compré _________: aretes, un collar y una _________.

Para conversar

5. **Buenas ideas** Get together with a partner. Play the roles of two friends who are telling each other what clothes and footwear to buy for some members of their families. Include details such as the material things are made of, etc. **(A tu... , cómprale... / regálale...).**

6. **De compras** With your partner, play the roles of a customer and a store clerk. Discuss sizes, colors, prices, etc. The customer should buy clothes and shoes.

7. **Mirando vidrieras** You and a partner are standing in front of the store window shown on page 367. Take turns saying what you are going to buy for yourselves and for a relative or friend.

CD3-3

Pronunciación

Pronunciation in context

In this lesson, there are some new words or phrases that may be challenging to pronounce. For further pronunciation practice of Spanish sounds, listen to your instructor and repeat the following sentences.

1. **Pruébate** esa blusa y esta falda. **Hacen juego** con tus sandalias.
2. ¡**Héctor**! Fíjate en el precio de los **zapatos** de tenis.
3. No te **preocupes.** Van a **durar** mucho tiempo.
4. Después de media **hora,** Fabio va a la caja.
5. Por fin **se encuentran** con Mireya y Nora.
6. Están en un **restaurante** de comida **rápida, cargadas** de bolsas.
7. **Además,** tuvimos que cambiar unos **zapatos** que no me gustaban.
8. ¿**Qué te parece** si nunca más volvemos al centro comercial?

¿Lo sabía Ud.?

Actualmente (*Nowadays*), los empleados de las tiendas a menudo tutean (*use the **tú** form of address*) a los clientes en España y en algunos países de Hispanoamérica.

ESTRUCTURAS

1 The familiar commands (tú) (*Las formas imperativas de* ***tú***)

Unlike other commands in Spanish, the familiar affirmative command does not use the subjunctive.

A. *Tú* commands[1]

› The affirmative command form for **tú** has exactly the same form as the third-person singular form of the present indicative.

Verb	Present Indicative	Familiar Command (*tú*)[1]
hablar	él habla	**habla** (tú)
comer	él come	**come** (tú)
abrir	él abre	**abre** (tú)
cerrar	él cierra	**cierra** (tú)
volver	él vuelve	**vuelve** (tú)

—Teresa, **trae** el vestido. — *Teresa, bring the dress.*
—**Espera** un momento. Estoy ocupada. — *Wait a moment. I'm busy.*
—Me voy. — *I'm leaving.*
—**Vuelve** temprano y **cierra** la puerta de calle. — *Return early and close the front door.*

› Spanish has eight irregular **tú** command forms.

decir	**di**	salir	**sal**
hacer	**haz**	ser	**sé**
ir	**ve**	tener	**ten**
poner	**pon**	venir	**ven**

—Carlitos, **ven** aquí; **hazme** un favor. **Ve** a la casa de Rita y **dile** que la fiesta es hoy. — *Carlitos, come here; do me a favor. Go to Rita's house and tell her the party is today.*

—Muy bien. En seguida vuelvo. — *Okay. I'll be right back.*

Un dicho

Crea fama y acuéstate a dormir.
Equivalent: *Once you build a reputation, it stays forever.*

LEARNING TIP

To remember the eight verbs that are irregular in the **tú** command, memorize the following:

Ana, *sé* buena y *ve* al mercado con Rosa. *Ven* a casa y *ponlo* todo en el refrigerador. *Haz* una ensalada y *dile* a Luis que coma con ustedes. *Sal* con los niños, pero *ten* paciencia con ellos.

As you say aloud and/or write down this text, visualize it as a movie you are starring in. This will aid you in memorizing it.

[1]The affirmative command form for **vosotros** is formed by changing the final **r** of the infinitive to **d:** hablar → **hablad,** comer → **comed,** vivir → **vivid.**

B. Negative forms

› The negative **tú**[1] commands use the corresponding forms of the present subjunctive.

hablar	no **hables** tú
vender	no **vendas** tú
decir	no **digas** tú

—¿Voy con Julia?	*Shall I go with Julia?*
—No, no **vayas** con ella.	*No, don't go with her.*
—¿Pongo las faldas aquí?	*Do I put the skirts here?*
—No, no las **pongas** aquí.	*No, don't put them here.*

Un dicho

No cantes victoria antes de tiempo.

Equivalent: *Don't count your chickens before they're hatched.*

Pon**lo** aquí.	*Put it here.*
No **lo** pongas allí.	*Don't put it there.*
Vénde**nosla.**	*Sell it to us.*
No **nos la** vendas.	*Don't sell it to us.*

¡Atención! Object and reflexive pronouns are positioned with familiar commands just as they are with the formal commands.

Práctica

8. **Órdenes** Play the role of an older sibling giving instructions to a younger brother or sister, using the cues provided.
   1. levantarse temprano, bañarse y vestirse
   2. ponerse los pantalones negros y la camisa de cuadros y salir antes de las siete
   3. lavar su ropa interior y sus calcetines
   4. ir a la biblioteca y devolver los libros
   5. llamar por teléfono a su tía y decirle que la necesitamos
   6. no ponerse las botas negras
   7. no ir al centro comercial; quedarse en casa y estudiar
   8. no preocuparse si llegamos un poco tarde
   9. limpiar su cuarto y pasarle la aspiradora a la alfombra
   10. no acostarse antes de terminar la tarea (*homework*)

[1]The negative **vosotros** commands also use the present subjunctive: **no habléis.**

9. ¿Qué hago? Juana always has a hard time deciding what to do. Give her some suggestions, using the cues provided.

Modelo No sé qué clase tomar. (francés)
Toma una clase de francés.

1. No sé adónde ir esta noche. (cine)
2. No sé con quién salir. (Mauricio)
3. No sé qué hacer mañana. (ir de compras)
4. No sé qué comprar. (un traje de baño)
5. No sé qué regalarle a papá. (una corbata)
6. No sé qué comprarle a mamá. (un vestido)
7. No sé qué hacer para comer. (sopa y pollo)
8. No sé qué decirle a Jorge. (que te lleve al centro comercial)
9. No sé en qué banco poner mi dinero. (en el Banco Nacional)
10. No sé qué hacer con las botas. (cambiarlas)

10. Haz esto... No hagas eso. (*Do this . . . Don't do that.*) Say two commands, one affirmative and one negative, that the following people would be likely to give.

1. una madre a su hijo de quince años
2. un(a) estudiante a su compañero(a) de cuarto
3. una muchacha a su novio
4. un hombre a su esposa
5. un profesor a un estudiante

11. Las órdenes de Lucía Lucía and David are moving into their new apartment and some friends are helping them. Based on the illustration, what does Lucía tell each person to do? Use familiar commands.

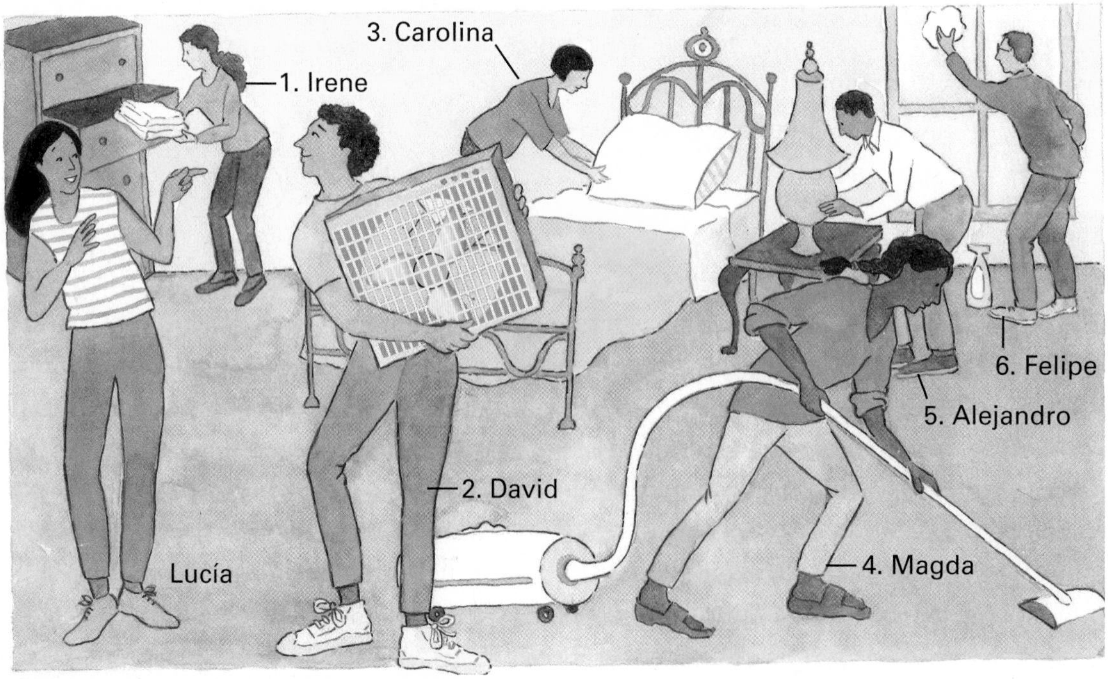

Para conversar

12. De compras With a partner, play the role of two friends who are at a shopping mall helping a third friend shop for clothes, shoes, jewelry, etc., and telling him/her what to do and what not to do. Use informal commands.

¿Lo sabía Ud.?

Aunque ahora hay muchos grandes almacenes, todavía existen en los países hispanos muchas tiendas pequeñas especializadas en un solo producto. Por ejemplo, se vende **perfume** en la **perfumería, joyas** en la **joyería** y **relojes** en la **relojería.**

› **En este país, ¿la mayoría de las tiendas especializadas están en centros comerciales o en edificios independientes?**

2 *¿Qué?* and *¿cuál?* used with *ser* (*Qué* y *cuál* usados con el verbo *ser*)

› *What?* translates as **¿qué?** when it is used as the subject of the verb and it asks for a definition.

—¿**Qué** es el pisco?	*What is pisco?*
—Es una bebida chilena.	*It's a Chilean drink.*

› *What?* translates as **¿cuál?** when it is used as the subject of a verb and it asks for a choice. **Cuál** conveys the idea of selection from among several or many available objects, ideas, and so on.

—¿**Cuál** es su número de teléfono?	*What is your phone number?*
—792-4856.	*792-4856.*
—¿**Cuál** es su tienda favorita?	*Which is your favorite store?*
—La tienda París, pero yo tengo una modista.	*The Paris Store, but I have a dressmaker.*

¿Lo sabía Ud.?

En las ciudades hispanas hay excelentes tiendas donde se puede comprar ropa hecha (*ready-to-wear*), pero muchas personas prefieren utilizar los servicios de un sastre (*tailor*) o de una modista (*dressmaker*).

› **En general, ¿dónde prefieren comprar la ropa los estadounidenses?**

Práctica

13. Preguntas Write the questions you would ask to get the following information. Use **qué** or **cuál,** as needed.

1. —____________________
   —Mi apellido es Velázquez.
   —____________________
   —Calle Rosales, número 420.
   —_________________________
   —835-2192.

2. —¿Quiere un pisco?
   —____________________
   —Es una bebida chilena. ¿Quiere comer una cazuela de ave?
   —____________________
   —Es un plato chileno que se prepara con pollo.

Para conversar

14. ¡Habla con tu compañero(a)! With a partner, take turns asking and answering the following questions.

1. ¿Cuál es la fecha de tu cumpleaños?
2. ¿Cuál es tu color favorito?
3. ¿Cuál es la estación del año que más te gusta?
4. ¿Cuál es tu programa de televisión favorito?
5. ¿Cuál es el título de tu libro favorito?
6. ¿Cuál es la ciudad más grande de tu estado?
7. ¿Cuál es la tienda que más te gusta?
8. ¿Cuál es tu día favorito?

3 The subjunctive to express indefiniteness and nonexistence

(*El subjuntivo para expresar lo indefinido y lo inexistente*)

› The subjunctive is always used when the subordinate clause refers to someone or something that is indefinite, unspecified, or nonexistent.

Quiero una cartera que **haga** juego con estos zapatos.	*I want a purse that matches these shoes.*
Busco un disco compacto que le **guste** a Eva.	*I'm looking for a CD that Eva will like.*
No hay ninguna blusa que **sea** de mi talla.	*There is no blouse that's my size.*

LEARNING TIP
These are words or phrases that you might use to express indefiniteness: **quiero, busco, prefiero, ¿hay?, ¿tienen ustedes?, ¿conoces?** Use each one to make a statement or ask a question. For example: ***Quiero* un par de zapatos que me *queden* bien.**

› If the subordinate clause refers to existing, definite, or specific persons or things, the indicative is used instead of the subjunctive.

Tengo una cartera que **hace** juego con estos zapatos.	*I have a purse that matches these shoes.*
Busco el disco que le **gusta** a Eva.	*I'm looking for the CD that Eva likes.*
Hay una blusa que **es** de mi talla.	*There is a blouse that's my size.*

Práctica

15. En esta clase Indicate that there is nobody in your class to whom the circumstances below apply. Follow the model.

Modelo En mi clase... hay una chica que baila flamenco.
En mi clase no hay nadie que baile flamenco.

En mi clase...

1. ... hay dos chicas que son de Paraguay.
2. ... hay un muchacho que conduce un Mercedes Benz.
3. ... hay un muchacho que habla francés.
4. ... hay tres estudiantes que tienen solamente quince años.
5. ... hay una chica que sabe tocar el violín.
6. ... hay dos muchachos que dan fiestas todos los sábados.
7. ... hay una chica que va a Europa todos los veranos.
8. ... hay dos muchachas que vienen a la universidad los domingos.
9. ... hay tres estudiantes que siempre están ocupados.
10. ... hay una chica que sale de su casa a las cinco de la mañana.

16. Información With a partner, play the roles of a newcomer to Santiago and a helpful long-time resident who is able to offer solutions to all of the newcomer's needs. Have a conversation based on your needs: for example, a house, a car, a job, places to go for leisure, etc. Follow the model.

Modelo una casa – tener piscina
—Quiero (Necesito, Busco) una casa que tenga piscina.
—En mi barrio hay una casa que tiene piscina.

1. una casa – tener tres dormitorios
2. una casa – estar cerca de la universidad
3. una casa – no costar un ojo de la cara
4. un coche – tener aire acondicionado
5. muebles – ser baratos
6. un empleo – pagar bien
7. alguien – ayudarme a mudarme
8. un restaurante – servir hamburguesas

17. Quiero saber A friend of yours is planning to move to your city or town and wants some information about it. Answer his or her questions as completely as possible.

1. ¿Hay alguna casa en un buen barrio que sea barata?
2. ¿Hay alguna casa que tenga piscina?
3. ¿Hay algún apartamento que esté cerca del centro (*downtown*)?
4. Yo necesito una secretaria. ¿Conoces a alguien que sepa hablar alemán y japonés?
5. A mí me gusta la comida chilena. ¿Hay algún restaurante que sirva comida chilena?
6. A mis padres les gusta la comida mexicana. ¿Hay algún restaurante que sirva comida mexicana?

18. ¿Subjuntivo o indicativo? Complete the following sentences logically, using the subjunctive or indicative as appropriate.

1. Necesito unos zapatos que...
2. En esta tienda no hay ningún pantalón que...
3. Aquí venden unas botas que...
4. Rosa tiene una falda que...
5. Busco una tienda que...
6. En esta clase no hay nadie que...
7. Mi novio(a) necesita un empleo que...
8. ¿Hay alguien aquí que...?

¿Lo sabía Ud.?

En la mayoría de los países hispanos, la talla de la ropa se basa en el sistema métrico.

› **¿Se usa el sistema métrico en este país?**

Para conversar

19. Díganme... You and your classmates want to know more about other people. Take turns asking whether there is anybody there who speaks German, vacations in a foreign country, or needs new clothes, jewelry, etc. The answers should imply indefiniteness and nonexistence.

Modelo *—¿Hay alguien en la clase que hable alemán?*
—No, no hay nadie que hable alemán.

¡Vamos a ver!

Antes de ver el video

20. Preguntas You and a partner take turns asking and answering the following questions.

1. ¿Tú te encuentras con tus amigos en el centro comercial a veces?
2. Cuando tú vas a un centro comercial, ¿cuánto tiempo tardas en hacer tus compras?
3. ¿Prefieres conducir un coche o un camión?
4. ¿Es verdad que tú no tienes nada que ponerte?
5. ¿Siempre te pruebas la ropa antes de comprarla?
6. ¿Cuándo fue la última vez que fuiste a la zapatería? ¿Qué compraste? Si compras un par de botas y ves que te quedan chicas, ¿las cambias?
7. ¿Prefieres usar sandalias o zapatos de tenis?
8. ¿Tú siempre compras zapatos de buena marca? ¿Los zapatos te duran mucho tiempo?
9. ¿Tú comes en restaurantes de comida rápida a menudo?
10. ¿Es verdad que tú exageras a veces? ¿Bromeas con tus amigos?

El video: Vamos de compras

—Fernando, ¿qué te parece si Rebeca y yo vamos a los Almacenes París, y Gonzalo y tú van a la zapatería?

—Buena idea. Yo quiero cambiar un par de botas que me quedan chicas y Gonzalo necesita zapatos.

—Ven acá, Rebeca. Mira esta falda. Hace juego con la blusa que compré ayer.

—¿Tienen botas como estas que sean más anchas? Estas son un poco estrechas... Yo calzo el número cuarenta.

—(*A su novia*) No hay nadie que pueda comprar tanto como ustedes dos en un par de horas.
—Hazme un favor... ¡Llama un taxi!
—(*Bromeando*) ¡Necesitamos un camión!

Después de ver el video

© Cengage Learning
Ángela

© Cengage Learning
Fernando

© Cengage Learning
Gonzalo

© Cengage Learning
Rebeca

21. ¿Quién lo dice? Identify the person who said the following in the dialogues.

1. También quiero ir a la librería. _________
2. Llámame para saber a qué hora nos encontramos. _________
3. ¡Pruébatelo! Pero la falda te va a quedar grande. _________
4. Yo quiero cambiar un par de botas que me quedan chicas. _________
5. Mira esta falda. Hace juego con la blusa que compré ayer. _________
6. No te preocupes. Él sabe tu número mejor que el suyo. _________
7. ¡Necesitamos un camión! _________
8. A ver... ¿cuál es tu número de teléfono? _________

22. Hablemos With a partner, take turns asking and answering the following questions. Base your answers on the dialogue.

1. ¿Con quiénes van de compras Ángela y Rebeca?
2. ¿Qué quiere cambiar Fernando?
3. ¿Qué quiere comprar Fernando para su hermanita?
4. ¿Cuánto tiempo van a tardar las chicas en hacer sus compras?
5. ¿Qué quiere Ángela que haga Fernando?
6. ¿Con qué hace juego la falda?
7. ¿Qué talla usa Ángela?
8. ¿Qué problema tiene Rebeca?
9. ¿Qué número calza Fernando?
10. ¿Qué dice Gonzalo que necesitan para llevar todos los paquetes?

23. ¿Qué pasa después? You and a partner use your imagination to say what the characters do. In Spanish, discuss the following.

1. Whether Gonzalo's little sister liked the CD that he bought her.
2. What Gonzalo bought at the bookstore and whether he bought something for his girlfriend.
3. The four of them had dinner together. Did they go to a fast-food restaurant again or to a good restaurant? Who paid the bill?
4. Whether Rebeca is still saying that she has nothing to wear and whether she and Ángela plan to go shopping again.
5. Whether Fernando and Ángela plan to get married (When?) or she wants to find a new boyfriend (*un nuevo novio*).

Now compare your ideas to those of the members of another group.

¡Vamos a escuchar!

ESTRATEGIA **Listening for the order of events** You have already read about the words **primero, luego, después,** and **finalmente** to indicate sequence. When listening to a narration of events, biographical information, or other text in which a series of events comes into play, pay particular attention to sequencing words in order to understand the chronology of events.

CD3-4 **24. La cronología** You are going to hear a short narration about a shopping trip. Listen and number the activities according to the order in which they occurred. Then listen again and write the sequencing word or phrase used to indicate the order of each event. There may be a sequencing phrase that you have not heard before. Can you identify it?

_____ Fueron a la zapatería. _______________

_____ Fueron a la tienda La Francia. _______________

_____ Fueron a la joyería. _______________

_____ Almorzaron. _______________

¡Vamos a conversar!

ESTRATEGIA **Expressing ideas and opinions** Here is a series of phrases and expressions that are useful for discussing ideas and introducing your opinions or point of view on a topic.

Introducing an opinion or idea:

(No) Me parece que...
(No) Creo que...
(No) Pienso que...

Adding ideas or changing the direction of a conversation:

Sin embargo,... *However, . . .*
Por el contrario... *On the contrary . . .*
Por otro lado... *On the other hand . . .*

Reacting to ideas:

De acuerdo. *I'm in agreement.*
¡Ya lo creo! *I'll say!*
No exactamente. *Not exactly.*
No creo eso por lo siguiente: ... *I don't think so for the following reason: . . .*
No creo eso porque... *I don't think so because . . .*
No estoy de acuerdo contigo (en eso, en ese punto, con esa idea). *I disagree with you (on that, on that point, with that idea).*

25. A discutir In groups of three or four, discuss the following issue for five minutes. Use the phrases for expressing opinions and be ready to report at least two arguments in favor and two against to the class.

26. ¿Qué dice Ud.? What would you say in the following situations? What might the other person say? Act out the scenes with a partner. Take turns playing each role.

1. You are shopping in a large department store. You need a pair of gloves, pantyhose, and a wallet. You also see a brown suit that you like for your father, and you want to know how much it costs.
2. You are a clerk. A customer is admiring an evening gown. Ask her what size she wears, and tell her the fitting room is on the left next to the cash register.
3. A clerk is showing you a pair of boots. They are too tight on you.
4. Your friend is going to the store. Ask her to buy you a pair of socks and a T-shirt.

27. Para conocernos mejor To do this activity, work with a classmate whom you would like to get to know. Take turns asking and answering these questions.

1. ¿Prefieres comprar tu ropa en una boutique o en una tienda por departamentos? ¿Prefieres usar ropa de algodón, de seda o de rayón? ¿Gastas mucho dinero en ropa?
2. Para el cumpleaños de tu mejor amiga, ¿planeas regalarle aretes, un collar o una pulsera? ¿Recibiste muchos regalos en tu cumpleaños? ¿Cuál te gustó más?
3. ¿Usas talla grande, pequeña o mediana? ¿Qué número calzas? ¿Tus zapatos son de cuero? ¿Prefieres usar botas o zapatos de tenis? ¿Por qué?
4. Si tienes la oportunidad de ir de compras o al cine, ¿adónde vas? ¿Prefieres ir de compras solo(a) o con un(a) amigo(a)? ¿Vas de compras por lo menos una vez al mes?

28. Una encuesta Interview your classmates to identify who fits the following descriptions. Include your instructor, but remember to use the **Ud.** form when addressing him/her. After finishing the survey, get together with two or three classmates and discuss the results.

1. Va de compras cada semana. ____________
2. Solamente va de compras cuando hay rebajas. ____________
3. Siempre dice que no tiene nada que ponerse. ____________
4. Se encuentra con sus amigos en el centro comercial. ____________
5. Tiene mucho dinero en la cartera (en la billetera). ____________
6. Usa zapatos de tenis todos los días. ____________
7. A veces consigue buenas gangas. ____________
8. A menudo devuelve las cosas que le regalan. ____________

29. Para crear Get together in groups of three or four and "create" the scenario for this photo. Who are these children? What is their relationship to each other? What are they wearing? Whose clothes are they wearing? Are they having fun? And so on.

Rincón literario

Gabriela Mistral (Chile: 1889–1957)

Gabriela Mistral es una de las poetisas más famosas de Hispanoamérica. Nació en Vicuña, Chile. Su verdadero nombre era Lucila Godoy. Gabriela Mistral es un pseudónimo o nombre de pluma (*pen name*). Dejó una amplia obra tanto en (*both in*) prosa como en (*and in*) verso. Los temas principales de su poesía son la maternidad (*motherhood*), el dolor (*pain*) del amor y la justicia. Además del libro *Ternura*, donde muestra su inmenso amor por los niños y de donde es el siguiente poema, Gabriela Mistral escribió otros libros de poemas: *Desolación, Tala* y *Lagar*. En 1945 recibió el premio Nobel de Literatura, siendo (*being*) la primera entre los escritores latinoamericanos en recibirlo.

Antes de leer

ESTRATEGIA **Reading poetry** When reading poetry you can use some of the same strategies you have used with other types of texts. Looking at the title and skimming the poem for the main idea or recurring phrases can provide clues to the subject of the poem. Remember that poetry often conveys strong feelings and frequently makes use of images and symbols. Here are a few elements to look for to aid your comprehension and appreciation of a poem.

- **la rima** (*rhyme*) or **el verso libre** (*blank verse*)
- **la repetición** of sounds, words, or phrases
- **los símbolos** or **las imágenes** (*images*)
- **el ritmo** (*rhythm*)

30. El lenguaje poético In this poem a mother rocks a baby. With a partner, skim the poem and identify the words or phrases that are repeated in each stanza. What impression or sensation do you think this might convey?

¡A leer!

Meciendo

El mar sus millares° de olas°
mece,° divino.
Oyendo a los mares amantes°
mezo a mi niño.

El viento errabundo° en la noche
mece los trigos.°
Oyendo a los vientos amantes
mezo a mi niño.

Dios° Padre sus miles de mundos
mece sin ruido.°
Sintiendo su mano en la sombra°
mezo a mi niño.

thousands / waves
rocks
loving
wandering
wheat
God
sin... *silently*
shadow

31. Comprensión As you read the poem, find the answers to the following questions.

1. ¿A quién está dedicado este poema?
2. Mientras el **yo** del poema mece a su niño, ¿qué mecen el mar y el viento?
3. ¿Qué mece Dios Padre?
4. ¿Qué siente la madre que mece a su niño?

Después de leer… reflexiones

32. **Reacciones** In groups of three, have a conversation using the following questions as guidelines.

1. ¿Por qué sentimos ternura al mecer a un niño?
2. ¿Qué sensación recordamos al pensar en el mar y en las olas?
3. ¿Experimentamos alguna vez una noche de tranquilidad y de silencio, lejos de los ruidos de la ciudad?
4. El **yo** del poema "siente" una "mano en la sombra". ¿Sentimos algunas veces una presencia que no podemos explicar?
5. ¿En qué ocasiones nos sentimos parte de la naturaleza?
6. ¿Qué podemos hacer para poder experimentar esos sentimientos (*feelings*) más frecuentemente?

Otro poema de Gabriela Mistral

Antes de leer

As you will recall, sometimes the title of a story or a poem will suggest something about the topic. What does the word **"piececitos"** (*little feet*) bríng to mind? Does it evoke tenderness?

Read the first verse. Does it give you an idea about what the rest of the poem will be like? Skim the poem, reading it aloud. You will notice that the author uses the **vosotros** form. Thus, the pronoun **os** means "you."

¡A leer!

33. Comprensión As you read the poem, find the answers to the following questions.

1. ¿Por qué están azulosos los piececitos? ¿Qué es lo que la gente no hace?
2. ¿Qué es lo que hiere a[1] los piececitos?
3. ¿Qué es lo que ignora el hombre?
4. Donde los piececitos sangran, ¿qué flor nace más fragante?
5. La autora dice que los piececitos son perfectos. ¿Qué más deben ser?
6. ¿Qué es lo que la gente no hace al pasar?

[1]The personal "**a**" is used here because the author personifies "**piececitos**".

PIECECITOS

Piececitos de niño,
azulosos de frío,
¡cómo os ven y no os cubren
Dios mío!

¡Piececitos heridos° — *wounded*
por los guijarros° todos, — *pebbles*
ultrajados de nieves
y lodos°! — *mud*

El hombre ciego° ignora — *blind*
que por donde pasáis,
una flor de luz viva
dejáis;

que allí donde ponéis
la plantita sangrante,° — *bleeding*
el nardo nace más
fragante.

Sed,° puesto que marcháis — *Be*
por los caminos rectos,° — *straight*
heroicos como sois.
perfectos.

Piececitos de niño,
dos joyitas° sufrientes, — *little jewels*
¡cómo pasan sin veros
las gentes°! — *people*

Después de leer… reflexiones

34. Reacciones In groups of three or four, discuss the following.

1. Muchos niños pobres andan descalzos (*go barefoot*) porque sus padres no tienen dinero para comprarles zapatos. ¿Qué puede hacer la gente para ayudarlos?
2. ¿Qué organizaciones de caridad ayudan a los pobres? ¿Uds. pertenecen a alguna iglesia o institución que tenga un programa especial para este fin?
3. ¿Uds. creen que el gobierno (*government*) debe encargarse (*take charge*) de ayudar a la gente pobre? ¿Por qué sí o por qué no?

¡Vamos a escribir!

Antes de escribir

ESTRATEGIA **Writing an advice column** When giving advice, you need to draw on a few strategies:

1. State the purpose or the main idea of the advice.
2. Brainstorm ideas, possible solutions, and how to's.
3. Organize the advice according to categories or subtopics relating to the main topic.
4. Write an outline that includes details.
5. Summarize.

35. Consejos para una madre You will write an advice column in which you tell mothers how to raise a healthy, happy child. First brainstorm about the following topics, jotting down all the ideas that come to you.

1. What to do for a baby's physical and emotional well-being.
2. How to involve the father in the caring of the baby.
3. How to help a child develop intellectually.
4. How to help a child feel loved and secure.

¡A escribir!

36. La columna Write the **primer borrador** of your column.

Después de escribir

37. A revisar Before writing the final version of your advice column, exchange your first draft with a classmate's, and peer edit each other's work, making sure that the guidelines have been followed.

Chile

Chile nos da la posibilidad de esquiar en junio o julio. ¿Recuerdas? Chile está en el hemisferio sur, y en junio y julio el país está en pleno invierno.

Es una zona de montañas altas y tiene los centros de esquí más famosos, como Portillo y Farallones.

La economía del país depende principalmente de la exportación de minerales, frutas y vinos. Chile tiene tratados de libre comercio con más de 50 países.

Puntos de interés turístico

© Gary yim /Shutterstock.com

Santiago de Chile

Santiago, la capital, se distingue por el contraste de sus modernos rascacielos y las pocas construcciones coloniales que los terremotos han dejado en pie (*have left standing*), como el Palacio de La Moneda (actual Palacio Presidencial).

Viña del Mar

Viña del Mar es la ciudad balnearia (*seaside resort*) más famosa de Chile, con playas y barrios residenciales de gran belleza. Aquí se celebra todos los años el Festival Internacional de la Canción, donde participan artistas de todo el mundo. Los ganadores reciben, como trofeo, la Gaviota (*Sea Gull*) de Oro o de Plata.

© Kord.com/Age Fotostock

© Andrzej Gibasiewicz/Shutterstock.com

La isla de Pascua

Situada en medio del océano Pacífico, esta isla pertenece a Chile y es famosa por tener aproximadamente 600 estatuas gigantes de piedra (moáis): único vestigio de una misteriosa cultura ancestral.

Los viñedos (*vineyards*) de Chile producen uvas para hacer uno de los vinos más famosos del mundo. Chile exporta vinos a más de 100 países.

© Leo Rosenthal/Pix Inc./Time Life Pictures/Getty Images

Tres grandes escritores

Gabriela Mistral es la más conocida de las poetisas de Chile y una de las más famosas de Latinoamérica. Fue la primera, entre los escritores latinoamericanos, en recibir el Premio Nobel de Literatura (1945). Además de su labor poética, fue educadora y diplomática en distintos países de América y de Europa.

Pablo Neruda es el poeta chileno más famoso internacionalmente. Su obra más leída es *20 poemas de amor y una canción desesperada*, pero la mayor parte de sus obras reflejan sus ideas políticas. Entre ellas sobresalen las dedicadas a la Guerra Civil Española. Recibió el Premio Nobel de Literatura en 1971 y ocupó cargos diplomáticos en diferentes países.

© AP Photo/Michel Lipchitz

© AP Photo/Jakub Mosur

Isabel Allende es una de las escritoras actuales más famosas. Antes de cumplir 20 años, comenzó a escribirle una carta a su abuelo, un anciano de 99 años. La carta se fue extendiendo hasta convertirse en su primera novela, *La casa de los espíritus,* llevada al cine con el nombre *House of Spirits.* Más tarde publicó, entre otras, los *Cuentos de Eva Luna* y *Paula*, dedicada a su hija muerta (*dead*).

Ahora dime...

In groups of three, take turns asking and answering the following questions.

1. ¿Prefieres los deportes de invierno o las actividades típicas del verano? ¿Qué deportes practicas en cada estación?
2. ¿Qué lugares de los Estados Unidos son famosos por sus pistas de esquí?
3. ¿Qué sabes de los moáis y qué ejemplos de otras estructuras misteriosas de culturas antiguas conoces?
4. *La casa de los espíritus,* de Isabel Allende, fue llevada al cine. ¿Qué otras novelas de autores hispanos fueron llevadas al cine?
5. ¿Qué opinas de los poetas que, como Neruda, usan su arte para hablar de política? ¿Crees que puede ser útil? ¿Crees que la política y la poesía no se deben mezclar? ¿Por qué?

iLrn

To learn more about Chile, watch the cultural footage in the Media Library.

AUTOPRUEBA

¿Cuánto sé ahora?

Take this test. When you have finished, check your answers in the answer key provided in Appendix D. Then use a red pen to correct any mistakes you may have made. Are you ready?

A. Familiar commands (*tú*) Give the Spanish equivalent of the words in parentheses.

1. ________, Paco, ¿pusiste el dinero en la billetera? (Tell me)
2. ________ la comida y luego ________ las camisetas. (Do / wash)
3. ________ de mi cuarto, Carlitos. (Leave)
4. ¿Los guantes? ________ en el cuarto. (Put them)
5. ________ conmigo. (Come)
6. Anita, ________ buena y ________ los aretes. (be / bring me)
7. Julia, ________ con Sara y ________ el vestido para la niña. (go / buy)
8. ________ la fiesta hoy. (Have)
9. ________ el camisón si no está en rebaja, Anita. (Don´t buy)
10. ¿Los zapatos? ________, Elena. (Don´t exchange them)
11. ________, Silvia. (Don't go away)
12. ________ a las siete y ________ a las diez. (Get up / go to bed)

B. *Qué* and *cuál* used with *ser* Supply the questions that elicited the following responses. Begin each one with **qué** or **cuál,** as appropriate.

1. Mi número de teléfono es 862-4031.
2. El apellido de mi abuela es Álvarez.
3. Una pulsera es una joya.
4. Las lecciones que necesitamos son la once y la doce.
5. Su dirección es calle Universidad, número treinta.
6. Una enchilada es un plato mexicano.

C. The subjunctive to express indefiniteness and nonexistence Complete the following sentences, using the present subjunctive or the present indicative of the verbs given.

1. ¿Hay alguien aquí que ________ (saber) hablar español?
2. Tengo unos zapatos que Uds. ________ (tener) que devolver.
3. No conozco a nadie que ________ (ser) chileno.
4. ¿Ud. quiere una blusa que ________ (tener) rayas?
5. Necesito una falda que ________ (hacer) juego con esta blusa.
6. Aquí hay una chica que ________ (hablar) francés, pero no hay nadie que ________ (hablar) italiano.
7. Busco una casa que ________ (estar) cerca de la universidad.
8. En esta tienda hay un vestido de noche que me ________ (gustar) mucho.

D. Just words . . .

a. Complete the following sentences, using the vocabulary from **Lección 13.**

1. Voy a ir al centro _________ para _________ unos zapatos de tenis.
2. No tengo nada que _________; por eso voy a _________ de compras.
3. Estas botas no son estrechas; son muy _________.
4. ¿Qué número _________ Ud.?
5. La caja está al _________ del probador.
6. Voy a devolver este vestido porque me _________ grande. Yo uso _________ mediana.
7. Ernesto está en el _________ de caballeros porque necesita comprar _________ interior.
8. No me gustan las camisas de _________. Prefiero las de cuadros.
9. Voy a la _________ para comprar unos libros.
10. Tengo que comprar un _________ de zapatos negros.
11. ¿Qué les _________ si vamos de compras hoy?
12. Esta cartera cuesta solamente diez dólares; es una _________.
13. Ellos volvieron de las tiendas _________ de paquetes.
14. No sé qué número necesita el niño. ¿Puede _________ los pies?
15. Estos zapatos son muy buenos. Van a _________ mucho tiempo.
16. Para llevar todas las cosas que compramos vamos a necesitar un _________.

b. Write the word or phrase that corresponds to the following.

1. combinar
2. persona de Chile
3. kilo
4. estrecho
5. talla
6. lino
7. cambiar
8. rebaja
9. muy, muy bonito
10. opuesto de **quedar chico**
11. lugar donde compramos libros
12. almacén
13. la usamos con una blusa
14. zapatos que usamos en el verano
15. ni grande ni pequeño

E. Culture

1. Complete the following sentences, based on the information found in the **¿Lo sabía Ud.?** section.
   a. Aunque en los países hispanos ahora hay muchos grandes _______, todavía existen tiendas pequeñas donde se vende un solo producto.
   b. En la mayoría de los países hispanos, la talla de la ropa se basa en el sistema _________.
2. Answer these questions, based on the information found in the **El mundo hispánico y tú** section.
   a. ¿En qué país encontramos algunas de las montañas más altas de Sudamérica?
   b. ¿Cuáles son dos de los poetas chilenos más famosos del siglo pasado?
   c. ¿Por qué es famosa la isla de Pascua?

F. Un dicho Do you remember the Spanish saying that is equivalent to "You can´t make a silk purse out of a sow's ear"? Find it in this lesson.

LECCIÓN 14

LAS CARRERAS UNIVERSITARIAS

La Facultad de Derecho en Buenos Aires

OBJETIVOS COMUNICATIVOS

You will learn vocabulary related to college activities and careers.

SITUACIONES

¿Qué carrera me interesa?

ESTRUCTURAS

1 The subjunctive or indicative after certain conjunctions

2 The past participle

3 The present perfect and the past perfect (pluperfect)

ASÍ SOMOS

¡Vamos a ver!

Watching and understanding situations

¡Vamos a escuchar!

Guessing meaning practice I

¡Vamos a conversar!

Paraphrasing practice IV

Rincón literario

Using your experience as context

Lecciones de inglés by Germán Arciniegas

¡Vamos a escribir!

Writing about opinions or experiences

EL MUNDO HISPÁNICO Y TÚ...

› Argentina

AUTOPRUEBA

You will review what you learned in this lesson.

ARGENTINA, por su extensión, es el país de habla española más grande del mundo, y ocupa el octavo lugar entre los países más extensos. Sin embargo, la población del país es de solo unos 40 millones de habitantes, la mayor parte de origen europeo, principalmente italianos, españoles, alemanes e ingleses. Argentina es uno de los principales países exportadores de carne vacuna y de vinos.

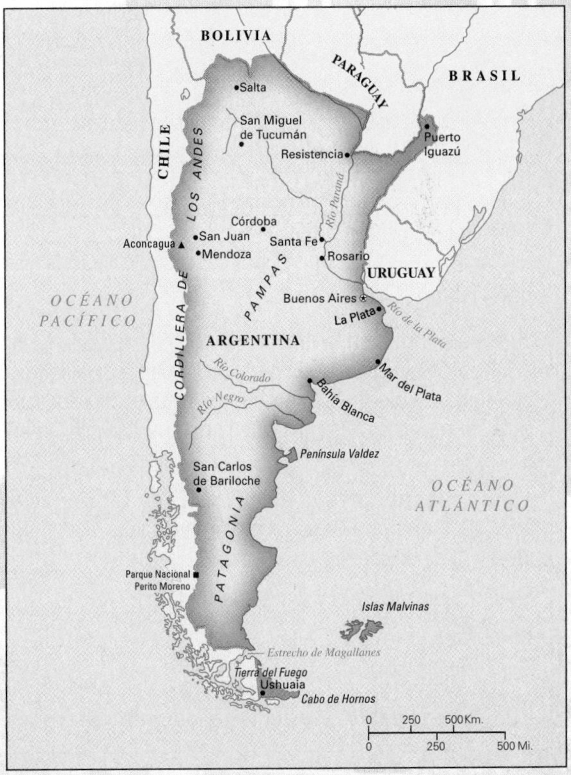

Recursos iLrn video audio web playlist

SITUACIONES

¿Qué carrera me interesa?

CD3-5

¡Ubíquela!

Elizabeth can't wait to be in Buenos Aires, the capital of Argentina, and visit all the very interesting places that are shown in the video, which make this city "the Paris of South America."

Laura, una chica porteña,[1] *está leyendo un correo electrónico de su amiga estadounidense, Elizabeth Ugarte, una muchacha de ascendencia española. Laura había pasado un año con la familia de Elizabeth y después continuaron siendo amigas. Ahora, Elizabeth va a ir a visitar a Laura a Argentina.*

Send Mail: Message Composition

A: Laura

De: Elizabeth

Asunto: Mi viaje a Argentina

Hola, Laura:

Ya me matriculé en la universidad. Como todavía no he decidido cuál va a ser mi especialización, voy a tomar varios requisitos: química, física, biología y sicología. Mi materia favorita es la educación física, pero no sirve de mucho... a menos que la use para ponerme en forma.

En fin, voy a tomar una decisión cuando vuelva a los Estados Unidos, ¡y espero que sea antes de graduarme! ¡Ay, Laura! ¡Esta mañana me di cuenta de que pronto voy a estar en Buenos Aires! No veo la hora de verte y... de conocer a tu hermano.

Envíame un mensaje y dime qué tal te va.

Un abrazo,

Elizabeth

P.D.[2] ¿Qué te parece si estudio periodismo? ¡Necesito ideas!

Laura y su hermano Sergio están sentados en el comedor, hablando durante el almuerzo. Sergio estudia para abogado, pero también le gusta la idea de ser escritor.

[1]**porteña** = *from Buenos Aires; literally, of the port* (*of Buenos Aires*)
[2]P.D. (Postdata) = P.S.

Laura: Bueno, mi amiga Elizabeth está matriculada para el otoño y pronto termina el semestre. Llega dentro de tres semanas.

Sergio: Yo propongo que, en cuanto llegue, la llevemos a Mar del Plata.

Laura: Yo no sé si podemos ir… a menos que tía Graciela insista en que nos quedemos en su casa…

Sergio: ¡Vamos, Laura! Lo único que tienes que hacer es llamarla y ella nos va a invitar. Tú siempre has sido su sobrina favorita. ¡Siempre te lo he dicho!

Laura: (*Se ríe.*) ¡Tienes razón! Oye, ¿quieres ir al gimnasio conmigo? Después tengo que estudiar para mi clase de sociología y ayudar a Pablito con su deber de matemáticas.

Sergio: ¡Ah, sí! La futura maestra… Lo siento, hermanita, pero no puedo. Tengo que ir a la facultad, y después tengo que ir al médico para que me haga un chequeo… ¡No te enojes! Vamos a pasar mucho tiempo juntos cuando venga Elizabeth. Con tal que, a veces, ella y yo podamos salir solos…

¿Lo sabía Ud.?

En la mayoría de las universidades hispanas no existe el concepto de "*major*" usado en los Estados Unidos. Los estudiantes españoles y latinoamericanos toman muy pocas clases optativas (*electives*), ya que la mayoría comienza a especializarse en la universidad a partir de su primer año.

› **¿Cuáles son algunas clases optativas que se toman en la universidad?**

1. Hablemos With a partner, take turns asking and answering the following questions. Base your answers on the dialogue and on your own circumstances.

En el diálogo

1. ¿De quién es el correo electrónico?
2. ¿Cuánto tiempo había pasado Laura con la familia de Elizabeth?
3. ¿Qué no ha decidido Elizabeth todavía?
4. ¿Qué requisitos va a tomar Elizabeth?
5. ¿De qué se dio cuenta Elizabeth?
6. ¿Qué idea le gusta a Sergio?
7. ¿Para qué semestre está matriculada Elizabeth?
8. ¿Qué propone Sergio?
9. Según Sergio, ¿quién ha sido siempre la sobrina favorita de su tía Graciela?
10. ¿Para qué tiene que ir Sergio al médico?

¿Y tú?

1. ¿Tú recibes muchos correos electrónicos?
2. ¿Tú quieres pasar unos meses con una familia de otro país?
3. ¿Cuál es tu especialización?
4. ¿Estás tomando algún requisito?
5. ¿Qué ciudad extranjera (*foreign*) quieres visitar tú?
6. ¿Tú quieres ser escritor(a)?
7. ¿Tú estás matriculado(a) para el próximo semestre?
8. ¿Adónde llevas tú a tus amigos?
9. ¿Quién ha sido siempre tu tía favorita?
10. ¿Tú necesitas un chequeo?

¿Lo sabía Ud.?

En España y en Latinoamérica, las universidades se dividen en "facultades", donde los estudiantes toman clases directamente relacionadas con su especialización (por ejemplo, la Facultad de Medicina, la Facultad de Ingeniería, la Facultad de Arquitectura, etcétera). No existen requisitos generales, pues estos se toman en la escuela secundaria.

› **¿Cuáles son algunos de los requisitos generales que se toman en las universidades de su país?**

VOCABULARIO

En el diálogo

Cognados

la biología	*biology*
la física	*physics*
futuro(a)	*future*
el gimnasio	*gym*
la sicología	*psychology*
la sociología	*sociology*

Nombres

el (la) abogado(a)	*lawyer*
el abrazo	*hug*
la ascendencia	*ancestry*
la carrera	*career*
el chequeo	*check-up*
el deber, la tarea	*homework*
la educación física	*physical education*
el (la) escritor(a)	*writer*
la especialización	*major*
la facultad	*college, school*
la materia, la asignatura	*subject (in school)*
el (la) médico(a)	*doctor, M.D.*
el periodismo	*journalism*
el requisito	*requirement*

Verbos

continuar, seguir[1] (e:i)	*to continue*
enojarse, enfadarse	*to get angry*
graduarse	*to graduate*
insistir (en)	*to insist (on)*
interesar	*to interest*
matricularse	*to register*
proponer (yo propongo)	*to propose*

Adjetivos

matriculado(a)	*registered*
querido(a)	*dear*
sentado(a)	*seated, sitting*
varios(as)	*several*

Otras palabras y expresiones

a menos que	*unless*
como	*since, being that*
con tal (de) que	*provided that, as long as*
darse cuenta (de)	*to realize*
lo único	*the only thing*
no servir de mucho	*not to be much good*
No veo la hora de...	*I can't wait to . . .*
ponerse en forma	*to get in shape*
pronto	*soon*
¿Qué tal te va?	*How's it going for you?*
tomar una decisión	*to make a decision*

© Petrenko Andriy/Shutterstock.com

[1] continuar, seguir + gerundio *to continue to do (something)*
Laura sigue leyendo = *Laura continues to read.*

Más sobre el tema

Profesiones y oficios (*Trades*)

El bombero

El carpintero

El cocinero

El electricista

La ejecutiva

El ingeniero

El plomero

El programador

Para hablar de los estudios

la administración de empresas	*business administration*
aprobar (o:ue)	*to pass (an exam or course)*
la beca	*scholarship*
el (la) bibliotecario(a)	*librarian*
la ciencia	*science*
el (la) consejero(a)	*advisor*
la contabilidad	*accounting*
entregar	*to turn in, to deliver*
el horario	*schedule*
la investigación	*research*
el laboratorio	*laboratory*
mantener	*to maintain (conj. like* tener*)*
la matrícula	*registration, tuition*
la nota	*grade*
el promedio	*grade point average*
quedar suspendido(a)	*to fail (an exam or course)*
sacar	*to get, to receive (a grade)*
el título	*title*

VOCABULARIO

Práctica

2. Preguntas y respuestas Match the questions in column A with the answers in column B.

A		B
1. ¿Cuáles son tus materias favoritas?	______	a. Hemingway.
2. ¿Eres americano?	______	b. Sí, ya lo entregué.
3. ¿Tomas educación física?	______	c. Sí, es cocinero.
4. ¿Quién es tu escritor favorito?	______	d. Sí, de ascendencia italiana.
5. ¿Cuándo vienes a verme?	______	e. Sí, todas mis clases son por la mañana.
6. ¿Trabaja en un restaurante?	______	f. Una B.
7. ¿Escribiste el informe?	______	g. Biología y física.
8. ¿Qué promedio mantienes?	______	h. Si tengo tiempo, pronto.
9. ¿Tienes un buen horario?	______	i. ¡Sí! ¡No veo la hora de estar allí!
10. ¿Vas a viajar a Buenos Aíres?	______	j. Sí, porque quiero ponerme en forma.
11. ¿Qué tal te fue en el examen?	______	k. Todavía no lo sé.
12. ¿Cuál es tu especialización?	______	l. Muy bien. Creo que voy a sacar una A.

3. ¿Qué es? Write the words or phrases that correspond to the following.

1. opuesto de **pasado** ______________
2. tarea ______________
3. materia ______________
4. doctor en medicina ______________
5. materia obligatoria ______________
6. continuar ______________
7. decidir ______________
8. opuesto de **aprobar** ______________
9. persona que trabaja en una biblioteca ______________
10. persona que escribe ______________
11. enojarse ______________
12. terminar los estudios ______________

4. Para completar Complete the following sentences, using vocabulary from this lesson.

1. Voy a estudiar contabilidad y administración de ________.
2. No quiero tomar química porque no me gustan las ________.
3. Los chicos están ________ cerca de la puerta.
4. Estudiamos a Freud en la clase de ________ y a Isaac Newton en la clase de ________.
5. Yo no me di ________ de que tú estabas enferma.
6. Yo creo que voy a sacar una buena ________ en el próximo examen.
7. Como el inodoro no funcionaba, llamé un ________.
8. Voy a escribir un informe. Tengo que hacer ________ en la biblioteca.
9. Voy al ________ para hacer ejercicio.
10. Estudiamos los problemas de las ciudades en la clase de ________.
11. No me interesa la ________ de abogada.
12. Ellos vuelven ________ de diez días.
13. No puedo terminar el trabajo ________ tú me ayudes.
14. Puedes mirar la tele con ________ que hagas los deberes primero.
15. Tomo educación física para ________ en forma.
16. Lo ________ que le gusta es comer.

Para conversar

5. **En este país...** With a partner, play the roles of a counselor and a student from Argentina who is attending your college. Tell the student what classes to take (**Puede tomar...**) and suggest some extracurricular activities. Also, ask the student what professions or trades and related courses he/she likes.

Puede tomar una clase de contabilidad.

6. **Nuestras clases...** You and your partner discuss your class schedule and talk about your favorite classes and the classes you don't like. Give reasons. Talk also about the classes you plan to take next semester.

7. **Profesiones** Taking into account the professions and trades presented on page 393, discuss, with a partner, the ones you like and don't like, and say why. State the possible places to work. Give details.

Un pensamiento

La educación empieza en la cuna y termina en la tumba.
Equivalent: *Education begins in the womb and ends in the tomb.*

CD3-6

Pronunciación

Pronunciation in context

In this lesson, there are some new words or phrases that may be challenging to pronounce. For further pronunciation practice of Spanish sounds, listen to your instructor and repeat the following sentences.

1. Laura está leyendo un **correo electrónico** de su amiga **estadounidense**.
2. Como **todavía no he decidido** cuál va a ser mi **especialización**, voy a tomar **varios requisitos**.
3. Mi materia **favorita** es la **educación física**, pero no **sirve** de mucho.
4. Voy a tomar una **decisión** cuando vuelva a los Estados Unidos.
5. Yo **propongo** que, en cuanto **llegue**, la **llevemos** a Mar del Plata.
6. Yo no sé si podemos ir... a menos que tía **Graciela** insista en que nos **quedemos** en su casa.
7. Tú siempre **has sido** su sobrina **favorita**. Siempre te lo **he dicho**.
8. Tengo que ir a la **facultad**, y después tengo que ir al médico para que me **haga un chequeo**.

ESTRUCTURAS

1 The subjunctive or indicative after certain conjunctions

(*El subjuntivo o el indicativo después de ciertas conjunciones*)

A. Conjunctions that are always followed by the subjunctive

› Some conjunctions, by their meaning, imply uncertainty or condition. They are, therefore, always followed by the subjunctive. Here are some of them.

en caso de que	*in case*
sin que	*without*
con tal (de) que	*provided that*
a menos que	*unless*
para que	*in order that*
antes de que	*before*

—Voy a ir al gimnasio **con tal que** los chicos **vayan** conmigo. — *I'm going to go to the gym provided that the boys go with me.*

—Llámelos **antes de que salgan**. — *Call them before they leave.*

—No me van a dar la beca **a menos que** ella me **dé** una carta. — *They're not going to give me the scholarship unless she gives me a letter.*

—Yo puedo dársela **en caso de que** ella no **quiera** hacerlo. — *I can give it to you in case she doesn't want to do it.*

—Te voy a dar dinero **para que puedas** matricularte. — *I'm going to give you money so that you can register.*

—No puedo matricularme **sin que** el consejero **firme** la tarjeta. — *I can't register without the advisor signing the card.*

B. Conjunctions that are followed by the subjunctive or indicative

› The subjunctive follows certain conjunctions when the main clause refers to the future or is a command. Some of these conjunctions are:

cuando	*when*
hasta que	*until*
tan pronto como, en cuanto	*as soon as*

—¿Lo van a esperar? — *Are you going to wait for him?*

—Sí, **hasta que llegue**. — *Yes, until he arrives.*

—**En cuanto llegue**, díganle que me llame. — *As soon as he arrives, tell him to call me.*

› If there is no indication of a future action, the conjunction of time is followed by the indicative.

—¿Siempre lo esperan? — *Do you always wait for him?*

—Sí, **hasta que llega**. — *Yes, until he arrives.*

Práctica

8. **Preparativos** Complete the following dialogue between two roommates who are expecting a houseguest, using **con tal que, sin que, en caso de que, a menos que, para que**, and **antes de que** and the verbs given. Then act it out with a partner, adding two original lines.

—Tenemos que limpiar el apartamento 1. ____________ (llegar) él.

—Yo voy a preparar unos sándwiches 2. ____________ (tener) hambre.

—Sí, ¿y por qué no compras unos refrescos 3. ____________ (poder) tomar algo en cuanto llegue?

—Bueno, pero yo no puedo ir al supermercado 4. ____________ tú me 5. ____________ (dar) el dinero.

—Está bien. Yo te voy a dar el dinero 6. ____________ tú me lo 7. ____________ (devolver) mañana.

—Voy ahora mismo. Voy a salir 8. ____________ me 9. ____________ (ver) Paco porque va a querer ir conmigo.

— ____

— ____

9. **Y en el futuro** Change the following, according to the new beginning.
    1. Todos los días yo llamo a mi amiga en cuanto llego a casa. Mañana,...
    2. Generalmente esperamos al profesor hasta que llega. El próximo viernes,...
    3. Todos los días, tan pronto como termina la clase, vamos a la cafetería. Esta tarde...
    4. Ud. se lo dice a los estudiantes cuando los ve. Dígaselo a los estudiantes...
    5. Cuando él va al laboratorio siempre se queda dos horas. La semana próxima...

Para conversar

10. **¡Habla con tu compañero(a)!** With a partner, ask each other the following questions. Answer the questions in complete sentences.
    1. Generalmente, ¿qué haces en cuanto llegas a tu casa? ¿Qué vas a hacer hoy en cuanto llegues? ¿Vas a estudiar o vas a descansar?
    2. ¿Tú puedes pagar la matrícula sin que tus padres te presten el dinero?
    3. ¿Qué promedio tienes que mantener para que te den una beca? ¿Una "A" o una "B"? ¿Es difícil mantener un promedio de A?
    4. ¿Tú puedes estudiar conmigo antes de que el profesor nos dé el próximo examen? ¿Qué días podemos estudiar?
    5. Por lo general, ¿adónde vas cuando termina la clase? ¿Adónde vas a ir hoy cuando termine la clase? ¿Vas a encontrarte con alguien?
    6. ¿Con quién puedo dejar un mensaje en caso de que tú no estés cuando yo te llame? ¿Puedes llamarme más tarde?

LEARNING TIP
Personalize each of these statements by talking about what *you* usually do and what *you* are going to do. For example: ***Todos los días*** **yo como algo en cuanto *llego* a casa.**

2 The past participle (*El participio pasado*)

A. Forms of the past participle

Past Participle Endings		
-ar *verbs*	-er *verbs*	-ir *verbs*
habl-**ado** (*spoken*)	com-**ido** (*eaten*)	decid-**ido** (*decided*)

› The following verbs have irregular past participles.

abrir	**abierto**	*opened*
cubrir	**cubierto**	*covered*
decir	**dicho**	*said*
escribir	**escrito**	*written*
hacer	**hecho**	*done, made*
morir	**muerto**	*died*
poner	**puesto**	*put*
romper	**roto**	*broken*
ver	**visto**	*seen*
volver	**vuelto**	*returned* (somewhere)
devolver	**devuelto**	*returned* (something)
envolver	**envuelto**	*wrapped*

LEARNING TIP
Write the list of infinitives and their corresponding past participles on a piece of paper. Fold the paper so you can only see the infinitives. Test your knowledge of the past participles by seeing how many times you have to unfold the paper.

¡Atención! Verbs ending in **-er** and **-ir** with stems that end in a strong vowel require an accent mark on the **i** of the **-ido** ending.

creer	**creído**	*believed*
leer	**leído**	*read*
oír[1]	**oído**	*heard*
traer	**traído**	*brought*

[1]Present tense: **oigo, oyes, oye, oímos, oís, oyen.**

Práctica

11. Participios Supply the past participle of each of the following verbs.

1. tener	________	13. entrar	________
2. traer	________	14. salir	________
3. cerrar	________	15. hacer	________
4. decir	________	16. poner	________
5. aprovechar	________	17. abrir	________
6. apretar	________	18. escribir	________
7. cortar	________	19. ver	________
8. volver	________	20. aceptar	________
9. romper	________	21. devolver	________
10. cubrir	________	22. leer	________
11. cambiar	________	23. dar	________
12. sentir	________	24. sacar	________

¿Lo sabía Ud.?

En lugar de letras, el sistema de calificaciones (*grading system*) en las universidades hispanas usa números. Por lo general, se califica asignando notas de 1 a 5 en Hispanoamérica y de 1 a 10 en España. Una nota de 3 o de 6 es normalmente la nota mínima para aprobar una clase o un examen.

› **En su país, ¿cuál es la nota mínima para aprobar una clase o un examen?**

B. Past participles used as adjectives

› In Spanish, most past participles may be used as adjectives. As such, they agree in number and gender with the nouns they modify.

La biblioteca está **abierta** hoy.	*The library is open today.*
El gimnasio está **abierto** hoy.	*The gym is open today.*
Las bibliotecas están **abiertas** hoy.	*The libraries are open today.*
No dejen los libros **abiertos**.	*Don't leave the books open.*
Le mandé dos tarjetas **escritas** en inglés.	*I sent him two cards written in English.*

Un dicho

En boca cerrada no entran moscas (*flies*).

Equivalent: *If you keep quiet, you won't get in trouble.*

Práctica

12. ¿Qué pasa? Complete the description of each illustration, using the verb **estar** and the appropriate past participle.

1. El coche ________ en la esquina.

2. Los niños ________.

3. La puerta ________.

4. La ventana ________.

5. El restaurante ________.

6. La carta ________ en español.

7. Los vestidos ________ en México.

8. El cuaderno ________.

9. La señora ________ cerca de la ventana.

Para conversar

13. ¿Cómo están...? In groups of three, talk about the state of the following things. After you finish, you may brainstorm and propose other possibilities.

1. En mi casa: la puerta, las ventanas, los muebles...
2. En la clase: el profesor, los estudiantes, los libros...
3. En la ciudad: el correo, los bancos, las tiendas...

3 The present perfect and the past perfect (pluperfect)

(*El pretérito perfecto y el pluscuamperfecto*)

A. The present perfect

› The present perfect tense is formed by using the present indicative of the auxiliary verb **haber** with the past participle of the verb that expresses the action or state. This tense is equivalent to the English present perfect (*have* + *past participle*, as in *I have spoken*).

Present Indicative of *haber*	
he	hemos
has	habéis
ha	han

Formation of the Present Perfect Tense			
	hablar	***tener***	***venir***
yo	**he** hablado	**he** tenido	**he** venido
tú	**has** hablado	**has** tenido	**has** venido
Ud. / él / ella	**ha** hablado	**ha** tenido	**ha** venido
nosotros(as)	**hemos** hablado	**hemos** tenido	**hemos** venido
vosotros(as)	**habéis** hablado	**habéis** tenido	**habéis** venido
Uds. / ellos / ellas	**han** hablado	**han** tenido	**han** venido

—¿**Has pagado** más de mil dólares por la matrícula?
—No, nunca **he pagado** tanto dinero.

Have you paid more than one thousand dollars for the tuition?
No, I've never paid that much money.

—¿**Has visto** a Teresa?
—No, no la **he visto**.

Have you seen Teresa?
No, I haven't seen her.

ESTRUCTURAS

Note that when the past participle is part of a perfect tense, it is invariable. The past participle only changes in form when it is used as an adjective.

Ella ha escrit**o** la cart**a**.	*She has written the letter.*
La cart**a** está escrit**a**.	*The letter is written.*

In the Spanish present perfect tense the auxiliary verb **haber** can never be separated from the past participle as it can in English.

Yo nunca **he estado** en Lima.	*I have never been in Lima.*

› Remember that when reflexive or object pronouns are used with compound tenses, the pronouns are placed immediately before the auxiliary verb.

Le ha dado mucho dinero a su hijo.	*He has given a lot of money to his son.*
María y José **se** han ido.	*María and José have left.*

Práctica

14. Lo que hemos hecho Look at the following illustrations and describe what these people have done today, using the present perfect.

1. Tú ____________________

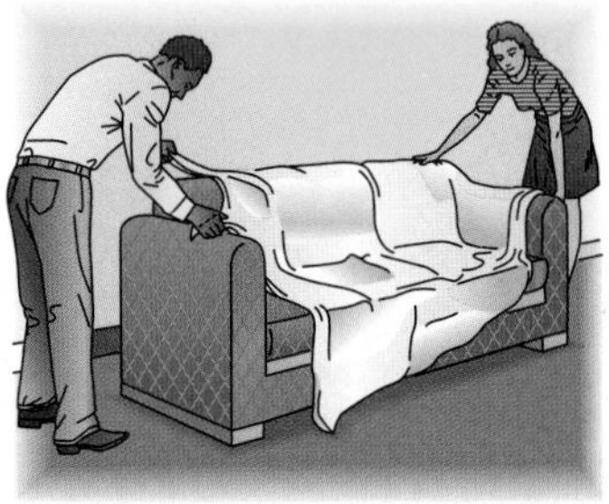

2. Tú y yo ____________________

3. Los chicos ____________________

4. Yo ____________________

5. Mi mamá ____________________

6. Ustedes ____________________

15. Últimamente With a partner, take turns asking each other what you have done lately.

Modelo ir al cine / con quién
—¿Has ido al cine últimamente?
—Sí, he ido al cine.
—¿Con quién has ido?
—He ido con mi novio(a).

1. comprar ropa / dónde
2. ver alguna película / cuál
3. dar una fiesta / dónde
4. mandar algún mensaje electrónico / a quién
5. tomar algún examen / en qué clase
6. visitar algún lugar interesante / cuál
7. escribir una carta / a quién
8. poner dinero en el banco / en cuál
9. leer un libro / cuál
10. recibir algún regalo / de quién

Para conversar

16. Nuestras experiencias With a partner, discuss five things that you or your family and friends have never done and five things you have done many times. Compare your own experiences with those of your partner.

Modelo *—Yo nunca he estado en Buenos Aires.*

—Yo tampoco he estado en Buenos Aires, pero he estado en...
(*Yo he estado en Buenos Aires dos veces.*)

Yo he estado en Buenos Aires dos veces.

17. Todavía... With a partner, use your imagination to indicate what these people haven't done yet.

Modelo mi hermana
Mi hermana todavía no ha aprendido a cocinar.

Yo
Mi padre
Mi madre
Mi hermano(a)
Mi mejor amigo(a)
Tú
Mi familia y yo
Mis amigos
El (La) profesor(a) de español

B. The past perfect (pluperfect)

› The past perfect tense is formed by using the imperfect tense of the auxiliary verb **haber** with the past participle of the verb that expresses the action or state.

› This tense is equivalent to the English past perfect (*had* + past participle, as in *I had spoken*). Generally, the past perfect tense expresses an action that had taken place before another action in the past.

Imperfect of *haber*	
había	habíamos
habías	habíais
había	habían

Formation of the Past Perfect Tense			
	estudiar	***beber***	***ir***
yo	**había** estudiado	**había** bebido	**había** ido
tú	**habías** estudiado	**habías** bebido	**habías** ido
Ud. / él / ella	**había** estudiado	**había** bebido	**había** ido
nosotros(as)	**habíamos** estudiado	**habíamos** bebido	**habíamos** ido
vosotros(as)	**habíais** estudiado	**habíais** bebido	**habíais** ido
Uds. / ellos / ellas	**habían** estudiado	**habían** bebido	**habían** ido

—¿No hablaste con tu abogada? — *Didn't you speak with your lawyer?*
—No, cuando yo llegué, ella ya se **había ido**. — *No, when I arrived, she had already left.*

—¿Uds. ya **habían estado** en Buenos Aires? — *Had you already been in Buenos Aires?*
—No, nunca **habíamos estado** allí. — *No, we had never been there.*

Práctica

18. Ya lo habíamos hecho One of your brothers is never around when there is work to be done. Say what you and other members of your family had already done by the time he got home last night.

Modelo nosotros / lavar los platos

Cuando él llegó, nosotros ya habíamos lavado los platos.

1. yo / barrer la cocina
2. los chicos / pasarle la aspiradora a la alfombra
3. Roberto y yo / hacer la comida
4. Elsa / planchar la ropa
5. tú / limpiar el refrigerador

6. Carmen y Elena / bañar al perro
7. Anita / poner la mesa
8. Raúl y Carlos / comprar las bebidas
9. Mirta / lavar las sábanas
10. Raúl y yo / envolver los regalos

19. Siempre o nunca Complete the following sentences logically, using the pluperfect tense.

1. Antes de venir a esta universidad, yo nunca...
2. Antes de tomar esta clase, mis compañeros y yo nunca...
3. Hasta el año pasado, mis amigos y yo siempre...
4. Hasta el semestre pasado, los estudiantes de esta clase nunca...
5. Hasta que yo cumplí dieciséis años, yo nunca...
6. Hasta el verano pasado, mi familia y yo siempre...
7. Antes de vivir en esta ciudad, yo nunca...
8. Antes de cumplir dieciocho años, yo siempre...

© Galina Barskaya/Shutterstock.com

Antes de vivir aquí, yo nunca había comido en un restaurante argentino.

Para conversar

20. ¡Habla con tu compañero(a)! With a partner, have a conversation about what other people in his/her family had done when he/she arrived home last night. Answer the questions in complete sentences. Be creative. Use the verbs in the word bank as a guide.

Modelo *Cuando llegaste a tu casa anoche, ¿las otras personas ya habían cenado?*
Mis padres ya habían cenado. Mi hermano no había comido todavía.

acostarse	hacer	mirar
preparar	bañarse	irse
llegar	comer	

21. Antes de cumplir los 16 años With a partner, discuss things you had done before you turned sixteen. Then talk to another classmate and tell him/her about your partner's experience. Use the pluperfect tense and answer the questions in complete sentences.

22. ¿Y nuestro(a) profesor(a)? In groups of three, prepare three questions to ask your professor about his/her experiences before turning sixteen. Use the questions for an interesting interview!

¡Vamos a ver!

Antes de ver el video

23. Preguntas With a partner, answer the following questions.

1. ¿En qué año te graduaste de la escuela secundaria?
2. ¿Qué tal te va en tus clases? ¿Son interesantes?
3. ¿Tú ya estás matriculado(a) para el próximo semestre? ¿Vas a tomar algunos requisitos?
4. ¿A qué hora termina tu última clase?
5. ¿Qué es algo que siempre te ha gustado hacer?
6. Si una persona quiere ponerse en forma, ¿le recomiendas que camine, que corra o que vaya al gimnasio?
7. ¿Tú haces ejercicio todos los días?
8. Si tú caminas o corres, ¿insistes en que alguien vaya contigo? ¿Tú corres cuando hace mucho calor?
9. En el verano, ¿adónde vas para escapar del calor?
10. ¿Te es fácil o difícil tomar decisiones?

El video: En un café al aire libre

—¿Ya has decidido cuál va a ser tu especialización?

—Bueno, todavía no he tomado ninguna decisión... Mi padre se enoja conmigo porque cuando él tenía mi edad, ya había decidido ser médico. Me gusta el periodismo, pero a veces quiero ser abogada, o arquitecta o escritora,...

—Bueno, cuando empieces a tomar clases, vas a darte cuenta de cuáles te gustan.

Después de ver el video

Mónica

Norma

24. ¿Quién lo dice? Identify the person who said the following in the dialogue.

1. Oye, ¿no vamos a encontrarnos con tu hermano? ________
2. Me gusta el periodismo, pero a veces quiero ser abogada. ________
3. Pronto vamos a comenzar a trabajar en el hospital. ________
4. Lo único que me ha gustado siempre ha sido ir al gimnasio. ________
5. ¿Por qué no invitas a mi hermano? A él le encanta correr. ________
6. Con tal de que no insistas en que yo corra... ________
7. ¡Me has dado una magnífica idea! ¡Profesora de educación física! ________
8. El único ejercicio que yo hago es ir de la sala de estar a mi cuarto. ________

25. Hablemos With a partner, take turns asking and answering the follwing questions. Base your answers on the dialogue.

1. ¿En qué mes se graduó Mónica de la escuela secundaria?
2. ¿Dónde están sentadas las chicas y de qué están hablando?
3. ¿Qué empezó a hacer Norma en marzo?
4. ¿Cómo le va a Norma en las clases?
5. ¿Cuántos requisitos está tomando Mónica?
6. ¿Cuándo va a llamar Mónica a su mamá?
7. ¿Ha decidido Mónica cuál va a ser su especialización?
8. ¿Por qué se enoja el padre de Mónica con ella a veces?
9. ¿Qué es lo único que siempre le ha gustado a Mónica?
10. ¿Qué quiere hacer Mónica mañana?
11. ¿Cuál es el único ejercicio que hace Norma?
12. ¿A quién va a invitar Mónica?

26. ¿Qué pasa después? You and a partner use your imagination to say what the characters do. In Spanish, discuss the following.

1. Whether or not Monica decided to specialize in physical education.
2. Whether Monica's mother can buy the books that Monica is going to need.
3. What Monica is going to do to get in shape.
4. Whether Monica is now Norma's brother's girlfriend.
5. What Monica is going to do when she returns to Arizona.
6. Whether Norma's brother plans to visit Monica in Arizona.
7. Whether Norma decides to start exercising.
8. Whether Norma still likes her classes and whether she started to work at the hospital.

Now compare your statements to those of another group.

¡Vamos a escuchar!

ESTRATEGIA **Guessing meaning practice I** You have already practiced guessing meaning from context while listening and reading. Remember to use cognates, word families (**aprender–aprendizaje–aprendiz**), the words you know, and the surrounding ideas to make informed guesses about unfamiliar words.

CD3-7 **27. Tres avisos** You are going to hear three brief commercials on institutions of higher learning and guess the meaning of the following words or phrases. Listen to each commercial first for the gist and then listen again for the specific words.

Aviso 1: 1. diseñados 2. extranjeras 3. enseñanza 4. docente

Aviso 2: 1. calendario 2. a partir de 3. publicada 4. avanzados

Aviso 3: 1. aprendizaje 2. sustituir 3. a través de

¡Vamos a conversar!

ESTRATEGIA **Paraphrasing practice IV** When paraphrasing, remember that your goal is to simplify what you hear while capturing the main idea. Aim to apply this technique in the future in speech and in writing when you report, summarize, or explain what you hear or read.

28. ¿Qué dijeron? Listen to five sentences and restate each in your own words. Then compare
CD3-8 your responses with those of a classmate.

29. ¿Qué dice Ud.? What would you say in the following situations? What might the other person say? Act out the scenes with a partner. Take turns playing each role.

1. Carlos is a new classmate. Ask him what his major is, what his favorite subjects are, and when he plans to graduate. Ask also how he's doing in his classes.
2. You tell a friend that you want to take a physical education class because you realize you need to get in shape.
3. A freshman asks you what courses to take. Find out something about his or her interests and plans, and make sure he/she takes the appropriate courses. Be sure to mention some of your school's requirements.
4. You are talking to a friend about classes you like, classes you don't like, and the reasons why.

30. Para conocernos mejor To do this activity, work with a classmate whom you would like to get to know. Take turns asking and answering these questions.

1. ¿Prefieres tomar una clase de matemáticas, una clase de nutrición o una clase de contabilidad? ¿Has tomado una clase de biología? ¿Cuál es tu asignatura favorita? ¿Cuál es la materia que menos te gusta?
2. ¿Has pensado en el futuro? ¿En qué año te vas a graduar? ¿Qué carrera te gusta? ¿Te gusta más la idea de ser ingeniero(a), arquitecto(a), bibliotecario(a) o profesor(a)?
3. ¿Qué tal te va en tus estudios hasta ahora? ¿Tienes un buen horario? ¿Qué requisitos has tomado? ¿Has aprobado todos tus exámenes o has quedado suspendido(a) en alguno? ¿En qué materia has sacado mejor nota?
4. ¿Te enojas a veces con tus profesores? ¿Por qué? ¿Con qué otras personas te enojas a veces? ¿Alguien se enoja contigo? ¿Quién?
5. ¿Ya estás matriculado(a) para el semestre que viene? ¿Qué clases vas a tomar?

31. Una encuesta Interview your classmates to identify who fits the following descriptions. Include your instructor, but remember to use the **Ud.** form when addressing him/her. After finishing the survey, get together with two or three classmates and discuss the results.

1. Ha conseguido una beca.	____________
2. Mantiene un buen promedio.	____________
3. Saca buenas notas en todas sus clases.	____________
4. Está haciendo investigación para una clase.	____________
5. Ha tomado clases de educación física.	____________
6. Ha hablado con un consejero últimamente.	____________
7. Se va a graduar pronto.	____________
8. Piensa estudiar periodismo.	____________

32. Para crear In groups of three or four, make up a story about the people in the photo. Say who they are, what subjects they are taking, their majors, their grade point averages, when they will graduate, and so forth. The woman in the middle is an advisor.

Rincón literario

Germán Arciniegas

(Colombia: 1900–1999)

Germán Arciniegas es uno de los grandes escritores colombianos. Es autor de más de 50 ensayos sobre la cultura, la sociología, la historia, el arte y la literatura de su país y de toda Latinoamérica. Su estilo es ligero (*light*) y ágil. Muchos de sus libros han sido traducidos al inglés, y uno de ellos, *Entre la libertad y el miedo*, donde explica la situación de América Latina a mediados del siglo pasado, fue publicado en inglés antes que en español.

Antes de leer

ESTRATEGIA **Using your experience as context** With a partner, make a list of some aspects of the English language that make it difficult to learn as a second language.

¡A leer!

33. Comprensión Read the selection and find the answers to the following questions.

1. ¿Qué deletrea (*spells*) un inglés cuando se presenta?
2. Según el autor, ¿de cuántas maneras puede escribirse una palabra?
3. ¿Es más difícil el deletreo cuando se hace por teléfono?
4. ¿Qué se puede decir como tesis fundamental?
5. ¿Cuál es el título de su libro en español? ¿Y en inglés?
6. Cuando Arciniegas habla de su libro en inglés, nadie sabe si él escribió un nocturno o un libro de caballería. ¿Por qué?
7. ¿Cómo anunciaron un día una conferencia de Arciniegas en el periódico?
8. Para el autor, ¿dónde está la dificultad del inglés?
9. ¿Qué causa el esfuerzo que un hispanohablante realiza para producir "eres" o "eses"?
10. ¿Qué explicación les da siempre el autor a sus colegas?

Lecciones de inglés (Adaptado)

Un inglés que en algo se estima° se presenta de esta manera: "Soy Mr. John Nielsen, Ene-i-e-ele-ese-e-ene". Esto es porque en inglés se supone que una palabra se pronuncia de un modo —cosa que no es exacta— pero que en todo caso puede escribirse de mil maneras. Aun el deletreo° puede no ser suficientemente claro, principalmente si se hace por teléfono. En este caso lo más discreto y usual es decir: "Mr. Arciniegas, A como en Argentina, R como en Rusia, C como en Colombia, I como en Irlanda---". De esta manera, siendo el idioma de Shakespeare tan conciso, un apellido puede extenderse indefinidamente.

que... *who has some self esteem*

spelling

Las confusiones no quedan limitadas° a los apellidos. Como tesis fundamental usted puede decir que toda palabra inglesa es un jeroglífico. Yo tengo un libro que, en la edición española, se llama El caballero° de El Dorado. Aquí, The Knight of El Dorado. Pero como en inglés "noche" y "caballero" se pronuncian

no... *are not limited*

knight

de un mismo modo,° cuando estoy hablando de mi libro nadie sabe si escribí un nocturno° o una obra de caballería.° En la cubierta° de este libro aparece la siguiente advertencia:° "Germán Arciniegas (se pronuncia Hair-máhn Ar-seen-yay-gus)". La advertencia es indispensable.

way
nocturne / chivalry / cover
warning

Pero si el lector° quiere saber más sobre los problemas de mi apellido en este país, puedo informarle que un día en el periódico anunciaron una conferencia mía así: "Hoy da una conferencia sobre la América Latina el doctor *Arthur Nagus*".

reader

La dificultad del inglés está en la emisión de los sonidos.° Cuando uno se da cuenta° de que cada letra de las vocales° se pronuncia de cuatro o cinco modos distintos, desfallece.° El esfuerzo que uno realiza para producir "eres" o "eses" no sólo causa una gran fatiga a quienes estamos acostumbrados al español, sino que deja en el rostro° una impresión de dolor o de gran torpeza.° Yo siempre les doy esta explicación a mis colegas: "Yo no soy bobo°; es que no sé inglés".

sounds
se... *realizes / vowels*
faints
face
stupidity
dumb

Después de leer... reflexiones

34. Opiniones In groups of three or four, discuss the following.

› Lo que ustedes encuentran difícil en español

› Cuánto tiempo hace que ustedes empezaron a estudiar español y si lo practican

¡Vamos a escribir!

Antes de escribir

ESTRATEGIA **Writing about opinions or experiences** When preparing to write about this, you need to draw on a number of strategies:

› Brainstorm ideas and then select the most important and interesting aspects

› Organize your writing by grouping ideas according to categories related to your main topic. You may want to create an outline. Provide details.

35. Lecciones de español You will write about your experiences in learning Spanish. First, brainstorm about what you find easy and what you find difficult about studying this language, and jot down all the ideas that come to you. Select the ones you want to use.

› Verb conjugations

› Pronunciation

¡A escribir!

36. Aprender el español Write the **primer borrador**.

Después de escribir

37. A revisar Before writing the final version, exchange your first draft with a classmate's and peer edit each other's work. Make sure to have followed the guidelines.

› formation and subject-verb agreement of all tenses used

› noun-adjective agreement and spelling and punctuation

EL MUNDO HISPÁNICO Y TÚ

Argentina

Argentina es un país con universidades muy importantes. ¿Qué tal te va en los estudios? ¿Te gusta leer buenos libros, visitar museos y galerías de arte? Al estudiar Argentina, vamos a hablar, entre otras cosas, del sistema de educación y de sus centros culturales.

Para muchos, Argentina es la tierra del tango, de Evita[1] y de los gauchos, pero en la actualidad la música argentina es muy variada, la política ha cambiado, y el campo y la ciudad están más unidos gracias a la tecnología.

Argentina exporta carne y cereales, pero su fuente de riqueza (*source of income*) actual depende principalmente de la industria y del sector de servicios.

© Peter Adams Photography Ltd/Alamy

Buenos Aires, la reina del Plata[2]

Buenos Aires, la ciudad capital, es la más grande del mundo hispano después de México. Allí vive casi la mitad de la población argentina. La ciudad tiene amplias avenidas, entre ellas, la Avenida 9 de Julio, una de las más anchas del mundo. Buenos Aires ha sido llamada "el París de Sudamérica" porque muchos de sus edificios tienen un estilo similar al de París.

La famosa calle Florida, arteria comercial y cultural a partir del (*since*) año 1900, es una calle peatonal (*only for pedestrians*) con algunas de las tiendas más elegantes del país.

© Robert Frerck and Odyssey Productions, Inc.

© Ken Durden/Shutterstock.com

El barrio de la Boca es famoso por su tradición italiana, sus casas de múltiples colores y su **Caminito**, que inspiró uno de los tangos más populares.

[1] Wife of former president Juan Perón and advocate of the working class.
[2] The queen of the Río de la Plata, the main, wide river betwen Argentina and Uruguay.

La educación en Argentina

Argentina tiene los niveles de educación más altos de Latinoamérica. Los niños de entre seis y catorce años deben asistir a la escuela por ley (*law*). La educación es gratis, y el número de personas que sabe leer y escribir pasa del 95%. Las universidades públicas son también gratis.

© Danita Delimont/Alamy

La Universidad de Buenos Aires (UBA) fue inaugurada en el año 1821, y tiene más de 300.000 estudiantes. La investigación científica es de gran importancia. Hombres de ciencia de muchas partes del mundo enseñan y hacen investigación en esta universidad.

© Winfield Parks/National Geographic/Getty Images

El Teatro Colón tiene fama internacional. Allí actuan (*perform*) algunos de los más grandes artistas del mundo.

© APEIRON-PHOTO/Alamy

El Centro Cultural Recoleta es uno de los principales de la ciudad. Tiene grandes salones de exhibición, con exposiciones excepcionales.

La música típica de Argentina es el tango, pero además, el país tiene una música folclórica muy rica.

Ahora dime...

In groups of three, take turns asking and answering the following questions.

1. El tango es un baile tradicional pero muy popular entre los jóvenes. ¿Qué danza típica crees que es popular entre los jóvenes de este país?
2. ¿La UBA y otras universidades reciben estudiantes extranjeros? ¿Te interesa la idea de tomar clases en esas universidades? ¿Por qué te parece útil?
3. ¿Vas al teatro frecuentemente? ¿Hay algún teatro en la ciudad donde tú vives que se pueda comparar con el teatro Colón?

iLrn™

To learn more about Argentina, watch the cultural footage in the Media Library.

AUTOPRUEBA

¿Cuánto sé ahora?

Take this test. When you have finished, check your answers in the answer key provided in Appendix D. Then use a red pen to correct any mistakes you may have made. Are you ready?

A. The subjunctive or indicative after certain conjunctions Complete the following sentences with the present subjunctive or the present indicative of the verbs given.

1. Tan pronto como Marta ________ (llegar) a casa, le voy a dar el dinero.
2. Voy a esperarlos hasta que ________ (volver).
3. Cuando ellos ________ (ir) a la facultad, siempre salen temprano.
4. Cuando lo ________ (ver), dile que me llame.
5. Vamos a hablar con ellos antes de que ________ (tomar) una decisión.
6. Ella va a ir al laboratorio con tal que tú ________ (ir) con ella.
7. No puedo matricularme a menos que tú me ________ (dar) el dinero.
8. En caso de que ella ________ (necesitar) el horario, yo puedo traérselo.
9. Voy a llamar a Raúl para que nos ________ (llevar) a la universidad.

B. The past participle Give the past participle of the following verbs.

1. escribir
2. abrir
3. ver
4. hacer
5. romper
6. ir
7. hablar
8. comer
9. recibir

C. Past participles used as adjectives Give the Spanish equivalent of the words in parentheses.

1. Los informes están ________ en español. (*written*)
2. ¿Están ________ las puertas del gimnasio? (*open*)
3. Ese escritor está ________. (*dead*)
4. El laboratorio está ________. (*closed*)
5. Los trabajos ya están ________. (*done*)
6. Los regalos ya están ________. (*wrapped*)

D. The present perfect Complete the sentences with the present perfect tense of the verbs given.

1. El arquitecto no ________ (venir) hoy.
2. Los abogados no me ________ (decir) nada.
3. ¿Tú ________ (escribir) el informe de biología?
4. Yo no ________ (hacer) el trabajo todavía.
5. ¿Uds. ________ (hablar) con la bibliotecaria?
6. Nosotros nunca ________ (enojarse) con ellos.

E. The past perfect (pluperfect) Complete the following sentences with the past perfect tense of the verbs given.

1. Cuando yo llegué, la clase ya ________ (terminar).
2. Elsa dijo que ellos ________ (ir) al laboratorio.
3. El carpintero me ________ (decir) que venía hoy.
4. Yo ya ________ (hacer) mi trabajo.
5. Nosotros todavía no nos ________ (matricular).
6. ¿Tú le ________ (preguntar) cuál era su especialización?

F. Just words . . .

a. Match the questions in column A with the answers in column B.

A			B
1. ¿Adónde vas?	_____	a.	Administración de empresas.
2. ¿Qué materias estás tomando?	_____	b.	El año próximo.
3. ¿Quién es tu consejero?	_____	c.	No, es plomero.
4. ¿Qué tal te va?	_____	d.	Al laboratorio.
5. ¿Qué tienes que escribir?	_____	e.	Sí, para pagar la matrícula.
6. ¿Qué nota sacaste?	_____	f.	Física, química y sociología.
7. ¿Estudia periodismo?	_____	g.	No, quedé suspendido.
8. ¿Necesitas dinero?	_____	h.	El Dr. Peña.
9. ¿Aprobaste el examen?	_____	i.	Un informe para mi clase de biología.
10. ¿Es carpintero?	_____	j.	No muy bien.
11. ¿Qué carrera estudia?	_____	k.	Una "B".
12. ¿Cuándo te gradúas?	_____	l.	Sí, quiere trabajar para el *Times*.

b. Complete the following, using vocabulary from **Lección 14**.

1. En la clase de __________ estudiamos a Newton.
2. Voy a ir al __________ todos los días porque necesito ponerme en __________.
3. Cuando vi a mi hijo le di un __________ y un beso (*kiss*).
4. Mi familia es de __________ española.
5. Ellos no se han __________ en la universidad todavía.
6. Lo __________ que me interesa es graduarme este año para que me den mi __________ de abogado.
7. Ayer hablé con mi __________ sobre las clases que debo tomar.
8. Tengo que terminar la __________ que estoy haciendo para mi informe porque tengo que __________ mañana.
9. ¿Qué __________ tienes que __________ en el examen para poder mantener un __________ de B?
10. No estudies esa materia. No te va a __________ de mucho.

G. Culture

1. Complete the following, based on the information found in the **¿Lo sabía Ud.?** section.
   a. En la mayoría de los países hispanos no existe el concepto de "____________".
   b. En lugar de letras, el sistema de calificación (*grading system*) en las universidades hispanas usa ____________.
2. Answer these questions, based on the information found in the **El mundo hispánico y tú** section.
   a. ¿Cuál es la música típica de Argentina? __________
   b. ¿Cuál es la ciudad más importante de Argentina? __________
   c. ¿Cuántos estudiantes tiene la Universidad de Buenos Aires? __________

H. Un dicho Do you remember the Spanish saying about keeping quiet to stay out of trouble? Find it in this lesson.

LECCIÓN 15

LA SALUD

En el consultorio de la médica

OBJETIVOS COMUNICATIVOS

You will learn vocabulary related to health problems.

SITUACIONES

Síntomas

ESTRUCTURAS

1 The future
2 The conditional
3 The future perfect and the conditional perfect

ASÍ SOMOS

¡Vamos a ver!

Watching and understanding situations

¡Vamos a escuchar!

Recognizing transitions

¡Vamos a conversar!

Practicing extended conversation

Rincón literario

Skimming and anticipation

El buen ejemplo by Vicente Riva Palacio

¡Vamos a escribir!

A review of different strategies

EL MUNDO HISPÁNICO Y TÚ...

› Paraguay
› Bolivia

AUTOPRUEBA

You will review what you learned in this lesson.

PARAGUAY es casi tan grande como el estado de California, pero su población es de menos de 6 millones de habitantes. La mayoría de los paraguayos hablan dos idiomas: español y guaraní.

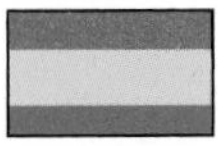

BOLIVIA, llamada así en honor del Libertador Simón Bolívar, es un país de superlativos. Tiene la capital (La Paz), el aeropuerto y el lago navegable (el lago Titicaca) más altos del mundo. También tiene unas de las ruinas más antiguas en Tiahuanaco.

Recursos iLrn video audio web playlist

SITUACIONES

Síntomas

CD3-9

© Cengage Learning

¡Ubíquelos!

César and Gloria live in Asunción, the capital of Paraguay. The video shows you some sights and tells you about the most important Paraguayan musical instrument, the harp. It also shows you places in La Paz, Cesar's place of birth.

© BananaStock/Jupiter Images

César Benítez y su esposa, Gloria, viven en Asunción, la capital de Paraguay. César es de La Paz, Bolivia, y Gloria es paraguaya. Viven en un barrio de casas antiguas y patios enormes con árboles frutales. César es un joven guapo, inteligente y simpático, pero tiene un defecto: ¡es hipocondriaco! Gloria es una mujer encantadora, pero a veces... ¡pierde la paciencia!

César: Ven acá, Gloria. Tócame la frente. Creo que tengo fiebre... debo tener como 39 grados;[1] como sabes, tengo catarro. También tengo otros síntomas: dolor de garganta y tos. (*Tose.*)

Gloria: (*Le toca la frente.*) Tendré que tomarte la temperatura. ¿Dónde está el termómetro? ¿Quieres que te haga una taza de té con miel de abeja?

César: (*Suspira.*) No... Me gustaría merendar. Quiero un cafecito bien caliente y pan tostado. Estoy un poco débil...

Gloria: De haber sabido que estabas tan enfermo, no habría invitado a tu amigo a cenar con nosotros. Puedo llamarlo por teléfono... ¡Qué lástima! Dijo que vendría a eso de las siete.

César: No, no... para esa hora ya habré tomado algún remedio casero y unas aspirinas y me sentiré perfectamente bien. ¡Ya verás!

Gloria: ¿Y si lo que tienes es contagioso? (*Un poco sarcástica*) A lo mejor tienes gripe... ¡o pulmonía! ¡O algo peor!

César: ¿Por qué no llamas al médico y le preguntas si necesito un antibiótico? Supongo que está en su consultorio.

Gloria: ¡El médico no te recetará nada sin verte!

César: Ahora me duele la cabeza. Creo que, en vez de mejorarme, me estoy empeorando...

[1]37°C = 98.6°F (*normal body temperature*)

A las siete suena el timbre y la criada abre la puerta. César se levanta y saluda a su amigo.

César: ¡Fernando! ¡Qué gusto de verte! ¡Pasa, pasa! ¿Un cafecito?

Fernando: ¡No te molestes...! Bueno... ¡acepto!

Gloria: (*Piensa.*) ¡Menos mal que vino Fernando! Él va a entretener a César y yo podré mirar mi telenovela en paz.

¿Lo sabía Ud.?

En los países de habla hispana se mide la temperatura en grados Celsius o centígrados. En la escala Celsius, 0° (temperatura de fusión del hielo) corresponde a 32° Fahrenheit. Por ejemplo, 40° Celsius corresponden a 104° Fahrenheit.

› **¿Sabe Ud. convertir grados Fahrenheit a centígrados?**

1. **Hablemos** With a partner, take turns asking and answering the following questions. Base your answers on the dialogue and on your own circumstances.

En el diálogo

1. ¿Cómo son las casas del barrio donde viven César y Gloria?
2. ¿Qué defecto tiene César? ¿Y Gloria?
3. ¿Qué le duele a César? ¿Tiene tos?
4. ¿Qué le ofrece Gloria a César?
5. ¿Qué quiere César? ¿Cómo se siente?
6. De haber sabido que César estaba tan enfermo, ¿qué no habría hecho Gloria?
7. ¿Qué habrá hecho César para las siete?
8. ¿A quién quiere César que Gloria llame? ¿Para qué?
9. ¿César cree que se está mejorando o que se está empeorando?
10. ¿Qué podrá hacer Gloria mientras Fernando entretiene a César?

¿Y tú?

1. ¿Las casas del barrio donde tú vives son modernas o antiguas?
2. ¿Tú pierdes la paciencia a veces? ¿En qué casos?
3. ¿Qué medicina tomas cuando tienes tos?
4. ¿Tú tomas té con miel de abeja? ¿Qué tomas generalmente cuándo estás enfermo(a)?
5. ¿Tú te sientes débil a veces?
6. ¿Tú invitas a tus amigos a cenar a veces? ¿Tú cocinas o van a un restaurante?
7. ¿Tú tomas remedios caseros a veces o prefieres que tu médico te recete algo?
8. ¿Tú llamas a tu médico frecuentemente?
9. Si estás enfermo(a) y no te mejoras, ¿qué haces?
10. ¿Qué haces tú para entretener a tus amigos?

VOCABULARIO

En el diálogo

Cognados

el antibiótico	*antibiotic*
la aspirina	*aspirin*
contagioso(a)	*contagious*
enorme	*enormous*
hipocondriaco	*hypochondriac*
la paciencia	*patience*
perfectamente	*perfectly*
sarcástico(a)	*sarcastic*
el síntoma	*symptom*
la temperatura	*temperature*
el termómetro	*thermometer*

Nombres

los árboles frutales	*fruit trees*
el cafecito	*small (cup of) coffee*
el catarro, el resfriado, el resfrío	*cold*
el consultorio	*doctor's office*
el defecto	*fault*
el dolor	*pain, ache*
______ **de garganta**	*sore throat*
la fiebre	*fever*
la frente	*forehead*
la garganta	*throat*
el grado	*degree*
la gripe	*influenza, flu*
el (la) joven	*young man (woman)*
la miel de abeja	*honey*
el patio	*backyard*
la pulmonía	*pneumonia*
el remedio, la medicina	*medicine*
la salud	*health*
el timbre	*doorbell*
la tos	*cough*

Verbos

doler[1] **(o:ue)**	*to hurt*
empeorarse	*to get worse*
entretener[2]	*to entertain*
mejorarse	*to get better*
merendar (e:ie)	*to have an afternoon snack*
molestarse	*to bother (doing something)*
preguntar	*to ask (a question)*
recetar	*to prescribe*
saludar	*to greet*
sonar (o:ue)	*to ring*
suponer (yo supongo)	*to suppose*
tocar	*to touch*
toser	*to cough*

Adjetivos

casero(a)	*homemade*
débil	*weak*

Otras palabras y expresiones

a eso de	*at about*
bien caliente	*nice and hot*
de haber sabido	*had I known*
en paz	*in peace*
en vez de	*instead of*
menos mal	*it's a good thing*
¡Qué gusto de verte!	*How nice to see you!*
¡Qué lástima!	*What a pity!*
tan	*so*
¡Ya verás!	*You'll see!*

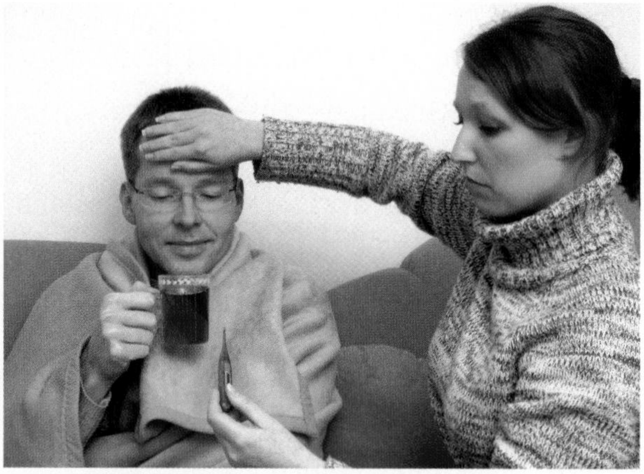

¿Lo sabía Ud.?

Especialmente en las grandes ciudades hispanas, la medicina está muy adelantada (*advanced*), pero en muchos pueblos remotos no hay médicos ni hospitales. En ese caso, mucha gente recurre a (*turn to*) los servicios de un curandero (*healer*). Muchas mujeres tienen sus bebés con la ayuda de una partera (*midwife*).

› **La mayoría de las mujeres de este país, ¿tienen sus bebés en un hospital o en casa con la ayuda de una partera?**

[1] Same construction as **gustar: Me duele** la cabeza. **Me duelen** los pies.
[2] Conjugated like **tener**.

Más sobre el tema

El cuerpo

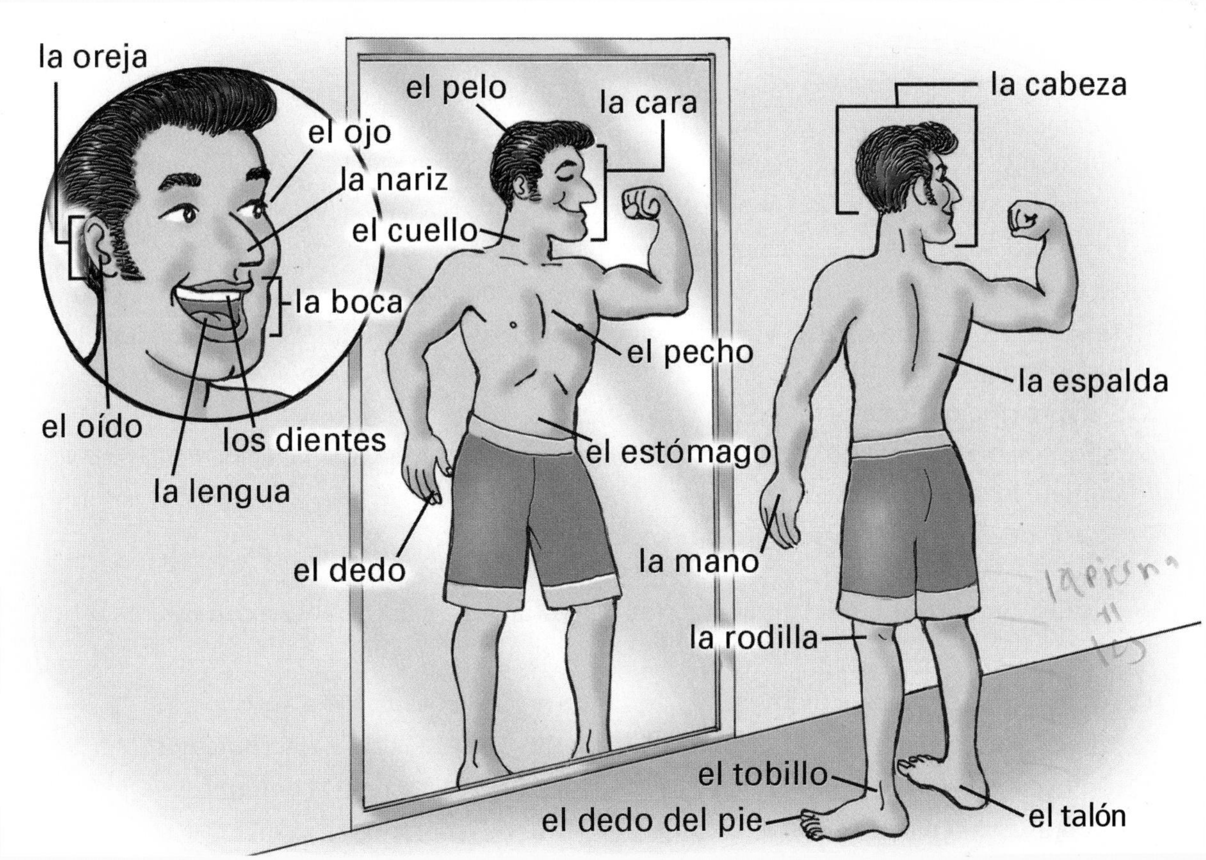

En el consultorio del médico

embarazada	*pregnant*
hacer una radiografía	*to take an X-ray*
la inyección antitetánica	*tetanus shot*
poner una inyección	*to give a shot*
la receta	*prescription*
la sala de rayos X	*X-ray room*
la vacuna	*vaccination*

En el hospital

el accidente	*accident*
el ataque al corazón	*heart attack*
la emergencia	*emergency*
romperse, quebrarse	*to break*
la silla de ruedas	*wheelchair*

¿Lo sabía Ud.?

En España y en algunos países latinoamericanos, las farmacias venden principalmente medicinas. En algunos países hispanos es posible comprar ciertas medicinas —como la penicilina— sin tener receta médica.

› **¿En este país se pueden comprar antibióticos sin receta médica?**

VOCABULARIO

Práctica

2. **Para completar** Complete the sentences, using vocabulary from this lesson.

   1. ¡Hola! ¡Qué ________ de verte! De haber ________ que venías, habría preparado algo de comer. Elena vuelve a ________ de las cinco.
   2. La casa no es moderna; es ________, con ________ frutales en el ________.
   3. Pásame el ________ porque quiero ver si tengo fiebre. También me duele la garganta. Creo que tengo ________... ¡O pulmonía! Espero que el médico me ________ un antibiótico.
   4. ¿Quieres una taza de té con miel de ________?
   5. La señora Rojas está ________; va a tener el bebé (*baby*) en abril.
   6. Tú tienes catarro; debes tomar la ________ que te compré en la farmacia.
   7. Tengo ________ de cabeza. Voy a tomar dos aspirinas. Le voy a ________ al médico si necesito algo más.
   8. Siempre cree que está enfermo. Yo creo que es ________ .
   9. Tiene una temperatura de 102 ________, pero no quiere ninguna medicina de la farmacia; prefiere los remedios ________.
   10. Yo creí que iba a mejorarse, pero la verdad es que ayer se ________.

3. **Preguntas y respuestas** Match the questions in column A with the answers in column B.

A		B
1. ¿Quieres que te prepare algo?	____	a. Sí, la criada fue a abrir.
2. ¿Quieres merendar?	____	b. Sí, pero no es nada contagioso.
3. ¿Sonó el timbre?	____	c. No, siempre está enfermo.
4. ¿Dónde está el médico?	____	d. Sí, y dolor de garganta.
5. ¿Tiene buena salud?	____	e. ¡Es enorme!
6. ¿Por qué me tocas la frente?	____	f. No, gracias. No tengo hambre.
7. ¿Estás enferma?	____	g. No... ¡qué lástima!
8. ¿El patio es grande?	____	h. ¡No! ¡Es perfecto!
9. ¿Tiene tos?	____	i. No, gracias. No te molestes.
10. ¿Cómo es Amanda?	____	j. Porque creo que tienes fiebre.
11. ¿Sergio tiene muchos defectos?	____	k. En su consultorio.
12. ¿Eva no puede ir con nosotros?	____	l. Es una joven muy bonita.

4. **¿Cuál escoge?** Choose the word or phrase that best completes each sentence.

   1. Mañana estaré perfectamente bien. Ya (verás, leerás, dirás).
   2. Elsa está mucho mejor. (¡Menos mal!, ¡Qué gusto de verte!, ¡Suena el timbre!)
   3. Murió de un ataque (al corazón, al accidente, a la receta).
   4. Le van a hacer una radiografía para ver si se (rompió, tosió, saludó) una pierna.
   5. Lo llevaron en una silla de (rodillas, ruedas, tobillos).
   6. Le van a (dar, enviar, poner) una inyección antitetánica.
   7. Lo van a llevar a la (vacuna, habitación, sala) de rayos X.
   8. Necesito comer algo porque me siento muy (antiguo, casero, débil).

5. ¿Cuál no va? Choose the word or phrase that does not belong in each group.

1. oído	oreja	lengua
2. boca	dedos	dientes
3. tobillo	cabeza	pelos
4. espalda	pie	talón
5. rodilla	pecho	estómago
6. ojo	nariz	dedo del pie
7. mano	cabeza	cuello
8. accidente	cara	emergencia

Para conversar

6. ¡Ay! (*Ouch!*) With a partner, play the roles of a doctor and a patient who is a hypochondriac. The patient describes symptoms and says what he/she thinks the problem is (**Yo creo que tengo...**). The doctor tells the patient what to do and what he/she is going to prescribe (**Tiene que... / Le voy a recetar...**). The patient keeps adding at least three more symptoms. Switch roles.

7. ¿Qué haces tú? With a partner, take turns asking each other what you do when different parts of your body hurt. When you answer, give some details.

8. ¡Bienvenido(a)! With a partner, play the roles of a guest and a gracious host (hostess). Express happiness at seeing each other. The host (hostess) offers something to eat and drink, including an afternoon snack. Use vocabulary from previous lessons.

CD3-10

Pronunciación

Pronunciation in context

In this lesson, there are some new words or phrases that may be challenging to pronounce. For further pronunciation practice of Spanish sounds, listen to your instructor and repeat the following sentences.

1. **César** es de La Paz, **Bolivia**, y Gloria es paraguaya.
2. Tiene un **defecto:** es **hipocondriaco**.
3. Tendré que tomarte la **temperatura**. ¿Dónde está el **termómetro**?
4. Para esa **hora** ya **habré** tomado algún **remedio casero**.
5. El médico no te **recetará** nada **sin verte**.
6. Creo que, **en vez de mejorarme,** me estoy **empeorando**.
7. **¡Fernando**! ¡Qué **gusto** de verte! ¡Pasa, pasa! ¿Un **cafecito**?
8. Él va a **entretener** a **César**.

1 The future (*El futuro*)

› Most Spanish verbs are regular in the future tense. The infinitive serves as the stem of almost all of them, and the endings are the same for all three conjugations.

The Future Tense				
	Infinitive	***Stem***	***Ending***	
yo	trabajar	trabajar-	**é**	trabajar**é**
tú	aprender	aprender-	**ás**	aprender**ás**
Ud.	escribir	escribir-	**á**	escribir**á**
él	hablar	hablar-	**á**	hablar**á**
ella	decidir	decidir-	**á**	decidir**á**
nosotros(as)	dar	dar-	**emos**	dar**emos**
vosotros(as)	ir	ir-	**éis**	ir**éis**
Uds.	caminar	caminar-	**án**	caminar**án**
ellos	perder	perder-	**án**	perder**án**
ellas	recibir	recibir-	**án**	recibir**án**

¡Atención! Note that all the endings, except the one for the **nosotros** form, have written accents.

—¿**Irás** al médico? — *Will you go to the doctor?*
—Sí, y ya **verás** que pronto me **sentiré** mejor. — *Yes, and you'll see that soon I'll feel better.*

The English equivalent of the Spanish future is *will* or *shall* + a verb. As you have already learned, Spanish also uses the construction **ir a** + *infinitive* or the present tense with a time expression to express future action, very much like the English present tense or the expression *going to*.

Vamos a ir al hospital esta noche.
or: **Iremos** al hospital esta noche. — *We're going (We'll go) to the hospital tonight.*

Anita **toma** el examen mañana.
or: Anita **tomará** el examen mañana. — *Anita is taking (will take) the exam tomorrow.*

¡Atención! The Spanish future is *not* used to express willingness, as is the English future. In Spanish, this is expressed with the verb **querer**.

¿**Quieres** llamar a Tomás? — *Will you call Tomás?*

¿Lo sabía Ud.?

En la mayoría de los países de habla hispana, los hospitales son gratis y subvencionados *(subsidized)* por el gobierno. Hay clínicas privadas para la gente de mejor posición económica que no quiere ir a un hospital público.

› **En este país, ¿los hospitales son gratis?**

› A small number of verbs are irregular in the future. These verbs use a modified form of the infinitive as a stem, but have the same endings as the regular verbs.

Irregular Future Stems		
Infinitive	***Modified form (Stem)***	***First-person singular***
decir	dir-	**diré**
hacer	har-	**haré**
querer	querr-	**querré**
saber	sabr-	**sabré**
poder	podr-	**podré**
caber	cabr-	**cabré**
poner	pondr-	**pondré**
venir	vendr-	**vendré**
tener	tendr-	**tendré**
salir	saldr-	**saldré**
valer[1]	valdr-	**valdré**

—¿Qué les **dirás** a tus padres? *What will you tell your parents?*

—Les **diré** que no **podremos** venir en enero y que **vendremos** en febrero. *I will tell them that we won't be able to come in January and that we will come in February.*

¡Atención! The future of **hay** (impersonal form of **haber**) is **habrá**.

¿Habrá una fiesta (hoy)? *Will there be a party (today)?*

Un brindis[2]

Salud, amor y pesetas... y tiempo para gastarlas.
Health, love, and money . . . and the time to enjoy them.

LEARNING TIP

Remember that you must create activities that will place information in your long-term memory. To help you do this, use each verb in short affirmative, interrogative, and negative sentences, varying the subjects. For example: ***Eva dirá* la verdad. *¿Tú dirás* la verdad? *Ellos* no *dirán* la verdad.**

[1] **valer** = *to be worth*
[2] This is a popular toast in Spain. The **peseta** is the former Spanish currency.

Práctica

9. La próxima semana Say what the following people will do next week, using the future tense.

1. Jorge / ir al consultorio del médico
2. mis padres / venir a visitarme / agosto
3. Ud. / ponerse / una inyección antitetánica
4. Uds. / pasar dos días / Asunción
5. Marta y yo / tener que hacernos una radiografía
6. yo / tomar / medicina todos los días
7. tú / visitar / un amigo en el hospital
8. yo / salir / para La Paz

10. ¿Qué haremos? Say what the following people *will do* in each situation.

1. Mauricio tiene pulmonía.
2. Eva y yo tenemos tos.
3. El doctor tiene dos pacientes que tienen gripe.
4. Yo tengo una temperatura de 103 grados de fiebre.
5. El médico cree que uno de sus pacientes se rompió una pierna.
6. A Paco y a Raquel les duele la garganta.
7. Uno de mis amigos está en el hospital.
8. Los niños están enfermos y están muy aburridos.

Un dicho

Dime con quién andas y te diré quién eres.
Equivalent: *You are known by the company you keep.*

11. Un viaje a Paraguay You and a friend will be attending a special program in Paraguay next year. Take turns asking and answering the following questions about your trip.

1. ¿A qué ciudad irán?
2. ¿Cuándo saldrán de viaje?
3. ¿Viajarán en barco o en avión?
4. ¿Cuánto tiempo estarán estudiando?
5. ¿Podrán visitar muchas ciudades?
6. ¿Qué lugares visitarán? (**HINT**: *see Internet*)
7. ¿Les enviarán tarjetas postales a sus amigos?
8. ¿Cuánto dinero necesitarán para el viaje?
9. ¿Se lo pedirán a sus padres?
10. ¿Cuándo volverán?

Para conversar

12. **¿Cuáles son tus planes?** Now, use questions similar to those in **Actividad 11** as a model to ask a classmate about his or her upcoming vacation plans.

13. **Tu horóscopo** You and your partner are in charge of the astrology section in a newspaper. Using the future tense, take turns making predictions for each sign. Your partner should write the predictions you say. Compare notes with other members of the class.

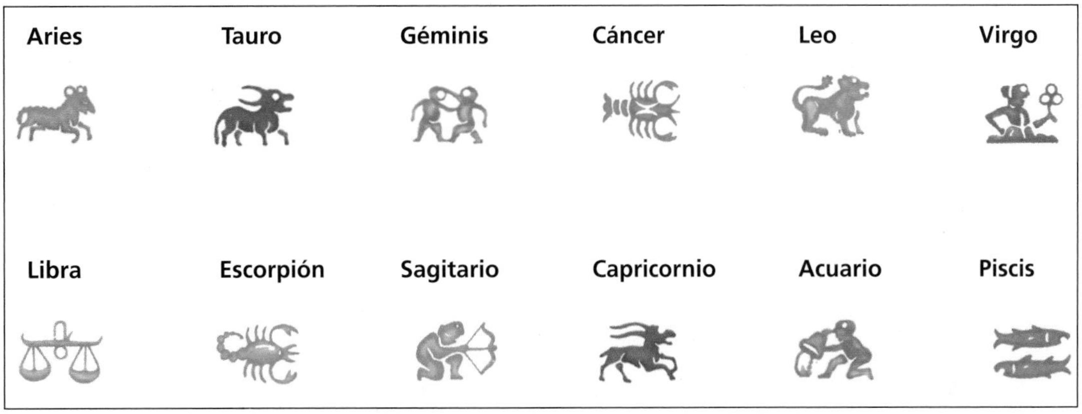

2 The conditional (*El condicional*)

› The conditional tense in Spanish is equivalent to the conditional in English, expressed by *should* or *would* + *a verb*.[1] Like the future tense, the conditional uses the infinitive as the stem and has only one set of endings for all three conjugations.

The Conditional Tense				
Infinitive		***Stem***	***Ending***	
trabajar	yo	trabajar-	**ía**	trabajar**ía**
aprender	tú	aprender-	**ías**	aprender**ías**
escribir	Ud.	escribir-	**ía**	escribir**ía**
ir	él	ir-	**ía**	ir**ía**
ser	ella	ser-	**ía**	ser**ía**
dar	nosotros(as)	dar-	**íamos**	dar**íamos**
hablar	vosotros(as)	hablar-	**íais**	hablar**íais**
servir	Uds.	servir-	**ían**	servir**ían**
estar	ellos	estar-	**ían**	estar**ían**
preferir	ellas	preferir-	**ían**	preferir**ían**

[1] The conditional is never used in Spanish as an equivalent of *used to*.
Cuando era pequeño, siempre **iba a la playa**. *When I was little, I would always go to the beach.*

› All of the conditional endings have written accents.

—Él dijo que **tomaría** esta medicina.	*He said that he would take this medicine.*
—Sí, y también dijo que **hablaría** con el médico.	*Yes, and he also said that he would speak with the doctor.*

› The conditional is also used as the future of a past action. The future states what *will* happen; the conditional states what *would* happen.

Future	**Conditional**
(states what *will* happen)	(states what *would* happen)
Él **dice** que **estará** aquí mañana.	Él **dijo** que **estaría** aquí mañana.
He says that he will be here tomorrow.	*He said that he would be here tomorrow.*

› The verbs that have irregular stems in the future tense are also irregular in the conditional. The endings are the same as those for regular verbs.

Irregular Future Stems		
Infinitive	***Modified form (Stem)***	***First-person singular***
decir	dir-	**diría**
hacer	har-	**haría**
querer	querr-	**querría**
saber	sabr-	**sabría**
poder	podr-	**podría**
caber	cabr-	**cabría**
poner	pondr-	**pondría**
venir	vendr-	**vendría**
tener	tendr-	**tendría**
salir	saldr-	**saldría**
valer	valdr-	**valdría**

—¿A qué hora te dijo que **vendría**?	*What time did he tell you he would come?*
—Dijo que **saldría** de casa a las dos.	*He said he would leave home at two.*

¡Atención! The conditional of **hay** (impersonal form of **haber**) is **habría**.

Dijo que **habría** un examen mañana.	*He said there would be an exam tomorrow.*

LEARNING TIP

Take all the affirmative and negative statements you created with verbs in the future, and change them to the conditional by starting with **"Yo te dije que..."** For example: **Yo te dije que *Eva diría* la verdad.**

Práctica

14. **No haríamos lo mismo** Nobody would do the things that Carlos does. With a partner, take turns saying what the following people would do instead.

Modelo Carlos come en la cafetería. (yo)
Yo comería en mi casa.

Carlos...

1. se levanta a las cinco. (Uds.)
2. estudia por la mañana. (Ana y Luis)
3. viene a la universidad en ómnibus. (Nosotros)
4. toma clases de alemán. (yo)
5. se baña por la noche. (Elsa)
6. se acuesta a las nueve de la noche. (Ud.)
7. va a las montañas los fines de semana. (Ellos)
8. sale con Margarita. (tú)

15. **¿Qué harías tú?** Describe what you would do in the following situations, using the conditional.

1. Su amigo cree que tiene pulmonía.
2. A Ud. le duele mucho la cabeza.
3. Son las cuatro de la tarde y Ud. tiene mucha hambre.
4. Suena el timbre.
5. Ud. nota (*notices*) que un niño está débil.
6. Ud. tiene un accidente.
7. A Ud. le duele el estómago.
8. Los zapatos le quedan chicos y le duelen los pies.
9. Ud. tiene dolor de espalda.
10. Ud. cree que su hermanito tiene fiebre.

Para conversar

16. **Buenos consejos** Using the following advice from a magazine article, take turns with your partner indicating what each person in the list on page 430 said he/she would or wouldn't do after reading it.

Buenos consejos para conservar la salud

DEBE	*NO DEBE*
✔ comer más vegetales y frutas	✖ fumar
✔ dormir lo suficiente	✖ consumir mucho alcohol
✔ visitar al médico periódicamente	✖ consumir mucha sal o azúcar
✔ hacer ejercicio	✖ usar drogas
✔ aprender a relajarse	✖ comer mucha grasa
✔ evitar la tensión *(stress)*	✖ trabajar en exceso
✔ pensar positivamente	
✔ tener una dieta balanceada	
✔ controlar su peso *(weight)*	

1. El Sr. Vega toma diez cervezas todos los días.
2. La Srta. Díaz está siempre sentada, mirando televisión.
3. Elsa come muchos dulces (*sweets*).
4. El Dr. Álvarez trabaja catorce horas cada día.
5. La Sra. Carreras duerme solo cuatro horas cada noche.
6. Estela se preocupa constantemente por todo.
7. Adela siempre come papas fritas, hamburguesas, mantequilla, pollo frito, etcétera.
8. Hace cinco años que Carlos no va a ver a su médico.
9. La dieta de Eduardo es de 5000 calorías al día.
10. Raúl pesa (*weighs*) 300 libras (*pounds*).
11. Raquel solamente come carne y pastas.
12. Jorge fuma muchísimo.

17. ¡Gané la lotería! With a partner, take turns telling each other what you would do if you won a million dollars in the lottery. Say at least five things each, and then compare your responses with those of other classmates.

3 The future perfect and the conditional perfect (*El futuro perfecto y el condicional perfecto*)

A. The future perfect

› The future perfect in Spanish corresponds closely in formation and meaning to the same tense in English. The Spanish future perfect is formed with the future tense of the auxiliary verb **haber** + *the past participle* of the main verb.

Future Tense of *haber*	
habré	habremos
habrás	habréis
habrá	habrán

Formation of the Future Perfect Tense		
yo	**habré terminado**	*I will have finished*
tú	**habrás vuelto**	*you will have returned*
Ud. / él / ella	**habrá comido**	*you (he, she) will have eaten*
nosotros(as)	**habremos escrito**	*we will have written*
vosotros(as)	**habréis dicho**	*you (fam.) will have said*
Uds. / ellos / ellas	**habrán salido**	*you (they) will have left*

› Like its English equivalent, the future perfect is used to indicate an action that will have taken place by a certain time in the future.

—¿Tus padres estarán aquí para el dos de junio? — *Will your parents be here by June second?*
—Sí, para esa fecha ya **habrán vuelto** de Madrid. — *Yes, by that date they will have returned from Madrid.*

Práctica

18. **Minidiálogos** Complete the following dialogues, using the future perfect forms of the verbs listed. Then act them out with a partner.

acostarse	salir	terminar (2)
cenar	limpiar	volver

1. —Esta noche a las once voy a llamar a Quique.
   —¿Estás loco(a)? Para esa hora él ya ____________. Llámalo mañana a las siete.
   —Para esa hora ya _________ de su casa.
2. —¿Uds. _________ de México para el 4 de julio?
   —No, todavía no. Vamos a estar allí hasta agosto.
3. —Tú y yo podemos salir para España el 12 de diciembre porque ya estaremos de vacaciones.
   —Bueno, tú ___________ las clases para entonces, pero yo no las ___________ todavía.
4. —No podemos traer a mis amigos esta noche porque la casa está muy sucia (*dirty*).
   —No te preocupes. Para cuando Uds. vengan, las chicas ya la _________.
5. —¿Quieres cenar con nosotros hoy?
   —Gracias, pero para cuando yo vuelva, Uds. ya ___________.

Para conversar

19. **Para entonces** With a partner, discuss things that you will or will not have done by certain times.

1. para las once de la noche
2. para mañana a las cinco de la mañana
3. para mañana a las seis de la tarde
4. para el sábado próximo
5. para junio del año próximo
6. para el año 2015
7. para diciembre
8. para el mes próximo
9. para el verano que viene
10. para el año 2020

B. The conditional perfect

› The conditional perfect is formed with the conditional tense of the auxiliary verb **haber** + *the past participle* of the main verb.

Conditional Tense of *haber*	
habría	habríamos
habrías	habríais
habría	habrían

Formation of the Conditional Perfect Tense		
yo	**habría vuelto**	*I would have returned*
tú	**habrías comido**	*you would have eaten*
Ud. / él / ella	**habría salido**	*you (he, she) would have left*
nosotros(as)	**habríamos estudiado**	*we would have studied*
vosotros(as)	**habríais hecho**	*you* (fam.) *would have done*
Uds. / ellos / ellas	**habrían muerto**	*you (they) would have died*

› Like the English conditional perfect, the Spanish conditional perfect is used to indicate an action that would have taken place but didn't.

—Lo llevé al hospital en mi coche. *I took him to the hospital in my car.*
—Yo **habría llamado** una ambulancia. *I would have called an ambulance.*

Práctica

20. ¿Qué habrías hecho? Following are some things that my family and I and a couple of friends did last week. Based on what I tell you, say what you and every member of your family and two of your friends would have done *differently*.

1. Mi mamá tomó té con miel de abeja.
2. Mis hermanos merendaron a las cuatro.
3. Mi papá volvió a casa a eso de las ocho.
4. Mi abuela no se sentía bien y tomó un remedio casero.
5. A mi amiga Nora le dolía mucho la cabeza y tomó dos aspirinas.
6. Mi amigo Sergio tuvo un ataque de alergia y tomó Benadryl.
7. Mi hermano tenía fiebre, tos y dolor de garganta, pero no fue al médico.
8. Yo tenía una enfermedad (*sickness*) contagiosa, pero no me quedé en mi casa.
9. Mi mamá se lavó las manos con jabón Dove.
10. Yo le toqué la frente a mi hermanito para ver si tenía fiebre.

Para conversar

21. ¡No los esperábamos! You and your family had unannounced guests last Saturday. You were not prepared! You and your partner take turns saying what you and other members of your family or the maid would have done had you known that they were coming.

Modelo mi mamá
E1: *De haber sabido que vendrían, mi mamá habría limpiado la casa.*
E2: *Mi mamá habría...*

1. yo
2. mi papá
3. mi hermana y yo
4. mis hermanos
5. mis padres
6. mi mamá y yo
7. la criada
8. mi tía
9. mi abuela
10. mi prima

Summary of the Tenses of the Indicative			
Simple tenses			
	-ar	***-er***	***-ir***
Presente	hablo	como	vivo
Pretérito	hablé	comí	viví
Imperfecto	habl**aba**	com**ía**	viv**ía**
Futuro	hablaré	comeré	viviré
Condicional	hablaría	comería	viviría
Compound tenses			
Pretérito perfecto	**he** hablado	**he** comido	**he** vivido
Pretérito pluscuamperfecto	**había** hablado	**había** comido	**había** vivido
Futuro perfecto	**habré** hablado	**habré** comido	**habré** vivido
Condicional perfecto	**habría** hablado	**habría** comido	**habría** vivido

¡Vamos a ver!

Antes de ver el video

22. Preguntas You and a partner take turns asking and answering the following questions.

1. Si te duele la cabeza y la garganta y tienes fiebre y tos, ¿vienes a clase? ¿Y si tienes algo contagioso?
2. Si tú no te sientes bien, y alguien te ofrece una taza de té bien caliente con miel de abeja, ¿tú la aceptas?
3. Si tú tienes gripe, ¿vas al médico para que te recete un antibiótico o te quedas en tu casa y descansas?
4. Tengo una temperatura de 102 grados. ¿Será necesario que el doctor me vea?
5. A eso de las cuatro, ¿te gustaría mirar la tele y merendar? ¿Qué prepararías para comer?
6. ¿Tú tendrás que salir o tendrás que quedarte en tu casa el domingo?
7. Cuando suena el timbre en tu casa, ¿quién abre la puerta, generalmente?
8. ¿Tienes árboles frutales en tu patio? ¿Qué flores tienes en tu jardín? ¿Qué flores te gustaría tener?
9. ¿Preferirías vivir en una casa moderna o en una casa de tipo colonial?
10. Para las once de la noche, ¿tú ya te habrás acostado?
11. La próxima vez que tengas fiebre, ¿vendrás a clases?
12. ¿Qué le dirías a un amigo que está enfermo?
13. Tu mejor amigo(a) estaba enfermo con un virus contagioso. ¿Lo (La) habrías invitado a tu fiesta de cumpleaños?
14. Tus amigos te invitan a una fiesta cuando estás con un poco de fiebre. ¿Qué harás? ¿Qué les dirás?
15. Imagina que ayer tu amigo te llamó y te dijo que tenía una temperatura de 102 grados. ¿Qué habrías hecho?
16. Para las once de la noche de hoy, ¿tú ya te habrás acostado?

El video ¿Qué síntomas tiene Adriana?

—¿Anabel? Habla Adriana. Hoy no quiero ir a la facultad, de modo que le voy a decir a mi mamá que no me siento bien.

—No, Adriana... podrías empeorarte. Necesitas descansar... Voy a llamar a Carolina, a ver si ella puede ir conmigo. ¡Ojalá que te mejores pronto!

Después de ver el video…

Adriana

Doña Eva

Criada

Ignacio

23. ¿Quién lo dice? Identify the person who said the following in the dialogues.

1. No, gracias, señora. ¡No se moleste!
2. ¡Ojalá que te mejores pronto!
3. Para el lunes ya se habrá curado y podrá volver a la universidad.
4. Mamá, tendré que quedarme en casa hoy.
5. Voy a llamar a Carolina, a ver si ella puede ir conmigo.
6. ¡Ignacio! ¡Qué gusto de verte!
7. ¿Te gustaría venir a visitarme?
8. Señora, aquí hay un joven que quiere hablar con la señorita Adriana.

24. Hablemos With a partner, take turns asking and answering the following questions. Base your answers on the dialogue.

1. Para no ir a la facultad, ¿qué le va a decir Adriana a su mamá?
2. ¿Qué síntomas dice Adriana que tiene?
3. ¿Qué tomará Adriana para mejorarse?
4. ¿Qué dice la mamá de Adriana que su hija tendrá que hacer?
5. ¿Quién abre la puerta cuando suena el timbre?
6. ¿Qué habría hecho doña Eva de haber sabido que Ignacio venía?
7. ¿Qué quiere preguntarle Ignacio a Adriana?
8. ¿Cuándo dice doña Eva que Adriana podrá volver a la universidad?

25. ¿Qué pasa después…? You and a partner use your imagination to say what the characters do. In Spanish, discuss the following.

1. Whether or not Anabel comes to visit Adriana and what they do.
2. What Adriana tells Anabel about Ignacio. Give details.
3. Whether Dr. Viñas will see Adriana and what he will prescribe.
4. Whether Adriana would like to drink tea with honey, or something else.
5. What doña Eva would have prepared for an afternoon snack.
6. Whether later Adriana told her mother that she wasn't sick.
7. Carolina accepted Ignacio's invitation. Say whether they had a good time at the party. Did Ignacio call Adriana the next day? Does he like Carolina better?

Now compare your answers with those of the members of another group.

¡Vamos a escuchar!

ESTRATEGIA **Recognizing transitions** You have already seen that certain words establish links or transitions between one idea and the next. Review the transition words listed in **¡Vamos a escuchar!, Lección 11**. Here are other transition words you have seen. The lesson number where each was introduced is shown in parentheses.

bueno (1)	en ese caso (2)	en fin (8)
a pesar de (esto, lo anterior) (9)	es que (13)	por ejemplo (13)
en cuanto (14)	si (14)	de haber(lo) sabido (15)

CD3-11 **26. Estoy muy mal** Listen to a conversation between Rosa and Sergio. Listen specifically for the transitional markers and write them on a piece of paper. Try to list ten different ones.

¡Vamos a conversar!

ESTRATEGIA **Practicing extended conversation** As you continue your study of Spanish, it is important that you develop your conversational skills beyond brief oral exchanges. When you make a statement, try to elaborate with details. For example, on the topic *Hoy voy al médico*, you can talk about the time of the appointment, why you are going, your symptoms, how long you have had the problem, etc.

27. Anécdotas personales Think of three simple statements to tell your partner and expand on each with as much information as you can. You might talk about something you plan to do, a friend, a recent medical problem, a movie you saw, etc.

28. ¿Qué dice Ud.? What would you say in the following situations? What might the other person say? Act out the scenes with a partner. Take turns playing each role.

1. You tell a friend that you were sick but the doctor has prescribed some medicine, and you are now feeling perfectly well.
2. You tell a friend that an ambulance has taken his dad to the emergency room because he had a heart attack.
3. You tell a friend that, had you known that he/she was sick, you would have taken him/her to the doctor.
4. Someone offers to do something for you. Tell him/her not to bother.

29. Para conocernos mejor To do this activity, work with a classmate whom you would like to get to know. Take turns asking and answering these questions.

1. ¿Has tenido algún problema últimamente? ¿Cuántas veces al año vas al médico? ¿Cuándo fue la última vez que te hicieron un chequeo? ¿Cómo se llama tu médico? ¿Cómo te sientes hoy?
2. ¿Tú te quedas en tu casa cuando estás enfermo(a)? ¿Has tenido pulmonía alguna vez? ¿Cuándo fue la última vez que tuviste catarro? ¿Qué hiciste?
3. ¿Tú eres alérgico(a) a alguna medicina? ¿Qué tomas cuando tienes tos? ¿Tu médico te receta antibióticos a veces? ¿Cuáles?

4. ¿Te has roto una pierna o un brazo alguna vez? ¿Cuándo fue la última vez que te hicieron una radiografía? ¿De qué parte del cuerpo? ¿Te pusieron una inyección antitetánica? ¿Cuándo?
5. ¿Tú conoces a alguien que sea hipocondriaco? ¿Qué haces tú si tienes una temperatura de 102 grados? Si un niño está enfermo y no puede jugar, ¿qué puedes hacer para entretenerlo? Cuando un buen amigo viene a visitarte, ¿qué le dices para saludarlo?
6. Mañana, ¿te habrás acostado para las once de la noche?

30. Una encuesta Interview your classmates to identify who fits the following descriptions. Include your instructor, but remember to use the **Ud.** form when addressing him/her. After finishing the survey, get together with two or three classmates and discuss the results.

1. Tiene buena salud.	________________
2. Necesita descansar más.	________________
3. Toma una taza de té cuando no se siente bien.	________________
4. Le gustaría tomar un cafecito bien caliente.	________________
5. A veces le duele la espalda.	________________
6. Toma aspirina cuando le duele la cabeza.	________________
7. Se habrá acostado para las once de la noche.	________________
8. Tendrá que quedarse en su casa este fin de semana.	________________

31. Para crear Get together in groups of three or four and "create" the scenario for this photo. Who are the people? Give them names. What is their relationship to each other? What happened to the young man, and what did the doctor do? What symptoms is the patient describing? What is the doctor saying? What will he prescribe? What are some things that the patient won't be able to do?

(**Hint:** muletas = *crutches*)

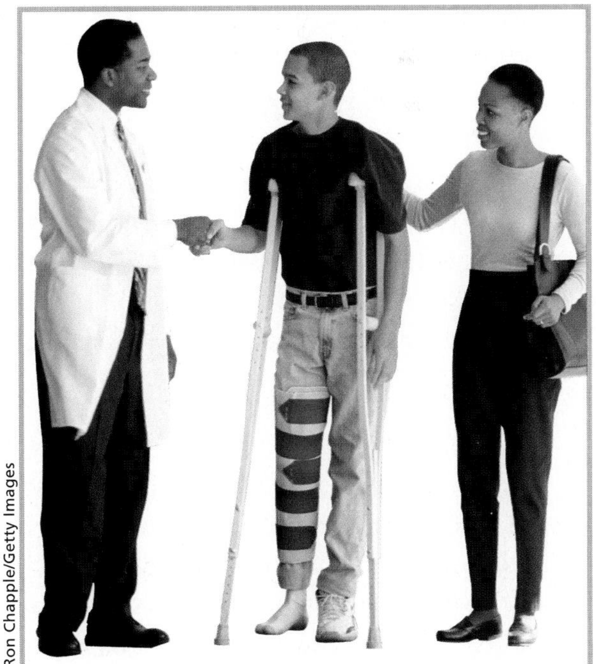

© Ron Chapple/Getty Images

Rincón literario

Vicente Riva Palacio (México: 1832–1896)

Además de escritor, Vicente Riva Palacio fue diputado, militar, periodista y magistrado. Escribió novelas, poesía y obras teatrales. De su obra narrativa, *Los cuentos del general* está considerada la mejor. Fue representante de México en España, donde murió en 1896. El estilo de Riva Palacio es satírico y lleno de gracia.

Antes de leer

ESTRATEGIA **Skimming and anticipation** Especially with short narrations, these strategies allow the reader to get the gist of what the story is about. It may be by reading a part of it—the first few lines or the first couple of paragraphs—or the whole story. The main topic, the main character, the important ideas come through even if we don't worry about details. This strategy, coupled with anticipating based on the title of the narration, will make our understanding and appreciation of the story much easier.

¡A leer!

32. Comprensión Read the story for the second time, and answer the following questions.

1. ¿Quién es don Lucas? ¿Dónde enseña? ¿Es fácil ser maestro en una escuela de pueblo?
2. ¿Qué pasaba siempre a las cinco de la tarde? ¿Cuál era la relación entre don Lucas y su loro?
3. ¿Por qué no le cortaba don Lucas las alas a su loro? ¿Qué pasó una mañana?
4. ¿Adónde fue don Lucas un día, después de varios meses? ¿Qué creyó oír a lo lejos?
5. ¿Qué salió de los árboles cercanos? ¿Qué cantaban? ¿Qué le dijo el loro a don Lucas?

El buen ejemplo (Adaptado)

En la parte sur de la República Mexicana, y en las faldas° de la Sierra Madre, hay un pueblito con casitas blancas. En este pueblo había una escuela que don Lucas gobernaba. ¡Qué vocación de mártires necesitan los maestros de escuela de los pueblos!

slopes

En esta escuela, el estudio para los muchachos era una especie de orfeón°, y en diferentes tonos, pero siempre con monotonía. En coro estudiaban y en coro cantaban las letras° y sílabas, la doctrina cristiana y la tabla de multiplicar y todos los días don Lucas soportaba con heroica resignación aquella ópera.

singing society
letters

A las cinco de la tarde los chicos salían de la escuela. Un criado le traía a don Lucas una taza de chocolate y un pedazo de pan, que compartía con su loro°.

parrot

Don Lucas tenía un loro que era su debilidad°. Estaba siempre en una percha a la puerta de la escuela. Aquel loro y don Lucas se entendían perfectamente.

weakness

Todos los días cuando la escuela estaba desierta y don Lucas salía a tomar su chocolate, aquellos dos amigos daban expansión libre a sus afectos.

Pasaron así varios años, y don Lucas tenía tanta confianza° en su querido Perico°, como lo llamaban los muchachos, que no le cortaba las alas°.

faith
parrot / wings

Una mañana, uno de los chicos gritó —¡Perico se va!— y a lo lejos se veía al loro volando para ganar refugio en el cercano bosque.

Como era imposible distinguir a Perico entre la multitud de loros que viven en aquellos bosques, don Lucas volvió, resignado, a sus tareas escolares.

Pasaron varios meses y don Lucas hizo un viaje a uno de los pueblos cercanos.

Eran las dos de la tarde y hacía sol; los pájaros cantaban en medio de aquel terrible silencio a la mitad del día.

De pronto°, don Lucas creyó oír a lo lejos el canto de los niños de la escuela cuando estudiaban las letras y sílabas.

De... *Suddenly*

Al principio° aquello le pareció una alucinación producida por el calor, pero mientras avanzaba, aquellos cantos se hacían más claros y aquello era una escuela en medio del bosque desierto.

Al... *At first*

Don Lucas se detuvo asombrado°, cuando de los árboles cercanos salió una bandada° de loros que cantaban acompasadamente ba, be, bi, bo, bu, la, le, li, lo, lu; y tras ellos, volando majestuosamente, un loro, que al pasar cerca del maestro, volvió la cabeza y le dijo alegremente: —Don Lucas, ya tengo escuela.

astonished

flock

Desde esa época los loros de aquella región, muy avanzados para su siglo, han visto desaparecer las sombras° de la ignorancia.

shadows

Después de leer... reflexiones

33. Opiniones In groups of three, discuss the following questions.

1. ¿Cuál es la diferencia entre la manera de enseñar de don Lucas y la metodología de los maestros de la escuela primaria en este país?
2. ¿Los maestros son "mártires"? ¿Por qué sí o por qué no? Den detalles y ejemplos.

¡Vamos a escribir!

Antes de escribir

ESTRATEGIA **A review of different strategies** Think of the strategies used before. Which one proved most helpful to you? Which one is better when trying to narrate, summarize, or explain? Can you come up with a new way of organizing your thoughts and ideas?

34. Don Lucas escribe sobre lo que pasó You will write a letter to one of the parents in the town, explaining what happened when don Lucas last saw his parrot, as if you were don Lucas. Add details, and express the way you felt when you saw the flock of parrots.

¡A escribir!

35. Lo que pasó aquel día Write the *primer borrador* of your letter.

Después de escribir

36. A revisar Before writing the final version of your letter, exchange your first draft with a classmate's and peer edit each other's work, using the following guidelines:

- formation and subject-verb agreement of all tenses
- correct use of the preterit and imperfect tenses
- organization of the sequence of events

EL MUNDO HISPÁNICO Y TÚ

Paraguay

Paraguay tiene dos idiomas importantes: el guaraní y el español. Los paraguayos van generalmente de uno a otro idioma, según el tema de la conversación. ¿Te gustaría aprender una palabra en guaraní? Aquí va: Para decir "vámonos", di "yajhá". Los niños aprenden el guaraní en las escuelas.

Paraguay es un país principalmente agrícola y su economía depende de sus bosques y tierras (*lands*). Sin embargo, desde la construcción de la planta hidroeléctrica de Itaipú, la más grande del mundo, el país ha comenzado a industrializarse y empieza a convertirse en un centro de atracción turística.

Asunción, la capital de Paraguay, es también su principal puerto. Paraguay no tiene salida al mar, pero tiene más de 1800 millas de ríos navegables, que son sus principales vías de transporte. Desde Asunción salen los barcos que, a través del río Paraná, transportan los productos del país hasta el río de la Plata.

En la frontera de Paraguay, Argentina y Brasil están las famosas cataratas de Iguazú, nombre guaraní que significa "agua grande". Estas cataratas son una de las mayores atracciones turísticas.

La danza y la música

Esta muchacha baila la "danza de la botella", un baile típico de Paraguay. Una mujer baila con una, dos o, a veces, más botellas en la cabeza, lo cual requiere increíble habilidad y gracia.

El arpa paraguaya es el instrumento nacional. Es más pequeña que el arpa clásica y tiene 32 cuerdas. Se escuchan en el arpa las melódicas guaranias y las alegres polcas paraguayas.

Bolivia

Bolivia tiene dos capitales: La Paz, situada a 12 000 pies de altura, es la capital administrativa. Sucre es la capital política. Bolivia es tan grande como los estados de California y Texas juntos, pero apenas (*barely*) puede explotar sus riquezas naturales porque no tiene salida al mar y su territorio es muy montañoso. Los indios quechua y aymará, que constituyen más de la mitad de su población, mantienen su cultura y sus lenguas tradicionales. El resto de la población lo constituyen las personas de ascendencia europea y los mestizos.

La Plaza Murillo está en el lugar más céntrico de La Paz y está dedicada a don Pedro Domingo Murillo, patriota y precursor de la lucha por la independencia. En la plaza está el Palacio Presidencial.

Una manada de alpacas pace (*grazes*) en las montañas de Bolivia. La alpaca pertenece a la familia de las llamas. La llama se usa principalmente como animal de transporte, mientras que la lana (*wool*) de la alpaca se utiliza para hacer alfombras y diferentes artículos de ropa.

La música boliviana se toca con instrumentos típicos del altiplano, como la quena, que es una flauta de caña, y el charango, un instrumento de cuerdas hecho con el cuerpo del armadillo.

Ruinas milenarias

Tiahuanaco es un importante sitio arqueológico precolombino situado en el oeste (*west*) de Bolivia. Las ruinas de esta antigua (*ancient*) ciudad están cerca del lago Titicaca, el segundo lago más grande de Suramérica. Las esculturas típicas de Tiahuanaco son como columnas de piedra, con ojos enormes y cuadrados (*square*).

Ahora, dime...

In groups of three, take turns asking and answering the following questions.

1. Se ha dicho que Paraguay es el corazón (*heart*) de Sudamérica. Mira un mapa y di por qué es eso. ¿Qué estado sería el corazón de los Estados Unidos?
2. Piensa en el guaraní. ¿Hay alguna región de este país donde la gente cambie de un idioma a otro normalmente?

iLrn™

To learn more about Paraguay and Bolivia, watch the cultural footage in the Media Library.

AUTOPRUEBA

¿Cuánto sé ahora?

Take this test. When you have finished, check your answers in the answer key provided in Appendix D. Then use a red pen to correct any mistakes you may have made. Are you ready?

A. The future Rewrite the following sentences using the future tense.

1. Le vamos a decir que debe tomar antibióticos.
2. ¿Qué van a hacer Uds. con las recetas?
3. Ellos no van a querer ir al consultorio ahora.
4. Mañana voy a saber el resultado del examen.
5. Ellos no van a venir hoy.
6. Vamos a ir al hospital ahora.
7. ¿Te van a poner la inyección hoy?
8. Nosotros vamos a venir con el médico.
9. Voy a tener que comprar un termómetro.
10. Vamos a salir mañana temprano.
11. Vamos a tomar aspirina para el dolor de garganta.
12. Le van a preguntar si tiene una enfermedad contagiosa.

B. The conditional Rewrite the following sentences, using the conditional tense.

1. Yo voy a Paraguay.
2. Nosotros les recetamos antibióticos.
3. ¿Tú se lo dices?
4. Ellos hablan con Dora.
5. ¿Ud. lo pone en el consultorio?
6. ¿Uds. vienen el domingo?
7. Julio pide miel.
8. Nosotros lo hacemos hoy.
9. Tú no sales con ella.
10. Ella no va sola.
11. Aurora y yo podemos ir a eso de las diez.
12. Me gusta tomar un cafecito bien caliente.

C. The future perfect Complete the following sentences, using the future perfect of the verbs given.

1. Para mañana, el médico me __________ (decir) qué medicina debo tomar.
2. Para las cuatro de la tarde, ellos __________ (volver) del consultorio.
3. Para el domingo, yo ____________ (mejorarse).
4. Para las cinco, nosotras ya _______________ (merendar).
5. ¿Tú me __________ (traer) la silla de ruedas para el mediodía?
6. ¿Ud. se __________ (poner) la inyección antitétanica para el viernes?
7. Para las ocho de la noche, los niños ____________ (cepillarse) los dientes.
8. Para la próxima semana, Elena ____________ (curarse) de la gripe.

D. The conditional perfect Complete the following sentences, using the conditional perfect of the verbs given.

1. Yo ______________ (tomar) aspirinas.
2. Ellos ______________ (venir) a eso de las tres.
3. La enfermera te ______________ (poner) una inyección antitetánica.
4. De haber sabido que estabas enferma, nosotros ______________ (ir) a verte.
5. ¿Qué ______________ (hacer) tú?
6. ¿Ud. le ______________ (preguntar) cuáles eran sus síntomas?
7. ¿Uds. le ______________ (dar) miel de abeja para la tos?
8. Ellos no ______________ (decir) que él era hipocondriaco.

E. Just words . . . Choose the word or phrase in parentheses that best completes each sentence.

1. Ella es alérgica a la (radiografía, penicilina, clase).
2. Comemos con (los oídos, los dientes, el pecho).
3. Hablamos con (la espalda, los dedos, la lengua).
4. Vemos con (los ojos, la boca, las orejas).
5. Caminamos con (las manos, el cuello, los pies).
6. Tuvo un accidente. Lo llevaron al hospital en una (garganta, salud, ambulancia).
7. ¿Te (rompiste, quejaste, evitaste) el brazo alguna vez?
8. Me dolía mucho (la pierna, el pelo, el consultorio).
9. ¿Cuándo fue la última vez que le (cortaron, quebraron, pusieron) una inyección antitetánica?
10. ¿Por qué tomaste aspirina? ¿Tenías (dolor de cabeza, tos, frío)?
11. ¿Tienes Alka Seltzer? Es para (el pecho, el estómago, los dedos de los pies).
12. Va a tener un bebé. Está (cansada, enferma, embarazada).

F. Culture

1. Complete the following, based on the information found in the **¿Lo sabía Ud.?** section.
   a. En los países de habla hispana se mide la temperatura en grados Celsius, también llamados ______________.
   b. En la mayoría de los países de habla hispana, los hospitales son ______________.
2. Answer the following questions, based on the information found in the **El mundo hispánico y tú** section.
   a. ¿Cuál es la mayor planta hidroeléctrica del mundo? ______________
   b. ¿Cuál es el segundo lago más grande de Suramérica? ______________

G. Un dicho Do you remember the Spanish saying that is equivalent to "You are known by the company you keep"? Find it in this lesson.

LECCIÓN 16

LAS ACTIVIDADES AL AIRE LIBRE

Un jugador va a patear (*kick*) la pelota durante un partido de fútbol.

© Rodolfo Buhrer/FotoArena/LatinContent/Getty Images

OBJETIVOS COMUNICATIVOS

You will learn vocabulary related to sports and outdoor activities.

SITUACIONES

¡Que se diviertan!

ESTRUCTURAS

1 The imperfect subjunctive

2 Some uses of the prepositions **a**, **de**, and **en**

3 The present perfect subjunctive

ASÍ SOMOS

¡Vamos a ver!

Watching and understanding situations

¡Vamos a escuchar!

Identifying word boundaries practice I

¡Vamos a conversar!

Transitioning between ideas

Rincón literario

Skimming and predicting

Tres cartas… y un pie by Horacio Quiroga

¡Vamos a escribir!

Exchanging ideas and experiences

EL MUNDO HISPÁNICO Y TÚ…

› Uruguay

› Brasil

AUTOPRUEBA

You will review what you learned in this lesson.

URUGUAY, el país más pequeño de Sudamérica, está situado entre Brasil y Argentina, en la costa oriental *(east)* de este continente. Su nombre oficial es República Oriental del Uruguay.

BRASIL es el país más grande y más rico de Latinoamérica. Limita con todos los países de Sudamérica, excepto Chile y Ecuador. El idioma del país es el portugués, porque Brasil fue colonizado por Portugal.

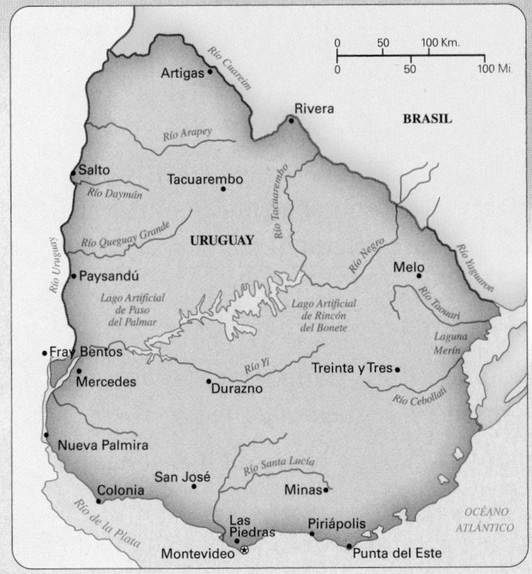

Recursos iLrn video audio web playlist

SITUACIONES

¡Que se diviertan!

CD3-12

© Cengage Learning

¡Ubíquelo!

David lives with his parents in Montevideo, the capital of Uruguay. When you watch the video, you will see the places that David's Uruguayan friends want him to get to know, and the "parrillada" that he gets a sample of.

© Fuse/Getty Images

Marcelo y Julia Estévez y sus hijos, Graciela y Mario, están hablando con David, un chico norteamericano que vive con sus padres en Montevideo. David es alto y atlético.

DAVID: Un día de estos me gustaría ir a acampar y hacer un picnic en la playa. Yo tengo dos tiendas de campaña...

GRACIELA: Me gusta la idea de hacer un picnic y quizás jugar al voleibol... Y, por supuesto, quiero broncearme, pero, ¿acampar...?

MARIO: Podemos hacer surfing. ¡Eso es divertido!

DAVID: ¿Les gustaría ir de pesca?

GRACIELA: ¿Estás loco? ¡Mamá y yo nos aburriríamos como ostras!

JULIA: (*Se ríe.*) David, en nuestra familia no hay nadie que haya ido de pesca ni que haya acampado. ¿Para qué son los hoteles?

MARCELO: Yo fui a pescar una vez... cuando estuve en Argentina. Mi tío me obligó a que fuera. ¡No me gustó nada!

DAVID: Pues cuando yo era chico, mi familia y yo íbamos a Colorado a esquiar en el invierno y en el verano íbamos a acampar. Mi papá y yo armábamos las tiendas de campaña y después íbamos a nadar en un lago o en un río. No había actividad al aire libre que no nos gustara. Tengo muy buenos recuerdos de todo eso...

MARIO: Bueno, pero ahora vas a comportarte como un buen uruguayo.

MARCELO: Sí, el domingo vamos a ir al estadio a ver un partido de fútbol. Ya tenemos las entradas. Juega nuestro equipo favorito, que el año pasado salió campeón. ¡Apuesto a que gana!

MARIO: Después vamos a venir a casa a comer asado y empanadas.[1] Luego te vamos a enseñar a tomar mate.

JULIA: Pero por la mañana vamos a ir a misa. ¡Ah! ¿Te gustaría ir a ver una obra teatral el sábado por la noche?

[1]empanadas = *meat turnovers*

Graciela: ¡Ay, sí! ¡Con un actor español buenísimo! ¡Es divino! ¡Y dicen que es muy amable y no es nada orgulloso…!

Mario: Graciela está un poco enamorada de él…

David: ¡Acepto! Bueno, unos amigos míos me invitaron a que fuera a patinar con ellos el sábado por la tarde. ¿Te gustaría ir con nosotros, Graciela?

Graciela: Sí, a pesar de que la última vez que fui a patinar me caí como diez veces…

David: (*Se ríe.*) Bueno, si tú vas a patinar conmigo… ¡yo voy a aprender a tomar mate!

¿Lo sabía Ud.?

Tomar **mate** es una costumbre típica en Uruguay, Argentina, Paraguay y el sur de Brasil. El mate es una especie de té que se bebe en un recipiente especial con una bombilla (*straw*) que generalmente es de plata. Compartir con alguien el mate es una señal (*sign*) de amistad. En Uruguay se ve gente tomando mate en todas partes y a todas horas.

› **¿Qué bebidas son muy populares en este país?**

1. Hablemos With a partner, take turns asking and answering the following questions. Base your answers on the dialogue and on your own circumstances.

En el diálogo

1. ¿Cómo es David y cuál es su nacionalidad?
2. ¿Qué le gustaría hacer a David un día de estos?
3. ¿Qué dice Graciela que pasaría si fueran de pesca?
4. Según Julia, ¿hay alguien en su familia que haya ido de pesca?
5. ¿Qué hizo Marcelo cuando estuvo en Argentina? ¿Por qué?
6. ¿Qué hacían David y su familia cuando él era chico?
7. ¿Había alguna actividad al aire libre que no les gustara a él y a su familia?
8. Según Mario, ¿cómo se va a comportar David ahora?
9. ¿Adónde van a ir todos el domingo?
10. ¿Qué van a hacer el sábado por la noche?
11. ¿A quién invita David a ir a patinar?
12. ¿Qué le pasó a Graciela la última vez que fue a patinar?

¿Y tú?

1. ¿Cómo eres tú y cuál es tu nacionalidad?
2. ¿Qué te gustaría hacer un día de estos?
3. ¿Qué pasaría si tú fueras de pesca?
4. ¿Has ido de pesca alguna vez?
5. ¿Alguien te obligó a hacer algo? ¿Qué?
6. ¿Qué hacían tú y tu familia cuando tú eras chico(a)?
7. ¿Qué actividades al aire libre prefieres tú?
8. ¿Cómo te comportas cuando vas a la playa en grupo?
9. ¿Adónde vas a ir tú el domingo?
10. ¿Te gustaría ver una obra teatral, una comedia o un drama?
11. ¿Te gustaría ir a patinar o preferirías jugar al fútbol?
12. ¿Cuántos años tenías cuando aprendiste a patinar?

VOCABULARIO

En el diálogo

Cognados

la actividad	*activity*
atlético(a)	*athletic*
divino(a)	*divine*
el estadio	*stadium*
uruguayo(a)	*Uruguayan*
el voleibol	*volleyball*

Nombres

la actividad al aire libre	*outdoor activity*
el asado	*barbecue*
el (la) campeón (campeona)	*champion*
la entrada	*ticket (to an event)*
el fútbol	*soccer*
el lago	*lake*
la misa	*mass (Catholic service)*
la obra teatral	*play*
la ostra	*oyster*
el recuerdo	*memory*
el río	*river*
la tienda de campaña	*tent*

Verbos

aburrirse	*to be bored*
acampar	*to camp*
apostar (o:ue)	*to bet*
armar	*to pitch (a tent)*
broncearse	*to get a tan*
caerse (yo me caigo)	*to fall*
comportarse	*to behave*
enseñar	*to teach*
esquiar	*to ski*
ganar	*to win*
jugar (u:ue)	*to play*
obligar (a)	*to make (someone do something)*
patinar	*to skate*
pescar	*to fish, to catch (a fish)*

Adjetivos

divertido(a)	*fun*
enamorado(a) (de)	*in love (with)*
loco(a)	*crazy*
último(a)	*last*

Otras palabras y expresiones

aburrirse como una ostra	*to be bored to death*
como	*about, like*
hacer (tener) un picnic	*to have a picnic*
ir a acampar	*to go camping*
ir a pescar, ir de pesca	*to go fishing*
la última vez	*the last time*
no es nada orgulloso(a)	*he (she) is not proud at all*
no me gustó nada	*I didn't like it at all*
¡Que se diviertan!	*(May you) have fun!*
un día de estos	*one of these days*
una vez	*once*

¿Lo sabía Ud.?

Aunque el básquetbol, el voleibol, el tenis, el ciclismo y la natación son muy populares en Uruguay, el fútbol es el deporte nacional. Generalmente se juega los domingos, día en que los estadios están llenos de fanáticos de este deporte. Los niños comienzan a jugar al fútbol desde pequeños.

› **En este país, ¿cuáles son los deportes favoritos?**

Más sobre el tema

Deportes y actividades al aire libre (*Sports and outdoor activities*)

Las actividades al aire libre

andar en patineta	*to skateboard*
la cabaña	*cabin*
el campo	*country, countryside*
la canoa	*canoe*
cazar	*to hunt*
escalar	*to climb*
la escopeta	*shotgun*
jugar al golf	*to play golf*
jugar al tenis	*to play tennis*
la nieve	*snow*
el palo de golf	*golf club*
el pino	*pine tree*
la raqueta	*racquet*

¿Lo sabía Ud.?

En Uruguay, en cualquier reunión familiar, están siempre presentes el asado y las empanadas, comidas típicas de los países del Cono Sur (*Southern Cone*). La comida italiana es también muy popular allí.

› **¿Cuáles son las comidas típicas de este país?**

Práctica

2. Para completar Complete the following, using vocabulary from this lesson.

1. ¿Te gustan las actividades al aire _______? ¿Tienes una tienda de _______? ¿Te gusta _______ montañas?
2. ¿Prefieres montar a _______ o montar en _______?
3. ¿Te gusta _______ surfing? ¿Tienes una _______ de mar?
4. Ellos se divirtieron, pero yo me aburrí como una _______.
5. Quiero broncearme; voy a tomar el _______.
6. Voy a _______ al tenis; necesito una _______.
7. Un día de _______ voy a ir de pesca con Uds. Voy a comprar una _______ de pescar.
8. Compré una _______ porque quiero ir a cazar.
9. Tenemos una canoa, pero no sabemos _______.
10. ¿Tú vives en el norte, en el sur, en el este o en el _______ de los Estados Unidos?

3. ¿Cuál no va? Select the word or phrase that does not belong in each group.

1. uruguayo / argentino / enamorado
2. arena / árbol / pino
3. lago / nieve / río
4. palo de golf / raqueta / salvavidas
5. ir a acampar / hacer un picnic / caerse
6. simpático / loco / divertido
7. obligar / armar / acampar
8. No me gustó nada. / Me aburrí. / Me comporté bien.
9. Que lo pasen bien. / Que se diviertan. / Que se vayan.
10. primero / orgulloso / último

4. Preguntas y respuestas Match the questions in column A with the responses in column B.

A		B
1. ¿Qué van a comer?	____	a. Un traje de baño.
2. ¿Uds. ganaron?	____	b. Te apuesto a que van a misa.
3. ¿Qué compraste?	____	c. No, alquilamos una cabaña.
4. ¿Te gusta vivir en la ciudad?	____	d. Sí, son los campeones.
5. ¿Se hospedaron en un hotel?	____	e. No, prefiero patinar.
6. ¿Adónde van los domingos?	____	f. No, no tenemos entradas.
7. ¿Te gusta esquiar?	____	g. Sí, ¡es divino!
8. ¿Ellos ganaron todos los partidos?	____	h. Asado.
9. ¿Es alto, guapo y atlético?	____	i. Yo puedo enseñarte.
10. ¿Van a ir al estadio?	____	j. No, prefiero el campo.
11. Tú sabes que yo no sé jugar al golf, ¿no?	____	k. No, un velero.
12. ¿Tienen un bote?	____	l. No, perdimos.

Para conversar

5. **Una semana inolvidable** With a partner, play the roles of two activity directors for a children's camp. Discuss the activities that you will have for a week and the equipment you will need.

6. **Cada cual con su gusto**[1] With a partner, discuss the outdoor activities that you love (**Me encanta...**) and the ones you don't like at all (**No me gusta nada...**). Give details.

CD3-13

Pronunciación

Pronunciation in context

In this lesson, there are some new words or phrases that may be challenging to pronounce. For further pronunciation practice of Spanish sounds, listen to your instructor and repeat the following sentences.

1. Mamá y yo **nos aburríamos** como **ostras**.
2. No hay nadie que **haya ido** de pesca **ni que haya acampado**.
3. Mi tío **me obligó** a que **fuera**.
4. **Íbamos** a **Colorado** a esquiar en el **invierno**.
5. Mi papá y yo **armábamos** las tiendas de **campaña**.
6. No **había actividad** al **aire libre** que no nos gustara.
7. Ahora vas a **comportarte** como un buen **uruguayo**.
8. La **última vez** que fui a patinar **me caí** como diez veces.

Un dicho

No te ahogues en un vaso de agua.
Equivalent: *Don't make a mountain out of a mole hill.*

[1]To each his own

ESTRUCTURAS

1 The imperfect subjunctive *(El imperfecto de subjuntivo)*

A. Forms

› To form the imperfect subjunctive of all Spanish verbs—regular and irregular—drop the **-ron** ending of the third-person plural of the preterit and add the following endings to the stem.[1]

Imperfect Subjunctive Endings	
-ra *form*	
-ra	-ramos
-ras	-rais
-ra	-ran

LEARNING TIP
Review the forms of the preterit before you attempt to learn the forms of the imperfect subjunctive.

Formation of the Imperfect Subjunctive			
Verb	***Third-person plural preterit***	***Stem***	***First-person singular imperfect subjunctive***
hablar	habla**ron**	habla-	**hablara**
aprender	aprendie**ron**	aprendie-	**aprendiera**
vivir	vivie**ron**	vivie-	**viviera**
dejar	deja**ron**	deja-	**dejara**
ir	fue**ron**	fue-	**fuera**
saber	supie**ron**	supie-	**supiera**
decir	dije**ron**	dije-	**dijera**
poner	pusie**ron**	pusie-	**pusiera**
pedir	pidie**ron**	pidie-	**pidiera**
estar	estuvie**ron**	estuvie-	**estuviera**

¡Atención! The **nosotros** form of the imperfect subjunctive always takes an accent on the vowel that precedes the **-ra** ending: **habláramos**.

LEARNING TIP
Not all learning takes place in class or while you are "studying." To help you assimilate the use of this tense, do the following: Each time someone tells you or asks you to do something, think of what it was. For example: Someone asked you to call him. (**Me pidió que lo llamara.**) Make sure you use correct forms.

[1] A second form of the imperfect subjunctive ends in **-se** rather than **-ra: hablase, hablases, hablase, hablásemos, hablaseis, hablasen**. The two forms are interchangeable, but the -ra form is more commonly used.

Práctica

7. Formas Give the imperfect subjunctive forms of the following verbs.

1. yo: ganar, volver, pedir, decir, recibir
2. tú: ser, dormir, querer, dar, conocer
3. él: ir, estar, poner, conducir, servir
4. nosotros: saber, poder, regresar, conseguir, hacer
5. ellos: tener, recetar, comenzar, seguir, mentir

B. Uses

The imperfect subjunctive is used in a subordinate clause when the verb of the main clause is in the past and calls for the subjunctive.

—¿Qué te dijo René?	*What did René tell you?*
—Me dijo que **leyera** el artículo.	*He told me to read the article.*
—¿Qué le pediste a tu mamá?	*What did you ask your mom?*
—Le pedí que **hiciera** empanadas.	*I asked her to make empanadas.*

When the verb of the main clause is in the present, but the subordinate clause refers to the past, the imperfect subjunctive is used.

—Es una lástima que no **fueras** al teatro ayer.	*It's a pity that you didn't go to the theater yesterday.*
—No me sentía bien.	*I wasn't feeling well.*

Práctica

8. Minidiálogos Complete the following dialogues, using the imperfect subjunctive of the verbs given. Then act them out with a partner.

1. —¿Qué te dijo Cristina?
   —Me dijo que ________ (comprar) las entradas y se las ________ (llevar) a su casa.
2. —¿Qué quería Eduardo?
   —Quería que nosotros lo ________ (llevar) al estadio y que ________ (ir) con él a esquiar.
3. —¿Por qué no te llevaron a escalar la montaña?
   —Porque temían que yo ________ (caerse) y ________ (romperse) una pierna.
4. —Yo quería que tú ________ (poner) la bolsa de dormir en la tienda de campaña.
   —Sí, pero yo no creí que tú la ________ (necesitar) hoy mismo.
5. —Siento que Uds. no ________ (poder) venir a la cabaña ayer.
   —Yo no me sentía bien. Le dije a Jorge que te ________ (llamar) y que te lo ________ (decir).

9. **Mis padres y yo** Describe all the things your parents did and did not want you to do at college, using the cues provided and the imperfect subjunctive.

Mis padres querían que yo...

1. *escribirles* todas las semanas
2. *llamarlos* por teléfono los domingos
3. *tomar* varias clases el primer semestre
4. *estudiar* mucho
5. *abrir* una cuenta corriente en el banco
6. *hacer* la tarea todos los días
7. *levantarme* temprano
8. *visitarlos* en las vacaciones

Mis padres no querían que yo...

9. *vivir* lejos de la universidad
10. *ir* a muchas fiestas
11. *comer* hamburguesas todos los días
12. *gastar* mucho
13. *pedirles* dinero extra todos los meses
14. *conducir* muy rápido
15. *olvidarme* de tomar la medicina
16. *acostarme* muy tarde

Para conversar

10. **Esperanzas y temores** With a partner, talk about what your parents and other people in your life hoped you would do and what they feared you would do.

2 Some uses of the prepositions *a*, *de*, and *en*

(Algunos usos de las preposiciones **a, de** *y* **en***)*

A. a

The preposition **a** (*to, at, in*) expresses direction toward a point in space or a moment in time. It is used for the following purposes.

› to indicate the time (hour) of day

A las cinco salimos para Montevideo.	*At five we leave for Montevideo.*

› after verbs of motion, when followed by an infinitive, a noun, or a pronoun

Siempre venimos **a** caminar aquí.	*We always come to walk here.*

› after the verbs **empezar, comenzar, enseñar,** and **aprender,** when followed by an infinitive

Ellos **empezaron a** esquiar.	*They started skiing.*
Yo puedo **enseñarte a** patinar.	*I can teach you to skate.*

› after the verb **llegar**

¿Cuándo **llegaron a** Río?	*When did they arrive in Río?*

› before a direct object noun that refers to a specific person. It may also be used to personify an animal or a thing.

Yo no conozco a tu padrino.	*I don't know your godfather.*
Bañé a mi perro.	*I bathed my dog.*

¡Atención! If the direct object is not a definite person, the personal **a** is not used.

Busco un buen médico	*I'm looking for a good doctor.*

B. de

The preposition **de** (*of, from, about, with, in*) indicates possession, material, and origin. It is also used in the following ways.

› to refer to a specific period of the day or night when telling time

Ayer buceamos hasta las tres **de** la tarde.	*Yesterday we dove until three in the afternoon.*

› after the superlative to express *in* or *of*

Orlando es el más simpático **de** la familia.	*Orlando is the nicest in the family.*

› to describe personal physical characteristics

Es morena, **de** ojos negros.	*She is brunette, with dark eyes.*

› as a synonym for **sobre** or **acerca de** (*about*)

Hablaban **de** todo menos **de** deportes.	*They were talking about everything except about sports.*

C. en

The preposition **en** (*at, in, on, inside, over*) in general situates someone or something within an area of time or space. It is used for the following purposes.

› to refer to a definite place

Están **en** el campo de golf.	*They are at the golf course.*

› as a synonym for **sobre** (*on*)

Está sentada **en** la silla.	*She is sitting on the chair.*

› to indicate means of transportation

Nunca he viajado **en** avión.	*I have never traveled by plane.*

Práctica

11. Una carta Complete the following letter, adding the missing prepositions.

Querida Alicia:

Como te prometí, te escribo en seguida. Ayer llegamos a Río. Es una ______ las ciudades más hermosas ______ Brasil. Llegamos ______ las tres ______ la tarde y fuimos a buscar hotel.

______ el hotel conocimos ______ unos chicos muy simpáticos que nos invitaron ______ salir con ellos. Yo salí con Carlos, que es alto, moreno, ______ ojos verdes. Me ha dicho que me va ______ enseñar ______ bailar la samba. Espero aprender ______ bailar otros bailes también. Mañana vamos ______ ir ______ visitar el Pan de Azúcar. Vamos ______ ir ______ el coche ______ Carlos. Bueno, ______ la próxima carta espero poder contarte más ______ mi vida ______ esta hermosa ciudad.

Isabel

12. Preposiciones Look at the illustrations and complete the following sentences with logical answers, using an appropriate preposition.

1. Delia va a... ___________

2. Sergio y Toña están... ___________

3. Beatriz es rubia... ___________

4. Teresa se quedó... ___________

5. Rogelio quiere ir al club... ___________

6. Tito salió de su casa... ___________

7. Julio es... grupo. ___________

8. Eva llega... ___________

Para conversar

13. Una cita With a partner, talk about someone you met recently or someone you went out with. Include information about where you went, what time you left and returned home, what the person is like, and what you talked about. Use the appropriate prepositions.

3 The present perfect subjunctive *(El pretérito perfecto de subjuntivo)*

› The present perfect subjunctive is formed with the present subjunctive of the auxiliary verb **haber** + *the past participle* of the main verb.

Present Subjunctive of *haber*	
haya	hayamos
hayas	hayáis
haya	hayan

Formation of the Present Perfect Subjunctive			
yo	**haya cambiado**	nosotros(as)	**hayamos hecho**
tú	**hayas temido**	vosotros(as)	**hayáis puesto**
Ud. / él / ella	**haya salido**	Uds. / ellos / ellas	**hayan visto**

› The present perfect subjunctive is used in the same way as the present perfect tense in English, but only in sentences that require the subjunctive in the subordinate clause. It is used to describe events that have ended prior to the time indicated in the main clause.

—Me alegro de que **hayas venido**.	*I'm glad you have come.*
—Es una lástima que papá no **haya podido** venir conmigo.	*It is a pity that Dad has not been able to come with me.*
—¿Hay alguien aquí que **haya estado** en Punta del Este?	*Is there anyone here who has been in Punta del Este?*
—No, no hay nadie que **haya viajado** a Uruguay.	*No, there's no one who has traveled to Uruguay.*

Práctica

14. Minidiálogos Complete the following dialogues, using the present perfect subjunctive forms of the verbs given. Then act them out with a partner.

1. —¿Dices que no hay nadie que te ________ (ganar) jugando al tenis?
   —No es verdad que yo ________ (decir) eso.
2. —Dudo que Olga ________ (leer) ese artículo.
   —Bueno... si lo ha leído, no creo que lo ________ (entender).
3. —¿Dónde están los chicos?
   —No sé, pero espero que ya ________ (volver) a casa.
4. —Siento que tú no ________ (ir) a esquiar con tus amigos.
   —Y yo me alegro de que tú y yo ________ (poder) conversar un rato.
5. —¿Aquí hay alguien que ________ (hacer) un viaje a Uruguay?
   —No, no hay nadie que ________ (estar) allí.

Para conversar

15. ¡Habla con tu compañero(a)! With a partner, take turns asking and answering the following questions.

1. ¿Tú conoces a alguien que haya escalado el Monte Everest?
2. ¿Es verdad que tú has trabajado de salvavidas?
3. ¿Es verdad que tú y tus amigos han comprado un velero?
4. ¿Tú crees que tus padres te han comprado una tabla de mar recientemente?
5. ¿Es verdad que tú y tu familia han hecho un picnic últimamente?
6. ¿Hay alguien en tu familia que haya escrito un libro sobre deportes?
7. ¿Es verdad que tú y tus amigos han aprendido a tomar mate?
8. ¿Tú conoces a alguien que haya estado en Uruguay?

16. Díganos... With a partner, prepare two questions to ask your classmates about their life experiences and what they have done. Use the present subjunctive and always begin with **"¿Hay alguien aquí que...?"**

Un dicho

El que no haya trabajado, que no coma.
He who hasn't worked, shouldn't eat.

¡Vamos a ver!

Antes de ver el video

17. Preguntas With a partner, take turns asking and answering the following questions.

1. ¿Todavía ves a los amigos que tenías en el jardín de infantes (*kindergarten*)?
2. ¿Qué revista te gusta leer? ¿Comentas a veces los artículos con un(a) amigo(a)?
3. ¿Te gusta ir a acampar con tus amigos o con tu familia? ¿Te gusta ir a pescar? ¿Te gusta hacer un picnic? (¿Dónde?)
4. Cuando tu equipo de fútbol favorito juega, ¿tú prefieres ver el partido en la tele o ir al estadio? ¿Son caras las entradas?
5. ¿Tú preferirías esquiar en Bariloche, escalar montañas en Chile o hacer surfing en Río de Janeiro?
6. La primera vez que fuiste a patinar, ¿te caíste?
7. Si tú fueras a pescar, ¿lo pasarías bien o te aburrirías como una ostra?
8. ¿Has comido empanadas alguna vez? ¿Te gustaría comerlas?
9. ¿Es verdad que tú has tomado mate?
10. ¿Qué harías si te encontraras con tus amigos del jardín de infantes (*kindergarten*)?
11. ¿Qué revista te gusta leer? ¿Lees en tu casa, en el autobús o en el parque?
12. Cuando tus padres no están en su casa, ¿tú tienes la casa a tu disposición? ¿Qué haces cuando estás solo(a)?
13. ¿Prefieres practicar deportes en la playa o en un gimnasio?
14. ¿Alguien te ofreció que fueras parte de un equipo o de un torneo importante?
15. ¿Conoces a alguien que haya tomado mate? ¿Quién era?
16. Si tú fueras a pescar, ¿preferirías hacerlo en un bote o en un muelle (*dock*)?

El video: Ramón no es muy atlético

—El artículo es una charla sobre cómo viven los millonarios, especialmente cuando van de vacaciones... A esquiar a Bariloche, a escalar montañas en Chile, a hacer surfing en Río de Janeiro...
—Yo traté de hacer surfing una vez... ¡Casi me ahogo!

—Aquí hay otro artículo sobre Fernando Peñarreal, el campeón de tenis... ¡Es divino! ¡Y no hay nadie que haya viajado tanto como él... ni ganado tantos partidos!
—Todas las chicas están enamoradas de él. ¡Y dicen que no es nada orgulloso!

Despúes de ver el video

© Cengage Learning

Isabel

© Cengage Learning

Ramón

© Cengage Learning

Estrella

© Cengage Learning

Néstor

18. ¿Quién lo dice? Identify the person who said the following in the dialogue.

1. Yo traté de hacer surfing una vez... ¡Casi me ahogo!
2. ¡Dejen tranquilo al pobre Ramón!
3. ¡Tenemos el televisor a nuestra disposición!
4. Todas las chicas están enamoradas de él.
5. Yo tengo una tienda de campaña, pero es de plástico...
6. El artículo es sobre cómo viven los millonarios, sobre todo cuando se van de vacaciones...
7. ¿Por qué no hacemos un picnic en Pocitos mañana?
8. Y aquella vez que fuimos a patinar, ¡te caíste como diez veces!

19. Hablemos With a partner, take turns asking and answering the following questions. Base your answers on the dialogue.

En el diálogo

1. ¿Desde cuándo se conocen los cuatro amigos?
2. ¿Sobre qué es el artículo que están leyendo las chicas?
3. ¿Qué pasó cuando Ramón trató de hacer surfing?
4. ¿Ramón sabe patinar?
5. ¿Dónde van a ver los chicos el partido de fútbol?
6. ¿Qué les gusta comer a Isabel y a Estrella?
7. ¿Cómo se llama el campeón de tenis?
8. ¿Qué le gusta hacer a Fernando Peñarreal los fines de semana?
9. ¿Les gusta a las chicas la idea de ir a pescar? ¿Por qué?
10. ¿Qué puede enseñarle Néstor a Ramón?

20. ¿Qué pasa después? You and a partner use your imagination to say what the characters do. In Spanish, discuss the following.

1. Whether Isabel talks about the article again and whether she would like to go skiing or surfing.
2. Whether or not Ramón learned how to skate or whether he fell again.
3. Whether or not they watched the soccer game on TV and what they ate.
4. Whether or not they went to Mass on Sunday.
5. Whether or not Peñarol won the game and what the four friends did to celebrate.
6. The girls talk about Fernando Peñarreal again. What do they say about him?
7. They went to Pocitos the next day. Say what they did there and whether they had fun.
8. Whether or not Ramón and Néstor went fishing or camping and what happened.

¡Vamos a escuchar!

ESTRATEGIA **Identifying word boundaries practice I** In **Lección 10** you practiced recognizing units of meaning, that is, detecting where one word ends and the next one begins. Developing this skill takes practice. Remember to be aware of linking—a final vowel or consonant is linked with an initial vowel of the following word—to help you distinguish words and listen for key words and phrases.

CD3-14 **21. Una noticia** Imagine that you work at a radio station. You need to prepare the transcript of what you hear for a press conference. Listen to several sentences that appear transcribed without spacing between words. Mark the divisions between words and punctuate the sentences.

Lanuevacampeonadetenisdeuruguayesmaríaalonsonadiehaganadotantospartidoscom
oellamaríaesunajovenmuyatractivaynoesnadaorgullosaademásdeltenisellapracticaotr
osdeportescomoelesquíacuáticoyelgolf

¡Vamos a conversar!

ESTRATEGIA **Transitioning between ideas** In earlier lessons you practiced listening for Spanish transition words and expressions. Using transition words when speaking helps you sound more fluent. Linking your ideas together creates smoother sentences and avoids a choppy feel in your speech.

22. De una idea a otra In pairs, tell your partner about a sports event you attended, watched on TV, or participated in. Try to use as many of the following words as possible to create smooth transitions in your narrative.

primero	además	pero	
después (luego)	entonces	de modo que	a pesar de
en fin	en cuanto	porque	si

23. ¿Qué dice Ud.? What would you say in the following situations? What might the other person say? Act out the scenes with a partner. Take turns playing each role.

1. On your vacation, you learned how to swim and ride a horse, and you caught a fish. Someone asks whether you had a good time. Say what else you did.
2. A friend invites you to go camping. You don't have a tent or a sleeping bag, and you want to know what else you will need.
3. You are trying to convince a friend to go camping. Tell him or her how much fun it can be and all the things you can do together.
4. You tell a group of people to have a good time. Add that, one of these days, you would like to go camping with them.
5. You ask a friend if he/she would prefer to play volleyball or to play tennis.
6. You tell someone on what occasions you are bored to death.

24. Para conocernos mejor To do this activity, work with a classmate whom you would like to get to know. Take turns asking and answering these questions.

1. ¿Tú eres atlético(a)? Cuando tú eras chico(a), ¿tus padres te obligaban a que practicaras algún deporte? ¿Qué buenos recuerdos tienes de tu niñez? Si alguien te invitara a ir a patinar, ¿aceptarías? ¿Por qué sí o por qué no? Si alguien no sabe patinar, ¿tú puedes enseñarle?
2. ¿Prefieres ir a la montaña o a la playa? Cuando vas a la playa, ¿tomas el sol para broncearte o prefieres nadar todo el tiempo? ¿Te gusta hacer surfing? ¿Has trabajado de salvavidas alguna vez? ¿Te gustaría ir a pasear en velero?
3. ¿Cuál es tu deporte favorito? ¿Has jugado al golf alguna vez? ¿Prefieres el fútbol o el fútbol americano? ¿Qué crees que es más divertido, jugar al tenis o al béisbol? ¿Prefieres patinar o esquiar?
4. Si fueras a pescar, ¿te divertirías o te aburrirías como una ostra? ¿Qué cosas te aburren? ¿Cuál es tu actividad favorita para divertirte?
5. Si tú fueras a acampar, ¿preferirías dormir en una tienda de campaña o al aire libre, en una bolsa de dormir? ¿Preferirías acampar cerca de una montaña o cerca de un lago? ¿Has ido a acampar alguna vez? ¿Te divertiste?

25. Una encuesta Interview your classmates to identify who fits the following descriptions. Include your instructor, but remember to use the **Ud.** form when addressing him/her. After finishing the survey, get together with two or three classmates and discuss the results.

1.	Le gusta tomar el sol en la arena.	________________
2.	Le gusta escalar montañas.	________________
3.	Siempre apuesta a que su equipo favorito va a ganar.	________________
4.	Tiene una tabla de mar.	________________
5.	Practica esquí acuático.	________________
6.	Se cayó la última vez que fue a patinar.	________________
7.	Está enamorado(a) de alguien.	________________
8.	Tiene una escopeta para ir a cazar.	________________

26. Para crear Get together in groups of three or four and "create" the scenario for this photo. Say who these people are, how long they have been on vacation, how they are getting along, what they did already, and what their plans are for the next few days. Indicate whether they are staying at a hotel or whether they have rented cabins.

Rincón literario

Horacio Quiroga

(*Uruguay*: 1878–1937)

Horacio Quiroga, cuentista, dramaturgo y poeta, fue el maestro del cuento latinoamericano. Sus relatos breves, que a menudo retratan la naturaleza como enemiga del ser humano, le valieron ser comparado con Edgar Allan Poe.

Quiroga es conocido por el dramatismo de sus cuentos y por su fino sentido del suspenso. Sus temas preferidos presentan aspectos extraños de la naturaleza, y están llenos de terror, enfermedad y sufrimiento de los seres humanos.

En casi toda su obra vemos la influencia de las tragedias que experimentó en su vida. Sin embargo, en su cuento "Tres cartas... y un pie", que aparece a continuación, Quiroga experimenta con la comunicación epistolar (intercambio de cartas) para dar estructura a este relato (*story*) que, a diferencia de los demás, es humorístico.

Antes de leer

ESTRATEGIAS Before reading the complete story that follows, you will look at different aspects with different goals for each.

1. **Skimming:** The title of this story seems puzzling at first: One wonders: What does a foot have to do with letters? With a partner, skim through as much of the reading as you need to in order to figure out a possible reason for this title.
2. **Predicting:** Skim the first letter from M.R. and briefly discuss with your partner what kind of response you think M.R. will get, how you would respond, and how you think M.R. would respond to you.

¡A leer!

27. Comprensión As you read the complete story, find the answers to the following questions.

1. ¿Por qué quiere M.R. que el autor publique con el nombre de él lo que ella escribió?
2. ¿Cuánto tiempo hace que M.R. hace el mismo recorrido?
3. ¿Cómo se describe M.R.?
4. ¿Qué sabe M.R. desde que un hombre se acerca al coche?
5. Según M.R., ¿qué hacen los hombres antes de subir a un tranvía?
6. ¿Qué hace M.R. cuando un hombre se sienta a su lado?
7. Mientras algunos hombres parecen estar pensando en la luna, ¿qué hacen en realidad?
8. ¿Qué hace M.R. cuando el pie de su vecino está a medio camino del suyo?
9. Cuando los hombres se dan cuenta de su fracaso, ¿qué hacen quince de diecisiete veces?
10. Cuando H.Q. le pregunta si alguna vez le ha sido difícil alejar su pie, ¿qué le contesta ella?

Tres cartas... y un pie (Adaptado)

Señor:

Le envío estas líneas, esperando que tenga la amabilidad de publicarlas con su nombre, pues sé que no las admitirían en un periódico firmadas por mí.

Dos veces por día tomo el tranvía° y hace cinco años que hago el mismo recorrido. Tengo veinte años, soy alta, delgada y no mal parecida°. Creo saber juzgar° a la mayoría de los hombres.

Usted sabe que es costumbre de ustedes, antes de subir al tranvía, echar una ojeada° hacia adentro para estudiar las caras de las mujeres. Después suben y se sientan. Pues bien, desde que el hombre se acerca al coche y mira hacia adentro,° yo sé perfectamente qué clase de hombre es. Sé si es serio, o si quiere aprovechar bien los diez centavos, con una rápida conquista. Sé quiénes quieren ir cómodos, y nada más, y quiénes prefieren la incomodidad al lado de una chica.

Cuando el asiento a mi lado está vacío, sé cuáles son los indiferentes que se sentarán en cualquier lado y cuáles son los que dejarán siete asientos libres para buscar la incomodidad a mi lado. Cuando esto sucede, yo me corro° hacia la ventanilla para dejarle amplio lugar a mi vecino.

¡Amplio lugar! Ésta es una simple expresión, pues si una persona lo observa, nota que el cuerpo del hombre empieza a deslizarse° poco a poco hacia la ventanilla, donde está la chica que él no mira ni parece importarle en lo más mínimo. Así son: podría jurarse° que están pensando en la luna. Entre tanto, el pie derecho (o el izquierdo) continúa deslizándose imperceptiblemente.

Confieso que en estos casos tampoco me aburro. Mi diversión consiste en lo siguiente: desde el momento en que el seductor ha apreciado con perfecta exactitud la distancia a recorrer con el pie, raramente baja los ojos. La gracia para él está en el contacto, no en la visión. Pues bien: cuando él está a medio camino,° yo comienzo la maniobra que él ejecutó, también con aire distraído, solamente que en la dirección inversa. No mucho, diez centímetros son suficientes.

Imagínese la sorpresa de mi vecino cuando al llegar por fin al lugar exactamente localizado, no encuentra nada. Nada; su zapato está perfectamente solo. Es demasiado para él; echa una ojeada al piso primero, y a mi cara después... y se da cuenta.

street car

no... *not bad looking*

judge

echar... *have a quick look*

inside

yo... *I move over*

slide

podría... *one could swear*

a... *half way*

De diecisiete veces, quince, el incómodo señor no insiste más. En los dos casos restantes tengo que recurrir a una mirada de advertencia°. A veces basta con un movimiento de cabeza hacia él, pero sin mirarlo. El encuentro con la mirada de un hombre que podría interesarnos real y profundamente es algo que conviene evitar° en estos casos.

warning
avoid

Su segura servidora,

M.R.

Señorita:

Gracias por su amabilidad. Firmaré con mucho gusto sus impresiones, pero me interesaría, como coautor, saber lo siguiente: Aparte de los diecisiete casos que usted menciona, ¿no ha sentido nunca el menor enternecimiento° por algún vecino? ¿No ha tenido jamás un vago sentimiento° de abandono que le hiciera particularmente difícil alejar su propio pie?

tenderness
feeling

Es lo que desearía saber,

H.Q.

Señor:

Sí, una vez, una sola vez en mi vida, he sentido ese enternecimiento por una persona, o esa falta° de fuerzas en el pie a que usted se refiere. Esa persona era usted. Pero usted no supo aprovecharlo.

lack

M.R.

Después de leer... reflexiones

28. ¿Qué harían? The central topic of this story is flirting and, specifically, playing footsie. In groups of three, talk about what kinds of things you do, in several circumstances, when you spot someone you find attractive.

1. ¿Tratan de atraer su atención? ¿Cómo?
2. ¿Qué dicen para iniciar una conversación con esa persona?
3. ¿Sonríen?
4. Si alguien se les acerca, ¿Uds. son amistosos(as) o se hacen los (las) difíciles (*play hard to get*)?
5. ¿Uds. piensan que van a actuar de la misma forma en el futuro? ¿Por qué sí or por qué no?

¡Vamos a escribir!

Antes de escribir

ESTRATEGIA **Exchanging ideas and experiences** In "Tres cartas... y un pie," Horacio Quiroga writes an epistolary story, that is, an exchange of letters between two people.

You will be inventing two characters who e-mail each other (a la 21st century!) to exchange ideas, observations, and experiences about meeting people they might date or with whom they might develop a serious relationship.

Here are some aspects to consider as you tackle this task.

- Who are the characters? What are they like?
- Where do they meet these people: in church, at school, at work, in a bar, in a chat room?
- What do the cyber friends observe about these people? What experiences do they have? What are their conclusions?
- Do they think that "encounter" might lead to marriage?

29. ¿Habrá romance...? Using your imagination, write two e-mails that a young man and a young woman send each other about their experiences trying to meet Mr. or Miss Right.

- Brainstorm about the guidelines presented above and think about your own experiences or those of people you know.
- Share a couple of those experiences.
- Ask questions about the qualities that you consider important.
- Ask for opinion or advice.
- Offer advice.

¡A escribir!

30. Dos mensajes electrónicos Write the **primer borrador** of your e-mails.

Después de escribir

31. A revisar Before writing the final version of your e-mails, exchange your first draft with a classmate's and peer edit each other's work, using the following guidelines.

- subject-verb agreement and correct formation of tenses
- description of characters
- ideas and opinions of characters
- expectations
- advice offered
- use of guidelines

Something to think about:

Would you include your photograph when writing the e-mail?

Would you request a photo from your cyber friend?

Uruguay

Uruguay está prácticamente rodeado de agua. ¿Cuándo fue la última vez que tú nadaste en el mar y te bronceaste? ¿Cuándo fue la última vez que comiste algo sabrosísimo y después un postre fabuloso? ¡Puedes hacer eso y mucho más en este pequeño país suramericano, bañado por el Atlántico!

La superficie total es casi igual a la del estado de Washington. Sus aguas y su tierra son sus mejores recursos naturales. La mayor parte de la población es de ascendencia europea, especialmente española e italiana.

Ciudades y balnearios

Montevideo es la capital, la ciudad más importante y el puerto principal de Uruguay. Tiene magníficas playas y una arquitectura que combina lo colonial con lo moderno. Se dice que esta ciudad provee la calidad de vida más alta de Latinoamérica.

La playa de Pocitos es la favorita de los jóvenes, quienes practican fútbol, voleibol y deportes acuáticos.

La población de Punta del Este es de unos 12.000 habitantes, pero en el verano, con los turistas, llega a los 500.000. Aquí se lleva a cabo el Festival Internacional de Cine.

La cocina uruguaya y el mate

En Uruguay se come mucha carne de res (*beef*) y, debido a la tradición italiana, también se come pasta y pizza. Los postres son muy variados: algunos son los alfajores (sándwiches de galletitas con dulce de leche),[1] budín inglés, flan y strudel.

El mate es una infusión hecha con hojas secas (*dried leaves*) de yerba mate y agua caliente. Se bebe con una bombilla (*straw*) de metal. Esta bebida es, prácticamente, la bebida nacional del país.

[1]Hecho con leche y azúcar

Brasil

Brasil, colonizado por los portugueses, no es un país de habla hispana, pero está incluido aquí porque es parte de Latinoamérica y… ¡es demasiado grande para que lo ignoremos! Como tú hablas español, podrás entender un poco de portugués, pues estos dos idiomas son similares.

Brasil es famoso por sus hermosas playas, su música y su carnaval. Es un gran productor de café.

© Frontpage/Shutterstock.com

Brasilia, la nueva capital, es una ciudad ultramoderna.

© artincamera/Shutterstock.com

Río de Janeiro, la antigua capital, es famosa por sus hermosas playas, como Ipanema y Copacabana.

© Eduardo Garcia/Taxi/Getty Images

La formación rocosa, el Pan de Azúcar, de granito, tiene 400 metros de alto, y es el símbolo de Río de Janeiro. Es una de las mayores atracciones turísticas de Brasil, y es visitada por miles de personas todos los años.

Ahora, dime…

In groups of three, take turns asking and answering the following questions.

1. Uruguay es el país de habla hispana más pequeño de Sudamérica. ¿Cuál es el estado (la provincia) más pequeño(a) de este país?
2. ¿Crees que en Uruguay hay mucha gente vegetariana? ¿Qué tipo de carne come el estadounidense típico?
3. Los idiomas español y portugués son similares porque vienen del latín. Si tú sabes español, ¿qué otro idioma crees que podrías entender?

iLrn™

To learn more about Uruguay and Brasil, watch the cultural footage in the Media Library.

AUTOPRUEBA

¿Cuánto sé ahora?

Take this test. When you have finished, check your answers in the answer key provided in Appendix D. Then use a red pen to correct any mistakes you may have made. Are you ready?

A. The imperfect subjunctive Rewrite the following sentences, using the new beginnings.

1. Quiero que traigas la escopeta y se la des a Luis. Quería…
2. Espero que jueguen y que no se aburran. Esperaba…
3. ¿Hay alguien aquí que sepa armar la tienda de campaña? ¿Había…
4. Te sugiero que vayas a patinar o a esquiar. Te sugerí…
5. No hay nadie que pueda ir a misa conmigo. No había…
6. Les aconsejo que hagan un picnic y que coman asado. Les aconsejé…
7. Me alegro de que ella gane siempre y de que sea la campeona. Me alegré…
8. No creo que ella esté enamorada. No creí…
9. No es verdad que nosotros te obliguemos a ir al estadio. No era verdad…
10. Yo temo que los chicos se caigan. Yo temía…
11. Mis padres quieren que veamos esa obra teatral. Mis padres querían…
12. Me gusta que ellos vengan a acampar con nosotros. Me gustaría…

B. Some uses of the prepositions *a*, *de*, and *en* Complete the following sentences, using **a**, **de**, or **en** as necessary.

1. Nora y Luisa fueron ________ Brasil ________ junio y ahora solo hablan ________ su viaje. Dicen que cuando llegaron ________ Río conocieron ________ dos chicos muy simpáticos.
2. Ricardo está ________ el estadio desde las tres ________ la tarde. Va ________ volver ________ su casa ________ las cinco.
3. Anoche conocí ________ Teresa. Es una chica morena ________ ojos verdes y es la más simpática ________ su familia.
4. El mes pasado empecé ________ aprender ________ jugar al tenis.
5. A Rita no le gusta viajar ________ avión; prefiere viajar ________ tren.
6. Sergio me va ________ enseñar ________ bailar salsa.
7. Yo compré palos de golf ________ esa tienda.
8. Puse la raqueta ________ la mesa.

C. The present perfect subjunctive Complete these sentences with the present perfect subjunctive form of the verbs given.

1. Es una lástima que ellos no ________ (ir) al estadio hoy.
2. Me alegro de que tú ________ (aprender) a jugar al golf.
3. ¿Hay alguien aquí que ________ (leer) ese artículo?
4. Los padres de Clara esperan que ella no ________ (aburrirse) en la fiesta.
5. No creo que Ud. ________ (saber) armar la tienda de campaña.
6. No es verdad que nosotros nos ________ (divertir) en la fiesta.
7. Aquí no hay nadie que ________ (jugar) con el campeón de tenis.
8. Temo que ellos no ________ (poder) ir al río.

D. Just words... Complete the following, using vocabulary from **Lección 16**.

1. Teresa es ________; es de Montevideo. A ella le gustan las ________ al aire ________, especialmente hacer surfing. Le vamos a regalar una ________ de mar.
2. A mí me gusta montar a ________ y montar en ________. También me gusta ________ montañas.
3. ¿Te gusta el ________ acuático? Yo tengo una canoa. ¿Te gusta ________? ¿Te gusta tomar el ________ y broncearte?
4. ¿Prefieres vivir en el norte, en el ________, en el este o en el ________ de los Estados Unidos?
5. Ellos quieren ir de ________ y quieren que yo vaya con ellos. Yo prefiero no ir, porque la ________ vez que fui a pescar, no me gustó ________. Entonces... ¿________ qué voy a ir...?
6. Fui al cine y me aburrí como una ________. Un día de ________ voy a ir a ver una ________ teatral.
7. ¿Te gusta ________ en patineta? Yo prefiero esquiar o ir a la playa. ¡Ah! Ahora me acuerdo de que necesito un ________ de baño nuevo.
8. ¿Prefieres vivir en la ciudad o en el ________?
9. Marisa Vargas es la nueva ________ de tenis. Ha ________ todos los juegos. Es muy simpática y no es ________ orgullosa.
10. Espero que los chicos hayan ido hoy al ________ a ver el partido de ________, porque hoy ________ su equipo favorito.
11. Espero que haya mucha ________ en la montaña porque queremos ir a esquiar.
12. ¡Te ________ a que mi equipo gana hoy!

E. Culture

1. Complete the following, based on the information found in the **¿Lo sabía Ud.?** section.
   a. El ________ es una especie de té que se bebe en un recipiente especial con una bombilla.
   b. El asado y las ________ son comidas típicas de los países del Cono Sur.
2. Answer the following questions, based on the information found in the **El mundo hispánico y tú** section.
   a. ¿Cuáles son los dos únicos países suramericanos de habla hispana que no lindan (*border*) con Brasil?
   b. ¿Qué ciudad de Uruguay es uno de los centros turísticos más famosos de Latinoamérica?

F. Un dicho Do you remember the Spanish saying that states that people should work for a living? Find it in this lesson.

LECCIÓN 17

EL MUNDO DE LOS NEGOCIOS

Una reunión de negocios

OBJETIVOS COMUNICATIVOS

You will learn vocabulary related to business, job interviews, and job-related technology.

SITUACIONES

¿Asistente… o víctima?

ESTRUCTURAS

1 The pluperfect subjunctive

2 *If* clauses

3 Summary of the uses of the subjunctive

ASÍ SOMOS

¡Vamos a ver!

Watching and understanding situations

¡Vamos a escuchar!

Guessing meaning practice II

¡Vamos a conversar!

Giving a presentation

Rincón literario

Interacting with a reading

El tiempo y el espacio by Julio Camba

¡Vamos a escribir!

Writing to persuade

EL MUNDO HISPÁNICO Y TÚ…

› España

AUTOPRUEBA

You will review what you learned in this lesson.

ESPAÑA forma con Portugal la Península Ibérica, y es el tercer país europeo en cuanto a extensión. Con las islas Baleares en el Mediterráneo, las islas Canarias en el Atlántico, y Ceuta y Melilla en el continente africano, llega a una extensión de 770.750 kilómetros cuadrados. Por su situación entre el resto de Europa y África, siempre ha poseído considerable valor (*value*) estratégico. En su suelo se mezclaron (*mixed*) y fundieron (*melted*) diversos grupos étnicos provenientes (*coming*) de una gran variedad de civilizaciones; entre ellas, las más importantes fueron la romana, la judía y la árabe (*Arabic*).

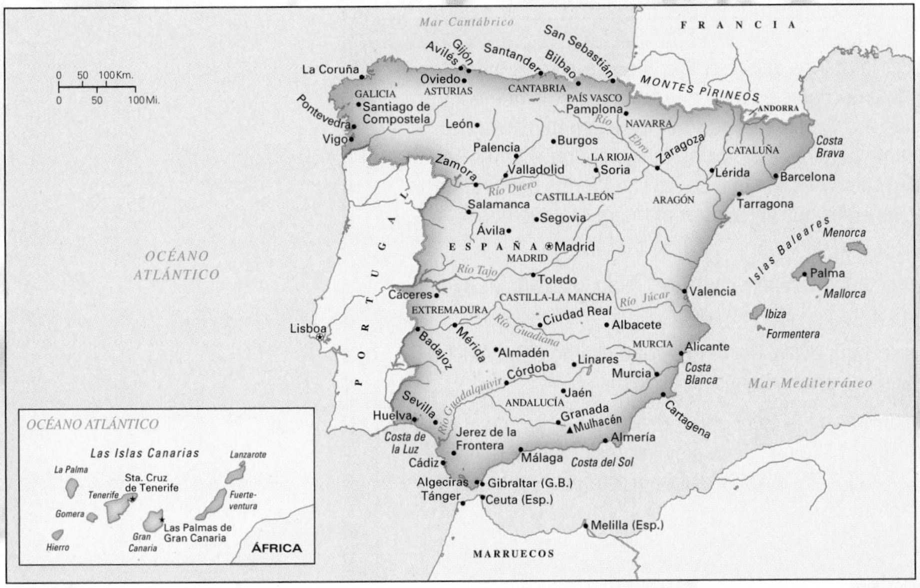

Recursos iLrn video audio web playlist

¿Asistente... o víctima?

CD3-15

¡Ubíquela!

The company for which Mrs. Guerra works is in Madrid, the capital of Spain. As you watch the video, you might imagine yourself enjoying the innumerable attractions that this magnificent city has to offer.

La Sra. Guerra es la jefa de compras de una compañía de importación en Madrid. Ella está encargada de la selección, evaluación y compra de los equipos electrónicos que vende la compañía: computadoras, grabadoras de DVD, fotocopiadoras, sistemas de comunicación telefónica, etcétera. La Sra. Guerra es contadora pública, especializada en mercadeo. Es inteligente, tiene mucha experiencia y es extremadamente eficiente, pero... tiene fama de ser una tirana. En este momento Magda, su asistente, está leyendo un correo electrónico de la Sra. Guerra.

Send Mail: Message Composition

A: Magda

De: A. Guerra

Asunto: Instrucciones

Magda: Necesito que traduzcas las cartas que te di ayer y que escuches todos los mensajes que están en mi máquina contestadora y que me digas solamente los que sean importantes. Después, archiva las carpetas que están en mi escritorio y lee la correspondencia. Durante la hora de almorzar, te sugiero que comas un bocadillo en la oficina. Lee el resumé de cada uno de los candidatos para el puesto de traductor e intérprete que tenemos que entrevistar mañana. (Te dije que la entrevista era mañana, ¿no?)

Yo sé que tenemos cuarenta candidatos, pero, si hubieras leído los resumés ayer, cuando te pedí que los leyeras...

Te pedí que entrenaras a la secretaria del Sr. Roca. Yo sé que ella no tiene mucha experiencia, sobre todo en el uso de procesadores de textos.

¡Ah! ¿Les escribiste a los accionistas de la compañía? ¿Leíste las cartas de recomendación sobre los candidatos? Yo no quedé muy impresionada con algunas de ellas. Mándale un fax al Sr. Varela y después llámalo por teléfono y dile que venga a verme mañana mismo.

Magda, que está frustrada, le manda un mensaje muy breve a su jefa.

Send Mail: Message Composition

A: Sra. A. Guerra

De: Magda

Asunto: Instrucciones

¿Cuándo voy a hacer todo eso? ¡El sueldo que yo gano no compensa todo el trabajo que hago!

Mensaje electrónico no tan breve, de A. Guerra:

Send Mail: Message Composition

A: Magda

De: A. Guerra

Asunto: Tus responsabilidades

Magda: Si tú no puedes desempeñar tu trabajo y aceptar tus responsabilidades, yo puedo hablar con el jefe de personal y con el presidente de la compañía y decirles que no te den el aumento que pediste. ¡No te olvides de que tú trabajas bajo mi supervisión! ¡Yo tengo la última palabra!

Último correo electrónico de Magda, que ahora está realmente furiosa:

Send Mail: Message Composition

A: A. Guerra

De: Magda

Asunto: Últimas palabras

Creo que la última palabra es mía: ¡Renuncio!

1. Hablemos With a partner, take turns asking and answering the following questions. Base your answers on the dialogue and on your own circumstances.

En el diálogo

1. ¿Qué puesto tiene la Sra. Guerra?
2. ¿De qué está encargada ella?
3. ¿Qué fama tiene la Sra. Guerra?
4. De los mensajes en su máquina contestadora, ¿cuáles quiere ella?
5. ¿Qué le sugiere a Magda que haga durante la hora del almuerzo?
6. ¿Qué tuvo que hacer Magda con respecto a la secretaria del Sr. Roca?
7. ¿Qué quiere la Sra. Guerra que Magda le diga al Sr. Varela?
8. ¿Con quiénes dice la Sra. Guerra que ella puede hablar?
9. ¿De qué no debe olvidarse Magda?
10. ¿Qué decisión ha tomado Magda?

¿Y tú?

1. ¿Qué puesto tienes tú? Cuando tu familia da una fiesta, ¿de qué estás encargado(a) tú?
2. ¿Eres famoso(a) o conocido(a) por algo en especial?
3. ¿Cuántos mensajes por día tienes en tu máquina contestadora?
4. ¿Tú trabajas a veces durante la hora del almuerzo? ¿Qué haces?
5. ¿Tú has tenido que entrenar a alguien alguna vez? ¿En qué?
6. ¿Tú piensas terminar esta lección mañana mismo?
7. ¿Con qué personas de tu trabajo o de tu clase puedes hablar tú?
8. ¿Adónde vas a ir tú el domingo?
9. ¿De qué no debes olvidarte tú?
10. ¿Te es fácil o difícil tomar decisiones?

VOCABULARIO

En el diálogo

Cognados

el (la) asistente	*assistant*
el (la) candidato(a)	*candidate*
la compañía	*company*
la comunicación	*communication*
la correspondencia	*correspondence*
eficiente	*efficient*
especializado(a)	*specialized*
la evaluación	*evaluation*
extremadamente	*extremely*
el fax (facsímile)	*fax*
la importación	*import*
impresionado(a)	*impressed*
el (la) intérprete	*interpreter*
el personal	*personnel*
el (la) presidente(a)	*president*
la recomendación	*recommendation*
la responsabilidad	*responsibility*
el resumé, el currículum vitae	*résumé, curriculum vitae*
la selección	*selection*
la supervisión	*supervision*
el (la) supervisor(a)	*supervisor*
el (la) tirano(a)	*tyrant*
el uso	*use*
la víctima[1]	*victim*

Nombres

el (la) accionista	*shareholder*
el aumento	*increase*
el bocadillo	*sandwich (Spain)*
la carpeta	*folder*
la carta	*letter*
la compra	*purchase*
el (la) contador(a) público(a)	*certified public accountant*
la entrevista	*interview*
el equipo electrónico	*electronic equipment*
la fama	*reputation, fame*
la fotocopiadora	*photocopy machine*
el (la) jefe(a)	*boss, chief*
—de compras	*purchasing manager*
la máquina contestadora	*answering machine*
el mercadeo	*marketing*
la palabra	*word*
el procesador de textos	*word processor*
el puesto	*position, job*
el sistema de comunicación telefónica	*telephone system*
el sueldo, el salario	*salary*
el (la) traductor(a)	*translator*
la grabadora de DVD	*DVD recorder*

Verbos

archivar	*to file*
compensar	*to compensate*
desempeñar	*to perform (a job)*
entrenar	*to train*
entrevistar	*to interview*
renunciar	*to resign*

Adjetivo

encargado(a)	*in charge*

Otras palabras y expresiones

bajo	*under*
cada	*each*
la hora de almorzar	*lunch time*
mañana mismo	*tomorrow and not a day later*
quedar impresionado(a)	*to be impressed*

[1]The word **víctima** is always feminine.

Más sobre el tema

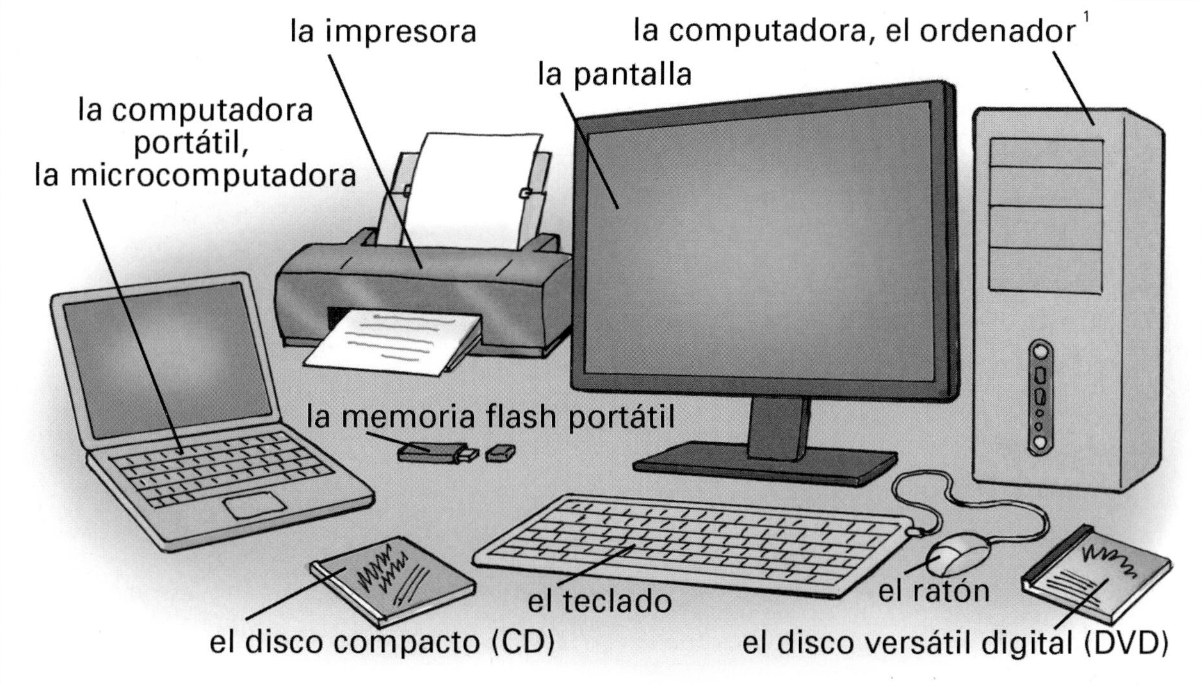

El mundo de los negocios

el (la) administrador(a)	*administrator*
el (la) agente de bienes raíces	*real estate agent*
el (la) agente de relaciones públicas	*public relations agent*
el (la) agente de seguros	*insurance agent*
el (la) bolsista	*stockbroker*
el (la) comprador(a)	*buyer*
el despacho, la oficina	*office*
el (la) empleado(a) bancario(a)	*bank employee*
el (la) gerente	*manager*

¿Lo sabía Ud.?

En los países de habla hispana, generalmente las transacciones comerciales son menos formales que en los Estados Unidos y tienen un toque (*touch*) más personal. Nuestro "*businesslike approach*" puede parecerles brusco a las personas del mundo hispano.

› **Las transacciones comerciales entre este país y los países de habla hispana, ¿son más o menos frecuentes hoy en día? ¿Puedes dar ejemplos?**

[1] Used in Spain

Práctica

2. ¿Qué es? Write the words or phrases that correspond to the following.

1. computadora ____________
2. computadora portátil ____________
3. opuesto de **vendedor** ____________
4. oficina ____________
5. persona que trabaja en un banco ____________
6. todas las cartas ____________
7. opuesto de **exportación** ____________
8. currículum vitae ____________
9. sándwich ____________
10. reputación ____________
11. máquina de hacer fotocopias ____________
12. sueldo ____________

3. Para completar Complete the following sentences, using vocabulary from this lesson.

1. Ella no va a ________ muy impresionada con las ________ de recomendación, incluyendo la del Sr. Peña, que es uno de los ________ de la compañía.
2. Teresa es agente de ________ raíces y su esposo es agente de ________ públicas.
3. Fernando es ________ e intérprete y es ________ público, ________ en mercadeo.
4. Vamos a ________ a todos los candidatos. La entrevista es mañana ________.
5. Ella está encargada de la selección, ________ y compra de los ________ electrónicos que vende la compañía.
6. Tengo que ________ estas carpetas, llamar al ________ de compras y dejarle un mensaje en su máquina ________.
7. Necesitamos un sistema de comunicación ________.
8. Yo no tengo experiencia en ese trabajo; me tienen que ________.

4. Preguntas y respuestas Match the questions in column A with the responses in column B.

A		B
1. ¿Qué vas a hacer?	______	a. El de gerente.
2. ¿El Sr. Paz va a decidir?	______	b. ¡Sí! ¡Sus empleados son sus víctimas!
3. ¿Qué puesto desempeña?	______	c. No, es la hora de almorzar.
4. ¿Es agente de seguros?	______	d. No, voy a renunciar.
5. ¿No vas a trabajar?	______	e. Una grabadora de DVD.
6. ¿Le ofrecieron el puesto?	______	f. Sí, él tiene la última palabra.
7. ¿Es verdad que él es un tirano?	______	g. Sí, pero no sé usarlo.
8. ¿Qué compraste para la sala de estar?	______	h. Sí, trabaja para Allstate.
9. ¿Tienes un procesador de textos?	______	i. Voy a solicitar el puesto.
10. ¿No vas a seguir trabajando aquí?	______	j. Sí, pero él no lo aceptó.
11. ¿Pidió un aumento de sueldo?	______	k. Su asistente.
12. ¿Quién va a ayudar al jefe de personal?	______	l. Sí, pero no se lo dieron.

Para conversar

5. **Una entrevista** With a partner, play the roles of two friends who are helping a third friend to get ready for an interview with a big company. Ask him/her what type of company it is, details about his/her résumé, and tell him/her how he/she should dress.

6. **Un aumento de sueldo** With a partner, play the roles of an employee who wants a raise and a boss who doesn't think he/she deserves it. The employee should emphasize what he/she does for the company.

7. **Sueldos...** With a partner, talk about the different kinds of jobs a person may have, and try to figure out what yearly salary they might earn. Give reasons why. Decide which profession would be the best.

CD3-16

Pronunciación

Pronunciation in context

In this lesson, there are some new words or phrases that may be challenging to pronounce. For further pronunciation practice of Spanish sounds, listen to your instructor and repeat the following sentences.

1. Es jefa de **compras** de una **compañía** de **exportación** de Madrid.
2. Está **encargada** de la selección, evaluación y compra de los **equipos electrónicos**.
3. La Sra. Guerra es **contadora pública**, especializada en **mercadeo**.
4. Necesito que **traduzcas** las cartas que te di ayer.
5. Durante la hora de almorzar, te sugiero que comas **un bocadillo** en la oficina.
6. Ella no tiene mucha **experiencia**, sobre todo en el uso de **procesadores de textos**.
7. ¿Les escribiste a **los accionistas** de la compañía?
8. Creo que la última palabra es mía: ¡**Renuncio!**

ESTRUCTURAS

1 The pluperfect subjunctive (*El pluscuamperfecto de subjuntivo*)

› The pluperfect subjunctive is formed with the imperfect subjunctive of the auxiliary verb **haber** + *the past participle* of the main verb. It is used in the same way that the past perfect is used in English, but only in sentences in which the main clause calls for the subjunctive.

Imperfect Subjunctive of *haber*	
hubiera	hubiéramos
hubieras	hubierais
hubiera	hubieran

Formation of the Pluperfect Subjunctive	
yo	**hubiera hablado**
tú	**hubieras comido**
Ud. / él / ella	**hubiera vivido**
nosotros(as)	**hubiéramos visto**
vosotros(as)	**hubierais hecho**
Uds. / ellos / ellas	**hubieran vuelto**

—Yo me alegré de que ellos le **hubieran dado** el puesto.
—Sí, porque ella tenía mucha experiencia.

I was glad that they had given her the job.
Yes, because she had a lot of experience.

—¿No había nadie que **hubiera visto** al jefe de personal?
—Sí, Eva ya lo había visto.

Wasn't there anybody who had seen the personnel director?
Yes, Eva had already seen him.

¡Atención! The pluperfect subjunctive of **hay** (impersonal form of **haber**) is **hubiera habido.**
Yo te dije que no era verdad que **hubiera habido** una reunión en mi despacho.

Práctica

8. La Sra. Díaz Indicate what Mrs. Díaz, the supervisor, had expected everyone in the office to do by the time she got back from a business trip.

Modelo su secretaria / archivar la correspondencia

Ella esperaba que su secretaria hubiera archivado la correspondencia.

1. yo / leer los currículums de los candidatos
2. Álvaro y yo / hacer la evaluación de la nueva empleada
3. tú / ir al despacho del Sr. Gómez
4. su asistente / devolver la microcomputadora nueva
5. Víctor y Omar / escribir las cartas de recomendación
6. la Sra. López / limpiar su oficina

9. Reacciones With a partner, take turns deciding how Mrs. Díaz reacted (**se alegró, lamentó, sintió**) to what happened during her absence. Use the pluperfect subjunctive.

Modelo El presidente de la compañía le había dado un aumento de sueldo.

Ella se alegró de que el presidente le hubiera dado un aumento de sueldo.

1. Su asistente había terminado todo el trabajo.
2. El jefe de compras se había enfermado.
3. Yo había hecho la selección de los equipos electrónicos.
4. Los traductores habían traducido todos los documentos.
5. Tú no habías entrevistado a los candidatos.
6. Su secretaria había renunciado.

Para conversar

10. El año pasado... In groups of three, talk about the things that you hoped (**esperaba**) would happen, the things that you feared (**temía**) would happen, and the things that you were glad (**me alegré**) happened last year.

Modelo *Yo me alegré de que mis padres me hubieran comprado una computadora.*

2 *If* clauses (*Cláusulas con* si)

› In Spanish, the imperfect subjunctive is used in *if* clauses when a contrary-to-fact statement is made.

—Si **tuviera** dinero, **compraría** una grabadora de DVD.	*If I had money, I would buy a DVD recorder.*
—Usa tu tarjeta de crédito.	*Use your credit card.*

LEARNING TIP
Think of several ways in which you might finish these questions: **¿Qué haría yo si (no)...?** and **¿Qué habría hecho yo si (no)...?**

› Note that the imperfect subjunctive is used in the *if* clause and the conditional is used in the main clause. When a statement expresses a contrary-to-fact situation in the past, the pluperfect subjunctive is used in the *if* clause and the conditional perfect is used in the main clause.

—No pude comprar la impresora.	*I wasn't able to buy the printer.*
—Si **hubieras ahorrado** dinero, **habrías podido** comprarla.	*If you had saved money, you would have been able to buy it.*

› The imperfect subjunctive is also used in *if* clauses that express an unlikely fact, or simply the Spanish equivalent of the English *if . . . were to. . . .*

—Si me **ofrecieran** el puesto, lo aceptaría.	*If they were to offer me the job, I would accept it.*
—No creo que te lo ofrezcan.	*I don't think they will offer it to you.*

› The imperfect subjunctive is also used after the expression **como si** (*as if*).

—Pepe se compró otra computadora.	*Pepe bought himself another computer.*
—Ese hombre gasta dinero **como si fuera** millonario.	*That man spends money as if he were a millionaire.*

› When an *if* clause refers to something that is possible or likely to happen, the indicative is used.

—¿Me vas a comprar la fotocopiadora?	*Are you going to buy me the photocopy machine?*
—Si **tengo** dinero, te la compro.	*If I have money, I'll buy it for you.*

¡Atención! The present subjunctive is *never* used in an *if* clause.

Práctica

11. En estos casos... Complete the following sentences, using the imperfect subjunctive, the pluperfect subjunctive, or the present indicative, as appropriate.

1. Si yo ____________ (hablar) con el agente de bienes raíces antes, habría podido vender mi casa.
2. Si tú ____________ (estudiar) inglés, podrás trabajar de intérprete.
3. Si nosotros ____________ (encontrar) un comprador, podríamos vender el coche mañana mismo.
4. Si el presidente de la compañía ____________ (leer) tu resumé, habría quedado muy impresionado.
5. Olga habla como si ____________ (saber) mucho de mercadeo.
6. Si nosotros ____________ (saber) lo que había pasado, te habríamos avisado.
7. Si ellos ____________ (tener) la entrevista hoy, podremos ir.
8. Si tú ____________ (querer), podrías ayudarme con mi informe.
9. Si todos los accionistas ____________ (venir) mañana, podemos tener la reunión.
10. Si Pablo ____________ (tener) experiencia, podría conseguir un puesto en el departamento de compras.
11. Esa mujer tiene cincuenta años, pero actúa como si ____________ (ser) muy joven.
12. Si nosotros ____________ (conseguir) bastante dinero, podemos mejorar el sistema de comunicación telefónica.

12. **Según la situación** Say what the following people are going to do, would do, or would have done according to each situation.

Modelo María quiere comprar una computadora, pero no tiene dinero.

Si María tuviera dinero, compraría una computadora.

1. Yo no trabajé mucho el año pasado y no me dieron un aumento de sueldo.
2. Teresa quiere hablar con el administrador, pero no tiene tiempo.
3. Nosotros queremos comprar un procesador de textos nuevo. Es posible que tengamos suficiente dinero.
4. Juan quiere que yo le dé la dirección del agente de seguros, pero yo no la sé.
5. Mi madre quería que yo fuera contador público, pero no me gustaban las matemáticas.
6. Tú quieres estudiar para programador(a), pero no tienes computadora. Es posible que tus padres te regalen una.
7. Yo habría llevado a Marta a hablar con el gerente, pero tuve que trabajar.
8. Nosotros habríamos hablado con el bolsista, pero él no estaba en su despacho hoy.

Para conversar

13. **Si...** With a partner, take turns asking each other what you would do or what would happen if the following were true.

Modelo tener mucho dinero

—¿Qué harías tú si tuvieras mucho dinero?

—Si yo tuviera mucho dinero, viajaría mucho.

1. no ganar un buen sueldo
2. necesitar una microcomputadora
3. ser la hora de almorzar
4. tener que trabajar los domingos
5. no sentirse bien
6. tener que entrenar a alguien
7. quedar suspendido(a) en un examen
8. querer comprar libros en español
9. tener un examen
10. no poder viajar en avión

¿Lo sabía Ud.?

En los países hispanos, las mujeres trabajan cada vez más fuera de su hogar (*home*), y tienen carreras y puestos importantes en el mundo de los negocios.

› **¿Qué problemas tienen en este país las mujeres que trabajan fuera de su hogar, y son esposas y madres?**

3 Summary of the uses of the subjunctive (*Resumen de los usos del subjuntivo*)

Use the subjunctive . . .	Use the infinitive . . .
a. after verbs of volition (when there is change of subject). **Yo** quiero que **él salga**.	**a.** after verbs of volition (when there is no change of subject). **Yo** quiero **salir**.
b. after verbs of emotion (when there is change of subject). **Me alegro** de que **tú estés** aquí.	**b.** after verbs of emotion (when there is no change of subject). **Me alegro** de **estar** aquí.
Use the subjunctive . . .	**Use the indicative . . .**
a. to express doubt, denial, and disbelief. **Dudo** que **pueda** venir. **Niego** que él **esté** aquí. **No creo** que él **vaya** con Eva.	**a.** when there is no doubt, denial, or disbelief. **No dudo** que **puede** venir. **No niego** que él **está** aquí. **Creo** que él **va** con Eva.
b. to refer to the indefinite or nonexistent. **Busco** una casa que **sea** cómoda. No **había nadie** que lo **supiera**.	**b.** to refer to something specific. **Tengo** una casa que **es** cómoda. **Había alguien** que lo **sabía**.
c. with certain conjunctions when referring to a future action.[1] Lo **llamaré** cuando **llegue**.	**c.** with certain conjunctions when there is no indication of future action. Lo **llamo** cuando **llego**.
d. in an *if* clause to refer to something contrary-to-fact or to something impossible or very improbable. Si **pudiera**, iría. Si el presidente me **invitara** a la Casa Blanca, yo aceptaría.	**d.** in an *if* clause when not referring to anything that is contrary-to-fact, impossible, or very improbable. Si **puedo**, iré. Si Juan me **invita** a su casa, aceptaré.

Un dicho

Si el sabio no aprueba, malo; si el necio aplaude… peor.
(*If the wise man does not approve, that's bad; if the stupid man applauds . . . that's worse.*)

[1]The subjunctive is always used after the conjunctions **con tal que, sin que, en caso de que, a menos que, para que,** and **antes de que**, which by their very meaning imply uncertainty or condition: **Puedo salir *sin que* los chicos me *vean, a menos que estén* en la sala.**

Subjunctive or Infinitive . . . ? / Subjunctive or Indicative . . . ?

Práctica

14. Minidiálogos Complete the following dialogues using the subjunctive, indicative, or infinitive of the verbs given. Then act them out with a partner.

1. —¿Qué vas a hacer cuando _________ (llegar) a la oficina?
   —Yo quiero _________ (archivar) las carpetas, pero mi jefe quiere que _________ (trabajar) con el agente de relaciones públicas.
2. —No creo que _________ (valer) la pena continuar usando ese equipo.
   —Es verdad, pero dudo que nosotros _________ (poder) comprar uno nuevo.
3. —Yo espero _________ (poder) hablar con mi antiguo (*former*) jefe hoy.
   —No creo que _________ (estar) en su oficina. Mándale un correo electrónico.
4. —¿Tú conoces a alguien que _________ (estar) especializado en mercadeo?
   —Sí, conozco a un hombre que _________ (trabajar) en la compañía Mirabal. Si tú _________ (querer), podemos ir a verlo mañana.
   —Si _________ (poder), iría, pero tengo que trabajar.
5. —Yo llamé al electricista para que _________ (venir) a arreglar las luces de la oficina.
   —Cuando él _________ (venir), quiero hablar con él.

15. Los negocios With a partner, take turns completing the following.

1. La supervisora quiere que su asistente...
2. El jefe de personal les ha pedido a los candidatos...
3. Los accionistas habrían comprado más acciones...
4. Yo temía que el sueldo...
5. Cora va a llamar al traductor para que él...
6. Yo espero que el agente de bienes raíces...
7. El jefe de compras no conocía a nadie que...
8. Ojalá que el presidente de la compañía...
9. Nosotros no creíamos que la nueva secretaria...
10. Yo buscaba una asistente que...

Esperamos que nuestro agente de bienes raíces nos ayude a vender nuestra casa.

Para conversar

16. ¡Habla con tu compañero(a)! With a partner, take turns asking each other the following questions. Answer the questions in complete sentences.

1. ¿A quién llamarías si tu computadora no funcionara?
2. Tengo que arreglar mi computadora, ¿adónde me recomiendas que la lleve?
3. Si vas a comprar una computadora, ¿qué marca prefieres comprar?
4. ¿Es cierto que siempre tienes tu teléfono celular contigo?
5. ¿Crees que es una buena idea tener una microcomputadora?
6. ¿Qué esperas que tus padres te regalen para tu cumpleaños?
7. ¿Tú podrías comprar una casa sin que tus padres te ayudaran?
8. ¿Es verdad que gastas dinero como si fueras millonario(a)?
9. ¿Siempre tratas de llegar a la clase antes de que llegue el profesor?
10. ¿Qué vas a hacer hoy tan pronto como llegues a tu casa?

17. Responde... With a partner, take turns reacting to the following statements. Use the subjunctive.

Modelo —*Un traductor habla solo un idioma.*
—*No es verdad que un traductor hable solo un idioma.*

1. El gerente tiene dieciocho años.
2. Busco a alguien que hable japonés y chino.
3. El sueldo que ganan los maestros compensa su trabajo.
4. Me dieron un aumento de sueldo.
5. No sé qué quiere el jefe que hagan los empleados.
6. Las secretarias escriben a máquina; no usan computadoras.
7. Ella habla inglés y él habla ruso. No necesitan un intérprete.
8. Le encanta su trabajo; piensa renunciar.
9. El jefe de personal es muy comprensivo. Es un tirano.
10. Busco un esposo (una esposa) que tenga mucho dinero.

¿Lo sabía Ud.?

El uso de "Internet" o la "Red", como se llama en español, es hoy muy popular en el mundo hispano, y la mayoría de las instituciones (empresas y organizaciones) tienen su propia página (*home page*).

› **En general, ¿cuáles son algunas de las transacciones comerciales que se pueden hacer a través de Internet?**

¡Vamos a ver!

Antes de ver el video

18. Preguntas You and a partner take turns asking and answering the following questions.

1. Si te entrevistaran para el puesto de asistente del supervisor del departamento de compras, ¿crees que te lo darían?
2. ¿Te gustaría ser contador(a) público(a) especializado(a) en mercadeo o preferirías ser traductor(a)? ¿Por qué o por qué no?
3. ¿Tú tienes conocimiento de ordenadores? ¿Sabes escribir a máquina? ¿Sabes usar un procesador de textos?
4. ¿Tú tienes experiencia en el mundo de los negocios?
5. ¿Qué equipos electrónicos puedes nombrar (*name*)?
6. La última vez que pediste un aumento de sueldo, ¿te lo dieron?
7. Si tú trabajas, ¿compensa el sueldo que te pagan todo el trabajo que tú haces?
8. Si alguien leyera tu currículum vitae y una carta de recomendación sobre ti, ¿quedaría impresionado?
9. ¿Te gustaría ser uno(a) de los (las) principales accionistas de una compañía multinacional?
10. Si yo te llamo y tú no estás en casa, ¿puedo dejarte un mensaje en la máquina contestadora?
11. ¿Preferirías ser empleado(a), bancario(a) o agente de relaciones públicas?
12. En tu familia, ¿quién tiene la última palabra?

El video: Dos entrevistas

—Si le ofreciéramos el puesto, ¿cuándo podría empezar a trabajar?

—La semana próxima.

—Perfecto. Si hoy termino las entrevistas, espero poder avisarle sobre mi decisión mañana mismo.

—¿Le va a dar el puesto al Sr. Menéndez? Leí su resumé y las cartas de recomendación de sus antiguos jefes. ¡Quedé muy impresionada!

—¡Yo también! Voy a hablar con el Sr. Valdivia, que es el que tiene la última palabra. Si él está de acuerdo conmigo, le ofrecemos el puesto.

Después de ver el video

© Cengage Learning
Pablo

© Cengage Learning
Elena

© Cengage Learning
Sra. Vigo

© Cengage Learning
Luis

19. ¿Quién lo dice? Identify the person who said the following in the dialogues.

1. ¡Mucha responsabilidad para un hombre tan joven como usted!
2. Si me hubieran dado el aumento, habría continuado trabajando allí.
3. Parece muy inteligente y encantador.
4. Si él está de acuerdo conmigo, le ofrecemos el puesto.
5. Además de mi trabajo, servía de traductor de toda la correspondencia en inglés.
6. A veces voy a visitar a mi tío, el señor José Ariet.
7. ¿Le va a dar el puesto al Sr. Menéndez?
8. Sé escribir a máquina... con dos dedos...

20. Hablemos With a partner, take turns asking and answering the following questions. Base your answers on the dialogue.

En el diálogo

1. ¿Qué puesto tiene la Sra. Vigo?
2. ¿De qué quiere la Sra. Vigo que le hable Luis?
3. ¿De qué estaba encargado Luis en la compañía Telelux?
4. ¿Por qué dejó Luis el puesto?
5. ¿Qué habría hecho Luis si le hubieran dado el aumento?
6. ¿Qué título tiene Pablo Casas?
7. ¿Qué sabe hacer Pablo?
8. ¿Dónde puede dejarle la Sra. Vigo un mensaje a Pablo?
9. ¿Con qué quedó muy impresionada Elena?
10. ¿Qué puesto le van a ofrecer a Pablo?

21. ¿Qué pasa después? You and a partner use your imagination to say what the characters do. In Spanish, discuss the following.

1. Whether or not the Telelux Company called Luis to offer him a salary increase.
2. Whether Mr. Valdivia does have the last word or whether Mrs. Vigo can make the decision.
3. Whether or not Luis will serve as a translator and interpreter for the company.
4. How many employees will be working under Luis's supervision.
5. Whether Pablo calls his uncle to tell him about the interview and what he wants his uncle to do.
6. Whether Mrs. Vigo calls Pablo and leaves a message on his answering machine or whether she sends him an e-mail.
7. Whether Pablo Casas accepts the job that Mrs. Vigo offers him.
8. Whether Pablo goes back to college to study marketing.

¡Vamos a escuchar!

CD3-17

ESTRATEGIA **Guessing meaning practice II** When listening, keep in mind the topic to help orient you to the nature of unfamiliar words. Also remember to use cognates, word families, the words you know, and the surrounding ideas to make informed guesses about unfamiliar words.

22. Avisos de empleo You will listen to three announcements about job openings. Listen for context and guess the meaning of the following words or phrases.

Aviso 1: 1. estar dispuesto 2. dominar
Aviso 2: 1. ambos 2. capacidad
Aviso 3: 1. empresa 2. se encarga de 3. adiestramiento

¡Vamos a conversar!

ESTRATEGIA **Giving a presentation** When speaking formally about a topic in a foreign language, preparation is especially important. Here are some general guidelines for the delivery of a sound presentation.

- Know your subject as well as possible.
- Organize your presentation so that your audience is able to follow your thoughts easily.
- Establish a comfortable balance between following a script and improvising.
- Do a "dry run" in front of people you know and get feedback from them.
- Rehearse further if you think that this will strengthen your actual delivery.

23. Para mejorar la universidad Imagine that you have been asked to present to the president of your college your ideas on how to improve student services. In pairs, brainstorm ideas; then, individually, prepare your presentation and rehearse it with your partner. As you develop your ideas, ask yourself the following questions.

- What specific measures am I proposing to achieve the suggested improvements?
- How am I going to persuade my audience (the president) about these measures?

24. ¿Qué dice Ud.? What would you say in the following situations? What might the other person say? Act out the scenes with a partner. Take turns playing each role.

1. Someone wants you to help him get a job at the company where you work. Tell him that you work under the supervision of Mrs. Rojas, and she has the last word.
2. You complain to your boss, saying that the salary you get doesn't compensate for all the work you do because you have too many responsibilities.
3. You tell someone that, if you had money, you would buy a printer.
4. Tell a friend to leave you a message on your answering machine or to send you a fax.

25. Para conocernos mejor To do this activity, work with a classmate whom you would like to get to know. Take turns asking and answering these questions.

1. ¿Qué preferirías tú, ser empleado(a) bancario(a) o trabajar en una oficina? Si pudieras escoger una profesión, ¿cuál escogerías? ¿Por qué? ¿Qué es más importante para ti, tener un buen sueldo o desempeñar un trabajo que te guste?
2. ¿Crees que es importante que una persona tenga conocimiento de ordenadores? ¿Qué marca de computadora tienes tú? ¿Usas la computadora principalmente para escribir informes o para mandar y recibir mensajes?
3. Si tuvieras que escribir tu resumé para solicitar un trabajo, ¿qué podrías decir sobre tu experiencia? ¿Y sobre tu educación?
4. Si el sueldo que tú recibes no compensa el trabajo que tú haces, ¿continúas trabajando en el mismo lugar o tratas de conseguir otro trabajo? ¿Cuál crees tú que debe ser el sueldo mínimo?
5. ¿Vas a tratar de conseguir un trabajo en cuanto te gradúes o piensas tomarte unas vacaciones en vez de comenzar a trabajar enseguida?

26. Una encuesta Interview your classmates to identify who fits the following descriptions. Include your instructor, but remember to use the **Ud.** form when addressing him/her. After finishing the survey, get together with two or three classmates and discuss the results.

1. Ha tenido que entrenar a alguien.	______________
2. Usa la computadora todos los días.	______________
3. No sabe usar un procesador de textos.	______________
4. Sabe lo que va a hacer en cuanto se gradúe.	______________
5. Puede conseguir muy buenas cartas de recomendación.	______________
6. Tiene muchas responsabilidades en su trabajo.	______________
7. Tiene un jefe antipático.	______________
8. Siempre tiene la última palabra en una discusión.	______________

27. Para crear In groups of three or four, look at the photo and use your imagination to create a story about the people in the picture. Who are they? Give them names and say where they work. What are their responsibilities? What do they do best? How much money do they make? What are their plans for the future?

Rincón literario

Julio Camba (*España: 1882–1962*)

Julio Camba es un verdadero observador de culturas y sociedades, incluida la suya propia: España. Escritor humorístico y satírico, viajó por el mundo y escribió sus impresiones sobre la manera de ser de la gente, y sobre la vida y la cultura de los países que visitó. El artículo que ofrecemos a continuación es de su libro *La rana viajera*. Otros libros de Camba son *Alemania; Londres; Aventura de una peseta; Lúculo o el arte de comer*; *Esto, lo otro y lo de más allá; La ciudad automática* y *Millones al horno*.

Antes de leer

ESTRATEGIA **Interacting with a reading** Training yourself to read includes, above all else, establishing a dialogue between what you read and what you think. Noting or jotting down your impressions, key information, and questions you have serves as an aid when later discussing a reading. By engaging with and reacting to a text you will be able to better understand and appreciate it.

28. La puntualidad The essay you are going to read takes a critical look at the concept of punctuality. Read the first seven lines of the text and note your reactions from the point of view of the narrator (**yo**). Then, in groups of three, discuss your impressions and talk about the personal issues that arise from meeting people who have a standard of punctuality that differs substantially from yours. Use the following questions to guide your conversation.

1. Para ti, ¿es importante la puntualidad? ¿Eres puntual o generalmente llegas tarde?
2. Si tienes una cita y la persona llega tarde, ¿cuánto tiempo la esperas? ¿Cómo te sientes? ¿Piensas que quizás te dejó plantado(a) (*stood you up*)?

¡A leer!

29. Comprensión As you read the essay, find the answers to the following questions.

1. Cuando el autor le dice a su amigo que tiene algo urgente que discutir con él, ¿cuál es la respuesta del amigo?
2. ¿Por qué dice el autor que "después de almorzar" es algo demasiado elástico?
3. ¿Tiene el amigo del autor una hora exacta para almorzar?
4. ¿A qué hora dice el amigo del autor que estará sin falta en el café?
5. ¿Qué sucede (*happens*) al día siguiente a las ocho?
6. ¿Qué piensa el amigo del autor sobre la puntualidad?
7. ¿Qué cosas hacen la vida imposible?
8. ¿Por qué es una buena idea acudir (*to show up*) puntualmente a una cita?

El tiempo y el espacio

(Adaptado)

Tengo algo urgente que discutir con un amigo. Por supuesto el amigo dice que hoy no puede ser.

—¿Mañana...?

—Muy bien. ¿A qué hora?

—A cualquier hora. Después de almorzar, por ejemplo... Yo digo que eso no es una hora. "Después de almorzar" es algo demasiado vago, demasiado elástico.

—¿A qué hora almuerza usted? —pregunto.

—A la hora de almorzar.

—Pero ¿qué hora es la hora de almorzar para usted? ¿El mediodía? ¿La una de la tarde? ¿Las dos...?

—Más o menos... —dice mi amigo—. Yo almuerzo de una a dos. A veces a las tres... De todos modos° a las cuatro siempre estoy libre.

De... *Anyway*

—Entonces, ¿a las cuatro?

—Sí, claro que, si llego unos minutos tarde —añade° —usted me puede esperar, ¿verdad? Quien dice a las cuatro, dice a las cuatro y media. En fin, de cuatro a cinco yo estoy sin falta° en el café.

he adds

sin... *without fail*

Yo quiero ser exacto.

—¿A las cinco?

—Muy bien. A las cinco... Es decir,° de cinco a cinco y media... Uno no es un tren, ¡qué diablo!°

Es... *That is to say*

qué... *what the heck*

—Pues podemos decir a las cinco y media —propongo yo. Entonces mi amigo tiene una idea brillante.

—¿Por qué no decimos a la hora del aperitivo? —sugiere.

Finalmente, decidimos reunirnos° de siete a ocho. Al día siguiente son las ocho y, claro está, mi amigo no viene. Llega a las ocho y media echando el bofe° y no me encuentra.

to get together

echando... *out of breath*

—No es justo —exclama días después al encontrarnos en la calle—. Me hace usted fijar una hora, me hace usted correr, y no me espera ni diez minutos. Yo llego a las ocho y media en punto,° y usted no está esperándome.

en... *on the dot*

Y lo más curioso es que la indignación de mi amigo es auténtica. Para él, la puntualidad es algo completamente absurdo.

—Pero —digo yo— una cita° es una cosa que tiene que estar tan limitada en el tiempo como en el espacio.

appointment

De despreciar° el tiempo, podemos despreciar también el espacio. Y de respetar el espacio, ¿por qué no considerar también el tiempo?

De... *If we scorn*

—Pero con esa precisión, con esa exactitud,° la vida es imposible —opina mi amigo.

accuracy

—¿Cómo explicarle que esa exactitud y esa precisión sirven, al contrario, para simplificar la vida? ¿Cómo convencerle de que, llegando puntualmente a las citas, uno ahorra mucho tiempo para hacer otras cosas?

Después de leer... reflexiones

30. ¿Con quién está de acuerdo? In groups of four, debate the two positions in the essay: **¿Está Ud. de acuerdo con el autor o con el amigo del autor? Defienda su postura** (*position*) **preferida o la que le asigne su profesor(a).**

La puntualidad es muy importante

1. Las ventajas (*advantages*) que tienen las personas puntuales
2. Las desventajas (*disadvantages*) de llegar tarde
3. La puntualidad es una virtud y la falta (*lack*) de puntualidad es un defecto.
4. La mayoría de la gente asocia la falta de puntualidad con la falta de responsabilidad.

La puntualidad es a veces una obsesión

1. Puede producir tensión
2. Las ventajas de no tener que preocuparse por llegar a tiempo (*on time*) a todas partes
3. Las personas que no viven "mirando el reloj" son más felices.
4. Muchas personas piensan que llegar un poco tarde a una fiesta, por ejemplo, puede ser visto como algo "elegante".

¿Otras ideas? ¡Defiendan su punto de vista (*point of view*)!

Algunos ejemplos de la vida diaria que pueden discutir:

1. Nora llegó tarde a un examen y perdió la parte oral.
2. Roberto llegó tarde al aeropuerto y perdió el avión.
3. Eva y Luis llegaron tarde al cine y la película ya había comenzado.
4. Fernando llegó tarde a la biblioteca y ya se había cerrado.
5. Olga y Sergio llegaron tarde a una conferencia y no les permitieron entrar.

Ahora hablen de las consecuencias que estas personas tuvieron que sufrir, pero también imaginen por qué llegaron tarde en cada caso. ¡Quizás habían estado haciendo algo muy importante! ¿Qué...?

¡Vamos a escribir!

Antes de escribir

ESTRATEGIA **Writing to persuade** When writing a persuasive essay, your task is not only to convince your reader, but to state your arguments clearly and in an organized manner. Support your point of view with strong evidence and offer examples and details.

31. ¿Deben casarse o no? You will write an essay in which you will present a man and a woman (**Daniel and Sara**) who are total opposites. Sara is very disciplined and punctual. She is never late and expects others to be punctual as well. Daniel, her fiancé, has no sense (*sentido*) of time and is always late. Describe both people and give some examples of their habits.

The question is this: **Should they get married or not?** Would they be happy together or would they have to get a divorce (*divorciarse*)? Would you say that opposites attract, or would you consider that a myth?

Choose one position and state your arguments. As you write the essay, give reasons that support your point of view.

¿Se atraen los opuestos?

¡A escribir!

32. Ensayo Write the **primer borrador** of your essay.

Después de escribir

33. A revisar Before writing the final version of your letter, exchange your first draft with a classmate's and peer edit each other's work. Have the guidelines been followed? How persuasive were your arguments?

España (I)

¿Recuerdas la canción que aprendiste en la lección 1? Españoles y turistas de otros países la cantan el Día de San Fermín, en la ciudad de Pamplona, conocida por sus encierros y sus corridas de toros.

En el norte del país están también Barcelona, la segunda ciudad más importante de España, y Santiago de Compostela.

En el centro del país está Madrid, la capital, una ciudad moderna de gran vitalidad, visitada cada año por más de 60 millones de turistas.

El Prado es uno de los mejores museos del mundo. Allí se conserva la colección más grande de las obras de pintores españoles, como Goya, Murillo y Velázquez (incluida *Las Meninas*, su obra maestra).

El Parque del Buen Retiro es notable por su estanque y sus muchas fuentes. En una de ellas está la famosa estatua del Ángel Caído, que representa al diablo cuando fue arrojado del paraíso. En el parque están también la Rosaleda y el Palacio de Cristal.

Otros puntos de interés turístico

En Barcelona está la Iglesia de la Sagrada Familia, la obra maestra (*masterpiece*) del arquitecto catalán Antonio Gaudí.

La Mancha es la región de España más conocida en todo el mundo, debido a la novela **Don Quijote de la Mancha**, de Miguel de Cervantes.

Los idiomas de España

En España llaman castellano al idioma español, que todos los españoles hablan y entienden. Además, se hablan otras lenguas: el catalán en Cataluña; el gallego en Galicia; el vascuence en el País Vasco, etc.

Dos universidades españolas

©Vlas 2000.shutterstock.com

La Universidad de Salamanca, fundada en 1218, es la más antigua de España y una de las cuatro más antiguas del mundo. Tiene programas especiales de español para extranjeros.

© Pepe Franco/Cover/Getty Images

La Universidad Complutense de Madrid está situada en la Ciudad Universitaria de Madrid y ha tenido, desde su fundación, un papel importante en el desarrollo político de España.

La política: del pasado al presente

© Alberto Pizzoli/Sygma/Corbis

El Rey Juan Carlos de Borbón y la Reina Sofía, los Reyes de España.

El Gobierno de España es una monarquía constitucional.

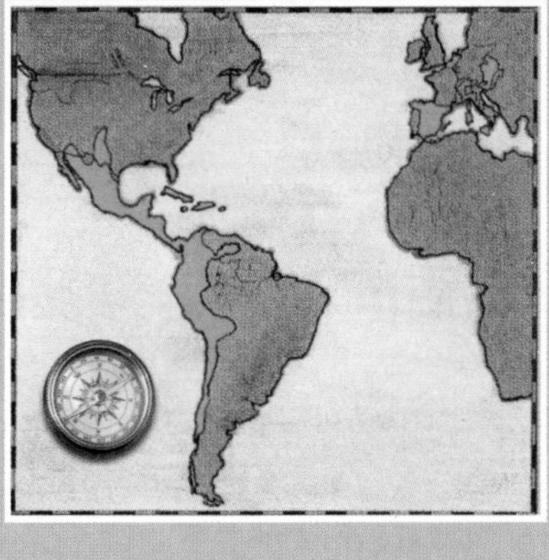

© Cengage Learning/Trigg/Shutterstock.com

Mapa que señala los territorios que pertenecían al imperio de Carlos V (Siglo XVI).

Ahora dime...

In groups of three, talk about the following.

1. Si estuvieran en Pamplona el 7 de julio, ¿correrían delante de los toros? Y aquí, ¿participarían en un rodeo? ¿Por qué o por qué no?
2. Madrid es visitada por millones de turistas cada año. ¿Qué ciudades de este país son visitadas por personas de otros países? ¿Por qué creen ustedes que esas ciudades les resultan interesantes?
3. ¿A cuál de las universidades mencionadas aquí les gustaría asistir? ¿Por qué?

iLrn™

To learn more about Spain, watch the cultural footage in the Media Library.

AUTOPRUEBA

¿Cuánto sé ahora?

Take this test. When you have finished, check your answers in the answer key provided in Appendix D. Then use a red pen to correct any mistakes you may have made. Are you ready?

A. The pluperfect subjunctive Complete the following sentences with the pluperfect subjunctive of the verbs in parentheses.

1. No había nadie que ______________ (ver) al presidente de la compañía.
2. Yo me alegré de que ellos no ______________ (tener) que entrevistarme.
3. Ellos no creían que nosotros ya ______________ (archivar) todos los documentos.
4. Yo temía que Ud. no le ______________ (ofrecer) el puesto.
5. Ellos se alegraron de que yo ______________ (escribir) las cartas a máquina.
6. Yo temía que tú ______________ (renunciar).
7. Nosotros esperábamos que Uds. ______________ (recibir) un aumento de sueldo.
8. ¿Había alguien que ______________ (trabajar) bajo la supervisión del jefe de compras?

B. *If* clauses Complete the following sentences with the imperfect subjunctive, the pluperfect subjunctive, or the present indicative of the verbs given.

1. Si yo ______________ (tener) tiempo, hablaré con el jefe.
2. Nosotros trabajaríamos con ellos si ______________ (poder).
3. Si ellos ______________ (ir) al despacho, habrían visto al supervisor.
4. Si Uds. ______________ (necesitar) un traductor, pueden emplearlo.
5. Tú habrías hablado con el jefe de personal si lo ______________ (ver).
6. Elsa habla como si lo ______________ (saber) todo.
7. Si Amanda ______________ (entrenar) al nuevo empleado, él va a aprender mucho.
8. Nosotros compraríamos una impresora si ellos nos ______________ (prestar) el dinero.
9. Si nosotros ______________ (hablar) con el administrador, él nos habría dicho la verdad.
10. Fernando actúa (*acts*) como si él ______________ (ser) el jefe.

C. Summary of the uses of the subjunctive Complete the following sentences, using the verbs in parentheses in the appropriate tense of the subjunctive or the indicative.

1. Yo quería que ellos me __________ (entrevistar) hoy.
2. Esperamos que tú __________ (poder) hablar mañana con los accionistas.
3. Dile que me __________ (avisar) esta tarde.
4. Yo no creo que nosotros __________ (poder) desempeñar ese puesto, pero creo que Carlos __________ (poder) hacerlo.
5. ¿Hay alguien aquí que __________ (haber) visto al gerente hoy?
6. Voy a usar la fotocopiadora en cuanto __________ (llegar) a la oficina.
7. Le di dinero para que __________ (poder) comprar la videograbadora.
8. No es verdad que nosotros le __________ (pagar) ese sueldo.
9. Yo te sugiero que le __________ (preguntar) al candidato si tiene su resumé.
10. Yo dudaba que nosotros __________ (tener) dinero para comprar una microcomputadora.
11. Yo niego que mi padre __________ (ser) un tirano, y dudo que nosotros __________ (ser) sus víctimas.
12. No había nadie que __________ (estar) encargado de ese programa.

D. Just words . . . Match the questions in column A with the responses in column B.

A		B
1. ¿Quién es Ana Vega?	____	a. Las voy a archivar.
2. ¿Qué hizo con las cartas de recomendación?	____	b. En su despacho.
3. ¿Qué puesto desempeña él?	____	c. Mañana mismo.
4. ¿Cuál es tu especialización?	____	d. Es contador público.
5. ¿Tiene un buen sueldo?	____	e. Sí, trabaja para Geico.
6. ¿Qué vas a hacer con las carpetas?	____	f. Sí, y traductor.
7. ¿Cuál es su profesión?	____	g. Mercadeo.
8. ¿Qué quieres que compre?	____	h. Sí, yo tengo la última palabra.
9. ¿Cuándo lo va a hacer?	____	i. El de gerente.
10. ¿Vende casas?	____	j. Sí, voy a comer un bocadillo.
11. ¿Dónde está el jefe?	____	k. Sí, cien mil dólares al año.
12. ¿Es agente de seguros?	____	l. Sí, trabaja para Wells Fargo.
13. ¿Tú siempre decides?	____	m. La asistente del jefe de compras.
14. ¿Tú eres intérprete?	____	n. Sí, es agente de bienes raíces.
15. ¿Elsa es empleada bancaria?	____	o. Una fotocopiadora.
16. ¿Es la hora de almorzar?	____	p. Se las dio al supervisor.

E. Culture

1. Complete the following, based on the information found in the **¿Lo sabía Ud.?** sections.
   a. En los países de habla hispana, generalmente las transacciones comerciales son menos ________ que en los Estados Unidos.
   b. En los países hispanos, las mujeres trabajan cada vez más fuera de su ________.
2. Answer the following questions, based on the information found in the **El mundo hispánico y tú** section.
   a. ¿Cuál es el sistema de gobierno de España?
   b. ¿Cuál es la segunda ciudad más grande de España?

F. Un dicho Do you remember the Spanish saying that suggests that it is better to have a wise man disapprove of what you do than to have a stupid man applaud your actions? Find the saying in this lesson.

LECCIÓN 18

TEATRO... CINE... TELEVISIÓN...

Pedro Almodóvar, famoso director de cine español, junto a Penélope Cruz, actriz de muchas de sus películas. Esta es otra actriz española que ha triunfado en Hollywood.

OBJETIVOS COMUNICATIVOS

You will learn vocabulary related to media and the arts, communication, and entertainment.

SITUACIONES

La futura actriz

ESTRUCTURAS

1 Uses of some prepositions after certain verbs
2 Uses of **por** and **para** in certain expressions
3 Some idiomatic expressions

ASÍ SOMOS

¡Vamos a ver!

Watching and understanding situations

¡Vamos a escuchar!

Identifying word boundaries and punctuating sentences

¡Vamos a conversar!

Expressing idiomatic language

Rincón literario

Using prior knowledge

Los deseos by Fernán Caballero

¡Vamos a escribir!

Writing a dialogue

EL MUNDO HISPÁNICO Y TÚ...

› España (Cont.)

AUTOPRUEBA

You will review what you learned in this lesson.

ESPAÑA (Cont.) En el sur de España se encuentran Granada, Sevilla y Córdoba, ciudades de gran belleza donde se ve la influencia árabe. La Alhambra de Granada, la Giralda de Sevilla y la Mezquita (*Mosque*) de Córdoba son verdaderas joyas arquitectónicas. Sevilla tiene además el maravilloso Parque de María Luisa, donde se encuentra la gran Plaza de España. En esta plaza, construida enteramente de azulejos (*ceramic tiles*) de tipo andaluz, están representadas escenas históricas de las cincuenta provincias de España.

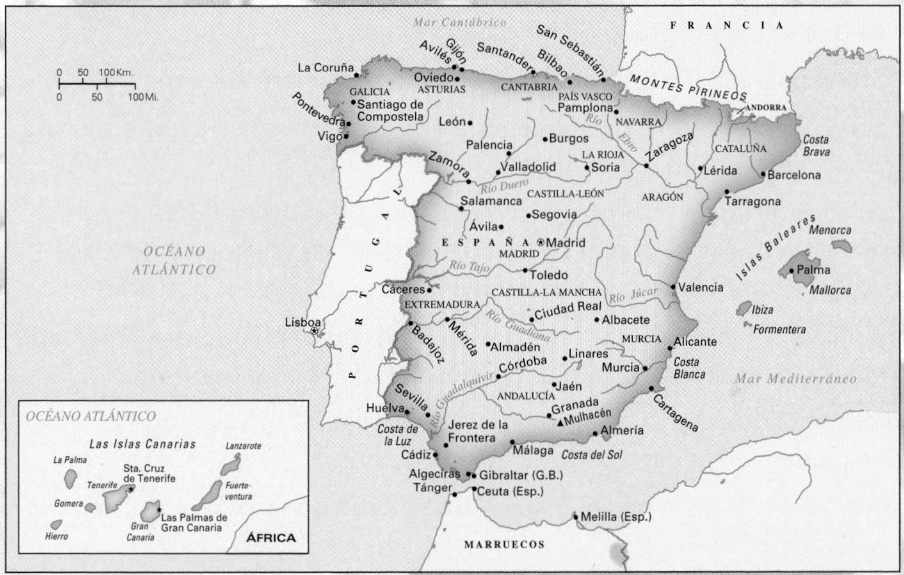

Recursos iLrn video audio web playlist

La futura actriz

CD3-18

© Cengage Learning

¡Ubíquelos!

Don Luis Burés and his family live in Toledo, a city near Madrid. As you watch the video, you will appreciate the cultural importance of this very interesting city.

© PhotoAlto/Alamy

Don Luis Burés está hablando con Paloma, su nieta, sobre los planes de la muchacha. Ella está decidida a ser actriz, y quiere empezar a estudiar arte dramático inmediatamente. A su abuelo le gustaría que ella se casara con el nieto de su mejor amigo, que es médico y gana muchísimo dinero... Por desgracia, no pueden ponerse de acuerdo.

Paloma: Abuelo, tú sabes que yo pertenezco a un grupo de teatro de aficionados. Ahora estamos ensayando una obra de teatro de Alejandro Casona.[1] ¡El director dice que tengo mucho talento!

Don Luis: ¡Y puedes seguir haciendo eso! Pero tú quieres ser actriz de cine. Quieres filmar películas... seguir los pasos de Penélope Cruz... en vez de casarte con tu prometido, ¡que está loco por ti!

Paloma: ¡Pablo y yo no estamos comprometidos! Y él piensa irse para Nueva York el mes entrante, así que él no se acuerda de que está enamorado de mí, como tú crees...

Don Luis: ¡Ahora te estás burlando de mí! ¡Le estás tomando el pelo a tu pobre abuelo!

Paloma: (*Se ríe.*) No, no... pero yo estoy segura de que tendría éxito como actriz... Estoy dispuesta a estudiar, a trabajar duro. ¡Al fin y al cabo soy tu nieta!

Don Luis: ¡Pero es que las películas de hoy en día no son como las de antes! Películas de ciencia ficción con efectos especiales... Películas de acción en las que la trama no es importante... Los actores no tienen que "actuar". ¡Bah! Desde que murió John Wayne... ¡Ya no hay actores!

Paloma: ¡Hoy en día tenemos actores fabulosos! ¡Y directores de cine como Almodóvar y Spielberg! Hay buenas películas de guerra, de misterio, musicales... y documentales buenísimos...

Don Luis: Yo siempre leo la columna de ese crítico... ¿cómo se llama? El que critica a todo el mundo... ¡Él piensa lo mismo que yo! Por eso, yo nunca me la pierdo.

Paloma: Norberto Santacruz. ¡A él no le gusta nadie! Según él, Spielberg no sabe dirigir... Abuelo, yo sé que va a ser difícil...

[1] Famous Spanish playwright

DON LUIS: ¡Exactamente! Nadie se hace famoso de la noche a la mañana. De hecho, la mayoría no tiene éxito, pero... yo tengo fe en ti. (*Tocan el timbre.*) Ah, tus amigos están aquí...

PALOMA: ¡Que esperen! ¡Yo voy a darle un abrazo a mi abuelo favorito!

DON LUIS: Bueno, bueno... quizás yo puedo ser uno de los extras en tu primera película... un caballero distinguido, sentado en un restaurante... o algo por el estilo...

PALOMA: (*Se ríe.*) ¡Por supuesto!

¿Lo sabía Ud.?

En España, Cuba, México y Argentina, entre otros países, la producción de películas tiene gran importancia. Algunos directores hispanohablantes famosos son Almodóvar y Buñuel, de España; Tomás Gutiérrez Alea, de Cuba; Guillermo del Toro, de México; y Juan José Campanella, de Argentina.

› **¿Pasan películas extranjeras en los cines de su ciudad? ¿Están dobladas (*dubbed*) o tienen subtítulos?**

1. **Hablemos** With a partner, take turns asking and answering the following questions. Base your answers on the dialogue and on your own circumstances.

En el diálogo

1. ¿A qué está decidida Paloma?
2. ¿Qué le gustaría a su abuelo que ella hiciera?
3. ¿Qué están ensayando Paloma y su grupo?
4. Según don Luis, ¿qué está haciendo Paloma?
5. ¿Qué está dispuesta a hacer Paloma?
6. ¿Qué dice don Luis de las películas de hoy en día?
7. ¿Qué dice don Luis de las películas de acción?
8. Según don Luis, ¿quién era un buen actor?
9. ¿Qué no se pierde nunca don Luis? ¿Por qué?
10. ¿Qué tipo de personaje dice don Luis que él puede ser?

¿Y tú?

1. ¿A qué estás decidido(a) tú?
2. ¿Qué te gustaría a ti que hiciera tu mejor amigo(a)?
3. ¿Te gustaría actuar en una obra teatral?
4. ¿Tú les tomas el pelo a tus amigos a veces? ¿Ellos te toman el pelo a ti?
5. ¿Tú estás dispuesto(a) a trabajar duro?
6. ¿Tú crees que hoy en día se filman buenas películas o que las de antes eran mejores?
7. ¿Qué tipos de películas prefieres tú?
8. ¿Quién es tu actor favorito? ¿Y tu actriz favorita?
9. ¿Tú siempre estás de acuerdo con los críticos?
10. ¿Te gustaría ser uno de los extras en una película? ¿Por qué sí o por qué no?

Un dicho

Si quieres acertar, cásate con tu igual.
If you want to succeed (in marriage), marry your equal.

VOCABULARIO

En el diálogo

Cognados

la acción	*action*
el actor	*actor*
la actriz	*actress*
el arte dramático	*dramatic art*
la columna	*column*
el (la) crítico(a)	*critic*
distinguido(a)	*distinguished*
el (la) director(a)	*director*
el documental	*documentary*
el efecto especial	*special effect*
exactamente	*exactly*
el (la) extra	*extra*
inmediatamente	*immediately*
la mayoría	*majority*
musical	*musical*
el plan	*plan*
el talento	*talent*

Nombres

el caballero	*gentleman*
la ciencia ficción	*science fiction*
el (la) director(a) de cine	*movie director*
la fe	*faith*
la guerra	*war*
la película de misterio	*mystery movie, murder mystery*
el teatro de aficionados	*amateur theater*
la trama	*plot*

Verbos

actuar	*to perform, to act*
burlarse (de)	*to make fun (of)*
criticar	*to criticize*
dirigir	*to direct*
ensayar	*to rehearse*
filmar	*to film, to make (a movie)*
perderse	*to miss out (on something)*
pertenecer (yo pertenezco)	*to belong*

Adjetivos

comprometido(a)	*engaged*
entrante	*next*

Otras palabras y expresiones

al fin y al cabo	*after all*
algo por el estilo	*something like that*
así que	*so*
de hecho	*in fact*
de la noche a la mañana	*overnight*
desde	*since*
estar decidido(a)	*to be determined*
estar loco(a) por	*to be crazy about*
hoy en día	*nowadays*
las de antes	*the ones in the olden days*
el mes entrante	*next month*
¡Que esperen!	*Let them wait!*
seguir los pasos	*to follow in the footsteps*
tener éxito	*to be successful*
todo el mundo	*everybody*
tomarle el pelo (a alguien)	*to pull someone's leg, to tease*
trabajar duro	*to work hard*
ya no	*no longer*

Más sobre el tema

© Denis Babenko/Shutterstock.com

En L'Hemisfèric de Valencia, España, hay un cine IMAX.

El cine

la actuación	*acting*
el avance	*preview*
la banda sonora	*soundtrack*
la cartelera	*movie section*
los dibujos animados	*cartoons*
el espectáculo	*show*
estrenar	*to show for the first time*
el estreno	*première*
el festival de cine	*film festival*
el guión, el libreto	*script, screenplay*
la música	*music*
el músico	*musician*
la orquesta	*orchestra*
la pantalla	*movie screen*
el papel	*role*
la película de suspenso	*thriller*
la película del oeste (de vaqueros)	*western movie*
el personaje	*character*
el (la) productor(a)	*producer*
el (la) protagonista	*protagonist, main character*
el reparto (la distribución) de papeles	*casting, cast*
3-D	*three-dimensional*

¿Lo sabía Ud.?

Las películas norteamericanas son muy populares en España y en el resto del mundo hispánico. Generalmente tienen subtítulos en español o están dobladas. Muchos de los títulos en español suelen ser completamente diferentes de los de inglés; por ejemplo, la película *Where the Heart Is* se llamó ***La fuerza del amor***. Algunos títulos se dejan en inglés.

› **¿Tiene gran importancia la producción de películas en su país? Dé ejemplos.**

Práctica

2. ¿Cuál no va? Select the word or phrase that does not belong in each group.

1. guión / libreto / papel
2. banda sonora / música / avance
3. pantalla / protagonista / personaje
4. no asistir / criticar / perderse
5. caballero / estreno / festival de cine
6. del oeste / musical / de vaqueros
7. músico / productor / director de cine
8. dibujos animados / orquesta / documental

3. Preguntas y respuestas Match the questions in column A with the responses in column B.

A		B
1. ¿Nora y Luis están comprometidos?	_____	a. Una obra teatral de Casona.
2. ¿Quién dirigió la película?	_____	b. Las de ciencia ficción.
3. ¿Qué están ensayando los actores?	_____	c. Un famoso director de cine.
4. ¿Es una película de guerra?	_____	d. Sí, y tiene mucho talento.
5. ¿Quién es Almodóvar?	_____	e. Mi abuelo.
6. ¿Qué tipos de películas te gustan?	_____	f. ¡Que espere!
7. ¿Quién es ese caballero tan distinguido?	_____	g. Sí, se casan en mayo.
8. ¿Pertenece a un grupo de teatro de aficionados?	_____	h. Pienso trabajar duro.
9. ¿Qué planes tienes para este año?	_____	i. No, de misterio.
10. ¿Sergio te está esperando?	_____	j. Almodóvar.
11. ¿Qué estás leyendo?	_____	k. De la distribución de papeles.
12. ¿De qué está encargado él?	_____	l. La cartelera.

4. Para completar Complete the following, using vocabulary from this lesson.

1. Eva estudia arte _________. ¡Está _________ a ser actriz!
2. Mi prometido y yo no podemos _________ de acuerdo en nada, pero ¡yo estoy _________ por él!
3. ¡Te estás _________ de mí! ¡Me estás _________ el pelo!
4. Al fin y al _________, ¡nadie se hace famoso de la _________ a la mañana! Pero Luis va a tener _________. Yo tengo _________ en él.
5. Ese actor se llamaba Mario... Fabio... o algo por el _________. Antes, todo el _________ lo conocía, pero _________ no es famoso.
6. Las películas de _________ en día no son tan buenas como las de _________.
7. Ana está dispuesta a seguir los _________ de su mamá, que es actriz de cine. De _________, va a filmar una película el mes _________.
8. Yo nunca me _________ la columna de ese crítico. La leo todos los días.

Para conversar

5. **Algunas ideas** With a partner, play the roles of two producers who are discussing the possibility of collaborating on a movie. Talk about different types of movies, whom you would like to get to direct the movie, where you would film it, and who would play the main roles. Add any necessary details.

   Modelo —*Me gustaría hacer una película documental.*
   —*No, es mejor hacer una película de acción. Da más dinero.*

6. **Una película con la clase** Your class is making a movie. With a partner, decide what type of movie it will be, who will be the director, who will have the main roles, and what the theme of the movie is. Join another group and compare notes. Pick up the common elements, if any, and present your project to the class.

CD3-19

Pronunciación

Pronunciation in context

In this lesson, there are some new words or phrases that may be challenging to pronounce. For further pronunciation practice of Spanish sounds, listen to your instructor and repeat the following sentences.

1. Quiere empezar a estudiar arte dramático **inmediatamente**.
2. Abuelo, tú sabes que yo **pertenezco** a un grupo de teatro de **aficionados**.
3. Quieres **filmar películas...** seguir los pasos de Penélope Cruz...
4. Yo estoy segura de que **tendría éxito** como actriz.
5. Películas de **ciencia ficción** con efectos especiales...
6. Hay buenas películas de misterio, de **guerra, musicales...**
7. **De hecho**, la gran **mayoría** no tiene **éxito**.
8. **Quizás** yo puedo ser uno de las extras en tu **primera película**.

Un dicho

Tarde o temprano se descubre al mentiroso.
Equivalent: *Sooner or later the liar is discovered.*

ESTRUCTURAS

1 Uses of some prepositions after certain verbs (*Usos de algunas preposiciones con ciertos verbos*)

In Spanish, some verbs are used with prepositions that have no equivalent to or are different from the ones used in English. The prepositions used most often are **a, de, con,** and **en**.

› a

aprender a *to learn (how)*
asistir a *to attend*
ayudar a *to help*
empezar (comenzar) a *to begin, to start*
enseñar a *to teach*
invitar a *to invite*
ir a *to go*
venir a *to come*

—**¿Fuiste a** ensayar con Rafael? — *Did you go rehearse with Rafael?*
—Sí, **empezamos a** ensayar anoche. — *Yes, we started to rehearse last night.*

—Yo quiero **aprender a** bailar flamenco. — *I want to learn how to dance flamenco.*
—Yo te puedo **enseñar a** bailarlo. — *I can teach you to dance it.*

› de

acordarse de *to remember*
alegrarse de *to be glad*
enamorarse de *to fall in love with*
olvidarse de *to forget*

—No **te olvides de** llamar al productor. — *Don't forget to call the producer.*
—Bueno..., y tú, **acuérdate de** leer el guión. — *Okay . . . , and you, remember to read the script.*

› con

casarse con *to marry, to get married to*
soñar (o:ue) con *to dream about (of)*
comprometerse con *to get engaged to*

—Teresa **se comprometió con** Antonio. — *Teresa got engaged to Antonio.*
—Debe estar muy contenta. Siempre **soñó con casarse con** un actor de cine. — *She must be very happy. She always dreamed of marrying a movie actor.*

› en

fijarse en *to notice*
pensar en *to think about*
insistir en *to insist on*

—¿**En** qué estás **pensando**? — *What are you thinking about?*
—Estoy **pensando en** la boda de Beatriz. Ella **insistió en** invitar a Pablo y él siempre causa problemas... — *I am thinking about Beatriz's wedding. She insisted on inviting Pablo and he always causes problems . . .*

> **LEARNING TIP**
> Use each verb with its corresponding preposition to make a statement about yourself or people you know. For example: **Yo quiero *aprender a* tocar el piano.**

Práctica

7. Minidiálogos Complete the following dialogues with the Spanish equivalent of the words in parentheses. Then act them out with a partner.

1. —¿________________ llamar al director, Anita? (*Did you remember*)
   —Sí, pero ________________ a Julio para que viniera a verlo. (*I forgot to call*)
2. —¿Dónde ________________ flamenco, Rosita? (*did you learn to dance*)
   —En Sevilla. Y en Barcelona ________________ la sardana. (*they taught me how to dance*)
3. —Hola, vengo ________________ ir al estreno. (*to invite you*)
   —No puedo, porque tengo que ________________ una clase de drama. (*to attend*)
4. —Rubén ________________ Alicia, pero ella no ________________ él. (*fell in love with / notice*)
   —No, ella ________________ Mauricio. (*married*)
5. —¿Cuándo van a ________________ filmar la película? (*start*)
   —El mes entrante.

8. ¿Qué pasa aquí? With a partner, take turns asking and answering questions about the people in the following situations. Use the prepositions and verbs you learned in this section.

Para conversar

9. **¿Qué hacemos?** With a partner, discuss the following. Use the appropiate prepositions in your sentences.
   1. things you would like to learn to do or can teach others to do
   2. what time you start to work and to study
   3. what you always (never) remember to do and what you always (never) forget to do
   4. what you dream about doing
   5. what you insist on doing
   6. whom you think about every day

2 Uses of *por* and *para* in certain expressions

(*Usos de* por *y* para *en ciertas expresiones*)

A. Expressions with *por*

The following idiomatic expressions use **por**.

por aquí cerca *around here*
por desgracia *unfortunately*
por eso *that's why*
por fin *finally*
por lo general *generally*
por si acaso *just in case*
por suerte *luckily*
por supuesto *of course*

—¿Conseguiste la banda sonora de la película? *Did you get the movie soundtrack?*
—No, **por desgracia** no pude conseguirla. *No, unfortunately I wasn't able to get it.*
—Hay una tienda **por aquí cerca** que la tiene. ¿Quieres que te la compre? *There's a store around here that has it. Do you want me to buy it for you?*
—**Por supuesto.** *Of course.*

B. Expressions with *para*

The following idiomatic expressions use **para**.

para eso *for that* (said sarcastically or contemptuously)
¿para qué? *what for?*
sin qué ni para qué *without rhyme or reason*
para peor *to make matters worse*
para siempre *forever*

—¿**Para qué** te vas a poner un vestido tan elegante? *What are you going to wear such an elegant dress for?*
—Para ir a cenar con Beto. Me va a llevar a comer una hamburguesa. *To go to dinner with Beto. He's taking me out for a hamburger.*
—¿Y **para eso** te pones tu mejor vestido? Y **para peor**... ¡está lloviendo! *And for that you're wearing your best dress? And to make matters worse . . . it's raining!*

Práctica

10. ¿Por...? ¿Para...? Complete the following sentences, using the appropriate expressions with **por** or **para**.

1. Yo no tenía dinero para ir al estreno; ____________ mi papá me dio cien dólares.
2. ¡Esa actriz es tan temperamental! Nadie la criticó, pero ella se enojó ____________.
3. ¿____________ aceptaste ese papel? No es muy importante.
4. Hoy ponen una película de suspenso en un cine que hay ____________.
5. No creo que ellos puedan ir al festival de cine con nosotros pero, ____________, los voy a invitar.
6. El espectáculo fue muy aburrido y, ____________, cuando salí del teatro descubrí que me habían robado el auto.
7. ¡____________ René pudo conseguir un puesto en la orquesta!
8. El productor invirtió mucho tiempo y mucho dinero en esa película pero, ____________, no tuvo éxito.
9. Me ofrecieron el papel de protagonista y ____________ lo acepté.
10. ____________ vamos a ver películas musicales. Nos gustan mucho.
11. El día de la boda él le prometió amarla (*to love her*) ____________.
12. Armando admiraba mucho a ese director y ____________ quiso seguir sus pasos.

Para conversar

11. ¡Habla con tu compañero(a)! With a partner, take turns asking and answering the following questions using appropriate, logical expressions with **por** or **para**.

Modelo E1: *Si el cielo está nublado* (cloudy) *cuando sales de tu casa, ¿llevas un paraguas?*
E2: *Sí, llevo un paraguas por si acaso llueve.*

1. ¿Qué programas de televisión ves tú los sábados?
2. ¿Tú piensas quedarte a vivir en este estado?
3. Si te ofrecieran un aumento de sueldo, ¿lo aceptarías?
4. ¿Hay algún restaurante mexicano cerca de la universidad?
5. ¿Sacaste una buena nota en el último examen?
6. ¿Puedes ir al cine esta noche o tienes que trabajar?

3 Some idiomatic expressions (*Algunas expresiones idiomáticas*)

› **a más tardar** *at the latest*

Van a estrenar la película la próxima semana **a más tardar**.

The movie will be shown for the first time next week at the latest.

› **a principios de** *the first part of* (*a month, a year, etc.*)

El grupo musical de Sevilla viene **a principios de mes**.

The musical group from Sevilla is coming during the first part of the month.

› **dar las gracias** *to express gratitude*

El actor **dio las gracias** cuando recibió el Óscar.

The actor expressed gratitude when he received the Oscar.

ESTRUCTURAS

› **darle rabia a uno** *to be furious*

Me dio rabia cuando el crítico dijo que la película era mala.

I became furious when the critic said (that) the movie was bad.

› **de repente, de pronto** *suddenly*

De repente decidieron cambiar la programación del canal.

They suddenly decided to change the channel's programming.

› **dejar plantado(a) a alguien** *to stand somebody up*

La novia **lo dejó plantado** en el altar.

The bride stood him up at the altar.

› **hacerse ilusiones** *to dream, to fool oneself*

¡No **te hagas ilusiones!** Tú no puedes pertenecer a ese club tan exclusivo.

Don't fool yourself! You can't belong to such an exclusive club.

› **hacer las paces** *to make up* (*after a fight*)

Ayer Nora se enojó con Luis, pero hoy **hicieron las paces**.

Yesterday Nora got angry at Luis, but today they made up.

› **importarle a uno** *to matter, to concern*

La trama es interesante. No **me importa** lo que digan los críticos.

The plot is interesting. It doesn't matter to me what the critics say.

› **llevar puesto(a)** *to have on, to be wearing* (*clothes*)

El vestido que la actriz **llevaba puesto** era horrible.

The dress the actress was wearing was horrible.

› **sin falta** *without fail*

Elba es muy puntual, así que tenemos que estar allí a las seis **sin falta**.

Elba is very punctual, so we have to be there at six o'clock without fail.

› **tarde o temprano** *sooner or later*

No te preocupes. **Tarde o temprano** él admitirá que tú tienes razón.

Don't worry. Sooner or later he'll admit that you're right.

Práctica

12. Esto es idiomático Complete the following sentences, using the appropriate idiomatic expressions.

1. Ana estaba furiosa con Raúl, pero yo creo que van a ____________.
2. ____________ cuando mi novio insiste en ver una película de guerra. No me gustan esas películas.
3. Lo esperé por tres horas y no vino. ____________.
4. Tenemos que estar allí a las cinco ____________. No podemos llegar más tarde.
5. Julián ____________ un traje azul que le quedaba muy bien.
6. Yo les ____________ por todos los favores que me han hecho.
7. Clara va a hacer lo que ella quiera porque no ____________ lo que tú digas.
8. Van a estrenar la obra ____________ junio.
9. Mi padre me dice que no ____________ porque él no me va a comprar un coche.

13. ¿Qué me dices? With a partner, take turns using appropriate idiomatic expressions to respond to the following.

1. ¿Tú quieres que yo esté en el teatro a las siete y media?
2. ¿Tú esperaste al crítico por dos horas y él no vino?
3. ¿Tú dices que estrenan esa película el cuatro o el cinco de febrero?
4. ¿Tú siempre esperas que te den el papel de protagonista y nunca te lo dan?
5. ¿El director se levantó y se fue sin decir nada?

Para conversar

14. ¡Habla con tu compañero(a)! With a partner, take turns asking and answering the following questions in complete sentences. Use the corresponding idiomatic expressions.

1. ¿Adónde tienes que ir mañana sin falta?
2. ¿A qué hora tienes que estar en la universidad, a más tardar?
3. ¿Qué llevabas puesto la última vez que fuiste a una fiesta?
4. ¿Qué cosa te da rabia?
5. ¿A quién tienes que darle las gracias? ¿Por qué?
6. ¿Qué va a pasar en tu vida tarde o temprano?

15. In groups of three, talk about the following.

1. Si hay alguien que tenga que darles las gracias a Uds. y por qué.
2. Si Uds. han dejado plantado a alguien alguna vez. ¿Qué excusa dieron?
3. Si hay algo que Uds. hagan que le dé rabia a alguien. ¿A quién?
4. Con quiénes se enojan Uds. a veces y cómo hacen las paces.
5. Si a Uds. les importa o no lo que la gente piense de Uds. Den razones.
6. Si Uds. se hacen ilusiones a veces. Den detalles.

¡Vamos a ver!

Antes de ver el video

16. Preguntas You and a partner take turns asking and answering the following questions.

1. ¿Conoces a alguien que pertenezca a un grupo de teatro de aficionados?
2. ¿Prefieres las comedias musicales, las películas de misterio, las películas de guerra o las películas de ciencia ficción?
3. ¿Te gustan las películas que tienen efectos especiales o solo te interesa la trama?
4. ¿Te gustaría dirigir una película? ¿Preferirías seguir los pasos de Almodóvar o de Spielberg?
5. ¿Preferirías estar a cargo de la programación de un canal o ser crítico y tener tu propia columna en un periódico?
6. Si tú no puedes ver un programa, ¿lo grabas (*record*) para verlo más tarde?
7. ¿Tú te burlas de tus amigos a veces? ¿Les tomas el pelo?
8. Si tus padres te regalaran un coche, ¿te vendría de perillas?
9. ¿Es verdad que tú estás comprometido(a) para casarte?
10. ¿A cuánto estamos hoy?

El video: El futuro director

—Me gusta el teatro, pero creo que sería interesante filmar una película. Cuando era chica no me perdía una, especialmente si era una comedia musical o una película de misterio.

—Yo prefería las de guerra, las de acción o las de ciencia ficción, especialmente si tenían efectos especiales.

—No sabía que te interesaba el baile flamenco...

—Bueno... al fin y al cabo tengo dos hermanas que son bailarinas... tus futuras cuñadas...

—Es verdad. Oye, ¿y cuándo van a ser mis cuñadas...?

Después de ver el video

© Cengage Learning

Marisol

© Cengage Learning

Ángel

17. ¿Quién lo dice? Identify the person who said the following in the dialogue.

1. ¡Yo creo que tendría éxito!
2. A mí me dijeron que tú criticabas a todo el mundo.
3. Me gusta tomarte el pelo a veces.
4. A mí me gustaría dirigir.
5. Eran las dos cuando hablé con Álvaro.
6. ¡Que esperen!
7. ¿Qué te parece si la boda es en diciembre?
8. ¿A cuánto estamos hoy?

18. Hablemos With a partner, take turns asking and answering the following questions. Base your answers on the dialogue.

1. ¿Con quién está comprometido Ángel Estévez?
2. ¿Dónde conoció Ángel a su prometida?
3. ¿Qué van a ensayar Ángel y sus amigos?
4. ¿Qué tipo de películas le gustaban a Marisol?
5. ¿A qué famoso director español admira Ángel?
6. ¿Por qué dice Ángel que no le habla de sus ilusiones a Marisol?
7. ¿Qué documental quiere ver Ángel?
8. ¿Qué hacen las dos hermanas de Ángel?
9. ¿En qué mes va a ser la boda de Ángel y Marisol?
10. ¿Qué hace Marisol cuando Ángel le propone casamiento (*marriage*)?

19. ¿Qué pasa después...? You and a partner, use your imagination to say what the characters do. In Spanish, discuss the following.

1. Whether the play that they were rehearsing was a musical comedy or a drama.
2. How long their friends had to wait before Marisol opened the door.
3. Whether or not they recorded the documentary about flamenco dancing.
4. Whether Marisol and Ángel told their friends that they were going to get married.
5. Whether or not Marisol continued to pull Ángel's leg. Did he pull *her* leg?
6. If the next time Marisol and Ángel went to the movies, they saw a murder mystery, a war movie, or an action movie with special effects.
7. What the exact wedding date is. Were their parents happy?
8. Whether Ángel followed in Almodóvar's footsteps or in Spielberg's footsteps. Was he successful?

¡Vamos a escuchar!

ESTRATEGIA **Identifying word boundaries and punctuating sentences practice II** When identifying where words and sentences begin and end, you may be dealing with narration or dialogue, or a combination of both. Spanish punctuation is similar to English; however, differences occur, not just with exclamations and questions, but also with dialogue and the use of the colon.

- A colon introduces a list, a quote, and the heading of a letter, and precedes the completion of a thought.
- Dialogue dashes (—) often precede a quote in Spanish.

CD3-20 **20. Un guión** Listen to an excerpt from a soap opera script. Mark the divisions between words and punctuate the sentences. Keep in mind the format of a script.

llegóelmomentodecisivocristinanoteníalamenorideadesusituación
estertocóalapuertadelahabitacióndecristinaestabapálida
adelanteestercristinadebodecirtelaverdadluisitonoestuhijo

¡Vamos a conversar!

ESTRATEGIA **Expressing idiomatic language** As you develop your ability to express yourself in Spanish, try not to "think" in English, because you can run into trouble if you translate idiomatic English word for word. Instead, think in simple, basic terms about what you want to say. For example:

- Analyze the basic message behind *Can you give me a ride home?* You are actually asking the person to take you home in his or her car: **¿Puedes llevarme a casa (en tu coche)?**
- The idiomatic phrase *Are we on for tonight?* is asking if you are going to meet tonight: **¿Vamos a encontrarnos esta noche?** or **¿Nos veremos esta noche?**

21. ¿Cómo se dice...? With a partner, express the following ideas.

1. We had a ball!
2. I need to get dinner ready.
3. I'll walk you home.
4. I would rather take a taxi.
5. Keep quiet!

22. ¿Qué dice Ud.? What would you say in the following situations? What might the other person say? Act out the scenes with a partner. Take turns playing each role.

1. Someone tells you that there are people waiting for you. Tell him/her "let them wait, because, after all, it's still early."
2. You tell a friend what kind of movies you like and what kind you don't like.
3. You tell a friend two things that he/she must do to be successful.
4. You tell someone what you want to accomplish and what you are willing to do to achieve your goal (*meta*).

23. **Para conocernos mejor** To do this activity, work with a partner whom you would like to get to know. Take turns asking and answering these questions.

1. ¿Tú perteneces a algún club universitario? ¿A cuál? ¿Qué clubes de los que hay aquí te parecen interesantes? ¿A cuál te gustaría pertenecer?
2. Si te ofrecieran un papel en una obra teatral, ¿lo aceptarías? ¿Tendrías tiempo para ensayar o estás demasiado ocupado(a)? ¿Preferirías el papel de protagonista o uno menos importante? ¿Crees que tienes talento para actuar?
3. ¿Vas al cine a menudo? ¿Con quién? ¿Qué tipo de películas te gusta ver? De las películas que has visto últimamente, ¿cuál crees que puede ganar un Óscar? Por lo general, ¿estás de acuerdo con la opinión de los críticos?
4. Si tú estuvieras a cargo de la programación de un canal de televisión, ¿qué tipo de programas pondrías? ¿Cuáles suprimirías (*would you eliminate*)? ¿Crees que hay demasiada violencia en la televisión? ¿Estás de acuerdo con la censura (*censorship*) en la televisión? ¿Por qué?
5. ¿Has asistido alguna vez a un festival de cine? Cuando vas al cine, ¿te gusta ver los avances? Si tú estuvieras a cargo de la distribución de papeles para una película musical, ¿a qué actores escogerías (*would you choose*)? ¿Por qué?

24. **Una encuesta** Interview your classmates to identify who fits the following descriptions. Include your instructor, but remember to use the **Ud.** form when addressing him/her. After finishing the survey, get together with two or three classmates and discuss the results.

1. Cree que tendría éxito como actor (actriz).	______________
2. Le gusta ver dibujos animados.	______________
3. Le gustan los documentales.	______________
4. Ha visto una película de suspenso últimamente.	______________
5. Por lo general asiste a los estrenos.	______________
6. Tiene la banda sonora de algunas películas.	______________
7. Le gustaría tener su propia columna en un periódico.	______________
8. A veces les toma el pelo a sus amigos.	______________

25. **Para crear** These girls are going to get movie tickets. Get together in groups of three and "create" the scenario for this photo. Who are the people? Give them names. What is the relationship between them? What types of movies are they going to see? Are they going to enjoy the movies? What are they going to do afterwards?

Rincón literario

Fernán Caballero (*España: 1796–1877*)

A Fernán Caballero —quien en realidad era una mujer y cuyo verdadero nombre era Cecilia Böhl de Fáber— corresponde la gloria de haber iniciado el realismo en España y de haber señalado el camino para el renacimiento de la novela en su país. Su idea de lo que debe ser una novela queda expresada al decir: "La novela no se inventa; se observa". Su obra es el resultado de la fusión de dos elementos románticos: lo sentimental y el costumbrismo. Su primera novela, y quizás la mejor de todas, fue *La gaviota*.

Los cuentos de Fernán Caballero tienen una temática muy variada, que va desde la exquisita espiritualidad poética hasta lo vulgar. Siente especial predilección por el relato de tipo moral, y su estilo es sencillo y natural. Sus cuentos fueron publicados en la colección que lleva el título de *Cuadros de costumbres andaluzas*.

Antes de leer

ESTRATEGIA **Using prior knowledge** You will be reading a story that has some of the aspects of a fable, especially because it is didactic, which means that it has as its object to teach a lesson, which is expressed in the "**moraleja.**" The characters in the story are an old married couple and a fairy godmother. Keeping this in mind, what does the title suggest to you? Do you know or have you heard about some people who have won the lottery or have inherited a great deal of money? What happened to them afterwards? Did their lives improve?

26. ¿Necesidades o deseos? This story is about two people who are not satisfied with what they have and envy their neighbors. Read the first paragraph of the text and note your reaction to their feelings. Have you at times experienced similar thoughts? Are you perfectly happy with what you have and you don't wish for material things?

¡A leer!

27. Comprensión As you read the text, find the answers to the following questions.

1. ¿Qué hacía el matrimonio mientras estaba sentado junto al fuego?
2. ¿Qué le envidiaba el marido al tío Polainas?
3. ¿Qué le envidiaba la mujer a su vecina?
4. ¿Quién bajó por la chimenea y cómo era?
5. ¿Qué le concede el hada al matrimonio?
6. ¿Por qué no decidió el matrimonio inmediatamente lo que deseaba pedirle al hada?
7. ¿Qué vio el marido en la casa de los vecinos?
8. ¿Cómo desperdició la mujer el primer deseo?
9. ¿Por qué perdieron el segundo deseo?
10. ¿Qué querían hacer el perro y el gato?
11. ¿Cómo se sentía la mujer?
12. ¿Cuál fue el tercer deseo del matrimonio?

Los deseos (Adaptado)

Había un matrimonio anciano° que, aunque pobre, había tenido una buena vida, trabajando y cuidando de su pequeña hacienda°. Una noche de invierno, marido y mujer estaban sentados junto al fuego, y en lugar de° darle gracias a Dios por el bien y la paz de que disfrutaban, estaban enumerando los bienes° que tenían otros, y que ellos deseaban poseer también.

—Yo quiero un rancho como el del tío Polainas —decía el viejo.

—Y yo —añadía su mujer— quiero una casa como la de nuestra vecina, que es más nueva que la nuestra.

—Yo —continuaba el viejo— en lugar de la burra°, quiero un mulo como el del tío Polainas.

—Yo —añadía su mujer— ¡quiero matar un puerco° de doscientas libras como la vecina! Esa gente, para tener las cosas, sólo necesita desearlas. ¿Cuándo voy a ver yo cumplidos° mis deseos°?

Apenas° dijo estas palabras, vieron que bajaba por la chimenea una mujer hermosísima; era pequeña y traía, como una reina°, una corona° de oro en la cabeza y tenía un cetro° de oro en la mano.

—Soy el hada° Fortunata —les dijo—; pasaba por aquí, y oí sus quejas°. Vengo a concederles° tres deseos: uno a ti —le dijo a la mujer—; otro a ti —le dijo al marido—, y el tercero para los dos; este último lo voy a otorgar mañana a esta misma hora. Hasta entonces, tienen tiempo de pensar qué es lo que quieren.

Después de decir esto, desapareció.

La alegría del buen matrimonio fue muy grande y pensaron en tantos deseos que, no pudiendo decidir, dejaron la elección° definitivamente para la mañana siguiente, y toda la noche para consultarlo con la almohada°, y se pusieron a conversar de otras cosas.

Empezaron a hablar otra vez de sus afortunados vecinos.

—Hoy estuve allí —dijo el marido—. Estaban haciendo las morcillas°. ¡Eran magníficas!

—¡Mmm! Quiero comer una de esas morcillas —dijo la mujer—. Inmediatamente apareció sobre las brasas° la morcilla más hermosa del mundo.

elderly
property
en... *instead of*
assets
donkey
pig
fulfilled / wishes
Barely
queen
crown / wand
fairy
complaints / grant you
choice
consultarlo... *sleep on it*
blood sausages
coals

La mujer se quedó mirándola con la boca abierta. El marido se levantó, desesperado.

—Por ti, que eres tan comilona°, desperdiciamos uno de los deseos. ¡Qué mujer tan tonta! ¿Por qué no se te pega° una morcilla en la naríz?

Al terminar de decirlo, ya estaba la morcilla colgando° de la nariz de la mujer. —¡Yo no quiero esta morcilla en mi nariz!

—Mujer, ¿y el rancho?

—Nada.

—¿Y la casa?

—Nada.

—Te puedo hacer una funda de oro para la morcilla.

—¿Estás loco?

—Pues qué, ¿nos vamos a quedar como estábamos?

—Ése es todo mi deseo.

El marido siguió rogando, pero no convenció a su mujer, que estaba más y más desesperada por su doble nariz y tratando de apartar° al perro y al gato, que querían comerse la morcilla.

Cuando, a la noche siguiente, apareció el hada y le dijeron cuál era su último deseo, ella les respondió:

—Ya ven cuán ciegos° y necios° son los hombres, creyendo que la satisfacción de sus deseos trae felicidad. La dicha° no está en el cumplimiento de los deseos; la dicha está en no tenerlos; porque rico es el que posee, pero feliz el que nada desea.

gluttonous
sticks
hanging
push away
blind / foolish
happiness

Después de leer... reflexiones

28. Gente que conocen In groups of three or four, talk about some people you know who are never satisfied with what they have.

1. ¿Quiénes son estas personas? ¿Piensan incluir Uds. a personas famosas?
2. ¿Cuán importante son las cosas materiales para Uds.? ¿Qué cosas consideran necesarias?
3. ¿Qué harían si tuvieran muchísimo dinero? ¿Usarían parte de ese dinero para ayudar a los pobres?
4. ¿Hay algún talento que Uds. no posean y deseen tener?
5. ¿Cuál es la moraleja del cuento? ¿Están Uds. de acuerdo con esta idea?

¡Vamos a escribir!

Antes de escribir

ESTRATEGIA **Writing a dialogue** When writing a dialogue, you have to "think" as your characters would think; you have to "become" that person. This would allow you to decide what they would say, and how they would say it. Follow these guidelines.

- Identify the people participating in the dialogue.
- Decide whether the people are educated or lack education.
- Decide whether they are young or old.
- Is one of them trying to persuade the other or are they in agreement?
- Is there a problem to solve?

29. Mi hada madrina y yo You will use your imagination to write a dialogue between you and your fairy godmother in which you ask her for three wishes and explain to her why you need or want the things that you ask for. Are they material things? Are they talents you would like to possess? How does your fairy godmother react?

¡A escribir!

30. El diálogo Write the **primer borrador** of your dialogue. Remember how a dialogue is presented in Spanish:

—Hola. ¿Cómo está?

—Bien, ¿y usted?

Después de escribir

31. A revisar Before writing the final version of your dialogue, exchange your first draft with a classmate's and peer edit each other's work. Make sure the guidelines have been followed.

España (Cont.)

¡Salud, amor y pesetas[1]! Asi brindamos con vino, que sea de Andalucía, que produce uno de los mejores vinos de España y el famoso Jerez. Andalucía es también la tierra de los olivos y del flamenco.

Como sabrás, el sur de España estuvo en poder de los árabes por más de 700 años. Su influencia se ve principalmente en la arquitectura de las ciudades más conocidas: Sevilla, Córdoba y Granada.

La Torre de la Giralda es una de las construcciones más famosas de Sevilla. Fue construida por los moros entre 1170 y 1200. En 1401 fue destruida y en el siglo XVI se convirtió en campanario.

En la Mezquita-Catedral de Córdoba se mezclan la arquitectura islámica y la cristiana.

La mezquita fue construida en el siglo VIII, y convertida en la Catedral de Santa María en el siglo XVIII.

La Alhambra está en Granada. Es un inmenso palacio construido por los árabes en el siglo XIV. Son notables allí el Patio de los Leones y sus hermosos jardines.

Los personajes principales de la novela Don Quijote: Sancho Panza, a la izquierda, y don Quijote, a la derecha. Plaza de España, Sevilla.

[1]Former Spanish currency.

La Feria de Abril, en Sevilla, es color, alegría y fiesta. Dura seis días, y se celebra una o dos semanas después de la Semana Santa. En estos días, los sevillanos visten sus trajes típicos.

La Semana Santa de Sevilla es una de las más famosas del mundo hispano. Durante la semana hay procesiones con las imágenes de Jesucristo y de la Virgen María, entre otras.

Tapas y música

Una costumbre muy española es "ir de tapas". La gente se reúne en los bares y restaurantes para charlar, comer y beber. Las tapas son pequeñas muestras (*samples*) de diferentes comidas típicas.

La música moderna española ha llegado a muchos países del mundo. Cantantes como Enrique Iglesias, David Bisbal, Rosario y Joaquín Sabina actúan en espectáculos en toda Latinoamérica y en Estados Unidos.

Ahora dime...

In groups of three, talk about the following.

1. ¿En qué lugar de los Estados Unidos se produce muy buen vino? ¿Qué tipos de vino conocen ustedes?
2. ¿Celebran ferias en la ciudad donde tú vives? ¿Cómo son?
3. ¿Hay alguna costumbre en este país que sea similar a la de "ir de tapas"? ¿Cuál?
4. ¿Han escuchado música española? ¿Conocen ustedes algunos cantantes españoles?

iLrn

To learn more about Spain, watch the cultural footage in the Media Library.

AUTOPRUEBA

¿Cuánto sé ahora?

Take this test. When you have finished, check your answers in the answer key provided in Appendix D. Then use a red pen to correct any mistakes you may have made. Are you ready?

A. Uses of some prepositions after certain verbs Complete the following sentences, using the verbs listed and the appropriate prepositions.

casarse	invitar	pensar	fijarse
insistir	enseñar	asistir	empezar

1. Yo los quiero ________ cenar conmigo.
2. Nosotros ________ ensayar a las siete y terminamos a las diez.
3. Ellos ________ todos los estrenos.
4. Yo te puedo ________ bailar el tango, porque yo lo bailo muy bien.
5. Ana va a ________ Julio. La boda es en septiembre.
6. Yo nunca ________ la ropa de la gente.
7. Elena siempre ________ trabajar duro, aunque esté cansada.
8. Yo siempre estoy ________ mi novia. ¡Estoy loco por ella!

B. Uses of *por* and *para* in certain expressions Complete the following sentences, using the appropriate expressions with **por** or **para**.

1. ________, yo estoy dispuesto a ayudarte, pero hoy no puedo hacer nada por ti.
2. ________, mis padres ya no me dan dinero.
3. Yo me perdí el festival de cine y, ________, estuve enferma toda la semana.
4. ¿________ quieres ver los avances? ¡Son muy aburridos!
5. ¿Tu papá te compró la banda sonora de la película que tú le pediste el año pasado?
   ¡________!
6. Me llevó a un restaurante de comida rápida. ¡________ me puse un vestido tan elegante!
7. ________ yo puedo empezar a trabajar el mes entrante.
8. No quiero irme de Madrid. Quiero quedarme aquí ________.

C. Complete the following, using the appropriate idiomatic expressions.

1. Tengo que estar allí a las cinco __________.
2. __________ cuando él no me devolvió el dinero que yo le había prestado.
3. __________ se levantó y se fue, sin decir nada.
4. __________. Lo esperé hasta las diez y no vino.
5. __________ vas a casarte con tu prometido; si no es este año, será el próximo año.
6. Me tienes que traer todos los documentos mañana __________.
7. Las chicas __________ un abrigo negro.
8. No me van a dar el papel principal; yo __________.
9. Ella se enojó con él, pero esta mañana __________.
10. __________ la opinion de la gente. Yo hago lo que quiero.

D. Just words . . . Match the questions in column A with the answers in column B.

A		B
1. ¿Es una película de guerra?	____	a. Sí, desde las cuatro.
2. ¿Quién dirigió la película?	____	b. La cartelera.
3. ¿Fuiste al estreno?	____	c. No, no lo han estrenado.
4. ¿Están comprometidos?	____	d. No, él dice sí y ella dice no.
5. ¿Se llama Ada?	____	e. Del reparto de papeles.
6. ¿Los actores están aquí?	____	f. Sí, toca el contrabajo.
7. ¿Se hizo famoso?	____	g. No, me lo perdí.
8. ¿No se ponen de acuerdo?	____	h. Las de suspenso.
9. ¿Hablas en serio?	____	i. Sí... o Ana, o algo por el estilo.
10. ¿Qué estás leyendo?	____	j. No, te estoy tomando el pelo.
11. ¿Viste esa película?	____	k. No, de ciencia ficción.
12. ¿Roberto es músico?	____	l. Sí, va a seguir los pasos de su mamá.
13. ¿Qué tipo de películas te gustan?	____	m. ¡Sí! ¡Está loco por ella!
14. ¿De qué estás encargado?	____	n. Almodóvar.
15. ¿Está enamorado de Nora?	____	o. Sí, de la noche a la mañana.
16. ¿Va a ser actriz?	____	p. Sí, se casan en mayo.

E. Culture

1. Answer the following questions, based on the information found in the **¿Lo sabía Ud.?** section.
   a. ¿Cuál es el baile típico de la región de Andalucía?
   b. ¿De qué país son los directores Almodóvar y Buñuel?
2. Complete the following, based on the information found in the **El mundo hispánico y tú** section.
   a. En la Mezquita, la Catedral de Córdoba, se mezclan la arquitectura ________ y la ________.
   b. La Feria de Abril se celebra una o dos semanas después de la ______________.

F. Un dicho Do you remember the Spanish saying that states that liars are always found out? Find it in this lesson.

SPANISH SOUNDS Vowels

There are five distinct vowels in Spanish: **a, e, i, o,** and **u.** Each vowel has only one basic, constant sound. The pronunciation of each vowel is constant, clear, and brief. The length of the sound is practically the same whether it is produced in a stressed or unstressed syllable.[1]

While producing the sounds of the English stressed vowels that most closely resemble the Spanish ones, the speaker changes the position of the tongue, lips, and lower jaw, so that the vowel actually starts as one sound and then glides into another. In Spanish, however, the tongue, lips, and jaw keep a constant position during the production of the sound.

English: ban*a*na **Spanish:** ban**a**na

The stress falls on the same vowel and syllable in both Spanish and English, but the English stressed *a* is longer than the Spanish stressed **a.**

English: ban*a*na **Spanish:** ban**a**na

Note also that the English stressed *a* has a sound different from the other *a*'s in the word, while the Spanish **a** sound remains constant.

a The Spanish **a** sounds similar to the English *a* in the word *father.*

alta	casa	palma	Ana
cama	Panamá	alma	apagar

e The Spanish **e** is pronounced like the English *e* in the word *eight.*

mes	entre	este	deje
ese	encender	teme	prender

i The Spanish **i** has a sound similar to the English *ee* in the word *see.*

fin ir sí sin dividir Trini difícil

o The Spanish **o** is similar to the English *o* in the word *no,* but without the glide.

toco	como	poco	roto
corto	corro	solo	loco

u The Spanish **u** is pronounced like the English *oo* sound in the word *shoot* or the *ue* sound in the word *Sue.*

su	Lulú	Úrsula	cultura
un	luna	sucursal	Uruguay

Diphthongs and Triphthongs

When unstressed **i** or **u** falls next to another vowel in a syllable, it unites with that vowel to form what is called a *diphthong*. Both vowels are pronounced as one syllable. Their sounds do not change; they are only pronounced more rapidly and with a glide. For example:

tr**ai**ga	Lid**ia**	tr**ei**nta	s**ie**te	**oi**go	ad**ió**s
Aurora	ag**ua**	b**ue**no	antig**uo**	c**iu**dad	L**ui**s

[1] In a stressed syllable, the prominence of the vowel is indicated by its loudness.

A triphthong is the union of three vowels: a stressed vowel between two unstressed ones (**i** or **u**) in the same syllable. For example: Parag**uay,** estud**iéi**s.

Note: Stressed **i** and **u** do not form diphthongs with other vowels, except in the combinations **iu** and **ui.** For example: **rí**-o, sa-**bí**-ais.

In syllabication, diphthongs and triphthongs are considered a single vowel; their components cannot be separated.

Consonants

p Spanish **p** is pronounced in a manner similar to the English *p* sound, but without the puff of air that follows after the English sound is produced.

pesca	pude	puedo	parte	papá
postre	piña	puente	Paco	

k The Spanish **k** sound, represented by the letters **k, c** before **a, o, u** or a consonant, and **qu,** is similar to the English *k* sound, but without the puff of air.

casa	comer	cuna	clima	acción	que
quinto	queso	aunque	kiosko	kilómetro	

t Spanish **t** is produced by touching the back of the upper front teeth with the tip of the tongue. It has no puff of air as in the English *t.*

todo	antes	corto	Guatemala	diente
resto	tonto	roto	tanque	

d The Spanish consonant **d** has two different sounds depending on its position. At the beginning of an utterance and after **n** or **l,** the tip of the tongue presses the back of the upper front teeth.

día	doma	dice	dolor	dar
anda	Aldo	caldo	el deseo	un domicilio

In all other positions the sound of **d** is similar to the *th* sound in the English word *they,* but softer.

medida	todo	nada	nadie	medio
puedo	moda	queda	nudo	

g The Spanish consonant **g** is similar to the English *g* sound in the word *guy* except before **e** or **i.**

goma	glotón	gallo	gloria	lago	alga
gorrión	garra	guerra	angustia	algo	Dagoberto

j The Spanish sound **j** (or **g** before **e** and **i**) is similar to a strongly exaggerated English *h* sound.

gemir	juez	jarro	gitano	agente
juego	giro	bajo	gente	

b, v There is no difference in sound between Spanish **b** and **v.** Both letters are pronounced alike. At the beginning of an utterance or after **m** or **n, b** and **v** have a sound identical to the English *b* sound in the word *boy.*

vivir	beber	vamos	barco	enviar
hambre	batea	bueno	vestido	

When pronounced between vowels, the Spanish **b** and **v** sound is produced by bringing the lips together but not closing them, so that some air may pass through.

sábado	autobús	yo voy	su barco

y, ll In most countries, Spanish **ll** and **y** have a sound similar to the English *y* sound in the word *yes*.

el llavero	trayecto	su yunta	milla
oye	el yeso	mayo	yema
un yelmo	trayectoria	llama	bella

NOTE: When it stands alone or is at the end of a word, Spanish **y** is pronounced like the vowel **i**.

rey	hoy	y	doy	buey
muy	voy	estoy	soy	

r The sound of Spanish **r** is similar to the English *dd* sound in the word *ladder*.

crema	aroma	cara	arena	aro
harina	toro	oro	eres	portero

rr Spanish **rr** and also **r** in an initial position and after **n, l,** or **s** are pronounced with a very strong trill. This trill is produced by bringing the tip of the tongue near the alveolar ridge and letting it vibrate freely while the air passes through the mouth.

rama	carro	Israel	cierra	roto
perro	alrededor	rizo	corre	Enrique

s Spanish **s** is represented in most of the Spanish world by the letters **s, z,** and **c** before **e** or **i.** The sound is very similar to the English sibilant *s* in the word *sink*.

sale	sitio	presidente	signo
salsa	seda	suma	vaso
sobrino	ciudad	cima	canción
zapato	zarza	cerveza	centro

h The letter **h** is silent in Spanish.

hoy	hora	hilo	ahora
humor	huevo	horror	almohada

ch Spanish **ch** is pronounced like the English *ch* in the word *chief*.

hecho	chico	coche	Chile
mucho	muchacho	salchicha	

f Spanish **f** is identical in sound to the English *f*.

difícil	feo	fuego	forma
fácil	fecha	foto	fueron

l Spanish **l** is similar to the English *l* in the word *let*.

dolor	lata	ángel	lago	sueldo
los	pelo	lana	general	fácil

m Spanish **m** is pronounced like the English *m* in the word *mother*.

mano	moda	mucho	muy
mismo	tampoco	multa	cómoda

n In most cases, Spanish **n** has a sound similar to the English *n*.

nada	nunca	ninguno	norte
entra	tiene	sienta	

The sound of Spanish **n** is often affected by the sounds that occur around it. When it appears before **b, v,** or **p,** it is pronounced like an **m**.

tan bueno	toman vino	sin poder
un pobre	comen peras	siguen bebiendo

ñ Spanish **ñ** is similar to the English *ny* sound in the word *canyon*.

señor	otoño	ñoño	uña
leña	dueño	niños	años

x Spanish **x** has two pronunciations depending on its position. Between vowels the sound is similar to English *ks*.

examen	exacto	boxeo	éxito
oxidar	oxígeno	existencia	

When it occurs before a consonant, Spanish **x** sounds like *s*.

expresión	explicar	extraer	excusa
expreso	exquisito	extremo	

NOTE: When **x** appears in **México** or in other words of Mexican origin, it is pronounced like the Spanish letter **j.**

Rhythm

Rhythm is the variation of sound intensity that we usually associate with music. Spanish and English each regulate these variations in speech differently because they have different patterns of syllable length. In Spanish the length of the stressed and unstressed syllables remains almost the same, while the English stressed syllables are considerably longer than unstressed ones. Pronounce the following Spanish words, enunciating each syllable clearly.

es-tu-dian-te	bue-no	Úr-su-la
com-po-si-ción	di-fí-cil	ki-ló-me-tro
po-li-cí-a	Pa-ra-guay	

Because the length of the Spanish syllables remains constant, the greater the number of syllables in a given word or phrase, the longer the phrase will be.

Linking

In spoken Spanish, the different words in a phrase or a sentence are not pronounced as isolated elements but are combined together. This is called *linking*.

Pepe come pan.	Pe-pe-co-me-pan
Tomás toma leche.	To-más-to-ma-le-che
Luis tiene la llave.	Luis-tie-ne-la-lla-ve
La mano de Roberto.	La-ma-no-de-Ro-ber-to

› The final consonant of a word is pronounced together with the initial vowel of the following word.

Carlos anda	Car-lo-san-da
un ángel	u-nán-gel
el otoño	e-lo-to-ño
unos estudios interesantes	u-no-ses-tu-dio-sin-te-re-san-tes

› A diphthong is formed between the final vowel of a word and the initial vowel of the following word. A triphthong is formed when there is a combination of three vowels (see rules for the formation of diphthongs and triphthongs on pages A-1 and A-2).

su hermana	suher-ma-na
tu escopeta	tues-co-pe-ta
Roberto y Luis	Ro-ber-toy-Luis
negocio importante	ne-go-cioim-por-tan-te
lluvia y nieve	llu-viay-nie-ve
ardua empresa	ar-duaem-pre-sa

- When the final vowel of a word and the initial vowel of the following word are identical, they are pronounced slightly longer than one vowel.

Ana alcanza	A-n*a*l-can-za
lo olvido	l*o*l-vi-do
tiene eso	tie-n*e*-so
Ada atiende	Ad*a*-tien-de

- The same rule applies when two identical vowels appear within a word.

crees	cres
Teherán	Te-rán
coordinación	cor-di-na-ción

- When the final consonant of a word and the initial consonant of the following word are the same, they are pronounced as one consonant with slightly longer than normal duration.

el lado	e-*l*a-do
Carlos salta	Car-lo-*s*al-ta
tienes sed	tie-ne-*s*ed

Intonation

Intonation is the rise and fall of pitch in the delivery of a phrase or a sentence. In general, Spanish pitch tends to change less than English, giving the impression that the language is less emphatic.

As a rule, the intonation for normal statements in Spanish starts in a low tone, rises to a higher one on the first stressed syllable, maintains that tone until the last stressed syllable, and then goes back to the initial low tone, with still another drop at the very end.

Tu amigo viene mañana.	José come pan.
Ada está en casa.	Carlos toma café.

Syllable Formation in Spanish

General rules for dividing words into syllables:

Vowels

- A vowel or a vowel combination can constitute a syllable.

a-lum-no a-bue-la Eu-ro-pa

- Diphthongs and triphthongs are considered single vowels and cannot be divided.

bai-le puen-te Dia-na es-tu-diáis an-ti-guo

- Two strong vowels (**a**, **e**, **o**) do not form a diphthong and are separated into two syllables.

em-ple-ar vol-te-ar lo-a

- A written accent on a weak vowel (**i** or **u**) breaks the diphthong, separating the vowels into two syllables.

trí-o dú-o Ma-rí-a

Consonants

- A single consonant forms a syllable with the vowel that follows it.

po-der ma-no mi-nu-to

NOTE: Spanish **ch, ll,** and **rr** are considered single consonants: **a-ma-ri-llo, co-che, pe-rro.**

- When two consonants appear between two vowels, they are separated into two syllables.

  al-fa-be-to   cam-pe-ón   me-ter-se   mo-les-tia

  EXCEPTION: When a consonant cluster composed of **b, c, d, f, g, p,** or **t** with **l** or **r** appears between two vowels, the cluster joins the following vowel: **so-bre, o-tros, ca-ble, te-lé-gra-fo.**

- When three consonants appear between two vowels, only the last one goes with the following vowel.

  ins-pec-tor   trans-por-te   trans-for-mar

  EXCEPTION: When there is a cluster of three consonants in the combinations described in rule 2, the first consonant joins the preceding vowel and the cluster joins the following vowel: **es-cri-bir, ex-tran-je-ro, im-plo-rar, es-tre-cho.**

Accentuation

In Spanish, all words are stressed according to specific rules. Words that do not follow the rules must have a written accent to indicate the change of stress. The basic rules for accentuation are as follows.

- Words ending in a vowel, **n**, or **s** are stressed on the next-to-last syllable.

hi-jo	**ca**-lle	**me**-sa	fa-**mo**-sos
flo-**re**-cen	**pla**-ya	**ve**-ces	

- Words ending in a consonant, except **n** or **s**, are stressed on the last syllable.

  ma-**yor**   a-**mor**   tro-pi-**cal**   na-**riz**   re-**loj**   co-rre-**dor**

- All words that do not follow these rules must have a written accent.

ca-**fé**	**lá**-piz	**mú**-si-ca	sa-**lón**
án-gel	**lí**-qui-do	fran-**cés**	**Víc**-tor
sim-**pá**-ti-co	rin-**cón**	a-**zú**-car	de-**mó**-cra-ta
sa-**lió**	**dé**-bil	e-**xá**-me-nes	

- Pronouns and adverbs of interrogation and exclamation have a written accent to distinguish them from relative pronouns.

¿**Qué** comes?	*What are you eating?*
La pera que él no comió.	*The pear that he did not eat.*
¿**Quién** está ahí?	*Who is there?*
El hombre a quien tú llamaste.	*The man whom you called.*
¿**Dónde** está él?	*Where is he?*
En el lugar donde trabaja.	*At the place where he works.*

- Words that have the same spelling but different meanings take a written accent to differentiate one from the other.

el	*the*	él	*he, him*	te	*you*	té	*tea*
mi	*my*	mí	*me*	si	*if*	sí	*yes*
tu	*your*	tú	*you*	mas	*but*	más	*more*

VERBS Regular Verbs

Model *-ar, -er, -ir* verbs

	Infinitive	
amar *(to love)*	**comer** *(to eat)*	**vivir** *(to live)*
	Present Participle	
amando *(loving)*	**comiendo** *(eating)*	**viviendo** *(living)*
	Past Participle	
amado *(loved)*	**comido** *(eaten)*	**vivido** *(lived)*

SIMPLE TENSES

Indicative Mood

Present

(I love)		*(I eat)*		*(I live)*	
amo	amamos	como	comemos	vivo	vivimos
amas	amáis	comes	coméis	vives	vivís
ama	aman	come	comen	vive	viven

Imperfect

(I used to love)		*(I used to eat)*		*(I used to live)*	
amaba	amábamos	comía	comíamos	vivía	vivíamos
amabas	amabais	comías	comíais	vivías	vivíais
amaba	amaban	comía	comían	vivía	vivían

Preterit

(I loved)		*(I ate)*		*(I lived)*	
amé	amamos	comí	comimos	viví	vivimos
amaste	amasteis	comiste	comisteis	viviste	vivisteis
amó	amaron	comió	comieron	vivió	vivieron

Future

(I will love)		*(I will eat)*		*(I will live)*	
amaré	amaremos	comeré	comeremos	viviré	viviremos
amarás	amaréis	comerás	comeréis	vivirás	viviréis
amará	amarán	comerá	comerán	vivirá	vivirán

Conditional

(I would love)		*(I would eat)*		*(I would live)*	
amaría	amaríamos	comería	comeríamos	viviría	viviríamos
amarías	amaríais	comerías	comeríais	vivirías	viviríais
amaría	amarían	comería	comerían	viviría	vivirían

Subjunctive Mood

Present

([that] I [may] love)		*([that] I [may] eat)*		*([that] I [may] live)*	
ame	amemos	coma	comamos	viva	vivamos
ames	améis	comas	comáis	vivas	viváis
ame	amen	coma	coman	viva	vivan

Imperfect (two forms: -ra, -se)

([that] I [might] love)	*([that] I [might] eat)*	*([that] I [might] live)*
amara(-ase)	comiera(-iese)	viviera(-iese)
amaras(-ases)	comieras(-ieses)	vivieras(-ieses)
amara(-ase)	comiera(-iese)	viviera(-iese)
amáramos(-ásemos)	comiéramos(-iésemos)	viviéramos(-iésemos)
amarais(-aseis)	comierais(-ieseis)	vivierais(-ieseis)
amaran(-asen)	comieran(-iesen)	vivieran(-iesen)

Imperative Mood

(love)	*(eat)*	*(live)*
ama (tú)	come (tú)	vive (tú)
ame (Ud.)	coma (Ud.)	viva (Ud.)
am**emos** (nosotros)	com**amos** (nosotros)	viv**amos** (nosotros)
am**ad** (vosotros)	com**ed** (vosotros)	viv**id** (vosotros)
am**en** (Uds.)	com**an** (Uds.)	viv**an** (Uds.)

COMPOUND TENSES

Perfect Infinitive

haber amado	haber comido	haber vivido

Perfect Participle

habiendo amado	habiendo comido	habiendo vivido

Indicative Mood

Present Perfect

(I have loved)	*(I have eaten)*	*(I have lived)*
he amado	he comido	he vivido
has amado	has comido	has vivido
ha amado	ha comido	ha vivido
hemos amado	hemos comido	hemos vivido
habéis amado	habéis comido	habéis vivido
han amado	han comido	han vivido

Pluperfect

(I had loved)	*(I had eaten)*	*(I had lived)*
había amado	había comido	había vivido
habías amado	habías comido	habías vivido
había amado	había comido	había vivido
habíamos amado	habíamos comido	habíamos vivido
habíais amado	habíais comido	habíais vivido
habían amado	habían comido	habían vivido

Future Perfect

(I will have loved)	*(I will have eaten)*	*(I will have lived)*
habré amado	habré comido	habré vivido
habrás amado	habrás comido	habrás vivido
habrá amado	habrá comido	habrá vivido
habremos amado	habremos comido	habremos vivido
habréis amado	habréis comido	habréis vivido
habrán amado	habrán comido	habrán vivido

Conditional Perfect

(I would have loved)	*(I would have eaten)*	*(I would have lived)*
habría amado	habría comido	habría vivido
habrías amado	habrías comido	habrías vivido
habría amado	habría comido	habría vivido
habríamos amado	habríamos comido	habríamos vivido
habríais amado	habríais comido	habríais vivido
habrían amado	habrían comido	habrían vivido

Subjunctive Mood

Present Perfect

([that] I [may] have loved)	*([that] I [may] have eaten)*	*([that] I [may] have lived)*
haya amado	haya comido	haya vivido
hayas amado	hayas comido	hayas vivido

haya amado	haya comido	haya vivido
hayamos amado	hayamos comido	hayamos vivido
hayáis amado	hayáis comido	hayáis vivido
hayan amado	hayan comido	hayan vivido
	Pluperfect (two forms: -ra, -se)	
([that] I [might] have loved)	*([that] I [might] have eaten)*	*([that] I [might] have lived)*
hubiera(-iese) amado	hubiera(-iese) comido	hubiera(-iese) vivido
hubieras(-ieses) amado	hubieras(-ieses) comido	hubieras(-ieses) vivido
hubiera(-iese) amado	hubiera(-iese) comido	hubiera(-iese) vivido
hubiéramos(-iésemos) amado	hubiéramos(-iésemos) comido	hubiéramos(-iésemos) vivido
hubierais(-ieseis) amado	hubierais(-ieseis) comido	hubierais(-ieseis) vivido
hubieran(-iesen) amado	hubieran(-iesen) comido	hubieran(-iesen) vivido

Stem-changing verbs

The *-ar* and *-er* stem-changing verbs

Stem-changing verbs are those that have a spelling change in the root of the verb. Stem-changing verbs that end in **-ar** and **-er** change the stressed vowel **e** to **ie,** and the stressed **o** to **ue.** These changes occur in all persons, except the first- and second-persons plural, of the present indicative, present subjunctive, and imperative.

Infinitive	Indicative	Imperative	Subjunctive
cerrar	cierro	——	cierre
(to close)	cierras	cierra	cierres
	cierra	cierre	cierre
	cerramos	cerremos	cerremos
	cerráis	cerrad	cerréis
	cierran	cierren	cierren
perder	pierdo	——	pierda
(to lose)	pierdes	pierde	pierdas
	pierde	pierda	pierda
	perdemos	perdamos	perdamos
	perdéis	perded	perdáis
	pierden	pierdan	pierdan
contar	cuento	——	cuente
(to count; to tell)	cuentas	cuenta	cuentes
	cuenta	cuente	cuente
	contamos	contemos	contemos
	contáis	contad	contéis
	cuentan	cuenten	cuenten
volver	vuelvo	——	vuelva
(to return)	vuelves	vuelve	vuelvas
	vuelve	vuelva	vuelva
	volvemos	volvamos	volvamos
	volvéis	volved	volváis
	vuelven	vuelvan	vuelvan

Verbs that follow the same pattern:

acordarse	*to remember*	cocer	*to cook*
acostar(se)	*to go to bed*	colgar	*to hang*
almorzar	*to have lunch*	comenzar	*to begin*
atravesar	*to go through*	confesar	*to confess*

costar	*to cost*	negar	*to deny*
demostrar	*to demonstrate, show*	nevar	*to snow*
despertar(se)	*to wake up*	pensar	*to think; to plan*
empezar	*to begin*	probar	*to prove; to taste*
encender	*to light; to turn on*	recordar	*to remember*
encontrar	*to find*	rogar	*to beg*
entender	*to understand*	sentar(se)	*to sit down*
extender	*to stretch*	soler	*to be in the habit of*
llover	*to rain*	mover	*to move*
mover	*to move*	soñar	*to dream*
mostrar	*to show*	torcer	*to twist*

The *-ir* stem-changing verbs

There are two types of stem-changing verbs that end in **-ir:** one type changes stressed **e** to **ie** in some tenses and to **i** in others, and stressed **o** to **ue** or **u;** the second type changes stressed **e** to **i** only in all the irregular tenses.

Type 1: -ir: e > ie *or* i / o > ue *or* u

These changes occur as follows.

Present Indicative: all persons except the first- and second-persons plural change **e** to **ie** and **o** to **ue.** *Preterit:* third person, singular and plural, changes **e** to **i** and **o** to **u.** *Present Subjunctive:* all persons change **e** to **ie** and **o** to **ue,** except the first- and second-persons plural, which change **e** to **i** and **o** to **u.** *Imperfect Subjunctive:* all persons change **e** to **i** and **o** to **u.** *Imperative:* all persons except the first- and second-persons plural change **e** to **ie** and **o** to **ue;** first-person plural changes **e** to **i** and **o** to **u.** *Present Participle:* changes **e** to **i** and **o** to **u.**

Infinitive	**Indicative**		**Imperative**	**Subjunctive**	
sentir *(to feel)*	**PRESENT**	**PRETERIT**		**PRESENT**	**IMPERFECT**
	siento	sentí		sienta	sintiera(-iese)
	sientes	sentiste	siente	sientas	sintieras
	siente	sintió	sienta	sienta	sintiera
PRESENT PARTICIPLE sintiendo	sentimos	sentimos	sintamos	sintamos	sintiéramos
	sentís	sentisteis	sentid	sintáis	sintierais
	sienten	sintieron	sientan	sientan	sintieran
dormir *(to sleep)*	duermo	dormí		duerma	durmiera(-iese)
	duermes	dormiste	duerme	duermas	durmieras
	duerme	durmió	duerma	duerma	durmiera
PRESENT PARTICIPLE durmiendo	dormimos	dormimos	durmamos	durmamos	durmiéramos
	dormís	dormisteis	dormid	durmáis	durmierais
	duermen	durmieron	duerman	duerman	durmieran

Other verbs that follow the same pattern:

advertir	*to warn*	herir	*to wound, hurt*
arrepentirse	*to repent*	mentir	*to lie*
consentir	*to consent; to pamper*	morir	*to die*
convertir(se)	*to turn into*	preferir	*to prefer*
discernir	*to discern*	referir	*to refer*
divertir(se)	*to amuse oneself*	sugerir	*to suggest*

Type II: -ir: e > i

The verbs in the second category are irregular in the same tenses as those of the first type. The only difference is that they have only one change: **e** > **i** in all irregular persons.

Infinitive	Indicative		Imperative	Subjunctive	
pedir *(to ask for, request)*	PRESENT	PRETERIT		PRESENT	IMPERFECT
	pido	pedí		pida	pidiera(-iese)
PRESENT PARTICIPLE	pides	pediste	pide	pidas	pidieras
	pide	pidió	pida	pida	pidiera
pidiendo	pedimos	pedimos	pidamos	pidamos	pidiéramos
	pedís	pedisteis	pedid	pidáis	pidierais
	piden	pidieron	pidan	pidan	pidieran

Verbs that follow this pattern:

concebir	*to conceive*
competir	*to compete*
despedir(se)	*to say good-bye*
elegir	*to choose*
impedir	*to prevent*
perseguir	*to pursue*
repetir	*to repeat*
reñir	*to fight*
seguir	*to follow*
servir	*to serve*
vestir(se)	*to dress*

Orthographic-Changing Verbs

Some verbs undergo a change in the spelling of the stem in some tenses in order to maintain the sound of the final consonant. The most common ones are those with the consonants **g** and **c.** Remember that **g** and **c** in front of **e** or **i** have a soft sound, and in front of **a, o,** or **u** have a hard sound. In order to keep the soft sound in front of **a, o,** or **u, g** and **c** change to **j** and **z,** respectively. In order to keep the hard sound of **g** or **c** in front of **e** and **i, u** is added to the **g** (**gu**) and the **c** changes to **qu.** The most important verbs that are regular in all the tenses but change in spelling are the following.

1. Verbs ending in **-gar** change **g** to **gu** before **e** in the first person of the preterit and in all persons of the present subjunctive.

   pagar *to pay*
   Preterit: pa**gué,** pagaste, pagó, etc.
   Pres. Subj.: pa**gue**, pa**gues**, pa**gue**, pa**guemos**, pa**guéis**, pa**guen**

   Verbs that follow the same pattern: **colgar, llegar, navegar, negar, regar, rogar, jugar.**

2. Verbs ending in **-ger** or **-gir** change **g** to **j** before **o** and **a** in the first person of the present indicative and in all the persons of the present subjunctive.

   proteger *to protect*
   Pres. Ind.: prote**jo**, proteges, protege, etc.
   Pres. Subj.: prote**ja**, prote**jas**, prote**ja**, prote**jamos**, prote**jáis**, prote**jan**

   Verbs that follow the same pattern: **coger, corregir, dirigir, elegir, escoger, exigir, recoger.**

3. Verbs ending in **-guar** change **gu** to **gü** before **e** in the first person of the preterit and in all persons of the present subjunctive.

   averiguar *to find out*
   Preterit: averi**güé**, averiguaste, averiguó, etc.
   Pres. Subj.: averi**güe**, averi**gües**, averi**güe**, averi**güemos**, averi**güéis**, averi**güen**

   The verb **apaciguar** follows the same pattern.

4. Verbs ending in **-guir** change **gu** to **g** before **o** and **a** in the first person of the present indicative and in all persons of the present subjunctive.

   conseguir *to get*
   Pres. Ind.: consi**g**o, consigues, consigue, etc.
   Pres. Subj.: consi**g**a, consi**g**as, consi**g**a, consi**g**amos, consi**g**áis, consi**g**an

   Verbs that follow the same pattern: **distinguir, perseguir, proseguir, seguir.**

5. Verbs ending in **-car** change **c** to **qu** before **e** in the first person of the preterit and in all persons of the present subjunctive.

   tocar *to touch; to play (a musical instrument)*
   Preterit: to**qu**é, tocaste, tocó, etc.
   Pres. Subj.: to**qu**e, to**qu**es, to**qu**e, to**qu**emos, to**qu**éis, to**qu**en

   Verbs that follow the same pattern: **atacar, buscar, comunicar, explicar, indicar, pescar, sacar.**

6. Verbs ending in **-cer** or **-cir** preceded by a consonant change **c** to **z** before **o** and **a** in the first person of the present indicative and in all persons of the present subjunctive.

   torcer *to twist*
   Pres. Ind.: tuer**z**o, tuerces, tuerce, etc.
   Pres. Subj.: tuer**z**a, tuer**z**as, tuer**z**a, tor**z**amos, tor**z**áis, tuer**z**an

   Verbs that follow the same pattern: **convencer, esparcir, vencer.**

7. Verbs ending in **-cer** or **-cir** preceded by a vowel change **c** to **zc** before **o** and **a** in the first person of the present indicative and in all persons of the present subjunctive.

   conocer *to know, be acquainted with*
   Pres. Ind.: cono**zc**o, conoces, conoce, etc.
   Pres. Subj.: cono**zc**a, cono**zc**as, cono**zc**a, cono**zc**amos, cono**zc**áis, cono**zc**an
   Verbs that follow the same pattern: **agradecer, aparecer, carecer, entristecer** *(to sadden),* **establecer, lucir, nacer, obedecer, ofrecer, padecer, parecer, pertenecer, reconocer, relucir.**

8. Verbs ending in **-zar** change **z** to **c** before **e** in the first person of the preterit and in all persons of the present subjunctive.

   rezar *to pray*
   Preterit: re**c**é, rezaste, rezó, etc.
   Pres. Subj.: re**c**e, re**c**es, re**c**e, re**c**emos, re**c**éis, re**c**en

   Verbs that follow the same pattern: **abrazar, alcanzar, almorzar, comenzar, cruzar, empezar, forzar, gozar.**

9. Verbs ending in **-eer** change the unstressed **i** to **y** between vowels in the third-persons singular and plural of the preterit, in all persons of the imperfect subjunctive, and in the present participle.

   creer *to believe*
   Pres. Part: cre**y**endo
   Preterit: creí, creíste, cre**y**ó, creímos, creísteis, cre**y**eron
   Imp. Subj.: cre**y**era(-ese), cre**y**eras, cre**y**era, cre**y**éramos, cre**y**erais, cre**y**eran
   Past Part.: creído

   Verbs that follow the same pattern: **leer, poseer.**

10. Verbs ending in **-uir** change the unstressed **i** to **y** between vowels (except **-quir,** which has the silent **u**) in the following tenses and persons.

    huir *to escape, flee*
    Pres. Part.: hu**y**endo
    Pres. Ind.: hu**y**o, hu**y**es, hu**y**e, huimos, huís, hu**y**en
    Preterit: huí, huiste, hu**y**ó, huimos, huisteis, hu**y**eron
    Imperative: hu**y**e, hu**y**a, hu**y**amos, huid, hu**y**an
    Pres. Subj.: hu**y**a, hu**y**as, hu**y**a, hu**y**amos, hu**y**áis, hu**y**an
    Imp. Subj.: hu**y**era(-ese), hu**y**eras, hu**y**era, hu**y**éramos, hu**y**erais, hu**y**eran

Verbs that follow the same pattern: **atribuir, concluir, constituir, construir, contribuir, destituir, destruir, disminuir, distribuir, excluir, incluir, influir, instruir, restituir, sustituir.**

11. Verbs ending in **-eír** lose the **e** in the third-person singular and plural of the preterit, in all persons of the imperfect subjunctive, and in the present participle.

reír *to laugh*
Pres Ind.: río, ríes, ríe, reímos, reís, ríen
Preterit: reí, reíste, rio, reímos, reísteis, rieron
Pres. Subj.: ría, rías, ría, riamos, riáis, rían
Imp. Subj.: riera(-ese), rieras, riera, riéramos, rierais, rieran
Pres. Part.: riendo

Verbs that follow the same pattern: **freír, sonreír.**

12. Verbs ending in **-iar** add a written accent to the **i,** except in the first- and second-persons plural of the present indicative and subjunctive.

fiar(se) *to trust*
Pres. Ind.: (me) fío, (te) fías, (se) fía, (nos) fiamos, (os) fiáis, (se) fían
Pres. Subj.: (me) fíe, (te) fíes, (se) fíe, (nos) fiemos, (os) fiéis, (se) fíen

Verbs that follow the same pattern: **ampliar, criar, desviar, enfriar, enviar, guiar, telegrafiar, vaciar, variar.**

13. Verbs ending in **-uar** (except **-guar**) add a written accent to the **u,** except in the first- and second-persons plural of the present indicative and subjunctive.

actuar *to act*
Pres. Ind.: actúo, actúas, actúa, actuamos, actuáis, actúan
Pres. Subj.: actúe, actúes, actúe, actuemos, actuéis, actúen

Verbs that follow the same pattern: **acentuar, continuar, efectuar, exceptuar, graduar, habituar, insinuar, situar.**

14. Verbs ending in **-ñir** lose the **i** of the diphthongs **ie** and **ió** in the third-person singular and plural of the preterit and all persons of the imperfect subjunctive. They also change the **e** of the stem to **i** in the same persons in the present indicative and present subjunctive.

teñir *to dye*
Pres. Ind.: tiño, tiñes, tiñe, teñimos, teñís, tiñen
Preterit: teñí, teñiste, tiñó, teñimos, teñisteis, tiñeron
Pres. Subj.: tiña, tiñas, tiña, tiñamos, tiñáis, tiñan
Imp. Subj.: tiñera(-ese), tiñeras, tiñera, tiñéramos, tiñerais, tiñeran

Verbs that follow the same pattern: **ceñir, constreñir, desteñir, estreñir, reñir.**

Some Common Irregular Verbs

Only those tenses with irregular forms are given below.

adquirir *to acquire*
Pres. Ind.: adquiero, adquieres, adquiere, adquirimos, adquirís, adquieren
Pres. Subj.: adquiera, adquieras, adquiera, adquiramos, adquiráis, adquieran
Imperative: adquiere, adquiera, adquiramos, adquirid, adquieran

andar *to walk*
Preterit: anduve, anduviste, anduvo, anduvimos, anduvisteis, anduvieron
Imp. Subj.: anduviera (anduviese), anduvieras, anduviera, anduviéramos, anduvierais, anduvieran

avergonzarse *to be ashamed, to be embarrassed*
Pres. Ind.: me avergüenzo, te avergüenzas, se avergüenza, nos avergonzamos, os avergonzáis, se avergüenzan
Pres. Subj: me avergüence, te avergüences, se avergüence, nos avergoncemos, os avergoncéis, se avergüencen
Imperative: avergüénzate, avergüéncese, avergoncémonos, avergonzaos, avergüéncense

caber *to fit, to have enough room*
Pres. Ind.: quepo, cabes, cabe, cabemos, cabéis, caben
Preterit: cupe, cupiste, cupo, cupimos, cupisteis, cupieron
Future: cabré, cabrás, cabrá, cabremos, cabréis, cabrán
Conditional: cabría, cabrías, cabría, cabríamos, cabríais, cabrían
Imperative: cabe, quepa, quepamos, cabed, quepan
Pres. Subj.: quepa, quepas, quepa, quepamos, quepáis, quepan
Imp. Subj.: cupiera (cupiese), cupieras, cupiera, cupiéramos, cupierais, cupieran

caer *to fall*
Pres. Ind.: caigo, caes, cae, caemos, caéis, caen
Preterit: caí, caíste, cayó, caímos, caísteis, cayeron
Imperative: cae, caiga, caigamos, caed, caigan
Pres. Subj.: caiga, caigas, caiga, caigamos, caigáis, caigan
Imp. Subj.: cayera (cayese), cayeras, cayera, cayéramos, cayerais, cayeran
Past Part.: caído

conducir *to guide; to drive*
Pres. Ind.: conduzco, conduces, conduce, conducimos, conducís, conducen
Preterit: conduje, condujiste, condujo, condujimos, condujisteis, condujeron
Imperative: conduce, conduzca, conduzcamos, conducid, conduzcan
Pres. Subj.: conduzca, conduzcas, conduzca, conduzcamos, conduzcáis, conduzcan
Imp. Subj.: condujera (condujese), condujeras, condujera, condujéramos, condujerais, condujeran
(All verbs ending in **-ducir** follow this pattern.)

convenir *to agree (see* **venir***)*

dar *to give*
Pres. Ind.: doy, das, da, damos, dais, dan
Preterit: di, diste, dio, dimos, disteis, dieron
Imperative: da, dé, demos, dad, den
Pres. Subj.: dé, des, dé, demos, deis, den
Imp. Subj.: diera (diese), dieras, diera, diéramos, dierais, dieran

decir *to say, to tell*
Pres. Ind.: digo, dices, dice, decimos, decís, dicen
Preterit: dije, dijiste, dijo, dijimos, dijisteis, dijeron
Future: diré, dirás, dirá, diremos, diréis, dirán
Conditional: diría, dirías, diría, diríamos, diríais, dirían
Imperative: di, diga, digamos, decid, digan
Pres. Subj.: diga, digas, diga, digamos, digáis, digan
Imp. Subj.: dijera (dijese), dijeras, dijera, dijéramos, dijerais, dijeran
Pres. Part.: diciendo
Past Part.: dicho

detener *to stop; to hold; to arrest (see* **tener***)*

entretener *to entertain, amuse (see* **tener***)*

errar *to err; to miss*
Pres. Ind.: yerro, yerras, yerra, erramos, erráis, yerran
Imperative: yerra, yerre, erremos, errad, yerren
Pres. Subj.: yerre, yerres, yerre, erremos, erréis, yerren

estar *to be*
Pres. Ind.: estoy, estás, está, estamos, estáis, están
Preterit: estuve, estuviste, estuvo, estuvimos, estuvisteis, estuvieron
Imperative: está, esté, estemos, estad, estén
Pres. Subj.: esté, estés, esté, estemos, estéis, estén
Imp. Subj.: estuviera (estuviese), estuvieras, estuviera, estuviéramos, estuvierais, estuvieran

haber *to have*
Pres. Ind.: he, has, ha, hemos, habéis, han
Preterit: hube, hubiste, hubo, hubimos, hubisteis, hubieron
Future: habré, habrás, habrá, habremos, habréis, habrán
Conditional: habría, habrías, habría, habríamos, habríais, habrían
Pres. Subj.: haya, hayas, haya, hayamos, hayáis, hayan
Imp. Subj.: hubiera (hubiese), hubieras, hubiera, hubiéramos, hubierais, hubieran

hacer *to do; to make*
Pres. Ind.: hago, haces, hace, hacemos, hacéis, hacen
Preterit: hice, hiciste, hizo, hicimos, hicisteis, hicieron
Future: haré, harás, hará, haremos, haréis, harán
Imperative: haz, haga, hagamos, haced, hagan
Pres. Subj.: haga, hagas, haga, hagamos, hagáis, hagan
Imp. Subj.: hiciera (hiciese), hicieras, hiciera, hiciéramos, hicierais, hicieran
Past Part.: hecho

imponer *to impose; to depose (see* **poner***)*

ir *to go*
Pres. Ind.: voy, vas, va, vamos, vais, van
Imp. Ind.: iba, ibas, iba, íbamos, ibais, iban
Preterit: fui, fuiste, fue, fuimos, fuisteis, fueron
Imperative: ve, vaya, vayamos, id, vayan
Pres. Subj.: vaya, vayas, vaya, vayamos, vayáis, vayan
Imp. Subj.: fuera (fuese), fueras, fuera, fuéramos, fuerais, fueran

jugar *to play*
Pres. Ind.: juego, juegas, juega, jugamos, jugáis, juegan
Imperative: juega, juegue, juguemos, jugad, jueguen
Pres. Subj.: juegue, juegues, juegue, juguemos, juguéis, jueguen

obtener *to obtain (see* **tener***)*

oír *to hear*
Pres. Ind.: oigo, oyes, oye, oímos, oís, oyen
Preterit: oí, oíste, oyó, oímos, oísteis, oyeron
Imperative: oye, oiga, oigamos, oíd, oigan
Pres. Subj.: oiga, oigas, oiga, oigamos, oigáis, oigan
Imp. Subj.: oyera (oyese), oyeras, oyera, oyéramos, oyerais, oyeran
Pres. Part.: oyendo
Past Part.: oído

oler *to smell*
Pres. Ind.: huelo, hueles, huele, olemos, oléis, huelen
Imperative: huele, huela, olamos, oled, huelan
Pres. Subj.: huela, huelas, huela, olamos, oláis, huelan

poder *to be able to*
Preterit: pude, pudiste, pudo, pudimos, pudisteis, pudieron
Future: podré, podrás, podrá, podremos, podréis, podrán
Conditional: podría, podrías, podría, podríamos, podríais, podrían
Imperative: puede, pueda, podamos, poded, puedan
Pres. Subj.: pueda, puedas, pueda, podamos, podáis, puedan
Imp. Subj.: pudiera (pudiese), pudieras, pudiera, pudiéramos, pudierais, pudieran
Pres. Part.: pudiendo

poner *to place, to put*
Pres. Ind.: pongo, pones, pone, ponemos, ponéis, ponen
Preterit: puse, pusiste, puso, pusimos, pusisteis, pusieron
Future: pondré, pondrás, pondrá, pondremos, pondréis, pondrán
Conditional: pondría, pondrías, pondría, pondríamos, pondríais, pondrían
Imperative: pon, ponga, pongamos, poned, pongan
Pres. Subj.: ponga, pongas, ponga, pongamos, pongáis, pongan
Imp. Subj.: pusiera (pusiese), pusieras, pusiera, pusiéramos, pusierais, pusieran
Past Part.: puesto

querer *to want, to wish; to like, to love*
Preterit: quise, quisiste, quiso, quisimos, quisisteis, quisieron
Future: querré, querrás, querrá, querremos, querréis, querrán
Conditional: querría, querrías, querría, querríamos, querríais, querrían
Imp. Subj.: quisiera (quisiese), quisieras, quisiera, quisiéramos, quisierais, quisieran

resolver *to decide on, to solve*
Past Part.: resuelto

saber *to know*
Pres. Ind.: sé, sabes, sabe, sabemos, sabéis, saben
Preterit: supe, supiste, supo, supimos, supisteis, supieron

Future:	sabré, sabrás, sabrá, sabremos, sabréis, sabrán
Conditional:	sabría, sabrías, sabría, sabríamos, sabríais, sabrían
Imperative:	sabe, sepa, sepamos, sabed, sepan
Pres. Subj.:	sepa, sepas, sepa, sepamos, sepáis, sepan
Imp. Subj.:	supiera (supiese), supieras, supiera, supiéramos, supierais, supieran

salir *to leave; to go out*

Pres. Ind.:	salgo, sales, sale, salimos, salís, salen
Future:	saldré, saldrás, saldrá, saldremos, saldréis, saldrán
Conditional:	saldría, saldrías, saldría, saldríamos, saldríais, saldrían
Imperative:	sal, salga, salgamos, salid, salgan
Pres. Subj.:	salga, salgas, salga, salgamos, salgáis, salgan

ser *to be*

Pres. Ind.:	soy, eres, es, somos, sois, son
Imp. Ind.:	era, eras, era, éramos, erais, eran
Preterit:	fui, fuiste, fue, fuimos, fuisteis, fueron
Imperative:	sé, sea, seamos, sed, sean
Pres. Subj.:	sea, seas, sea, seamos, seáis, sean
Imp. Subj.:	fuera (fuese), fueras, fuera, fuéramos, fuerais, fueran

suponer *to assume; to suppose (see* **poner***)*

tener *to have*

Pres. Ind.:	tengo, tienes, tiene, tenemos, tenéis, tienen
Preterit:	tuve, tuviste, tuvo, tuvimos, tuvisteis, tuvieron
Future:	tendré, tendrás, tendrá, tendremos, tendréis, tendrán
Conditional:	tendría, tendrías, tendría, tendríamos, tendríais, tendrían
Imperative:	ten, tenga, tengamos, tened, tengan
Pres. Subj.:	tenga, tengas, tenga, tengamos, tengáis, tengan
Imp. Subj.:	tuviera (tuviese), tuvieras, tuviera, tuviéramos, tuvierais, tuvieran

traducir *to translate (see* **conducir***)*

traer *to bring*

Pres. Ind.:	traigo, traes, trae, traemos, traéis, traen
Preterit:	traje, trajiste, trajo, trajimos, trajisteis, trajeron
Imperative:	trae, traiga, traigamos, traed, traigan
Pres. Subj.:	traiga, traigas, traiga, traigamos, traigáis, traigan
Imp. Subj.:	trajera (trajese), trajeras, trajera, trajéramos, trajerais, trajeran
Pres. Part.:	trayendo
Past Part.:	traído

valer *to be worth*

Pres. Ind.:	valgo, vales, vale, valemos, valéis, valen
Future:	valdré, valdrás, valdrá, valdremos, valdréis, valdrán
Conditional:	valdría, valdrías, valdría, valdríamos, valdríais, valdrían
Imperative:	vale, valga, valgamos, valed, valgan
Pres. Subj.:	valga, valgas, valga, valgamos, valgáis, valgan

venir *to come*

Pres. Ind.:	vengo, vienes, viene, venimos, venís, vienen
Preterit:	vine, viniste, vino, vinimos, vinisteis, vinieron
Future:	vendré, vendrás, vendrá, vendremos, vendréis, vendrán
Conditional:	vendría, vendrías, vendría, vendríamos, vendríais, vendrían
Imperative:	ven, venga, vengamos, venid, vengan
Pres. Subj.:	venga, vengas, venga, vengamos, vengáis, vengan
Imp. Subj.:	viniera (viniese), vinieras, viniera, viniéramos, vinierais, vinieran
Pres. Part.:	viniendo

ver *to see*

Pres. Ind.:	veo, ves, ve, vemos, veis, ven
Imp. Ind.:	veía, veías, veía, veíamos, veíais, veían
Preterit:	vi, viste, vio, vimos, visteis, vieron
Imperative:	ve, vea, veamos, ved, vean
Pres. Subj.:	vea, veas, vea, veamos, veáis, vean
Imp. Subj.:	viera (viese), vieras, viera, viéramos, vierais, vieran
Past Part.:	visto

volver *to return*

Past Part.:	vuelto

GLOSSARY OF GRAMMATICAL TERMS

adjective: A word that is used to describe a noun: *tall* girl, *difficult* lesson.

adverb: A word that modifies a verb, an adjective, or another adverb. It answers the questions "How?" "When?" "Where?": She walked *slowly.* She'll be here *tomorrow.* She is *here.*

agreement: A term applied to changes in form that nouns cause in the words that surround them. In Spanish, verb forms agree with their subjects in person and number (**yo** habl**o**, **él** habl**a**, etc.). Spanish adjectives agree in gender and number with the noun they describe. Thus, a feminine plural noun requires a feminine plural ending in the adjective that describes it (cas**as** amarill**as**) and a masculine singular noun requires a masculine singular ending in the adjective (libr**o** negr**o**).

auxiliary verb: A verb that helps in the conjugation of another verb: I *have* finished. He *was* called. She *will* go. He *would* eat.

command form: The form of the verb used to give an order or a direction: *Go! Come* back! *Turn* to the right!

conjugation: The process by which the forms of the verb are presented in their different moods and tenses: I *am,* you *are,* he *is,* she *was,* we *were,* etc.

contraction: The combination of two or more words into one: *isn't, don't, can't.*

definite article: A word used before a noun indicating a definite person or thing: *the* woman, *the* money.

demonstrative: A word that refers to a definite person or object: *this, that, these, those.*

diphthong: A combination of two vowels forming one syllable. In Spanish, a diphthong is composed of one *strong* vowel (**a, e, o**) and one *weak* vowel (**u, i**) or two weak vowels: **ei, ua, ui.**

exclamation: A word used to express emotion: *How* strong! *What* beauty!

gender: A distinction of nouns, pronouns, and adjectives, based on whether they are masculine or feminine.

indefinite article: A word used before a noun that refers to an indefinite person or object: *a* child, *an* apple.

infinitive: The form of the verb generally preceded in English by the word *to* and showing no subject or number: *to do, to bring.*

interrogative: A word used in asking a question: *Who? What? Where?*

main clause: A group of words that includes a subject and a verb and by itself has complete meaning: *They saw me. I go now.*

noun: A word that names a person, place, or thing: *Ann, London, pencil.*

number: Refers to singular and plural: *chair, chairs.*

object: Generally a noun or a pronoun that is the receiver of the verb's action. A direct object answers the question *"What?"* or *"Whom?":* We know *her.* Take *it.* An indirect object answers the question *"To whom?"* or *"To what?":* Give *John* the money. Nouns and pronouns can also be objects of prepositions: The letter is *from Rick.* I'm thinking *about you.*

past participle: Past forms of a verb: *gone, worked, written.*

person: The form of the pronoun and of the verb that shows the person referred to: *I* (first-person singular), *you* (second-person singular), *she* (third-person singular), and so on.

possessive: A word that denotes ownership or possession: This is *our* house. The book isn't *mine.*

preposition: A word that introduces a noun or pronoun and indicates its function in the sentence: They were *with* us. She is *from* Nevada.

present participle: A verb form in English that ends in *-ing: eating, sleeping, working.* In Spanish, this form cannot be used as a noun or after a preposition.

pronoun: A word that is used to replace a noun: *she, them, us,* and so on. A **subject pronoun** refers to the person or thing spoken of: *They* work. An **object pronoun** receives the action of the verb: They arrested *us* (direct object pronoun). She spoke to *him* (indirect object pronoun). A pronoun can also be the object of a preposition: The children stayed with *us.*

reflexive pronoun: A pronoun that refers back to the subject: *myself, yourself, himself, herself, itself, ourselves,* and so on.

subject: The person, place, or thing spoken of: *Robert* works. *Our car* is new.

subordinate clause: A clause that has no complete meaning by itself but depends on a main clause: They knew *that I was here.*

tense: The group of forms in a verb that show the time in which the action of the verb takes place:
I go (present indicative), *I'm going* (present progressive), *I went* (past), *I was going* (past progressive), *I will go* (future), *I would go* (conditional), *I have gone* (present perfect), *I had gone* (past perfect), *that I may go* (present subjunctive), and so on.

verb: A word that expresses an action or a state: We *sleep.* The baby *is* sick.

AUTOPRUEBA: Answer key to *¿Cuánto sé ahora?*

Lección 1

A. 1. efe-o-equis 2. doble ve-i-ele-ese-o-ene 3. ka-u-ere-te 4. jota-a-ce-ka-ese-o-ene 5. be-u-de-ge-e 6. hache-i-ele-ele 7. eme-ce-de-e-ve-i-te 8. pe-e-erre-y griega 9. cu-u-e-ene-te-i-ene 10. zeta-e-ele-ele-e-ere
B. 1. cero 2. once 3. veinte 4. catorce 5. diez 6. siete 7. doce 8. treinta 9. trece 10. quince 11. treinta y ocho 12. veinticinco
C. 1. amarillo 2. anaranjado 3. negro 4. verde 5. marrón 6. morado 7. rosado 8. gris 9. rojo, blanco y azul 10. rojo, verde, amarillo
D. domingo / martes / jueves / sábado
E. 1. el treinta y uno de octubre 2. el cuatro de julio 3. el primero (uno) de enero 4. el catorce de febrero 5. el veinticinco de diciembre 6. el once de noviembre
F. 1. verano 2. primavera 3. invierno 4. otoño
G. son / somos / eres / soy / son / es / es
H. 1. Buenos / está / Bien / nuevo / mucho
2. Buenas / Universidad / Mucho / mío / Tome / favor
3. tal / Muy / tú / fecha / Es / Feliz / vemos / hasta / Saludos
I. 1 a. María b. Lola c. Quique
2 a. Unos cuarenta millones. b. Una escritora mexicoamericana.
J. El tiempo es oro.

Lección 2

A. 1. las 2. el 3. la 4. la 5. los 6. el 7. la 8. los 9. las 10. la 11. la 12. la 13. las 14. los
B. 1. una 2. una 3. unos 4. un 5. unas 6. un 7. unos 8. una 9. unos 10. una 11. una 12. unos
C. 1. cuarenta y dos 2. cien 3. cincuenta y tres 4. sesenta y uno 5. ochenta 6. setenta y nueve 7. noventa 8. ochenta y seis 9. cincuenta 10. sesenta
D. 1. La clase de español es a las nueve y diez de la mañana 2. La clase de inglés es a la una y cuarto de la tarde. 3. La clase de literatura es a las ocho y veinticinco de la noche.
E. 1. toman / tomamos / toma 2. practico / necesitas 3. llegan / llega / llegamos 4. Estudian / estudiamos 5. desea / deseo
F. 1. La dirección de las chicas / muchachas 2. Las clases de Carmen 3. Los padres de Alina
G. 1. k 2. n 3. h 4. a 5. m 6. d 7. c 8. l 9. f 10. e 11. i 12. g 13. b 14. j
H. 1. a. calle / avenida b. 24
2. a. económicas b. español
I. El saber no ocupa lugar.

Lección 3

A. 1. mi / mis 2. nuestra / su 3. tus 4. sus 5. nuestra / nuestros 6. Su
B. 1. ciento noventa y cinco 2. doscientos ochenta y seis 3. trescientos setenta y uno 4. cuatrocientos sesenta 5. quinientos cincuenta y tres 6. seiscientos cuarenta y cuatro 7. setecientos treinta y dos 8. ochocientos veintisiete 9. novecientos dieciocho 10. mil
C. 1. una chica (muchacha) muy bonita 2. una mujer encantadora 3. altos, morenos y guapos 4. inglesa / alemana
D. 1. aprendemos 2. comes 3. creo 4. leen 5. bebe 6. debe 7. venden 8. abro 9. reciben 10. escribimos
E. 1. vengo / tengo 2. tienes / viene 3. venimos / tenemos 4. viene / vienen 5. tienen
F. 1. llamo a mis amigos 2. lleva a su hermano 3. llamamos a Nora y a Alicia
G. 1. solicitud 2. informe 3. mensaje 4. ganar 5. llenar 6. alta 7. mi escritorio 8. Con ella habla 9. rubio 10. Bebo mucho.
H. 1. a. Bueno b. Castellano
2. a. béisbol b. actor / productor
I. Debes comer para vivir, no vivir para comer.

Lección 4

A. 1. contigo / conmigo 2. ti / mí 3. él / ella 4. usted / nosotros 5. ti
B. 1. del zoológico / de la playa 2. a la fiesta de Navidad / al teatro 3. al hijo del Sr. Vega 4. a los hijos de mi vecino(a)
C. 1. voy 2. damos 3. está 4. está 5. van 6. dan 7. estoy 8. van 9. estás 10. doy

D. 1. Yo no voy a hablar con mi mamá hoy. 2. Mis hijos van a estudiar en Guadalajara. 3. Mi amiga va a leer un libro. 4. Uds. van a traer los discos compactos. 5. Tú vas a bailar en la fiesta. 6. Nosotros no vamos a beber vino.
E. 1. quieren 2. empiezan (comienzan) 3. prefieres 4. entiende 5. pierde 6. pienso 7. cerramos
F. 1. tienen prisa 2. no tengo hambre / tengo mucha sed 3. tenemos calor 4. tienen mucho sueño 5. tienes miedo 6. tiene razón / tiene diez años
G. 1. contento 2. hambre 3. sacar 4. fin de semana 5. ¡Salud! 6. preocupado 7. enojada 8. cantan 9. sed 10. acabamos
H. 1. a. José b. santo
2. a. Guadalajara b. Autónoma c. pintora
I. Ojos que no ven, corazón que no siente.

Lección 5

A. 1. mucho más rico (sabroso) que 2. más de veinte 3. tan hermosa como 4. tantos problemas como 5. el más inteligente de 6. tanto helado como
B. 1. mucho mayor que 2. mejor que / el mejor de 3. mucho peor 4. la menor de
C. 1. cuesta 2. pueden 3. Recuerda 4. cuento 5. almorzamos 6. vuelves 7. llueve 8. Duerme
D. 1. Ella está diciendo que nosotros necesitamos más dinero. 2. Yo estoy hablando con mi abuela en español. 3. Nosotros estamos leyendo un libro muy bueno. 4. ¿Qué estás comiendo tú? ¿Biftec? 5. Luis está durmiendo en su cuarto. 6. Los chicos están pidiendo dinero. 7. El camarero está sirviendo la comida. 8. ¿Uds. están estudiando en la biblioteca?
E. 1. Elsa es la mamá de Marcela. 2. El restaurante Miramar está en la calle Siete. 3. ¡Mmm! El pollo está delicioso. 4. Roberto es de México, pero ahora está en Guatemala. 5. El café está frío. 6. El escritorio es de metal. 7. Hoy es lunes. 8. Elvira es profesora de español. 9. La fiesta es en la casa de Armando. 10. Mariana es muy inteligente. 11. Ellos están cansados. 12. Mi suegra es salvadoreña.
F. 1. Está lloviendo 2. Hace frío 3. Hace calor 4. nieva 5. hace sol 6. lluvia
G. 1. plato 2. servilleta 3. cordero 4. volver 5. leche 6. pescado 7. mantel 8. al mediodía 9. tinto 10. verdura
H. 1. a. propina b. euro
2. a. El quetzal b. Antigua
I. A mal tiempo, buena cara.

Lección 6

A. 1. este / esta / esos 2. Aquel / aquellas 3. Eso
B. 1. sigue 2. digo / dice 3. servimos / sirve 4. consigo 5. piden
C. 1. No, yo nunca trapeo el piso. 2. No, nosotros no limpiamos ni el baño ni la cocina. 3. No, no hay ninguna revista española en mi casa. 4. No, no hay nadie en la casa de mis suegros.
D. 1. conduzco 2. sé 3. quepo 4. salgo 5. traduzco 6. veo 7. hago 8. pongo 9. conozco 10. traigo
E. 1. Nosotros sabemos que ella es su novia. 2. Yo conozco a Teresa, pero no sé dónde vive. 3. Peter conoce Madrid, pero no sabe hablar español. 4. Los chicos no saben los poemas de memoria.
F. 1. Sí, yo la conozco. 2. Sí, mis tíos lo saben. 3. Sí, nuestros abuelos nos llevan al teatro. 4. Sí, mis primos me llaman por teléfono. 5. Sí, yo puedo llevarte. 6. Sí, yo las escondo en mi cuarto. 7. Sí, yo los lavo. 8. Sí, nosotros la sacamos todos los días.
G. 1. aspiradora / sacudir / césped / ropa 2. abrir / sé
3. escoba / huéspedes 4. sala / planchar 5. taxi / agencia
6. salgo 7. cuñado 8. montón 9. artículos
H. 1. a. trabajos b. soltera
2. a. Tegucigalpa b. En la agricultura
I. Nadie es profeta en su tierra.

Lección 7

A. 1. les da 2. le digo 3. le va a traer 4. nos sirve 5. comprarme 6. nos hablan 7. les hablamos
B. 1. A Elsa le gusta tomar una siesta. 2. A ellos les gusta caminar por el jardín. 3. A mí me gusta una habitación con vista al mar. 4. A nosotros nos gusta más ese colchón. 5. ¿A ti te gusta más nadar en la piscina? 6. ¿A Uds. les gusta viajar en el verano?
C. 1. Hace dos días que yo no duermo. 2. Hace un mes que tú no me llamas. 3. Hace media hora que nosotras estamos aquí. 4. Hace un año que ellos viven en Panamá. 5. Hace doce horas que Eva no come. 6. Hace 15 minutos que Uds. hablan por teléfono.

D. 1. llamé / reservé / pagué 2. llegué / empecé 3. leyó / dejaste / leyeron 4. volvió / gustaron / visitó 5. salí / almorcé / Regresé / nadé / miré 6. busqué / mandaron / encontré
E. 1. tercer 2. quinto 3. cuarto 4. décimo 5. octavo 6. primer
F. a. 1. maleta 2. elevador 3. mandar 4. bañera 5. alberca 6. reserva 7. descansar 8. a la izquierda
b. 1. cámara / tienda / al lado 2. puedo / reservación / nombre / doble 3. hacer / caminar 4. servicio / desayunar 5. colchón / cómodo 6. ducha 7. lista 8. cancelar 9. cambio 10. pasaporte / tarjeta
G. 1. a. pensiones / comida b. planta
2. a. economías b. Canal
H. Salió de Guatemala y entró en Guatepeor.

Lección 8

A. 1. se lo / dárselo 2. me la 3. nos la / dárnosla 4. me los 5. te lo / regalártelo 6. Se los
B. 1. fuimos / dimos 2. fueron 3. diste 4. fui 5. dieron 6. fueron 7. fue 8. fue / dio 9. fuiste / dio 10. fuimos
C. 1. Durmieron 2. siguieron 3. servimos 4. mintió 5. consiguió 6. pidieron 7. murió 8. repitió 9. dormí / durmió 10. pidió
D. para / por / por / para / por / para / para / para / por / por / para
E. 1. especialmente 2. frecuentemente 3. lenta / claramente 4. recientemente 5. Generalmente 6. Desafortunadamente
F. 1. tintorería 2. préstamo 3. robaron 4. una multa 5. gratis 6. violetas 7. fechar 8. regalo 9. encanta 10. suerte 11. estacionó 12. peces 13. equivocado 14. a plazos 15. tonterías
G. 1. a. martes b. familia
2. a. Viejo San Juan b. bosque
H. Todo tiempo pasado fue mejor.

Lección 9

A. 1. se afeita / nos afeitamos 2. me levanto / me acuesto 3. se divirtieron 4. te bañas 5. se lava 6. me olvidé 7. nos acordamos 8. se quitan 9. se despierta 10. nos preocupamos 11. te sientas 12. me visto
B. 1. ¿Tú te quitas el abrigo? 2. Ellos están en la escuela. 3. Mi mamá me lava la cabeza. 4. Uds. no se lavan las manos. 5. Los padres se preocupan por sus hijos. 6. Nosotros preferimos el café. 7. La educación es lo más importante. 8. ¿Tú vas a ir a la iglesia hoy? 9. Me gusta mucho el té. 10. La Sra. Díaz llega el lunes a las ocho de la noche.
C. 1. El mío 2. las suyas 3. las nuestras 4. las tuyas 5. los nuestros 6. El suyo (El de él) 7. La nuestra 8. el suyo (el de Uds.) 9. la mía 10. la suya (la de Ud.)
D. 1. tuve / estuvieron 2. trajeron / pusieron 3. vino / tradujo 4. pudo / tuvo 5. dijimos 6. supiste 7. vinieron / quisieron 8. condujeron 9. hizo 10. dijeron
E. 1. Hace media hora que llegué. 2. Hace tres días que vi a Carlos. 3. Hace cuatro meses que conocí a Eva. 4. Hace tres años que compré mi coche. 5. Hace quince minutos que Carlitos empezó a tocar el piano.
F. a. 1. infancia 2. bolso 3. melocotón 4. bote 5. medianoche 6. carnicería 7. órgano 8. naranja
b. 1. h 2. j 3. k 4. e 5. l 6. i 7. b 8. g 9. d 10. f 11. c 12. a
G. 1. a. productos b. música
2. a. pintores b. merengue
H. El amor todo lo puede.

Lección 10

A. 1. era / Eran 2. vivías / eras / vivía / íbamos / veías / vivían 3. era / quejaba 4. gustaba
B. 1. dijo / necesitaba / podía / tenía 2. compramos / éramos / llevábamos / íbamos 3. tenía / vinimos / hablábamos / estudiábamos 4. fue / Tuve / sentía 5. iba / vio / murieron 6. Eran / salimos / Llovía / hacía / Volvimos
C. 1. conocías / conocí 2. sabían / supimos 3. quiso / quería
D. 1. que se queja 2. que se mudaron 3. que nos gusta 4. a quien conocí 5. para quien
E. a. 1. alquiler 2. vecindad 3. subterráneo 4. lejos 5. venezolano(a) 6. avisar
b. 1. incluye / electricidad 2. amueblado 3. único 4. centro / mesita 5. desocupados 6. acondicionado / ventiladores 7. queda / estación 8. lavadora 9. tostadora 10. tratar
F. 1. a. barrio b. pisos
2. a. petróleo b. joropo
G. El que ríe último, ríe mejor.

Lección 11

A. 1. estemos 2. camines 3. saque 4. sugiera 5. den 6. sepa 7. vuelvas 8. me queje 9. sean 10. vaya 11. recoja 12. reciba
B. 1. ir / vayamos 2. venga / estés 3. ir / compre 4. hacer / hagamos 5. viajar / viajemos 6. quedarnos / se queden / visiten
C. 1. hagan una excursión. 2. venga este verano. 3. no sepas cuánto cuesta el vuelo. 4. esté enferma. 5. no podamos ir en ese viaje. 6. vayan a Colombia. 7. haga escala en Panamá.
D. a. 1. f 2. d 3. c 4. e 5. a 6. b 7. h 8. g 9. j 10. i
b. 1. excursión 2. compañera 3. frunce 4. incluyen 5. centavo 6. describen 7. fila 8. azafata 9. facturar 10. bosques
E. 1. a. comprometidas b. padrino
2. a. el Museo del Oro b. de Colombia c. Juanes y Shakira
F. Si quieres que los demás te respeten, empieza por respetar a los demás.

Lección 12

A. a. 1. Estén 2. Tráigamelo 3. Salgan 4. Désela a él 5. Vaya 6. Quédese 7. Mandémosla 8. No los ponga 9. pregúntenle 10. Cómprenlas
b. 1. Vaya al taller de mecánica 2. Dígale al mecánico que haga lo siguiente a. Cambie el aceite del coche. b. Revise los frenos. c. Arregle el neumático pinchado. d. Limpie el sistema de inyección.
B. 1. sea 2. esté 3. necesiten 4. está 5. se encuentran 6. necesitamos 7. cuesta 8. gusta
C. 1. ¿Qué idiomas se hablan en Perú? 2. ¿A qué hora se cierran las gasolineras? 3. ¿Por dónde se sale de aquí? 4. ¿Cómo se llega a la estación de servicio? 5. ¿Cómo se dice *manejar* en inglés? 6. ¿Dónde se compran piezas de repuesto?
D. a. 1. arranca 2. de cambios mecánicos 3. costó 4. bolsas 5. los frenos 6. chapa 7. la cajuela 8. vacío
b. 1. clasificados 2. compactos 3. correos / pie 4. descompuesto 5. autopista / velocidad 6. lleno 7. millas 8. taller 9. vale 10. acostumbrarme / cambios
E. 1. a. cara b. identidad
2. a. Machu Picchu b. las islas Galápagos c. Quito
F. Se sufre, pero se aprende.

Lección 13

A. 1. Dime 2. Haz / lava 3. Vete (Sal) 4. Ponlos 5. Ven 6. sé / tráeme 7. ve / compra 8. Ten 9. No compres 10. No los cambies 11. No te vayas 12. Levántate / acuéstate
B. 1. ¿Cuál es tu número de teléfono? 2. ¿Cuál es el apellido de tu abuela? 3. ¿Qué es una pulsera? 4. ¿Cuáles son las lecciones que necesitan? 5. ¿Cuál es su dirección? 6. ¿Qué es una enchilada?
C. 1. sepa 2. tienen 3. sea 4. tenga 5. haga 6. habla / hable 7. esté 8. gusta
D. a. 1. comercial / comprar 2. ponerme / ir 3. anchas 4. calza 5. lado 6. queda / talla 7. departamento / ropa 8. rayas 9. librería 10. par 11. parece 12. ganga 13. cargados 14. medirle 15. durar 16. camión
b. 1. hacer juego 2. chileno(a) 3. kilogramo 4. angosto 5. medida 6. hilo 7. devolver 8. liquidación 9. precioso 10. quedar grande 11. librería 12. tienda por departamentos 13. falda 14. sandalias 15. mediano
E. 1. a. almacenes b. métrico
2. a. En Chile b. Gabriela Mistral y Pablo Neruda c. Por sus gigantescas estatuas de piedra
F. Aunque la mona se vista de seda, mona se queda.

Lección 14

A. 1. llegue 2. vuelvan 3. van 4. vea 5. tomen 6. vayas 7. des 8. necesite 9. lleve
B. 1. escrito 2. abierto 3. visto 4. hecho 5. roto 6. ido 7. hablado 8. comido 9. recibido
C. 1. escritos 2. abiertas 3. muerto 4. cerrado 5. hechos 6. envueltos
D. 1. ha venido 2. han dicho 3. has escrito 4. he hecho 5. han hablado 6. nos hemos enojado
E. 1. había terminado 2. habían ido 3. había dicho 4. había hecho 5. habíamos matriculado 6. habías preguntado
F. a. 1. d 2. f 3. h 4. j 5. i 6. k 7. l 8. e 9. g 10. c 11. a 12. b
b. 1. física 2. gimnasio / forma 3. abrazo 4. ascendencia 5. matriculado 6. único / título 7. consejero 8. investigación / entregarlo 9. nota / sacar / promedio 10. servir
G. 1. a. "*major*" b. números
2. a. El tango. b. Buenos Aires. C. Más de 300 000.
H. En boca cerrada no entran moscas.

Lección 15

A. *Verb forms* 1. diremos 2. harán 3. querrán 4. sabré 5. vendrán 6. Iremos 7. pondrán 8. vendremos 9. tendré 10. saldremos 11. tomaremos 12. preguntarán
B. *Verb forms* 1. iría 2. recetaríamos 3. dirías 4. hablarían 5. pondría 6. vendrían 7. pediría 8. haríamos 9. saldrías 10. iría 11. podríamos 12. gustaría
C. 1. habrá dicho 2. habrán vuelto 3. Me habré mejorado 4. habremos merendado 5. habrás traído 6. habrá puesto 7. se habrán cepillado 8. se habrá curado
D. 1. habría tomado 2. habrían venido 3. habría puesto 4. habríamos ido 5. habrías hecho 6. habría preguntado 7. habrían dado 8. habrían dicho
E. 1. penicilina 2. los dientes 3. la lengua 4. los ojos 5. los pies 6. ambulancia 7. rompiste 8. la pierna 9. pusieron 10. dolor de cabeza 11. el estómago 12. embarazada
F. 1. a. centígrados b. gratis
2. a. Itaipú b. el lago Titicaca
G. Dime con quién andas y te diré quién eres.

Lección 16

A. 1. que trajeras la escopeta y se la dieras a Luis. 2. que jugaran y que no se aburrieran. 3. alguien aquí que supiera armar la tienda de campaña? 4. que fueras a patinar o a esquiar. 5. nadie que pudiera ir a misa conmigo. 6. que hicieran un picnic y que comieran asado. 7. de que ella ganara siempre y de que fuera la campeona. 8. que ella estuviera enamorada. 9. que nosotros te obligáramos a ir al estadio. 10. que los chicos se cayeran. 11. que viéramos esa obra teatral. 12. que ellos vinieran a acampar con nosotros.
B. 1. a / en / de / a / a 2. en / de / a / a / a 3. a / de / de 4. a / a 5. en / en 6. a / a 7. en 8. en
C. 1. hayan ido 2. hayas aprendido 3. haya leído 4. se haya aburrido 5. haya sabido 6. hayamos divertido 7. haya jugado 8. hayan podido
D. 1. uruguaya / actividades / libre / tabla 2. caballo / bicicleta / escalar 3. esquí / remar / sol 4. sur / oeste 5. pesca / última / nada / para 6. ostra / estos / obra 7. andar / traje 8. campo 9. campeona / ganado / nada 10. estadio / fútbol / juega 11. nieve 12. apuesto
E. 1. a. mate b. empanadas
2. a. Chile y Ecuador b. Punta del Este
F. El que no haya trabajado, que no coma.

Lección 17

A. 1. hubiera visto 2. hubieran tenido 3. hubiéramos archivado 4. hubiera ofrecido 5. hubiera escrito 6. hubieras renunciado 7. hubieran recibido 8. hubiera trabajado
B. 1. tengo 2. pudiéramos 3. hubieran ido 4. necesitan 5. hubieras visto 6. supiera 7. entrena 8. prestaran 9. hubiéramos hablado 10. fuera
C. 1. entrevistaran 2. puedas 3. avise 4. podamos / puede 5. haya 6. llegue 7. pudiera 8. paguemos 9. preguntes 10. tuviéramos 11. sea / seamos 12. estuviera
D. 1. m 2. p 3. i 4. g 5. k 6. a 7. d 8. o 9. c 10. n 11. b 12. e 13. h 14. f 15. l 16. j
E. 1. a. formales b. hogar
2. a. Una monarquía constitucional b. Barcelona
F. Si el sabio no aprueba, malo; si el necio aplaude... peor.

Lección 18

A. 1. invitar a 2. empezamos a 3. asisten a 4. enseñar a 5. casarse con 6. me fijo en 7. insiste en 8. pensando en
B. 1. Por lo general 2. Por desgracia 3. para peor 4. Para qué 5. Por fin 6. Para eso 7. Por suerte 8. para siempre
C. 1. a más tardar 2. Me dio rabia 3. De repente 4. Me dejó plantado(a) 5. Tarde o temprano 6. sin falta 7. llevaban puesto 8. yo no me hago ilusiones 9. hicieron las paces 10. No me importa
D. 1. k 2. n 3. g 4. p 5. i 6. a 7. o 8. d 9. j 10. b 11. c 12. f 13. h 14. e 15. m 16. l
E. 1. a. el flamenco b. de España
2. a. Costa del sol b. Pablo Picasso
F. Tarde o temprano se descubre al mentiroso.

PROFESSIONS AND TRADES

accountant **contador(a)**
actor **actor**
actress **actriz**
administrator **administrador(a)**
agent **agente**
architect **arquitecto(a)**
artisan **artesano(a)**
artist **artista**
baker **panadero(a)**
bank officer **empleado(a) bancario(a)**
bank teller **cajero(a)**
banker **banquero(a)**
barber **barbero(a)**
bartender **barman, cantinero(a)**
bill collector **cobrador(a)**
bookkeeper **tenedor(a) de libros**
brickmason (bricklayer) **albañil**
butcher **carnicero(a)**
buyer **comprador(a)**
camera operator **camarógrafo(a)**
carpenter **carpintero(a)**
cashier **cajero(a)**
chiropractor **quiropráctico(a)**
clerk **dependiente(a)** *(store)*, **oficinista** *(office)*
computer operator **computista**
construction worker **obrero(a) de la construcción**
constructor **constructor(a)**
contractor **contratista**
cook **cocinero(a)**
copilot **copiloto** *(masc., fem.)*
counselor **consejero(a)**
dancer **bailarín(-ina)**
decorator **decorador(a)**
dental hygienist **higienista dental**
dentist **dentista**
designer **diseñador(a)**
detective **detective**
dietician **especialista en dietética**
diplomat **diplomático(a)**
director **director(a)**
dockworker **obrero(a) portuario(a)**
doctor **doctor(a), médico(a)**
draftsman **dibujante**
dressmaker **modista**
driver **conductor(a)**
economist **economista**
editor **editor(a)**
electrician **electricista**
engineer **ingeniero(a)**
engineering technician **ingeniero(a) técnico(a)**
eye doctor **oculista**
farmer **agricultor(a)**
fashion designer **diseñador(a) de alta costura**
fire fighter **bombero(a)**
fisherman **pescador(a)**
flight attendant **auxiliar de vuelo**
foreman **capataz, encargado(a)**
funeral director **empresario(a) de pompas fúnebres**
garbage collector **basurero(a)**
gardener **jardinero(a)**
guard **guardia**
guide **guía**
hairdresser **peluquero(a)**
home economist **economista doméstico(a)**
housekeeper **mayordomo, ama de llaves**
inspector **inspector(a)**
instructor **instructor(a)**
insurance agent **agente de seguros**
interior designer **diseñador(a) de interiores**
interpreter **intérprete**
investigator **investigador(a)**
janitor **conserje**
jeweler **joyero(a)**
journalist **periodista**
judge **juez(a)**
lawyer **abogado(a)**
librarian **bibliotecario(a)**
machinist **maquinista**
maid **criada**
mail carrier **cartero(a)**
manager **gerente**
mechanic **mecánico(a)**
midwife **comadrona, partera**
miner **minero(a)**
model **modelo**
musician **músico(a)**
nurse **enfermero(a)**
optician **óptico(a)**
optometrist **optometrista**
painter **pintor(a)**
paramedic **paramédico(a)**
pharmacist **farmacéutico(a)**
photographer **fotógrafo(a)**
physical therapist **terapista físico(a)**
physician **médico(a)**
pilot **piloto** *(masc., fem.)*, **aviador(a)**
plumber **plomero(a)**
police officer **policía, agente de policía**
printer **impresor(a)**
psychologist **psicólogo(a)**
public relations agent **agente de relaciones públicas**
real estate agent **agente de bienes raíces**
receptionist **recepcionista**
reporter **reportero(a), periodista**
sailor **marinero(a)**
sales representative **vendedor(a)**
scientist **científico(a)**
secretary **secretario(a)**
security guard **guardia**
social worker **trabajador(a) social**
sociologist **sociólogo(a)**
soldier **soldado, militar**
stenographer **estenógrafo(a)**
stockbroker **bolsista**
student **estudiante**
supervisor **supervisor(a)**
surgeon **cirujano(a)**
systems analyst **analista de siste-mas**
tailor **sastre**
taxi driver **chofer de taxi, taxista**
teacher **maestro(a)** *(elem. school)*, **profesor(a)** *(high school and college)*
technician **técnico(a)**
telephone operator **telefonista**
television and radio announcer **locutor(a)**
television and radio technician **técnico(a) de radio y televisión**
teller **cajero(a)**
therapist **terapista**
travel agent **agente de viajes**
truck driver **camionero(a)**
typist **mecanógrafo(a), dactilógrafo(a)**
undertaker **director(a) de pompas fúnebres**
veterinarian **veterinario(a)**
waiter **mozo, camarero**
waitress **camarera**
watchmaker **relojero(a)**
worker **obrero(a)**
writer **escritor(a)**

The Spanish-English vocabulary contains all active and passive vocabulary that appears in the student text. Active vocabulary includes words and expressions that appear in the vocabulary lists that follow the dialogues, and in charts and word lists that are part of the grammar explanations. Passive vocabulary consists of words and expressions that are given an English gloss in textual material throughout the book: readings, photo captions, exercises, activities, and authentic documents.

The English-Spanish Vocabulary contains both active and passive words and expressions. The following abbreviations are used in the vocabularies:

abbr.	abbreviation	*indir. obj.*	indirect object	*poet.*	poetic
adj.	adjective	*inf.*	infinitive	*prep.*	preposition
adv.	adverb	*lang.*	language	*pron.*	pronoun
aux.	auxiliary	*m.*	masculine	*p.p.*	past participle
dir. obj.	direct object	*Mex.*	Mexico	*sing.*	singular
f.	feminine	*obj.*	object	*Sp.*	Spain
fam.	familiar	*pl.*	plural	*Sp. Am.*	Spanish America
form.	formal				

Spanish-English

a at, 2; to, 16; in, 16; **— casa** home; **¿— cómo está el cambio de moneda?** What is the exchange rate?, 6; **¿— cuánto estamos hoy?** What's the date today?, 18; **— deshoras** untimely; **— eso de** at about, 15; **— la derecha (izquierda)** to the right (left), 12; **— la parrilla** grilled, 5; **— la vez** at a time; **— lo mejor** maybe, 12; **— más tardar** at the latest, 18; **— menos que** unless, 14; **— menudo** often, 12; **— nuestra disposición** at our disposal, 16; **— pesar de (que)** in spite of, 9; **— pie** on foot, 12; **— plazos** in installments, 11; **— principios de** at the first part of, 18; **¿— qué hora?** At what time?, 2; **— (en) todas partes** everywhere, 12; **— todos lados** everywhere, 12; **— veces** sometimes, 6; **— ver** let's see, 3
abierto(a) *(p.p. of* **abrir** *and adj.)* open(ed), 14
abogado(a) (*m., f.*) lawyer, 14
abrazar to hug, 4
abrazo (*m.*) hug, 4
abrigo (*m.*) coat
abril April, 1
abrir to open, 3; **— una cuenta** to open an account, 8
abuela (*f.*) grandmother, 4
abuelo (*m.*) grandfather, 4
aburrido(a) bored, 4
aburrirse (como una ostra) to be bored (to death), 16
acá here, 10
acabar de to have just, 4
acampar to camp, 16
accidente (*m.*) accident, 15
acción (*f.*) action, 18
accionista (*m., f.*) shareholder, 17
aceite (*m.*) oil, 9; **— de oliva** (*m.*) olive oil
aceituna (*f.*) olive
aceptar to accept, 3
acercarse to approach
aconsejar to advise, 11
acontecimiento (*m.*) event
acordarse (o:ue) (de) to remember, 9
acostar (o:ue) to put to bed, 9
acostarse to go to bed, 9
acostumbrarse (a) to get used to, 12
actividad (*f.*) activity, 16; **— al aire libre** (*f.*) outdoor activity, 16
actor (*m.*) actor, 18
actriz (*f.*) actress, 18
actualmente nowadays
actuación (*f.*) acting, 18
actuar to act
acumulador (*m.*) battery, 12
adelantado(a) advanced
además besides, 5
adicional additional
adiós good-bye, 1
adjetivo (*m.*) adjective
administración de empresas (*f.*) business administration, 14
administrador(a) administrator, 17
adolescente (*m., f.*) teenager, 7
¿adónde? where? (destination)
aduana (*f.*) customs, 7
advertencia (*f.*) warning
aerolínea (*f.*) airline, 11
aeropuerto (*m.*) airport, 4
afeitar(se) to shave, 9
agencia de viajes (*f.*) travel agency, 11
agente (*m., f.*) agent; **— de bienes raíces** (*m., f.*) real estate agent, 17; **— de policía** (*f.*) policewoman, 8; **— de relaciones públicas** (*m., f.*) public relations agent, 17; **— de seguros** (*m., f.*) insurance agent, 17; **— de viajes** (*m., f.*) travel agent, 11
agosto August, 1
agradecimiento (*m.*) gratefulness
agua (el) (*f.*) water, 4; **— mineral** (*f.*) mineral water, 5
aguardar to wait
ahijado(a) (*m., f.*) godson (daughter)
ahogarse to drown, 16
ahora now, 4
ahorrar to save, 8
ahorros (*m. pl.*) savings, 11
aire acondicionado (*m.*) air conditioning, 7
ajeno belonging to other people
al (*m. sing.*) (*contraction*) to the; **— aire libre** outdoor; **— contado** in cash, 8; **— fin y al cabo** after all, 18; **— horno** baked, cooked in the oven, 5; **— lado de** next to, 12; **— mes** a month, per month; **— teléfono** on the phone, 3
alacena (*f.*) pantry
alba (*f.*) dawn, daybreak
alberca (*f.*) swimming pool (*Mex.*), 7
alegrarse (de) to be glad, 11
alegre merry
alérgico(a) allergic, 8
alfabetizar to alphabetize
alfabeto (*m.*) alphabet
alfombra (*f.*) carpet, 10
alforja (*f.*) saddlebag
algo something, anything, 6
algodón (*m.*) cotton, 13
alguien someone, somebody, anyone, 6
alguno(a), algún any, some, 6
algunos(-as) some, 6
allí there
alma (*f.*) soul
almacén (*m.*) department store, 13
almohada (*f.*) pillow, 10
almorzar (o:ue) to have lunch, 5
almuerzo (*m.*) lunch, 7
alojamiento (*m.*) lodging
alquilar to rent, 10
alquiler (*m.*) rent, 10
altiplano (*m.*) plateau
alto(a) tall, 3
alumno(a) (*m., f.*) student
amable polite, courteous, 3; **Muy —.** Very kind (of you)., 1
amante (*adj.*) loving
amar to love
amarillo(a) yellow, 1
ambos(-as) both
ambulancia (*f.*) ambulance, 15
americano(a) American, 2
amigo(a) (*m., f.*) friend, 1
amistad (*f.*) friendship
amor (*m.*) love
amplio(a) large, ample, 10
amueblado(a) furnished, 10
anaranjado(a) orange, 1
ancho(a) wide, 13
andén (*m.*) platform
angosto(a) narrow, 13
anillo (*m.*) ring, 13
anoche last night, 7
anotar to write down, 2

anteayer the day before yesterday, 7
antes (de) before, 7; **— de que** before, 14
antibiótico (*m.*) antibiotic, 15
antiguo(a) former, 17
antipático(a) unpleasant, 3
antojársele a uno to seem to one
anuncio (*m.*) ad, 3
añadir to add
año (*m.*) year, 3; **— Nuevo** (*m.*) New Year, 4
aparato electrodoméstico (*m.*) home appliance, 10
aparcar to park, 8
apariencia (*f.*) appearance
apartamento (*m.*) apartment, 3
apellido (*m.*) last name, 3; **— de soltera** (*m.*) maiden name
apio (*m.*) celery, 9
aprender (a) to learn, 3
apretar (e:ie) to be tight, 15; to tie together
aprobar (o:ue) to pass (*an exam or course*), 14
aprovechar to take advantage of
aquel(los), aquella(s) (*adj.*) that, those (*distant*), 6
aquel(los), aquella(s) (*pron.*) that one, those (*distant*), 6
aquello (*neuter pron.*) that, 6
aquí here, 3; **¡— va!** Here it goes!
árbol (*m.*) tree; **— de Navidad** Christmas tree, 4; **— frutal** (*m.*) fruit tree, 15
archivar to file, 17
arena (*f.*) sand
arete (*m.*) earring, 13
argentino(a) Argentinian, 11
armar to pitch (*a tent*), 16
arquitecto(a) (*m., f.*) architect, 14
arrancar to start (*car*), 12
arreglar to tidy up, to fix, 6; to repair, 12
arreglo (*m.*) repair, 12
arroz (*m.*) rice, 5; **— con leche** (*m.*) rice pudding, 5
arte (*f.*) art
artículo (*m.*) article, 16
asado (*m.*) barbecue, 16
asado(a) roasted, barbecued, 9
ascendencia (*f.*) ancestry, 14
ascensor (*m.*) elevator, 7
Así es la vida. Such is life.
así que so, 18
asiento (*m.*) seat; **— de pasillo** (*m.*) aisle seat, 11; **— de ventanilla** (*m.*) window seat, 11
asignatura (*f.*) (school) subject, 14
asistente (*m., f.*) assistant, 17
asistir (a) to attend, 3
aspiradora (*f.*) vacuum cleaner, 6
aspirina (*f.*) aspirin, 15
ataque al corazón (*m.*) heart attack, 15
atlético(a) athletic, 16
atónito(a) aghast
atravesar (e:ie) to go through; **— con la mirada** to look right through
aturdido(a) dazed, confused, 4
aumento (*m.*) increase, 17
aunque although, 9
auto (*m.*) car, 10
autobús (*m.*) bus, 6
automático(a) automatic, 12
automóvil (*m.*) car, 10
autopista (*f.*) freeway, highway, 12
auxiliar de vuelo (*m., f.*) flight attendant, 11
avance (*m.*) preview, 18
avenida (*f.*) avenue, 12
avergonzado(a) ashamed
avión (*m.*) plane, 11
avisar to let know, to advise, 10
aviso (*m.*) ad, 3; **— clasificado** (*m.*) classified ad
ayer yesterday, 7
ayudar (a) to help, 6
azafata (*f.*) female flight attendant, 11
azúcar (*m.*) sugar, 9
azul blue, 1
azulejo (*m.*) tile

bailar to dance, 4
bailarín(-ina) (*m., f.*) dancer, 18
bajo(a) (*adj.*) short, 3; (*prep.*) under
balneario (*m.*) resort
banana (*f.*) banana, 9
banco (*m.*) bank, 18
banda sonora (*f.*) soundtrack, 18
bandera (*f.*) flag
bañadera (*f.*) bathtub, 7
bañar(se) to bathe (oneself), 9
bañera (*f.*) bathtub, 7
baño (*m.*) bathroom, 6
barato(a) inexpensive, 13
¡Bárbaro! Great!
barca (*f.*) boat, 16
barco (*m.*) ship, 11
barrer to sweep, **6**
barrio (*m.*) neighborhood, 10
bastante quite, 14
batería (*f.*) drums, 9; battery, 12; **— de cocina** (*f.*) cookware, 10
batir to beat
beber to drink, 3; **— algo** to have something to drink, 3
bebida (*f.*) drink, 5
beca (*f.*) scholarship, 14
belleza (*f.*) beauty
besar to kiss
beso (*m.*) kiss
biblioteca (*f.*) library, 2
bibliotecario(a) (*m., f.*) librarian, 14
bicicleta (*f.*) bicycle, 12
bien well, fine, 1; **— caliente** nice and hot, 15
bienvenido(a) welcome, 4
biftec (*m.*) steak, 5
billete (*m.*) ticket, 11; **— de ida** (*m.*) one-way ticket, 11; **— de ida y vuelta** (*m.*) round-trip ticket, 11
billetera (*f.*) wallet, 13
biología (*f.*) biology, 14
bisabuela (*f.*) great-grandmother
bisabuelo (*m.*) great-grandfather
bistec (*m.*) steak, 5
blanco(a) white, 1
blusa (*f.*) blouse, 13
boca (*f.*) mouth, 15; **— de incendios** (*f.*) fire hydrant, 8
bocina (*f.*) horn, 12
boda (*f.*) wedding, 18
bolígrafo (*m.*) pen, 2
bolsa de aire (*f.*) air bag, 12
bolsa de dormir (*f.*) sleeping bag, 10
bolso (*m.*) purse, handbag, 9; **— de mano** (*m.*) carry-on bag
bombilla (*f.*) straw (*for mate*)
bondad (*f.*) kindness
bonito(a) pretty, 3
borrador (*m.*) first draft
bosque (*m.*) forest, 11
bosquejo (*m.*) outline
bota (*f.*) boot, 13
bote (*m.*) (*Mex.*) can, 9; boat, 16
botones (*m.*) bellhop, 7
brillante brilliant, 11
bromear to joke, to kid, 12
broncearse to get a tan, 16
bucear to scuba dive, 16
buenísimo(a) extremely good, 11
bueno(a), buen good, 1
  ¡Buen viaje! Have a nice trip!, 11
  buenas noches good evening, good night, 1
  buenas tardes good afternoon, 1
  bueno... well..., okay, 1
  buenos días good morning, 1
burlarse de to make fun of, 18
burro(a) (*m., f.*) donkey
bus (*m.*) bus, 16
buscar to get, to pick up, 6; to look for; to find
búsqueda (*f.*) search
butaca (*f.*) armchair, 10

caballería (*f.*) chivalry
caballero (*m.*) knight
cabaña (*f.*) cabin, 16
cabello (*m.*) hair, 15
caber to fit, 6
cabeza (*f.*) head, 15
cacerola (*f.*) saucepan, 10
cada (*invariable adj.*) each, 13
caer(se) to fall, 16
café (*m.*) brown, 1; coffee, 3; café, 3
cafecito (*m.*) small (cup of) coffee, 15
cafetera (*f.*) coffee maker, 10
cafetería (*f.*) cafeteria, 1
caja (*f.*) cash register, 13
cajero automático (*m.*) automatic teller, 8
cajuela (*f.*) trunk (*car*), 12
calcetines (*m. pl.*) socks, 13
calculadora (*f.*) calculator
calefacción (*f.*) heating, 10
callar to be silent
calle (*f.*) street, 2
calor (*m.*) heat, 14
caloría (*f.*) calorie, 5
calzar to wear (a certain size in shoes), 13
cama (*f.*) bed, 16
cámara (fotográfica) (*f.*) camera, 7; **— de video** (*f.*) video camera, 7
camarero(a) (*m., f.*) waiter, waitress, 5
camarones (*m. pl.*) shrimp, 5
cambiar to change, 6; to exchange, 13
cambio de moneda (*m.*) exchange rate
cambios mecánicos (*m. pl.*) standard shift, 12
camelia (*f.*) camellia, 8
caminar to walk, 12
camión (*m.*) truck, 13
camisa (*f.*) shirt, 6
camiseta (*f.*) T-shirt, 13
camisón (*m.*) nightgown, 13
campeón(-ona) (*m., f.*) champion, 16
campo (*m.*) country, 16

canal (*m.*) channel, 7
canario (*m.*) canary, 8
cancelar to cancel, 7
canción (*f.*) song, 9; — **infantil** (*f.*) children's song
candidato(a) (*m., f.*) candidate, 17
canoa (*f.*) canoe, 16
cansado(a) tired, 4
cantar to sing, 4
caña de azúcar (*f.*) sugar cane
caña de pescar (*f.*) fishing rod, 16
capital (*f.*) capital (city)
capó (*m.*) hood, 12
capullo (*m.*) bud
cara (*f.*) face, 15
¡caramba! gee!, 2
carbón (*m.*) coal
carburador (*m.*) carburetor, 12
cárcel (*f.*) jail
cargado(a) (de) loaded with, 13
cargo (*m.*) position
cariño (*m.*) love
carnaval (*m.*) Mardi Gras
carne (*f.*) meat, 6; flesh; — **de res** (*f.*) beef
carnicería (*f.*) meat market, 9
caro(a) expensive, 5
carpeta (*f.*) folder, 17
carpintero(a) (*m., f.*) carpenter, 14
carrera (*f.*) career, 16
carro (*m.*) car, 10; carriage
carta (*f.*) letter, 17
cartelera (*f.*) movie (entertainment) section (of a newspaper), 18
cartera (*f.*) handbag, 9; wallet, 13
casa (*f.*) house, 2; home; — **de ancianos** (*f.*) nursing home
casado(a) married, 3
casarse (con) to get married (to), 11
casi almost, 8
catarro (*m.*) cold, 15
cátedra (*f.*) faculty appointment
catorce fourteen, 1
cazar to hunt, 16
cebolla (*f.*) onion, 9
cédula (*f.*) document
celebrar to celebrate, 9
cena (*f.*) dinner, 7
cenar to have dinner, to dine, 7
censura (*f.*) censorship
centro (*m.*) downtown; — **commercial** (*m.*) shopping mall, 13
cerca close to, near, 10; around; — **de** near
cereza (*f.*) cherry
cero zero, 1
cerradura (*f.*) lock
cerrar (e:ie) to close, 4
cerveza (*f.*) beer, 5
cesto de papeles (*m.*) wastebasket, 2
champán (*m.*) champagne, 5
chapa (*f.*) license plate, 12
Chau. Good-bye., 1
cheque (*m.*) check, 8; — **de viajero** (*m.*) traveler's check, 8
chequeo (*m.*) checkup, 15
chequera (*f.*) checkbook, 8
¡Chévere! Great!
chica (*f.*) girl, young woman, 2
chico (*m.*) boy, young man, 2
chico(a) small, 10
chino Chinese (*lang.*)
chocolate (*m.*) chocolate, 5; — **caliente** (*m.*) hot chocolate, 5
chorizo (*m.*) sausage
cielo (*m.*) sky, heaven
cien, ciento one hundred, 2
ciencia (*f.*) science, 14; — **ficción** (*f.*) science fiction, 18
cierto true
cinco five, 1
cincuenta fifty, 2
cine (*m.*) movie (theater), 4
cita (*f.*) appointment
ciudad (*f.*) city, 3
clarinete (*m.*) clarinet, 9
claro(a) light; clear
clase (*f.*) class, 1; — **optativa** (*f.*) elective; — **turista** (*f.*) tourist class, 11
clasificado(a) classified, 12
clavel (*m.*) carnation, 8
cliente (*m., f.*) customer
cobardía (*f.*) cowardice
cobrar un cheque to cash a check, 8
cobre (*m.*) copper
coche (*m.*) car, 10
cocina (*f.*) kitchen, 5
cocinar to cook, 6
cocinero(a) (*m., f.*) cook, chef, 14
cognado (*m.*) cognate
col (*f.*) cabbage
cola (*f.*) tail
colchón (*m.*) mattress, 7
colega (*m., f.*) colleague
collar (*m.*) necklace, 13
colonial colonial, 15
color (*m.*) color, 1
colorado(a) red
columna (*f.*) column, 18
combinar (con) to match, 13
comedia (*f.*) comedy, 7
comedor (*m.*) dining room, 6
comenzar (e:ie) (a) to begin, to start, 4
comer to eat, 3; — **algo** to have something to eat, 3
comida (*f.*) food, 4; meal, 5
como since, 7; about, 16; — **si** as if, 17
¿cómo? how?, 1; what?; **¿ — está usted?** How are you? (*form.*), 1; **¿ — estás?** How are you? (*fam.*); **¿ — están ustedes?** How are you?, 1; **¿ — le va?** How is it going (for you)? (*form.*), 1; **¿ — se dice...?** How do you say . . . ?, 2; **¿ — se escribe...?** How do you write . . .?; **¿ — se llama usted?** What's your name? (*form.*), 1; **¿ — te llamas tú?** What's your name? (*fam.*), 1; **¿ — te va?** How is it going (for you) (*fam.*)?
cómoda (*f.*) bureau, chest of drawers, 10
cómodo(a) comfortable, 7
compacto(a) compact, 12
compañero(a) (*m., f.*) partner; — **de clase** (*m., f.*) classmate, 4; — **de cuarto** (*m., f.*) roommate, 3
compañía (*f.*) company, 3
comparar to compare, 14
comparativo(a) comparative
compartir to share, 9
compensar to compensate, 17
complicado(a) complicated, 12
compra (*f.*) purchase, 17
comprador(a) (*m., f.*) buyer, 17
comprar to buy, 6
comprometerse con to get engaged to, 18
comprometido(a) engaged, 18
computadora (*f.*) computer, 2 ; — **portátil** (*f.*) laptop computer, 17
con with, 1; **¿ — cuánta anticipación?** How far in advance?; — **él (ella) habla.** This is he (she) speaking., 3; — **permiso.** Excuse me., 1; — **razón** no wonder, 3; — **tal (de) que** provided that, as long as, 14; — **vista a** overlooking, 7
concierto (*m.*) concert, 4
concordancia (*f.*) agreement
condicional conditional
conducir to drive (*Sp.*), 6
conejillo de Indias (*m.*) Guinea pig, 8
conejo (*m.*) rabbit, 8
conferencia (*f.*) lecture
confiar to trust
confirmar to confirm, 7
conmigo with me, 2
conocer to know, to be acquainted, 6; to meet, 10
conocimiento (*m.*) knowledge, 3
conseguir (e:i) to get, to obtain, 6
consejero(a) (*m., f.*) advisor, 14
consejo (*m.*) advice
consulado (*m.*) consulate, 7
consultorio (*m.*) doctor's office, 15
contabilidad (*f.*) accounting, 14
contado: al — in cash, 8
contador(a) (*m., f.*) accountant, 5; — **público(a)** (*m., f.*) certified public accountant, 17
contagioso(a) contagious, 15
contaminación del aire (*f.*) smog
contar (o:ue) to count, 5; to tell, 18
contento(a) happy, 4
contestar to answer, 3
contigo (*fam. sing.*) with you, 4
continente (*m.*) continent, 11
continuar to continue, 17
contra against
contrabajo (*m.*) bass, 9
contracción (*f.*) contraction
convencer to convince, 10
conversación (*f.*) conversation, 2
conversar to talk, to converse, 4
convivencia (*f.*) coexistence
copa (*f.*) glass, goblet, 5
corbata (*f.*) tie, 13
cordero (*m.*) lamb, 5
correo (*m.*) post office, 12; — **electrónico** (*m.*) e-mail, 17
correr to run, 3
corrida de toros (*f.*) bullfight
correspondencia (*f.*) correspondence, 17
corsario (*m.*) privateer
cortar(se) to cut (oneself), 9; — **el césped** to mow the lawn, 6
corte de pelo (*m.*) haircut, cut, 12
cortés polite, courteous, 3
cortina (*f.*) curtain, 10
cosa (*f.*) thing, 6
costar (o:ue) to cost, 5; — **un ojo de la cara** to cost an arm and a leg, 12
costumbre (*f.*) custom, 4
crear to create
crecer to grow, 9
creer to believe, to think, 3

creído (*p.p. of* **creer**) believed, 14
crema (*f.*) cream, 5
crepúsculo (*m.*) twilight
criada (*f.*) maid, 10
criticar to criticize, 18
crítico(a) (*m., f.*) critic, 18
cuaderno (*m.*) notebook, 2
cuadro (*m.*) picture, painting, 10
de cuadros plaid, 13
¿cuál? what?, which?, 1; **¿ — es tu (su) número de teléfono?** What is your telephone number?, 1
cuando when, 14
¿cuándo? when?, 2
¿cuánto(a)? how much?; **¿ — tiempo hace que...?** How long . . . ?, 7
¿cuántos(-as)? how many?
cuarenta forty, 2
cuarto (*m.*) room, 4; **— de baño** (*m.*) bathroom, 6; **menos —** quarter of/ to (*time*), 2; **y —** quarter after/past (*time*), 2
cuarto(a) fourth, 7
cuatro four, 1
cuatrocientos(-as) four hundred, 3
cubano(a) Cuban, 2
cubierto(a) (*p.p. of* **cubrir** *and adj.*) covered, 14
cubiertos (*m. pl.*) silverware, 5
cubrir to cover
cuchara (*f.*) spoon, 5
cucharada (*f.*) spoonful
cucharita (*f.*) teaspoon, 5
cuchillo (*m.*) knife, 5
cuello (*m.*) neck, 15; collar
cuenta (*f.*) bill, check, 5; account, 8; **— conjunta** (*f.*) joint account, 8; **— corriente** (*f.*) checking account, 8; **— de ahorros** (*f.*) savings account, 8
cuero (*m.*) leather, 13
cuerpo (*m.*) body, 15
cuidado (*m.*) care
cumbre (*f.*) pinnacle
cumpleaños (*m.*) birthday, 1
cumplir... años to turn . . . years old, 9
cuñada (*f.*) sister-in-law, 6
cuñado (*m.*) brother-in-law, 6
curandero(a) (*m, f.*) healer
curarse to cure oneself, to get better, 15
currículum vitae (*m.*) curriculum vitae, 17
curtido(a) weatherbeaten

dar to give, 4; **— alimento (a)** to feed; **— hacia** to overlook; **— la mano** to shake hands; **— las gracias** to express gratitude, 18; **— un beso** to kiss; **— una multa** to give a ticket (fine), 8; **— una película** to show a movie, 7; **— le rabia a uno** to be furious, 18; **—se cuenta (de)** to realize, 14
datos personales (*m. pl.*) personal data
de from, 1; of, 1; about, with, in, 16; **— acuerdo** in agreement, 13; **— acuerdo con** according to; **— cuadros** plaid, 13; **— estatura mediana** of medium height, 5; **— haber sabido** had I known, 15; **— la mañana** A.M., 2; **— la tarde** P.M., 2; **— lunares** polka-dotted, 13; **— manera que** so, 9; **— memoria** by heart; **— modo que** so, 9; **— nada.** You're welcome., 1; **— postre** for dessert, 5; **— pronto** suddenly, 18; **— rayas** striped, 13; **— repente** suddenly, 18; **— todos modos** anyway
debajo de under, 6
deber (+ *infinitive*) must, should, 3
deberse a to be due to
debidamente duly
decidir to decide, 3
décimo(a) tenth, 7
decir (e:i) to say, to tell, 6
decisión (*f.*) decision, 17
dedo (*m.*) finger, 15; **— del pie** (*m.*) toe, 15
dejar to leave behind, 5; **— plantado(a) a alguien** to stand somebody up, 18; **— tranquilo(a)** to leave alone, 16
deletrear to spell
deletreo (*m.*) spelling
delgado(a) thin, slender, 3
demás: los (las) — others
demasiado(a)(s) too
demostrativo(a) demonstrative
dentro inside
departamento (*m.*) department, section; **— de (ropa para) caballeros** (*m.*) men's department, 13; **— de (ropa para) damas** (*m.*) women's department, 13
depender to depend, 14
deporte (*m.*) sport, 16
depositar to deposit, 8
derecho (*m.*) right; **derecho(a)** (*adj.*) right; **— ajeno** (*m.*) the other person's right; **a la derecha** to the right, 12
derretir (e:i) to melt
desafortunadamente unfortunately, 8
desafortunado(a) unfortunate, 8
desagradecido(a) (*adj.*) ungrateful
desamparo (*m.*) abandonment
desastre (*m.*) disaster, 8
desayuno (*m.*) breakfast, 7
descansar to rest, 15
descomponerse to break down, 12
descompuesto(a) (*p.p. of* **descomponer** *and adj.*) out of order, not working, 12
desconcertado(a) bewildered
describir to describe, 11
desde since, 6; from, 10
desear to want, to wish, 11
desempeñar to perform (a job), 17
desesperanza (*f.*) despair
desfallecer to faint
desocupado(a) vacant, 10
desocupar el cuarto to vacate the room, 7
despacho (*m.*) office, 17
despacio slowly
despedazar to tear
despedida (*f.*) farewell, 1
despertarse (e:ie) to wake up, 9
desposar to marry, to betroth
despreciar to scorn
después afterwards, 3
desvestirse (e:i) to get undressed, 9
destacar to emphasize
destacarse to stand out
detener to stop (something); **— se** to stop
determinado(a) definite
devolver (o:ue) algo to return (something), 13
devuelto(a) (*p.p. of* **devolver** *and adj.*) returned, 14
día (*m.*) day, 1
diamante (*m.*) diamond
diariamente daily
diario (*m.*) newspaper, 3
dibujos animados (*m. pl.*) cartoons, 18
diccionario (*m.*) dictionary, 8
diciembre December, 1
dicho (*m.*) saying
dicho(a) (*p.p. of* **decir** *and adj.*) said, told, 15
diecinueve nineteen, 1
dieciocho eighteen, 1
dieciséis sixteen, 1
diecisiete seventeen, 1
diente (*m.*) tooth, 15
dieta (*f.*) diet, 5
diez ten, 1
difícil difficult, 2
diligencia (*f.*) errand, 11
dinero (*m.*) money, 2
Dios God
dirección (*f.*) address, 2
directo(a) direct, 11
director(a) (*m., f.*) director, 18; **— de cine** (*m., f.*) movie director, 18
dirigir to direct, 18
disco compacto (*m.*) compact disc (CD), 4
discoteca (*f.*) discotheque, 4
diseño (*m.*) design, 13
disfrutar to enjoy
disquete (*m.*) diskette, 17
distinto(a) different
distribución de papeles (*f.*) casting, 18
divertido(a) fun, 16
divertirse (e:ie) to have a good time, to enjoy oneself, 6
divino(a) divine, 16
divorciado(a) divorced, 3
doblado(a) dubbed
doblar to turn, 12; to dub; **— la ropa** to fold the clothes, 6
doble double, 7
doce twelve, 1
doctor(a) (*m., f.*) doctor, 1
documental (*m.*) documentary, 18
doler (o:ue) to hurt, 15
dolor (*m.*) pain
domicilio (*m.*) address, 2
domingo (*m.*) Sunday, 1
don (*m.*) gift
¿dónde? where?, 1
dorado(a) golden
dormir (o:ue) to sleep, 5
dormirse to fall asleep, 9
dormitorio (*m.*) bedroom, 6
dos two, 1
doscientos(-as) two hundred, 3
dramaturgo(a) (*m., f.*) playwright
ducha (*f.*) shower, 7
dudar to doubt, 12
dulce fresh (*water*); sweet
dulces (*m. pl.*) sweets
durar to last, 13
durazno (*m.*) peach, 9

echar el bofe to be out of breath
económico(a) financial, 3
edad (*f.*) age, 14

edificio (*m.*) building, 10
educación física (*f.*) physical education, 14
efectivo (*m.*) cash, 8; **en —** in cash, 8
efecto especial (*m.*) special effect, 18
ejecutivo(a) (*m., f.*) executive, 14
ejército (*m.*) army
el the (*m. sing.*), 2; **— (la) que** he (she) who
él he, 1; him, 4
electricidad (*f.*) electricity, 10
electricista (*m., f.*) electrician, 14
elevador (*m.*) elevator, 7
ella she, 1; her, 4
ellas (*f. pl.*) they, 1; them, 4
ellos (*m. pl.*) they, 1; them, 4
embajada (*f.*) embassy, 7
embarazada pregnant, 15
embarcarse to get on a boat
emergencia (*f.*) emergency, 15
empanada (*f.*) meat turnover
empeorarse to get worse, 15
empezar (e:ie) (a) to begin, to start, 4
empleado(a) (*m., f.*) clerk, 13; **— bancario** (*m., f.*) bank employee, 17
empleo (*m.*) job, 3
empresarial (*adj.*) business
en in, at, 1; on, inside, over, 16; **— casa** at home, 4; **— caso de que** in case, 14; **— cuanto** as soon as, 14; **— cuanto a** regarding; **— efectivo** in cash, 11; **— ese caso** in that case, 2; **— este momento** at this moment, 5; **— fin...** anyway . . ., 8; **— la actualidad** nowadays, 18; **— ningún lado** nowhere, 11; **— ninguna parte** nowhere, 11; **— parte** in part, 14; **¿ — qué puedo servirle?** How can I help you?, 7; **— punto** on the dot; **— seguida** right away, 6; **— seguida vuelvo** I'll be right back, 6; **¿ — serio?** seriously?, 2; **— vez de** instead of, 17
enamorado(a) (de) in love (with), 16
enamorarse de to fall in love with, 18
encantado(a) charmed
encantador(a) charming, 3
encantarle a uno to love, 8
encargado(a) (*m., f.*) super-(intendent), 10
encargado(a) de in charge of, 17
enciclopedia (*f.*) encyclopedia, 8
encontrar (o:ue) to find, 5
encontrarse (con) to meet, 10
encuesta (*f.*) survey
enderezarse a to be for, to exist for
enero January, 1
enfriar to cool down
enojarse to get angry, 14
enorme enormous, 15
ensalada (*f.*) salad, 5
ensangrentado(a) blood-stained
ensayar to rehearse, 18
ensayo (*m.*) essay
enseñar (a) to teach, 18
entablar to start
entender (e:ie) to understand, 4
enterrado(a) buried
entonces then, in that case, 4
entrada (*f.*) entrance, 11; ticket (*to an event*), 16
entrante next, 18; **el mes —** (*m.*) next month, 18
entrar to enter, to come in, 12
entre among, between, 9
entregar to turn in, to deliver, 14
entrevista (*f.*) interview, 17
entrevistar to interview, 17
enviar to send, 7
envolver (o:ue) to wrap, 14
envuelto(a) (*p.p. of* **envolver** *and adj.*) wrapped, 14
enyesar to put in a cast, 15
equipaje (*m.*) luggage, 7
equipo electrónico (*m.*) electronic equipment, 17
equipo estereofónico (*m.*) stereo system, 4
equivocado(a) wrong, 4
errabundo wandering
es decir that is to say
es que... the fact is . . . , 13
escalar to climb, 16
escalera (*f.*) stairs, 7; **— mecánica** (*f.*) escalator, 7
escapar to escape, 14
esclavo(a) (*m., f.*) slave
escoba (*f.*) broom, 6
escoger to choose
esconder to hide, 6
escopeta (*f.*) shotgun, 16
escribir to write, 3; **— a máquina** to type, 17
escrito(a) (*p.p. of* **escribir** *and adj.*) written, 14
escritor(a) (*m., f.*) writer, 14
escritorio (*m.*) desk, 2
escuchar to listen (to)
escuela (*f.*) school, 10; **— secundaria** (*f.*) high school, 18
ese(os), esa(s) (*adj.*) that, those, (nearby), 6
ese(os), esa(s) (*pron.*) that one, those (*nearby*), 6
esfuerzo (*m.*) effort
eso (*neuter pron.*) that, 6
espada (*f.*) sword
espalda (*f.*) back, 15
España Spain
español (*m.*) Spanish (*lang.*), 2
especial special, 5
especialización (*f.*) major (*field of study*), 14
especializado(a) specialized, 17
especialmente especially, 8
espectáculo (*m.*) show, 18
espejo (*m.*) mirror, 10
esperanza (*f.*) hope
esperar to wait (for), to expect, 6; to hope, 11
esposa (*f.*) wife, 5
esposo (*m.*) husband, 5
espuma (*f.*) foam
esquí acuático (*m.*) water ski, 16
esquiar to ski, 16
esquina (*f.*) corner
esta noche tonight, 2
estación (*f.*) season, 1; station, 12; **— de la seca** (*f.*) dry season; **— de servicio** (*f.*) gas (service) station, 12
estacionar to park, 8
estadio (*m.*) stadium, 16
estado (*m.*) state; **— civil** (*m.*) marital status, 3
Estados Unidos (*m. pl.*) United States
estampado(a) print (fabric), 13
estar to be, 4; **— a cargo** to be in charge, 18; **— de acuerdo** to agree, 6; **— de vacaciones** to be on vacation, 7; **— equivocado(a)** to be wrong, 4; **— loco(a) por** to be crazy about, 18; **— muerto(a) de hambre** to be starving, 15
¿Está... (*name*)? Is . . . (*name*) there?, 3
estatura (*f.*) height, 5
este east, 16
este(os), esta(s) (*adj.*) this, 6; these, 6
este fin de semana (*m.*) this weekend, 4
este(os) esta(s) (*pron.*) this one; these, 6
estimarse to have self-esteem
estirar to stretch
esto (*neuter pron.*) this, 6
estómago (*m.*) stomach, 15
estrechar to hold
estrecho(a) narrow, 13
estrenar to show for the first time, 18
estreno (*m.*) première, 18
estribillo (*m.*) refrain
estrofa (*f.*) stanza
estudiante (*m., f.*) student, 1
estudiar to study, 2
etapa (*f.*) period
evaluación (*f.*) evaluation, 17
evitar to avoid, 17
exactamente exactly, 17
exactitud (*f.*) accuracy
examen (*m.*) exam, 3; checkup, 15; **— parcial (de mitad de curso)** (*m.*) midterm examination, 3
excelente excellent, 11
exceso de equipaje (*m.*) excess baggage, 11
excursión (*f.*) excursion, 11
exigir to demand
éxito (*m.*) success
experiencia (*f.*) experience, 3
experto(a) (*m., f.*) expert, 14
expresión (*f.*) expression
extranjero(a) foreign; **en el extranjero** abroad
extrañar to miss, 9
extraño(a) (*m., f.*) stranger

fábrica (*f.*) factory, 5
fácil easy, 2
fácilmente easily
facsímile (*m.*) fax, 17
factoría (*f.*) factory, 5
facturar el equipaje to check luggage, 11
facultad (*f.*) college, school, 14
falda (*f.*) skirt, 13
fallecer to pass away, 9
falta (*f.*) lack
familia (*f.*) family, 4
fantasma (*m.*) ghost
farmacia (*f.*) pharmacy, 9
fastidiado(a) annoyed
favorito(a) favorite, 7
fax (*m.*) fax , 17
febrero February, 1
fecha de nacimiento (*f.*) date of birth, 3

fechar to date (*check or letter*), 8
feliz happy, 1
femenino(a) feminine
feo(a) ugly, 3
ferretería (*f.*) hardware store, 9
festejar to celebrate, 9
festival de cine (*m.*) film festival, 18
fiebre (*f.*) fever, 15
fiesta (*f.*) party, 1
fijarse en to notice, 18
filmar to film (make) a movie, 18
filosofía (*f.*) philosophy, 17
fin (*m.*) end; **— de semana** (*m.*) weekend, 4
fingir to pretend
firma (*f.*) signature, 8
firmar to sign, 8
física (*f.*) physics, 14
flan (*m.*) caramel custard, 5
flauta (*f.*) flute, 9
flor (*f.*) flower, 8
florería (*f.*) flower shop, 8
folleto (*m.*) brochure, 11
fortaleza (*f.*) fortress
foto (*f.*) photo, photograph, 4
fotocopiadora (*f.*) photocopy machine, 17
fotografía (*f.*) photo, photograph, 4
francamente frankly, 12
francés (*m.*) French (*lang.*), 2
frecuentar to visit frequently
frecuente frequent
frecuentemente frequently, 12
fregar (e:ie) los platos to wash the dishes, 6
freno (*m.*) brake, 12
frente a in front of, 8
fresa (*f.*) strawberry, 9
frijoles (*m. pl.*) beans, 5
frito(a) fried, 5
frondoso(a) leafy
fruta (*f.*) fruit, 9
fuego (*m.*) fire, 8
fuente (*f.*) source
fuera (*adv.*) outside
fumar to smoke
funcionar to work, to function, 12
funda (*f.*) pillowcase, 10
fundir to melt
fusilar to shoot
fútbol (*m.*) soccer, 16
futuro (*m.*) future, 14

ganadería (*f.*) livestock
ganar to earn, 3; to win, 16
ganga (*f.*) bargain, 13
garaje (*m.*) garage, 6
garganta (*f.*) throat, 15
gasolina (*f.*) gasoline, 12
gasolinera (*f.*) gas (service) station, 12
gato (*m.*) cat, 8; car jack, 12
general general, 8
generalmente generally, 8
género (*m.*) gender
gente de negocio (*f.*) businesspeople
geranio (*m.*) geranium, 8
gerente (*m., f.*) manager, 17
gimnasio (*m.*) gym, 14
goma de borrar (*f.*) eraser, 2
gordo(a) fat, 3
grabar to tape, 18
gracias thank you, thanks, 1
grado (*m.*) degree, 15
graduarse to graduate, 14
grande big
gratis free (of charge), 8
gratuito(a) free
gripe (*f.*) flu, 15
gris gray, 1
grúa (*f.*) tow truck, 12
grupo (*m.*) group, 18
guante (*m.*) glove, 13
guapo(a) handsome, good-looking, 3
guatemalteco(a) (*m., f.*) Guatemalan, 5
guerra (*f.*) war, 18
guía telefónica (*f.*) telephone book
guión (*m.*) script, screenplay, 18
guitarra (*f.*) guitar, 9
gustar to like, to be pleasing to, 7
gusto (*m.*) pleasure, joy; **El — es mío.** The pleasure is mine., 1

haber (*aux.*) to have
habitación (*f.*) room, 4; **— doble** (*f.*) double room, 7; **— sencilla** (*f.*) single room, 7
hablar to speak, 2
hace + *time* + **que** + *verb* (*present*) to have been doing something for a length of time, 7
hace + *time* + **que** + *verb* (*preterit/imperfect*) to have done something in the past (ago), 9
hacer to do, 4; to make, 6; **— buen tiempo** to be good weather, 5; **— calor** to be hot, 5; **— diligencias** to run errands, 8; **— ejercicio** to exercise, 7; **— escala** to make a stopover, 11; **— frío** to be cold, 5; **— juego (con)** to match, 13; **— las compras** to do the shopping, 6; **— las maletas** to pack; **— mal tiempo** to be bad weather, 5; **— sol** to be sunny, 5; **— surfing** to surf, 16; **— un crucero** to take a cruise, 11; **— un picnic** to have a picnic, 16; **— una radiografía** to take an X-ray, 15; **— viento** to be windy, 5; **—se cargo** to take charge; **—se ilusiones** to dream, to fool oneself, 18
hacia towards, 5
hambre (*f.*) hunger, 4; **tener —** to be hungry, 4
hamburguesa (f.) hamburger, 5
hasta until, 7; **— ahora** up to now, 14; **— la vista.** Good-bye., 1; **— mañana.** See you tomorrow., 1; **— que** until, 14
hay there is, there are, 1
hecho (*m.*) happening
hecho(a) (*p.p. of* **hacer** *and adj.*) done, made, 14
helado (*m.*) ice cream, 5
herir (e:ie) to hurt
hermana (*f.*) sister, 4
hermanastra (*f.*) stepsister, 6
hermanastro (*m.*) stepbrother, 6
hermanita(-o) (*m., f.*) little sister (brother), 13
hermano (*m.*) brother, 4
hermoso(a) beautiful, 5
hidrante (*m.*) fire hydrant, 8
hija (*f.*) daughter, 4
hijastra (*f.*) stepdaughter, 6
hijastro (*m.*) stepson, 6
hijito(a) darling, 4
hijo (*m.*) son, 4
hijos (*m. pl.*) children
hilo (*m.*) linen, 13
historia (*f.*) history, 3
hogar (*m.*) home
hogareño(a) family oriented
hoja (*f.*) leaf; **— de papel** (*f.*) sheet of paper, 2
hola hello, 1
hombre (*m.*) man; **— de negocios** (*m.*) businessman, 7
honrado(a) honest, honorable
hora (*f.*) time (of day), 2; hour; **¿A qué —...?** (At) what time . . . ?, 2; **¿Qué — es?** What time is it?, 2
horario (*m.*) schedule, 14
horno (*m.*) oven, 10
hospedaje (*m.*) lodging, 11
hospedarse en to stay, to lodge (at a hotel), 11
hospital (*m.*) hospital, 2
hotel (*m.*) hotel, 7
hoy today, 1; **— en día** nowadays, 18

idea (*f.*) idea, 2
ideal (*adj.*) ideal, 11
idioma (*m.*) language, 2
iglesia (*f.*) church
igualmente likewise, 1
ilusión (*f.*) dream, 18
impaciencia (*f.*) lack of patience; **—s** (*f. pl.*) pressures
imperativo (*m.*) command
imperfecto (*m.*) imperfect
impermeable (*m.*) raincoat
importación (*f.*) import, 17
importarle a uno to matter, to concern
imposible impossible, 5
impresionado(a) impressed, 17
impresora (*f.*) printer, 17
incendio (*m.*) fire, 8
incluir to include, 10
indeterminado(a) indefinite
indicativo(a) indicative
infancia (*f.*) childhood, 9
informe (*m.*) report, 3
ingeniero(a) (*m., f.*) engineer, 14
inglés (*m.*) English (*lang.*), 2
ingreso(s) (*m. pl.*) income
insistir en to insist on, 14
instantáneo(a) instant, 7
instrumento musical (*m.*) musical instrument, 9
inteligente intelligent, 3
interesante interesting, 11
interesar to interest, 18
Internet (*f.*) the World Wide Web, 7
intérprete (*m., f.*) interpreter, 17
interrogativo(a) interrogative
investigación (*f.*) research, 14
invierno (*m.*) winter, 1
invitación (*f.*) invitation, 3
invitado(a) (*m., f.*) guest, 10
invitado(a) invited, 4
invitar (a) to invite, 18
inyección antitetánica (*f.*) tetanus shot, 15; **poner una —** to give a shot, 15

ir to go, 4; **ir a** + *infinitive* to be going (to) + *infinitive*, 4; **— a acampar** to go camping, 16; **— a pescar** to go fishing, 16; **— a pie** to go on foot, to walk, 12; **— caminando** to go on foot, to walk, 12; **— de pesca** to go fishing, 16
irse to go away, to leave, 9
isla (*f.*) island, 9
italiano (*m.*) Italian (*lang.*), 2
izquierdo(a) left; **a la —** to (on, at) the left, 12

jabón (*m.*) soap, 7
jactarse (de) to brag (about)
jamás never, ever 6
jamón (*m.*) ham, 5
jardín (*m.*) garden, 13; **— de infantes (infancia)** (*m.*) kindergarten, 16
jefe(a) (*m., f.*) boss, chief, 17; **— de compras** purchasing manager, 17
joven (*m., f.*) young man, young woman, 15; (*adj.*) young, 17
jóvenes (*m., f.*) young people
joyas (*f. pl.*) jewels, jewelry, 13
joyería (*f.*) jewelry store, 9
juego (*m.*) game, 4
jueves (*m.*) Thursday, 1
jugar (u:ue) to play (*game, sport*); **— al golf** to play golf, 16; **— al tenis** to play tennis, 16
jugo (*m.*) juice; **— de frutas** fruit juice, 5
julio July, 1
junio June, 1
juntos(-as) together, 7
justo(a) fair
juventud (*f.*) youth, 9

la (*f. sing.*) the, 2; (*pron.*) her, it, you (*form.*), 6
labio (*m.*) lip
laboratorio (*m.*) laboratory, 14
labrador(a) (*m., f.*) farmer
ladera (*f.*) hillside
lago (*m.*) lake
lámpara (*f.*) lamp, 10
lana (*f.*) wool, 13
langosta (*f.*) lobster, 5
lápiz (*m.*) pencil, 2
las (*f. pl.*) the, 2; (*pron.*) them, you (*form.*), 6
lástima (*f.*) pity, shame; **es una —** it's a pity, 11; **¡Qué —!** What a pity!, 15
lata (*f.*) can, 9
lavadora (*f.*) washing machine, 10
lavar(se) to wash (oneself), 9; **— la cabeza** to wash one's hair, 9; **— la ropa** to do the laundry, 6; **— los platos** to wash dishes, 6
le (to, for) her, (to, for) him, (to, for) you (*form.*), 7
leal loyal
leche (*f.*) milk, 5
lecho (*m.*) bed
lechón (*m.*) pork, 5
lechuga (*f.*) lettuce, 9
lector(a) (*m., f.*) reader
leer to read, 3
legumbre (*f.*) vegetable, 5
leído (*p.p. of* **leer**) read, 14
lejano(a) far away
lejos (*adv.*) far, 10
lengua (*f.*) language, 2; tongue, 15
lentamente slowly, 8
lento(a) slow, 8
les (to, for) them, (to, for) you, (*form. pl.*), 7
levantar to lift, to raise, 9; **—se** to get up, 9
libertad (*f.*) liberty, freedom, 2
libra (*f.*) pound
libre vacant, 7; free, available, 13
librería (*f.*) bookstore, 13
libreta de ahorros (*f.*) savings passbook, 8
libreto (*m.*) script, screenplay, 18
libro (*m.*) book, 2
licencia para conducir (*f.*) driver's license, 12
licuadora (*f.*) blender, 10
liga (*f.*) league
ligero(a) light
lila (*f.*) lilac, 8
limpiar el baño to clean the bathroom, 6
limpio(a) clean
lino (*m.*) linen, 13
liquidación (*f.*) sale, 13
lista (*f.*) list; **— de espera** (*f.*) waiting list, 7
literatura (*f.*) literature, 3
llama (*f.*) flame
llamar to call, 3; **—se** to be called, 9; **¿Cómo se llama usted?** What is your name? (*form.*), 1; **¿Cómo te llamas?** What's your name? (*fam.*), 1; **Me llamo...** My name is . . . , 1
llano (*m.*) plain
llanta (*f.*) tire, 12; **— pinchada** (*f.*) flat tire, 12
llanura (*f.*) plain
llave (*f.*) key, 7
llegada (*f.*) arrival
llegar to arrive, 4
llenar to fill, to fill out, 3
lleno(a) full, 12
llevar to take (*someone or something someplace*), 3; **— puesto(a)** to have on, to be wearing (clothes), 18
llover (o:ue) to rain, 5
lluvia (*f.*) rain, 5
lo him, it, you (*form.*), 6; **— que** what, which, 6; **— siguiente** the following; **— soy.** Indeed I am.; **— +** *adj.* that which is + *adj.*
loco(a) crazy, 16
logro (*m.*) achievement
loquito(a) crazy
loro (*m.*) parrot, 8
los (*m. pl.*) the, 2; (*pron.*) them, you (*form.*), 6
luchar to fight
lugar (*m.*) place, 6; **— de nacimiento** (*m.*) place of birth, 3; **— donde trabaja** (*m.*) place of employment, 3
lujo (*m.*) luxury
luna (*f.*) moon, 11; **— de miel** (*f.*) honeymoon, 11
lunares: de — polka-dotted, 13
lunes (*m.*) Monday, 1
luz (*f.*) light, 2; headlight, 12
madera (*f.*) wood
madrastra (*f.*) stepmother, 6
madre (*f.*) mother, 1
madrina (*f.*) godmother
maestro(a) (*m., f.*) teacher (elementary school), 7
magnífico(a) excellent, 14; great, 4
mal bad, badly
maleta (*f.*) suitcase, 7
maletero (*m.*) (car) trunk, 12
maletín (*m.*) briefcase
maligno(a) evil
malo(a) bad
mamá mom, 1
mancha (*f.*) blemish, spot
mandar to send, 7; to order
manejar to drive
manga (*f.*) sleeve
mango (*m.*) mango, 9
mano (*f.*) hand, 15
mantel (*m.*) tablecloth, 5
mantener to maintain, 14; **— la conversación** to keep the conversation going
mantequilla (*f.*) butter, 9
manzana (*f.*) apple, 9; (*Sp.*) city block
mañana (*f.*) tomorrow; **— mismo** tomorrow and not a day later, 17
mapa (*m.*) map, 2
máquina contestadora (*f.*) answering machine, 17
máquina de afeitar (*f.*) razor
mar (*m.*) sea, 7
marca (*f.*) brand, 13
margarina (*f.*) margarine, 9
margarita (*f.*) daisy, 8
marido (*m.*) husband, 5
mariposa (*f.*) butterfly
mariscos (*m. pl.*) shellfish, 8
marrón brown, 1
martes (*m.*) Tuesday, 1
marzo March, 1
más more, 2; plus; **— allá** beyond; **— o menos** more or less, 3
mascota (*f.*) pet, 8
masculino male
matemáticas (*f. pl.*) math, mathematics, 14
materia (*f.*) (school) subject, 14
maternidad (*f.*) motherhood
matrícula (*f.*) registration, tuition, 14
matricularse to register, 14
matrimonio (*m.*) marriage
mayo May, 1
mayor older, 5; bigger, 5; **el (la) —** the oldest, 5
me me, 6; (to, for) me, 7; (to) myself, 9; **— llamo...** My name is . . . , 1
mecánico (*m.*) mechanic, 12
mecer to rock
mediano(a) medium, 13
medicina (*f.*) medicine, 15
médico(a) (*m., f.*) physician, doctor, 14
medida (*f.*) size, 13; measure
medio(a) half; **medio** (*m.*) means; **medio hermana** (*f.*) half sister, 6; **medio hermano** (*m.*) half brother, 6; **y media** half-past (*telling time*), 2
mejor best; better, 5; **el (la) —** the best, 5
mejorar to improve, 9; **—se** to get better, 15
melocotón (*m.*) peach, 9

menor younger, 5; **el (la) —** youngest, 5
menos to, till (*telling time*), 2; less, 5; minus; **— mal** it's a good thing, 15
mensaje electrónico (*m.*) e-mail, 3
menú (*m.*) menu, 5
mercadeo (*m.*) marketing, 17
mercado (*m.*) market, 6
merecer la pena to be worth it, 12
merendar (e:ie) to have an afternoon snack, 15
mes (*m.*) month, 1
mesa (*f.*) table, 4; **— de centro** (*f.*) coffee table, 10
mesita de noche (*f.*) night table, 10
meta (*f.*) goal
métrica (*f.*) meter (*poetry*)
metro (*m.*) subway, 10
mexicano(a) Mexican, 1
mexicanoamericano(a) Mexican American, 1
mezcla (*f.*) mixture
mezclar to mix
mi (*sing.*) my, 3; **— amor** my love, 3; **— vida** (*f.*) darling, (my life), 3
mí (*obj. of prep.*) me, 4
microcomputadora (*f.*) laptop computer, 17
microondas (*m.*) microwave, 10
miedo (*m.*) fear, 4
miel de abeja (*f.*) honey, 15
mientras while, 3
miércoles (*m.*) Wednesday, 1
mil one thousand, 3
milla (*f.*) mile, 12
millar (*m.*) thousand
millonario(a) (*m., f.*) millionaire, 16
mío(s), mía(s) (*pron.*) mine, 9
mirar to look (at), 5; to watch (*i.e., TV*), 5; **— por la ventana** to look out the window, 6; **— vidrieras** to window shop, 13
mis (*pl.*) my, 3
misa (*f.*) mass (*Catholic service*), 16
mismo(a) same, 10
misterio (*m.*) mystery
mitad (*f.*) half
mochila (*f.*) backpack, 2
moda (*f.*) fashion
moderno(a) modern, 12
modista (*f.*) dressmaker
modo (*m.*) way
molestarse to bother (doing something), 15
momento (*m.*) moment, 3
moneda (*f.*) currency
mono (*m.*) monkey, 8
montaña (*f.*) mountain, 4
montar to ride, 16; **— a caballo** to ride a horse, 16; **— en bicicleta** to ride a bicycle, 16
monte (*m.*) mountain
montón (*m.*): **un montón de** a bunch of, 6
morado(a) purple, 1
moreno(a) dark, brunette, 3
morir (o:ue) to die, 5
mostrar (o:ue) to show
moto (*f.*) motorcycle, 8
motocicleta (*f.*) motorcycle, 8
mozo (*m.*) waiter, 5
muchacha (*f.*) girl, young woman, 2
muchacho (*m.*) boy, young man, 2
muchísimo a lot, 7
mucho(a) much, 1
Mucho gusto. How do you do? Nice to meet you., 1
mucho tiempo a long time, 7
muchos(-as) many, 4
Muchas gracias. Thank you very much., 1
mudarse to move (from one house to another), 10
muebles (*m. pl.*) furniture, 10
muelle (*m.*) dock
muerte (*f.*) death
muerto(a) (*p.p. of* **morir** *and adj.*) died, 14
mujer (*f.*) wife, 5; woman; **— de negocios** (*f.*) businesswoman, 7
multa (*f.*) fine, ticket, 8
mundo (*m.*) world, 17
museo (*m.*) museum, 4
música (*f.*) music
musical musical, 18
músico (*m.*) musician, 18
muy very, 1; **— bien** very well, 1

nacer to be born
nacido(a) born
nacimiento (*m.*) birth
nacionalidad (*f.*) nationality
nada nothing, 1
nadar to swim, 7
nadie nobody, no one, not anyone, 6
naranja (*f.*) orange, 9
nariz (*f.*) nose, 15
Navidad (*f.*) Christmas, 4
necesario(a) necessary, 3
necesitar to need, 2
negarse (e:ie) to refuse
negativo(a) negative
negocio (*m.*) business, 17
negro(a) black, 1
neumático (*m.*) tire, 12; **— pinchado** (*m.*) flat tire, 12
nevado(a) snowed
nevar (e:ie) to snow, 5
ni nor, 6; **—... ni...** neither . . . nor . . . , 6
niebla (*f.*) fog, 5
nieta (*f.*) granddaughter, 6
nieto (*m.*) grandson, 6
nieve (*f.*) snow, 16
ninguno(a), ningún no, none, not any, 6
niño(a) (*m., f.*) child, 5
no no, not, 1; **—... más que** nothing but; **— muy bien** not very well, 1
noche (*f.*) evening, night, 3
nocturno (*m.*) nocturne
nombre (*m.*) (first) name, 1; noun; **— de pluma** (*m.*) pen name
norte north, 16
norteamericano(a) North American, 2
nos us, 6; (to, for) us, 7; (to, for) ourselves, 9; **— vemos.** See you., 1
nosotros(-as) we, 1; us, 4
nota (*f.*) grade, 14
noticia(s) (*f. pl.*) (piece of) news, 7
novecientos(-as) nine hundred, 3
noveno(a) ninth, 7
noventa ninety, 2
novia (*f.*) girlfriend, 3
noviembre November, 1
novio (*m.*) boyfriend, 3
nublado(a) cloudy
nuera (*f.*) daughter-in-law, 5
nuestro(a) our, 3; (*pron.*) ours, 9
nuestro(-as) our (*pl.*), 3
nueve nine, 1
nuevo(a) new, 1
número (*m.*) number, 1; size (*of shoes*), 13; **— de identidad** (*m.*) I.D. number, 3; **— de la licencia de conducir** (*m.*) driver's license number, 3; **— de seguro social** (*m.*) social security number, 3; **— de teléfono** (*m.*) phone number, 1
nunca never, 6
nutrición (*f.*) nutrition, 14

o or, 6; **—... o...** either . . . or . . . , 6
objeto (*m.*) object
obligar to force, to make, 12
obra (*f.*) work (*of art*); **— teatral (de teatro)** (*f.*) play, 18
obrero(a) (*adj.*) labor
ochenta eighty, 2
ocho eight, 1
ochocientos(-as) eight hundred, 3
octavo(a) eighth, 7
octubre October, 1
ocultar to hide
ocupación (*f.*) occupation, 3
ocupado(a) busy, 4
ocurrir to happen, 8
oeste west, 16
oficina (*f.*) office, 13; **— de correos** (*f.*) post office, 12
oficio (*m.*) trade, 14
ofrecer to offer, 17
oído (*m.*) (*p.p. of* **oír**) heard, 14; ear (inner), 17
oír to hear
ojalá I hope, God grant, 11
ojo (*m.*) eye, 15
ola (f.) wave
olvidar(se) (de) to forget, 9
ómnibus (*m.*) bus, 6
once eleven, 1
oportunidad (*f.*) opportunity, 13
oprimir to hold tightly
optativo(a) elective
optimista (*invariable adj.*) optimistic, 3
opuesto(a) opposite
oración (*f.*) sentence
orden (*f.*) order
ordenador (*m.*) computer (*Sp.*), 3
oreja (*f.*) ear, 15
orgulloso(a) proud, 16; **no ser nada —** not to be proud at all, 16
oro (*m.*) gold
orquesta (f.) orchestra, band, 18
orquídea (*f.*) orchid, 8
os you (*fam. pl.*), 6; (to, for) you, 7; (to) yourselves, 9
oscuro(a) dark
ostra (*f.*) oyster, 16
otoño (*m.*) autumn, fall, 1
otro(a) another, other, 2
otra vez again
oveja (*f.*) sheep
oye listen, 1

padrastro (*m.*) stepfather, 6
padre (*m.*) father, 1
padres (*m. pl.*) parents, 6
padrino (*m.*) godfather, 11
pagar to pay, 5
país (*m.*) country, 9

pájaro (*m.*) bird
palabra (*f.*) word, 17
palma (*f.*) palm, palm tree, 9
palo de golf (*m.*) golf club, 16
pan (*m.*) bread, 14
panadería (*f.*) bakery, 9
pantalla (*f.*) screen, 17; movie screen, 18
pantalones (*m. pl.*) pants, trousers, 8
pantimedias (*f. pl.*) pantyhose, 13
pañuelo (*m.*) handkerchief, 13
papa (*f.*) potato, 5
papá dad, 1
papel (*m.*) paper; role; **— higiénico** (*m.*) toilet paper, 9
paquete (*m.*) package, 11
par (*m.*) pair, 13
para in order, 2; for, 3; to, in order to, 8; by, 8; **— beber** to drink, 5; **— eso** for that, 18; **— peor** to make matters worse, 18; **— que** in order that, 14; **¿ — qué?** What for?; **— siempre** forever, 18; **— ver** to see, 5
parabrisas (*m.*) windshield, 12
parada de autobuses (*f.*) bus stop, 6
paraguas (*m.*) umbrella
paraíso terrenal (*m.*) Garden of Eden
parecer to seem, 18
pared (*f.*) wall, 2
pareja (*f.*) couple
pariente (*m., f.*) relative, 6
parque (*m.*) park, 4; **— de diversiones** (*m.*) amusement park, 4
parquear to park, 8
partera (*f.*) midwife
partido (*m.*) game, 4
partir to leave
pasado(a) last, 7
pasado mañana the day after tomorrow, 4
pasaje (*m.*) ticket, 11; **— de ida** (*m.*) one-way ticket, 11; **— de ida y vuelta** (*m.*) round-trip ticket, 11
pasaporte (*m.*) passport, 7
pasar to spend (*time*), 4; to happen, 8; **— la aspiradora** to vacuum, 6; **— por la aduana** to go through customs, 7; **— por las armas** to shoot; **— una película** to show a movie, 7
pasarlo bien to have a good time, 5
Pase. Come in., 1
pastel (*m.*) pie, 5
patinar to skate, 16
patio (*m.*) backyard, 15
patria (*f.*) homeland
pavo (*m.*) turkey, 8
paz (*f.*) peace
pecho (*m.*) chest, 15
pedazo (*m.*) piece, 5
pedido (*m.*) order, 5
pedir (e:i) to order, 5; to ask for, to request, 6; **— un préstamo** to apply for a loan, 8
película (*f.*) movie, 7; **— de misterio** (*f.*) mystery, murder mystery, 18; **— de suspenso** (*f.*) thriller, 18; **— de vaqueros** (*f.*) western, 18; **— del oeste** (*f.*) western, 18
peligroso(a) dangerous
pelirrojo(a) red-headed, 3
pelo (*m.*) hair, 15
peluquería (*f.*) beauty salon, 12
pena (*f.*) sorrow
pensamiento (*m.*) pansy, 8; thought
pensar (e:ie) to think, 4; (+ *inf.*) to plan (*to do something*), 4; **— en** to think about, 18
pensión (*f.*) boarding house, 10
peor worse, 5; **el (la)** — the worst, 5
pepino (*m.*) cucumber, 9
pequeño(a) small, little
perder (e:ie) to lose, 4; **— se (algo)** to miss (*out on something*), 18
Perdón. Pardon me., 1
perfectamente perfectly, 15
perfecto(a) perfect, 2
periódico (*m.*) newspaper, 3
periodismo (*m.*) journalism, 14
pero but, 1
perro(a) (*m., f.*) dog, 8; **— caliente** (*m.*) hot dog, 5
persona (*f.*) person, 4
personaje (*m.*) character, 18
personal (*m.*) personnel, 17
pertenecer to belong, 18
pesar to weigh
pescadería (*f.*) fish store, 9
pescado (*m.*) fish, 5
pescar to fish, to catch (*a fish*), 16
pesimista (*invariable adj.*) pessimistic, 3
pez (*m.*) fish; **— de color** (*m.*) goldfish, 8
piano (*m.*) piano, 9
pie (*m.*) foot, 15
piedra (*f.*) stone
pierna (*f.*) leg
pieza de repuesto (*f.*) spare part, 12
pimienta (*f.*) pepper, 5
pino (*m.*) pine tree, 16
pintor(a) (*m., f.*) painter
piña (*f.*) pineapple, 9
piscina (*f.*) swimming pool, 7
piso (*m.*) floor, 6
placa (*f.*) license plate, 12
plancha (*f.*) iron, 10
planchar to iron, 6
planear to plan, 11
plástico (*m.*) plastic, 16
plata (*f.*) silver
plátano (*m.*) banana, 9
platicar to talk, to converse, 2
platillo (*m.*) saucer, 5
plato (*m.*) plate, 5; dish, 5
playa (*f.*) beach, 4
plomero(a) (*m., f.*) plumber, 14
pluma (*f.*) pen, 2
pluscuamperfecto (*m.*) pluperfect
pobre poor (*unfortunate*), 4
pobrecito(a) poor thing, 8
pobreza (*f.*) poverty
poder (o:ue) to be able to, can, 5; (*m.*) power
poema (*m.*) poem, 2
poesía (*f.*) poetry
policía (*m.*) policeman, 8
poliéster (*m.*) polyester, 13
pollo (*m.*) chicken, 5
ponche (*m.*) punch, 4
poner to put, to place, 6; **— una inyección** to give an injection, shot, 15; **— una multa** to give a ticket (*fine*), 8; **—se** to put on, 9; **—se en forma** to get into shape, 14; **no tener nada que —** not to have anything to wear, 13
por along, 8; around, 8; because of, 8; by, 8; during, 8; for, 8; in, 8; in exchange for, 8; in search of, 8; on account of, 8; on behalf of, 8; per, 8; through, 8; **— aquí cerca** around here, 18; **— desgracia** unfortunately, 8; **— ejemplo** for example, 13; **— el contrario** on the contrary, 13; **— eso** that is why, 18; **— favor** please, 1; **— fin** finally, 18; **— la mañana** in the morning, 2; **— la noche** in the evening, at night, 2; **— la tarde** in the afternoon, 2; **— lo general** generally, 18; **— lo menos** at least, 13; **— mes** a month, per month, 12; **— primera vez** for the first time, 4; **¿ — qué?** why?; **— si acaso** just in case, 18; **— suerte** luckily, 18; **— supuesto** of course, 18; **— teléfono** on the phone, 3; **— un tiempo** for a while, 12
porque because
postre (*m.*) dessert, 5
porteño(a) from Buenos Aires
portugués (*m.*) Portuguese (*lang.*), 2
practicar to practice, 2
precioso(a) pretty, beautiful, 13
preferir (e:ie) to prefer, 4
pregunta (*f.*) question, 4
preguntar to ask (a question), 15
preocuparse (por) to worry (about), 9
preparar to prepare, 4
presentar to introduce, 18
presente present
presidente(a) (*m., f.*) president, 17
préstamo (*m.*) loan, 8
prestar to lend, 8
presuroso(a) in haste
prevalecer to prevail
primaria (*f.*) elementary school
primavera (*f.*) spring, 1
primera clase (*f.*) first class, 11
primero(a), primer first, 2; — (*poet., pl.*) basic (i.e., elemental)
primo(a) (*m., f.*) cousin, 4
principal main, 17
probable probable, 8
probablemente probably, 18
probador (*m.*) fitting room, 13
probar (o:ue) to try, 9; to taste, 9; **—se** to try on, 9
problema (*m.*) problem, 2
procesador de textos (*m.*) word processor, 17
productor(a) (*m., f.*) producer, 18
profesión (*f.*) profession, 3
profesor(a) (*m., f.*) professor, teacher, instructor, 1
profundidad (*f.*) depth
programa (*m.*) program, 2
programación (*f.*) programming, 18
programador(a) (*m., f.*) programmer, 14
promedio (*m.*) grade point average, 14
prometer to promise, 7

prometido(a) fiancé(e), 11
pronóstico del tiempo (*m.*) weather forecast
pronto soon, 14
propina (*f.*) tip, 5
propio(a) own, 16; **propia página** (*f.*) home page
proponer to propose; **—se** to set out to
proporcionar to furnish
proseguir (e:i) to continue
protagonista (*m., f.*) protagonist, main character, 18
próximo(a) next, 6
publicar to publish
pueblo (*m.*) town, 11; (*community, nation*) people
puente (*m.*) bridge
puerta (*f.*) door, 2; **— de calle** (*f.*) front door, 12; **— de salida** (*f.*) airline departure gate, 11
puertorriqueño(a) (*m., f.*) Puerto Rican
pues... well . . ., 6
puesto(a) (*p.p. of* **poner** *and adj.*) put, 14; (*m.*) position, job, 17
pulmonía (*f.*) pneumonia, 15
pulsera (*f.*) bracelet, 13
punto (*m.*) dot
puré de papas (*m.*) mashed potatoes, 5

que (*rel. pron.*) that, who, 4; than, 5; which, 10; (*conj.*) than, 5; **— viene** coming, next, 11
¿qué? what?, 1; **¿A — hora?** (At) what time?, 2; **¡— Diablo!** What the heck!; **¡— esperen!** Let them wait!, 18; **¡ — gusto de verte!** How nice to see you!, 15; **¿ — hay (de nuevo)?** What's up (new)?, 1; **¿ — hora es?** What time is it?, 2; **¡— lástima!** What a pity!, 15; **¿ — les parece si...?** What do you think about . . .? 13; **¡— mala suerte!** Such bad luck!, 8; **¿ — quiere decir...?** What does . . . mean?; **¿ — tal?** How are you?, 1; **¿ — tal te va?** How's it going for you? (*fam.*), 14
quebrar(se) (e:ie) to break, 15
quedar to fit, to be; **— impresionado(a)** to be impressed, 17; **—le grande (chico) a uno** to be too big (small) on someone, 13; **— suspendido(a)** to fail (*an exam or a course*), 14; **—se** to stay, 11; **—se con** to keep; **—se sentado(a)** to remain seated
quehaceres de la casa (*m. pl.*) housework, 6
quejarse to complain, 10
quemar to burn
querer (e:ie) to want, to wish, 4; **— decir** to mean; **no quise** I refused, 10
queso (*m.*) cheese, 5
quien(es) who, whom, that, 10
¿quién? who?; **¿de —?** whose?
química (*f.*) chemistry, 14
quince fifteen, 1
quinientos(-as) five hundred, 3
quinto(a) fifth, 7

quitar to take away, 9; **—se** to take off, 9
quizás perhaps, 13

radiografía (*f.*) X-ray
raíz (*f.*) root
rama (*f.*) branch
ramo (*m.*) bouquet, 8
rápidamente rapidly, 8
rápido(a) (*adv.*) quick, 6; rapid, 8; (*adj.*) fast, 13
raqueta (*f.*) racket, 16
rascacielos (*m. sing.*) skyscraper
rato (*m.*) while, 4
ratón (*m.*) mouse, 17
raya (*f.*) stripe, 13
rayón (*m.*) rayon, 13
razón (*f.*) reason; **tener** — to be right, 4
realista (*invariable adj.*) realistic, 3
realizar to make
rebaja (*f.*) sale, 13
rebajar to mark down, 13
recámara (*f.*) bedroom (*Mex.*), 6
recepción (*f.*) registration, 7
receta (*f.*) recipe, 9; prescription, 15
recetar to prescribe, 15
recibir to receive, 3
reciente recent, 8
recientemente recently, 8
recoger to pick up, 6
recomendación (*f.*) recommendation, 17
recomendar (e:ie) to recommend, 11
recompensa (*f.*) reward
recordar (o:ue) to remember, 5
recurrir a to turn to
Red (*f.*) the World Wide Web
refresco (*m.*) soft drink, soda pop, 5
refugiado(a) (*m., f.*) refugee
regalar to give (*as a gift*), 8
regalo (*m.*) gift, 8
regatear to bargain
regla (*f.*) ruler
regresar to return, 2
reina (*f.*) queen
reírse (e:i) to laugh, 12
reloj (*m.*) clock, 2
remar to row, 16
remedio (*m.*) medicine, 15
remolcador (*m.*) tow truck, 12
renglón (*m.*) line
renunciar to resign
reparto de papeles (*m.*) casting, 18
repetir (e:i) to repeat
repollo (*m.*) cabbage, 9
represa (*f.*) dam
reproductor de discos (*m.*) CD player, 4
requisito (*m.*) requirement, 14
reserva (*f.*) reservation, 7
reservación (*f.*) reservation, 7
resfriado (*m.*) cold, 15
resfrío (*m.*) cold, 15
resoplar to blow
responsabilidad (*f.*) responsibility, 17
respuesta (*f.*) answer
restaurante (*m.*) restaurant, 4
resto (*m.*) the rest, 10
resumé (*m.*) résumé, curriculum vitae, 17
resumen (*m.*) summary

retrato (*m.*) portrait
reunirse to get together
revista (*f.*) magazine, 6
revolución (*f.*) revolution, 9
revolver (o:ue) to stir
revuelo (*m.*) fluttering
rey (*m.*) king
rico(a) tasty, 5
risa (*f.*) laughter
robar to steal, 8
rodaja (*f.*) slice
rodeado(a) surrounded
rodilla (*f.*) knee, 15
rogar (o:ue) to beg, to plead, 11
rojo(a) red, 1
romántico(a) romantic, 11
romper(se) to break, 15
ropa (*f.*) clothes, 6; clothing, 13; **— hecha** (*f.*) ready-to-wear clothes; **— interior** (*f.*) underwear, 13
rosa (*f.*) rose, 8
rosado(a) pink, 1
rostro (*m.*) face
roto(a) (*p.p. of* **romper** *and adj.*) broken, 14
rubio(a) blond, 3
ruido (*m.*) noise

sábado (*m.*) Saturday, 1
sábana (*f.*) sheet, 6
saber to know, 6; to find out, 10
sabroso(a) tasty, 5
sacapuntas (*m.*) pencil sharpener, 2
sacar to get, to receive (*a grade*), 14; **— la basura** to take out the garbage, 6; **— una foto** to take a picture, 4
saco de dormir (*m.*) sleeping bag, 10
sacudir los muebles to dust the furniture, 6
sal (*f.*) salt, 5
sala de estar (*f.*) living room, 3
sala de rayos X (equis) (*f.*) X-ray room, 15
salario (*m.*) salary, 17
salida (*f.*) exit, departure, 11
salir to go out, 6; leave; **— de casa** to leave the house, 8
salón de belleza (*m.*) beauty salon, 12
salsa (*f.*) sauce, 9
salud (*f.*) health, 15
¡Salud! Cheers!
saludo (*m.*) greeting, 1; **—s a...** Say hello to . . ., 1
salvavidas (*m., f.*) lifeguard, 16
sandía (*f.*) watermelon, 9
sándwich (*m.*) sandwich, 3
santo (*m.*) saint's day
sartén (*f.*) frying pan, skillet, 10
sastre (*m.*) tailor
se (to) himself, (to) herself, (to) yourself (*form.*), (to) yourselves, (to) themselves, 9; **— dice...** You say . . ., One says . . ., 2
Sea. So be it.
secadora (*f.*) dryer, 10
secar to dry, 6
sección de (no) fumar (*f.*) (no) smoking section, 11
seco(a) dry
sed (*f.*) thirst, 4; **tener** — to be thirsty, 4
seda (*f.*) silk, 13

seguir (e:i) to follow, 6; to continue, 6; **— derecho** to continue straight ahead, 12; **— los pasos** to follow in the footsteps, 18
según according to
segundo(a) second, 7; **Segunda Guerra Mundial** (*f.*) Second World War; **segundo nombre** (*m.*) middle name
seguro(a) sure, 8
seis six, 1
seiscientos(-as) six hundred, 3
selección (*f.*) selection, 17
selva (tropical) (*f.*) jungle, 11
semana (*f.*) week, 4; **la semana que viene** (*f.*) next week, 4; **la semana próxima** (*f.*) next week, 4
sendero (*m.*) path
sensibilidad (*f.*) sensitivity
sentado(a) seated, sitting, 14
sentarse (e:ie) to sit (down), 9
sentir(se) (e:ie) to feel, 9; to be sorry, to regret
señal (*f.*) sign
señor (Sr.) mister, Mr., sir, gentleman, 1
señora (Sra.) madam, Mrs., lady, 1
señorita (Srta.) Miss, young lady, 1
septiembre September, 1
séptimo(a) seventh, 7
sepulcro (*m.*) tomb
ser to be, 1
servicio (*m.*) service, 7; **— de habitación (cuarto)** (*m.*) room service, 7
servilleta (*f.*) napkin, 5
servir (e:i) to serve, 6; **— de** to serve as, 17; **no — de mucho** to not be much good, 14
sesenta sixty, 2
setecientos(-as) seven hundred, 3
setenta seventy, 2
sexo (*m.*) gender
sexto(a) sixth, 7
si if, 14
sí yes, 1
sicología (*f.*) psychology, 14
siempre always, 6
sierra (*f.*) mountain
siete seven, 1
siglo (*m.*) century
signo (*m.*) sign
siguiente following
silla (*f.*) chair, 2; **— de ruedas** (*f.*) wheelchair, 15
sillón (*m.*) armchair, 10
simpatía (*f.*) charm
simpático(a) nice, charming, 3
sin without; **— embargo** however, nevertheless, 13; **— falta** without fail, 18; **— que** without, 14; **— qué ni para qué** without rhyme or reason, 18
sincero(a) sincere, 9
síntoma (*m.*) symptom, 15
sistema (*m.*) system. 2; **— de calificaciones** (*m.*) grading system; **— de comunicación telefónica** (*m.*) telephone system, 17
sitio (*m.*) room
sobre about, 11; **— todo** above all, especially, 17
sobrecama (*f.*) bedspread, 10
sobrenombre (*m.*) nickname
sobrina (*f.*) niece, 4
sobrino (*m.*) nephew, 4
sociología (*f.*) sociology, 14
sofá (*m.*) sofa, 6
sol (*m.*) sun
solamente only, 10
soledad (*f.*) loneliness; solitude
solicitar un préstamo to apply for a loan, 8
solicitud (*f.*) application (form), 3; **— de empleo** (*f.*) job application, 3
solo(a) alone, 5
solo only, 10
soltar (o:ue) amarras to untie lines
soltero(a) single, 3
sombra (*f.*) shadow
sombrero (*m.*) hat
sonar (o:ue) to ring, 15
sonido (*m.*) sound
sonreír to smile
soñar (o:ue) con to dream about (of), 18
sopa (*f.*) soup, 5; **— de fideos** (*f.*) noodle soup, 5
sorprender to surprise, 11
sótano (*m.*) basement, 6
su his, her, its, your (*form.*), their, 3
subterráneo (*m.*) subway, 10
subvencionado(a) subsidized
sucio(a) dirty
sucursal (*f.*) branch (office)
suegra (*f.*) mother-in-law, 6
suegro (*m.*) father-in-law, 6
sueldo (*m.*) salary, 17
sueño (*m.*) dream; **tener —** to be sleepy, 4
suerte (*f.*) luck, 8
suéter (*m.*) sweater, 15
sugerir (e:ie) to suggest, 11
supermercado (*m.*) supermarket, 9
supersticioso(a) superstitious, 8
supervisión (*f.*) supervision, 17
supervisor(a) (*m., f.*) supervisor, 17
sur south, 16
sus his, her, its, your (*form.*), their, 3
suspirar to sigh, 6
sustantivo (*m.*) noun
suyo(s), suya(s) (*pron.*) his, hers, theirs, yours, 9

tabla de mar (*f.*) surfboard, 16
tablilla de anuncios (*f.*) bulletin board, 2
talla (*f.*) size, 13
taller de mecánica (*m.*) car repair shop, 12
talonario de cheques (*m.*) checkbook, 8
tamaño (*m.*) size
también also, too, 2
tampoco neither, not either, 6
tan as, 5; so, 17; **— pronto como** as soon as, 14
tanque (*m.*) tank, 12
tanto(a) as much, 5; so much, 11; **— como** as much as, 5; **— en... como en...** both in . . . and in . . .
tantos(-as) as many, 5; **— como** as many as, 5
tardar to take (*time to do something*), 13
tarde (*f.*) afternoon, 2; (*adv.*) late, 7; **— o temprano** sooner or later, 18; **por la —** in the afternoon, 2
tarjeta (*f.*) card, 7; **— de crédito** (*f.*) credit card, 8; **— de embarque** (*f.*) boarding pass, 11; **— de turista** (*f.*) tourist card, 7; **— postal** (*f.*) postcard, 7
taxi (*m.*) taxi, 6
taza (*f.*) cup, 5
te (*pron.*) you (*fam.*), 6; (to, for) you, 7; (to) yourself, 9
té (*m.*) tea, 5; **— frío (helado)** (*m.*) iced tea, 5
teatro (*m.*) theater, 4; **— de aficionados** (*m.*) amateur theatre, 18
teclado (*m.*) keyboard, 17
teja (*f.*) tile
tela (*f.*) material, 13
teléfono (*m.*) telephone, 1; **— celular** (*m.*) cellular phone, 12
telenovela (*f.*) soap opera, 5
televisión (*f.*) television, 2
televisor (*m.*) TV, 7
tema (*m.*) subject, theme, 2
temblar to tremble
temer to fear, to be afraid, 11
temperatura (*f.*) temperature, 17
templado(a) mild
temprano early, 9
tenedor (*m.*) fork, 5
tener to have, 3; **—... años (de edad)** to be . . . years old, 4; **— calor** to be hot, 4; **— cuidado** to be careful, 4; **— ... de retraso (atraso)** to be . . . behind schedule, 11; **— en cuenta** to keep in mind; **— éxito** to be successful, 18; **— frío** to be cold, 4; **— hambre** to be hungry, 4; **— lugar** to take place; **— miedo** to be afraid, 4; **— prisa** to be in a hurry, 4; **— que** (+ *inf.*) to have to (+ *inf.*), 3; **— razón** to be right, 4; **— sed** to be thirsty, 4; **— sueño** to be sleepy, 4; **— un picnic** to have a picnic, 16; **— un pinchazo** to have a flat tire, 18; **no — razón** to be wrong, 4
tenis (*m.*) tennis, 16
tercero(a), tercer third, 7
terco(a) stubborn, 3
terminar to finish, to end, 14
ternura (*f.*) tenderness
terreno (*m.*) land
ti you (*obj. of prep.*), 4
tía (*f.*) aunt, 4
tiburón (*m.*) shark
tiempo (*m.*) time, 2; weather, 5
tienda (*f.*) store, 4; **— por departamentos** (*f.*) department store, 13
tierra (*f.*) land
timbre (*m.*) doorbell, 15
tinto red (wine), 5
tintorería (*f.*) dry cleaner's, 8
tío (*m.*) uncle, 4
tipo (*m.*) type, 15
tirano(a) (*m., f.*) tyrant
tirar to throw (away), to abandon ; **— basura** to litter
título (*m.*) degree, 14; title
toalla (*f.*) towel, 7
tobillo (*m.*) ankle, 15
tocador (*m.*) dresser, 10
tocar to play (*a musical instrument*), 9; **— a la puerta** to knock on the door, 6

todo(a) all, 6
todo all, everything, 8; — **el mundo** everybody, 18
todos(-as) everybody
todos los días every day
tomar to take, 2; to drink, 3; — **algo** to have something to drink, 3; — **el sol** to sunbathe, 16; — **una decisión** to make a decision, 14; — **una foto** to take a picture, 4
Tome asiento. Have a seat., 1
tomate (*m.*) tomato, 9
toque (*m.*) touch
torpeza (*f.*) stupidity
torre (*f.*) tower
torta (*f.*) cake, 5
tortuga (*f.*) turtle, 8
tos (*f.*) cough, 15
toser to cough, 15
tostadora (*f.*) toaster, 10
trabajar to work, 2
trabajo (*m.*) job, 3; work, 3; — **de la casa** (*m.*) housework, 6
tradición (*f.*) tradition, 4
traducir to translate, 6
traductor(a) (*m., f.*) translator, 17
traer to bring, 6
trágico(a) tragic
traído (*p.p. of* **traer**) brought, 14
traje (*m.*) suit, 13; — **de baño** (*m.*) bathing suit, 16
trama (*f.*) plot, 18
tranquilidad (*f.*) tranquility
trapear el piso to mop the floor, 6
tratar de to deal with
trece thirteen, 1
treinta thirty, 1
tren (*m.*) train, 11
tres three, 1
trescientos(-as) three hundred, 3
trigo (*m.*) wheat
trompeta (*f.*) trumpet, 9
tropezar (e:ie) to trip
trozo (*m.*) piece, 5
tu your (*fam. sing.*), 3
tú you (*fam. sing.*), 1
tulipán (*m.*) tulip, 8
turbio(a) muddy
turismo (*m.*) tourism, 7
turista (*m., f.*) tourist, 6
tus your (*fam. pl.*), 3
tuyo(s), tuya(s) (*pron.*) yours (*fam. sing.*), 9

ubicación (*f.*) location
ubicar to locate
último(a) last, 17
última vez last time, 17

un a, an, 1; — **poco** + *adj.* a little + *adj.*, 4; — **poco (de)** a little, 2; — **rato** (*m.*) a while, 4
una a, an 1; — **vez** (*f.*) once, 16
único: **lo** — the only thing, 14
universidad (*f.*) university, 1
universitario(a) (*adj.*) university, 14
uno(a) one, 1
unos(-as) a few, some, 2; about
usado(a) used, 12
usar to use, 6; to wear
usted (Ud.) you (*form., sing.*), 1; (*obj. of prep.*), 4
ustedes (Uds.) you (*form. pl.*), 1; (*obj. of prep.*), 4
utilidad (*f.*) usefulness
uva (*f.*) grape, 9

vacaciones (*f. pl.*) vacation, 7
vacío(a) empty, 12
valer to be worth; **(no) vale la pena** it's (not) worth the trouble, 12
valeroso(a) brave
valija (*f.*) suitcase, 7
valor (*m.*) value
¡vamos! let's go!, 2; — **de compras** let's go shopping, 13
vaso (*m.*) glass, 4
vecindad (*f.*) neighborhood, 10
vecino(a) (*m., f.*) neighbor, 4
veinte twenty, 1
veinticinco twenty-five, 1
veinticuatro twenty-four, 1
veintidós twenty-two, 1
veintinueve twenty-nine, 1
veintiocho twenty-eight, 1
veintiséis twenty-six, 1
veintisiete twenty-seven, 1
veintitrés twenty-three, 1
veintiuno twenty-one, 1
velero (*m.*) sailboat, 16
velocidad máxima (*f.*) speed limit, 12
vendedor(a) (*m., f.*) salesperson, 14; merchant
vender to sell, 3
venir (a) to come, 3; —**le de perillas a uno** to suit one to perfection, 18
ventaja (*f.*) advantage
ventana (*f.*) window, 2
ventanilla (*f.*) window (of a vehicle or booth), 12
ventilador (*m.*) fan, 10
ver to see, 6
verano (*m.*) summer, 1
verbo (*m.*) verb
verdad (*f.*) truth; **¿verdad?** right?, 1
verdadero(a) real, 18; true
verde green, 1

verdura (*f.*) vegetable, 5
versión (*f.*) draft
verso (*m.*) line (of poetry)
vestido (*m.*) dress, 13; — **de noche** (*m.*) evening gown, 13
vestido(a) dressed; — **de gala** dressed up
vestirse (e:i) to get dressed, 9
vez (*f.*) time (*in a series*), 4; **a veces** at times, 6; **en** — **de** instead of, 17
viajar to travel, 7
viaje (*m.*) trip, 4
viajero(a) (*m., f.*) traveler, 11
vida (*f.*) life
videograbadora (*f.*) VCR, 17
vidriera (*f.*) shop window, 18
viejo(a) old
viento (*m.*) wind, 5; **hacer** — to be windy; **viernes** (*m.*) Friday, 1
vileza (*f.*) vileness
vinagre (*m.*) vinegar, 9
vino (*m.*) wine, 4; — **tinto** (*m.*) red wine, 8
violeta (*f.*) violet, 8
violín (*m.*) violin, 9
visitar to visit, 4
visto(a) (*p.p. of* **ver** *and adj.*) seen, 14; **vista** (*f.*) eyes
viudo(a) widowed, 3
vivir to live, 3
vocabulario (*m.*) vocabulary
volante (*m.*) steering wheel, 12
volar (o:ue) to fly, 5
vóleibol (*m.*) volleyball, 16
voltear to turn over
voluntad (*f.*) will power
volver (o:ue) to return, 5
vosotros(-as) (*subject pron.*) you (*fam. pl.*), 1; (*obj. of prep.*), you (*fam. pl.*), 4
vuelo (*m.*) flight, 11
vuelto(a) (*p.p. of* **volver** *and adj.*) returned, 14
vuestro(a) your (*fam. sing.*), 3; (*pron.*) yours (*fam. pl.*), 9
vuestros(-as) your (*fam. pl.*), 3

y and, 1; past, after (time), 2
ya already, 2; now, 7; — **lo creo** I'll say, 13; **¡— verás!** You'll see!, 15
yerno (*m.*) son-in-law, 6
yo I, 1

zanahoria (*f.*) carrot, 9
zapatería (*f.*) shoe store, 9
zapato (*m.*) shoe, 13; — **de tenis** (*m.*) tennis shoe, 13
zona postal (*f.*) zip code, 3
zoológico (*m.*) zoo, 4

English-Spanish

a, an un(a), 1
abandonment desamparo (*m.*)
about de, 16; como, 16
abroad en el extranjero
accept aceptar, 3
accident accidente (*m.*), 15
according to de acuerdo con; según, 3
account cuenta (*f.*), 8
accountant contador(a) (*m., f.*), 5
accounting contabilidad (*f.*), 14
accuracy exactitud (*f.*)
act actuar
acting actuación (*f.*), 18
action acción (*f.*), 18
activity actividad (*f.*), 16
actor actor (*m.*), 18
actress actriz (*f.*), 18
ad anuncio (*m.*), aviso (*m.*), 3
add añadir
address dirección (*f.*), domicilio (*m.*), 2
adjective adjetivo (*m.*)
advanced adelantado(a)
advice consejo (*m.*)
advise avisar, 10; aconsejar, 11
advisor consejero(a) (*m., f.*), 14
after (*time*) y, 2; **— all** al fin y al cabo, 18
afternoon tarde (*f.*), 2; **— snack** merienda (*f.*), 7; **good —** buenas tardes, 1; **in the —** por la tarde, 2
again otra vez
against contra
age edad (*f.*), 3
agency agencia (*f.*), 16
agent agente (*m., f.*)
aghast atónito(a)
agree estar de acuerdo, 6
agreement concordancia (*f.*)
aha! ¡ajá!, 3
air bag bolsa de aire (*f.*), 12; **air conditioning** aire acondicionado (*m.*), 7
airline aerolínea (*f.*), 11; **— departure gate** puerta de salida, 11
airport aeropuerto (*m.*), 11
aisle seat asiento de pasillo (*m.*), 11
alcoholic beverage bebida (*f.*) alcohólica, 5
all todo(a), 6; (*pron.*) todo, 8
allergic alérgico(a), 8
allergy alergia (*f.*), 8; **— attack** ataque (*m.*) de alergia, 8
almost casi, 8
alone solo(a), 5
along por, 8
alphabet alfabeto (*m.*)
alphabetize alfabetizar
also también, 2
always siempre, 6
A.M. de la mañana, 2
amateur theatre teatro de aficionados (*m.*), 18
ample amplio(a), 10
amusement park parque de diversiones (*m.*), 4
an un(a), 1
ancestry ascendencia (*f.*), 14
and y, 1
angry enfadado(a), enojado(a), 4
animated animado(a), 4
ankle tobillo (*m.*), 15

anniversary aniversario (*m.*), 9
annoyed fastidiado(a)
another otro(a), 2
answer contestar, 3; respuesta (*f.*)
answering machine máquina contestadora (*f.*), 17
antibiotic antibiótico (*m.*), 15
any alguno(a), algún, 6; **not —** ninguno(a), ningún, 6
anyone alguien, 6; **not —** nadie, 6
anything algo, 6
anyway en fin, 8; de todos modos
apartment apartamento (*m.*), 3
appearance apariencia (*f.*)
apple manzana (*f.*), 9
application (*form*) solicitud (*f.*), 3
apply for a loan pedir (e:i) un préstamo, solicitar un préstamo, 8
appointment cita (f.)
approach acercarse, 11
April abril, 1
armchair butaca (*f.*); sillón (*m.*), 10
army ejército (*m.*)
around por, 8; cerca de; **— here** por aquí cerca, 18
arrival llegada (*f.*), 4
arrive llegar, 4
article artículo (*m.*), 6
as tan, 5; **— . . . —** tan... como, 5; **— long as** con tal de que, 14; **— many** tantos(as), 5; **— many . . . —** tantos(as)... como, 5; **— much** tanto, 5; **— much —** tanto como, 5; **— soon —** en cuanto, tan pronto como,14
ashamed avergonzado(a)
ask (*a question*) preguntar, 15; **— (for)** pedir (e:i), 6
aspirin aspirina (*f.*), 15
assistant asistente (*m., f.*), 17
at en, 1; a, 2; **— a time** a la vez, 4; **— about** a eso de, 15; **— least** por lo menos, 13; **— night** por la noche, 2; **— the latest** a más tardar, 18; **— this moment** en este momento, 5; **at +** *time* a la (las) + *time*, 2
athletic atlético(a), 16
attend asistir (a), 3
August agosto, 1
aunt tía (*f.*), 4
automatic automático(a), 12; **— teller (ATM)** cajero automático (*m.*), 8
autumn otoño (*m.*), 1
available libre, 13
avenue avenida (*f.*), 8
avocado aguacate (*m.*), 9

back espalda (*f.*), 15
backpack mochila (*f.*), 2
backyard patio (*m.*), 15
bad malo(a), 8
bag bolsa (*f.*), 13
baked al horno, 5
bakery panadería (*f.*), 9
banana plátano (*m.*), 9
bank banco (*m.*), 8; **— employee** empleado(a) bancario(a) (*m., f.*), 17

barbeque asado (*m.*), 16
bargain regatear; ganga (*f.*), 13
basement sótano (*m.*), 6
bass contrabajo (*m.*), 9
bathe (oneself) bañar(se), 9
bathing suit traje de baño (*m.*), 16
bathroom baño (*m.*), 6; cuarto de baño (*m.*), 6
bathtub bañadera (*f.*), bañera, 7
battery acumulador (*m.*), batería (*f.*), 12
be ser, 1; estar, 4; **— able to** poder (o:ue), 5; **— acquainted with** conocer, 6; **— afraid** tener miedo (de), 4; temer, 11; **— at fault** tener la culpa, 9; **— bad weather** hacer mal tiempo, 5; **— . . . behind schedule** tener... de retraso (atraso), 11; **— bored (to death)** aburrirse (como una ostra), 16; **— called** llamarse, 9; **— careful** tener cuidado, 4; **— cold** tener frío, 5; (*weather*) hacer frío, 5; **— crazy about** estar loco(a) por, 18; **— determined** decidido(a), 18; **— due to** debido a; **— for,** *to exist for* enderezarse a; **— furious** darle rabia a uno, 18; **— glad** alegrarse (de), 11; **— going to** + *inf.* ir a + *inf.*, 4; **— good weather** hacer buen tiempo, 5; **— hot** tener calor, 5; (*weather*) hacer calor, 5; **— hungry** tener hambre, 4; **— impressed** quedar impresionado(a), 17; **— in a hurry** tener prisa, 4; **— in agreement** estar de acuerdo, 6; **— late** llegar tarde, 2; **— named** llamarse, 9; **— not much good** no servir de mucho, 14; **— on vacation** estar de vacaciones, 5; **— pleasing to** gustar, 7; **— right** tener razón, 4; **— right back** volver en seguida, 6; **— scared** tener miedo, 4; **— silent** callar; **— sleepy** tener sueño, 4; **— sorry** sentir (e:ie), 11; **— starving** estar muerto(a) de hambre, 5; **— successful** tener éxito, 18; **— sunny** hacer sol, 5; **— thirsty** tener sed, 4; **— too big (small) on someone** quedarle grande (chico) a uno, 13; **— wearing** llevar puesto(a), 18; **— worth it** valer (merecer) la pena, 12; **— wrong** no tener razón, 4; **— . . . years old** tener. . . años, 4
beach playa (*f.*), 4
beans frijoles (*m. pl.*), 5
beat batir
beautiful hermoso(a), 5; precioso(a), 13
beauty belleza (*f.*); **— salon** peluquería (*f.*), salón de belleza (*m.*), 12
because porque; **— of** por, 8
bed cama (*f.*), 6; lecho (*m.*); **to go to —** acostarse (o:ue), 9; **to put to —** acostar (o:ue), 9
bedroom dormitorio (*m.*); recámara (*f.*) (*Mex.*), 6; pieza, 6
bedspread sobrecama (*f.*), 10
beef carne de res (*f.*)
beer cerveza (*f.*), 5

before antes (de), 7; antes de que, 14
beg rogar (o:ue), 11
begin comenzar (e:ie), empezar (e:ie) (a), 4
behave comportarse, 16
being that como, 14
believe creer, 3
believed creído (*p.p. of* creer), 14
bellhop botones (*m.*), 7
belong pertenecer, 18
besides además, 2
best el (la) mejor, 5
bet apostar (o:ue), 16
betroth desposar
better mejor, 5
beverage bebida (*f.*), 5
bewildered desconcertado(a)
beyond más allá
bicycle bicicleta (*f.*), 12
big grande
bill cuenta (*f.*), 5
biology biología (*f.*), 14
bird pájaro (*m.*)
birth nacimiento (*m.*), 3
birthday cumpleaños (*m.*), 4
black negro(a), 1
blanket frazada (*f.*), 10
blemish mancha (*f.*)
blender licuadora (*f.*), 10
block (city) manzana (*f.*) (*Sp.*), cuadra (*f.*)
blond(e) rubio(a), 3
blood-stained ensangrentado(a)
blouse blusa (*f.*), 13
blow resoplar
blue azul, 1
boarding house pensión (*f.*), 10
boarding pass tarjeta de embarque (*f.*), 11
boat barca (*f.*), bote (*m.*), 16
book libro (*m.*), 2
bookstore librería (*f.*), 13
boot bota (*f.*), 13
bored aburrido(a), 4
born nacido(a); **be —** nacer, 9
borrow pedir (e:i) prestado, 11
boss jefe(a) (*m., f.*), 17
both ambos(as); **— in . . . and in . . .** tanto en. . . como en. . .; **both of them** los (las) dos, 2
bother (*doing something*) molestarse, 15
bouquet ramo (*m.*), 8
boy chico (*m.*), muchacho (*m.*), 2
boyfriend novio (*m.*), 3
bracelet pulsera (*f.*), 13
brake freno (*m.*), 12
branch rama (*f.*); (*office*) sucursal (*f.*)
brand marca (*f.*), 13
brave valeroso(a)
bread pan (*m.*), 9
break romper(se), quebrar(se) (e:ie), 17; **— down** (*car*) descomponerse, 12
breakfast desayuno (*m.*), 7
bridge puente (*m.*)
brilliant brillante, 7
bring traer, 6
brochure folleto (*m.*), 11
broken roto(a), 14
broom escoba (*f.*), 6
brother hermano (*m.*), 3
brother-in-law cuñado (*m.*), 6
brown marrón, café, 1
brought traído (*p.p. of* traer), 14
brunette moreno(a), 3
brush one's teeth cepillarse los dientes, 9
bud capullo (*m.*)
bulletin board tablilla de anuncios (*f.*), 2
bullfight corrida de toros (*f.*)
bunch: a — of un montón de (*m.*), 6
bureau cómoda (*f.*), 10
buried enterrado(a)
burn quemar
bus autobús (*m.*), ómnibus (*m.*), bus (*m.*), 6; colectivo, 12; **— stop** parada de autobuses (*f.*), 6
business (*adj.*) empresarial; **— administration** administración de empresas (*f.*), 14
businesspeople gente de negocio (*f.*)
busy ocupado(a), 4
but pero, 1; sino
butter mantequilla (*f.*), 9
butterfly mariposa (*f.*)
buy comprar, 6
buyer comprador(a) (*m., f.*), 17
by para, 8; por, 8; **— heart** de memoria
bye chau, 1

cabbage repollo (*m.*), 9; col (*f.*)
cabin cabaña (*f.*), 16
cafe café (*m.*), 3
cafeteria cafetería (*f.*), 1
cake torta (*f.*), 5
calculator calculadora (*f.*), 2
calender calendario (*m.*), 8
call llamar, 3
calorie caloría (*f.*), 5
camellia camelia (*f.*), 8
camera cámara (fotográfica) (*f.*), 7
camp acampar, 16
can poder (o:ue), 5; bote (*m.*) (*Mex.*), lata (*f.*), 9
canary canario (*m.*), 8
cancel cancelar, 7
candidate candidato(a) (*m., f.*), 17
canoe canoa (*f.*), 16
capital (city) capital (*f.*), 8
car auto (*m.*), automóvil (*m.*), carro (*m.*), coche (*m.*), 10; **— jack** gato (*m.*), 12; **— repair shop** taller (*m.*) de mecánica, 12
caramel custard flan (*m.*), 5
carburetor carburador (*m.*), 12
card tarjeta (*f.*), 7
care cuidado (*m.*)
career carrera (*f.*), 14
carnation clavel (*m.*), 8
carpet alfombra (*f.*), 10
carpenter carpintero(a), (*m., f.*), 14
carriage carro (*m.*)
carrot zanahoria (*f.*), 9
carry-on bag bolso de mano (*m.*)
cartoons dibujos animados (*m. pl.*), 18
carved tallado(a)
case: in — en caso de que, 14
cash efectivo (*m.*), 8; **— a check** cobrar un cheque, 8; **— register** caja (*f.*), 13; **in —** en efectivo, 8
casting reparto de papeles (*m.*), distribución de papeles (*f.*), 18
cat gato (*m.*), 8
catch a fish pescar, 16
CD player reproducor de discos (*m.*), 4
celebrate celebrar, festejar, 9
celery apio (*m.*), 9
cellular phone teléfono celular (*m.*), 12
censorship censura (*f.*)
cent centavo (m.), 11
ceramic tile azulejo (*m.*)
certified public accountant contador(a) público(a) certificado(a), 17
chair silla (*f.*), 2
chalk tiza (*f.*), 2
chalkboard pizarra (*f.*), 2
champagne champán (*m.*), 5
champion campeón(-ona) (*m., f.*), 16
change cambiar, 6
channel canal (*m.*), 7
character personaje (*m.*), 18
charge: in — encargado(a), 17
charm simpatía (*f.*)
charmed encantado(a), 1
charming simpático(a), encantador(a), 3
chat charlar, 4
check cuenta (*f.*), 5; cheque (*m.*), 8; **— luggage** facturar el equipaje, 11
checkbook talonario de cheques (*m.*), chequera (*f.*), 8
checking account cuenta corriente (*f.*), 8
checkup chequeo (*m.*), 15
Cheers! ¡Salud!
cheese queso (*m.*), 5
chef cocinero(a), (*m., f.*), 14
chemistry química (*f.*), 14
cherry cereza (*f.*)
chest pecho (*m.*), 15; **— of drawers** cómoda (*f.*), 10
chicken pollo (*m.*), 5; **— and rice** arroz (*m.*) con pollo, 5
chief jefe(a) (*m., f.*), 17
child niño(a) (*m., f.*), 5; **only —** hijo(a) único(a), 11
childhood infancia (*f.*), niñez (*f.*), 9
children hijos (*m. pl.*); **—'s** (*adj.*) infantil
Chilean chileno(a), 13
Chinese (*lang.*) chino (*m.*), 2
chivalry caballería (*f.*)
chocolate chocolate (*m.*), 5
choose escoger
Christmas Navidad (*f.*), 4; **— tree** árbol de Navidad (*m.*), 4
church iglesia (*f.*)
cider sidra (f.), 5
city ciudad (*f.*), 3; **— block** manzana (*f.*) (*Sp.*), cuadra (*f.*)
clarinet clarinete (*m.*), 9
class clase (*f.*), 1
classified clasificado(a), 12; **— ad** aviso clasificado (*m.*)
clean limpio(a); limpiar, 6
clerk empleado(a) (*m., f.*), 7
climate clima (*m.*), 2
climb escalar, 16
clock reloj (*m.*), 2
close cerrar (e:ie), 4; (*adv.*) cerca, 10

closed cerrado(a), 12
cloudy nublado(a)
coal carbón (*m.*)
coat abrigo (*m.*)
coffee café (*m.*), 3; (*small cup of*) cafecito (*m.*), 15; **— maker** cafetera (*f.*), 10; **— table** mesa (*f.*) de centro, 10
cognate cognado (*m.*), 1
cold catarro (*m.*), resfriado (*m.*), resfrío (*m.*), 15; **to be —** tener frío, 4; (*weather*) hacer frío, 5
collar cuello (*m.*)
colleague colega (*m., f.*)
college facultad (*f.*), 14; (*adj.*) universitario(a), 14
color color (*m.*), 1
column columna (*f.*), 18
comb one's hair peinarse, 9
come venir (a), 3; **— in.** Pase., 1
comfortable cómodo(a), 7
communication comunicación (*f.*), 17
compact compacto(a); **— disc** disco compacto (*m.*), 4; **— disc player reproductor de discos** (*m.*), 4
company compañía (*f.*), 3
compensate compensar, 17
complain quejarse, 9
computer computadora, (*f.*), 2; ordenador (*m.*) (*Sp.*), 3
concern importarle a uno, 18
concert concierto (*m.*), 4
condition condición (*f.*), 12
conditional condicional (*m.*)
conduct conducir, 6
confirm confirmar, 7
confused aturdido(a), 4
consulate consulado (*m.*), 7
contagious contagioso(a), 15
continue seguir (e:i), continuar, 14; proseguir (e:i); **— straight ahead** seguir derecho, 12
contraction contracción (*f.*)
conversation conversación (*f.*), 2
converse conversar, platicar, 2
convince convencer, 10
cook cocinar, 6; cocinero(a) (*m., f.*), 14
cool (down) enfriar
copper cobre (*m.*)
corner (*street*) esquina (*f.*), 12
correspondence correspondencia (*f.*), 17
cost an arm and a leg costar (o:ue) un ojo de la cara, 12
cotton algodón (*m.*), 13
cough tos (*f.*), 15; toser, 15
count contar (o:ue), 5
country país (*m.*), 9; campo (*m.*), 16
couple pareja (*f.*)
courteous amable, 3
cover cubrir
cousin primo(a) (*m., f.*)
covered cubierto(a), 14
cowardice cobardía (*f.*)
co-worker compañero(a) de trabajo, 11
crazy loco(a), 16; loquito(a)
cream crema (*f.*), 5
create crear
credit card tarjeta de crédito (*m.*), 8
critic crítico(a) (*m., f.*), 18
criticize criticar, 18
crowd muchedumbre (*f.*), 2
cruise crucero (*m.*), 11
cry llorar, 13
Cuban cubano(a), 2
Cuban American cubanoamericano(a), 2
cucumber pepino (*m.*), 9
cup taza (*f.*), 5
currency moneda (*f.*)
curriculum vitae currículum vitae (*m.*), 17
curtain cortina (*f.*), 10
customer cliente (*m., f.*)
customs aduana (*f.*), 7
cut cortar(se), 9

dad papá (*m.*), 1
daily diariamente
daisy margarita (*f.*), 8
dam represa (*f.*)
dance bailar, 4; baile (*m.*), 4
dancer bailarín(ina) (*m., f.*), 4
dangerous peligroso(a)
dark moreno(a), 3; oscuro(a)
darling mi amor (*m.*), mi vida, (*f.*), 3
date fechar, poner la fecha, 8; fecha; **— of birth** fecha de nacimiento (*f.*), 3
daughter hija (*f.*), 4; **— in-law** nuera (*f.*), 6
dawn alba (*f.*)
day día (*m.*), 1; **— before yesterday** anteayer, 8; **one of these days** un día de estos, 16
dazed aturdido(a), 4
deal with tratar de
dear querido(a), 14
death muerte (*f.*)
debit card tarjeta de débito, 7
December diciembre, 1
decide decidir, 3
definite determinado(a)
degree título (*m.*), 14; grado (*m.*), 15
deliver entregar, 14
demand exigir, 11
demonstrative demostrativo(a)
denial negación (*f.*)
deny negar (e:ie), 12
department store almacén (*m.*), tienda por departamentos (*f.*), 13
departure salida (*f.*), 11; **— gate** puerta de salida (*f.*), 11
deposit depositar, 8
depth profundidad (*f.*)
describe describir, 11
desk escritorio (*m.*), pupitre (*m.*), 2
despair desesperanza (*f.*)
dessert postre (*m.*), 5
diamond diamante (*m.*)
die morir(se) (o:ue), 8
died muerto(a), 14
diet dieta (*f.*), 5; dietético(a), 5
different distinto(a)
difficult difícil, 2
dine cenar, 7
dining room comedor (*m.*), 6
dinner cena (*f.*), 7; **have —** cenar, 7
direct directo(a), 11; dirigir, 18
director director(a) (*m., f.*), 18
dirty sucio(a)
disaster desastre (*m.*), 4
discotheque discoteca (*f.*), 4
discount descuento (*m.*), 13
dish plato (*m.*), 5
distinguished distinguido(a), 18
divine divino(a), 16
divorced divorciado(a), 3
do hacer, 4; **— the laundry** lavar la ropa, 6; **— the shopping** hacer las compras, 6
dock muelle (*m.*)
doctor (Dr.) doctor(a) (*m., f.*), 1; médico(a) (*m., f.*), 14; **—'s office** consultorio (*m.*), 15
document documento (*m.*), 12; cédula (*f.*)
documentary documental (*m.*), 18
dog perro(a) (*m., f.*), 8
done hecho (*p.p. of* hacer), 14
donkey burro(a) (*m., f.*)
door puerta (*f.*), 2
doorbell timbre (*m.*), 15
dot punto (*m.*); **on the —** en punto
double doble, 7; **— bed** cama doble, 7; **— room** habitación doble (*f.*), 7
doubt dudar, 12
draft borrador (*m.*), versión (*f.*)
dramatic art arte (*f.*) dramático, 18
dream hacerse ilusiones, 18; **— about (of)** soñar (o:ue) con, 18
dress vestido (*m.*), 13
dressed: to get — vestirse (e:i), 9; **— up** vestido(a) de gala
dressmaker modista (*f.*)
drink beber, tomar, 3; bebida (*f.*), 5
drive conducir, 6; manejar, 12
driver's license licencia para conducir (*f.*), 12; **— number** número de la licencia de conducir, 3
drums batería (*f.*), 9
dry secar; seco(a); **— cleaner's** tintorería (*f.*), 8; **— season** estación de la seca (*f.*)
dryer secadora (*f.*), 10
dubbed doblado(a)
duly debidamente
during durante, 7; por, 8
dust the furniture sacudir los muebles, 6
DVD disco (*m.*) versátil digital, 17

each cada, 17
ear (*inner*) oído (*m.*), 17; (*external*) oreja (*f.*), 17
early temprano, 9
earn ganar, 3
earring arete (*m.*), 13
easily fácilmente
east este, 16
easy fácil, 2
eat comer, 3; **— soup** tomar sopa, 5
efficient eficiente, 17
effort esfuerzo (*m.*)
egg huevo (*m.*), 5
eight ocho, 1; **— hundred** ochocientos(as), 3
eighteen dieciocho, 1
eighth octavo(a), 7
eighty ochenta, 2
either . . . or o. . . o, 6; **not —** tampoco, 6
elective clase optativa (*f.*); optativo(a)
electricity electricidad (*f.*), 10
electronic equipment equipo electrónico (*m.*), 17
elegant elegante, 13

elevator ascensor (*m.*), elevador (*m.*), 7
eleven once, 1
e-mail mensaje electrónico (*m.*), 3; correo electrónico (*m.*), 17
embassy embajada (*f.*), 7
emergency emergencia (*f.*), 15
emphasize destacar
employee empleado(a), 7
employment office agencia de empleos, 6
empty vacío (a), 12
end terminar, 14; fin (*m.*)
engaged comprometido(a), 18
engineer ingeniero(a) (*m., f.*), 14
English (*lang.*) inglés (*m.*), 2
enjoy disfrutar; **— oneself** divertirse (e:ie), 9
enormous enorme, 15
entertain entretener, 15
entertainment section (*of newspaper*) cartelera (*f.*), 18
enthused entusiasmado(a), 4
entrance entrada (*f.*), 11
eraser borrador (*m.*), 2
errand diligencia (*f.*), 8
to run —s hacer diligencias, 8
escalator escalera mecánica (*f.*), 7
especially especialmente, 8
essay ensayo (*m.*)
evaluation evaluación (*f.*), 17
evening noche (*f.*), 2; **— gown** vestido de noche (*m.*), 13
event acontecimiento (*m.*)
ever alguna vez
every day todos los días, 2
everybody todo el mundo, 18
everything todo, 8
everywhere a (de) todas partes, a todos lados, 12
evil maligno(a)
exactly exactamente, 17
exaggerate exagerar, 13
exam examen (*m.*), 3
excellent excelente, 11
exercise hacer ejercicio, 7
excess baggage exceso de equipaje (*m.*), 11
exchange cambiar, 13
excursion excursión (*f.*), 11
excuse: Excuse me. Con permiso., 1
executive ejecutivo(a) (*m., f.*), 14
exercise hacer ejercicio, 7
exit salida (*f.*), 11
expect esperar, 6
expensive caro(a), 5
experience experiencia (*f.*), 3
express gratitude dar las gracias, 18
expression expresión (*f.*)
extremely extremadamente, 17; **— good** buenísimo(a), 11
eye ojo (*m.*), 15; **with brown eyes** de ojos castaños, 5

face cara (*f.*), 15; rostro (*m.*)
fact: the — is . . . es que. . . , 13
faculty appointment cátedra (*f.*)
fail (*course or exam*) quedar suspendido(a), 14
faint desfallecer
fair justo(a)
faith fe (*f.*), 18
fall otoño (*m.*), 1; caer, 16; **— asleep** dormirse (o:ue), 9; **— in love with** enamorarse de, 18
false falso(a)
fame fama (*f.*), 17
family familia (*f.*), 4; **— oriented** hogareño(a); **— room** salón de estar (*m.*), 6
fan ventilador (*m.*), 10
far lejos, 10; **— away** lejano(a)
farewell despedida (*f.*), 1
farmer labrador(a) (*m., f.*)
fashion moda (*f.*)
fast rápido(a), 13
fat gordo(a), 3
father padre (*m.*), 1
father-in-law suegro (*m.*), 6
fault defecto (*m.*), 15
favorite favorito(a), 7
fear temer, 11
February febrero, 1
feed dar alimento (a), dar de comer
feel sentir(se) (e:ie), 9
fever fiebre (*f.*), 15
few unos(as), 2
fiancé(e) prometido(a) (*m., f.*), 11
fifteen quince, 1
fifth quinto(a), 7
fifty cincuenta, 2
fight luchar
file archivar, 17
fill, fill out llenar, 3
film película (*f.*), 7; filmar, 18; **— festival** festival de cine (*m.*), 18
finally por fin, 18
financial económico(a), 3
find encontrar (o:ue), 5; **— out** saber, 10
fine (*adv.*), bien, 1; multa (*f.*), 8; (*verb*) dar (poner) una multa, 8
finger dedo (*m.*), 15
finish terminar, 14
fire fuego (m.), incendio, 8
fire fighter bombero, 14
fire hydrant boca de incendios (*f.*), hidrante (*m.*), 8
first primero(a), primer, 2; **— class** primera clase, 11; **— name** nombre (*m.*), 3; **— part of** a principios de, 18
fish pescado (*m.*), 5; pez; pescar, 16; **— store** pescadería (*f.*), 9
fishing rod caña de pescar (*f.*), 16
fit caber, 6; quedar
fitting room probador (m.), 13
five cinco, 1; **— hundred** quinientos(as), 3
fix arreglar, 6
flame llama (*f.*)
flash memory card memoria (*f.*) flash portátil, 17
flat tire llanta pinchada (*f.*), neumático pinchado (*m.*), 12
flesh carne (*f.*)
flight vuelo (*m.*), 11; **— attendant** auxiliar de vuelo (*m., f.*), 11; azafata (*f.*), 11
floor piso (*m.*), 7
flower flor (*f.*), 8; **— shop** florería (*f.*), 8
flu gripe (*f.*), 15
flute flauta (*f.*), 9
fly volar (o:ue), 5
foam espuma (*f.*)
fog niebla (*f.*), 5
fold doblar, 6
folder carpeta (*f.*), 17
follow seguir (e:i), 6; **— in the footsteps** seguir los pasos, 18
following siguiente
food comida (*f.*), 4
fool oneself hacerse ilusiones, 18
foolishness tontería (*f.*), 8
foot pie (*m.*), 13; **on —** a pie, 12
for para, 3; por, 8; **— example** por ejemplo, 13; **— that** para eso, 18
force obligar, 12
forehead frente (*f.*), 15
foreign extranjero(a)
forest bosque (*m.*), 11
forever para siempre, 18
forget olvidar(se) (de), 9
fork tenedor (*m.*), 5
fortress fortaleza (*f.*)
forty cuarenta, 2
four cuatro, 1; **— hundred** cuatrocientos(as), 3
fourteen catorce, 1
fourth cuarto(a), 7
frankly francamente, 12
free (*of charge*) gratis, 8, gratuito(a); libre, 13
freedom libertad (*f.*), 2
freeway autopista (*f.*), 12
French (*lang.*) francés (*m.*), 2; **— fries** papas fritas, 5
frequent frecuente
frequently a menudo, frecuentemente, 12
fresh (*water*) dulce
Friday viernes (*m.*), 1
fried frito(a), 5
friend amigo(a) (*m., f.*), 1
friendship amistad (*f.*)
from de, 1; desde, 10; **— now on** de ahora en adelante, 9
front: in — of frente a, 8; **— door** puerta de calle (*f.*), 12
frown fruncir el ceño, 11
fruit fruta (*f.*), 9
fruit juice jugo de frutas (*f.*), 5
fruit tree árbol frutal (*m.*), 15
frustrated frustrado(a), 4
frying pan sartén (*f.*), 10
full lleno(a), 12
fun (*adj.*) divertido(a), 16
function funcionar, 12
furious furioso(a), 4
furnish proporcionar
furnished amueblado(a), 10
furniture muebles (*m. pl.*), 10
future futuro (*m.*), 14

game partido (*m.*), 4
garage garaje (*m.*), 6
garden jardín (*m.*), 7; **— of Eden** paraíso terrenal (*m.*)
gas station gasolinera (*f.*), estación de servicio (*f.*), 12
gasoline gasolina (*f.*), 12
gee! ¡caramba!, 2
gender género (*m.*), sexo (*m.*)
general general, 8
generally generalmente, 8; por lo general, 18

gentleman señor (*m.*), 1; caballero (*m.*)
geranium geranio (*m.*), 8
German *(lang.)* alemán (*m.*), 2
get buscar, 6; conseguir (e:i), 6; (*grade*) sacar, 14; **— a tan** broncearse, 16; **— angry** enojarse, enfadarse, 14; **— better** mejorarse, 15; **— dressed** vestirse (e:i), 9; **— engaged to** comprometerse con, 18; **— in shape** ponerse en forma, 14; **— married** casarse con, 11; **— together** reunirse; **— undressed** desvestirse (e:i), 9; **— up** levantarse, 9; **— used to** acostumbrarse a, 12; **— worse** empeorarse, 15
ghost fantasma (*m.*)
gift regalo (*m.*), 8; don (*m.*); **— shop** tienda de regalos, 7
girl chica (*f.*), muchacha (*f.*), 2
girlfriend novia (*f.*), 3
give dar, 4; (*as a gift*) regalar, 8; **— a shot** poner una inyección, 15
glass vaso (*m.*), 4; copa (*f.*), 5
glove guante (*m.*), 13
go ir (a), 4; **— away** irse, 9; **— camping** acampar, ir a acampar, 16; **— down** bajar, 12; **— fishing** ir de pesca, ir a pescar, 16; **— on an excursion** hacer una excursión, 11; **— on foot** ir a pie, ir caminando, 12; **— on vacation** ir de vacaciones, 11; **— out** salir, 6; **— through** atravesar (e:ie); **— through customs** pasar por la aduana, 7; **— to bed** acostarse (o:ue), 9
goal meta (*f.*)
goblet copa (*f.*), 5
God Dios; **— grant** ojalá, 11
goddaughter ahijada (*f.*)
godfather padrino (*m.*), 11
godmother madrina (*f.*)
godson ahijado (*m.*)
gold oro (*m.*)
golden dorado(a)
goldfish pez de color (*m.*), 8
golf club palo de golf (*m.*), 16
good bueno(a), buen, 1; **— afternoon** buenas tardes, 1; **— evening** buenas noches, 1; **— morning** buenos días, 1; **— night** buenas noches, 1
good-bye adiós, 1; chau, 1
good-looking guapo(a), 3
gosh! ¡caramba!, 1
grade nota (*f.*), 14; **— point average** promedio (*m.*), 14
grading system sistema de calificaciones (*m.*)
graduate graduar(se), 14
granddaughter nieta (*f.*), 6
grandfather abuelo (*m.*), 4
grandmother abuela (*f.*), 4
grandson nieto (*m.*), 6
grape uva (*f.*), 9
gratefulness agradecimiento (*m.*)
gray gris, 1
great magnífico(a), 14
Great! ¡Chévere!, ¡Bárbaro!
great-grandfather (mother) bisabuelo(a) (*m., f.*)
green verde, 1
greet saludar, 15
greeting saludo (*m.*), 1
grilled a la parrilla, 5
group grupo (*m.*), 7
guest invitado(a) (*m., f.*), 4; **— room** cuarto (m.) de huéspedes, 6
guilty culpable
Guinea pig conejillo de Indias (*m.*), 8
guitar guitarra (*f.*), 9
gym gimnasio (*m.*), 14

hair pelo (*m.*), cabello (*m.*)
half medio(a); mitad (*f.*); **— past** y media (*time*), 2
ham jamón (*m.*), 5
hamburger hamburguesa (*f.*), 5
hand mano (*f.*), 15
handbag bolso (*m.*), cartera (*f.*), 9
handkerchief pañuelo (*m.*), 13
handsome guapo(a), 3
happen pasar, ocurrir, 8
happening hecho (*m.*)
happy feliz, 1; contento(a), 4
hardware store ferretería (*f.*), 9
hardworking trabajador(a), 3
hat sombrero (*m.*)
have tener, 3; haber (*aux.*); **— a good time** pasarlo bien, 5; divertirse (e:ie), 9; **— a lot to do** tener mucho que hacer, 3; **— a nice trip** buen viaje, 11; **— a picnic** hacer un picnic, 16; **— a seat.** Tome asiento., 1; **— breakfast** desayunar, 5; **— dinner** cenar, 5; **— just . . .** acabar de. . . , 4; **— lunch** almorzar (o:ue), 5; **— self-esteem** estimarse; **— nothing to wear** no tener nada que ponerse, 13; **— something to drink (eat)** tomar (beber) algo, 3; **— to** tener que + *inf.*, 3
he él, 1; **— (she) who** el (la) que
head cabeza (*f.*), 15
headlight luz (*f.*), 12
healer curandero(a) (*m., f.*)
health salud (*f.*), 15
hear oír
heard oído (*p.p. of* oír), 15
heart corazón (*m.*); **— attack** ataque al corazón (*m.*), 15
heating califacción (*f.*), 10
heaven cielo (*m.*)
height estatura (*f.*), 3
hello hola, 1; **say — to . . .** saludos a. . . , 1
help ayudar (a), 6; ayuda (*f.*), 2
her su(s), 3; ella, 4; la, 6; le, 7
here aquí, 3; **— it is.** Aquí está., 3; **— it goes.** Aquí va.
hers suyo(a)(s), 9
herself se, 9
hide esconder, 6; ocultar
highway autopista (*f.*), 12
hillside ladera (*f.*)
him él, 4; lo, 6; le, 7
himself se, 9
his su(s), 3; suyo(a)(s), 9
history historia (*f.*), 3
holidays fiestas, 4
hold estrechar; **— tightly** oprimir
home casa (*f.*), hogar (*m.*); **— page** propia página (*f.*); **(related to) —** casero(a), 15
homework deber (*m.*), tarea (*f.*), 14
honest honrado(a)
honey miel de abeja (*f.*), 15
honeymoon luna de miel (*f.*), 11
honorable honorable
hood capó (*m.*), 12
hope esperar, 11; esperanza (*f.*); **I —** ojalá, 11
horn bocina (*f.*), 12
horse caballo (*m.*); **— rider** jinete (*m., f.*)
hospital hospital (*m.*), 2
hot caliente; **— chocolate** chocolate caliente (*m.*), 5; **— dog** perro caliente (*m.*), 5; **to be —** tener calor, 4; (*weather*) hacer calor, 5; **nice and —** bien caliente, 15
hotel hotel (*m.*), 5
hour hora (*f.*)
house casa (*f.*), 2
housework quehaceres (trabajos) de la casa, 6
how? ¿cómo?, 1; **— are you?** ¿Cómo está Ud.? (*form. sing.*),1; ¿Cómo están ustedes? (*form. pl.*), 1; ¿Cómo estás? (*fam.*), 1; **— do you do?** Mucho gusto., 1; **— does one say . . . ?** ¿Cómo se dice. . . ?, 2; **— far in advance?** ¿Con cuánta anticipación?; **— is it going (for you)?** ¿Qué tal (te va)?, 14; ¿Cómo le va? (*form.*), ¿Cómo te va? (*fam.*); **— many?** ¿cuántos(as)?; **— may I help you?** ¿En qué puedo servirle?, 7; **— much?** ¿cuánto(a)?; **— nice to see you!** ¡Qué gusto de verte!, 15
hug abrazo (*m.*), 14; abrazar, 8
hundred cien, ciento, 2
hunger hambre (*f.*), 5
hungry: to be — tener hambre, 4
hunt cazar, 16
hurt doler (o:ue), 15; herir (e:ie)
husband esposo (*m.*), marido (*m.*), 5
hypochondriac hipocondriaco (m.), 15

I yo, 1
ice cream helado (*m.*), 5
iced tea té helado, 5
I.D. number número de identidad (*m.*), 3
idea idea (*f.*), 2
ideal (*adj.*) ideal, 11
if si, 12
immediately inmediatamente, 18
imperfect imperfecto(a)
import importación (*f.*), 17
important importante, 17
impossible imposible
impressed impresionado(a), 17
improve mejorar, 9
in en, 1; por, 8; de, 16; a, 16; **— case** en caso de que, 14; **— charge** encargado(a), 17; **— exchange for** por, 8; **— fact** de hecho, 18; **— front of** frente a, 8; **— haste** presuroso(a); **— order** para, 2; **— order that** para que, 14; **— order to** a, 3; para, 8; **— search of** en busca de, 8; **— spite of** a pesar de (que), 9; entonces, 4; **— the afternoon** de (por) la tarde, 2; **— the evening** de (por) la

noche, 2; — **the morning** de (por) la mañana, 2
include incluir, 10
income ingreso (*m.*)
increase aumento (*m.*), 17
indefinite indeterminado(a)
indicative indicativo(a)
inexpensive barato(a), 11
influenza gripe (*f.*), 15
injection inyección (*f.*), 15; **to give an —** poner una inyección, 15
inside en, 16; dentro
insist on insistir en, 14
installments plazos (*m. pl.*), 8; **in (on) —** a plazos, 8
instructor profesor(a), 1
insurance agent agente de seguros (*m., f.*), 17
intelligent inteligente, 3
interest interesar, 18
interesting interesante, 11
international internacional, 2
Internet Internet (*m., f.*), 7
interpreter intérprete (*m., f.*), 17
interrogative interrogativo(a)
interview entrevista (*f.*), 17; entrevistar, 17
invitation invitación (*f.*), 3
invite invitar (a), 18
invited invitado(a), 4
iron planchar, 6; plancha (*f.*), 10
ironing board tabla de planchar, 10
Is. . . (*name*) there? ¿Está... (*name*)?, 3
it la, 6; lo, 6
Italian (*lang.*) italiano (*m.*), 2
its su(s), 3
itself se, 9

jack gato (*m.*), 12
jail cárcel (*f.*)
January enero, 1
Japanese (*lang.*) japonés (*m.*), 2
jewelry joyas (*f. pl.*), 13; **— store** joyería (*f.*), 9
job empleo (*m.*), trabajo (*m.*), 3; puesto (*m.*), 17; **— application** solicitud de trabajo (*f.*), 3
joint account cuenta conjunta (*f.*), 8
joke bromear, 12
journalism periodismo (*m.*), 14
joy gusto (*m.*)
juice jugo (*m.*), 5
July julio, 1
June junio, 1
jungle selva (tropical) (*f.*), 11
just in case por si acaso, 18

keep quedarse con; (*something going*) mantener; **— in mind** tener en cuenta
key llave (*f.*), 6
keyboard teclado (*m.*), 17
kid: to — (*joke*) bromear, 12
kilo, kilogram kilogramo (*m.*), 13
kindergarten jardín de infantes (infancia) (*m.*)
kindness bondad (*f.*)
king rey (*m.*)
kiss beso (*m.*); besar
kitchen cocina (*f.*), 6
knee rodilla (*f.*), 15
knife cuchillo (*m.*), 5
knight caballero (*m.*)
knock on the door tocar a la puerta, 6
know conocer, 6; saber, 6
knowledge conocimiento (*m.*)

labor (*adj.*) obrero(a)
laboratory laboratorio (*m.*), 14
lobster langosta (*f.*), 5
lack falta (*f.*); **— of patience** impaciencia (*f.*)
lady señora (*f.*), 1
lake lago (*m.*)
lamb cordero (*m.*), 5
lamp lámpara (*f.*), 10
land tierra (*f.*), terreno (*m.*)
language idioma (*m.*); lengua (*f.*), 2
laptop computer microcomputadora (*f.*), computadora portátil (*f.*), 17
large grande, amplio, 10
last pasado(a), 7; último(a), 16; durar, 13; **— name** apellido (*m.*), 3; **— night** anoche, 7; **— time** última vez (*f.*), 16
later después, más tarde, 3
laugh reírse (e:i), 10
laughter risa (*f.*)
lawyer abogado(a) (*m., f.*), 14
leaf hoja (*f.*)
leafy frondoso(a)
league liga (*f.*)
learn aprender (a), 3
leather cuero (*m.*), 13
leave (behind) dejar, 5; salir, 6; irse, 9; partir; **— alone** dejar tranquilo(a), 16; **— the house** salir de casa, 8
lecture conferencia (*f.*)
left izquierdo(a); **to the —** a la izquierda, 12
leg pierna (*f.*)
lemon limón (*m.*), 5
lend prestar, 8
less menos, 5; **— . . . than** menos. . . que, 5; **— than** + *number* menos de + *number*, 5; **more or —** más o menos, 3
let know avisar, 10
Let them wait! ¡Que esperen!, 18
let's go vamos, 2; **— shopping** vamos de compras, 13
let's see a ver, 3
letter carta (*f.*), 17
lettuce lechuga (*f.*), 9
liberty libertad (*f.*), 2
librarian bibliotecario(a) (*m., f.*), 14
library biblioteca (*f.*), 2
license licencia; **— plate** chapa (*f.*), placa (*f.*) (*Mex.*), 12
life vida (*f.*)
lifeguard salvavidas (*m., f.*), 16
lift levantar, 9
light luz (*f.*), 2; (*adj.*) claro(a), ligero(a)
likable simpático(a), 3
like gustar, 7; como, 16
likewise igualmente, 1
lilac lila (*f.*), 8
line renglón (*m.*); (*of poetry*) verso (*m.*)
linen hilo (*m.*), lino (*m.*), 13
lip labio (*m.*)
list lista (*f.*), 9
listen oye, 1; escuchar, 13
literature literatura (*f.*), 3
litter tirar basura
little pequeño(a); **— sister (brother)** hermanita(-o) (*f., m.*), 4; **a —** un poco (de), 2; **a —** + *adjective* un poco + *adjective*, 4
live vivir, 3
livestock ganadería (*f.*)
living room sala (*f.*), 6
loaded (with) cargado(a) (con), 13
loan préstamo (*m.*), 8
lobster langosta (*f.*), 5
locate ubicar
located: to be . . . quedar, 10
location ubicación (*f.*)
lock cerradura (*f.*)
lodge (at a hotel) hospedarse en, 11
lodging hospedaje (*m.*), 11; alojamiento (*m.*)
loneliness soledad (*f.*)
long time mucho tiempo, 7
look (at) mirar, 5; **— for** buscar, 6; **— out the window** mirar por la ventana, 6; **— right through** atravesar (e:ie) con la mirada
lose perder (e:ie), 4
love encantarle a uno, 8; amar; cariño (*m.*), 8; **in — (with)** enamorado(a) (de), 16
loving amante (*adj.*)
loyal leal
luck suerte (*f.*), 8
luckily por suerte, 18
luggage equipaje (*m.*), 7
lunch almuerzo (*m.*), 7; **to have —** almorzar (o:ue), 5; **— time** la hora de almorzar, 17
luxury lujo (*m.*)

madam señora (*f.*), 1
made hecho(a) (*p.p. of* hacer), 14
magazine revista (*f.*), 6
magnificent magnífico(a), 4
maid criada (*f.*), 10
maiden name apellido de soltera (*m.*)
main character protagonista (*m., f.*), 18
maintain mantener, 14
majority mayoría (*f.*), 18
make hacer, 6; obligar, 12; realizar; **— a decision** tomar una decisión, 14; **— a movie** filmar, 18; **— fun of** burlarse de, 18; **— matters worse** para peor, 18; **— a stopover** hacer escala, 11
man hombre (*m.*)
manager gerente (*m., f.*), 17
mango mango, 9
many muchos(as), 4
map mapa (*m.*), 2
March marzo, 1
Mardi Gras carnaval (*m.*)
margarine margarina (*f.*), 9
marital status estado civil (*m.*), 3
mark down rebajar, 13
marker marcador (*m.*), 2
market mercado (*m.*), 6
marketing mercadeo (*m.*), 17
marriage matrimonio (*m.*)
married casado(a), 3; **— couple** matrimonio (*m.*), 13

marry casarse (con), 18; desposar
mashed potatoes puré de papas (*m.*), 5
mass (*Catholic service*) misa (*f.*), 16
match combinar, hacer juego, 13
math(ematics) matemáticas (*f. pl.*), 2
matter importarle a uno, 18
mattress colchón (*m.*), 7
May mayo, 1
maybe a lo mejor, 12; tal vez
me mí, 4; me (*d.o.*), 6; me (*i.o.*), 7
meal comida (*f.*), 5
mean querer decir
means medio (*m.*)
measure medida (*f.*); medir (e:i), 13
meat carne (*f.*), 6; **— market** carnicería (*f.*), 9; **— turnover** empanada (*f.*)
mechanic mecánico (*m.*), 12
medicine medicina (*f.*), remedio (*m.*), 15
medium mediano(a), 13; **of — height** de estatura mediana, 3
meet conocer, 10; encontrarse (o:ue) (con), 10
melt fundir; derretir (e:i)
memory recuerdo (*m.*), 16
men hombres (*m. pl.*); **—'s department** departamento de (ropa para) caballeros (*m.*), 13
menu menú (*m.*), 5
merchant vendedor(a) (*m., f.*)
merry alegre
message mensaje (*m.*), 3
meter métrica (*f.*) (*poetry*)
Mexican mexicano(a), 1; **microwave** microondas (*m.*), 10
middle name segundo nombre (*m.*)
midnight medianoche (*f.*), 9
midterm exam examen parcial (*m.*), examen de mitad de curso (*m.*), 3
midwife partera (*f.*)
mild templado(a)
mile milla (*f.*), 12
milk leche (*f.*), 5
mine mío(a), míos(as), 9
mineral water agua mineral (*f.*), 5
minus menos
mirror espejo (*m.*), 10
miss extrañar, 9; (*out on something*) perderse (e:ie), 18
Miss señorita (Srta.) (f.), 1
mister señor (Sr.), 1
mix mezclar
mixture mezcla (*f.*)
modern moderno(a), 12
mom mamá (*f.*), 1
moment momento (*m.*), 3; **at this —** en este momento, 5
Monday lunes (*m.*), 1
money dinero (*m.*), 2
monkey mono (*m.*), 8
month mes (*m.*), 1; **a (per) —** al (por) mes, 12
moon luna (*f.*), 11
mop the floor trapear el piso, 6
more más, 2
most el (la) más, 5
mother madre (*f.*), 1
motherhood maternidad
mother-in-law suegra (*f.*), 6
motorcycle motocicleta (*f.*), moto (*f.*), 8
mountain montaña (f.), 4; sierra (f.), monte (m.)
mouse ratón (*m.*), 17
mouth boca (*f.*), 15
move (*from one house to another*) mudarse, 10
movie película (*f.*), 7; **— director** director(a) de cine (*m., f.*), 18; **— screen** pantalla cinematográfica (*f.*), 18; **— section** (*of newspaper*) cartelera (*f.*), 18; **— theater** cine (*m.*), 4
mow the lawn cortar el césped, 6
Mr. señor (*m.*), Sr., 1
Mrs. señora (*f.*), Sra., 1
much mucho(a), 1
muddy turbio(a)
murder mystery película de misterio (*f.*), 18
museum museo (*m.*), 4
music música (*f.*), 18
musical musical, 18
musician músico (*m.*), 18
must deber, 3
my mi(s), 1; **— love** mi amor; **— name is . . .** Me llamo..., 1
myself me, 9
mystery misterio (*m.*); **. . .** (*movie*) película de misterio (*f.*), 18

name nombre (*m.*), 3; nombrar; **My — is . . .** Me llamo. . . , 1; **first —** nombre (*m.*), 3; **What's your —?** ¿Cómo se llama Ud.? (*form.*), 1; ¿Cómo te llamas? (*fam.*), 1
nap siesta (*f.*), 7
napkin servilleta (*f.*), 5
narrow estrecho(a), angosto(a), 13
nation nación (*f.*); pueblo (*m.*)
nationality nacionalidad (*f.*), 3
natural ínsito(a)
necessary necesario(a), 3
neck cuello (*m.*), 15
necklace collar (*m.*), 13
need necesitar, 2
negative negativo(a)
neighbor vecino(a) (*m., f.*), 4
neighborhood barrio (*m.*), vecindad (*f.*), 10
neither tampoco, 6; **— . . . nor** ni. . . ni, 6
nephew sobrino (*m.*)
nervous nervioso(a), 4
never nunca, jamás, 6; **— again** nunca más, 13
new nuevo(a), 1
New Year Año Nuevo (*m.*), 4
newspaper diario (*m.*), periódico (*m.*), 3
next próximo(a), 2; que viene, 11; entrante, 18; **— to** al lado de, 7; **— month** el mes entrante (*m.*), 18
nice simpático(a), 3; **— to meet you.** Mucho gusto.,1; **nice and hot** bien caliente, 15
niece sobrina (*f.*)
night noche (*f.*), 2; **— table** mesita de noche (*f.*), 10
nightgown camisón (*m.*), 13
nine nueve, 1; **— hundred** novecientos(as), 3
nineteen diecinueve, 1
ninety noventa, 2
ninth noveno(a), 7
no no, 1; ningún, ninguna, 6; **— longer** ya no, 18; **— one** nadie, 6; **— smoking section** sección de no fumar (*f.*), 11; **— wonder** con razón, 3
nobody nadie, 6
nocturne nocturno (*m.*)
noise ruido (*m.*)
none ninguno(a), ningún, 6
noodles fideos (*m. pl.*), 5
nonsense tontería (*f.*), 8
noon mediodía (*m.*), 5; **at —** al mediodía, 5
nor ni, 6
normal normal, 8
north norte (*m.*), 16
nose nariz (*f.*), 15
not no, 1; **— any** ninguno(a), 6; **— either** tampoco, 6; **— working** descompuesto(a), 12
notebook cuaderno (*m.*), 2
nothing nada, 1; **— but** no... más que
notice fijarse en, 18
noun nombre (*m.*), sustantivo (*m.*)
November noviembre, 1
now ahora, 6
nowadays hoy en día, 18; actualmente
number número (*m.*), 1
nursing home casa de ancianos (*f.*)

object objeto (*m.*)
obtain conseguir (e:i), 6
occupation ocupación (*f.*), 3
October octubre, 1
of de, 1; **— course** por supuesto, 7
office oficina (*f.*), 13, despacho (*m.*), 17
often a menudo, frecuentemente, 12
Oh, no! ¡Ay, no!, 1
oil aceite (*m.*), 9
old viejo(a); antiguo(a),10; **to be . . . years —** tener. . . años, 4
older mayor, 5
oldest el (la) mayor, 5
olive aceituna (*f.*); **— oil** aceite de oliva (*m.*), 9
on en, 16; **— account of** por, 8; **— behalf of** por, 8; **— the other hand** por otro lado, 13; **— the phone** al (por) teléfono, 3
once una vez, 16
one uno, 1; **— says** se dice, 2; **— way (ticket)** de ida, 11
one thousand mil, 3
onion cebolla (*f.*), 9
online application form solicitud (*f.*) electrónica, 3
only solamente, sólo, 10 ; **— thing** lo único, 14
open abrir, 3; abierto(a), 12; **— an account** abrir una cuenta, 8
opened abierto (*p.p. of* abrir), 14
optimist(ic) optimista (*m., f.*), 3
or o, 6
orange anaranjado(a), 1; naranja (*f.*), 9
orchestra orquesta (*f.*), 18
orchid orquídea (*f.*), 8
order pedir (e:i), 5; mandar, 11; pedido (*m.*), 5; orden (*f.*)
organ órgano (*m.*), 9

other otro(a), 2; **— person's right** derecho ajeno (*m.*)
others los (las) demás
our nuestro(a)(os)(as), 3
ours nuestro(a)(s), 9
ourselves nos, 9
out of breath echando el bofe
out of order descompuesto(a), 12
outdoor activity actividad al aire libre, 16
outline bosquejo (*m.*)
outside fuera
oven horno (*m.*), 10
over en, 16
overlook dar hacia
overlooking con vista a, 6
own propio(a)
oyster ostra (*f.*), 16

pack hacer las maletas
package paquete (*m.*), 11
pain dolor (*m.*), 15
painter pintor(a)
painting cuadro (*m.*), 10
pair par (*m.*), 13
Panamanian panameño(a), 7
pansy pensamiento (*m.*), 8
pantry alacena (*f.*)
pants pantalones (*m. pl.*), 8
pantyhose pantimedias (*f. pl.*), 13
paper papel (*m.*), 2
Pardon me. Perdón., 1
parents padres (*m. pl.*)
park parque (*m.*), 4; aparcar, estacionar, parquear, 8
parrot loro (*m.*), 8
partner compañero(a) (*m., f.*)
party fiesta (*f.*), 4
pass (*an exam or course*) aprobar (o:ue), 14
passport pasaporte (*m.*), 7
past (*time*) y, 2
pastry pastel (*m.*), 5
path sendero (*m.*)
patience paciencia (*f.*), 15
pay pagar, 5; **— excess baggage** pagar exceso de equipaje, 11
peace paz (*f.*); **in —** en paz, 15
peach durazno (*m.*), melocotón (*m.*), 9
pen pluma (*f.*), 2; bolígrafo (*m.*), 2; **— name** nombre de pluma (*m.*)
pencil lápiz (*m.*), 2
people (*nation*) pueblo (*m.*)
pepper pimienta (*f.*), 5
per por, 8
perfect perfecto(a), 2
perfectly perfectamente, 15
perform (*a job*) desempeñar, 17
perhaps quizás, 13
period etapa (*f.*)
personnel personal, 17
Peruvian peruano(a), 12
pessimist(ic) pesimista (*m., f.*), 3
pharmacy farmacia (*f.*), 9
phone book guía telefónica (*f.*)
phone number número de teléfono (*m.*)
photocopy machine fotocopiadora (*f.*), 17
photo(graph) fotografía (*f.*), foto (*f.*), 4
physical education educación física (*f.*), 14
physician médico(a) (*m., f.*), 15
physics física (*f.*), 14
piano piano (*m.*), 9
pick up recoger, 6; buscar, 6
picture cuadro (*m.*), 10
pie pastel (*m.*), 5
piece pedazo (*m.*), trozo (*m.*), 5; **— of news** noticia (*f.*), 7
pillow almohada (*f.*), 10
pillowcase funda (*f.*), 10
pine tree pino (*m.*), 16
pineapple piña (*f.*), 9
pink rosado(a), 1
pinnacle cumbre (*f.*)
pitch (*a tent*) armar, 16
pity: it's a — es una lástima, 11; **What a —!** ¡Qué lástima!, 15
place lugar (*m.*), 6; poner, 6; **— of birth** lugar de nacimiento (*m.*), 3; **— of employment** lugar donde trabaja (*m.*), 3
plain llanura (*f.*), llano (*m.*)
plan pensar (e:ie) (+ *inf.*), 4; planear, 1; plan (*m.*), 18
plane avión (*m.*), 11
plateau altiplano (*m.*)
plate plato (*m.*), 5
platform andén (*m.*)
play (*instrument*) tocar, 9; jugar (u:ue), 16; obra teatral (de teatro) (*f.*), 16; **— golf** jugar (u:ue) al golf (*m.*), 16; **— tennis** jugar (u:ue) al tenis (*m.*), 16
playwright dramaturgo(a) (*m., f.*)
please por favor, 1
pleasure gusto; **The — is mine.** El gusto es mío., 1
plot trama (*f.*), 18
plumber plomero(a) (*m., f.*), 14
pluperfect pluscuamperfecto
P.M. de la tarde, de la noche, 2
pneumonia pulmonía (*f.*), 15
poem poema (*m.*), 2
poetry poesía (*f.*)
police officer policía (*m. f.*), 8
policewoman agente de policía (*f.*), 8
polite amable, 3
polyester poliéster (*m.*), 13
pool piscina (*f.*)
poor pobre (*unfortunate*), 4; **— thing** pobrecito(a) (*m., f.*), 8
portrait retrato (*m.*)
Portuguese (*lang.*) portugués (*m.*), 2
position puesto (*m.*), 17; cargo (*m.*)
possibility posibilidad (*f.*), 12
post office correo (*m.*), oficina de correos (*f.*), 12
postcard tarjeta postal (*f.*), 7
pot cacerola (*f.*), 10
potato papa (*f.*), 5
pound libra (*f.*)
poverty pobreza (*f.*)
power poder (*m.*)
practice practicar, 2
prefer preferir (e:ie), 4
pregnant embarazada, 15
première estreno (*m.*), 18
preparations preparativos, 4
prepare preparar, 4
prescribe recetar, 15
prescription receta (*f.*), 15
present regalo (*m.*), 8; presentar, 18; presente
president presidente(a) (*m., f.*), 17
pretend fingir
pretty bonito(a), lindo(a), 3; precioso(a), 13
prevail prevalecer
preview avance (*m.*), 18
price precio (*m.*), 11
print (*fabric*) estampado(a), 13
printer impresora (*f.*), 17
privateer corsario (*m.*)
probable probable, 8
probably probablemente, 8
problem problema (*m.*), 2; **There's no —.** No hay problema., 2
producer productor(a) (*m., f.*), 18
profession profesión (*f.*), 3
professor profesor(a) (*m., f.*), 1
program programa (*m.*), 2
programmer programador(a), (*m., f.*), 14
promise prometer, 7
propose proponer, 14
protagonist protagonista (*m., f.*), 18
proud orgulloso(a), 16
provided that con tal (de) que, 14
psychology sicología (*f.*), 14
public relations agent agente de relaciones públicas (*m., f.*), 17
publish publicar
Puerto Rican puertorriqueño(a) (*m., f.*), 3
pull someone's leg tomarle el pelo (a alguien), 18
punch ponche (*m.*), 4
punctual puntual, 2
purchase compra (*f.*), 17
purchasing department departmento de compras (*m.*), 17
purchasing manager jefe(a) de compras (*m., f.*), 17
purple morado(a), 1
purse bolso (*m.*), 9
put poner, 6; (*p.p. of* poner) puesto, 14; **— on** ponerse, 9; **— to bed** acostar (o:ue), 9

quarter after/past . . . y cuarto (*time*), 2
quarter of/to . . . menos cuarto (*time*), 2
queen reina (*f.*)
question pregunta (*f.*), 4
Quick! ¡Rápido!, 6
quite bastante, 5

rabbit conejo, 8
racket raqueta (*f.*), 16
rain lluvia (*f.*), 5; llover (o:ue), 5
raincoat impermeable (*m.*)
raise levantar, 9
rapid rápido(a), 8
rapidly rápidamente, 8
rare raro(a)
rate of exchange cambio de moneda (*m.*)
rayon rayón (*m.*), 13
razor máquina de afeitar (*f.*)
read leer, 3; (*p.p.*) leído, 14
reader lector(a) (*m., f.*)
ready listo(a), 8; **—-to-wear clothes** ropa hecha (*f.*)
real estate agent agente de bienes raíces (*m., f.*), 17
realist(ic) realista (*m., f.*), 3

realize darse cuenta (de), 14
receive recibir, 3; (*grade*) sacar, 14
recent reciente, 8
recently recientemente, 8
recite recitar, 9
recommend recomendar (e:ie), 11
recommendation recomendación (*f.*), 17
red rojo(a), 1
red-headed pelirrojo(a), 3
refrain estribillo (*m.*)
refugee refugiado(a) (*m., f.*)
refuse no querer (e:ie), 10; negarse (a) (e:ie)
regarding en cuanto a
register matricularse, 14
registered matriculado(a), 14
registration recepción (*desk*) (*f.*), 7; matrícula (*f.*), 14
regret sentir (e:ie), 11
rehearse ensayar, 18
relative pariente (*m., f.*), 6
remain seated quedar(-se) sentado (a)
remember recordar (o:ue), 5; acordarse (o:ue) (de), 9
rent alquiler (*m.*), 10; alquilar, 10
repair arreglar, 12; arreglo (*m.*), 12; **— shop** taller de mecánica (*m.*), 12
report informe (*m.*), 3
reputation fama (*f.*), 17
request pedir (e:i), 11
requirement requisito (*m.*), 14
research investigación (*f.*), 14
reservation reserva (*f.*), reservación (*f.*), 7
resign renunciar, 17
resort balneario
responsibility responsabilidad (*f.*), 17
rest descansar, 7
restaurant restaurante (*m.*), 5
résumé resumé (*m.*), 17
return regresar, 2; volver (o:ue), 5; (*some thing*) devolver (o:ue), 13
returned (*p.p.*) (de)vuelto(a), 14
revolution revolución (*f.*), 9
reward recompensa (*f.*)
rice arroz (*m.*), 5; **— pudding** arroz con leche (*m.*), 5
ride (*a bicycle*) montar en bicicleta, 16; (*a horse*) montar a caballo, 16
right derecho (*m.*); (*adj.*) derecho (a); **to the —** a la derecha, 7; **—?** ¿verdad?, 1; **— away** en seguida, 5
ring anillo (*m.*), 13; (*phone*) sonar (o:ue), 15
river río (*m.*), 16
rock mecer
role papel (*m.*)
romantic romántico(a), 11
room cuarto (*m.*), habitación (*f.*), 5; sitio (*m.*); **— service** servicio de habitación (cuarto) (*m.*), 7
roommate compañero(a) de cuarto (*m., f.*), 3
root raíz (*f.*)
rose rosa (*f.*), 8
round-trip de ida y vuelta, 11
row remar, 16; fila (*f.*), 11
run correr, 3; **— errands** hacer diligencias, 8
Russian (*lang.*) ruso (*m.*), 2

sad triste, 4
saddlebag alforja (*f.*)
said (*p.p. of* decir) dicho, 14
sailboat velero (*m.*), 16
saint's day santo (*m.*)
salad ensalada (*f.*), 5
salary salario (*m.*), sueldo (*m.*), 17
sale liquidación (*f.*), rebaja (*f.*), 13
salesperson vendedor(a) (*m., f.*), 1
salt sal (*f.*), 5
same mismo(a), 10; **— here** igualmente, 1; **— thing** lo mismo, 10
sand arena (*f.*), 16
sandel sandalia (*f.*), 13
sandwich sándwich (*m.*), 3; bocadillo (*Spain*), 17
sarcastic sarcástico(a), 15
Saturday sábado (*m.*), 1
sauce salsa (*f.*), 9
saucepan cacerola (*f.*), 10
saucer platillo (*m.*), 5
sausage chorizo (*m.*)
save ahorrar, 8
savings account cuenta de ahorros (*f.*), 8;
say decir (e:i), 6
schedule horario (*m.*), 14
scholarship beca (*f.*), 14
school escuela (*f.*), 10; facultad (*f.*), 14
science ciencia (*f.*), 14; **— fiction** ciencia ficción (*f.*), 18
scorn despreciar
scrambled revueltos(as), 5
screen pantalla (*f.*), 17; **— play** guión (*m.*), 18
script guión (*m.*), libreto (*m.*), 18
scuba dive bucear, 16
sea mar (*m.*), 7
search búsqueda (*f.*)
season estación (*f.*), 15
seat asiento (m.), 18
seated sentado(a), 14
second segundo(a), 6; **— World War** Segunda Guerra Mundial (*f.*)
see ver, 6; **— you.** Nos vemos., 1; **— you tomorrow.** Hasta mañana., 1
seem parecer, 18; **— to one** antojársele a uno
seen (*p.p. of* ver) visto(a), 14
selection selección (*f.*), 17
sell vender, 3
semester semestre (*m.*), 2
send enviar, mandar, 7
sensitivity sensibilidad (*f.*)
sentence oración (*f.*)
September septiembre, 1
seriously? ¿en serio?, 2
serve servir (e:i), 6
service servicio (*m.*), 7
set out to proponerse
seven siete, 1; **— hundred** setecientos(as), 3
seventeen diecisiete, 1
seventh séptimo(a), 7
seventy setenta, 2
several varios(as), 14
shadow sombra (*f.*)
shake hands darse la mano
shame: it's a — es una lástima, 11
share compartir, 10
shareholder accionista (*m., f.*), 17
shark tiburón (*m.*)
shave afeitar(se), 9

she ella, 1
sheep oveja (*f.*)
sheet sábana (*f.*), 6
ship barco (*m.*), 11
shirt camisa (*f.*), 6
shoe zapato (*m.*), 13; **— store** zapatería (*f.*), 9
shoot fusilar, pasar por las armas
shop tienda (*f.*), 7
shopping: to go — ir de compras, 13
shopping mall centro comercial (*m.*), 13
short bajo(a), 3; corto(a), 9
shot inyección (*f.*), 15; **to give a —** poner una inyección, 15
shotgun escopeta (*f.*), 16
should deber, 3
show mostrar (o:ue), 6; espectáculo (*m.*), 18; **— a movie** pasar (dar) una película, 7; **— for the first time** estrenar, 18
shower ducha (*f.*), 7
shrimp camarones (*m. pl.*), 5
sick enfermo(a), 4
sigh suspirar, 6
sign firmar, 8; señal (*f.*); signo (*m.*)
signature firma (*f.*), 8
silently sin ruido
silk seda (*f.*), 13
silver plata (*f.*)
silverware cubiertos (*m. pl.*), 5
since desde, 18; como, 7
sing cantar, 4
single soltero(a), 3; **— room** habitación sencilla (*f.*), 7; **— bed** cama sencilla (f.), 7
sink lavabo (*m.*), 7
sir señor, 1
sister hermana (*f.*), 4
sister-in-law cuñada (*f.*), 5
sit down sentarse (e:ie), 9; Siéntate., 1
sitting sentado(a), 14
six seis, 1; **— hundred** seiscientos(as), 3
sixteen dieciséis, 1
sixth sexto(a), 7
sixty sesenta, 2
size medida (*f.*), talla (*f.*), 13; (*of shoes*) número (*m.*), 13; tamaño (*m.*)
skate patinar, 16
skateboard andar en patineta, 16
ski esquiar, 16
skillet sartén (*f.*), 10
skirt falda (*f.*), 13
sky cielo (*m.*)
skyscraper rascacielos (*m. sing.*)
slave esclavo(a) (*m., f.*)
sleep dormir (o:ue), 5
sleeping bag saco de dormir (*m.*), bolsa de dormir (*f.*), 10
sleepy: to be — tener sueño, 4
sleeve manga (*f.*)
slender delgado(a), 3
slice rodaja (*f.*)
slippers zapatillas (*f., pl.*), 15
slow lento(a), 8
slowly lentamente, 8; despacio
small chico(a), 10; pequeño(a); **to be too — (on someone)** quedar(le) chico(a) (a uno), 13
smile sonreír
smog contaminación del aire (*f.*)
smoke fumar

smoking: (no) smoking section sección de (no) fumar (*f.*), 11
snow nevar (e:ie), 5; nieve (*f.*), 16
so tan, 17; así que, 18; **— be it.** Sea.; **— much** tanto, 11
soap jabón (*m.*), 7; **— opera** telenovela (*f.*), 5
soccer fútbol (*m.*), 16
social security number número de seguro social (*m.*), 3
sociology sociología (*f.*), 14
sock calcetín (*m.*), 13
soda pop refresco (*m.*), 5; soda (*f.*), 4
sofa sofá (*m.*), 6
solitude soledad (*f.*)
some unos(as), 2; algunos(as), 6; alguno(a), algún, 6
somebody alguien, 6
someone alguien, 6
something algo, 6; **something like that** algo por el estilo, 18
sometimes a veces
son hijo (*m.*), 4
son-in-law yerno (*m.*), 6
song canción (*f.*), 9
soon pronto, 14; **as — as** en cuanto, tan pronto como, 14; **—er or later** tarde o temprano, 18
sore throat dolor (*m.*) de garganta, 15
sorrow pena (*f.*)
soul alma (*f.*)
sound sonido (*m.*)
soundtrack banda sonora (*f.*), 18
soup sopa (*f.*), 5
source fuente (*f.*)
south sur (*m.*), 16
Spain España
Spanish (*lang.*) español (*m.*), 2
spare part pieza de repuesto (*f.*), 12
speak hablar, 2
special especial, 8; **— effect** efecto especial (*m.*), 18
specialized especializado(a), 17
speed limit velocidad máxima (*f.*), 12
spell deletrear
spelling deletreo (*m.*)
spend (*time*) pasar, 4; gastar, 12
spoil malcriar, 10
spoon cuchara (*f.*), 5
spoonful cucharada (*f.*)
spot mancha (*f.*)
sport deporte (*m.*)
spring primavera (*f.*), 1
stadium estadio (*m.*), 16
stairs escalera (*f.*), 7
stand out destacarse
stand somebody up dejar plantado (a) a alguien, 18
standard shift de cambios mecánicos, 12
stanza estrofa (*f.*)
start comenzar (e:ie), empezar (e:ie), 4; arrancar (*car*), 12; entablar
state estado (*m.*)
station estación (*f.*), 10
stay quedarse, 11; hospedarse (en) (*at a hotel*), 11
steak bistec (*m.*), biftec (*m.*), 5
steal robar, 8
steering wheel volante (*m.*), 12
stereo system equipo estereofónico (*m.*), 4
still todavía, 10
stingy tacaño(a), 11
stir revolver (o:ue)
stockbroker bolsista (*m., f.*), 17
stomach estómago (*m.*), 15
stone piedra (*f.*)
stop detenerse; **— (something)** detener + *d.o.*
stopover escala (*f.*), 11; **to make a —** hacer escala, 11
store tienda (*f.*), 8
stranger extraño(a) (*m., f.*)
straw (*for mate*) bombilla (*f.*)
strawberry fresa (*f.*), 9
street calle (*f.*), 2
stretch estirar
stripe raya (*f.*), 13
stubborn terco(a), 3
student estudiante (*m., f.*), 1; alumno(a), 3
study estudiar, 2
stupidity torpeza (*f.*)
subject tema (*m.*), 2; (*course*) asignatura, materia, 14
subsidized subvencionado(a)
subway metro (*m.*), subterráneo (*m.*), 10
success éxito (*m.*)
Such bad luck! ¡Qué mala suerte!, 8
Such is life. Así es la vida.
suddenly de pronto, de repente, 18
suffer sufrir, 8
sugar azúcar (*m.*), 9; **— cane** caña de azúcar (*f.*)
suggest sugerir (e:ie), 11
suit traje (*m.*), 13; **— one to perfection** venirle de perillas a uno, 18
suitcase maleta (*f.*); valija (*f.*), 7
summary resumen (*m.*)
summer verano (*m.*), 1
sun sol (*m.*)
sunbathe tomar el sol, 16
Sunday domingo (*m.*), 1
sunny: to be — hacer sol, 5
supermarket supermercado (*m.*), 9
superstitious supersticioso(a), 8
supervision supervisión (*f.*), 17
supervisor supervisor(a) (*m., f.*), 17
supper cena (*f.*), 7
suppose suponer, 15
sure seguro(a), 8
surf hacer surfing, 5
surfboard tabla de mar (*f.*), 16
surprise sorpresa (*f.*), 8; sorprender, 11
surrounded rodeado(a)
sweater suéter (*m.*)
sweep barrer, 6
sweet dulce
sweets dulces (*m. pl.*)
swim nadar, 7
swimming pool piscina (*f.*), alberca (*f.*) (*Mex.*), 7
sword espada (*f.*)
symptom síntoma (*m.*), 15
system sistema (*m.*)

T-shirt camiseta (*f.*), 13
table mesa (*f.*), 4
tablecloth mantel (*m.*), 5
tail cola (*f.*)
tailor sastre (*m.*)
take tomar, 2; (*someone or something someplace*) llevar, 3; (*a taxi*), 6; **— a cruise** hacer un crucero, 11; **— a picture** sacar (tomar) una foto, 4; **— advantage of** aprovechar, 15; **— an X-ray** hacer una radiografía, 15; **— away** quitar, 9; llevarse, 11; **— charge** hacerse cargo; **— off** quitarse, 9; **— out the garbage** sacar la basura, 6; **— place** tener lugar
talent talento (*m.*), 18
talk conversar, platicar, 2; hablar, 2
tall alto(a), 3
tank tanque (*m.*), 12
tape grabar, 18
taste probar (o:ue), 9
tasty sabroso(a), 5
taxi taxi (*m.*), 6
tea té (*m.*), 5
teach enseñar (a), 16
teacher (*elementary school*) maestro(a) (*m., f.*), 10; profesor(a), 1
tear despedazar
tease tomarle el pelo (a alguien), 18
teaspoon cucharita (*f.*), 5
teeth dientes (*m. pl.*), 15
telephone teléfono (*m.*), 1; **— book** guía (*f.*) telefónica; **— system** sistema de comunicación telefónica (*m.*), 17; **on the —** al teléfono, 3
television televisión (*f.*), 2
tell decir (e:i), 6; contar (o:ue), 18
temperature temperatura (*f.*), 15
ten diez, 1
tenderness ternura (*f.*)
tennis shoe zapato de tenis (*m.*), 13
tent tienda de campaña (*f.*), 16
tenth décimo(a), 7
terrible terrible, 8
tetanus shot inyección antitetánica (*f.*), 15
than que, 5
thank you gracias, 1; **— very much.** Muchas gracias., 1
thanks gracias, 1
that (*adj.*) que, 4; aquel(la), 6; (*adj.*) ese, 6; (*adj.*) esa, 6; (*neuter pron.*) aquello, 6; (*neuter pron.*) eso, 6; **— is to say** es decir; **— one** aquel(la), 7; ese, 6; esa, 6; **—'s why** por eso, 18
the el, la, las, los, 2
theater teatro (*m.*), 4
their su(s), 3
theirs suyo(a)(s), 9
them ellas, ellos, 4; las, 6; los, 6; les, 7
theme tema (*m.*), 2
themselves se, 9
then entonces (*in that case*), 4
there allí; **— are, is** hay, 1
thermometer termómetro (*m.*), 15
these (*adj.*) estos(as), 6; (*pron.*) estos(as), 6
they ellos 1; ellas, 1
thin delgado(a), 3
think creer, 3; pensar (e:ie), 4; **— about** pensar en, 18
third tercero(a), tercer, 7
thirst sed (*f.*), 4
thirsty: to be — tener sed, 4
thirteen trece, 1
thirty treinta, 1

this (*adj.*) este, esta, 6; (*neuter pron.*), esto, 6; **— is he (she) speaking.** Con él (ella) habla., 3
those (*adj.*) aquellos(as), 6; (*pron.*) aquellos(as), 6; (*adj.*) esos(as), 6; (*pron.*) esos(as), 6
thought pensamiento (*m.*)
thousand mil, 3; millar (*m.*)
three tres, 1; **— hundred** trescientos(as), 3; **3-D** three-dimensional, 18
thriller película de suspenso (*f.*), 18
throat garganta (*f.*), 15; **sore —** dolor (*m.*) de garganta, 15
through por, 8
Thursday jueves (*m.*), 1
ticket (*for plane, train, bus*) pasaje (*m.*), billete (*m.*), 11; (*to an event*) boleto (*m.*), entrada (*f.*), 16; (*fine*) multa (*f.*), 8; **one-way —** billete (pasaje) de ida (*m.*), 11; **round-trip —** billete (pasaje) de ida y vuelta (*m.*), 11
tidy up arreglar, 6
tie corbata (*f.*), 13; **— together** apretar (e:ie)
tile teja (*f.*); (*ceramic*) azulejo (*m.*)
till menos (*telling time*), 2
time hora (*f.*), 2; tiempo, 2; vez (*in a series*) (*f.*), 4; **for the first —** por primera vez, 4; **this —** esta vez, 4; **have a good —** divertirse (e:ie), 16; **What — is it?** ¿Qué hora es?, 2
tip propina (*f.*), 5
tire llanta (*f.*), neumático (*m.*), 12
tired cansado(a), 4
title título (*m.*), 1
to (*telling time*) menos, 2; a, 1; para, 3
to the al (*contrac.*)
toast brindis (*m.*), 4; pan (*m.*) tostado, 5
toaster tostadora (*f.*), 10
today hoy, 1
toe dedo del pie (*m.*), 15
together juntos(as), 13
toilet inodoro (*m.*), 7; **— paper** papel higiénico (*m.*), 9
tomato tomate (*m.*), 9
tomb sepulcro (*m.*)
tomorrow mañana, 3; **— and not a day later** mañana mismo, 17
tongue lengua (*f.*), 15
tonight esta noche, 2
too también, 2; demasiado(a), 8
tooth diente (*m.*), 15
touch toque (*m.*); tocar, 15
tourist turista (*m., f.*), 11; **— card** tarjeta de turista (*f.*), 7; **— class** clase turista (*f.*), 11; turístico(a), 11
tow truck grúa (*f.*), remolcador (*m.*), 12
towards hacia, 5
towel toalla (*f.*), 7
tower torre (*f.*)
town pueblo (*m.*), 11
tragic trágico(a)
train tren (*m.*), 11; entrenar, 17
tranquility tranquilidad (*f.*)
translate traducir, 6
translator traductor(a) (*m., f.*), 17
travel viajar, 7; **— agency** agencia de viajes (*f.*), 11; **— agent** agente de viajes (*m., f.*), 11
traveler viajero(a) (*m., f.*), 11
traveler's check cheque de viajeros (*m.*), 8
traveling de viaje, 11
tree árbol (*m.*)
tremble temblar
trip viaje (*m.*), 4
trousers pantalón (*m.*), pantalones (*m. pl.*), 8
truck camión (*m.*), 13
true cierto
trumpet trompeta (*f.*), 9
true? ¿verdad?, 11
trunk (*car*) maletero (*m.*), cajuela (*f.*), 12
trust confiar
truth verdad (*f.*), 6
try probar (o:ue), 9; **— on** probarse (o:ue), 9
Tuesday martes (*m.*), 1
tuition matrícula (*f.*), 14
tulip tulipán (*m.*), 8
turkey pavo (*m.*), 5
turn . . . years old cumplir... años, 9; **— in** entregar, 14; **— over** voltear; **— to** recurrir a
turtle tortuga (*f.*), 8
TV set televisor (*m.*), 7
twelve doce, 1
twenty veinte, 1; **—-one** veintiuno, 1; **—-two** veintidós, 1; **—-three** veintitrés, 1; **—-four** veinticuatro, 1; **—-five** veinticinco, 1; **—-six** veintiséis, 1; **—-seven** veintisiete, 1; **—-eight** veintiocho, 1; **—-nine** veintinueve, 1
twilight crepúsculo (*m.*)
two dos, 1; **— hundred** doscientos(as), 3
tyrant tirano(a) (*m., f.*)

ugly feo(a), 3
umbrella paraguas (*m. sing.*)
uncle tío (*m.*), 4
under debajo de, 6; bajo, 17
understand entender (e:ie), 4
underwear ropa interior (*f.*), 13
unfortunate desafortunado(a), 8
unfortunately desgraciadamente, por desgracia, desafortunadamente, 8
ungrateful (*adj.*) desagradecido(a)
United States Estados Unidos (*m. pl.*)
university universidad (*f.*), 1
unless a menos que, 14
unpleasant antipático(a), 3
untie lines soltar (o:ue) amarras
until hasta, 7; hasta que, 14
untimely a deshoras
up to now hasta ahora, 14
Uruguayan uruguayo(a), 16
us (*obj. of prep.*) nosotros(as), 4; nos, 6, 7
use usar, 6; gastar, 12; uso (*m.*), 17
used usado(a), 12; **— to** acostumbrado(a), 10
usefulness utilidad (*f.*)

vacant libre, 7; desocupado(a), 10
vacate the room desocupar el cuarto, 7
vacation vacaciones (*f. pl.*), 7; **— package** paquete turístico, 11
vaccination vacuna (*f.*), 15
vacuum pasar la aspiradora, 6
value valor (*m.*)
vegetable verdura (*f.*), vegetal (*m.*), legumbre (*m.*), 5
Venezuelan venezolano(a), 10
verb verbo (*m.*)
very muy, 1; **(not) — well** (no) muy bien, 1
victim víctima (*f.*), 17
video camera cámara de video (*f.*), 7
vinegar vinagre (*m.*), 9
violet violeta (*f.*), 8
violin violín (*m.*), 9
visit visitar, 6 ; **— frequently** frecuentar
vocabulary vocabulario (*m.*)
volleyball vóleibol (*m.*), 16

wait (for) esperar, 9; aguardar
waiter camarero (*m.*), mozo (*m.*), 5
waiting list lista de espera (*f.*), 7
waitress camarera (*f.*), 5
wake up despertarse (e:ie), 9
walk caminar, 7; ir a pie, ir caminando, 12
wall pared (*f.*), 2
wallet billetera (*f.*), 9; cartera (*f.*), 13
waltz vals (*m.*), 4
wandering errabundo
want querer (e:ie), 4; desear, 11
war guerra (*f.*), 18
warning advertencia (*f.*)
wash lavar(se), 9; **— dishes** lavar los platos, fregar (e:ie) los platos, 6; **— one's hair** lavarse la cabeza, 9
washing machine lavadora (*f.*), 10
wastebasket cesto de papeles (*m.*), 2
watch mirar, 5
water agua (*f.*), 5; **— ski** esquí acuático (*m.*), 16
watermelon sandía (*f.*), 9
wave ola (*f.*)
way modo (*m.*)
we nosotros(as), 1
weak débil, 15
wear usar; **— a certain (shoe) size** calzar, 13; **not to have anything to —** no tener nada que ponerse, 13
weather tiempo (*m.*); **— forecast** pronóstico del tiempo; **to be good (bad) —** hacer buen (mal) tiempo, 6; **What's the weather like?** ¿Qué tiempo hace?, 6
weatherbeaten curtido(a)
wedding boda (*f.*), 9; **golden — (anniversary)** bodas de oro, 9
Wednesday miércoles (*m.*), 1
week semana (*f.*), 2; **a — ago** hace una semana, 9; **per —** por semana, 2
weekend fin de semana (*m.*), 4
weigh pesar
welcome bienvenido(a), 4; **You're —.** De nada., 1
well bien, 1; pues, 4; **— . . . okay** bueno. . . , 1
west oeste (*m.*), 16
western (movie) película del oeste (de vaqueros) (*f.*), 18

what cuál, 1; qué, 2; lo que, 6; **— a pity!** ¡Qué lástima!, 15; **— do you think about . . .?** ¿Qué les parece si. . . ?, 13; **— for?** ¿Para qué?, 18; **— is the rate of exchange?** ¿A cómo está el cambio de moneda?, 7; **— is your name?** ¿Cómo se llama Ud.? (*form.*), 1; ¿Cómo te llamas? (*fam.*), 1; **— is your phone number?** ¿Cuál es tu número de teléfono?, 1; **— the heck!** ¡Qué diablo!; **— time is it?** ¿Qué hora es?, 2; **—'s new?** ¿Qué hay (de nuevo)?, 1
wheat trigo (*m.*)
wheelchair silla de ruedas (*f.*), 15
when? ¿cuándo?, 2; cuando, 14
where? ¿dónde?, 1; ¿adónde?, 3
which? ¿cuál?, 1; (*rel. pron.*) que, 10
white blanco(a), 1
who (*rel. pron.*) que, 4; quien(es), 10
whom quien, quienes, 10
whose de quién
why? ¿por qué?
wide ancho(a), 13
widowed viudo(a), 3
wife esposa (*f.*), mujer (*f.*), 5
willpower voluntad (*f.*)
win ganar, 16
window ventana (*f.*), 2; (*of a vehicle or booth*) ventanilla (*f.*), 12; **— seat** asiento de ventanilla (*m.*), 11; **to — shop** mirar vidrieras, 13
windshield parabrisas (*m.*), 12
windy: to be — hacer viento, 6
wine vino (*m.*), 4
winter invierno (*m.*), 1
wish desear, 2; querer (e:ie), 4
with con, 2; de, 16; **— me** conmigo, 2; **— you** (*fam. sing.*) contigo, 4
without sin que, 14; sin; **— fail** sin falta, 18; **— rhyme or reason** sin qué ni para qué, 18
woman mujer (*f.*)
women's department departamento de (ropa para) damas, 13
wood madera (*f.*)
wool lana (*f.*), 13
word palabra (*f.*), 17; **— processor** procesador de textos (*m.*) (de arte), 17
work trabajar, 2; trabajo (*m.*), 3; funcionar, 12; (*of art*) obra (*f.*) (de arte); **— hard** trabajar duro, 18
world mundo (*m.*), 17; **— Wide Web** Internet (*f.*), Red (*f.*), 7
worried preocupado(a), 4
worry (about) preocuparse (por), 9
worse peor, 5
worst el (la) peor, 5
worth: to be — the trouble valer la pena, 12
wrap envolver (o:ue), 14
wrapped envuelto(a), 14
write escribir, 3; **— down** anotar, 2
writer escritor(a) (*m., f.*), 14
written escrito(a), 14
wrong equivocado(a), 8; **be —** estar equivocado(a), no tener razón, 4

X-ray radiografía (*f.*), 15; **— room** sala de rayos X (*f.*), 15

year año (*m.*), 3; **to be . . . —s old** tener. . . años, 4
yellow amarillo(a), 1
yes sí, 2
yesterday ayer, 7
yogurt yogur (*m.*), 5
you (*subj.*) tú (*fam.*), usted (Ud.) (*form.*); ustedes, vosotros(as), 1; (*d.o. pron.*) la(s), lo(s), os, te, 6; (*i.o. pron.*) le(s), os, te, 7; (*obj. of prep.*) ti, usted(es), vosotros(as), 4
You'll see! ¡Ya verás!, 15
young joven (*m., f.*), 17; **— man** chico (*m.*), muchacho (*m.*), 2; joven (*m.*), 15; **— lady** señorita (*f.*), 1; **— people** jóvenes (*m., f.*); **— woman** chica (*f.*), muchacha (*f.*), 2; joven (*f.*), 15
younger menor, 5
youngest el (la) menor, 5
your su(s), tu(s), vuestro(a)(os)(as), 3
yours suyo(a)(s), tuyo(a)(s), vuestro(a)(s), 9
yourself se, te, 9
yourselves os, se, 9
youth juventud (*f.*), 9

zero cero, 1
zip code zona postal (*f.*), 3
zoo zoológico (*m.*), 4

Index